CLYMER®

YAMAHA

OUTBOARD SHOP MANUAL
9.9-100 HP FOUR-STROKE • 1985-1999

The World's Finest Publisher of Mechanical How-to Manuals

INTERTEC PUBLISHING

P.O. Box 12901, Overland Park, KS 66282-2901

Copyright ©2001 Intertec Publishing

FIRST EDITION
First Printing April, 2001

Printed in U.S.A.

CLYMER and colophon are registered trademarks of Intertec Publishing.

ISBN: 0-89287-766-9

Library of Congress: 2001089116

Technical illustrations by Robert Caldwell.

COVER: Photograph courtesy of Yamaha Marine, Kennesaw, GA.

PRODUCTION: Shara Pierceall-Meyer.

Contents

Quick Reference Data

SPARK PLUG APPLICATION

Engine model year	Type	Gap mm (in)	Torque N•m (ft.-lb.)
F9.9 (K-Q) 1985-1992	(NGK) CR6HS	0.6-0.7 (0.024-0.028)	12 (9)*
F9.9 (R-W) 1993-1998	(NGK) CR6HS	0.6-0.7 (0.024-0.028)	13 (9.4)*
F15 (W) 1998	(NGK) DPR6EA-9	0.9 (0.04)	18 (13)*
F25 (W) 1998	(NGK) DPR6EA-9	0.9 (0.04)	17.2 (12.6)*
F25 (X) 1999	(NGK) DPR6EA-9	0.9-1.0 (0.035-0.039)	17.2 (12.6)*
F50 (T-W) 1995-1998	(NGK) DPR6EA-9	0.8-0.9 (0.031-0.035)	17.0 (12.5)*
F50 (X) 1999	(NGK) DPR6EA-9	0.9 (0.035)	18.0 (13)*
F80 (X) 1999	(NGK) LFR5A-11	1.1 (0.043)	25 (18)*
F100 (X) 1999	(NGK) LFR5A-11	1.1 (0.043)	25 (18)*

*Finger-tighten the spark plug (s) before reaching torque specification.

ENGINE OIL VISCOSITY

Engine model	Oil type	SAE	API
F9.9	4-Stroke	10W-30, 10W-40	SE, SF, SE-SF, SE-SF-CC
F15	4-Stroke	10W-30, 10W-40, 20W-40	SE, SF, SG, SH
F25	4-Stroke	10W-30, 10W-40, 20W-40	SE, SF, SG, SH
F50	4-Stroke	10W-30, 10W-40, 20W-40	SE, SF, SG, SH
F80	4-Stroke	10W-30, 10W-40	SE, SF, SG, SH
F100	4-Stroke	10W-30, 10W-40	SE, SF, SG, SH

FUEL GRADE SPECIFICATIONS

Fuel type	Fuel rating
Unleaded regular gasoline	86 PON[1] 91 RON[2]

1. PON: Pump Octane Number
2. RON: Research Octane Number

GENERAL TORQUE SPECIFICATIONS*

Nut	Bolt	N•m	ft.-lb.
8 mm	M5	5.0	3.6
10 mm	M6	8.0	5.8
12 mm	M8	18	13
14 mm	M10	36	25
17 mm	M12	43	31

*The torque specified in this chart is for standard fasteners with standard ISO pitch thread. Special components or assemblies that require a special torque are covered in the applicable chapter in this book.

RECOMMENDED GEARCASE LUBRICANTS

Model	Oil type	SAE	API	Capacity
T9.9 (MH)(EH)(ER)	Hypoid	90	–	320 cm (10.82 oz)
F9.9 (MH)(EH)	Hypoid	90	–	185 cm (6.25 oz)
F15 (MH)(EH)	Hypoid	90	–	250 cm (8.45 oz)
F25 (MH)(EH)(TH)(ER) (TR)	Hypoid	90	–	320 cm (10.8 oz)
F40 (TR)(ER)(TH)(EH)	Hypoid	90	GL-4	430 cm (14.5 oz)
F50 (TR)(ER)(TH)(EH)	Hypoid	90	GL-4	430 cm (14.5 oz)
T50 (TR)	Hypoid	90	GL-4	610 cm (20.6 oz)
F80 and F100	Hypoid	90	GL-4	670 cm (22.6 oz)

RECOMMENDED ENGINE SPEED

Idle speed
F9.9 — 900-1000 rpm
T9.9 — 1100-1200 rpm
F15 — 900-1000 rpm
F25 — 875-975 rpm
F40-F50-FT50 — 700-800 rpm
F80-F100 — 850-950 rpm

Full-throttle speed
F9.9-T9.9 and F15 — 4500-5500 rpm
F25-F100 — 5000-6000 rpm

Trolling range
F9.9 and T9.9 — 800-900 rpm

Maximum horsepower output
F9.9 and T9.9 — 5.9 kW (8 hp) @ 5000 rpm
F15 — 11 kW (15 hp) @ 5000 rpm
F25 — 18.4 kW (25 hp) @ 5500 rpm
F40 — 29.4 kW (40 hp) @ 5500 rpm
F50 and T50 — 36.8 kW (50 hp) @ 5500 rpm
F80 — 58.8 kW (80 hp) @ 5500 rpm
F100 — 73.6 kW (100 hp) @ 5500 rpm

MAINTENANCE SCHEDULE

10 hours (break-in)
Inspect cowl latches and drain hole(s)
Inspect/replace fuel filter
Inspect/adjust throttle link rod
Inspect/adjust start-in-gear protection
Inspect/change engine oil
Inspect/adjust valve clearance[1]
Inspect engine for water leakage
Inspect motor exterior
Inspect for exhaust leakage
Change lower unit gear oil
Inspect battery every month
Inspect/clean/change spark plug(s)
Check connection of wiring harness

50 hours (3 months)
Inspect/replace fuel filter
Inspect/change engine oil
Replace engine oil filter
Inspect/replace timing belt
Check engine for exhaust leakage
Inspect/clean cooling water passage(s)
Inspect propeller for damage
Inspect anode(s) for wear
Inspect battery
Inspect/clean/replace spark plug(s)
Inspect and retighten all fasteners
(continued)

MAINTENANCE SCHEDULE (continued)

100 hours (6 months)	Inspect fuel line(s)
	Inspect/replace fuel filter
	Inspect/adjust start-in-gear protection
	Inspect/change engine oil
	Replace engine oil filter
	Inspect/replace timing belt
	Inspect/adjust valve clearance[2]
	Inspect/replace thermostat[3]
	Inspect engine for exhaust leakage
	Inspect/clean cooling water passages
	Change lower unit gear oil
	Inspect water pump impeller
	Inspect lower unit for leakage
	Inspect propeller for damage
	Inspect anode(s) for wear
	Inspect battery
	Inspect/clean/replace spark plug(s)
	Inspect and retighten all fasteners
	Inspect and grease all grease points
200 hours (1 year)	Inspect cowl latches and drain hole(s)
	Inspect fuel line
	Inspect/adjust throttle cable(s)
	Inspect/adjust idle speed
	Inspect/adjust shift control cable
	Inspect spark timing
	Inspect/replace thermostat[4]
	Inspect lower unit for leakage
	Check/reconnect wiring harness
400 hours (2 year)	Inspect/adjust valve clearance[5]

1. Maintenance not required on F80 and F100 at this interval.
2. Maintenance is required only for F25, F40, F50 and T50 at this interval.
3. Maintenance is required only for F25 at this interval.
4. Maintenance is required only for F40, F50 and T50 at this interval.
5. Maintenance is suggested only for F80 and F100 at this interval.

RECOMMENDED ENGINE OIL FOR FOUR-STROKE

Model	SAE	API	Capacity
F9.9 and T9.9	10W-30, 10W-40	SE, SF, SE-SF-CC	1.0 L (1.06 qt)
F15	10W-30, 10W-40	SE, SF, SG or SH	1.0 L (1.06 qt)[1]
			1.2 L (1.27 qt)[2]
F25	10W-30, 10W-40	SE, SF, SG, SH	1.7 L (1.80 qt)[1]
			1.9 L (2.01 qt)[2]
F40 and F50	10W-30, 10W-40	SE, SF, SG, SH	2.0 L (2.11 qt)[1]
			2.2 L (2.32 qt)[2]
T50	10W-30, 10W-40	SE, SF, SG, SH	2.0 L (2.11 qt)[1]
			2.2 L (2.32 qt)[2]
F80 and F100	10W-30, 10W-40	SE, SF, SG, SH	4.5 L (4.75 qt)[1]
			4.8 L (4.96 qt)[2]

1. Quantity without filter.
2. Quantity with filter.

CLYMER®

YAMAHA

OUTBOARD SHOP MANUAL
9.9-100 HP FOUR-STROKE • 1985-1999

Introduction

This Clymer shop manual covers service, maintenance and repair of 9.9-100 hp four-stroke Yamaha outboard motors manufactured from 1985-1999. Coverage is provided for outboard motors designed for recreational use only; commercial models are not covered in this manual.

Step-by-step instructions and hundreds of illustrations guide you through tasks ranging from routine maintenance to complete overhaul.

This manual can be used by anyone from a first time owner to a professional technician. Easy-to-read type, detailed drawings and clear photographs provide all the information need to complete the procedure correctly.

Having a well-maintained outboard motor will increase your enjoyment of your boat as well as ensuring your safety offshore. Keep this shop manual handy and use it often. Performing routine, preventive maintenance will save time and money by helping prevent premature failure and unnecessary repairs.

Chapter One

General Information

This detailed, comprehensive manual contains complete information on maintenance, tune-up, repair and overhaul. Hundreds of photos and drawings guide you through every step-by-step procedure.

Troubleshooting, tune-up, maintenance and repair are not difficult if you know what tools and equipment to use and what to do. Anyone not afraid to get their hands dirty, of average intelligence and with some mechanical ability, can perform most of the procedures in this book. See Chapter Two for more information on tools and techniques.

A shop manual is a reference. You want to be able to find information fast. Clymer books are designed with you in mind. All chapters are thumb tabbed and important items are indexed at the end of the book. All procedures, tables, photos, etc., in this manual assume that the reader may be working on the machine or using this manual for the first time.

Keep this book handy in your tool box. It will help you to better understand how your machine runs, lower repair and maintenance costs and generally increase your enjoyment of your marine equipment.

MANUAL ORGANIZATION

This chapter provides general information useful to marine owners and mechanics.

Chapter Two discusses the tools and techniques for preventive maintenance, troubleshooting and repair.

Chapter Three describes typical equipment problems and provides logical troubleshooting procedures.

Following chapters describe specific systems, providing disassembly, repair, assembly and adjustment procedures in simple step-by-step form. Specifications concerning a specific system are included at the end of the appropriate chapter.

NOTES, CAUTIONS
AND WARNINGS

The terms NOTE, CAUTION and WARNING have specific meanings in this manual. A NOTE provides additional information to make a step or procedure easier or clearer. Disregarding a NOTE could cause inconvenience, but would not cause damage or personal injury.

A CAUTION emphasizes areas where equipment damage could result. Disregarding a CAUTION could cause permanent mechanical damage; however, personal injury is unlikely.

A WARNING emphasizes areas where personal injury or even death could result from negligence. Mechanical damage may also occur. WARNINGS *are to be taken seriously.* In some cases, serious injury or death has resulted from disregarding similar warnings.

TORQUE SPECIFICATIONS

Torque specifications throughout this manual are given in foot-pounds (ft.-lb.) and either Newton meters (N·m) or meter-kilograms (mkg). Newton meters are being adopted in place of meter-kilograms in accordance with the International Modernized Metric System. Existing torque wrenches calibrated in meter-kilograms can be used by performing a simple conversion: move the decimal point one place to the right. For example, 4.7 mkg = 47 N·m. This conversion is accurate enough for mechanics' use even though the exact mathematical conversion is 3.5 mkg = 34.3 N·m.

ENGINE OPERATION

All marine engines, whether 2- or 4-stroke, gasoline or diesel, operate on the Otto cycle of intake, compression, power and exhaust phases.

4-stroke Cycle

A 4-stroke engine requires two crankshaft revolutions (4 strokes of the piston) to complete the Otto cycle. **Figure 1** shows gasoline 4-stroke engine operation. **Figure 2** shows diesel 4-stroke engine operation.

2-stroke Cycle

A 2-stroke engine requires only 1 crankshaft revolution (2 strokes of the piston) to complete the Otto cycle. **Figure 3** shows gasoline 2-stroke engine operation. Although diesel 2-strokes exist, they are not commonly used in light marine applications.

FASTENERS

The material and design of the various fasteners used on marine equipment are not arrived at by chance or accident. Fastener design determines the type of tool required to work with the fastener. Fastener material is carefully selected to decrease the possibility of physical failure or corrosion. See *Galvanic Corrosion* in this chapter for more information on marine materials.

Threads

Nuts, bolts and screws are manufactured in a wide range of thread patterns. To join a nut and bolt, the diameter of the bolt and the diameter of the hole in the nut must be the same. It is just as important that the threads on both be properly matched.

The best way to determine if the threads on two fasteners are matched is to turn the nut on the bolt (or the bolt into the threaded hole in a piece of equipment) with fingers only. Be sure both pieces are clean. If much force is required, check the thread condition on each fastener. If the thread condition is good but the fasteners jam, the threads are not compatible.

Four important specifications describe every thread:

a. Diameter.
b. Threads per inch.
c. Thread pattern.
d. Thread direction.

Figure 4 shows the first two specifications. Thread pattern is more subtle. Italian and British

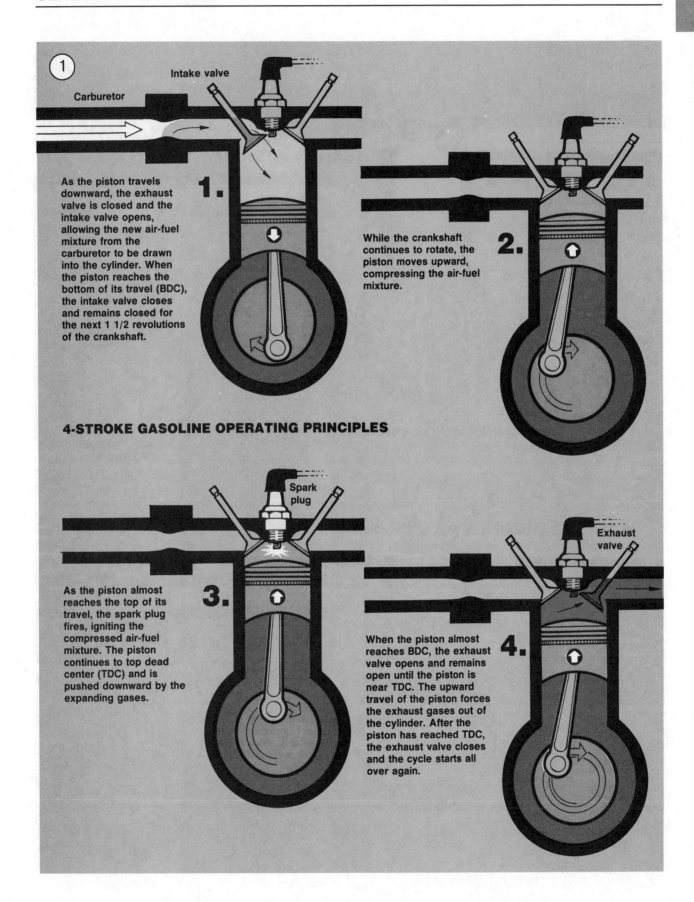

①

Intake valve

Carburetor

1.

As the piston travels downward, the exhaust valve is closed and the intake valve opens, allowing the new air-fuel mixture from the carburetor to be drawn into the cylinder. When the piston reaches the bottom of its travel (BDC), the intake valve closes and remains closed for the next 1 1/2 revolutions of the crankshaft.

2.

While the crankshaft continues to rotate, the piston moves upward, compressing the air-fuel mixture.

4-STROKE GASOLINE OPERATING PRINCIPLES

Spark plug

3.

As the piston almost reaches the top of its travel, the spark plug fires, igniting the compressed air-fuel mixture. The piston continues to top dead center (TDC) and is pushed downward by the expanding gases.

Exhaust valve

4.

When the piston almost reaches BDC, the exhaust valve opens and remains open until the piston is near TDC. The upward travel of the piston forces the exhaust gases out of the cylinder. After the piston has reached TDC, the exhaust valve closes and the cycle starts all over again.

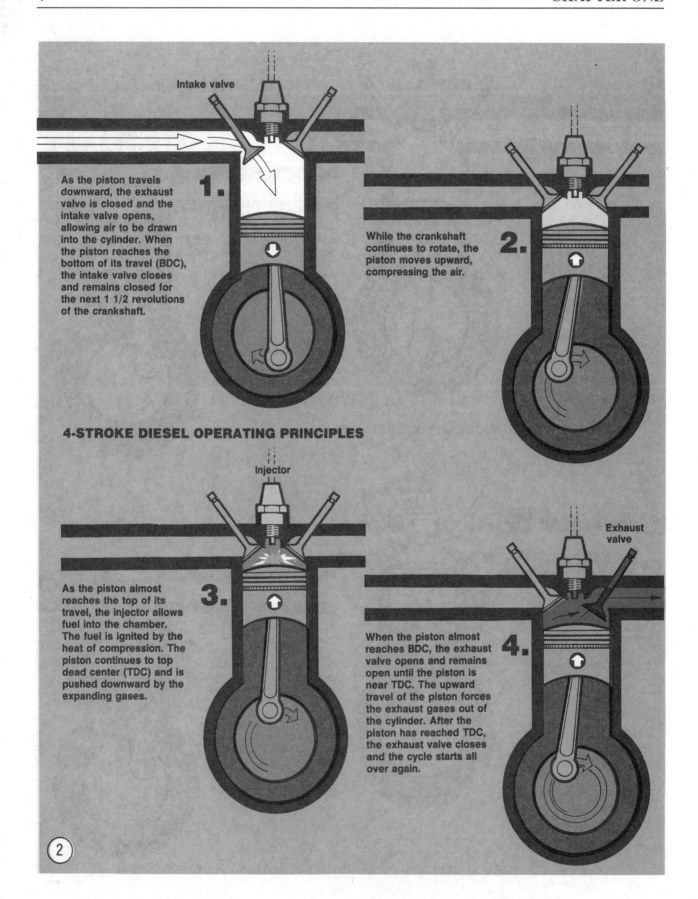

Intake valve

1.

As the piston travels downward, the exhaust valve is closed and the intake valve opens, allowing air to be drawn into the cylinder. When the piston reaches the bottom of its travel (BDC), the intake valve closes and remains closed for the next 1 1/2 revolutions of the crankshaft.

2.

While the crankshaft continues to rotate, the piston moves upward, compressing the air.

4-STROKE DIESEL OPERATING PRINCIPLES

Injector

3.

As the piston almost reaches the top of its travel, the injector allows fuel into the chamber. The fuel is ignited by the heat of compression. The piston continues to top dead center (TDC) and is pushed downward by the expanding gases.

Exhaust valve

4.

When the piston almost reaches BDC, the exhaust valve opens and remains open until the piston is near TDC. The upward travel of the piston forces the exhaust gases out of the cylinder. After the piston has reached TDC, the exhaust valve closes and the cycle starts all over again.

②

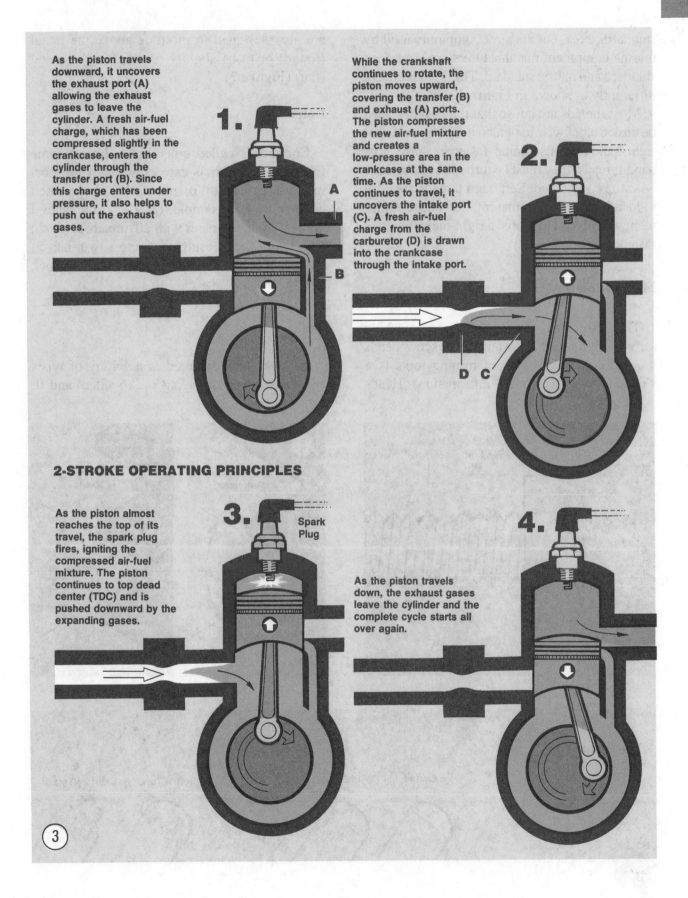

As the piston travels downward, it uncovers the exhaust port (A) allowing the exhaust gases to leave the cylinder. A fresh air-fuel charge, which has been compressed slightly in the crankcase, enters the cylinder through the transfer port (B). Since this charge enters under pressure, it also helps to push out the exhaust gases.

While the crankshaft continues to rotate, the piston moves upward, covering the transfer (B) and exhaust (A) ports. The piston compresses the new air-fuel mixture and creates a low-pressure area in the crankcase at the same time. As the piston continues to travel, it uncovers the intake port (C). A fresh air-fuel charge from the carburetor (D) is drawn into the crankcase through the intake port.

2-STROKE OPERATING PRINCIPLES

As the piston almost reaches the top of its travel, the spark plug fires, igniting the compressed air-fuel mixture. The piston continues to top dead center (TDC) and is pushed downward by the expanding gases.

Spark Plug

As the piston travels down, the exhaust gases leave the cylinder and the complete cycle starts all over again.

standards exist, but the most commonly used by marine equipment manufacturers are American standard and metric standard. The threads are cut differently as shown in **Figure 5**.

Most threads are cut so that the fastener must be turned clockwise to tighten it. These are called right-hand threads. Some fasteners have left-hand threads; they must be turned counterclockwise to be tightened. Left-hand threads are used in locations where normal rotation of the equipment would tend to loosen a right-hand threaded fastener.

Machine Screws

There are many different types of machine screws. **Figure 6** shows a number of screw heads requiring different types of turning tools (see Chapter Two for detailed information). Heads are also designed to protrude above the metal (round) or to be slightly recessed in the metal (flat) (**Figure 7**).

Bolts

Commonly called bolts, the technical name for these fasteners is cap screw. They are normally described by diameter, threads per inch and length. For example, 1/4-20 × 1 indicates a bolt 1/4 in. in diameter with 20 threads per inch, 1 in. long. The measurement across two flats on the head of the bolt indicates the proper wrench size to be used.

Nuts

Nuts are manufactured in a variety of types and sizes. Most are hexagonal (6-sided) and fit

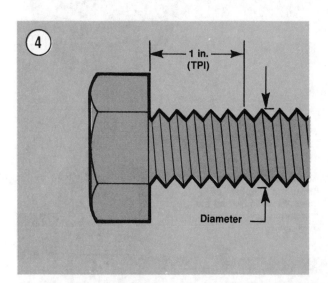

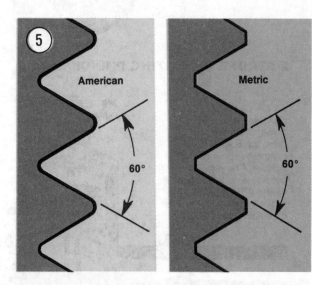

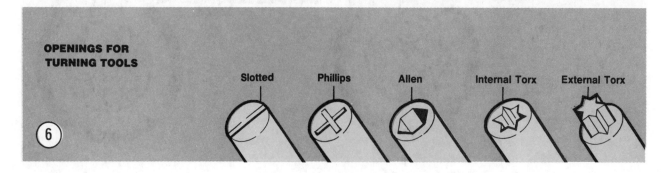

on bolts, screws and studs with the same diameter and threads per inch.

Figure 8 shows several types of nuts. The common nut is usually used with a lockwasher. Self-locking nuts have a nylon insert that prevents the nut from loosening; no lockwasher is required. Wing nuts are designed for fast removal by hand. Wing nuts are used for convenience in non-critical locations.

To indicate the size of a nut, manufacturers specify the diameter of the opening and the threads per inch. This is similar to bolt specification, but without the length dimension. The measurement across two flats on the nut indicates the proper wrench size to be used.

Washers

There are two basic types of washers: flat washers and lockwashers. Flat washers are simple discs with a hole to fit a screw or bolt. Lockwashers are designed to prevent a fastener from working loose due to vibration, expansion and contraction. **Figure 9** shows several types of lockwashers. Note that flat washers are often used between a lockwasher and a fastener to provide a smooth bearing surface. This allows the fastener to be turned easily with a tool.

Cotter Pins

Cotter pins (**Figure 10**) are used to secure special kinds of fasteners. The threaded stud

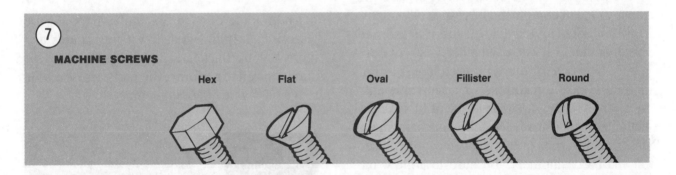

(7) MACHINE SCREWS

Hex   Flat   Oval   Fillister   Round

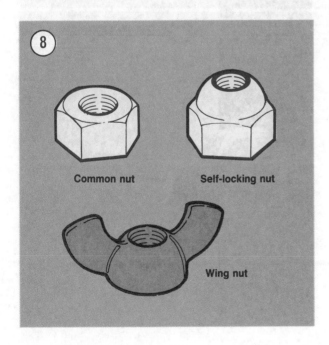

(8)

Common nut   Self-locking nut

Wing nut

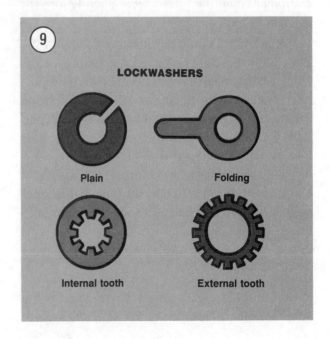

(9) LOCKWASHERS

Plain   Folding

Internal tooth   External tooth

must have a hole in it; the nut or nut lock piece has projections that the cotter pin fits between. This type of nut is called a "Castellated nut." Cotter pins should not be reused after removal.

Snap Rings

Snap rings can be of an internal or external design. They are used to retain items on shafts (external type) or within tubes (internal type). Snap rings can be reused if they are not distorted during removal. In some applications, snap rings of varying thickness can be selected to control the end play of parts assemblies.

LUBRICANTS

Periodic lubrication ensures long service life for any type of equipment. It is especially important to marine equipment because it is exposed to salt or brackish water and other harsh environments. The *type* of lubricant used is just as important as the lubrication service itself; although, in an emergency, the wrong type of lubricant is better than none at all. The following paragraphs describe the types of lubricants most often used on marine equipment. Be sure to follow the equipment manufacturer's recommendations for lubricant types.

Generally, all liquid lubricants are called "oil." They may be mineral-based (including petroleum bases), natural-based (vegetable and animal bases), synthetic-based or emulsions (mixtures). "Grease" is an oil which is thickened with a metallic "soap." The resulting material is then usually enhanced with anticorrosion, antioxidant and extreme pressure (EP) additives. Grease is often classified by the type of thickener added; lithium and calcium soap are commonly used.

4-stroke Engine Oil

Oil for 4-stroke engines is graded by the American Petroleum Institute (API) and the So-

ciety of Automotive Engineers (SAE) in several categories. Oil containers display these ratings on the top or label (**Figure 11**).

API oil grade is indicated by letters, oils for gasoline engines are identified by an "S" and oils for diesel engines are identified by a "C." Most modern gasoline engines require SF or SG graded oil. Automotive and marine diesel engines use CC or CD graded oil.

Viscosity is an indication of the oil's thickness, or resistance to flow. The SAE uses numbers to indicate viscosity; thin oils have low numbers and thick oils have high numbers. A "W" after the number indicates that the viscosity testing was done at low temperature to simulate cold weather operation. Engine oils fall into the 5W-20W and 20-50 range.

Multi-grade oils (for example, 10W-40) are less viscous (thinner) at low temperatures and more viscous (thicker) at high temperatures. This allows the oil to perform efficiently across a wide range of engine operating temperatures.

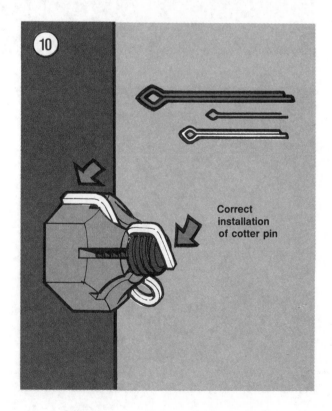

Correct installation of cotter pin

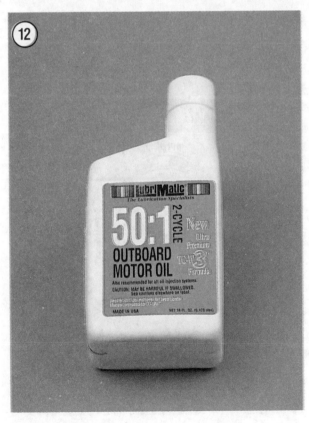

2-stroke Engine Oil

Lubrication for a 2-stroke engine is provided by oil mixed with the incoming fuel-air mixture. Some of the oil mist settles out in the crankcase, lubricating the crankshaft and lower end of the connecting rods. The rest of the oil enters the combustion chamber to lubricate the piston, rings and cylinder wall. This oil is then burned along with the fuel-air mixture during the combustion process.

Engine oil must have several special qualities to work well in a 2-stroke engine. It must mix easily and stay in suspension in gasoline. When burned, it can't leave behind excessive deposits. It must also be able to withstand the high temperatures associated with 2-stroke engines.

The National Marine Manufacturer's Association (NMMA) has set standards for oil used in 2-stroke, water-cooled engines. This is the NMMA TC-W (two-cycle, water-cooled) grade (**Figure 12**). The oil's performance in the following areas is evaluated:

a. Lubrication (prevention of wear and scuffing).
b. Spark plug fouling.
c. Preignition.
d. Piston ring sticking.
e. Piston varnish.
f. General engine condition (including deposits).
g. Exhaust port blockage.
h. Rust prevention.
i. Mixing ability with gasoline.

In addition to oil grade, manufacturers specify the ratio of gasoline to oil required during break-in and normal engine operation.

Gear Oil

Gear lubricants are assigned SAE viscosity numbers under the same system as 4-stroke engine oil. Gear lubricant falls into the SAE 72-250 range (**Figure 13**). Some gear lubricants are multi-grade; for example, SAE 85W-90.

Three types of marine gear lubricant are generally available: SAE 90 hypoid gear lubricant is designed for older manual-shift units; Type C gear lubricant contains additives designed for electric shift mechanisms; High viscosity gear lubricant is a heavier oil designed to withstand the shock loading of high-performance engines or units subjected to severe duty use. Always use a gear lubricant of the type specified by the unit's manufacturer.

Grease

Greases are graded by the National Lubricating Grease Institute (NLGI). Greases are graded by number according to the consistency of the grease; these ratings range from No. 000 to No. 6, with No. 6 being the most solid. A typical multipurpose grease is NLGI No. 2 (**Figure 14**). For specific applications, equipment manufacturers may require grease with an additive such as molybdenum disulfide (MOS^2).

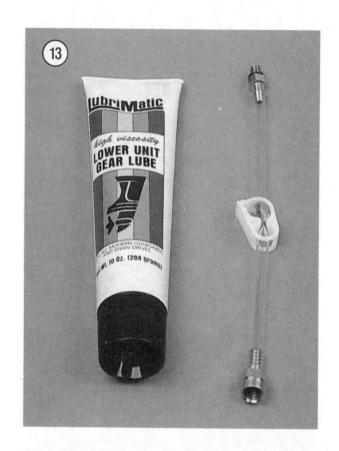

GASKET SEALANT

Gasket sealant is used instead of pre-formed gaskets on some applications, or as a gasket dressing on others. Two types of gasket sealant are commonly used: room temperature vulcanizing (RTV) and anaerobic. Because these two materials have different sealing properties, they cannot be used interchangeably.

RTV Sealant

This is a silicone gel supplied in tubes (**Figure 15**). Moisture in the air causes RTV to cure. Always place the cap on the tube as soon as possible when using RTV. RTV has a shelf life of one year and will not cure properly when the shelf life has expired. Check the expiration date

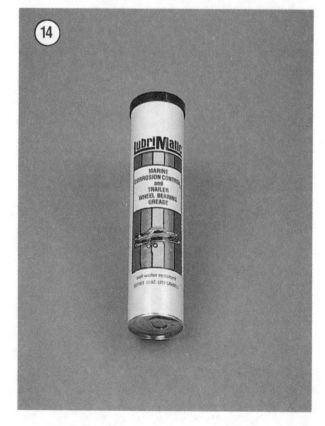

on RTV tubes before using and keep partially used tubes tightly sealed. RTV sealant can generally fill gaps up to 1/4 in. (6.3 mm) and works well on slightly flexible surfaces.

Applying RTV Sealant

Clean all gasket residue from mating surfaces. Surfaces should be clean and free of oil and dirt. Remove all RTV gasket material from blind attaching holes because it can create a "hydraulic" effect and affect bolt torque.

Apply RTV sealant in a continuous bead 2-3 mm (0.08-0.12 in.) thick. Circle all mounting holes unless otherwise specified. Torque mating parts within 10 minutes after application.

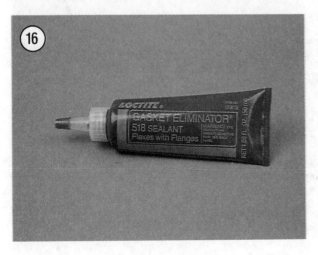

Anaerobic Sealant

This is a gel supplied in tubes (**Figure 16**). It cures only in the absence of air, as when squeezed tightly between two machined mating surfaces. For this reason, it will not spoil if the cap is left off the tube. It should not be used if one mating surface is flexible. Anaerobic sealant is able to fill gaps up to 0.030 in. (0.8 mm) and generally works best on rigid, machined flanges or surfaces.

Applying Anaerobic Sealant

Clean all gasket residue from mating surfaces. Surfaces must be clean and free of oil and dirt. Remove all gasket material from blind attaching holes, as it can cause a "hydraulic" effect and affect bolt torque.

Apply anaerobic sealant in a 1 mm or less (0.04 in.) bead to one sealing surface. Circle all mounting holes. Torque mating parts within 15 minutes after application.

GALVANIC CORROSION

A chemical reaction occurs whenever two different types of metal are joined by an electrical conductor and immersed in an electrolyte. Electrons transfer from one metal to the other through the electrolyte and return through the conductor.

The hardware on a boat is made of many different types of metal. The boat hull acts as a conductor between the metals. Even if the hull is wooden or fiberglass, the slightest film of water (electrolyte) within the hull provides conductivity. This combination creates a good environment for electron flow (**Figure 17**). Unfortunately, this electron flow results in galvanic corrosion of the metal involved, causing one of the metals to be corroded or eaten away by the process. The amount of electron flow (and, therefore, the amount of corrosion) depends on several factors:

a. The types of metal involved.

b. The efficiency of the conductor.

c. The strength of the electrolyte.

Metals

The chemical composition of the metals used in marine equipment has a significant effect on the amount and speed of galvanic corrosion. Certain metals are more resistant to corrosion than others. These electrically negative metals are commonly called "noble;" they act as the cathode in any reaction. Metals that are more subject to corrosion are electrically positive; they act as the anode in a reaction. The more noble metals include titanium, 18-8 stainless steel and nickel. Less noble metals include zinc, aluminum and magnesium. Galvanic corrosion

becomes more severe as the difference in electrical potential between the two metals increases.

In some cases, galvanic corrosion can occur within a single piece of metal. Common brass is a mixture of zinc and copper, and, when immersed in an electrolyte, the zinc portion of the mixture will corrode away as reaction occurs between the zinc and the copper particles.

Conductors

The hull of the boat often acts as the conductor between different types of metal. Marine equipment, such as an outboard motor or stern drive unit, can also act as the conductor. Large masses of metal, firmly connected together, are more efficient conductors than water. Rubber mountings and vinyl-based paint can act as insulators between pieces of metal.

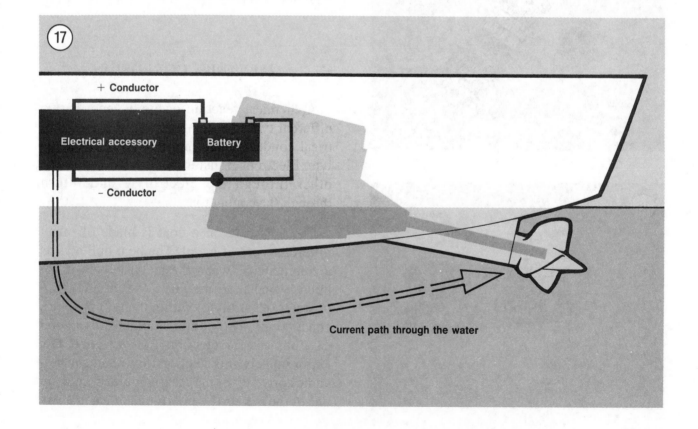

Electrolyte

The water in which a boat operates acts as the electrolyte for the galvanic corrosion process. The better a conductor the electrolyte is, the more severe and rapid the corrosion.

Cold, clean freshwater is the poorest electrolyte. As water temperature increases, its conductivity increases. Pollutants will increase conductivity; brackish or saltwater is also an efficient electrolyte. This is one of the reasons that most manufacturers recommend a freshwater flush for marine equipment after operation in saltwater, polluted or brackish water.

PROTECTION FROM GALVANIC CORROSION

Because of the environment in which marine equipment must operate, it is practically impossible to totally prevent galvanic corrosion. There are several ways by which the process can be slowed. After taking these precautions, the next step is to "fool" the process into occurring only where *you* want it to occur. This is the role of sacrificial anodes and impressed current systems.

Slowing Corrosion

Some simple precautions can help reduce the amount of corrosion taking place outside the hull. These are *not* a substitute for the corrosion protection methods discussed under *Sacrificial Anodes* and *Impressed Current Systems* in this chapter, but they can help these protection methods do their job.

Use fasteners of a metal more noble than the part they are fastening. If corrosion occurs, the larger equipment will suffer but the fastener will be protected. Because fasteners are usually very small in comparison to the equipment being fastened, the equipment can survive the loss of

material. If the fastener were to corrode instead of the equipment, major problems could arise.

Keep all painted surfaces in good condition. If paint is scraped off and bare metal exposed, corrosion will rapidly increase. Use a vinyl- or plastic-based paint, which acts as an electrical insulator.

Be careful when using metal-based antifouling paints. These should not be applied to metal parts of the boat, outboard motor or stern drive unit or they will actually react with the equipment, causing corrosion between the equipment and the layer of paint. Organic-based paints are available for use on metal surfaces.

Where a corrosion protection device is used, remember that it must be immersed in the electrolyte along with the rest of the boat to have any effect. If you raise the power unit out of the water when the boat is docked, any anodes on the power unit will be removed from the corrosion cycle and will not protect the rest of the equipment that is still immersed. Also, such corrosion protection devices must not be painted because this would insulate them from the corrosion process.

Any change in the boat's equipment, such as the installation of a new stainless steel propeller, will change the electrical potential and could cause increased corrosion. Keep in mind that when you add new equipment or change materials, you should review your corrosion protection system to be sure it is up to the job.

Sacrificial Anodes

Anodes are usually made of zinc, a far from noble metal. Sacrificial anodes are specially designed to do nothing but corrode. Properly fastening such pieces to the boat will cause them to act as the anode in *any* galvanic reaction that occurs; any other metal present will act as the cathode and will not be damaged.

Anodes must be used properly to be effective. Simply fastening pieces of zinc to your boat in random locations won't do the job.

You must determine how much anode surface area is required to adequately protect the equipment's surface area. A good starting point is provided by Military Specification MIL-A-818001, which states that one square inch of new anode will protect either:

a. 800 square inches of freshly painted steel.
b. 250 square inches of bare steel or bare aluminum alloy.
c. 100 square inches of copper or copper alloy.

This rule is for a boat at rest. When underway, more anode area is required to protect the same equipment surface area.

The anode must be fastened so that it has good electrical contact with the metal to be protected. If possible, the anode can be attached directly to the other metal. If that is not possible, the entire network of metal parts in the boat should be electrically bonded together so that all pieces are protected.

Good quality anodes have inserts of some other metal around the fastener holes. Otherwise, the anode could erode away around the fastener. The anode can then become loose or even fall off, removing all protection.

Another Military Specification (MIL-A-18001) defines the type of alloy preferred that will corrode at a uniform rate without forming a crust that could reduce its efficiency after a time.

Impressed Current Systems

An impressed current system can be installed on any boat that has a battery. The system consists of an anode, a control box and a sensor. The anode in this system is coated with a very noble metal, such as platinum, so that it is almost corrosion-free and will last indefinitely. The sensor, under the boat's waterline, monitors the potential for corrosion. When it senses that

corrosion could be occurring, it transmits this information to the control box.

The control box connects the boat's battery to the anode. When the sensor signals the need, the control box applies positive battery voltage to the anode. Current from the battery flows from the anode to all other metal parts of the boat, no matter how noble or non-noble these parts may be. This battery current takes the place of any galvanic current flow.

Only a very small amount of battery current is needed to counteract galvanic corrosion. Manufacturers estimate that it would take two or three months of constant use to drain a typical marine battery, assuming the battery is never recharged.

An impressed current system is more expensive to install than simple anodes but, considering its low maintenance requirements and the excellent protection it provides, the long-term cost may actually be lower.

PROPELLERS

The propeller is the final link between the boat's drive system and the water. A perfectly

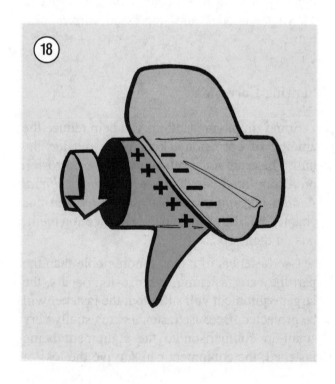

maintained engine and hull are useless if the propeller is the wrong type or has been allowed to deteriorate. Although propeller selection for a specific situation is beyond the scope of this book, the following information on propeller construction and design will allow you to discuss the subject intelligently with your marine dealer.

How a Propeller Works

As the curved blades of a propeller rotate through the water, a high-pressure area is created on one side of the blade and a low-pressure area exists on the other side of the blade (**Figure 18**). The propeller moves toward the low-pressure area, carrying the boat with it.

Propeller Parts

Although a propeller may be a one-piece unit, it is made up of several different parts (**Figure 19**). Variations in the design of these parts make different propellers suitable for different jobs.

The blade tip is the point on the blade farthest from the center of the propeller hub. The blade tip separates the leading edge from the trailing edge.

The leading edge is the edge of the blade nearest to the boat. During normal rotation, this is the area of the blade that first cuts through the water.

The trailing edge is the edge of the blade farthest from the boat.

The blade face is the surface of the blade that faces away from the boat. During normal rotation, high pressure exists on this side of the blade.

The blade back is the surface of the blade that faces toward the boat. During normal rotation, low pressure exists on this side of the blade.

The cup is a small curve or lip on the trailing edge of the blade.

The hub is the central portion of the propeller. It connects the blades to the propeller shaft (part of the boat's drive system). On some drive systems, engine exhaust is routed through the hub; in this case, the hub is made up of an outer and an inner portion, connected by ribs.

The diffuser ring is used on through-hub exhaust models to prevent exhaust gases from entering the blade area.

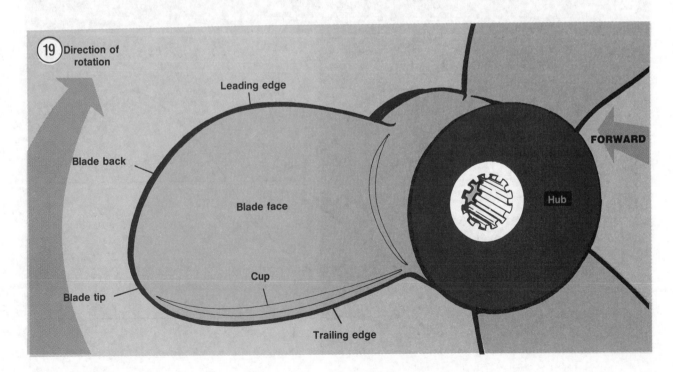

(19) Direction of rotation

Leading edge

FORWARD

Blade back

Blade face

Hub

Cup

Blade tip

Trailing edge

Propeller Design

Changes in length, angle, thickness and material of propeller parts make different propellers suitable for different situations.

Diameter

Propeller diameter is the distance from the center of the hub to the blade tip, multiplied by

2. That is, it is the diameter of the circle formed by the blade tips during propeller rotation (**Figure 20**).

Pitch and rake

Propeller pitch and rake describe the placement of the blade in relation to the hub (**Figure 21**).

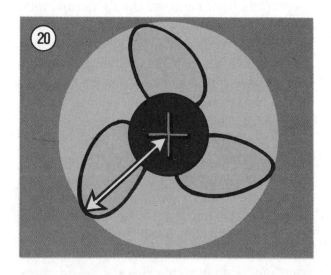

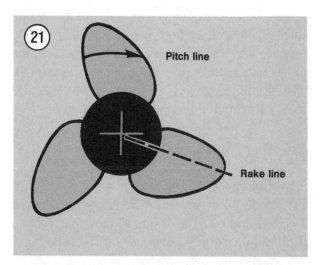

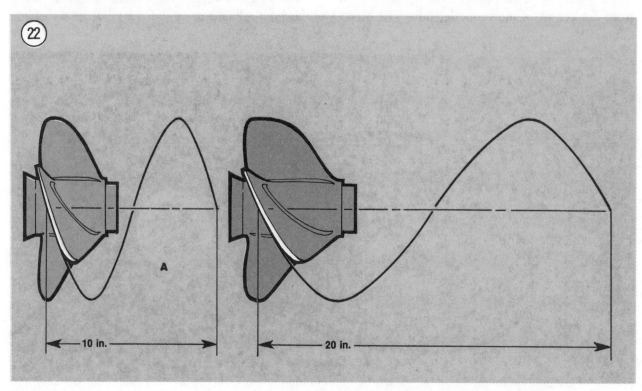

Pitch is expressed by the theoretical distance that the propeller would travel in one revolution. In A, **Figure 22**, the propeller would travel 10 inches in one revolution. In B, **Figure 22**, the propeller would travel 20 inches in one revolution. This distance is only theoretical; during actual operation, the propeller achieves about 80% of its rated travel.

Propeller blades can be constructed with constant pitch (**Figure 23**) or progressive pitch (**Figure 24**). Progressive pitch starts low at the leading edge and increases toward to trailing edge. The propeller pitch specification is the average of the pitch across the entire blade.

Blade rake is specified in degrees and is measured along a line from the center of the hub to the blade tip. A blade that is perpendicular to the hub (A, **Figure 25**) has 0° of rake. A blade that is angled from perpendicular (B, **Figure 25**) has a rake expressed by its difference from perpen-

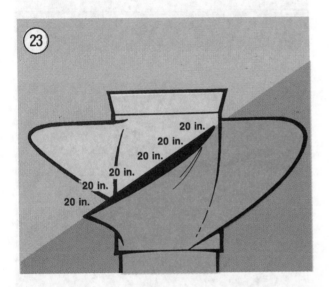

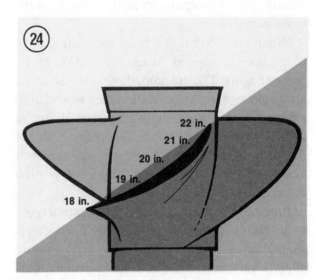

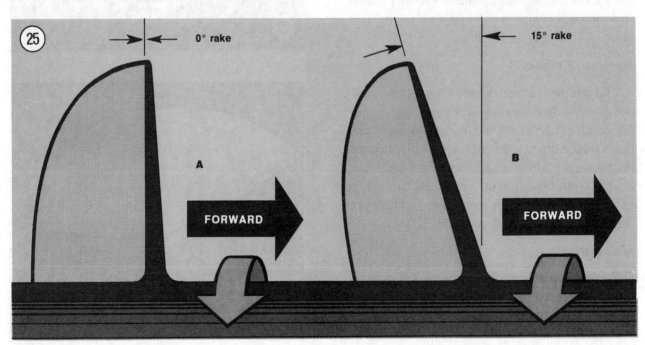

dicular. Most propellers have rakes ranging from 0-20°.

Blade thickness

Blade thickness is not uniform at all points along the blade. For efficiency, blades should be as thin as possible at all points while retaining enough strength to move the boat. Blades tend to be thicker where they meet the hub and thinner at the blade tip (**Figure 26**). This is to support the heavier loads at the hub section of the blade. This thickness is dependent on the strength of the material used.

When cut along a line from the leading edge to the trailing edge in the central portion of the blade (**Figure 27**), the propeller blade resembles an airplane wing. The blade face, where high pressure exists during normal rotation, is almost flat. The blade back, where low pressure exists during normal rotation, is curved, with the thinnest portions at the edges and the thickest portion at the center.

Propellers that run only partially submerged, as in racing applications, may have a wedge-shaped cross-section (**Figure 28**). The leading edge is very thin; the blade thickness increases toward the trailing edge, where it is the thickest. If a propeller such as this is run totally submerged, it is very inefficient.

Number of blades

The number of blades used on a propeller is a compromise between efficiency and vibration. A one-blade propeller would be the most efficient, but it would also create high levels of vibration. As blades are added, efficiency decreases, but so do vibration levels. Most propellers have three blades, representing the most practical trade-off between efficiency and vibration.

Material

Propeller materials are chosen for strength, corrosion resistance and economy. Stainless steel, aluminum and bronze are the most commonly used materials. Bronze is quite strong but

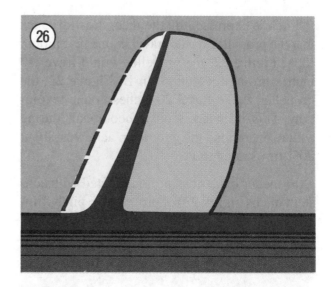

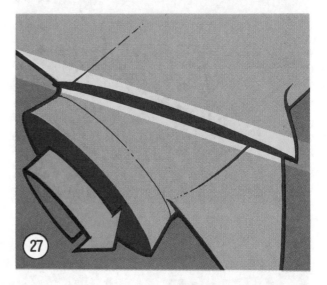

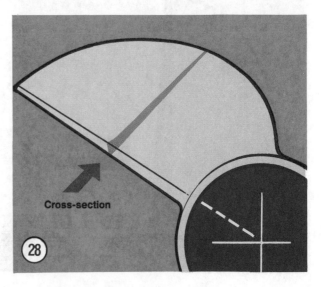

Cross-section

rather expensive. Stainless steel is more common than bronze because of its combination of strength and lower cost. Aluminum alloys are the least expensive but usually lack the strength of steel. Plastic propellers may be used in some low horsepower applications.

Direction of rotation

Propellers are made for both right-hand and left-hand rotation although right-hand is the most commonly used. When seen from behind the boat in forward motion, a right-hand propeller turns clockwise and a left-hand propeller turns counterclockwise. Off the boat, you can tell the difference by observing the angle of the blades (**Figure 29**). A right-hand propeller's blades slant from the upper left to the lower right; a left-hand propeller's blades are the opposite.

Cavitation and Ventilation

Cavitation and ventilation are *not* interchangeable terms; they refer to two distinct problems encountered during propeller operation.

To understand cavitation, you must first understand the relationship between pressure and the boiling point of water. At sea level, water will boil at 212° F. As pressure increases, such as within an engine's closed cooling system, the boiling point of water increases—it will boil at some temperature higher than 212° F. The opposite is also true. As pressure decreases, water will boil at a temperature lower than 212° F. If pressure drops low enough, water will boil at typical ambient temperatures of 50-60° F.

We have said that, during normal propeller operation, low-pressure exists on the blade back. Normally, the pressure does not drop low enough for boiling to occur. However, poor blade design

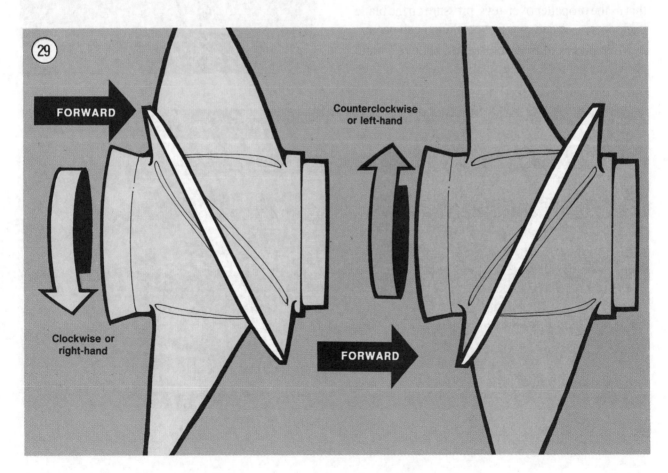

FORWARD

Counterclockwise or left-hand

Clockwise or right-hand

FORWARD

or selection, or blade damage can cause an unusual pressure drop on a small area of the blade (**Figure 30**). Boiling can occur in this small area. As the water boils, air bubbles form. As the boiling water passes to a higher pressure area of the blade, the boiling stops and the bubbles collapse. The collapsing bubbles release enough energy to erode the surface of the blade.

This entire process of pressure drop, boiling and bubble collapse is called "cavitation." The damage caused by the collapsing bubbles is called a "cavitation burn." It is important to remember that cavitation is caused by a decrease in pressure, *not* an increase in temperature.

Ventilation is not as complex a process as cavitation. Ventilation refers to air entering the blade area, either from above the surface of the water or from a through-hub exhaust system. As the blades meet the air, the propeller momentarily over-revs, losing most of its thrust. An added complication is that as the propeller over-revs, pressure on the blade back decreases and massive cavitation can occur.

Most pieces of marine equipment have a plate above the propeller area designed to keep surface air from entering the blade area (**Figure 31**). This plate is correctly called an "antiventilation plate," although you will often *see* it called an "anticavitation plate." Through hub exhaust systems also have specially designed hubs to keep exhaust gases from entering the blade area.

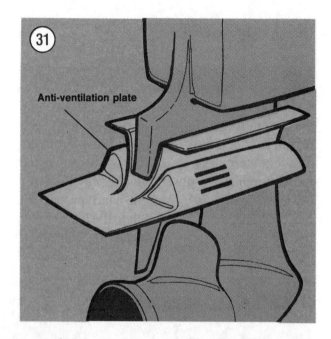

Anti-ventilation plate

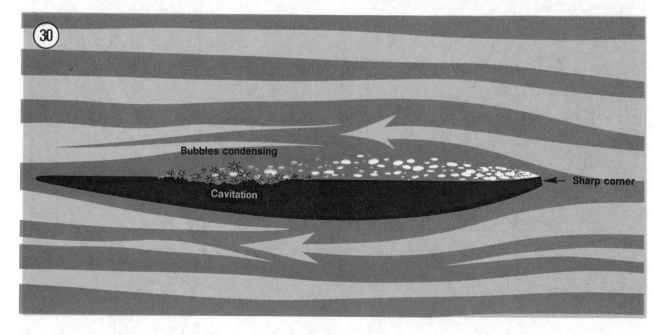

Bubbles condensing

Cavitation

Sharp corner

Chapter Two

Tools and Techniques

This chapter describes the common tools required for marine equipment repairs and troubleshooting. Techniques that will make your work easier and more effective are also described. Some of the procedures in this book require special skills or expertise; in some cases, you are better off entrusting the job to a dealer or qualified specialist.

SAFETY FIRST

Professional mechanics can work for years and never suffer a serious injury. If you follow a few rules of common sense and safety, you too can enjoy many safe hours servicing your marine equipment. If you ignore these rules, you can hurt yourself or damage the equipment.

1. Never use gasoline as a cleaning solvent.
2. Never smoke or use a torch near flammable liquids, such as cleaning solvent. If you are working in your home garage, remember that your home gas appliances have pilot lights.
3. Never smoke or use a torch in an area where batteries are being charged. Highly explosive hydrogen gas is formed during the charging process.

4. Use the proper size wrenches to avoid damage to fasteners and injury to yourself.
5. When loosening a tight or stuck fastener, think of what would happen if the wrench should slip. Protect yourself accordingly.
6. Keep your work area clean, uncluttered and well lighted.
7. Wear safety goggles during all operations involving drilling, grinding or the use of a cold chisel.
8. Never use worn tools.
9. Keep a Coast Guard approved fire extinguisher handy. Be sure it is rated for gasoline (Class B) and electrical (Class C) fires.

BASIC HAND TOOLS

A number of tools are required to maintain marine equipment. You may already have some of these tools for home or car repairs. There are also tools made especially for marine equipment repairs; these you will have to purchase. In any case, a wide variety of quality tools will make repairs easier and more effective.

Keep your tools clean and in a tool box. Keep them organized with the sockets and related drives together, the open end and box wrenches together, etc. After using a tool, wipe off dirt and grease with a clean cloth and place the tool in its correct place.

The following tools are required to perform virtually any repair job. Each tool is described and the recommended size given for starting a tool collection. Additional tools and some duplications may be added as you become more familiar with the equipment. You may need all standard U.S. size tools, all metric size tools or a mixture of both.

Screwdrivers

The screwdriver is a very basic tool, but if used improperly, it will do more damage than good. The slot on a screw has a definite dimension and shape. A screwdriver must be selected to conform with that shape. Use a small screwdriver for small screws and a large one for large screws or the screw head will be damaged.

Two types of screwdriver are commonly required: a common (flat-blade) screwdriver (**Figure 1**) and Phillips screwdrivers (**Figure 2**).

Screwdrivers are available in sets, which often include an assortment of common and Phillips blades. If you buy them individually, buy at least the following:

a. Common screwdriver—5/16 × 6 in. blade.
b. Common screwdriver—3/8 × 12 in. blade
c. Phillips screwdriver—size 2 tip, 6 in. blade.

Use screwdrivers only for driving screws. Never use a screwdriver for prying or chiseling. Do not try to remove a Phillips or Allen head screw with a common screwdriver; you can damage the head so that the proper tool will be unable to remove it.

Keep screwdrivers in the proper condition and they will last longer and perform better. Always keep the tip of a common screwdriver in good condition. **Figure 3** shows how to grind the tip to the proper shape if it becomes damaged. Note the parallel sides of the tip.

Pliers

Pliers come in a wide range of types and sizes. Pliers are useful for cutting, bending and crimping. They should never be used to cut hardened objects or to turn bolts or nuts. **Figure 4** shows several types of pliers.

Each type of pliers has a specialized function. General purpose pliers are used mainly for holding things and for bending. Locking pliers are used as pliers or to hold objects very tightly, like a vise. Needlenose pliers are used to hold or bend small objects. Adjustable or slip-joint pliers can

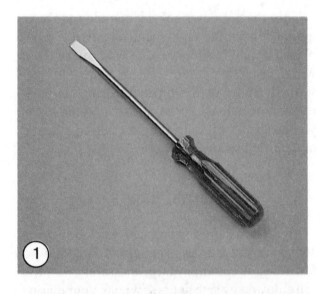

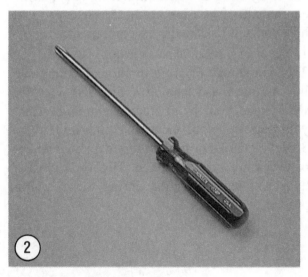

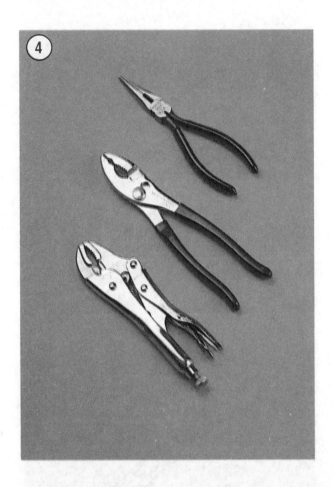

be adjusted to hold various sizes of objects; the jaws remain parallel to grip around objects such as pipe or tubing. There are many more types of pliers. The ones described here are the most commonly used.

Box and Open-end Wrenches

Box and open-end wrenches are available in sets or separately in a variety of sizes. See **Figure 5** and **Figure 6**. The number stamped near the end refers to the distance between two parallel flats on the hex head bolt or nut.

Box wrenches are usually superior to open-end wrenches. An open-end wrench grips the nut on only two flats. Unless it fits well, it may slip and round off the points on the nut. The box wrench grips all 6 flats. Both 6-point and 12-point openings on box wrenches are available. The 6-point gives superior holding power; the 12-point allows a shorter swing.

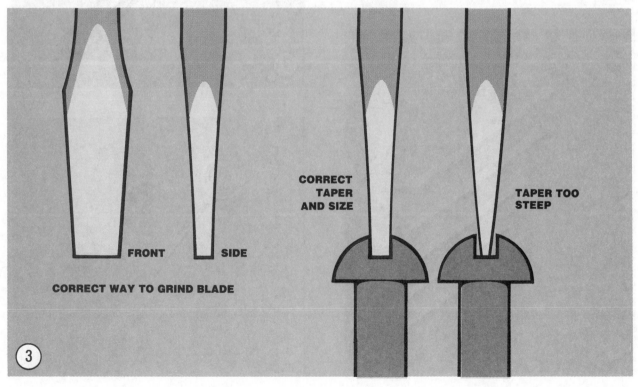

FRONT   SIDE

CORRECT WAY TO GRIND BLADE

CORRECT TAPER AND SIZE

TAPER TOO STEEP

Combination wrenches, which are open on one side and boxed on the other, are also available. Both ends are the same size.

Adjustable Wrenches

An adjustable wrench can be adjusted to fit nearly any nut or bolt head. See **Figure 7**. However, it can loosen and slip, causing damage to the nut and maybe to your knuckles. Use an adjustable wrench only when other wrenches are not available.

Adjustable wrenches come in sizes ranging from 4-18 in. overall. A 6 or 8 in. wrench is recommended as an all-purpose wrench.

Socket Wrenches

This type is undoubtedly the fastest, safest and most convenient to use. See **Figure 8**. Sockets, which attach to a suitable handle, are available with 6-point or 12-point openings and use 1/4, 3/8 and 3/4 inch drives. The drive size indicates

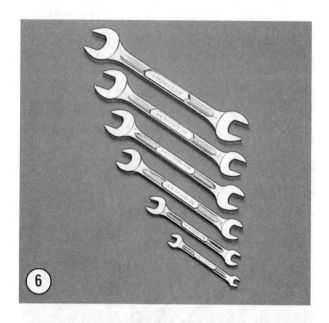

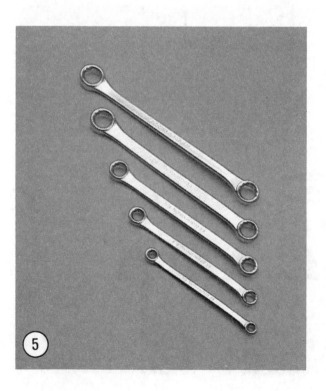

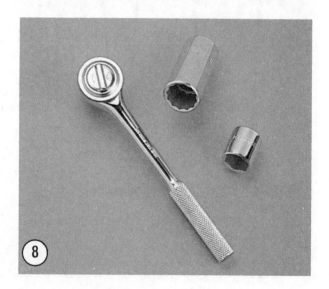

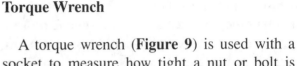

the size of the square hole that mates with the ratchet or flex handle.

Torque Wrench

A torque wrench (**Figure 9**) is used with a socket to measure how tight a nut or bolt is installed. They come in a wide price range and with either 3/8 or 1/2 in. square drive. The drive size indicates the size of the square drive that mates with the socket. Purchase one that measures up to 150 ft.-lb. (203 N•m).

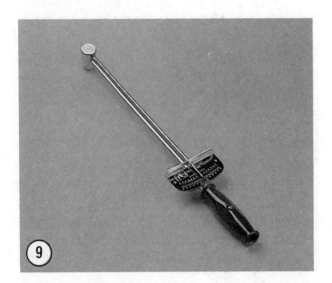

Impact Driver

This tool (**Figure 10**) makes removal of tight fasteners easy and eliminates damage to bolts and screw slots. Impact drivers and interchangeable bits are available at most large hardware and auto parts stores.

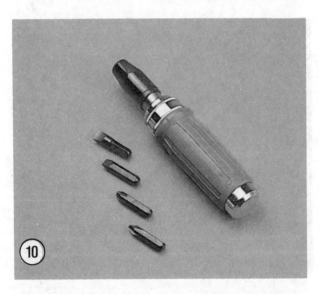

Circlip Pliers

Circlip pliers (sometimes referred to as snapring pliers) are necessary to remove circlips. See **Figure 11**. Circlip pliers usually come with several different size tips; many designs can be switched from internal type to external type.

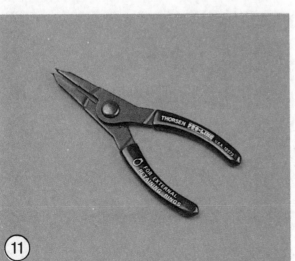

Hammers

The correct hammer is necessary for repairs. Use only a hammer with a face (or head) of rubber or plastic or the soft-faced type that is filled with buckshot (**Figure 12**). These are sometimes necessary in engine tear-downs. *Never* use a metal-faced hammer as severe damage will result in most cases. You can always produce the same amount of force with a soft-faced hammer.

Feeler Gauge

This tool has either flat or wire measuring gauges (**Figure 13**). Wire gauges are used to measure spark plug gap; flat gauges are used for all other measurements. A non-magnetic (brass) gauge may be specified when working around magnetized parts.

Other Special Tools

Some procedures require special tools; these are identified in the appropriate chapter. Unless otherwise specified, the part number used in this book to identify a special tool is the marine equipment manufacturer's part number.

Special tools can usually be purchased through your marine equipment dealer. Some can be made locally by a machinist, often at a much lower price. You may find certain special tools at tool rental dealers. Don't use makeshift tools if you can't locate the correct special tool; you will probably cause more damage than good.

TEST EQUIPMENT

Multimeter

This instrument (**Figure 14**) is invaluable for electrical system troubleshooting and service. It combines a voltmeter, an ohmmeter and an ammeter into one unit, so it is often called a VOM.

Two types of multimeter are available, analog and digital. Analog meters have a moving needle with marked bands indicating the volt, ohm and amperage scales. The digital meter (DVOM) is ideally suited for troubleshooting because it is easy to read, more accurate than analog, contains internal overload protection, is auto-ranging (analog meters must be recalibrated each time the scale is changed) and has automatic polarity compensation.

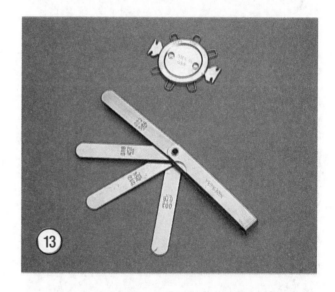

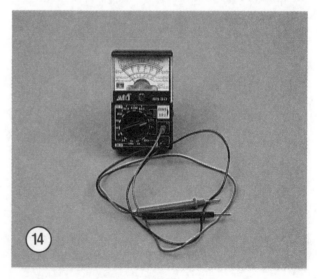

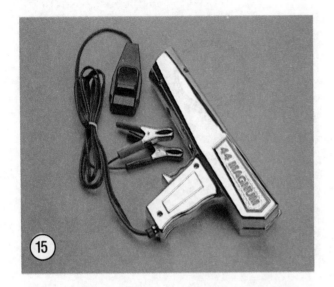

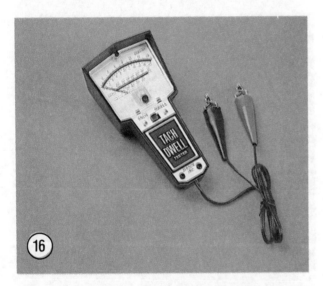

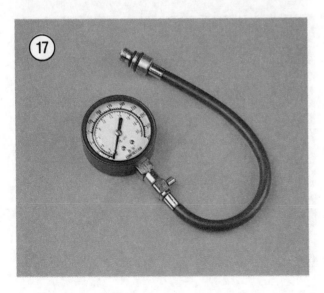

Strobe Timing Light

This instrument is necessary for dynamic tuning (setting ignition timing while the engine is running). By flashing a light at the precise instant the spark plug fires, the position of the timing mark can be seen. The flashing light makes a moving mark appear to stand still opposite a stationary mark.

Suitable lights range from inexpensive neon bulb types to powerful xenon strobe lights. See **Figure 15**. A light with an inductive pickup is best because it eliminates any possible damage to ignition wiring.

Tachometer/Dwell Meter

A portable tachometer is necessary for tuning. See **Figure 16**. Ignition timing and carburetor adjustments must be performed at the specified idle speed. The best instrument for this purpose is one with a low range of 0-1000 or 0-2000 rpm and a high range of 0-6000 rpm. Extended range (0-6000 or 0-8000 rpm) instruments lack accuracy at lower speeds. The instrument should be capable of detecting changes of 25 rpm on the low range.

A dwell meter is often combined with a tachometer. Dwell meters are used with breaker point ignition systems to measure the amount of time the points remain closed during engine operation.

Compression Gauge

This tool (**Figure 17**) measures the amount of pressure present in the engine's combustion chamber during the compression stroke. This indicates general engine condition. Compression readings can be interpreted along with vacuum gauge readings to pinpoint specific engine mechanical problems.

The easiest type to use has screw-in adapters that fit into the spark plug holes. Press-in rubber-tipped types are also available.

Vacuum Gauge

The vacuum gauge (**Figure 18**) measures the intake manifold vacuum created by the engine's intake stroke. Manifold and valve problems (on 4-stroke engines) can be identified by interpreting the readings. When combined with compression gauge readings, other engine problems can be diagnosed.

Some vacuum gauges can also be used as fuel pressure gauges to trace fuel system problems.

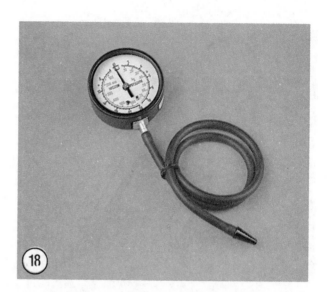

Hydrometer

Battery electrolyte specific gravity is measured with a hydrometer (**Figure 19**). The specific gravity of the electrolyte indicates the battery's state of charge. The best type has automatic temperature compensation; otherwise, you must calculate the compensation yourself.

Precision Measuring Tools

Various tools are needed to make precision measurements. A dial indicator (**Figure 20**), for example, is used to determine run-out of rotating parts and end play of parts assemblies. A dial indicator can also be used to precisely measure piston position in relation to top dead center; some engines require this measurement for ignition timing adjustment.

Vernier calipers (**Figure 21**) and micrometers (**Figure 22**) are other precision measuring tools used to determine the size of parts (such as piston diameter).

Precision measuring equipment must be stored, handled and used carefully or it will not remain accurate.

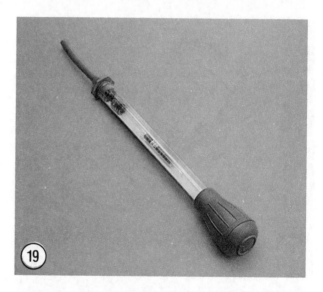

SERVICE HINTS

Most of the service procedures covered in this manual are straightforward and can be performed by anyone reasonably handy with tools.

It is suggested, however, that you consider your own skills and toolbox carefully before attempting any operation involving major disassembly of the engine or gearcase.

Some operations, for example, require the use of a press. It would be wiser to have these performed by a shop equipped for such work, rather than trying to do the job yourself with makeshift equipment. Other procedures require precise measurements. Unless you have the skills and

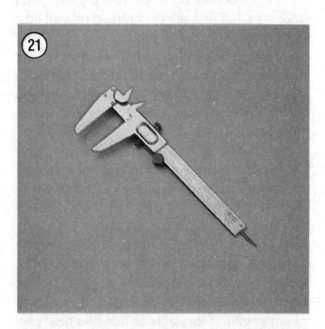

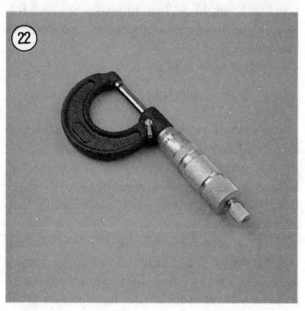

equipment required, it would be better to have a qualified repair shop make the measurements for you.

Preparation for Disassembly

Repairs go much faster and easier if the equipment is clean before you begin work. There are special cleaners, such as Gunk or Bel-Ray Degreaser, for washing the engine and related parts. Just spray or brush on the cleaning solution, let it stand, then rinse away with a garden hose. Clean all oily or greasy parts with cleaning solvent as you remove them.

> *WARNING*
> *Never use gasoline as a cleaning agent. It presents an extreme fire hazard. Be sure to work in a well-ventilated area when using cleaning solvent. Keep a Coast Guard approved fire extinguisher, rated for gasoline fires, handy in any case.*

Much of the labor charged for repairs made by dealers is for the removal and disassembly of other parts to reach the defective unit. It is frequently possible to perform the preliminary operations yourself and then take the defective unit in to the dealer for repair.

If you decide to tackle the job yourself, read the entire section in this manual that pertains to it, making sure you have identified the proper one. Study the illustrations and text until you have a good idea of what is involved in completing the job satisfactorily. If special tools or replacement parts are required, make arrangements to get them before you start. It is frustrating and time-consuming to get partly into a job and then be unable to complete it.

Disassembly Precautions

During disassembly of parts, keep a few general precautions in mind. Force is rarely needed to get things apart. If parts are a tight fit, such as a bearing in a case, there is usually a tool designed to separate them. Never use a screwdriver to pry apart parts with machined surfaces (such as cylinder heads and crankcases). You will mar the surfaces and end up with leaks.

Make diagrams (or take an instant picture) wherever similar-appearing parts are found. For example, head and crankcase bolts are often not the same length. You may think you can remember where everything came from, but mistakes are costly. There is also the possibility you may be sidetracked and not return to work for days or even weeks. In the interval, carefully laid out parts may have been disturbed.

Cover all openings after removing parts to keep small parts, dirt or other contamination from entering.

Tag all similar internal parts for location and direction. All internal components should be reinstalled in the same location and direction from which removed. Record the number and thickness of any shims as they are removed. Small parts, such as bolts, can be identified by placing them in plastic sandwich bags. Seal and label them with masking tape.

Wiring should be tagged with masking tape and marked as each wire is removed. Again, do not rely on memory alone.

Protect finished surfaces from physical damage or corrosion. Keep gasoline off painted surfaces.

Assembly Precautions

No parts, except those assembled with a press fit, require unusual force during assembly. If a part is hard to remove or install, find out why before proceeding.

When assembling two parts, start all fasteners, then tighten evenly in an alternating or crossing pattern if no specific tightening sequence is given.

When assembling parts, be sure all shims and washers are installed exactly as they came out.

Whenever a rotating part butts against a stationary part, look for a shim or washer. Use new gaskets if there is any doubt about the condition of the old ones. Unless otherwise specified, a thin coat of oil on gaskets may help them seal effectively.

Heavy grease can be used to hold small parts in place if they tend to fall out during assembly. However, keep grease and oil away from electrical components.

High spots may be sanded off a piston with sandpaper, but fine emery cloth and oil will do a much more professional job.

Carbon can be removed from the cylinder head, the piston crown and the exhaust port with a dull screwdriver. *Do not* scratch either surface. Wipe off the surface with a clean cloth when finished.

The carburetor is best cleaned by disassembling it and soaking the parts in a commercial carburetor cleaner. Never soak gaskets and rubber parts in these cleaners. Never use wire to clean out jets and air passages; they are easily damaged. Use compressed air to blow out the carburetor *after* the float has been removed.

Take your time and do the job right. Do not forget that the break-in procedure on a newly rebuilt engine is the same as that of a new one. Use the break-in oil recommendations and follow other instructions given in your owner's manual.

SPECIAL TIPS

Because of the extreme demands placed on marine equipment, several points should be kept in mind when performing service and repair. The following items are general suggestions that may improve the overall life of the machine and help avoid costly failures.

1. Unless otherwise specified, use a locking compound, such as Loctite Threadlocker, on all bolts and nuts, even if they are secured with lockwashers. Be sure to use the specified grade

of thread locking compound. A screw or bolt lost from an engine cover or bearing retainer could easily cause serious and expensive damage before its loss is noticed.

When applying thread locking compound, use a small amount. If too much is used, it can work its way down the threads and stick parts together that were not meant to be stuck together.

Keep a tube of thread locking compound in your tool box; when used properly, it is cheap insurance.

2. Use a hammer-driven impact tool to remove and install screws and bolts. These tools help prevent the rounding off of bolt heads and screw slots and ensure a tight installation.

3. When straightening the fold-over type lockwasher, use a wide-blade chisel, such as an old and dull wood chisel. Such a tool provides a better purchase on the folded tab, making straightening easier.

4. When installing the fold-over type lockwasher, always use a new washer if possible. If a new washer is not available, always fold over a part of the washer that has not been previously folded. Reusing the same fold may cause the washer to break, resulting in the loss of its locking ability and a loose piece of metal adrift in the engine.

When folding the washer, start the fold with a screwdriver and finish it with a pair of pliers. If a punch is used to make the fold, the fold may be too sharp, thereby increasing the chances of the washer breaking under stress.

These washers are relatively inexpensive and it is suggested that you keep several of each size in your tool box for repairs.

5. When replacing missing or broken fasteners (bolts, nuts and screws), always use authorized replacement parts. They are specially hardened for each application. The wrong 50-cent bolt could easily cause serious and expensive damage.

6. When installing gaskets, always use authorized replacement gaskets *without* sealer, unless designated. Many gaskets are designed to swell when they come in contact with oil. Gasket sealer will prevent the gaskets from swelling as intended and can result in oil leaks. Authorized replacement gaskets are cut from material of the precise thickness needed. Installation of a too thick or too thin gasket in a critical area could cause equipment damage.

MECHANIC'S TECHNIQUES

Removing Frozen Fasteners

When a fastener rusts and cannot be removed, several methods may be used to loosen it. First, apply penetrating oil, such as Liquid Wrench or WD-40 (available at any hardware or auto supply store). Apply it liberally and allow it penetrate for 10-15 minutes. Tap the fastener several times with a small hammer; do not hit it hard enough to cause damage. Reapply the penetrating oil if necessary.

For frozen screws, apply penetrating oil as described, then insert a screwdriver in the slot and tap the top of the screwdriver with a hammer. This loosens the rust so the screw can be removed in the normal way. If the screw head is too chewed up to use a screwdriver, grip the head with locking pliers and twist the screw out.

Avoid applying heat unless specifically instructed because it may melt, warp or remove the temper from parts.

Remedying Stripped Threads

Occasionally, threads are stripped through carelessness or impact damage. Often the threads can be cleaned up by running a tap (for internal threads on nuts) or die (for external threads on bolts) through threads. See **Figure 23**.

Removing Broken Screws or Bolts

When the head breaks off a screw or bolt, several methods are available for removing the remaining portion.

If a large portion of the remainder projects out, try gripping it with vise-grip pliers. If the projecting portion is too small, file it to fit a wrench or cut a slot in it to fit a screwdriver. See **Figure 24**.

If the head breaks off flush, use a screw extractor. To do this, centerpunch the remaining portion of the screw or bolt. Drill a small hole in the screw and tap the extractor into the hole. Back the screw out with a wrench on the extractor. See **Figure 25**.

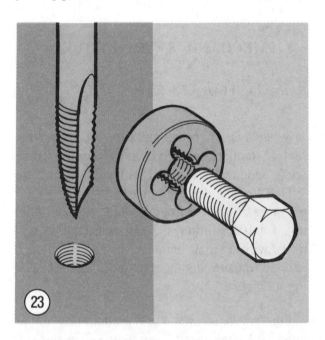

(23)

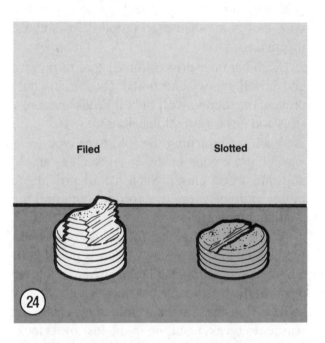

Filed   Slotted

(24)

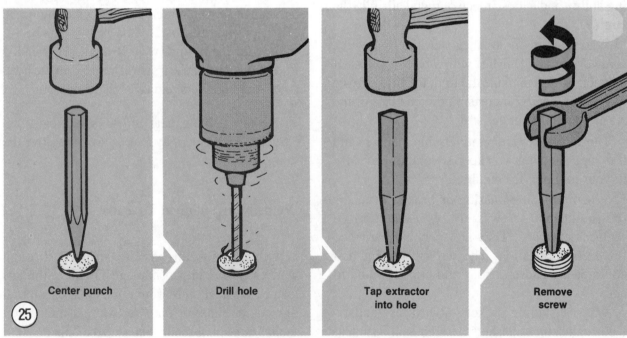

Center punch   Drill hole   Tap extractor into hole   Remove screw

(25)

Chapter Three

Troubleshooting and Testing

All internal combustion engines require ignition, an unrestricted supply of fuel and adequate compression to run. Without any one of these the engine will not run properly or will not run at all. Troubleshooting a problem can be accomplished by keeping it simple and thinking of the basic requirements. Define the symptom as closely as possible to one of the three functions, then isolate the problem.

Expensive equipment and complicated test gear are not needed to determine whether repairs can be attempted at home. A few simple checks could save a large repair bill and lost time. However, do not attempt repairs beyond your abilities. Service departments charge heavily for putting together a disassembled engine that may have been abused.

This chapter provides sections covering test equipment, starting problems, troubleshooting preparation, and systems or component testing.

Table 1 and **Table 2** list troubleshooting tips and a reference number to the correct chapter. **Tables 3-23** list specifications, ignition timing and engine identification. **Tables 1-23** are located at the end of this chapter.

NOTE
This manual provides procedures and specifications for standard products. It may not provide the necessary information if the product has been modified or has aftermarket equipment installed. The use of aftermarket equipment or the modification of the engine can affect engine performance and tuning requirements. For information on aftermarket equipment, consult a dealership that handles such equipment or is familiar with engine modification. If necessary, contact the manufacturer of the aftermarket equipment for information. If installing any aftermarket equipment, keep all instructions with the owner's manual for future reference.

TEST EQUIPMENT

The most common tools used to test components on a Yamaha outboard are the multimeter, pressure/vacuum gauge, fuel pressure gauge, compression gauge and gearcase pressure tester. A description of these tools and other equipment is in Chapter Two. Specific information on the use of this test equipment is provided in this chapter and throughout the manual.

Multimeter

Outboards today use advanced electronic engine control systems that improve the performance, reliability and fuel economy. The multimeter is a very important tool for troubleshooting the electrical system. It is a voltmeter, ohmmeter and ammeter combined into one unit.

A digital multimeter displays the readings on a screen on the meter. An analog multimeter displays readings with a needle on the face of the meter. In most cases, either type of meter can be used. Make sure that the meter has fresh batteries to avoid inaccurate readings and a false diagnosis. Refer to the instructions provided with the meter for features, specifications and specific instructions. Following are procedures for using a typical meter.

Meter functions

Most multimeters measure voltage, resistance and amperage. A LCD screen or the selector dial indicates what function is selected. For voltage, the meter displays voltage or V. For resistance, the meter displays ohms or resistance. For amperage, the meter displays amps. To select the proper function of the meter, refer to the tables that provide the desired test results. Volts, ohms or amps are listed near the specifications.

> *NOTE*
> *To avoid costly errors, always record the meter readings during testing. Note the wires colors, where the leads are connected and the actual readings. Perform the tests twice to verify results before replacing any component. This can save time and unnecessary expense.*

Test range

Before performing a test using the multimeter, determine the scale or range required for the test. Refer to the information provided in the tables for the test specifications. Available ranges on the meter vary by model and manufacturer. Check the instructions provided with the meter for specific instructions.

> *NOTE*
> *Some digital multimeters are automatically scaling and the selection of the range is not necessary. Not all meters provide accurate readings in the millivolt, milliohm and milliamp ranges. Check the instructions provided with the meter.*

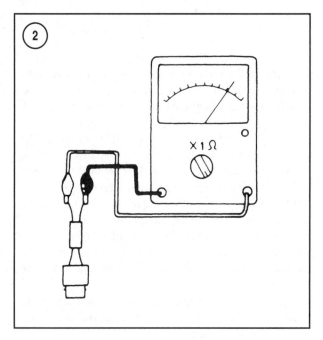

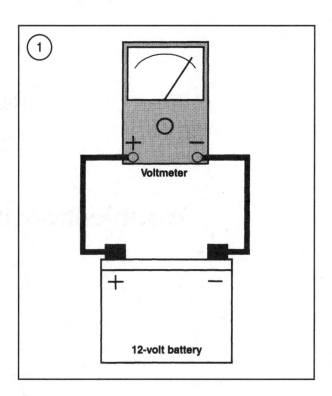

Measuring voltage

When measuring *voltage*, the negative lead is usually connected to the engine ground, negative battery terminal or another specified location (**Figure 1**). The positive lead is usually connected to the positive battery terminal or another specified lead/location. This connection arrange-

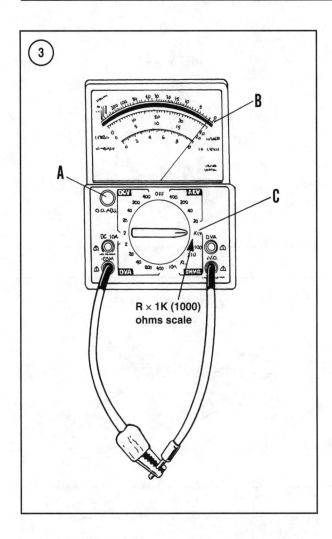

R × 1K (1000)
ohms scale

ment is commonly referred to as a parallel connection. Voltage values are typically used when troubleshooting the ignition system, charging system, starting system, instruments and controls. Voltage is the potential pressure of the current flowing in a circuit.

Measuring peak voltage

Some multimeters are provided with a peak voltage function. This feature allows the meter to measure voltage pulses that peak during a short duration. Most common meters are unable to accurately measure these short duration pulses. The use of the peak voltage adapter, Yamaha part No. YU-39991, gives most meters this capability. This is commonly used to test the ignition system.

> *WARNING*
> *Be extremely cautious when using any meter around high voltage. To avoid electric shock, do not allow the probe portion of the*

test leads to contact any portion of the body. Never perform the test near any source of fuel or vapor. Arcing may ignite the fuel or vapor and cause a fire or explosion.

Measuring ohms

Ohms are the measurement units for the resistance to current flow in a circuit. To measure *resistance*, the multimeter test leads are usually connected in a series connection (**Figure 2**). Resistance tests are generally performed on ignition system components, motor windings, wiring harness, switches and instruments.

Select the required scale and *calibrate* an analog meter before testing. To *calibrate* the meter, connect the two test leads together and rotate the adjusting knob (A, **Figure 3**) until a *0* reading (B, **Figure 3**) on the meter is attained. When an ohm value with a *K* is listed in the specifications, the resistance is 1000 times the displayed numerical value. For example (C, **Figure 3**), R × 1K (1000) would be selected if the specifications were in 1000 ohm increments. Connect the test leads to the specified locations and read the resistance on the meter. An open circuit, or infinity, is indicated if no needle movement is noted or the digital display flashes. Very little or no current can flow in this circuit. A closed circuit or continuity, is indicated if the needle moves all the way to *0*. Current easily flows in this circuit.

> *NOTE*
> *When using a digital multimeter to measure very low resistance values, select the proper scale, then connect the test leads together. A reading other than 0 indicates internal resistance in the meter or test leads. Subtract this value from the reading when testing components to determine the actual resistance in a circuit.*

> *CAUTION*
> *Never measure resistance on a circuit or component connected to the battery or any current. The meter can be permanently damaged.*

Measuring amperage

Amperage is the volume of current flowing in a circuit. To measure *amps*, connect the meter in a series connection. Pay close attention when connecting leads to avoid inaccurate readings or possible damage to engine components. Amperage readings are typically used when troubleshooting the battery charging system or the starting system.

> *WARNING*
> *Be extremely cautious when connecting meter leads to a battery terminal. Batteries may have explosive hydrogen gas in and around them. Never smoke around a battery, or allow any flame or spark to occur near a battery. If testing requires connecting a lead to a battery terminal, make certain that the final connection is made to a component other than the battery terminal. Follow all instructions carefully.*

> *NOTE*
> *Most multimeters cannot read above 10 amps. If the specification lists a value greater than 10 amps, obtain a meter capable of reading the required range(s).*

Checking diodes

A diode is essentially a one-way check valve for electricity. A diode typically allows current to flow through it in one direction only. Although some multimeters are equipped with a diode test function, an ohmmeter is most commonly used to test diodes.

To test a diode, connect the meter to the diode, note the meter reading, the reverse the meter leads. A good diode will have continuity with the meter connected one direction and no continuity with the meter connected in the opposite direction. If continuity or no continuity is noted in both connections, the diode has failed and must be replaced.

Vacuum/Pressure Gauge

Use a vacuum/pressure gauge to test the fuel pump and fuel delivery system. The manufacturer recommends using gauge part No. YB-35956 (**Figure 4**) on 9.9-50 hp models and part No. YU-08030 (**Figure 5**) on 80-100 hp models.

Compression gauge

Use a compression gauge to measure the pressure of the combustion chamber at a specified cranking speed. This chapter includes specific instructions for compression testing.

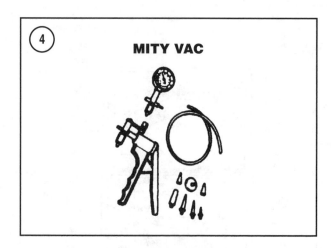

MITY VAC

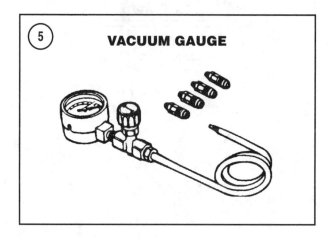

VACUUM GAUGE

YAMAHA SERIAL NUMBER TAG

1. Model name
2. Approval model code
3. Transom height
4. Serial number

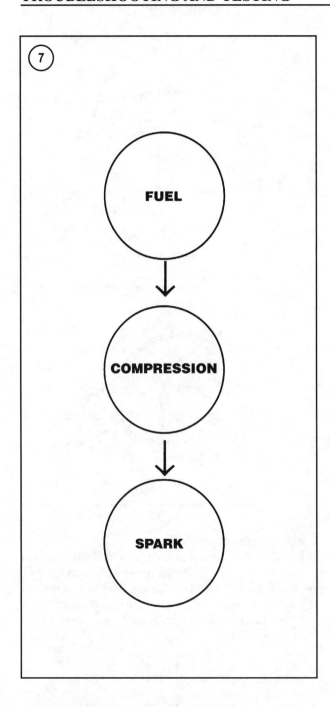

the engine. The model must be correctly identified before performing any service to the engine. In many cases, the tables list specifications by horsepower and/or model name. Identification tags for most models are located on the port side clamp bracket. Refer to **Figure 6** to review the various forms of information on this tag. To identify the horsepower, model name, model code, driveshaft length and starting serial number, refer to **Table 4**. The information provided on the tag is also required when purchasing replacement parts.

Preliminary inspection

Most engine problems can be resolved with a few basic checks. If the problem still exists, check the following tips and refer to **Tables 1** and **Table 2** at the end of this chapter for starting and fuel system troubleshooting. Additional troubleshooting tips are provided in this chapter for the specific system or component.

1. Inspect the engine for loose, corroded, broken/cracked or disconnected wires.
2. Fill the fuel tank with fresh fuel.
3. Check the battery for full charge, and make sure cable connections are secured tightly and free of corrosion.
4. Check for ignition spark at each cylinder using the proper tools.
5. Check spark plug condition and spark gap for correct setting.
6. Check the location of the lanyard switch. Make sure it is in the run position.
7. Make sure the boat hull is free of obstructions.

OPERATING REQUIREMENTS

An internal combustion engine requires an unrestricted supply of fresh fuel, adequate compression and ignition at the correct time (**Figure 7**) to run properly. Without any of requirements, the engine will not run properly, or will not run at all.

STARTING DIFFICULTY

Determining if a starting problem is caused by the fuel, ignition or starting system can be difficult. If the engine cranks normally, consider the starting system to be operating properly. Use a spark checker to determine if the ignition system is capable of producing adequate spark. Inspect the fuel system if the ignition system functions properly, but the engine is hard to start or will not start at all.

Gearcase pressure tester

Use a gearcase pressure tester to find the source of lubricant or water leakage. Procedures for the use of the pressure tester are provided in this chapter.

TROUBLESHOOTING PREPARATION

Before troubleshooting the engine, verify the model name, model number, horsepower and serial number of

Spark Test

1. Connect the ground lead (A, **Figure 8**) to a suitable engine ground.
2. Remove the spark plug(s) (B, **Figure 8**).
3. Attach the spark plug leads to the spark tester (C, **Figure 8**).
4. Crank the engine while observing the spark tester (**Figure 9**). A strong blue spark over a 9 mm (0.035 in.) gap indicates adequate spark.
5. Repeat Steps 1-4 for all cylinders. Install the spark plug(s) and connect the leads when the test is complete. Test the ignition system if the spark is weak or missing on any cylinder. Refer to **Table 1** for fuel system troubleshooting if the ignition system is working properly, but the engine will not start.

> *WARNING*
> *High voltage is present in the ignition system. Never touch wires or connections. Never perform this test in wet conditions. Electric shock can be fatal or can cause serious bodily injury. Never perform electrical testing if fuel or fuel vapor is present as arcing may cause a fire or explosion.*

Checking the Fuel System

Fuel related problems are common on outboard engines. Fuel available today has a relatively short shelf life. Gasoline can lose desirable qualities and become sour if stored for long periods. A sticky or gummy deposit may form in the carburetor and passages as the fuel evaporates. The fuel line and fuel filters may also clog with this deposit. Fuel stored in a tank can become contaminated with water from condensation or other sources. Water will cause the engine to run erratic or not run at all.

If the engine has been stored for a period of time and is difficult to start, check the condition of the fuel. Carefully drain the fuel from the carburetor float bowl into a suitable container. Chapter Six provides illustrations that locate the float bowl drain plugs (**Figure 10**). Contaminated fuel has a unique odor that indicates a problem. Debris, a cloudy appearance or water in the fuel also indicates a problem. If any of these problems are found, dispose of the old fuel in an environmentally safe manner. Contact a marine dealership or automotive repair center for information on proper disposal of fuel. If contaminants are found in the float bowl, clean the entire fuel system. Problems will occur if the entire fuel system is not clean. Replace all filters in the fuel system if contaminants are found in the fuel system. If no fuel drains from the float bowl, inspect the carburetor(s), fuel lines and fuel

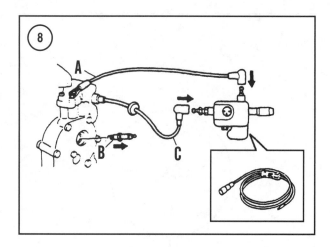

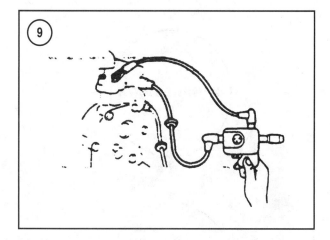

pump. If debris is found in the float bowl, then the needle is probably stuck closed or plugged with debris, and not allowing fuel to get to the carburetor. Carburetor repair procedures are provided in Chapter Six. For a hard-starting problem, check for a faulty enrichment valve, choke valve or electrothermal valve. These components are covered in Chapter Six.

FUEL SYSTEM COMPONENT TESTING

Fuel Pump and Fuel Tank

If the engine surges at higher speeds, there is usually a problem with the fuel pump or the fuel tank. Boats equipped with built-in fuel tanks have antisiphon valves installed by the boat manufacture. The antisiphon valve prevents fuel from being siphoned from the tank into the boat if a fuel line is cut or pinched. These devices are necessary for safety, but can cause problems if they malfunction. To test for a suspected problem with the fuel tank, temporarily run the engine with a portable fuel tank filled

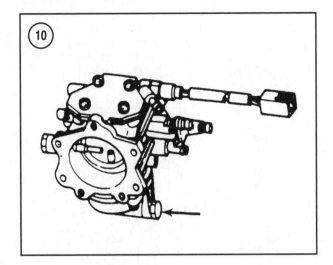

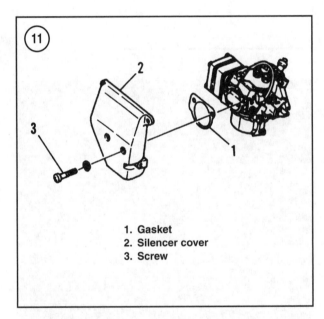

1. Gasket
2. Silencer cover
3. Screw

with fresh fuel. If the problem does not occur, check the fuel tank pickup. Replace the antisiphon valve if it is corroded or plugged.

When there is a problem with the fuel pump, squeeze the primer bulb gently while the problem is occurring. Perform a complete inspection of the fuel pump and fuel lines if the symptom improves when the primer bulb is squeezed. Complete fuel system repair procedures are provided in Chapter Six. Always check for and correct fuel leakage after working with fuel system components.

CAUTION
Never run an outboard without providing cooling water. Use either a test tank or flush/test device. Remove the propeller be-

fore running the engine. Install a test propeller to run the engine in a test tank.

Carburetor Malfunction

An engine that runs rough and smokes excessively usually indicates a rich fuel/air mixture. The typical causes are a flooding carburetor, stuck or closed choke, faulty puddle drain system, faulty enrichment valve or faulty electrothermal valve. The most common cause is a flooding carburetor or improper float level adjustment. A weak ignition spark can also cause rough running and excessive exhaust smoke.

Hesitation during acceleration usually indicates a lean condition.

Flooding carburetor

To check for a flooding carburetor, perform Steps 1-4. Refer to Chapter Six for specific instructions for all models.

1. Remove the attaching screw(s), silencer/cover and gasket (**Figure 11**) from the front of the engine. Replace the gasket as required.

2. Look into the throat of the carburetor and gently squeeze the primer bulb. Engines with an integral fuel tank are not equipped with a primer bulb. Open the fuel valve and look into the throat of the carburetor.

3. If fuel flows into the throat of the carburetor, remove the carburetor and repair it as described in Chapter Six.

4. Install the gasket, silencer/cover and screw(s) securely.

Plugged carburetor passages

Blocked jets, passages, orifices or vents can cause either a rich or lean condition. Operating the engine under a lean condition can lead to serious power head damage. Symptoms of an inadequate (lean) or excess (rich) fuel condition include hesitation or stalling during acceleration, rough idle, poor performance at high speed or surging. If the engine experiences a hesitation or stall during acceleration, push the key switch in or turn the choke switch ON to enrich the fuel mixture while accelerating the engine. The engine is operating excessively lean if the symptoms improve with the enriched fuel mixture. If the symptoms worsen, the engine is probably operating under a rich fuel condition. In either case, clean and inspect the carburetor(s) as described in Chapter Six.

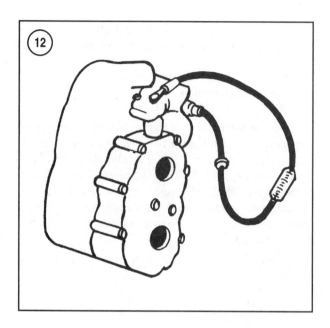

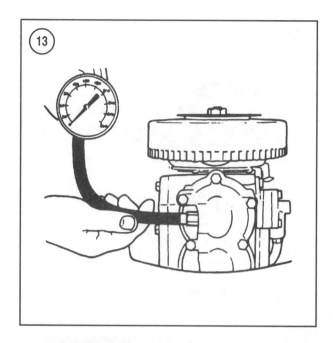

Altitude adjustments

In some instances, changes to carburetor jets or carburetor adjustments are required to correct engine malfunctions. If the engine is operated at higher elevation, carburetor jet changes may be required. Operation in some environments, such as extrememly hot or cold climates, may require carburetor adjustment or jet changes. Contact a Yamaha dealership in the area where the engine will be operated for recommendations.

> *WARNING*
> *Use extreme caution when working with the fuel system. Never smoke around fuel or fuel vapor. Make sure that no flame or source of ignition is present in the work area. Flame or sparks can ignite the fuel or vapor resulting in fire or explosion.*

Compression Test and Cylinder Condition

Check the cylinder compression if the engine is difficult to start and idles and runs poorly, but the fuel and ignition systems operate correctly.
1. Remove the spark plug(s) from the cylinder(s).
2. Connect the spark plug lead(s) to a good engine ground using jumper lead(s) (**Figure 12**).
3. Install the compression gauge into the No.1 cylinder spark plug hole (**Figure 13**).
4. Manually hold the throttle plate(s) in the wide-open position. Crank the engine at least six revolutions.
5. Record the compression reading.

6. Repeat Steps 3-5 for the remaining cylinders.

7. Install the spark plug(s) to the torque specification in Chapter Four.

8. Compare the highest and lowest compression readings. The lowest reading should be within 10% of the highest reading. One or more cylinders with significantly low readings indicate a problem. Fix the problem before

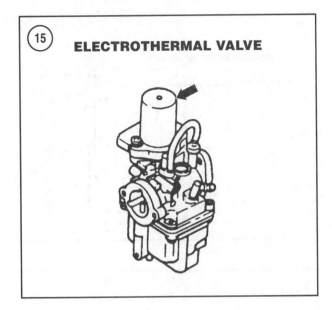

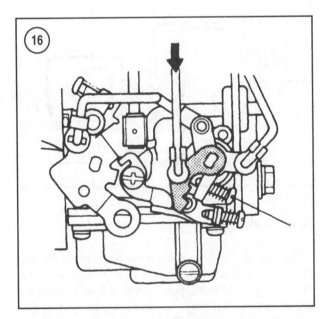

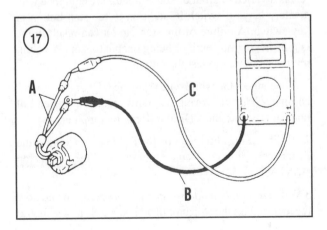

attempting to troubleshoot or tune the engine. Power head repair procedures are provided in Chapter Eight. An engine with inadequate compression cannot be tuned properly and will not perform correctly.

Enrichment Systems

Yamaha outboards are equipped with fuel enrichment systems to improve starting and cold engine operation. The systems include a manually operated choke valve, electrically operated choke valve (or an enrichment valve) or electrothermal valve. Manual start and tiller handle models are equipped with a manually operated choke valve.

Most electric start remote control models are equipped with a solenoid actuated choke valve (or an enrichment valve) (**Figure 14**). The choke valve restricts airflow into the front of the carburetor enriching the fuel mixture.

Electric start 9.9, 25, 80 and 100 hp models are equipped with an *electrothermal valve* (**Figure 15**). It allows fuel to flow from the carburetor directly into the engine, improving cold start/running conditions. An internal valve functions as a pump to move the fuel. The valve ceases fuel enrichment when the engine warms to operating temperature.

Test these devices if starting difficulty is noted and other systems are not at fault. Test the enrichment system as described in this chapter.

Enrichment valve/solenoid resistance test

Turn the key switch to the ON position, and activate the choke switch while observing the operation of the choke valve (**Figure 16**). The valve should move with a smooth, brisk motion. Check the resistance of the winding in the valve/solenoid following Steps 1-4 if the choke fails to operate. Check the wire harness and key switch if the resistance is within the specification. Replace the valve/solenoid if the wire harness, valve/solenoid resistance and key switch test properly.

1. Disconnect the leads from the harness of the fuel enrichment valve (A, **Figure 17**).
2. Connect the negative lead of the ohmmeter to one wire (B, **Figure 17**) of the fuel enrichment valve.
3. Connect the positive lead of the meter to the remaining (C, **Figure 17**) enrichment valve wire.
4. Resistance values are provided in **Table 14**. Replace the valve if its resistance is not within the specification.

NOTE
*The choke valve wire colors are different on many models. Refer to **Table 14** for wire col-*

ors and resistance specifications for all models.

Electrothermal valve resistance test

Use an ohmmeter to measure the resistance of the winding in the electrothermal valve (**Figure 18**). Resistance specifications are listed in **Table 14**. Refer to Chapter Six for electrothermal valve replacement. Check the valve operation by performing the *Electrothermal valve height test* described in this chapter.

1. Disconnect the wires from the electrothermal valve (**Figure 18**).

2. Connect the negative ohmmeter lead to one wire and the positive lead to the remaining electrothermal valve (**Figure 18**) wire.

3. Note the resistance of the valve. Replace the valve if its resistance is not within the specified range.

Electrothermal valve operational test

The engine must be cold for this test.

1. Remove the electrothermal valve from the carburetor (or bracket on some models). Refer to Chapter Six.

2. Measure the length of the electrothermal valve plunger at the points indicated in A, **Figure 19**.

3. Use jumper leads to connect the leads of the electrothermal valve to a 12-volt battery (**Figure 19**).

4. Maintain the connection for 5-7 minutes.

5. While the leads are still connected to the battery, measure the electrothermal valve at the points indicated in B, **Figure 19**.

6. Compare the measurement from Step 2 with the measurement from Step 5. Replace the electrothermal valve if there is no difference in the measurement.

> *NOTE*
> *The enrichment system will not operate properly unless the throttle is closed while starting a cold engine.*

IGNITION SYSTEM TESTING

The ignition system consists of the flywheel, charge coil, pulser coil, CDI unit, ignition coil and spark plugs. Except for the spark plugs, very little maintenance or adjustments are required. All components can be accurately tested using an ohmmeter or a peak-reading voltmeter. Refer to **Tables 5-13**.

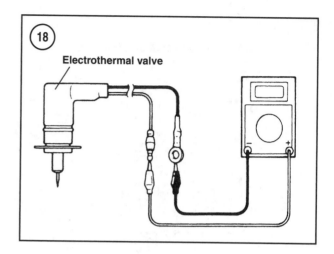

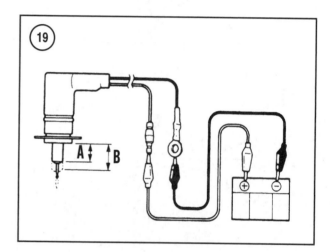

Stop Circuit Test

On tiller handle models, a stop button activates the stop circuit. On remote control models, a key switch activates the stop circuit. In both types, the engine stops running because the current required for operating the ignition system is diverted to ground. Some models are equipped with a safety lanyard switch in addition to the stop button or key switch. A failure of the stop circuit can result in the engine having no spark or being unable to stop. An ohmmeter is required to test the circuit.

1. Disconnect the white wire from the CDI unit or microcomputer. Use the wiring diagrams located at the end of manual to locate the CDI unit or microcomputer.

2. Calibrate the ohmmeter on the R × 1 scale. Connect the meter between a good engine ground and the white stop switch wire.

3A. *Tiller handle models*—Push the stop button and note the meter. With the stop circuit activated, the meter should

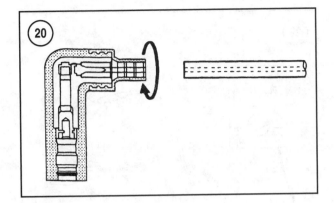

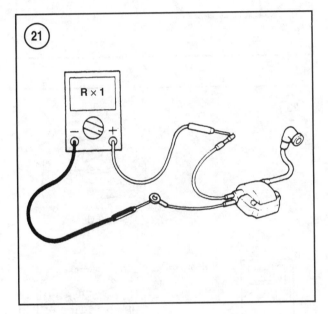

3

Spark Plug Cap

A defective spark plug cap can cause the short to ground causing a misfire. This type of failure often occurs during very humid conditions. Replace the spark plug cap if external arcing is noted at the spark plug. Corrosion at the spark plug cap and spark plug can also cause a misfire. Inspect the spark plug caps and replace the cap if corroded or if the insulation is cracked. To remove the spark plug cap, turn it counterclockwise and unscrew it from the wire (**Figure 20**).

Ignition Coil

A problem with an ignition coil can cause an intermittent or constant ignition misfire. Perform a visual inspection of all ignition coils. Replace coils that have corroded terminals or cracks on the body. A coil resistance test can be performed for the 9.9-100 hp models. Coil removal and installation are provided in Chapter Seven.

Ignition coil primary winding resistance

1. Disconnect the primary leads and the secondary lead from the ignition coil.
2. Connect the negative lead of an ohmmeter to the black wire (**Figure 21**) of the ignition coil.
3. Connect the positive ohmmeter lead to the orange wire (**Figure 21**) of the ignition coil.
4. Compare the reading with the primary resistance specification provided in **Tables 5-13**.
5. Repeat the test for all ignition coils on the engine. Replace coils that are not within specification.
6. Install the coil onto the power head and connect the leads to proper locations.

Ignition coil secondary winding resistance

1. Disconnect the primary the secondary lead from the ignition coil.
2. Connect the negative ohmmeter lead to the black wire (**Figure 22**) of the ignition coil.
3. Connect the positive meter lead to the secondary lead (**Figure 22**) of the ignition coil.
4. Compare the reading with the secondary resistance specification in the appropriate table.
5. Repeat the test for all ignition coils on the engine.
6. Install the coil onto the power head and connect the leads to the proper locations.

indicate continuity. Release the stop button and the meter should indicate no continuity.

3B. *Remote control models*—The meter should indicate continuity with the key and lanyard switches in the OFF positions. Place the key and lanyard switches in the ON positions and the meter should indicate no continuity.

4A. *Tiller handle models*—Replace the stop button and harness if the stop circuit fails to function as described.

4B. *Remote control models*—If the stop circuit fails to operate as described, test the key switch and lanyard switch as described in Chapter Seven. If the key and lanyard switches function correctly, inspect the stop circuit wire between the remote control and engine. Repair or replace the wire as required.

5. If all other components operate correctly, but the stop circuit is inoperative, the stop circuit inside the CDI unit may have failed. Replace the CDI unit and test the stop circuit again.

Pulser Coil (9.9-50 hp models)

The pulser coil is located under the flywheel. An electrical pulse is created as magnets attached to the flywheel pass near the coil. This electrical pulse is used to initiate a spark at the plug. If a pulser coil is faulty, remove the flywheel (**Figure 23**) to access the coil. Flywheel removal is *not* necessary to access the pulser coil leads. A faulty pulser coil can cause an intermittent or constant ignition misfire. Follow the test procedure carefully to avoid misdiagnosis and unnecessary flywheel removal. The pulser coil resistance test and the output voltage test specifications are provided for 9.9-50 hp models in **Tables 5-13**. A peak voltage adapter (YU-39991) and a digital voltmeter are required to test peak voltage on all models.

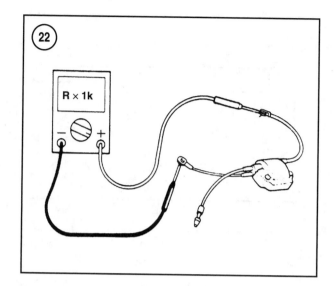

Pluser coil resistance (9.9-50 hp models)

1. Disconnect the pulser coil leads from the harness. Refer to the wiring diagrams at the end of the manual to identify the proper leads.
2. Connect the ohmmeter (**Figure 23**) to the pulser coil leads. Refer to the wiring diagrams at the end of the manual.

NOTE
The pulser coil resistance test is not affected by the polarity of the test leads.

3. Compare the reading with the specification provided in **Tables 5-13**. Replace the pulser coil if resistance is not within the specification. Removal and installation of the pulser coil are provided in Chapter Seven.
4. Reconnect the pulser coil when testing is complete.

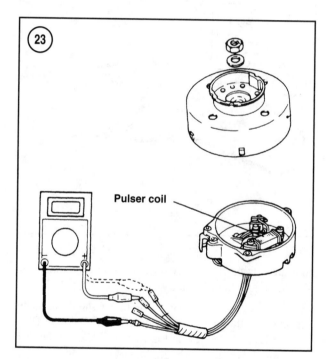

Pulser coil

Pulser coil peak voltage output (9.9-50 hp models)

Because a peak voltage test measures the output of the component while actually running, all components must remain connected to the main engine harness during a peak output test. Use a test harness or back-probe the wires (**Figure 24**) as necessary to connect the peak-reading voltmeter. On 9.9 and 15 hp models, refer to **Figure 25** for test connections. On 25 hp models, use test harness part No. YB-07678. On 40 and 50 hp models, use test harness part No. YB-06767.

1. Place the meter on the appropriate scale. Refer to the instructions provided with the meter and **Tables 5-13**.
2. Attach the test harness, if necessary, and connect the peak-reading voltmeter to the pulser coil wires (**Figure 26**).

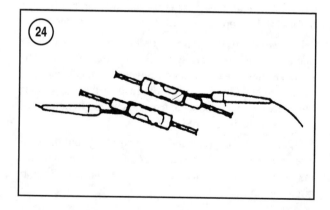

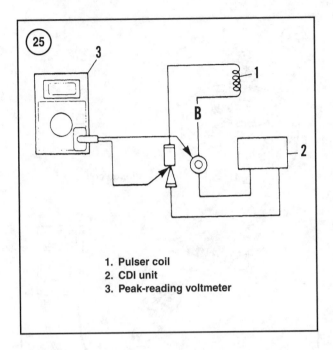

1. Pulser coil
2. CDI unit
3. Peak-reading voltmeter

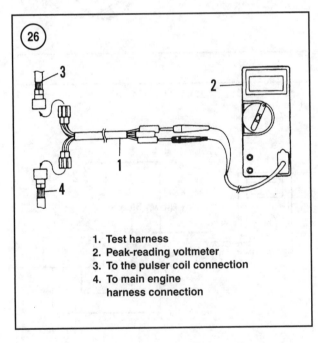

1. Test harness
2. Peak-reading voltmeter
3. To the pulser coil connection
4. To main engine
   harness connection

3. Run the engine on a flush device or in a test tank. Record the voltage at the indicated engine speed.

4. Compare the reading with the specification listed in **Tables 5-13**. Replace the CDI unit if the voltage reading is above the specification. Replace the pulser coil if the reading is below the specification. CDI unit and pulser coil replacement are provided in Chapter Seven.

5. Remove the test harness and attach all leads to the proper locations.

3

NOTE
If the peak voltage reading is excessively low, reverse the meter test leads and run the test again.

CAUTION
Never run an outboard without providing cooling water. Use either a test tank or flush/test device. Install a test propeller to run the engine in a test tank.

Ignition Charge Coil
(9.9-50 Hp)

The charge coil provides the CDI unit the voltage necessary to operate the ignition system. Charge coil failure can cause an intermittent misfire or no spark at all. Because charge coil output is alternating current, a peak-reading voltmeter (PRV) is required to test output. Resistance specifications and output specifications are listed in **Tables 5-13**. Refer to the wiring diagrams at the end of the manual to identify the charge coil wires. Check the coil resistance and output to ensure proper diagnosis.

Ignition charge coil resistance
(9.9-50 Hp)

1. Disconnect the ignition charge coil leads from the engine harness connection.
2. Connect the meter to the ignition charge coil leads (**Figure 27**) as specified in **Tables 5-13**.
3. Compare the resistance reading with the specification listed in **Tables 5-13**. Replace the ignition charge coil if it is not within the specification. Refer to Chapter Seven for coil removal and installation.
4. Connect all leads to the proper locations.

Ignition charge coil peak voltage output
(9.9-50 Hp)

A peak output test checks the charge coil output while running or cranking the engine. Therefore, when checking peak output, all components must remain connected. Use a test harness or back probe the wire connections (**Figure 24**) during the test.

On 9.9 and 15 hp models, refer to **Figure 28** for the test connections. Use test harness part No. YB-06768 on 25 hp models, test harness part No. YB-06767 on 40 and 50 hp models and test harness part No. YB-06770 on 80-100 hp models.

1. If necessary, attach the test harness to the engine harness at the charge coil connector. Connect the meter to the

test harness (**Figure 29**) at the specified wire colors. Refer to the wiring diagrams located at the back of the manual and the information provided in **Tables 5-13** to identify the connections and wire colors.

> *WARNING*
> *Remove the propeller shaft before running an engine on a flush/test device. Disconnect all spark plug lead(s) and battery connections before removing or installing the propeller.*

> *CAUTION*
> *Never run an outboard without providing cooling water. Use either a test tank or flush/test device. Install a test propeller to run the engine in a test tank.*

2. Run the engine on a test/flush device or in a test tank. Record the voltage at the indicated engine speed.

> *NOTE*
> *If the peak voltage reading is excessively low, reverse the meter test leads and run the test again.*

3. Compare the reading with the specification listed in **Tables 5-13**. Measure the pickup coil output if the reading is above specification. Replace the charge coil if the reading is below the specification. CDI unit and charge coil replacement procedures are provided in Chapter Seven.
4. Remove the test harness and attach all leads to the proper locations.

Pickup Coil (80-100 hp models)

The pickup coil provides a voltage signal to the CDI unit, which triggers the CDI unit output to the appropriate ignition coil. Test the pickup coil to determine of the coil is capable of producing a sufficient voltage signal and to ensure that the coil or coil wiring is not shorted to ground. A peak-reading voltmeter is required to check pickup coil output. A pickup coil failure can cause no spark or an intermittent misfire.

Resistance and output specifications are listed in **Tables 5-13**. Refer to the wiring diagrams at the end of the manual to identify the pickup coil wires.

Pickup coil resistance (80-100 hp models)

1. Disconnect the pickup coil from the engine harness.
2. Connect the ohmmeter to the pickup coil as specified in **Table 13**.

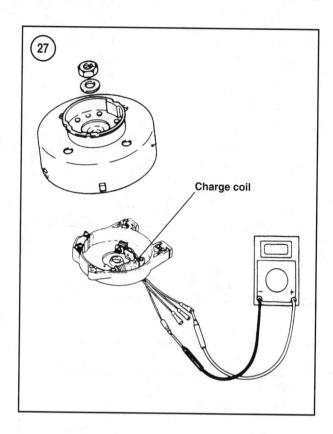

27

Charge coil

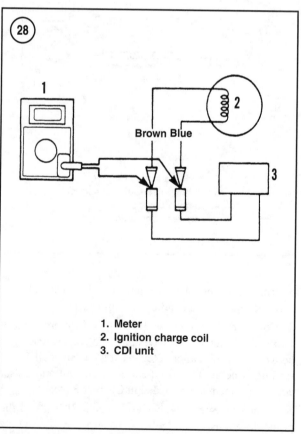

28

1

Brown Blue

2

3

1. Meter
2. Ignition charge coil
3. CDI unit

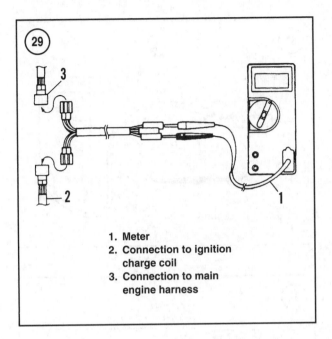

1. Meter
2. Connection to ignition charge coil
3. Connection to main engine harness

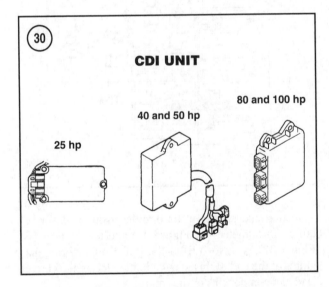

CDI UNIT

80 and 100 hp

40 and 50 hp

25 hp

3. Compare the resistance reading with specification in **Table 13**. Replace the pickup coil if it is not within the specification. Refer to Chapter Seven for pickup removal and installation.

4. Connect all leads to the proper location.

Pickup coil output voltage

A peak output test checks the pickup coil output while running or cranking the engine. Therefore, when checking peak output, all components must remain connected. Use test harness part No. YB-38832 or back probe the wire connections (**Figure 24**) during the test.

1. Attach the test harness to the engine harness at the pickup coil connector. Connect the peak-reading voltmeter to the test harness (**Figure 26**) at the specified wire colors. Refer to the wiring diagrams located at the back of the manual and the information provided in **Table 13** to identify the test lead connections and wire colors.

> *WARNING*
> *Remove the propeller before running an engine on a flush/test device. Disconnect all spark plug lead(s) and battery connections before removing or installing a propeller.*

2. Run the engine on a test/flush device or in a test tank. Record the voltage at the indicated engine speed.

3. Compare the reading with the specification listed in **Table 13**. Replace the CDI unit if the output is above specification. Replace the pickup coil if the output is below the specification. CDI unit and pickup coil replacement are provided in Chapter Seven.

4. Remove the test harness and attach all leads to the proper locations.

> *CAUTION*
> *Never run an outboard without providing cooling water. Use either a test tank or flush/test device. Remove the propeller before running the engine. Install a test propeller to run the engine in a test tank.*

CDI Unit

The primary function of the CDI unit (**Figure 30**) is to initiate spark to the correct cylinder at the correct time. As the flywheel magnets rotate past the charge coil, current is generated and stored in a capacitor within the CDI unit. Electrical pulses generated by the pulser or pickup coil trigger the release of the stored current, which is directed to the ignition coil. The ignition coil amplifies the current to the voltage needed to jump the gap at the spark plug.

The ignition timing is advanced at higher engine speeds to improve engine performance and efficiency. On some models, this is accomplished by rotating the pickup coil in relationship to the triggering magnets in the flywheel. On some models, the timing is advanced by the CDI unit. Automatic spark advance is provided with increased engine speed.

On 25-100 hp models, the CDI unit monitors input from various engine sensors to precisely control the ignition timing and fuel delivery. Testing procedures for the sensors are covered in this chapter. Ignition timing and linkage adjustment for all models are covered in Chapter Five.

A peak-reading voltmeter is required to check CDI unit output on all models.

CDI unit output voltage test

A peak output test checks CDI unit output while running or cranking the engine. Therefore, all components must remain connected when checking output. On 9.9 and 15 hp models, refer to **Figure 24** for test connections. Use test harness part No. YB-06768 for 25 hp models, test harness part No. YB-06767 on 40 and 50 hp models and test harness part No. YB-06770 on 80-100 hp models.

1. If necessary, attach the test harness to the engine harness at the CDI unit connector. Connect the peak-reading voltmeter to the test harness (**Figure 31**) at the specified wire colors. Refer to the wiring diagrams located at the back of the manual and the information provided in **Tables 5-19** to identify the test lead connections and wire colors.

> *WARNING*
> *Remove the propeller before running an engine on a flush/test device. Disconnect all spark plug lead(s) and battery connections before removing or installing a propeller.*

> *CAUTION*
> *Never run an outboard without providing cooling water. Use either a test tank or flush/test device. Remove the propeller before running the engine. Install a test propeller to run the engine in a test tank.*

2. Run the engine on a suitable test/flush device or in a test tank. Record the voltage at the indicated engine speed.
3. Compare the reading with the specification listed in **Tables 5-13**. Replace the ignition coil if the voltage reading is above the specification. If the reading is below specification, measure the charge coil output peak voltage on (9.9-50 hp models) and the lighting coil output voltage on (80-100 hp models). CDI unit, pickup coil and lighting coil replacement are provided in Chapter Seven.
4. Remove the test harness and attach all leads to the proper locations.

Throttle Position Sensor Test

The throttle position sensor is located on the lower port side of the power head (**Figure 32**). It provides a voltage signal to the CDI microcomputer, which indicates the position of the throttle plate. This information is used to set the timing advance.

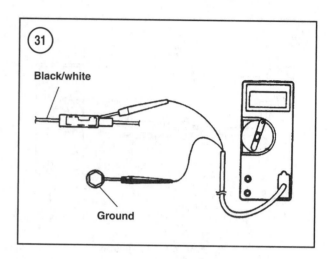

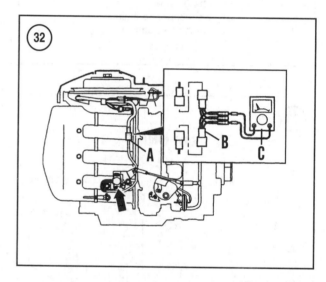

Testing and adjusting the throttle position sensor requires a voltmeter, (C, **Figure 32**) and test harness (B, **Figure 32**), part No. YB-06443. Refer to the wiring diagrams at the end of this manual to help locate the correct lead and components of the engine.

1. Disconnect the throttle position sensor from the main ending harness (A, **Figure 32**). Install a test harness between the disconnected leads as shown in B, **Figure 32**.
2. To check the throttle position sensor input voltage, connect the voltmeter to the orange and red test harness leads (**Figure 32**).
3. Start the engine and allow it to warm to normal operating temperature. Note the voltmeter while running at idle speed, then stop the engine. The voltmeter should indicate 4.75-5.25 volts. If not, replace the CDI microcomputer and retest the input voltage.
4. To test the throttle position sensor output voltage, connect the voltmeter to the pink and orange test harness leads.

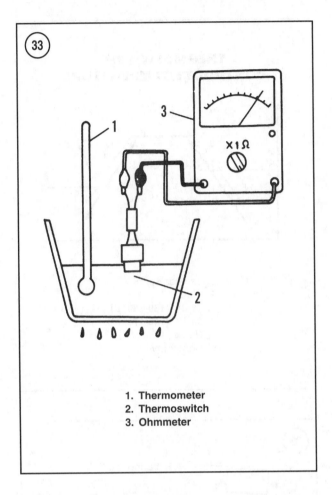

1. Thermometer
2. Thermoswitch
3. Ohmmeter

3. Oil pressure switch.
4. Low oil pressure warning lamp.
5. CDI microcomputer.

Thermoswitch Test

A thermoswitch is installed on 25-100 hp engines. The thermoswitch is designed to switch on at a predetermined temperature and switch off at a slightly lower temperature. This switch activatesthe warning lamp or buzzer if the power head overheats. One thermoswitch lead connects to the engine ground. The other lead connects to the warning lamp or buzzer. This lead may also connect to the CDI microcomputer. To test the thermoswitch, fill a container that can be heated with tap water. An ohmmeter and a liquid thermometer are also required for this test.

1. Disconnect the thermoswitch lead and remove it from the cylinder head. Fill the container with tap water and suspend the thermoswitch in the water.
2. Calibrate the ohmmeter to the R × 1 scale.

NOTE
Suspend the thermoswitch so only the tip of the switch is below the surface of the water. The reading may be inaccurate if the switch is totally immersed in the water.

3. Connect the ohmmeter between the pink and black thermoswitch wires.
4. Suspend the thermoswitch in the water so the tip is below the surface. Place a liquid thermometer in the container with the thermoswitch (**Figure 33**).
5. The meter should indicate no continuity. While heating the container, gently stir the water while observing the meter and thermometer.
6. When the meter indicates continuity, immediately record the temperature.
7. Discontinue the test if the water boils before the meter reading changes.
8. Allow the water in the container to cool and record the temperature when the meter reading indicates no continuity.
9. Compare the switching temperature with the values listed in **Figure 34**. Replace the thermoswitch if switching does not occur within the specified ranges.

Warning Lamp Test

A warning lamp is used on all models, except the 80 and 100 hp models, to alert the operator that the engine is over heating or the oil level is low. A 1.5-volt battery is required to test the lamp.

5. Start the engine and warm it to normal operating speed. Note the voltmeter while running at idle speed, then stop the engine. The sensor output voltage should be 0.68-0.72 volt. If not, adjust the throttle position sensor as described in Chapter Five.
6. Observe the voltmeter while slowly opening and closing the throttle. The voltage should increase and decrease smoothly. If the voltage changes abruptly, is erratic or does not change, replace the throttle position sensor as described in Chapter Seven.

WARNING SYSTEM

A warning system is used to warn the operator of a problem with the engine. Continued operation with the warning system activated can lead to serious and expensive engine damage. The low-oil warning is present on all models. An overheat warning system is available on 25-100 hp models.

The major components of the warning system include:
1. Thermoswitch/temperature switch/sensor.
2. Overheat warning lamp/buzzer.

1. Remove the warning lamp from the engine.

2. Using two jumper wires, connect the positive contact of the battery to the male terminal of the warning lamp. Connect the negative contact of the battery to the female terminal (**Figure 35**). The lamp should be lit.

3. Reverse the lead connections. The lamp should not be lit.

4. Replace the lamp if necessary.

> *CAUTION*
> *Use only an ordinary 1.5-volt battery to test the warning lamp. The use of a higher voltage battery or even an alkaline type battery will damage the lamp.*

Warning Buzzer Test

> *WARNING*
> *When performing tests using a battery, never make the final connection of a circuit at the battery terminal. Arcing may occur and ignite any explosive gasses near the battery.*

A warning buzzer is used on 80 and 100 hp models. On the tiller handle model, the horn is mounted on the lower cowling of the engine. On the remote control model, the warning horn is mounted inside the control box. Disassembly and assembly of remote control for access to the warning buzzer is covered in Chapter Twelve. The warning buzzer is used to indicate overheating and/or low oil level.

1. Remove the warning buzzer and attach the leads of the buzzer to a 12-volt battery using jumper leads as indicated in **Figure 36**.

2. Replace the buzzer if it fails to emit a loud warning.

Oil Pressure Switch Test

An oil pressure switch is used on 9.9-100 hp models. The oil pressure switch activates the warning system if insufficient oil pressure occurs. A suitable hand-held pressure/vacuum pump, such as a Mity-Vac pump and an ohmmeter are required to test the switch. It is necessary to apply a slight pressure, and be able to accurately measure the pressure during the switch test.

1. Attach an ohmmeter between the front of the oil pressure switch (A, **Figure 37**) and switch body (B, **Figure 37**).

2. Attach the pressure pump to the threaded end of the switch (C, **Figure 37**).

3. Slowly apply pressure to the oil pressure switch while observing the ohmmeter.

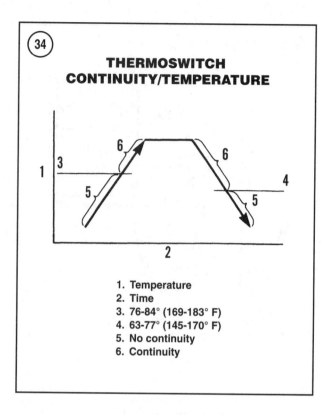

**THERMOSWITCH
CONTINUITY/TEMPERATURE**

1. Temperature
2. Time
3. 76-84° (169-183° F)
4. 63-77° (145-170° F)
5. No continuity
6. Continuity

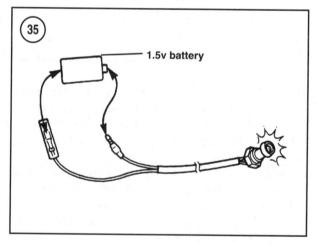

1.5v battery

4A. *9.9 hp:*

   a. At 0.0-10 kPa (0.0-1.4 psi), the meter should indicate continuity.

   b. At 50-70 kPa (7.1-9.9 psi), the meter should change to no continuity.

4B. *15, 40, 50, 80 and 100 hp:*

   a. At 0.0-14.7 kPa (0.0-2.13 psi), the meter should indicate continuity.

   b. The meter should change to no continuity when the pressure exceeds 14.7 kPa (2.13 psi).

4C. *25 hp:*

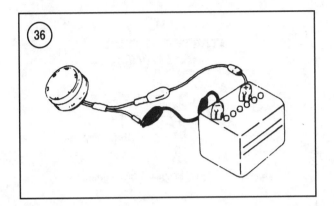

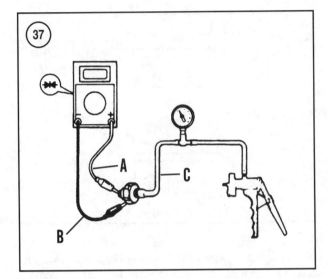

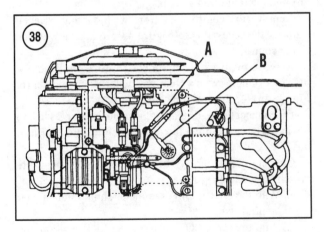

3

Thermoswitch and Oil Pressure Switch Input Voltage Test (40 and 50 hp Models)

This test measures the voltage input to the thermoswitch and oil pressure switch by the CDI unit. This test is valid for 40 and 50 hp models only.

1. Disconnect the gray/black thermoswitch wire (A, **Figure 38**).

2. Connect the positive lead of a voltmeter to the thermoswitch wire (not the thermoswitch) and the negative lead to a good engine ground.

3. Start the engine and run at idle speed. The voltage at the gray/black wire should be 4 volts.

4. Stop the engine, reconnect the thermoswitch and disconnect the pink/white (B, **Figure 38**) wire from the oil pressure switch. Attach the positive voltmeter lead to the pink/white wire (not the oil pressure switch).

5. Start the engine and run at idle speed. The voltmeter should indicate 4 volts.

6. Replace the CDI unit if the voltage is not as specified in Step 3 and Step 5.

STARTING SYSTEM

The starting system on Yamaha outboards consists of manual or electric start. Both systems are available on 9.9-40 hp models. The 50-100 hp models use only electric start.

The components of the electric starting system include the battery, start button or key switch, starter solenoid, starter motor, neutral switch and wires.

When activated, the starter motor (**Figure 39**) drive gear engages the flywheel ring gear and turns the engine crankshaft. A neutral start switch prevents the starting system from operating if the outboard motor is in gear.

The starter motor can produce considerable torque for a short time. Excessive cranking, however, will quickly overheat the starter motor. Never crank the engine for more than 10 seconds without allowing the motor to cool.

A fully charged battery of sufficient capacity is required to provide the current necessary to crank the engine. The minimum battery requirement is 380 cold-cranking amps. Weak or undercharged batteries are frequently the cause of a starting system malfunction. Battery maintenance and testing are covered in Chapter Seven.

The ignition switch or starter button (**Figure 40**) is connected to the positive terminal of the battery by the wire harness. When the switch or button is operated, current is directed first to the neutral switch (**Figure 40**), then to starter solenoid (**Figure 40**). The other terminal of the solenoid is connected to a terminal on the starter motor (**Figure 40**) with a large-diameter cable. When current is

a. 0.0-15.5 kPa (0.0-2.25 psi), the meter should indicate continuity.

b. When the pressure exceeds 15.5 kPa (2.25 psi), the meter should change to no continuity.

5. Replace the oil pressure switch if it fails to operate as specified.

supplied to the solenoid from the neutral switch it makes an internal connection that allows the current to flow from the battery directly to the starter motor. The solenoid allows the starter motor to be switched on or off using the shortest wires possible. The starter motor is attached and grounded to the power head. The power head is connected to the negative terminal of the battery (**Figure 40**) with a large-diameter cable, completing the circuit. Starter motor removal, disassembly, inspection, assembly and installation procedures are provided in Chapter Seven. Refer to **Table 1** for starting system troubleshooting. Starting system component testing is provided in the following sections.

CAUTION
Never operate the starter motor for over 10 seconds. Allow at least 2 minutes for the starter motor to cool between attempts. Attempting to start the engine with an insufficient or under-charged battery can result in starter motor overheating and subsequent failure.

Starter Cranking Voltage Test

This test measures the voltage available to the starter motor during cranking. Check and correct the battery condition before performing this test. Refer to Chapter Seven for battery maintenance. If the engine will not crank, check for a seized power head or gearcase before replacing any components.

1. Connect the positive voltmeter lead to the large terminal of the starter motor (**Figure 41**). Connect the negative lead to a good engine ground.
2. Disconnect the spark plug leads and connect them to ground. Crank the engine while observing the voltmeter.
3. Repair or replace the starter motor if the voltage indicated is 9.56 volts or greater, but the engine will not crank.
4. Test the starter solenoid and check all starting system wires for loose or corroded connections if the voltage is less than 9.5 volts. Charge the battery and test it again if all connections are in good condition.

Ignition Switch Test

The ignition switch is mounted in the dash or the remote control box (**Figure 42**) on all remote control models. Check the switch if the starter will not crank the engine, and the neutral switch, starter solenoid, connections, fuses and battery function correctly. If equipped with a dash-mounted switch, remove the switch and perform Steps 4-7. If the ignition switch is located in the control

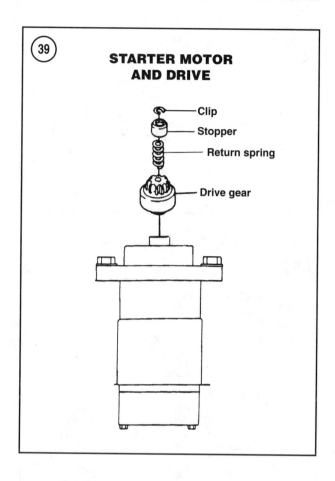

39

STARTER MOTOR AND DRIVE

- Clip
- Stopper
- Return spring
- Drive gear

box, partial disassembly of the control box is necessary to test the switch. Perform Steps 1-7 for a control box-mounted ignition switch.

1. Remove the control box from its mounting bracket. Remove the access cover (**Figure 43**) from the lower side of the control.
2. Remove the back cover screws (**Figure 44**). Remove the key from the switch. Remove the threaded retainer (6, **Figure 45**) for the ignition switch.
3. Disconnect the leads that connect the ignition switch to the harness and remove the key switch from the control box.
4. Connect the ohmmeter between the black and white switch terminals (**Figure 46**).
   a. With the switch OFF, the meter should indicate no continuity.
   b. With the switch ON or in the START position, the meter should indicate continuity.
5. Next, connect the ohmmeter between the yellow and red terminals (**Figure 47**).
   a. With the switch OFF, the meter should indicate no continuity.
   b. With the switch ON or in the START position, the meter should indicate continuity.

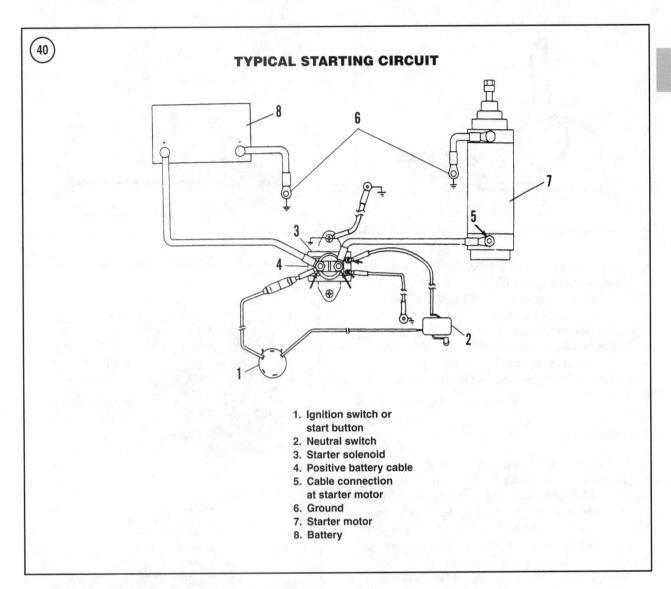

TYPICAL STARTING CIRCUIT

1. Ignition switch or
   start button
2. Neutral switch
3. Starter solenoid
4. Positive battery cable
5. Cable connection
   at starter motor
6. Ground
7. Starter motor
8. Battery

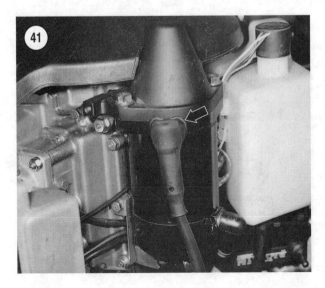

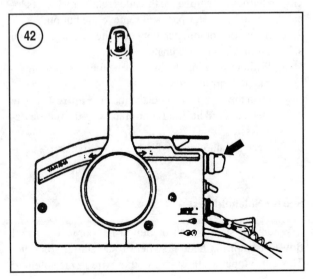

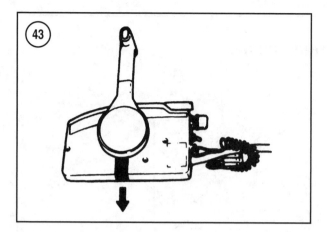

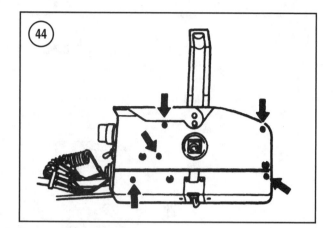

6. Connect the ohmmeter between the brown and red switch terminals (**Figure 48**).
   a. Place the switch in the START position. The meter should indicate continuity.
   b. Place the switch in the ON position, note the meter, then turn the switch to OFF. The meter should indicate no continuity in both positions.
7. Replace the ignition switch if it fails to operate as specified.

Start Button Test

On tiller controlled electric start models, the starter button (**Figure 49**) is mounted at the front of the lower cowling. One lead of the button connects to the positive battery terminal. The other lead connects to the neutral switch. When the button is depressed, current flows through the neutral switch to the starter solenoid. This activates the starter. A ohmmeter is required to test this component.
1. Disconnect the leads connecting the start button to the engine harness. Remove the threaded retainer which is located inside the motor pan, and remove the button.
2. Connect the ohmmeter between the red and brown start button wires or terminals.
   a. Without pushing the button, the meter should indicate no continuity.
   b. Push the button and note the meter (**Figure 49**). The meter should indicate continuity with the button depressed.
3. Replace the start button if it does not function as specified.

Starter Solenoid Test

When the start switch or button is operated, current flows through the neutral switch to the starter solenoid. This current passes through a coil of wire in the solenoid

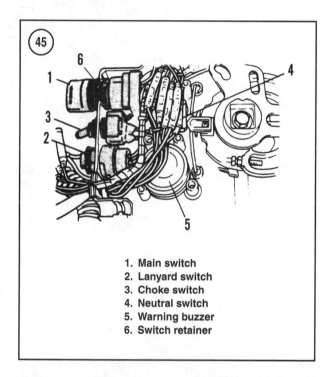

1. Main switch
2. Lanyard switch
3. Choke switch
4. Neutral switch
5. Warning buzzer
6. Switch retainer

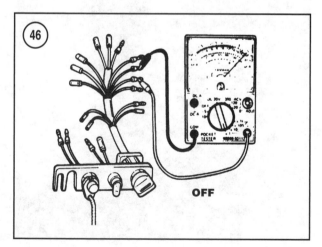

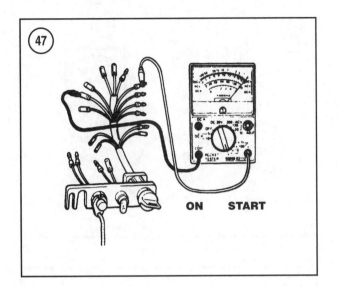

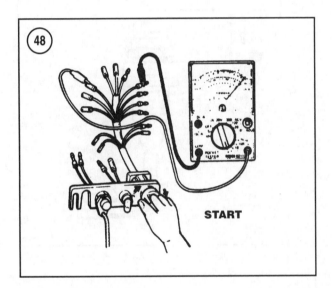

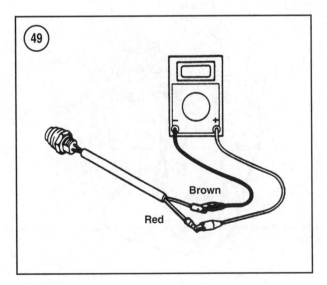

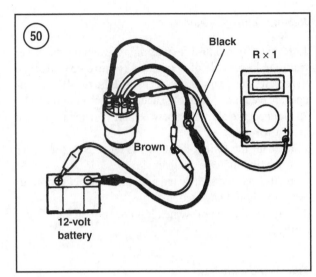

which creates a strong magnetic field. The magnetic field moves a plunger that closes contact points in the solenoid, allowing current to flow directly from the battery to the starter motor. An ohmmeter and jumper leads are required to test the solenoid.

1. Remove the solenoid as described in Chapter Seven.

2. Connect the ohmmeter between the two large solenoid terminals (**Figure 50**). No continuity should be noted.

3. Using jumper leads, connect the positive terminal of a 12-volt battery to the brown solenoid wire or terminal. Then attach a jumper lead to the negative terminal of the battery. While observing the ohmmeter, touch this jumper lead to the brown terminal or wire of the solenoid. See **Figure 50**.The meter should now indicate continuity.

4. Replace the solenoid if it does not function as described.

Neutral Switch Test

The neutral switch prevents the starter from operating when the engine is in forward or reverse gear. Manual start models (9.9 hp and larger) are equipped with a cable-operated locking mechanism that prevents the manual starter from operating if in gear. Refer to Chapter Ten to service the manual starter. Electric start models with a tiller control have a neutral switch mounted on the engine. Check for proper neutral switch adjustment on tiller models before testing or replacing the switch. On electric start models with remote control, the switch is located inside the remote control assembly. Partial disassembly of the control is required before testing the switch. A ohmmeter and a ruler are required to perform this test.

Remote-controlled models

1. Remove the control from its mount. Remove the cover from the lower side of the control (**Figure 43**). Remove the screws that retain the back cover (**Figure 44**). Disconnect the leads and remove the neutral switch (**Figure 51**).
2. Connect the ohmmeter between the two neutral switch brown wires.
   a. With the switch depressed (**Figure 51**), the meter should indicate continuity.
   b. Release the switch and note the meter. No continuity should be noted.
3. Replace the neutral switch if it does not operate as described.

Tiller handle models

1. Disconnect the neutral switch and remove it from the power head. See Chapter Seven.
2. Connect the ohmmeter between the neutral switch brown wires (**Figure 52**).
3. With the switch plunger released, the meter should indicate no continuity. With the plunger released, measure the distance (A, **Figure 52**). The distance must be 19.5-20.5 mm (0.77-0.81 in.).
4. While observing the ohmmeter, push the switch plunger. Continuity should now be present. Measure the distance (B, **Figure 52**) with the plunger pushed. The distance must be 18.5-19.5 mm (0.73-0.77 in.).
5. Replace the neutral switch if it fails to function as described or if the plunger lengths are incorrect.

Manual Start System

The manual start components include the recoil pulley, spring, drive pawls, drive pawl spring, rope and handle. The most common problem is a frayed or broken rope. If a manual or recoil starter is inoperable, make sure the gearcase and power head is not seized and the start lockout mechanism is functioning properly. Refer to Chapter Ten for complete manual starter repair procedures.

CHARGING SYSTEM

The components of the charging system are the flywheel, battery charging coil (**Figure 53**), rectifier (**Figure 54**) or rectifier/regulator (**Figure 55**), wires, and battery. The charging system maintains the battery charge level after starting the engine and when using onboard accessories. Accessories, such as depth finders and stereos, draw considerable current from the battery. The charging sys-

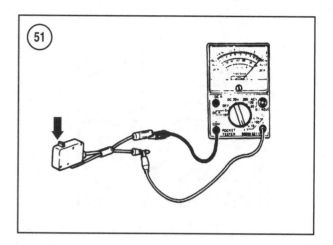

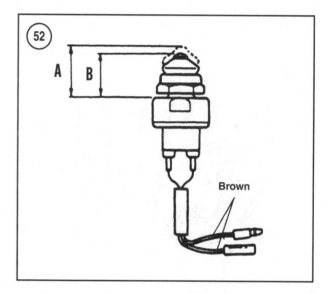

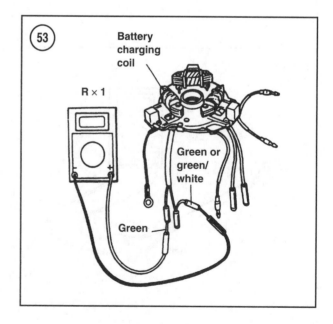

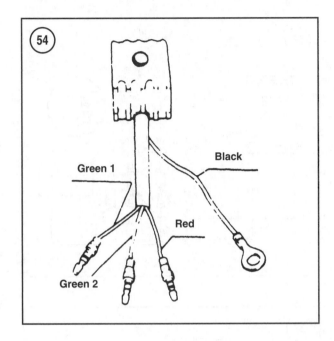

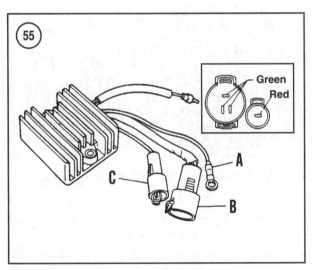

The lighting coil produces alternating current as the fly-wheel magnets rotate past it. The current produced by the lighting coil is only suitable for operating lights. Adding a *rectifier* to a similar circuit converts the current produced by the lighting coil to *direct current*. This allows the charging of the cranking battery. Models with the electric start use a rectifier/regulator unit. The rectifier converts the alternating current produced by the charging coil to direct current. The regulator senses the voltage at the battery and prevents overcharging of the battery.

Charging System Output

1. Connect the positive voltmeter lead to the battery positive terminal. Connect the negative lead to a good engine ground. Record the battery voltage.

2. With both test leads connected, start the engine. Record the battery voltage. A voltage equal to or less than the first measurement indicates that the charging system is not functioning. Further testing is required.

3. A voltage reading exceeding 14 volts indicates a likely overcharging also requires further testing.

> *WARNING*
> *Remove the propeller before running an engine on a flush/test device. Disconnect the spark plugs and the battery before removing or installing the propeller.*

> *CAUTION*
> *Never run an outboard motor without providing cooling water. Use either a test tank or flush/test device. Remove the propeller before running the engine. Install a test propeller to run the engine in a test tank.*

> *NOTE*
> *In most cases, the tachometer will not operate if a problem occurs in the charging system. Check all components as a precaution if the charging system is suspect, but the tachometer is operating.*

If a discharge or overcharge is indicated, test all components of the charging system. Both the charge coil and the rectifier/regulator may be faulty. Faulty flywheel magnets may cause decreased charging output and may cause ignition problems as well.

Check the resistance or voltage output of the lighting coil. Then check the resistance of the rectifier or rectifier/regulator.

tem may not be able to keep up with the demand and lead to a discharged battery. Check all components of the charging system if the battery fails to remain charged. Determine the total amperage draw of the accessories on the vessel and compare the total with the charging system output. The charging system delivers considerably less than the maximum output when the engine is operated at lower speeds. Adding additional batteries or installing a greater capacity battery is a possible solution. More frequent charging of the batteries may be required. Information on battery maintenance is provided in Chapter Seven.

Engines with a manual starter generally do not use a charging system. Some models have the option of a lighting coil.

Lighting/Battery Charge Coil
Resistance Test

Resistance specifications are provided for all models. While performing the lighting coil resistance test, remember that ambient temperature affects the measured resistance. The resistance values are specified in **Table 15**.

1. Disconnect the lighting coil from the main engine harness. Refer to the appropriate wiring diagram at the end of the manual.

2. Connect the ohmmeter to the lighting coil (**Figure 53**).

3. Compare lighting coil resistance to the specification in **Table 15**. Replace the coil if its resistance is not as specified. Refer to Chapter Seven for lighting coil replacement.

Lighting/battery charge coil
voltage output test

NOTE
The wire harness leads must remain connected to the lighting coil during a voltage output test. Back-probe connectors to make contact with the individual terminals.

1. A peak-reading voltmeter is required for this test.

2. Connect the peak-reading voltmeter to the coil. Refer to **Table 16** for the correct wire colors. See **Figure 56**.

3. Start the engine and run at the speed specified in **Table 16**.

4. Replace the coil if the output is less than specified in **Table 16**.

Rectifier/Regulator Output Test

Perform the rectifier/regulator voltage output test for all models. The 15-hp models are equipped two rectifier/regulators. One is a 6 amp and the other is a 10 amp. They have the same voltage specifications, but different color wires. Refer to **Table 17** and **Table 19** for the correct color code.

NOTE
The wire harness must remain connected to the rectifier/regulator during a voltage output test. Insert the meter test leads between the insulated connectors to make contact with the individual terminals.

1. Select the proper scale on the peak-reading voltmeter.

2. Connect the negative voltmeter lead to a good engine ground and the positive lead to the red terminal (**Figure 57**) of the rectifier/regulator.

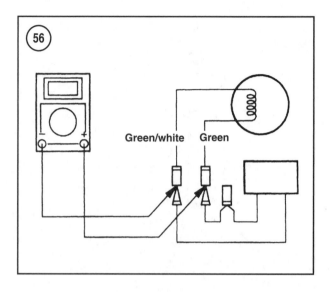

Green/white   Green

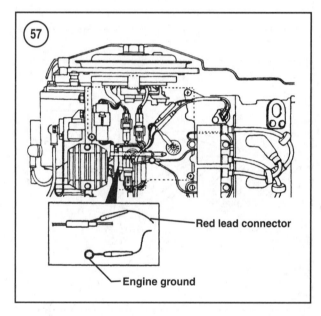

Red lead connector

Engine ground

3. Start the engine and run it at the speed specified in **Table 17**.

4. Note the voltage output. Replace the lighting coil if output is less than specified in **Table 17**. Replace the rectifier/regulator if the output exceeds the specification in **Table 17**.

FUSES AND WIRE HARNESS

Fuse Testing

Fuses on electric start models protect the wiring harness from a short circuit or overload. Never replace a fuse without performing a thorough check of the electrical sys-

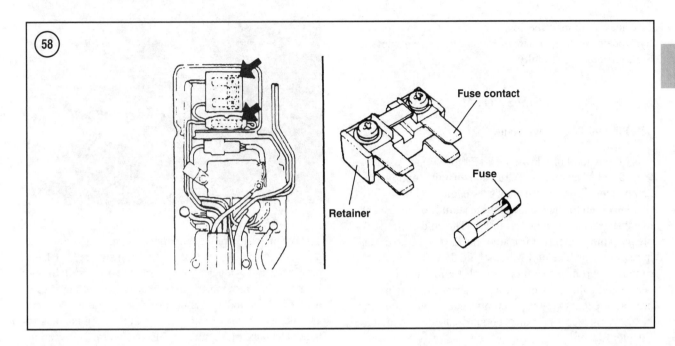

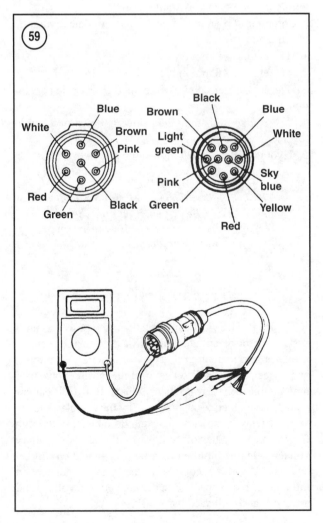

tem. Fuses are designed to open the circuit if an overload occurs. Never bypass a fuse or install a fuse with greater capacity than specified. Use an ohmmeter to test fuses. Note that different types of fuse retainers are used in the various models.

1. Remove the fuse (**Figure 58**) from the retainer.

2. Connect the ohmmeter to each of the fuse contacts (**Figure 58**).

3. The correct reading is continuity. Check all components connected to the wire harness the fuse serves. Correct any wire harness or component problems before installing a new fuse and returning engine to service.

Wire Harness Testing

If an electrical problem is evident, but all individual components test correctly, suspect the wiring harness. Check the engine and instrument harnesses on models equipped with remote control. Gently twist and pull the harness while checking the wires for continuity. Often this can locate the cause of an intermittent problem.

1. Disconnect the engine harness from the instrument harness if it is used. Disconnect the wire harness from the engine components or instruments.

2. Calibrate an ohmmeter on the R × 1 scale

3. Connect one of the meter or test light leads to a wire harness lead (**Figure 59**). Connect the other test lead to the connector pin that corresponds to the harness lead being tested. Refer to the wiring diagrams at the back of the manual to determine the proper connector pin.

4. The correct reading is continuity.

5. Check and repair the connector if there is no continuity. Repair the broken wire or replace the wire harness if the connector is not faulty.

TRIM SYSTEM

Tilt Pin and Lockdown Hook

A tilt pin and hold down hook (**Figure 60**) are used on 9.9, 15 and 25 hp models. A trim and tilt unit is optional on 25 hp model. The system allows the engine to run slightly tilted in or out to change the running attitude of the boat or to enhance shallow water operation. The hold down hook prevents the prop thrust from moving the engine up or out in reverse gear. The unit will not hold down in reverse or cannot tilt up in forward or neutral if a malfunction occurs. Check the adjustment, and inspect the system for broken or excessively worn components. Repair and adjustment procedures for these components are provided in Chapter Eleven.

Power Trim and Tilt

The single cylinder trim and tilt system is used on 25-100 hp models. The trim portion of this system moves the engine up/out against propeller thrust, allowing the operator to change the running attitude of the boat while underway. The tilt portion of this system allows the operator to tilt the engine up/out of the water, with the engine off, for mobility in shallow water. The tilt also allows the operator to raise or lower the engine completely when loading and unloading the boat. The major components are the electric motor, relays, hydraulic pump and hydraulic cylinder. A bi-directional electric motor (1, **Figure 61**) drives the hydraulic pump (8, **Figure 61**). The motor direction controls the direction of fluid movement to and from the pump and cylinder (8 and 11, **Figure 61**). Fluid moves from the pump to the UP side of the cylinder to trim the unit up. Fluid moves to the pump from the DOWN side of the cylinder to trim the unit down. Fluid returns to the pump from the UP side of the cylinder.

A manual relief valve (**Figure 62**) allows the engine to be moved up or down manually without running the electric motor. Always check this valve before performing other tests.

Follow the procedure provided in Chapter Four to check the fluid level before performing any test. Refer to *Electrical Testing* for electrical troubleshooting procedures. Trim electrical repair, and removal and installation procedures for major components of the trim system are in Chapter Eleven.

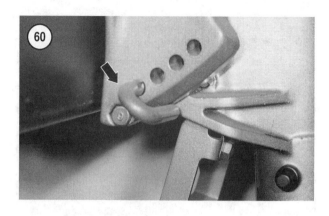

Have major hydraulic component repair performed at a dealership. Remove the trim system as instructed in Chapter Eleven and contact a Yamaha marine dealership for information. Removing the assembly before taking it to a dealership can reduce the cost of repair, and the expense and inconvenience of transporting and storing the boat at the dealership. Make sure the electric motor is operating before beginning any hydraulic test.

Common symptoms indicating a possible hydraulic malfunction are:
1. The engine will not move up.
2. The engine will not move down.
3. The engine leaks down while tilted up or during operation.
4. The engine trails out when slowing down or when in reverse.
5. Hydraulic fluid is leaking from the system.

> *WARNING*
> *The hydraulic system fluid may be under high pressure. Be extremely careful when removing valves or fittings. Always use eye protection when working with the hydraulic system.*

ELECTRICAL TESTING

The major electrical components of the power trim/tilt system are the electric motor, relays, trim position sender, switches and related circuitry. A blue wire (UP circuit) and a green wire (DOWN) connect the bi-directional trim motor to the trim relays. When unit is trimmed UP, battery voltage is supplied to the blue wire by the UP relay and the DOWN relay completes the ground connection through the green wire. When the unit is trimmed DOWN, battery voltage is applied to the green wire by the DOWN relay and the UP relay completes the ground connection through the blue wire. The switching between voltage and ground is accomplished by the trim relays.

POWER TRIM AND TILT ASSEMBLY

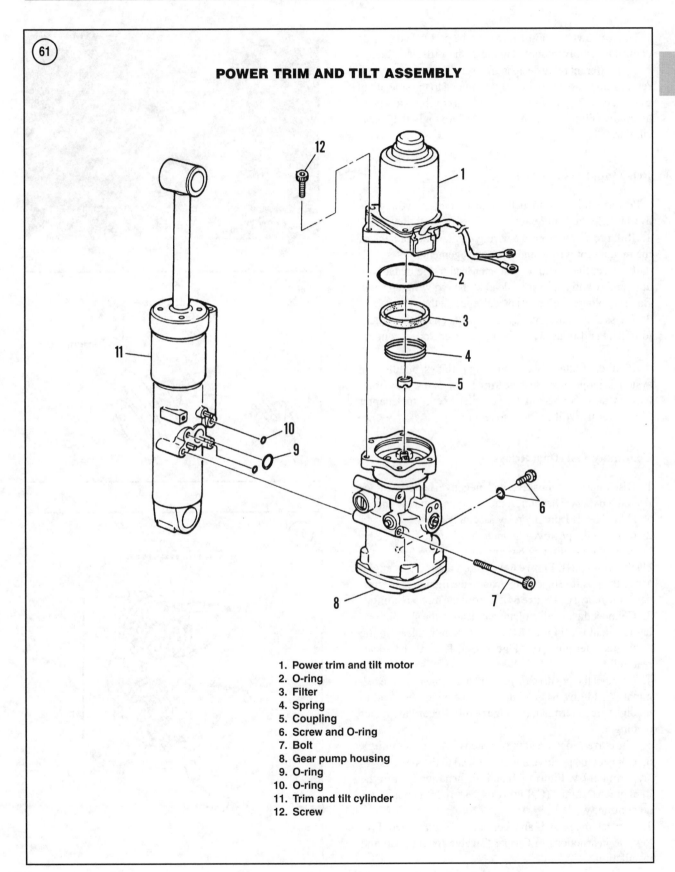

1. Power trim and tilt motor
2. O-ring
3. Filter
4. Spring
5. Coupling
6. Screw and O-ring
7. Bolt
8. Gear pump housing
9. O-ring
10. O-ring
11. Trim and tilt cylinder
12. Screw

The trim switch (**Figure 63**) can be part of the remote control assembly, mounted in the dash or tiller handle.

Two different relay designs are used. The most common relay arrangement is twin relays mounted to the side of the power head (**Figure 64**). Also used is a combination relay assembly (**Figure 65**). The test procedure for both types is similar.

Relay Input Voltage Test

Perform this test to determine of battery voltage is available to the trim relays.

1. Refer to the appropriate wiring diagram at the back of the manual for wiring and relay arrangement.

2. Connect the negative voltmeter lead to the black wire at the relay and the positive lead to the red wire terminal. Battery voltage should be noted. Repeat at the other relay.

3. If less than battery voltage is present, check the battery terminals and relay wires for loose or corroded connections.

4. If battery voltage is available to the relays, but the trim system is inoperative, test the trim motor, fuses and wiring harness as described in this chapter. Refer to Chapter Eleven for trim/tilt service procedures.

Continuity Test (Dual Relays)

1. Disconnect the positive and negative battery cables from the battery. Disconnect the sky blue, light green, red and black leads from the relay assembly.

2. Connect the positive ohmmeter lead to the sky blue relay terminal (A, **Figure 64**) and the negative lead to the black terminal (B, **Figure 64**). Record the meter reading. Move the positive ohmmeter lead to the light green terminal at the relay (C, **Figure 64**). Record the meter reading.

3. Connect the positive ohmmeter lead to the sky blue relay terminal (A, **Figure 64**) and the negative lead to the light green terminal (C, **Figure 64**). Record the meter reading.

4. Connect the positive meter test lead to the sky blue terminal (A, **Figure 64**) and the negative meter test lead to the light green terminal (C, **Figure 64**). Record the meter reading.

5. The correct meter readings in Steps 2-4 are continuity.

6. Connect the positive ohmmeter lead to the sky blue relay terminal (A, **Figure 64**) and the negative lead to the light green terminal (C, **Figure 64**). The correct reading is no continuity.

7. Replace the relay if an incorrect reading is noted. Follow the instructions in Chapter Twelve for removal and installation.

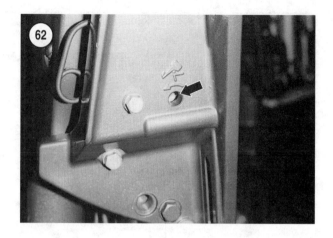

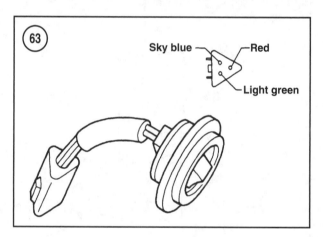

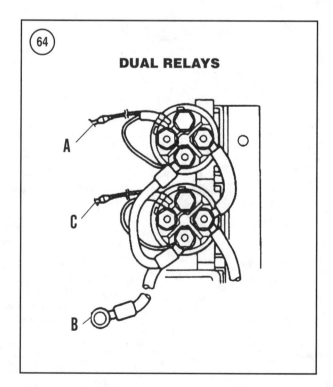

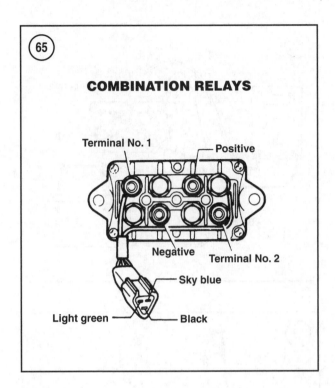

COMBINATION RELAYS

Terminal No. 1 — Positive

Negative — Terminal No. 2

— Sky blue

Light green — Black

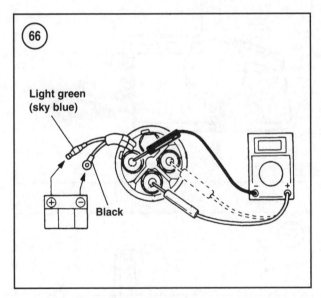

Light green (sky blue)

Black

3. Connect the positive ohmmeter lead to terminal No. 1 and the negative lead to the negative relay terminal (**Figure 65**). Record the meter reading. Move the ohmmeter lead to terminal No. 2 (**Figure 65**). Continuity should be noted.

4. Connect the positive ohmmeter lead to terminal No. 1 and the negative lead to the positive relay terminal (**Figure 65**). No continuity should be noted. Move the positive meter lead to terminal No. 2 and the negative lead to the positive relay terminal (**Figure 65**). No continuity should noted.

5. The correct readings for Steps 2 and 3 are a closed circuit or low resistance. The correct reading for Step 4 is an open circuit or high resistance. Replace the relays or relay unit if an incorrect reading is noted. Refer to Chapter Eleven for the removal and installation procedures. Install all leads to the proper locations. Replace the relay unit as described in Chapter Eleven if it fails to operate as specified.

Operational Test (Dual Relays)

1. Disconnect both battery cables from the battery. Remove the relay as described in Chapter Eleven.

2. Connect the ohmmeter positive lead to relay terminal No. 2. Connect the negative lead to relay terminal No. 1 (**Figure 66**). Next, using jumper leads, connect the positive battery terminal to the relay terminal for the sky blue wire and the negative battery terminal to the relay terminal for the black wire (**Figure 66**). With the battery connected as described, the ohmmeter should indicate continuity.

3. Move the jumper lead attached to the positive battery terminal to the relay terminal for the light green wire. Leave all other connections as described in Step 2. The ohmmeter should indicate continuity.

4. Connect the positive ohmmeter lead to relay terminal No. 1 and the negative meter lead to relay terminal No. 2. Allow all other connections to remain as described in Step 2. The meter should indicate no continuity.

5. Replace the relay if it does not function as described. See Chapter Eleven for relay removal and installation.

Operational Test (Combination Relay Assembly)

1. Disconnect the cables from the battery. Remove the combination relay assembly as described in Chapter Eleven.

2. Using a jumper lead, connect the negative battery terminal to the relay terminal for the light green wire. Then,

Continuity Test (Combination Relay Assembly)

1. Disconnect the positive and negative battery cables from the battery. Disconnect the relay harness connector or individual plug-in connectors.

2. Connect the positive ohmmeter lead to the sky blue relay terminal and the lead to the black terminal. Continuity should be noted. Move the positive ohmmeter lead to the light green relay terminal. Continuity should be noted.

connect the positive battery terminal to the relay terminal for the black wire (**Figure 67**).

3. Connect the ohmmeter positive lead to the positive relay terminal and the negative ohmmeter lead to the relay negative terminal. See **Figure 67**. The meter should indicate no continuity.

4. Move the jumper lead attached to the positive battery terminal to the relay terminal for the sky blue wire. Move the jumper lead attached to the negative battery terminal to the relay terminal for the black wire (**Figure 67**).

5. Connect the positive ohmmeter lead to the relay negative terminal and negative ohmmeter lead to the No. 1 relay terminal. The meter should now indicate continuity.

6. Replace the relay assembly if it fails to operate as described. See Chapter Eleven.

Trim Switch Test

The trim and tilt system is controlled by a three-position switch mounted on the remote control, dash panel or tiller handle. Some models have an additional switch mounted in the lower engine cowl for convenience. Testing procedures are similar for all switch locations. This rocker-type switch is spring loaded into the center or OFF position. The switch activates the UP or DOWN relay when toggled to the desired position. Battery voltage is supplied to the switch by a fused lead. Check the fuse or wire harness if the voltage is not supplied to the lead. Refer to *Fuse and Wire Harness Test* in this chapter. Follow Steps 1-7 for models with the trim switch mounted in the remote control. Follow Steps 3-7 for models with a dash-mounted switch.

1. Disconnect the cables from the battery. Remove the remote control from its mounting location. Remove the wire cover (**Figure 68**), then remove the screws from the back cover (**Figure 69**).

2. Remove the back cover and disconnect the tilt/trim switch connector.

3. On tiller models or models with an engine cover-mounted switch, unplug the switch connector (**Figure 70**).

4. Connect the positive ohmmeter lead to the red lead pin at the plug. Connect the negative lead to the sky blue lead pin at the plug. A correct reading is no continuity when the switch is in the middle position or in the DOWN position. A correct reading is continuity when the switch is in the UP position.

5. Connect the positive ohmmeter lead to the red lead pin at the switch plug. Connect the negative lead to the light green lead pin at the switch plug. A correct reading is no continuity when the switch is in the middle position or in

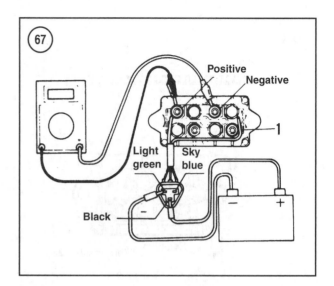

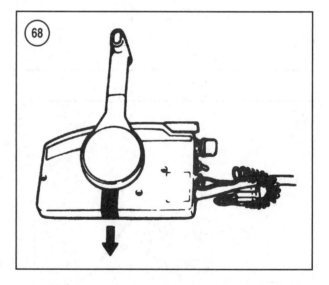

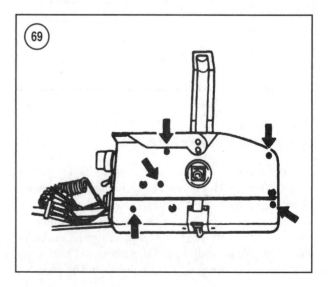

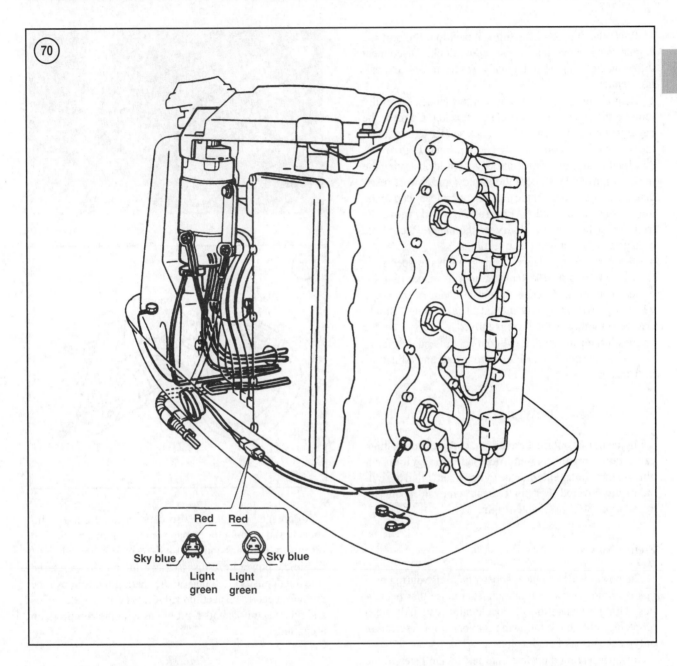

the UP position. The correct reading is continuity or low resistance when the switch is in the DOWN position.

6. Connect the negative ohmmeter lead to the sky blue lead at the switch plug and the positive lead to the light green lead at the switch plug. A correct reading is no continuity at *all* switch positions.

7. Replace the trim/tilt switch if an incorrect reading is noted.

NOTE
When testing a trim position sender, test the resistance at 20° C (68° F). Testing the unit at other temperatures can significantly affect the test result.

Trim Position Sender Test

A digital or analog engine trim position gauge is available on 40-100 hp models. A trim position sender (**Figure 71**) mounted on the engine clamp bracket operates the gauge. If the gauge reading is not correct, adjust the trim sender unit as instructed in Chapter Eleven. If adjustment does not correct the problem, perform Steps 1-5 to test the sender unit.

1. Raise the engine to the full UP position. Support the engine using an overhead cable and/or blocks. Disconnect the connector plug or individual wires from the trim position sender.

2. Remove the screw(s) that retain the sender. Carefully remove the sender from the clamp bracket. Connect the negative ohmmeter lead to the black sender terminal and the positive lead to the pink sender terminal (**Figure 72**).

3. Slowly move the trim sender lever while observing the meter (**Figure 73**). Record the highest and lowest resistance readings. Connect the positive ohmmeter lead to the orange sender connection (**Figure 73**). Slowly move the trim sender lever while observing the meter. Record the highest and lowest resistance readings.

4. Compare the resistance readings with the specifications listed in **Table 18**. Replace the trim sender if an incorrect reading is noted or if abrupt changes are noted when the lever is slowly moved. The readings should change smoothly as the lever is moved.

5. Install the trim sender and connect all leads. Refer to the procedure in Chapter Eleven to install and adjust the trim sender.

POWER HEAD

Engine noises, lubrication failure, compression testing, valve train component failure, detonation, preignition, engine seizure, water entering the cylinder and oil in the cylinders are covered. For power head removal, repair and installation, refer to Chapter Eight.

Engine Noises

The power head produces substantial noise during normal operation. However, any unusual noise that intensifies during acceleration or deceleration can indicate a problem. Refer to the following sections for a description of typical causes of engine noises.

Consider having a professional technician listen to the engine if a worn or damaged component is suspected of causing an unusual noise. Often, a trained technician can determine if a failure has occurred or if loose bracket or fastener is causing the noise.

Ticking noise

A ticking noise is common if valve adjustment is required or if a valve train component has failed. Valve adjustment procedures are provided in Chapter Four. See *Valve Train Component Failure* in this chapter for additional troubleshooting information.

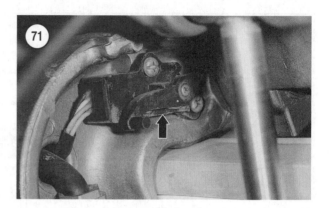

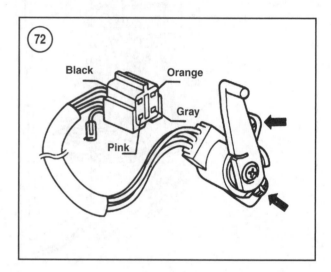

A damaged piston can also cause a ticking noise. Inspect the spark plug for damage or aluminum deposits and perform a compression test as described in this chapter. Complete power head disassembly and repair is required if metal deposits are found on the spark plug. Remove the cylinder head to inspect the valves, piston, cylinder walls and related components if problems with the compression are noted.

> *CAUTION*
> *If suspicious noises are ignored, damaged may be increased.*

Whirring noise

If a whirring noise is most pronounced when the throttle is *decreased*, it usually indicates a problem with the crankshaft and rod bearings.

Use a mechanic's stethoscope to identify the cylinder creating the noise. Compare the noise in one area of the engine with noise from the same area, but a different cylinder. Refer to *Oil Pressure Test* in this section to test the

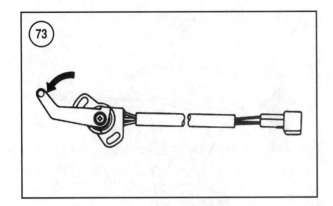

suspect cylinder. This is difficult and may result in damage to the electrical system if the spark plug leads are not properly grounded. Instead, remove one spark plug lead and attach it to an engine ground. Start the engine and listen to the noise. Install the spark plug lead and repeat the process for another cylinder. If, with one lead grounded, the noise is less than another cylinder, the grounded cylinder may be damaged.

Always perform an oil pressure check if there is a knocking noise. When combined with low or unstable oil pressure, knocking generally indicates a problem with the power head. Major repair may be required. Refer to *Oil Pressure Testing* in this section for repair procedures.

Detonation

Detonation damage is the result of the heat and pressure in the combustion chamber becoming too great for the fuel being used. Fuel normally burns at a controlled rate that causes the expanding gasses to drive the piston down. When conditions in the engine allow the heat and pressure to become excessive, the fuel may violently explode. These explosions in the combustion chamber cause serious damage to internal engine components. Carbon deposits, overheating, lean fuel mixture, over-advanced timing and lugging are conditions that may lead to detonation. Never use a fuel with a lower octane rating than recommended. This may cause detonation under normal operating conditions. The piston is subjected to the most damage from detonation. If detonation occurs, the engine will have a pinging noise similar to the pinging sometimes heard in automobiles. Outboards are considerably noisier than automobiles, so the pinging noise is seldom detected. The engine will have a rough idle and may seize if the damage is great enough. A compression test indicates if one or more cylinders is low on compression. Inspect the spark plug. The presence of aluminum deposits or melted electrodes (**Figure 74**) indicates probable detonation damage. To avoid repeat problems, address the listed causes for detonation prior to returning the engine to service.

oil pressure to ensure that the noise is not caused by insufficient lubrication.

> *WARNING*
> *Be extreme careful when working on or around a running engine. Never wear loose fitting clothing. Do not get near the flywheel or any drive belts, or near the propeller or propeller shaft while the engine is running.*

Knocking noise

Use a mechanic's stethoscope to determine if the noise is emanating from the power head or another component on the engine. If noise is more pronounced in the crankcase area, a problem exists in the crankshaft and connecting rod components. Special insulated pliers allow spark plug lead removal while running the engine. The noise may lessen when the spark plug lead is removed from the

Preignition

Preignition is the premature ignition of the air/fuel mixture in the combustion chamber. During preignition, combustion occurs before a spark initiates the combustion process. Basically, anything in the combustion chamber that gets hot enough to ignite the fuel/air charge can cause preignition. Glowing carbon deposits, inadequate cooling, improperly installed thread inserts, overheated spark plugs and nicks or scratches can all cause preignition. Preignition usually is first noticed as a power loss, but will eventually result in extensive damage to the internal engine components (especially pistons) because of excessive combustion chamber pressure and temperature. Preignition often melts the top of the piston. Sometimes the piston will actually have a hole melted through the crown. Spark plug inspection may reveal aluminum deposits (**Figure 74**) consistent with detonation failure. Correct the cause of preignition before returning the unit to service.

Engine Seizure

The power head can seize at any speed. Normally, the engine does not seize at high speed. The engine typically loses power gradually. The primary reason for the seizure is a faulty crankshaft or rod bearing, or detonation or preignition damage. An immediate seizure can result from a valve train component failure. In either case, the starter is unable to turn the engine over. Always inspect the gearcase before removing the power head. A gearcase failure can prevent the power head from rotating. Refer to *Gearcase* in this chapter to inspect the gearcase for metal contamination. Refer to Chapter Nine to remove the gearcase to check for gearcase seizure. Repair the gearcase if the power head turns freely with the gearcase removed. Refer to Chapter Eight for power head removal, repair and installation.

Water Entering the Cylinder

Water can enter the cylinder from the fuel, the front of the carburetor, a leaking exhaust cover/gaskets, a leaking cylinder head and/or gasket, and a cylinder block internal leak. The typical symptom of water in the cylinder is a rough running engine, particularly at idle. The engine may run correctly at higher speeds. Check for water leakage when the spark plugs are removed. Check for water a white deposit on the spark plugs. Remove the cylinder head following the instructions listed in Chapter Eight. Compare the wet cylinder(s) with the dry cylinder(s). A cylinder with water leakage usually has significantly less carbon deposits on the piston and combustion chamber. Rust or corrosion may be present on the valves or other components. Complete power head repair is not required if the cause and damage is confined to the cylinder head. Leakage in the cylinder block can be difficult to find. Casting flaws, pinholes and cracks may not be visible. Replace the cylinder block and/or cylinder head if water is entering the cylinder and visible gasket leakage cannot be

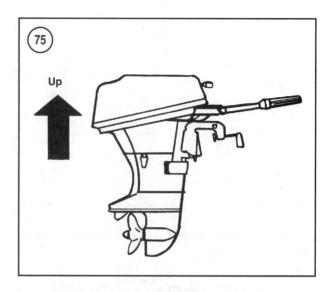

found. Continued operation with water intrusion will cause engine failure.

Oil Entering the Cylinder

Oil entering the cylinders is usually caused by improper storage of the engine. If positioned incorrectly, oil from the crankcase can flow past the piston rings and enter the combustion chambers. This can lead to a hydraulically locked engine, fouled spark plugs, low oil level and high oil consumption. Keep the engine upright (**Figure 75**) during storage.

To determine if excessive oil is entering the cylinders, remove the spark plugs and securely ground the spark plug leads to the engine. If the spark plugs are oily, place a shop towel over the spark plug holes and slowly rotate the flywheel to blow excess oil from the cylinders. Correct the oil level as described in Chapter Four. Clean and install the spark plugs.

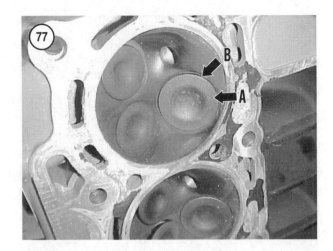

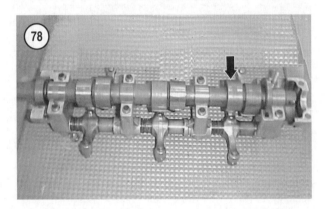

Start the engine and warm it to normal operating temperature. Stop the engine, allow it to cool and remove the spark plugs. If the plugs are oily or fouled, excessive oil is entering the cylinders. Refer to Chapter Four for spark plug inspection instructions.

Valve Train Components

Valve train problems can cause an inability to start the engine, rough engine operation, backfiring in the exhaust or intake, or a ticking noise. Timing belt failure, worn valve guides, sticking, worn or damaged valves, camshaft failure, and rocker arm failure are covered in this section.

Timing Belt Failure

CAUTION
Attempting to start the engine with incorrect valve timing or broken timing belt can cause piston and valve damage.

The crankshaft drives the camshaft(s) via the timing belt (**Figure 76**). If the timing belt is worn sufficiently to

jump over one or more teeth on the crankshaft or camshaft, the valve timing will be incorrect. If the valve timing is not correct, the engine will run poorly or not start at all. If the belt fails completely, the camshaft will not turn and engine will not start.

Refer to Chapter Five for timing belt and belt tensioner adjustment and Chapter Eight for belt replacement.

Sticking, Worn or Damaged Valves

Corrosion or heavy carbon deposits can cause a valve (A, **Figure 77**) to stick in the open position. Worn or damaged valves or valve seats (B, **Figure 77**) cause similar symptoms. Either condition causes a loss of compression, and rough running or backfiring. Backfiring through the intake is usually the result of a stuck, damaged or worn intake valve. A backfiring through the exhaust is usually the result of a stuck, damaged or worn exhaust valve.

If backfiring occurs, perform a compression test following the procedure in this chapter. Run the engine with one spark plug lead grounded at a time. The backfire will cease when the spark plug lead is grounded on the defective cylinder. Disassembly and inspection of the valve can verify this problem. In some cases, the valve contacts the top of the piston, causing a bent valve or damage to the top of the piston. Removal and inspection of the valves and related components are covered in Chapter Eight.

Stuck valves are generally the result of improper long-term storage, water entering the cylinders or submersion of the engine. Using the wrong type of oil, improper fuel system operation or lugging the engine can contribute to increased deposits, wear of the valve and seat area. Refer to Chapter Four for information regarding oil usage. Refer to Chapter One to select the correct propeller to prevent lugging the engine. Refer to Chapter Five and Chapter Six to make sure the fuel system is adjusted properly.

Camshaft Failure

Failure of a camshaft lobe (**Figure 78**) will cause a misfire and excessive valve lash on the affected cylinder. Typically the lobe becomes rounded off causing its corresponding valve to remain closed, or only open slightly.

The camshaft can be inspected without major disassembly of the power head. Removal of the rocker cover (**Figure 79**) allows inspection of the camshaft lobes. Refer to Chapter Eight for rocker cover removal and installation.

Insufficient lubrication or the wrong type or dirty oil generally causes camshaft failure. Continuous operation in cool water can increase oil dilution with fuel byproduct.

Diluted oil can contribute to camshaft lobe failure. Change the oil frequently to prevent this type of failure. See Chapter Four.

Rocker Arm Failure

Failure of a rocker arm (**Figure 79**) and related components can cause excessive noise in the rocker cover area or a loss of compression on the corresponding cylinder. Remove the rocker cover and inspect all rocker arms for broken or damaged components. Replace damaged components as described in Chapter Eight.

Rocker arm failure is generally due to the engine being run at higher than recommended engine speeds. Refer to **Table 20** for the maximum recommended engine speed. A different propeller may be required to correct excessive engine speed.

Lubrication System Failure

Problems in the lubrication system can result in severe engine damage. Problems in the system can be cause by an incorrect oil level, failure of the oil pumping system, the use of contaminated oil or inadequate oil. This section covers these conditions and provides oil pressure test procedures.

> *CAUTION*
> *Damage can occur in seconds if the lubrication system fails. To help prevent serious engine damage, slow down and stop the engine at once if the warning system indicates low oil pressure.*

Incorrect oil level

Improperly filling the engine with oil or checking the engine oil level improperly can cause an incorrect oil level.

An insufficient oil level can result in an inadequate supply of oil to the oil pump and/or overheating of the oil. The oil helps cool the crankshaft and other internal engine components.

An excessive oil level allows the crankshaft and other components to form bubbles or foam in the oil. Foam-contaminated oil may cause low oil pressure and activate the warning system. In some cases, the oil pressure is high enough not to activate the warning system, but the engine is not receiving adequate lubrication. Foam-contaminated oil does not provide the lubrication required by the engine.

Refer to Chapter Four to check or add engine oil.

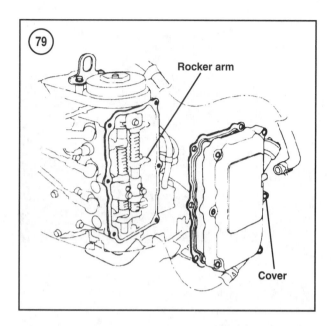

Most oil leaks are easily detected and corrected. Common leakage areas are the rocker cover (**Figure 79**), oil filter mounting surface, fuel pump mounting surface or crankcase mating surface (**Figure 80**). To locate a leak, carefully clean the engine with a degreasing agent. Run the engine until it reaches operating temperature. Turn the engine off, then inspect the mating surface for fresh oil leakage.

All engines consume some oil while running. Some of the oil that lubricates the cylinder walls or valves is drawn into the combustion chamber and burned. Oil consumption rates vary by model, condition of the engine and how the engine is used. Engines with worn internal components generally burn more oil than new engines. Damage to the piston and cylinder walls from detonation or preignition can cause increased oil consumption as well. New or recently rebuilt engines generally consume more oil during the break-in period. After the break-in period, the oil consumption should return to normal. Normal usage varies widely and oil usage specifications are not provided.

A typical symptom of excessive oil consumption is blue smoke coming from the exhaust during hard acceleration or high-speed operation. Inspection of the spark plug usually reveals oil fouling (**Figure 81**). Perform a compression test as described in this chapter. Worn or damaged components generally cause low compression results.

If oil levels are frequently low, and there is no indication of high oil consumption or external leak, check for a leakage at the oil pan area (**Figure 82**, typical). Inspect the oil pan and cylinder block mating surfaces and gaskets. Refer to Chapter Eight for engine removal and inspection.

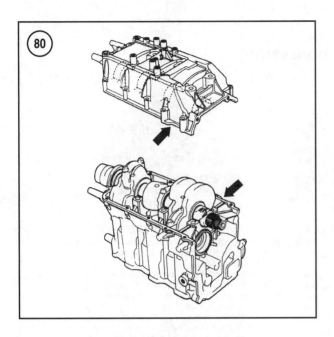

Failure of the Oil Pump System

Failure of the oil pump is cause by a worn or damaged oil pump (**Figure 83**), a worn or damaged bearing (**Figure 84**), or a blocked, damaged or loose oil screen (**Figure 82**).

Perform an oil pressure test to determine if a problem exists with the oil pumping system. See *Oil Pressure Test* in this chapter.

Oil Pressure Test

> *CAUTION*
> *Never run an outboard without first providing cooling water. Use either a test tank or flush/test device. Remove the propeller before running the engine. Install a test propeller to run the engine in a test tank.*

> *WARNING*
> *Stay clear of the propeller shaft while running an engine on a flush/test device. Remove the propeller before running the engine or while performing the test. Disconnect all spark plug lead(s) and battery connections before removing or installing a propeller.*

> *NOTE*
> *Oil pressure specifications are not available for F9.9, T9.9, F15 and F25 models. If the oil pressure warning system activates on these models, inspect the oil pump and*

pickup screen as described in Chapter Eight.

An oil pressure gauge (**Figure 85**) and an accurate shop tachometer are required to perform an oil pressure test. Perform the test while running the engine on a flush test device or in a test tank. Refer to *Oil Pressure Switch Test* in this chapter to determine the location of the oil pressure switch. Refer to **Table 21** for the oil pressure specification. Use an oil pressure gauge capable or reading $0\text{-}7$ kg/cm^2 (0-100 psi). Use an adapter with the same thread as the oil pressure switch to attach the gauge to engine.

1. Run the engine in a test tank or on a flush/test adapter until it reaches normal operating temperature.

2. With the engine switched off, note the wire location points and wire routing. Remove the wire from the oil pressure switch.

3. Use a suitable wrench to remove the oil pressure switch from the engine. Install the adapter (**Figure 85**) into the threaded hole for the oil pressure switch and tighten securely. Attach the oil pressure gauge to the adapter.

4. Following the manufacturer's instructions to attach the shop tachometer to the engine.

5. Start the engine and check for leakage at the gauge attaching points.

6. With the engine in neutral, advance the throttle until the tachometer indicates the engine speed specified in **Table 21**. Record the oil pressure reading on the gauge. Switch the engine off.

> *NOTE*
> *Oil pressure specifications are not available for F9.9, T9.9, F15 and F25 models. If the oil pressure warning system activates on these models, inspect the oil pump and pickup screen as described in Chapter Eight.*

7. Compare the oil pressure with the specification. Oil pressure below or above the listed specification indicates a problem with the oil pump system. Inspect the oil pump and related components as described in Chapter Eight.

8. Remove the shop tachometer, oil pressure gauge and adapter. Install the oil pressure switch and tighten securely.

9. Connect the wire to the oil pressure switch. Ensure that the wire is routed correctly. Start the engine and check for oil leakage at the oil pressure switch area. Correct any oil leakage before returning the engine to service.

(81)

SPARK PLUG CONDITION

NORMAL
- Identified by light tan or gray deposits on the firing tip.
- Can be cleaned.

GAP BRIDGED
- Identified by deposit buildup closing gap between electrodes.
- Caused by oil or carbon fouling. If deposits are not excessive, the plug can be cleaned.

OIL FOULED
- Identified by wet black deposits on the insulator shell bore and electrodes.
- Caused by excessive oil entering combustion chamber through worn rings and pistons, excessive clearance between valve guides and stems or worn or loose bearings. Can be cleaned. If engine is not repaired, use a hotter plug.

CARBON FOULED
- Identified by black, dry fluffy carbon deposits on insulator tips, exposed shell surfaces and electrodes.
- Caused by too cold a plug, weak ignition, dirty air cleaner, too rich fuel mixture or excessive idling. Can be cleaned.

LEAD FOULED
- Identified by dark gray, black, yellow or tan deposits or a fused glazed coating on the insulator tip.
- Caused by highly leaded gasoline. Can be cleaned.

WORN
- Identified by severely eroded or worn electrodes
- Caused by normal wear. Should be replaced.

FUSED SPOT DEPOSIT
- Identified by melted or spotty deposits resembling bubbles or blisters.
- Caused by sudden acceleration. Can be cleaned.

OVERHEATING
- Identified by a white or light gray insulator with small black or gray brown spots with bluish-burnt appearance of electrodes.
- Caused by engine overheating, wrong type of fuel, loose spark plugs, too hot a plug or incorrect ignition timing. Replace the plug.

PREIGNITION
- Identified by melted electrodes and possibly blistered insulator. Metallic deposits on insulator indicate engine damage.
- Caused by wrong type of fuel, incorrect ignition timing or advance, too hot a plug, burned valves or engine overheating. Replace the plug.

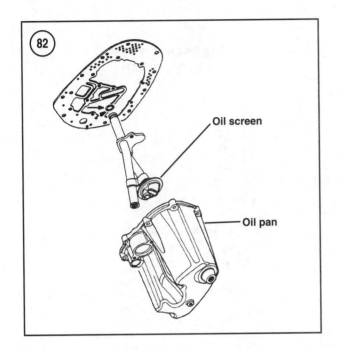

Oil screen

Oil pan

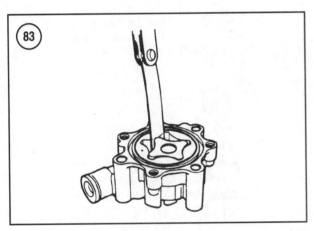

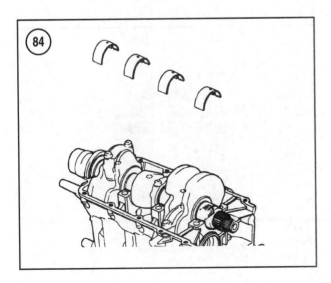

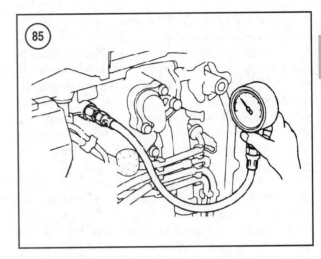

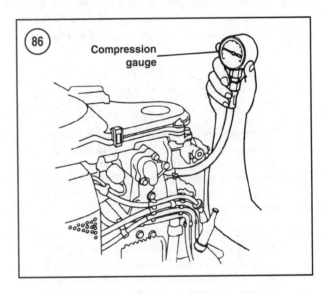

Compression gauge

Compression Test

A compression gauge (**Figure 86**) and adapter are required to perform a compression test. They are available at automotive parts stores and from tool suppliers. A small squirt can of engine oil may also be required.

1. Remove the spark plugs and connect the spark plug leads to an engine ground.

2. Install the adapter and compression gauge (**Figure 86**) into the No. 1 spark plug hole. Position the throttle in the wide-open position during testing.

3. Stand clear of the remaining spark plug openings during testing. Observe the compression gauge while operating the manual or electric starter. Make sure the engine has made a minimum of ten revolutions and the cranking speed is at or above 350 rpm. Record the compression reading.

4. Repeat Steps 2 and 3 for the remaining cylinders. Record all compression readings.

5. Compare the readings with the specification listed in **Table 23**. Perform Step 6 if any of the readings are below the specification. Go to Step 8 if all readings are within the listed specification.

6. Pour approximately one teaspoon of engine oil into any cylinder with low compression. Rotate the engine several revolutions to distribute the oil in the cylinder. Repeat Steps 2 and 3 for each suspect cylinder.

7. Compare the second compression reading with the first compression reading. A higher second reading indicates that low compression is the result of a problem with the piston, piston rings or cylinder walls. The valve or valve seat is faulty if no increase in compression is noted. Refer to Chapter Eight to repair the power head.

8. Position the throttle in the closed position. Remove the compression gauge and adapter. Install the spark plug leads.

COOLING SYSTEM

CAUTION
Never run an outboard without providing cooling water. Use either a test tank or flush/test device. Remove the propeller before running the engine on a flush/test device. Use a suitable test propeller to run the engine in a test tank.

WARNING
Stay clear of the propeller shaft while running an engine on a flush/test device. Remove the propeller before running the engine or while performing the test. Disconnect all spark plug lead(s) and battery connections before removing or installing a propeller.

System Description

The drive shaft in the gearcase drives the water pump mounted on the drive shaft. The water is pumped to the exhaust area of the power head, then to the cylinder block. The water exits the power head near the power head mounting surface through the drive shaft housing. As the water travels through the power head, it carries heat away. If the engine overheats, the water volume through the power head is insufficient or the water is not absorbing the heat. All models are equipped with a thermostat (**Figure 88**) to help maintain a minimum power head temperature and improve low speed running. They restrict exit water until a minimum water temperature is attained.

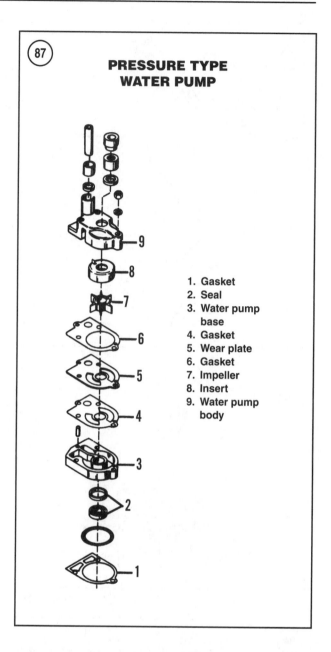

87

PRESSURE TYPE WATER PUMP

1. Gasket
2. Seal
3. Water pump base
4. Gasket
5. Wear plate
6. Gasket
7. Impeller
8. Insert
9. Water pump body

88

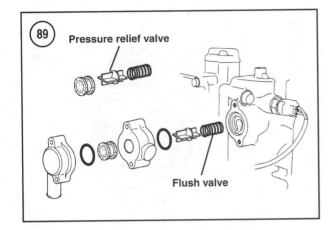

89

Pressure relief valve

Flush valve

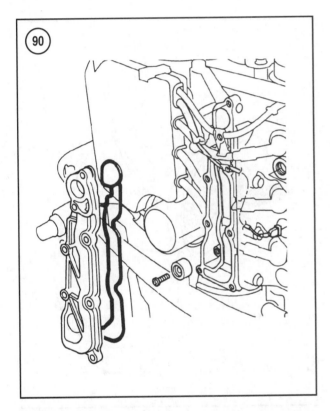

90

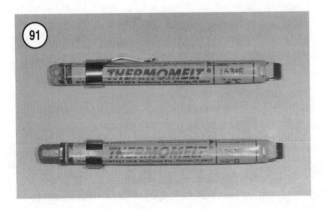

91

A stream of water is visible at the rear of the lower motor cover if the cooling system operates correctly. The fitting may become blocked with debris. Clean the passage with a small, stiff wire. Inspect the cooling system if the water stream is still not present. F80 and F100 hp models are equipped with a water pressure control valve (**Figure 89**) to provide adequate water pressure in the cylinder block at low speeds. Blockage in the valve can cause overheating at higher engine speeds. Never run the engine without supplying it with cooling water.

Cooling System Inspection

If the overheat warning horn sounds or if the water stream is not present at the rear of the engine, perform the following procedure

1. Inspect and repair the water pump. Refer to Chapter Nine.

2. Inspect and test the thermostat if overheating occurs and the water pump is in good condition. Refer to *Thermostat Test* in this chapter.

3. If no faults are found with the water pump, thermostat or water pressure relief valve (if so equipped), inspect the exhaust water jacket portion (**Figure 90**, typical) of the cooling system for debris and deposit buildup. Rocks, pieces of the water pump impeller, sand, shells or other debris may restrict water flow. Salt, calcium or other deposits can form in the cooling passages and restrict water flow.

4. Deposit buildup prevents the water from absorbing the heat from the power head. Use a cleaner specifically designed to dissolve this type of deposit. Make sure the cleaner is suitable for use on aluminum material. Always follow the manufacture's instructions when using these products. Cleaners are usually available at marine specialty stores.

5. It is necessary to remove the water jacket covers when inspecting cooling passages. Refer to Chapter Eight for water jacket removal and installation.

Verifying Engine Temperature

To verify the actual temperature of the engine, use Thermomelt Sticks (**Figure 91**). Thermomelt sticks resemble crayons and are designed to melt at a given temperature. Hold the sticks against the cylinder head near the temperature sender or switch. On smaller engines not equipped with an overheat alarm, hold the stick near the spark plug area. Check the temperature while the engine may be overheating, if possible. Hold different temperature sticks to the power head to determine the temperature

3

range the engine is reaching. Stop the engine if the temperature exceeds 90° C (194° F) to avoid damage to the power head. Perform a complete cooling system inspection if overheating is occurring. Test the overheat switch if the alarm or gauge indicates overheating, but the thermomelt sticks indicate normal temperature. Troubleshooting an overheating problem with a flush/test attachment is difficult. The water supplied through the hose masks problems with the cooling system. Perform this test with the engine in the water or use a test tank.

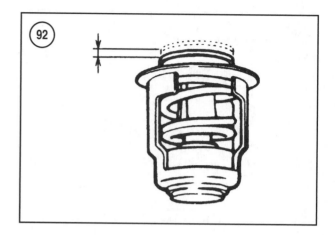

Thermostat Testing

Test the thermostat(s) if the engine is overheats or runs too cool. A thermometer, a piece of string and a container of water that can be heated is necessary to test the thermostat. Refer to Chapter Eight to locate the thermostat cover and related components.

1. Remove the thermostat(s) following the procedure in Chapter Eight. Discard the thermostat cover gasket. Tie a string to the thermostat and suspend the thermostat in the container of water.

2. Place the thermometer in the container and begin heating the water. Continue to heat the water while observing the temperature and thermostat.

3. The thermostat should begin to open at approximately 70° C (158° F). Measure the thermostat valve opening (A, **Figure 92**). The measurement should be a minimum of 3 mm (0.12 in.).

4. Replace the thermostat if it fails to operate as described.

5. Install the thermostat with a new gasket following the procedure in Chapter Eight.

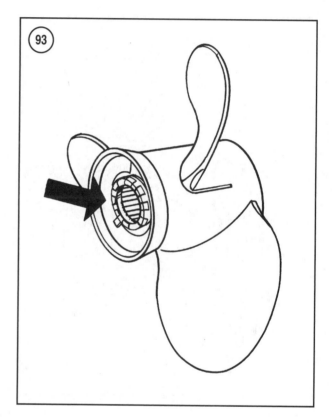

GEARCASE

Problems with the gearcase can include water or lubricant leakage, faulty internal components, noisy operation or shifting difficulty. To prevent gearcase problems, avoid contact with underwater objects, shift the engine into gear at idle speed only and perform regular maintenance. Maintenance procedures for the gearcase are in Chapter Four.

A slipping propeller hub can resemble a problem with the gearcase, while only minor repair to the propeller is required. Typical symptoms include an inability to accelerate the boat onto plane without over-speeding the engine and the engine seeming to not shifting into gear at all.

Propeller Hub Slipping

The propeller hub (**Figure 93**) in the propeller cushions the shifting action and helps absorb minor impacts. If the propeller hub spins in its bore, the engine speed increases as the throttle increases, but the boat speed does not increase. Some smaller engines use a shear pin (**Figure 94**) designed to break on impact. Symptoms indicating a broken cotter pin are similar to a slipping propeller hub.

To determine if the propeller hub slips, make a reference mark on the propeller shaft aligned with a reference

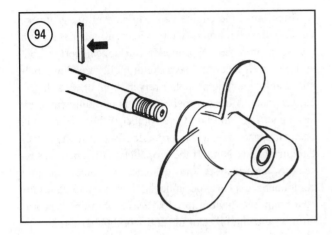

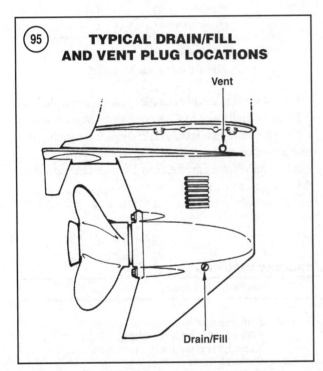

**TYPICAL DRAIN/FILL
AND VENT PLUG LOCATIONS**

Vent

Drain/Fill

mark on the propeller. Operate the boat, then compare the reference marks. Have the propeller repaired if the reference marks do not align after running the engine.

Water in the Gearcase

A small amount of water may be present in the gearcase lubricant if the gearcase has not received normal maintenance for several years and has been stored while submerged in water. Pressure test the gearcase to determine the source of water leakage if water is found in the gearcase lubricant. Refer to *Pressure Test* in this chapter. Failure to correct water leakage eventually causes exten-

sive damage to the internal components or complete failure of the gearcase. If repair is required, refer to Chapter Nine.

Lubricant Leakage

If gearcase lubricant is on the exterior or around the gearcase, perform a pressure test to determine the source of the leakage. Refer to *Pressure Testing* in this chapter. Failure to correct a leakage causes gear and bearing damage due to insufficient lubrication. Refer to Chapter Nine for gearcase repair procedures.

Pressure Test

A gearcase pressure tester is required to perform this test. Drain the gearcase lubricant and dispose of it properly. Apply air pressure to the internal cavities of the gearcase. The pressure gauge indicates if leakage is present. Submerge the entire gearcase in water and look for bubbles to determine the location of a leakage. Gearcase removal and installation are provided in Chapter Nine. Refer to Chapter Nine to locate the drain and vent plugs.
1. Place a suitable container below the gearcase. Position the gearcase so the drain (**Figure 95**) is as close as possible to the container. The engine may need to be tilted slightly. Remove the drain and vent plugs, (**Figure 95**) and allow the gearcase to drain completely.
2. Install the pressure tester into the vent opening. Install the drain plug.
3. Slowly apply pressure with the pressure tester. Push, pull and turn all shafts while observing the pressure gauge. Stop increasing pressure when it reaches approximately 100 kPa (14.5 psi).
4. If the gearcase does not hold this pressure for at least 10 seconds, remove the gearcase as described in Chapter Nine. Submerge the gearcase with pressure applied to locate the leak. Replace the seal and/or seal surface at the location where bubbles appear. Refer to Chapter Nine for repair procedures.
5. Loosen the drain plug to allow the air to slowly bleed from the gearcase. Refill the gearcase with fresh lubricant as described in Chapter Four.

Metal Contamination in the Lubricant

Fine metal particles form in the gearcase during normal usage. The gearcase lubricant may have a *metal flake* appearance when inspected during routine maintenance. Fine metal particles may cling to the end of the drain plug. Rub some of the material between your finger and thumb.

Inspect the gearcase if the material is large enough to feel. Removing the propeller shaft-bearing carrier allows a view of the internal components. Refer to Chapter Nine for removal, inspection and assembly procedures.

Gearcase Vibration or Noise

Normal gearcase noise is barely noticeable during operation. However, a rough, growling noise or a loud high-pitched whine may indicate damaged or faulty components.

If a knocking or grinding noise comes from the gearcase, gears or other components are probably damaged. Underwater impact or high speed shifting may have damaged the gears. A knocking noise from the gearcase can sometimes indicate the power unit (power head) is faulty. Always inspect the gearcase lubricant before inspecting the power unit. Inspect the gearcase lubricant for metal contamination. In most cases, the gearcase lubricant indicates if internal components are damaged. Refer to Chapter Nine for removal and repair procedures.

A high-pitched whine normally indicates a bearing problem or the gears are not properly aligned. Disassemble and inspect the internal components to check for a problem. Have a professional listen to the gearcase before proceeding with a repair.

Vibration in the engine can originate in the gearcase. Usually, the vibration is due to a bent propeller shaft or a damaged propeller. A propeller can appear perfect, but still be out of balance. Have the propeller trued and balanced at a reputable propeller repair shop, or try a different propeller. A bent propeller shaft is normally cause by an impact with an underwater object. When vibration is occurring, check for a bent propeller following the procedure in Chapter Nine. If the propeller shaft is bent, disassemble and inspect the gearcase as other internal components may also be damaged. Never operate the outboard motor with vibration. Excessive vibration can compromise the durability of the entire outboard motor.

WARNING
Remove all spark plug leads and disconnect both battery cables before removing, installing or working around the propeller.

Hard shifting is usually caused by an improper shift cable adjustment. Refer to Chapter Five to adjust the shift cables and linkage. Gearcase removal, disassembly and inspection are required if shifting problems are not corrected with adjustment. Refer to Chapter Nine to adjust the shift cable to linkage.

Table 1 STARTING SYSTEM TROUBLESHOOTING

Symptom	Causes	Corrective Action
Electric starter does not operate	Engine not in neutral	Shift into neutral
	Weak or discharged battery	Fully charge and test battery
	Dirty or corroded terminals	Thoroughly clean battery terminals
	Blown fuse in wire harness	Check all fuses
	Faulty neutral start switch	Test neutral switch operation
	Faulty starter button or switch	Test starter button or switch
	Faulty starter relay	Test starter relay
	Dirty or loose starter wires	Clean and tighten wire connections
	Faulty starter motor	Repair starter motor
	Improperly installed starter	Check for proper installation
	Improperly installed wires	Check for proper wire installation
Starter engages flywheel but rotates slowly	Weak or discharged battery	Fully charge and test battery
	Dirty or corroded battery	Thoroughly clean battery terminals terminals
	Loose or faulty starter wires	Clean, tighten and repair wire connections
	Faulty starter motor	Repair starter motor
	Improperly installed starter	Check for proper installation
	Engine is in gear	Check and correct shift system
	Water or oil in the cylinder(s)	Remove and inspect spark plug(s)
	Seized power head	Check for power head seizure
	Seized gearcase	Check for gearcase failure
	(continued)	

3

Table 1 STARTING SYSTEM TROUBLESHOOTING (continued)

Symptom	Causes	Corrective Action
Starter engages flywheel but flywheel does not rotate	Weak or discharged battery	Fully charge and test battery
	Dirty or corroded battery terminals	Thoroughly clean battery terminals
	Loose or faulty starter wires	Clean, tighten and repair wire connections
	Faulty starter motor	Repair starter motor
	Improperly installed starter	Check for proper installation
	Seized gearcase assembly	Check for gearcase failure
	Seized power head	Check for manual flywheel rotation
	Water in the cylinders	Check for water in the cylinders
	Oil in the cylinders	Remove and inspect the spark plugs
	Faulty starter motor	Repair starter motor
Noisy starter operation	Dirty or dry starter drive	Clean and lubricate starter drive
	Improperly installed starter	Check for proper installation
	Worn or dry starter bearings	Repair starter motor
	Corroded or damaged flywheel gear	Check condition of flywheel gear teeth
	Worn or damaged starter drive	Check condition of starter drive
	Internal power head damage	Check for problem in power head
	Internal gearcase damage	Check for problem in gearcase

Table 2 FUEL SYSTEM TROUBLESHOOTING

Symptom	Causes	Corrective Action
Engine will not start	Old or contaminated or fuel	Supply the engine with fresh fuel
	Fuel pump malfunction	Check for proper pump operation
	Plugged carburetor jets	See Plugged Carburetor Jets (Chapter Three)
	Improper carburetor adjustment	Check carburetor adjustment (Chapter Five)
	Blocked fuel filter	Check all fuel filters
	Closed fuel tank vent	Check for closed vent
	Air leakage in the fuel hoses	Check fuel hoses
	Faulty primer bulb	Test primer bulb
	Fuel leaking from system	Check for fuel leakage
	Flooding carburetor	Check for flooding carburetor
	Improper choke operation	Check for proper choke operation
	Faulty electrothermal valve	Test the electrothermal valve
Rough idle	Old or contaminated fuel	Supply the engine with fresh fuel
	Fuel pump malfunction	Check for proper pump operation
	Plugged carburetor jets	See plugged carburetor jets (Chapter Three)
	Improper carburetor adjustment	Correct carburetor adjustment (Chapter Five)
Air leakage in the fuel hoses	Check fuel hoses	
	Flooding carburetor	Check for flooding carburetor
	Improper choke operation	Check for proper choke operation
Engine dies at idle speed	Old or contaminated or fuel	Supply the engine with fresh fuel
	Fuel pump malfunction	Check for proper pump operation
	Plugged carburetor jets	See Plugged Carburetor Jets (Chapter Three)
	Improper carburetor adjustment	Check carburetor adjustment
	Blocked fuel filter	Check all fuel filters
	Closed fuel tank vent	Check for closed vent
	Air leakage in the fuel hoses	Check fuel hoses
	Fuel leaking from system	Check for fuel leakage
	Flooding carburetor	Check for flooding carburetor
	Improper choke operation	Check for proper choke operation
	Incorrect idle speed adjustment	Adjust idle speed (Chapter Five)
	Misadjusted throttle position sensor	Adjust sensor (Chapter Five)
	Faulty primer bulb	Test primer bulb

(continued)

Table 2 FUEL SYSTEM TROUBLESHOOTING (continued)

Symptom	Causes	Corrective Action
Idle speed too high	Improper carburetor adjustment	Check carburetor adjustment
	Improper idle speed adjustment	Adjust as required
	Improperly adjusted throttle cable	Check cable adjustment
	Binding throttle linkage	Check linkage
	Incorrect idle speed adjustment	Adjust idle speed (Chapter Five)
	Faulty electrothermal valve	Test electrothermal valve
Bogging on acceleration	Faulty accelerator pump	Check accelerator pump
	Old or contaminated or fuel	Supply the engine with fresh fuel
	Fuel pump malfunction	Check for proper pump operation
	Plugged carburetor jets	See Plugged Carburetor Jets (Chapter Three)
	Improper carburetor adjustment	Check carburetor adjustment
	Blocked fuel filter	Check all fuel filters
	Closed fuel tank vent	Check for and correct closed vent
	Air leakage in the fuel hoses	Check fuel hoses
	Fuel leaking from system	Check for fuel leakage
	Flooding carburetor	Check for flooding carburetor
	Improper choke operation	Check for proper choke operation
	Misadjusted throttle position sensor	Adjust sensor (see Chapter Five)
	Faulty electrothermal valve	Test electrothermal valve
Misfire at high engine speed	Old or contaminated or fuel	Supply the engine with fresh fuel
	Fuel pump malfunction	Check for proper pump operation
	Plugged carburetor jets	See Plugged Carburetor Jets (Chapter Three)
	Blocked fuel filter	Check all fuel filters
	Closed fuel tank vent	Check for and correct closed vent
	Air leaks in the fuel hoses	Check fuel hoses
	Fuel leaking from system	Check for fuel leakage
	Improper choke operation	Check for proper choke operation
	Faulty primer bulb	Test primer bulb
Excessive exhaust smoke	Improper carburetor adjustment	Check carburetor adjustment
	Fuel leaking from system	Check for fuel leaks
	Flooding carburetor	Check for flooding carburetor
	Improper choke operation	Check for proper choke operation

Table 3 IGNITION TIMING SPECIFICATIONS

Model	Full retard timing	Full advance timing
F9.9, T9.9	2-8° BTDC	32-38° BTDC
F15	2-8° BTDC	27-33° BTDC
F25	7-13° BTDC	27-33° BTDC
F40, F50, T50	5° BTDC	35° BTDC
F80, F100	5° ATDC	25° BTDC

Table 4 MODEL IDENIFICATION

Model	Year	Starting Serial No.
F9.9SK	1985-1990	000101
F9.9LK	1985-1990	300101
F9.9MSHP	1991	007080
F9.9MLHP	1991	304067
T9.9MHQ	1992	XL: 702322
T9.9EHQ	1992	L: 467478, XL: 784767
T9.9ERQ	1992	L: 405274
F9.9MHQ	1992	S: 007654, L: 304868
T9.9MHR	1993	L: 303184, XL: 702599
T9.9EHR	1993	L: 468608, XL: 785690
T9.9ERR	1993	S: 100536, L: 406983, XL: 761468

(continued)

TABLE 4 ENGINE MODEL IDENIFICATION (continued)

Model	Year	Starting Serial No.
F9.9MHR	1993	S: 008200 L: 305540
T9.9MHS	1994	L: 303492, XL: 702756
T9.9EHS	1994	L: 469307, XL: 786352
T9.9ERS	1994	S: 100690, L: 408272, XL: 761594
T9.9MHT	1995	L: 303720, XL: 702943
T9.9EHT	1995	L: 470253, XL: 786920
T9.9ERT	1995	S: 100839, L: 409897, XL: 761822
F9.9MHT	1995	S: 009053, L: 306647
T9.9MHU	1996	L: 303984, XL: 703193
T9.9EHU	1996	L: 471124, XL: 787490
T9.9ERU	1996	S: 100971, L: 411409, XL: 762032
F9.9MHU	1996	S: 009454, L: 307212
F9.9EHU	1996	S: 200321, L: 500329
T9.9MHW	1998	L: 304623, XL: 703474
T9.9EHW	1998	L: 472276, XL: 788442
T9.9ERW	1998	S: 101224, L: 413584, XL: 762552
F9.9MHW	1998	S: 010452, L: 308168
F9.9EHW	1998	S: 200421, L: 500514
F15MHW	1998	S: 000101, L: 300101
F15EHW	1998	S: 200101, L: 500101
F25EHW	1998	S: 050101, L: 350101
F25ERW	1998	S: 000101, L: 300101
F25ETW	1998	L: 400101
F25MHX	1999	S: 150101, L: 250101, XL: 550101
F25THX	1999	L: 450355
F25TRX	1999	L: 401032
F40TRX	1999	L: 400687
F40ERX	1999	L: 300135
F40THX	1999	L: 450201
F40EHX	1999	L: 350101
F50TRT	1995	L: 400101
F50THT	1995	L: 450101
F50TRU	1996	L: 401901
F50THU	1996	L: 450251
T50TRU	1996	L: 400122
F50TRW	1998	L: 406877
F50THW	1998	L: 451017
T50TRW	1998	L: 401951
F50TRX	1999	L: 409828
F50ERX	1999	L: 300837
F50THX	1999	L: 451272
F50EHX	1999	L: 350330
T50TRX	1999	L: 402765
F80TRX	1999	L: 300101, XL: 700101
F100TRX	1999	L: 300101, XL: 700101

S: Short shaft
L: Long shaft
XL: Extra Long shaft

Table 5 IGNITION SYSTEM RESISTANCE SPECIFICATIONS (1985-1990 F9.9 AND T9.9)*

Pulser coil resistance	173-211 ohms
Charge coil resistance	569-695 ohms
Ignition coil resistance	
Primary winding	0.085-0.115 ohm
Secondary winding	2890-3910 ohms
Lighting coil resistance	0.25-0.30 ohm

*At 20° C (68° F)

Table 6 IGNITION SYSTEM RESISTANCE SPECIFICATIONS (1991 F9.9 AND T9.9)*

Charge coil resistance	569-695 ohms (brown-blue)
Pulser coil resistance	162-198 ohms (white/red-black)
Ignition coil resistance	
Primary winding	0.078-0.106 ohm
Secondary winding	3480-4720 ohms
*At 20° C (68° F)	

Table 7 IGNITION SYSTEM RESISTANCE SPECIFICATIONS (1992-1995 F9.9 AND T9.9)*

Charge coil resistance	280-420 ohms (brown-blue)
Pulser coil resistance	168-152 ohms (white/red-black)
Ignition coil resistance	
Primary winding	0.074-0.110 ohm
Secondary winding	3280-4920 (k)
*At 20° C (68° F)	

Table 8 IGNITION SYSTEM VOLTAGE OUTPUT SPECIFICATIONS (1996-1997 F9.9 AND T9.9)

CDI voltage output	
Cranking speed	150 volts
1500 rpm	210 volts
Charge coil output	
Cranking speed	160 volts
1500 rpm	230 volts
Pulser coil output	
Cranking speed	7 volts
1500 rpm	10 volts

TABLE 9 IGNITION SYSTEM VOLTAGE OUTPUT SPECIFICATIONS (1998-1999 F9.9 AND T9.9)

CDI voltage output	
Cranking speed	90 volts
1500 rpm	205 volts
3500 rpm	195 volts
Charge coil output	
Cranking speed	150 volts
1500 rpm	220 volts
3500 rpm	210 volts
Pulser coil output	
Cranking speed	2.5 volts
1500 rpm	7.5 volts
3500 rpm	12.0 volts

TABLE 10 IGNITION SYSTEM SPECIFICATIONS (1998-1999 F15)

Charge coil output		
500 rpm	130 volts	Brown-blue
1500 rpm	180 volts	–
3500 rpm	180 volts	–
Pulser coil output		
500 rpm	4.0 volts	White/green-black
500 rpm	3.5 volts	White/green-black
1500 rpm	11.0 volts	–
3500 rpm	23.0 volts	–

(continued)

Table 10 IGNITION SYSTEM SPECIFICATIONS (1998-1999 F15) (continued)

CDI unit output		
500 rpm	120 volts	Orange-black
500 rpm	115 volts	Orange-black
1500 rpm	160 volts	–
3500 rpm	160 volts	–
Ignition coil resistance		
Primary winding	0.16-0.24 ohm	
Secondary winding	3940-5880 ohms	

Table 11 IGNITION SYSTEM VOLTAGE OUTPUT AND RESISTANCE SPECIFICATIONS (1998-1999 F25)

Charge coil output		
500 rpm	210 volts	Green/white-white/green
1500 rpm	210 volts	–
3500 rpm	210 volts	–
Pulser coil output		
500 rpm	90 volts	Red-white
500 rpm	90 volts	Red-white
1500 rpm	210 volts	–
3500 rpm	240 volts	–
CDI unit output		
500 rpm	180 volts	Black/white-orange
1500 rpm	190 volts	–
3500 rpm	190 volts	–
Charge coil resistance	660-710 ohms	White/green-green/white
Pulser coil resistance	300-350 ohms	–
Ignition coil resistance		
Primary winding	0.08-0.70 ohm	–
Secondary winding	3500-4700 ohms	–

Table 12 IGNITION SYSTEM SPECIFICATIONS (1999 F40-1995-1999 F50)

Charge coil output		
400 rpm	140 volts	Brown-blue
1500 rpm	150 volts	–
3500 rpm	135 volts	–
Pulser coil output		
400 rpm	7.0 volts	White/black-white/red
1500 rpm	14.0 volts	–
3500 rpm	20.0 volts	–
CDI output		
400 rpm	105 volts	Black/orange-black
		Black/white-black
1500 rpm	110 volts	–
3500 rpm	100 volts	–
Charge coil resistance*	272-408 ohms	Brown-blue
Pulser coil resistance*	340-510 ohms	White/black-white/red
Ignition coil resistance*		
Primary winding	0.078-0.106 ohm	–
Secondary winding	3500-4700 ohms	–

*At 20° C (68° F)

Table 13 IGNITION SYSTEM SPECIFICATIONS (F80 AND F100)

Pickup coil output		
400 rpm	4.5 volts	White/black-black
		White/red-black
1500 rpm	10.0 volts	–
3500 rpm	16.0 volts	–

(continued)

Table 13 IGNITION SYSTEM SPECIFICATIONS (F80 AND F100) (continued)

CDI unit output		
400 rpm	107 volts	Black/white-black
		Black/orange-black
1500 rpm	110 volts	–
3500 rpm	111 volts	–
Pickup coil resistance*	445-545 ohms	White/black-black
		White/red-black
Ignition coil resistance*		
Primary winding	0.078-0.106 ohm	–
Secondary winding	3500-4700 ohms	–
*At 20° C (68° F)		

Table 14 ENRICHMENT VALVE AND ELECTROTHERMAL VALVE RESISTANCE SPECIFICATIONS

Component	Ohms	Wire color
Electrothermal valve		
F9.9-T9.9	4.8-7.2	black-black
F25	6.7-7.1	yellow/black-yellow/black
F40-F50	not available	green/white-black
F80-F100	20	green/white-black
Enrichment valve		
F9.9-T9.9	0.24-0.36	yellow
F25	4	yellow

Table 15 LIGHTING COIL RESISTANCE SPECIFICATIONS*

Lighting coil resistance		
9.9 hp	6 amp	0.25-0.30 ohms
15 hp	6 Amp (G-G)	0.48-0.72 ohms
	10 amp (G-G/W)	0.24-0.36 ohms
25 hp	18 amp (Y-Y)	0.22-0.24 ohms
40 hp	15 amp (G-G)	1.20-1.80 ohms
50 hp	10 amp (G-G)	1.20-1.80 ohms
80-100 hp	20 amp (W-W)	0.32-0.48 ohms
*At 20° C (68° F)		

Table 16 LIGHTING COIL VOLTAGE OUTPUT

	Wire color	Volts
9.9 hp		
Cranking	G-G	9.0
	G/W-B	8.0
1500 rpm	G-G	35
	G/W-B	30
3500 rpm	G-G	75
	G/W-B	65
15 hp		
Cranking	G-G/W	6.5
1500 rpm	–	21
3500 rpm	–	46
25 hp		
Cranking	Y-Y	10
1500 rpm	–	25
3500 rpm	–	65
	(continued)	

3

Table 16 LIGHTING COIL VOLTAGE OUTPUT (continued)

	Wire color	Volts
40-50 hp		
Cranking	G-G	10
1500 rpm	–	16
3500 rpm	–	19
80-100 hp		
Cranking	W-W	7.0
1500 rpm	–	15
3500 rpm	–	18

Table 17 RECTIFIER/REGULATOR OUTPUT VOLTAGE

	Wire color (red-black)	Volts-circuit	Volts-loaded
9.9-15 hp (6 amp)			
Cranking	R-B	6.0	–
1500 rpm		20	–
3500 rpm		–	46
15 hp (10 amp)			
Cranking	R-B	6.0	–
1500 rpm		20	–
3500 rpm		–	46
25 hp			
Cranking	R-B	9.0	12
1500 rpm		35	12
3500 rpm		15	12
40-50 hp			
Cranking	R-B	–	9.5
1500 rpm		–	15
3500 rpm		–	15
80-100 hp			
Cranking	R-B	–	–
1500		–	14
3500		–	18

Table 18 TRIM SENDER RESISTANCE SPECIFICATIONS*

40-50 hp model	
Pink-black	360-540 ohms
Orange-black	800-1200 ohms
80-100 hp model	
Pink-black	582-873 ohms
Orange-black	800-1200 ohms

*At 20° C (68° F)

Table 19 WIRING COLOR CODE

B	Black
Br	Brown
L	Blue
G	Green
Gy	Gray
Lg	Light green
O	Orange
P	Pink
R	Red
Sb	Sky blue
W	White
	(continued)

Table 19 WIRING COLOR CODE (continued)

Y	Yellow
B/O	Black/orange
B/W	Black/white
B/Y	Black/yellow
G/W	Green/white
P/B	Pink/black
P/W	Pink/white
W/B	White/black
W/R	White/red

Table 20 RECOMMENDED ENGINE SPEED

Idle speed	
F9.9	900-1000 rpm
T9.9	1100-1200 rpm
F15	900-1000 rpm
F25	875-975 rpm
F40-F50-FT50	700-800 rpm
F80-F100	850-950 rpm
Full-throttle speed	
F9.9-T9.9 and F15	4500-5500 rpm
F25-F100	5000-6000 rpm
Trolling range	
F9.9 and T9.9	800-900 rpm
Maximum horsepower output	
F9.9 and T9.9	5.9 kW (8 hp) @ 5000 rpm
F15	11 kW (15 hp) @ 5000 rpm
F25	18.4 kW (25 hp) @ 5500 rpm
F40	29.4 kW (40 hp) @ 5500 rpm
F50 and T50	36.8 kW (50 hp) @ 5500 rpm
F80	58.8 kW (80 hp) @ 5500 rpm
F100	73.6 kW (100 hp) @ 5500 rpm

Table 21 OIL PRESSURE SPECIFICATIONS

Model	kPa (psi)	Temperature
40-50	150 (21)	55° C (131° F) at 850 rpm
80-100	320 (45.5)	65° C (149° F) at idle
	118 (16.78)	100° C (212° F) at 1000 rpm

Table 22 GENERAL TORQUE SPECIFICATIONS

Nut	N•m	in.-lb.	ft.-lb.
8 mm	5.0	44	–
10 mm	8.0	71	–
12 mm	18	–	13
14 mm	36	–	25
17 mm	43	–	32

Table 23 COMPRESSION PRESSURE

Model	Minimum pressure
F9.9 and T9.9 hp	785 kPa (114 psi)
F15 hp	1196 kPa (173 psi)
F25 hp	1180-1250 kPa (171-181 psi)
F50 hp	1270 kPa (184 psi)
F40 hp, F50 and T50 hp	900 kPa (130 psi)
F80 and F100 hp	950 kPa (138 psi)

Chapter Four

Lubrication, Maintenance and Tune-Up

A properly operating outboard provides smooth operation, reliable starting and excellent performance. Regular maintenance and frequent tune-ups help keep it running at its best. This chapter provides the procedures and information necessary to perform lubrication, maintenance and tune-up on the Yamaha four-stroke outboard.

During normal operation, certain components and fluids in the engine wear or become contaminated. unless these components and fluids are renewed, engine performance, reliability and engine life suffer. Performing routine lubrication, maintenance and tune-up helps ensure the outboard performs as it should and has a long and trouble free life.

This chapter provides lubrication and maintenance procedures for most systems and components on the engine. Certain components or systems on the engine require maintenance or inspection at more frequent intervals than others. **Table 1** lists the maintenance items and intervals for all engine systems and components. Maintenance intervals are also provided in the quick reference data section at the front of the manual. **Tables 1-7** are located at the end of this chapter.

This chapter also provides the procedures needed to perform an engine tune-up. A gradual decrease in performance and running quality occurs as certain components wear during normal operation. The operator does not notice as this occurs gradually. If not corrected, it will cause decreased performance, reduced fuel economy and a shortened engine life. A complete engine tune-up can restore most of the lost performance and improve fuel economy.

Because of their unique application, outboards may suffer complete or partial submersion. If this occurs, special procedures must be followed to minimize damage to the engine. Refer to *Special Maintenance Requirements* in this chapter for instructions.

Special procedures are required if the engine requires either short or long-term storage. Refer to the *Special Maintenance Requirements* in this chapter for instructions.

Engines used in salt laden or polluted water are especially susceptible to corrosion. Additional maintenance can minimize the damage caused by corrosion. Refer to *Special Maintenance Requirements* in this chapter for instructions.

LUBRICATION AND MAINTENANCE

The most common maintenance items are checking and/or changing the lubricating fluids, cleaning the engine, and applying grease or other lubricants to certain engine components. Lubrication is the most important maintenance item for any outboard. The outboard will not operate without proper lubrication. Lubricant for the power head, gearcase and other areas helps prevent component wear, guards against corrosion and provides smooth operation of turning or sliding surfaces.

Outboards operate in a corrosive environment and often require special types of lubricants. Using the incorrect type of lubricant can cause serious engine damage or substantially shorten the life of the engine. Lubricant specifications are provided in the applicable maintenance procedures. Special pumps (**Figure 1**) and lubricants are required to perform many of the maintenance items. These pumps are available from most automotive parts stores. The lubricants are available from most marine suppliers or marine dealerships.

Before Each Use

This section provides instructions for performing the following inspections:
1. Checking the oil level.
2. Checking the propeller.
3. Checking the engine mounting bolts/screws.
4. Checking the fuel system for leakage.
5. Checking the steering system for looseness or binding.
6. Checking the cooling system.
7. Checking the operation of the lanyard or stop switch.

> *CAUTION*
> *Never run the engine with the oil level over the full mark on the dipstick. Over filling the oil can result in oil foaming and inadequate lubrication of internal components.*

Checking the oil level

To prevent serious damage to the power head always check the engine oil level before starting the engine. To avoid over filling the oil, wait until the engine has been off for 30 minutes or more. This allows the oil in the engine to drain into the oil pan. Always check the oil level with the engine in a vertical position (**Figure 2**). The location and type of oil dipstick (**Figure 3**) varies by model. A yellow handle (on most models) allows easy identification of the dipstick.

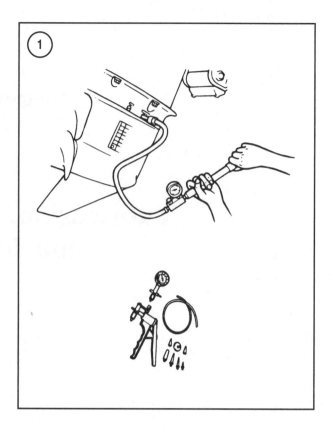

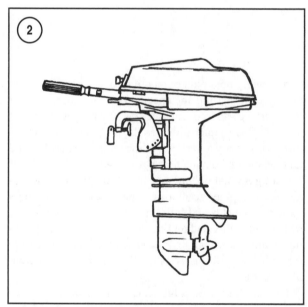

On 9.9, 15 and 25 hp models, the push-in type oil dipstick is located on the lower starboard side of the power head just below the intake manifold (**Figure 4**).

On 40 and 50 hp models, the push in type oil dipstick is located on the lower port side of the power head just below the electrothermal valve (**Figure 5**).

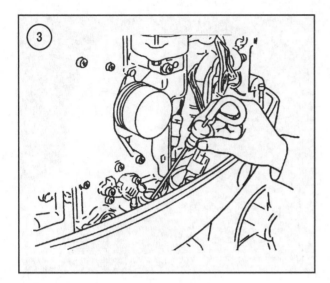

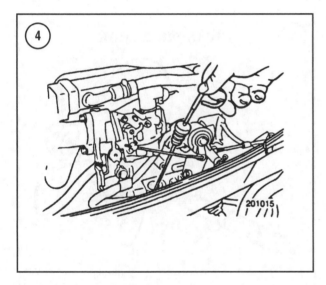

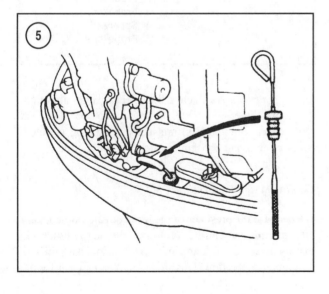

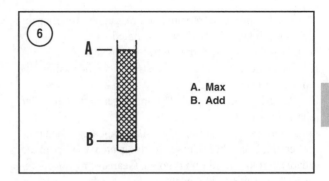

A. Max
B. Add

4

On 80 and 100 hp models, the push-in type oil dipstick (**Figure 3**) is located on the lower starboard side of the power head below the oil filter.

Check the oil level as follows:

1. Place the engine in the vertical position (**Figure 2**) with the ignition off.

2. To remove the dipstick from the engine, slightly turn it right to left while pulling straight up on it to pull it from its opening.

3. Wipe the dipstick with a clean shop towel.

4. Insert the oil dipstick fully into its opening.

5. Allow the dipstick to remain in position for 1 minute, then slowly pull the dipstick from the engine. Note the oil level relative to the *max and add* mark on the dipstick (**Figure 6**). Inspect the oil for water, a milky appearance or significant fuel odor. Refer to *Power Head* in Chapter Three if any of these conditions are noted.

6. Add a small quantity of oil to the engine following the instructions provided in this chapter under *Changing the engine oil*.

7. Repeat Steps 3-6 until the oil level is even with the *MAX* mark on the oil dipstick. Do not overfill the engine. It is far better for the oil level to be slightly below the *MAX* mark than to be above the mark. If necessary, drain excess oil from the engine as described in this chapter under *Changing the engine oil*.

8. Insert the dipstick fully into its opening. To secure it, slightly turn it right to left and push it into its opening until the cap portion of the dipstick contacts the dipstick tube opening.

Propeller Inspection

Inspect the propeller for cracked, damaged or missing blades (**Figure 7**). Operation with a damaged propeller results in decreased performance, excessive vibration and increased wear. Small bent areas can be easily straightened using locking pliers. Small nicks can be dressed with a metal file. To prevent imbalance, do not remove excessive amounts of material from the propeller.

Have the propeller repaired at a reputable propeller repair shop if significant damage is noted.

1. Place the engine in the neutral gear position.

2. Disconnect the battery on electric start models and disconnect all spark plug leads.

3. Carefully spin the propeller and observe the propeller shaft (**Figure 8**).

4. A noticeable wobbling of the shaft indicates a bent propeller shaft or other damage to the gearcase. Repair the gearcase if this condition is noted. Gearcase repair procedures are provided in Chapter Nine.

5. Install the spark plug wires. Clean the terminals, then connect the cables to the battery on electric start models.

Checking the mounting fasteners

> *WARNING*
> *Operating the engine with loose clamp screws or engine mounting bolts can result in serious bodily injury, death and/or loss of the engine. Always check and/or tighten all mounting bolts or screws before operating the engine.*

Tiller control 9.9-25 hp models are attached to the boat transom using lever type clamp screws (**Figure 9**). Tiller control 40-50 hp models are attached to the boat transom using bolts (**Figure 10**).

Check and tighten all transom bolts and lever type clamp screws before operating the outboard.

Fuel system inspection

1. Observe all fuel hoses, hose connections and the carburetor(s) while squeezing the primer bulb. Correct any leakage prior to starting the engine.

2. After starting the engine, check for a sheen on the water surface around the engine or fuel odor. Stop the engine and inspect the fuel system for leakage if either of these conditions is noted.

3. Fuel system repair procedures are provided in Chapter Six.

Steering system inspection

1. On tiller control models, move the tiller handle to full port and full starboard. Check for looseness of binding.

2. If looseness is noted, check for loose fasteners on the tiller handle, tiller handle mounting bracket or engine mounts. If binding is present, inspect the steering friction system (**Figure 11**) for correct adjustment or damage.

On remote control models, rotate the steering wheel to the clockwise and counterclockwise limits. Check for

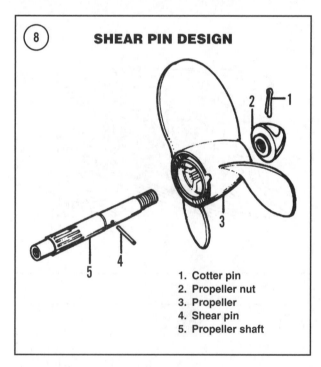

SHEAR PIN DESIGN

1. Cotter pin
2. Propeller nut
3. Propeller
4. Shear pin
5. Propeller shaft

binding or excessive slack as the wheel changes direction. A faulty steering cable, faulty helm or damaged midsection component(s) are likely if binding is noted. Midsection repair procedures are in Chapter Nine.

Cooling system inspection

Check for the presence of the water stream immediately after starting the engine. A stream of water (**Figure 12**) exiting the lower back area of the engine indicates the water pump is operating. This stream may not appear for the

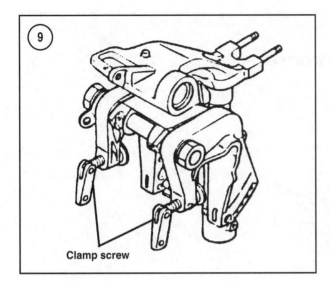

Clamp screw

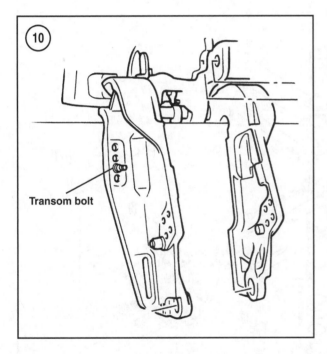

Transom bolt

first few seconds of operation, especially at idle speed. Stop the engine and check for a cooling system malfunction if the stream fails to appear. Refer to *Cooling System* in Chapter Three. Never run the engine if it is overheating or if the water stream fails to appear.

Lanyard or stop switch inspection

Check the operation of the lanyard and/or stop switch before each use. Press the stop button or switch the ignition off, on remote key switch models. Start the engine, then pull the lanyard cord from the lanyard switch (**Figure**

13). If the engine fails to stop, operate the choke, disconnect the fuel line or squeeze the fuel line until the engine stalls. Correct the faulty stop circuit before restarting the engine. The test procedure for the stop circuit is provided in Chapter Three.

After Each Use

As specified in **Table 1**, perform the following maintenance items after each use. Observing these requirements can dramatically reduce corrosion of engine components and extend the life of the engine.

Flushing the cooling system

Flush the cooling system after each use to help prevent corrosion and deposit buildup in the cooling system. This is extremely important if the engine is operated in salt, brackish or polluted water.

Some models are equipped with a power head flush fitting (**Figure 14**) at the front of the lower motor cover. This fitting allows the use of a garden hose to flush the power head. Connect the hose to this fitting, then run water through the power head for approximately 5 minutes. Never start the engine while using the power head flush fitting.

On engines stored on a trailer or boatlift, flush the engine using a flush/test adapter (**Figure 15**). These adapters are available from marine dealerships or marine supply stores. This method flushes the entire cooling system. Operating the engine in a test tank filled with clean water can also flush the entire cooling system.

The type of flush adapter used is determined by the location of the water inlets. All Yamaha engines have the water inlets located on the side of the gearcase (**Figure 16**).

Use a slide-on flush/test adapter (**Figure 15**) or a two piece adapter (**Figure 17**) on all models with side-mounted water inlets. The two piece design is preferred over the slide-on type flush/test adapter. It does not slip out of position during engine operation. Purchase the two piece adapter from a Yamaha dealership.

NOTE
Water may exit the auxiliary water pickup opening while the engine is running on a flush/test adapter. This is normal. To ensure adequate engine cooling, use full water pressure and never run the engine at high speed using a flush/test adapter.

Flush the cooling system as follows:

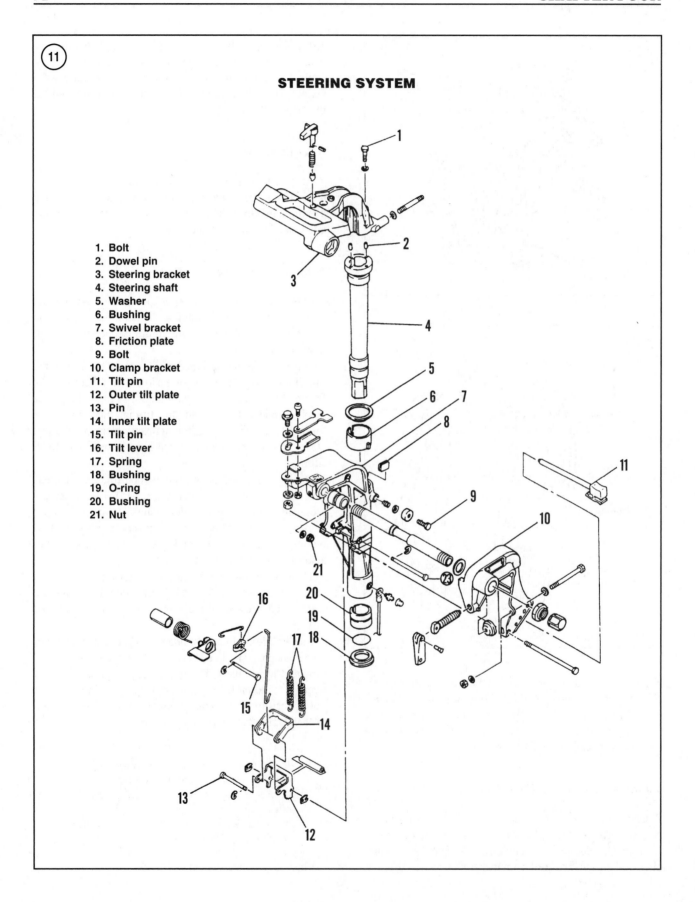

STEERING SYSTEM

1. Bolt
2. Dowel pin
3. Steering bracket
4. Steering shaft
5. Washer
6. Bushing
7. Swivel bracket
8. Friction plate
9. Bolt
10. Clamp bracket
11. Tilt pin
12. Outer tilt plate
13. Pin
14. Inner tilt plate
15. Tilt pin
16. Tilt lever
17. Spring
18. Bushing
19. O-ring
20. Bushing
21. Nut

4

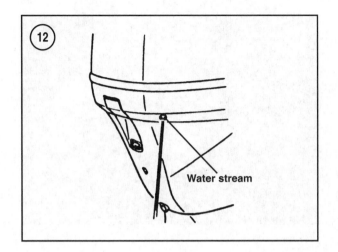

Water stream

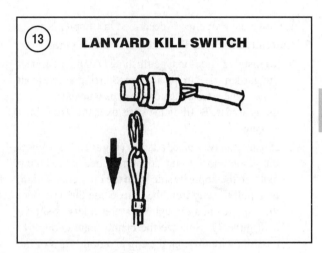

LANYARD KILL SWITCH

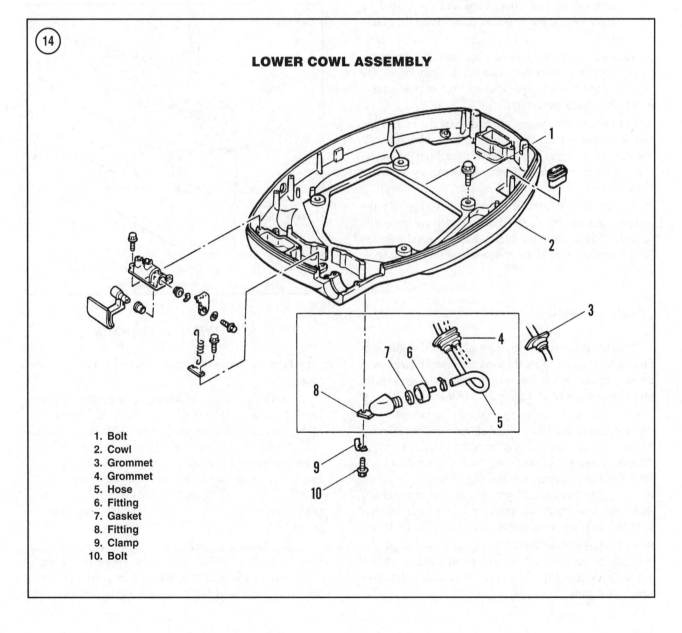

LOWER COWL ASSEMBLY

1. Bolt
2. Cowl
3. Grommet
4. Grommet
5. Hose
6. Fitting
7. Gasket
8. Fitting
9. Clamp
10. Bolt

1. Remove the propeller as described in Chapter Nine.
2. Carefully attach the flush adapter to the engine.
   a. To install a slide-on type flush/test adapter, connect the garden hose to the adapter. Starting at the front edge of the gearcase, slide the cups onto each side of the gearcase. Position the cups over the water inlet screens.
   b. If using the two-piece adapter (**Figure 17**), connect the garden hose to the adapter. Squeeze the clamp plate on the opposite side from the hose connection, then pull the cup from the wire. Slide the wire with the cup attached through the water inlets as shown in **Figure 17**. Squeeze the clamp plate enough to pass the wire through the cup and both sides of the clamp plate. Press both cups and the wire loop firmly against the gearcase, then release the clamp plate.
3. Turn the water on. Make sure the flush/test adapter is firmly positioned over the water inlets. Start the engine and run it at a fast idle in neutral until the engine reaches normal operating temperature.
4. Continue to run the engine until the water exiting the engine is clear and the engine has run for a minimum of 5 minutes. Monitor the engine temperature. Stop the engine if it begins to overheat or if water is not exiting the water stream fitting.
5. Throttle back to idle for a few minutes, then stop the engine. Remove the flush adapter. Install the propeller (Chapter Nine). Keep the engine in the vertical position for a few minutes to allow complete draining of the cooling system.

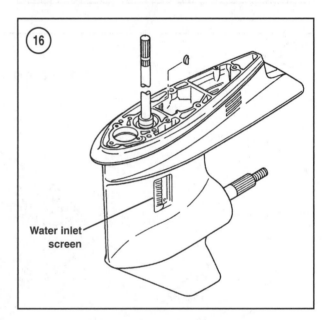

Water inlet
screen

Cleaning the engine

Clean all dirt or vegetation from all external engine surfaces after each use. This reduces corrosion, reduces wear on the gearcase and/or trim system seals and allows easier inspection for worn or damaged components.

Never use strong cleaning solutions or solvent to remove dirt or vegetation. Mild dish soap and pressurized water will clean most debris from the engine. To avoid contaminating power head components, never direct water toward any openings on the engine cover. Avoid directing spray from a high-pressure nozzle at openings, seals, plugs, wiring or wire grommets. The water may bypass the seals and contaminate the trim system, electric trim motor or trim fluid reservoir.

Rinse the external surfaces with clean water to remove any soap residue. Wipe the engine with a soft cloth to prevent water spots.

ROUTINE MAINTENANCE

Perform certain maintenance items at the specified time.

Always keep a log of maintenance items that were performed and when they were done. Try to log the number of running hours after each use. Without a maintenance/running hours log or a dash mounted hour meter, it is almost impossible to accurately determine the hours of usage. A dash mounted hour meter may run when the key switch is left in the ON position and the engine is not running. If this occurs, note it in the maintenance log should it occur.

Table 1 lists the required maintenance items and maintenance schedules. Some maintenance items do not apply to all models. The type of control system, starting system, and trim system used determines the maintenance require-

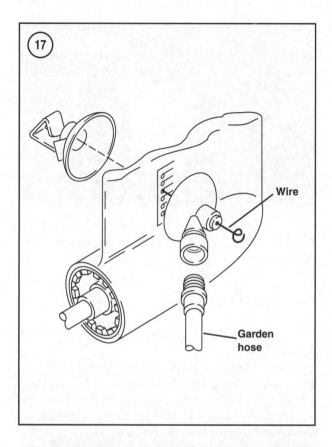

Wire

Garden hose

ments. Perform all applicable maintenance items listed in **Table 1**.

> *WARNING*
> *Use extreme caution when working with or around fuel. Never smoke around fuel or fuel vapor. Make sure that no flame or source of ignition is present in the work area. Flame or sparks can ignite the fuel or vapors and cause a fire or explosion.*

> *NOTE*
> *Fuel has a relatively short shelf life. Fuel begins to lose some of its desirable characteristics in as little as 14 days. Use the fuel within a few weeks after purchase.*

Fuel Requirements

Always use a major brand of fuel from a facility that sells a large amount of fuel. Fuels available today have a relatively short shelf life. Some fuels begin to lose potency in as little as 14 days. Plan on using the fuel in 60 days or less. This will reduce most fuel-related problems.

Use regular grade fuel with an average octane rating of 87 or higher for all models. This fuel meets the requirements for the engine when operated under normal operating conditions. Premium grade fuel offers little advantage over regular grade fuel under most operating conditions.

Purchase fuel from a busy fuel station. They usually have a higher turnover of fuel, providing a better opportunity to purchase fresh fuel. Always use the fuel well before it becomes stale. Refer to *Preparing the engine for storage* in this chapter for information on fuel additive recommendations.

> *CAUTION*
> *Never run the outboard on old or stale fuel. Engine damage could result from using fuel that has deteriorated. Varnish-like deposit form in the fuel system as fuel deteriorates. These deposits can block fuel passages and result in decreased fuel delivery. Decreased fuel delivery can cause a lean condition in the combustion chamber. Damage to the pistons, valve and other power head components can result from operating the engine under a lean fuel condition.*

Fuel Filter Inspection

Inspect and/or replace the fuel filter at the intervals specified in **Table 1**. An inline fuel filter (**Figure 18** and **Figure 19**) is used on 9.9, 15, 25, 80 and 100 hp models. A canister fuel filter (**Figure 20**) is used on 40 and 50 hp models. It is constructed of translucent material that allows detection of contamination inside its housing.

The filter is located in the fuel hose that connects the quick connector fitting (**Figure 21**) or fuel tank connectors to the fuel pump (**Figure 21**).

Direct light into the filter body to allow easier inspection for contamination. Replace the fuel filter if staining is noted inside the filter body. Fuel filter removal and installation are in Chapter Six.

NOTE
Some boats are equipped with a large spin-on fuel filter that resembles an oil filter in size. Most of these provide water-separating capabilities. They are located between the primer bulb and fuel tank on most applications. Service these units when servicing other fuel filters on the engine. Replacement elements for this type of filter are available from marine dealerships and marine supply stores. Follow the filter manufactures instructions to remove or install this type of filter.

CAUTION
Never use nondetergent oil or two-stroke outboard motor oil in a four-stroke outboard. It will not provide adequate lubrication of the internal engine components. Operating the engine without adequate lubrication results in severe power head damage.

Engine Oil Requirements

Yamaha recommends using Yamalube 4 engine oil or a premium quality four-stroke motor oil in all Yamaha four-stroke outboards. Four-stroke motor oil is available at Yamaha dealerships. Premium quality four-stroke oil is available from automotive parts stores.

Always use a good grade of oil in four-stroke outboards. Look for the SAE classification emblem (**Figure 22**) on the oil container when selecting oil for the engine. This label lists the service classification of the oil. Use only oil that meets or exceeds one the following service classifications: SH, SG, SF, SE-SF, SE or SF-CC.

Yamaha recommends using SAE approved 10W-30, 10W-40 or 20W-50 four-stroke motor oil. The oil viscosity rating is listed on the API classification emblem (**Figure 22**). Engine oil capacities are provided in **Table 2**.

The oil filter traps dirt, debris and other contaminants during engine operation. Always replace the filter or clean the screen when changing the oil. If the filter is not changed, contaminated oil remaining in the filter will

flow into the fresh oil. Oil filter change and filter cleaning are in this section.

Oil Drain and Fill Locations

Refer to the following information to locate the oil drain and oil fill.

On 9.9, 15 and 25 hp models, the oil drain plug (**Figure 23**) is located on the backside of the drive shaft housing. The oil fill cap (**Figure 24**) is located on the back of the power head. The dipstick (**Figure 25**) is located on the lower starboard side of the power head.

On 40 and 50 hp models, the oil drain plug (**Figure 26**) is located on the backside of the drive shaft housing. The oil fill cap (**Figure 26**) is located on the back of the power head and to the right of the fuel pump. The dipstick (**Figure 27**) is located on the lower starboard side of the power head.

On 80 and 100 hp models, the oil drain plug (**Figure 23**) is located on the backside of the drive shaft housing. The oil fill cap (**Figure 28**) is located on the upper port backside of the power head. The dipstick (**Figure 29**) is located on the lower starboard side of the power head.

Pumping the Oil From the Engine

If the boat is stored in the water or if the mounting arrangement makes accessing the drain plug difficult, the oil can be pumped from the oil pan or crankcase. Hand-operated pumps or electric pumps are available from most marine dealerships or marine supply stores. The required fittings and adapters are usually included with the pumps.

On 9.9 and 15 hp models, a tube inserted into the dipstick tube allows oil removal through the dipstick opening. The tube must reach the bottom of the crankcase or oil pan to remove all of the oil.

4

FUEL FILTER AND FUEL PUMP

1. Nut
2. Clip
3. Fuel hose
4. Clip
5. Bolt
6. Fuel pump
7. O-ring
8. Clip
9. Clip
10. Connector
11. Bolt
12. Seal
13. Fuel hose
14. Fuel hose
15. Clip
16. Fuel filter assembly

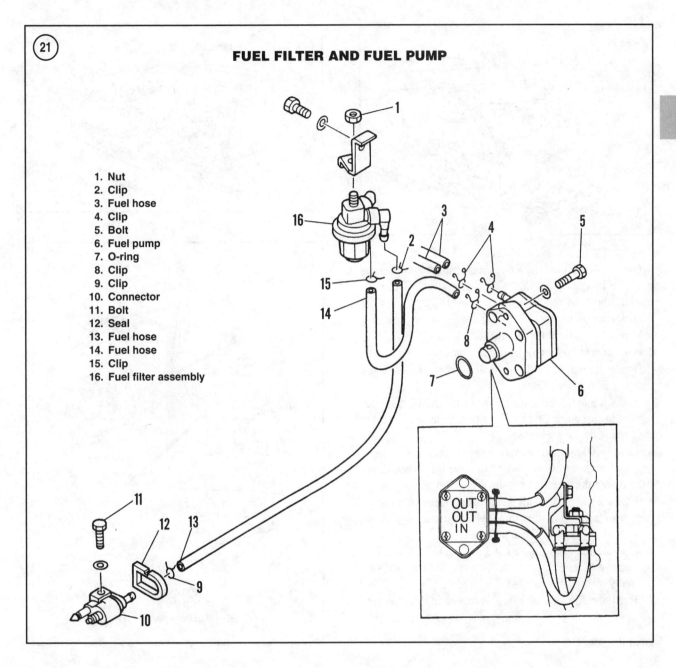

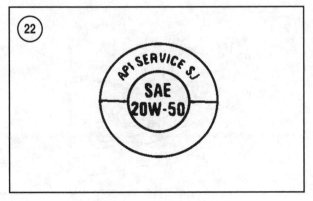

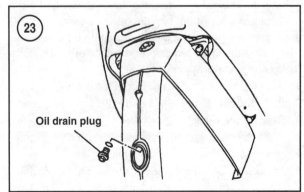

Oil drain plug

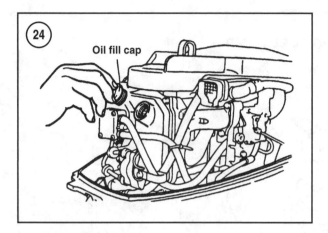

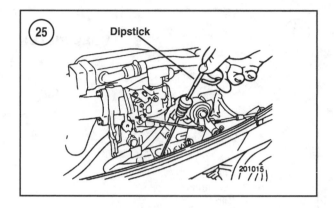

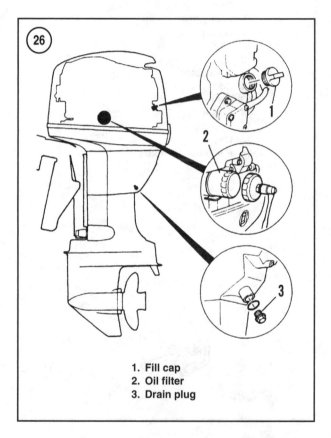

1. Fill cap
2. Oil filter
3. Drain plug

On 25-100 hp models, a threaded connector allows the pump to be connected to the oil dipstick tube. On these models, the dipstick tube is long enough to pump all of the oil from the oil pan.

Pump the oil from the engine as follows:

1. Disconnect both cables from the battery.

2. Place the engine in the vertical position. Remove the dipstick from the engine.

3. On 9.9 and 15 hp models, insert the small diameter tube of the oil pump into the dipstick tube until it contacts the bottom of the crankcase.

4. On 25-100 hp models, make sure the sealing washer is installed on the threaded adapter of the oil pump. Carefully thread the adapter onto the dipstick tube.

5. Operate the pump until all oil is removed. Stop the oil pump for a few minutes to allow any remaining oil to drain to the bottom of the crankcase.

6. Operate the pump to remove any remaining oil. Remove the oil pump. Dispose of the used oil in an environmentally responsible manner.

7. Refill the engine with oil as described in this chapter.

Draining the Oil

Refer to **Table 2** to determine the oil capacity. Find a container capable of holding the oil from the engine. Oil drain pans are available at most automotive parts stores. They are suitable for holding used engine oil and usually have enough capacity.

1. Remove both battery cables from the battery.

2. Place the engine upright (**Figure 30**).

3. Remove the fill cap.

4. Place the drain pan directly under the oil drain fitting. Remove the oil drain fitting from the engine.

5. Inspect the sealing washer or O-ring on the oil drain fitting for worn, torn or damaged areas. Replace if re-

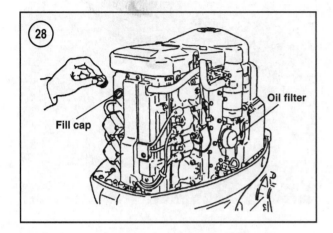

Fill cap

Oil filter

**OIL FILTER WRENCH
YU-38411**

4

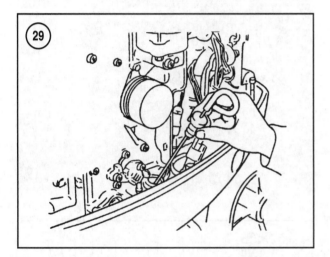

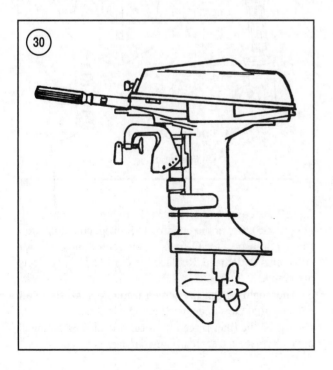

quired. Lubricate the seal or O-ring with a light coat of engine oil.

6. Install the drain fitting after all oil has drained from the engine. Securely tighten the oil drain fitting.

7. Refill the engine with oil as described in this chapter.

Filling the Engine with Oil

Refer to **Table 4** to determine the quantity of oil required. Fill the engine with oil as follows:

1. Place the engine upright (**Figure 30**). Clean the external surfaces, then remove the oil fill cap from the cylinder block.

2. Pour approximately 75% of the required oil into the oil fill opening.

3. Check the oil level. Add oil in small quantities until the oil level just reaches the MAX mark on the dipstick. Do not overfill the engine oil. Drain excess oil as required.

4. Clean and install the cap.

Oil Filter

All 15-100 hp models are equipped with a spin-on oil filter. Some 9.9 and 15 hp models are equipped with a serviceable oil screen. Refer to *Oil Screen* in this chapter. An oil filter removal tool is required to remove the oil filter. Yamaha offers a filter removal tool, part No.YU-38411 (**Figure 31**). They are also available from most automotive parts stores and tool suppliers. Take the filter with you when selecting the tool to ensure a correct fit.

Oil will drain from the engine after the filter is removed. Fashion an oil filter drain pan from a used plastic oil container. Cut the container to a depth that allows it to slide directly under the filter.

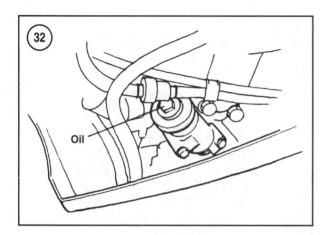

On 9.9 hp model, the oil filter (**Figure 32**) is located on the lower starboard side of the power head.

On 15, 25, 40 and 50 hp models, the oil filter (**Figure 26**) is located on the lower port side of the power head.

On 80 and 100 hp models, the oil filter (**Figure 28**) is located on the lower starboard side of the power head.

Change the oil filter as follows:

1. Use compressed air to blow all debris from the oil filter mounting area. Place a small container or shop towel under the oil filter.

2. Using the oil filter removal tool, rotate the oil filter one turn counterclockwise to loosen the filter. Remove the filter with a gloved hand. Wipe up any spilled oil.

3. Look for the gasket (**Figure 33**) on the removed oil filter. Remove the gasket from the cylinder block if it is not on the oil filter. Dispose of the oil filter in an environmentally responsible manner.

4. Carefully clean the oil filter mounting surface (**Figure 34**). Apply a light coat of engine oil to the gasket on the new oil filter (**Figure 33**). Thread the oil filter onto the cylinder block until the sealing ring just contacts the mating surface (**Figure 34**). Using the oil filter removal tool, tighten the filter to 17.5 N•m (12.9 ft.-lb.). Make sure the oil filter rotates a minimum of 3/4 turn clockwise after the gasket contacts the mating surface.

5. Fill the engine with oil following the instructions in this chapter.

6. Check for oil leakage immediately after starting the engine.

Oil Screen

Some early 9.9 and 15 hp models are equipped with an oil screen instead of an oil filter. Clean the screen at the intervals listed in **Table 1** as follows:

1. Clean the area around the oil screen cover (**Figure 32**), then unthread the cover from the oil screen housing.

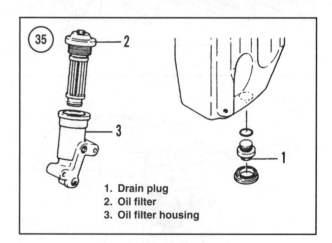

1. Drain plug
2. Oil filter
3. Oil filter housing

2. Lift the cover and oil screen from the screen housing (**Figure 35**). Cover the opening to prevent contamination of the oil. Inspect the O-rings on the screen and cover for wear, cuts or damage. Replace the O-rings if any defects are noted.

3. Thoroughly clean the screen using solvent. Blow all solvent from the screen using compressed air.

4. Inspect the filter screen for torn, corroded or damaged areas. Replace the screen if any damage is noted.

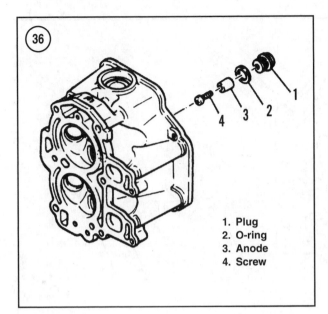

1. Plug
2. O-ring
3. Anode
4. Screw

5. Lubricate the O-rings with a light coat of engine oil. Make sure the O-rings are seated in their grooves at the bottom of the screen and the filter cover.

6. Carefully insert the oil screen into its housing (**Figure 35**). Make sure the O-rings are not dislodged during installation. Thread the cover into the oil screen housing. Tighten the cover to 8 N•m (70 in.-lb.).

Removing Carbon Deposits

Remove stubborn or heavy carbon deposits by manually scraping them from the pistons and combustion chambers. Cylinder head removal, cleaning and installation procedures are provided in Chapter Eight.

Prevent heavy carbon deposits by using good quality fuel and oil. Make sure the propeller is correct for the engine and boat combination. See Chapter One. Perform all applicable carburetor adjustments to minimize carbon deposits.

Power Head Anodes

Power head anodes help prevent corrosion damage to the power head cooling passages. The anodes are constructed of a material that is more corrosively active than the cylinder head or cylinder block. The anodes sacrifice themselves to protect the power head. Regular inspection and replacement help ensure continued protection against corrosion damage.

All 9.9 hp models are equipped with a single anode. This anode is mounted to a special plug (**Figure 36**) located beneath the rocker arm cover.

All 15 hp models are equipped with a single anode. This anode is located beneath a retaining clamp and cover (**Figure 37**) on the lower port side of the cylinder block.

All 25-50 hp models are equipped multiple anodes. They are mounted beneath a cover on the port side of the cylinder head (**Figure 38**). An anode is also located near each spark plug.

All 80 and 100 hp models are equipped with a pair of anodes. The anodes are mounted to special covers (**Figure 39**) located beneath the spark plug cover.

Inspect and replace the anode as follows:

1A. On 9.9 models, remove the anode as follows:

  a. Remove the rocker arm cover as described in Chapter Eight.

  b. Remove the bolt (1, **Figure 36**) from the cylinder head.

  c. Remove the screw (4, **Figure 36**) from the anode assembly.

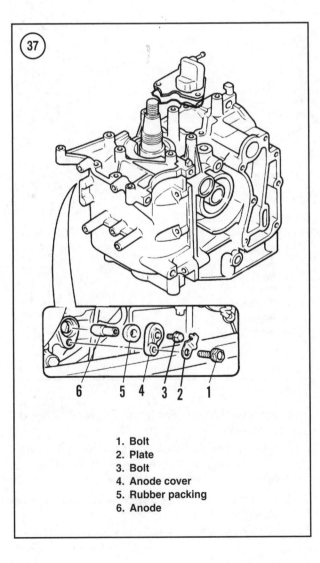

1. Bolt
2. Plate
3. Bolt
4. Anode cover
5. Rubber packing
6. Anode

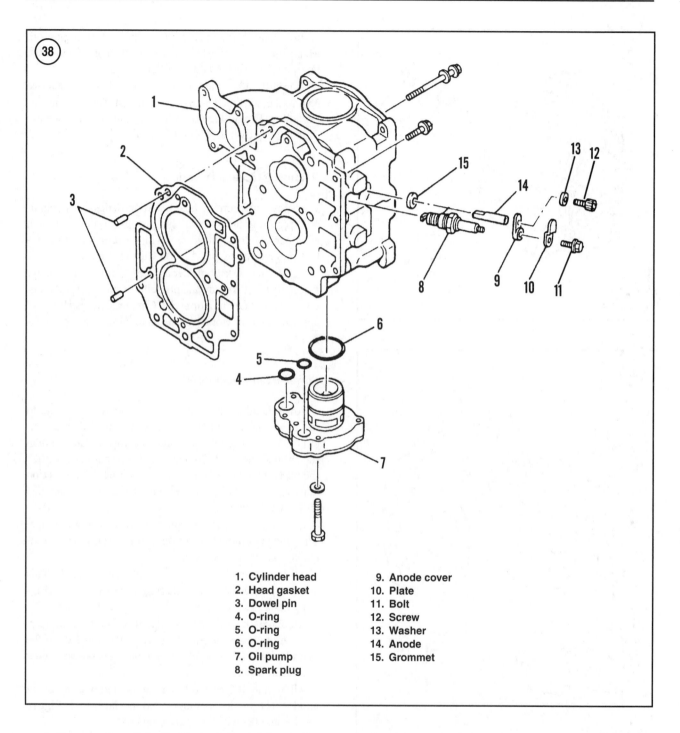

1. Cylinder head
2. Head gasket
3. Dowel pin
4. O-ring
5. O-ring
6. O-ring
7. Oil pump
8. Spark plug
9. Anode cover
10. Plate
11. Bolt
12. Screw
13. Washer
14. Anode
15. Grommet

d. Remove the anode (3, **Figure 36**), and the O-ring (2) from the bolt (1).

e. Inspect the O-ring for cuts or wear. Inspect the anode for wear. If the anode is worn to half its original size, replace it.

1B. On 15 hp models, remove the anode as follows:

a. Remove the bolt (1, **Figure 37**) and retainer (2) from the anode assembly.

b. Remove the bolt (3, **Figure 37**) from the anode cover (4).

c. Use a pair of needlenose pliers to remove the anode cover (4, **Figure 37**), rubber packing (5) and anode (6).

d. Inspect and/or replace any parts that are worn or damaged.

1C. On 25-50 hp models, remove the anode as follows:

4

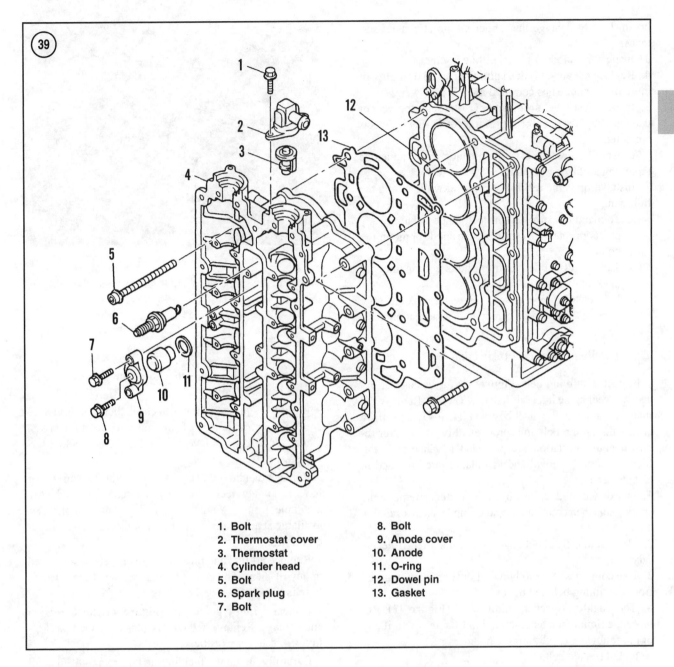

1. Bolt
2. Thermostat cover
3. Thermostat
4. Cylinder head
5. Bolt
6. Spark plug
7. Bolt
8. Bolt
9. Anode cover
10. Anode
11. O-ring
12. Dowel pin
13. Gasket

a. Remove the retaining screw (11, **Figure 38**) and retaining plate (10) from the anode cover.

b. Remove the anode cover screw (12, **Figure 38**) and washer (13).

c. Use needlenose pliers, if necessary to carefully pull the anode cover (9, **Figure 38**), anode (14) and rubber grommet (15) from the cylinder head (1).

d. Remove the rubber grommet from the anode.

e. Inspect and/or replace any worn or damaged parts.

1D. On 80 and 100 hp models, remove the anodes as follows:

a. Remove the spark plug cover as described in Chapter Eight.

b. Carefully loosen and remove each anode cover mounting bolt (7, **Figure 39**).

c. Carefully pry the cover loose, then lift it and the anode from the cylinder head (4, **Figure 39**).

d. Remove the single bolt (8, **Figure 39**), then pull the anode (10) and rubber grommet (11) from the anode cover (9).

2. Clean all corrosion, deposits or contamination from the anode and anode mounting surfaces using a wire

brush. Do not damage the rubber grommet contact surfaces.

3. Inspect the anode for deep pitting or cracks.

4. Replace the anode if deep pitting is noted or if 50% or more of the anode has corroded away.

5. Inspect the rubber grommet or O-ring seals for wear or damage. Replace the rubber grommet or O-ring if defects are noted.

6. Clean all corrosion or contamination from the anode mounting surface or opening.

7. Installation is the reverse of removal while noting the following:

   a. To maintain corrosion protection, do not apply any paint or protective coating to the anode or mounting bolts.

   b. Tighten all anode mounting bolts and retainers to the specification in Table ???.

   c. Inspect all anode covers for water leakage after starting the engine. Correct any leakage at once.

Timing Belt and Sprocket Inspection

Inspect the timing belt (**Figure 40**) for damage or excessive wear at the intervals listed in **Table 1**. Remove the manual starter or flywheel cover (**Figure 41**, typical) to access the timing belt and sprockets. Flywheel cover removal and installation are provided in Chapter Eight. Manual starter removal and installation are provided in Chapter Ten.

1. Disconnect both cables from the battery. Remove the spark plugs then connect the spark plug leads to a suitable engine ground.

2. Remove the flywheel cover, manual starter, if necessary.

3. Use compressed air to blow all dust or loose material from the timing belt and pulleys.

4. Thoroughly inspect the timing belt (**Figure 42**). Replace the timing belt as described in Chapter Eight if any of the following conditions are noted:

   a. Oil soaked belt.

   b. Deformed belt.

   c. Worn timing belt cogs.

   d. Cracked or worn belt.

   e. Cracked or missing timing belt cogs.

   f. Worn edges on the top or bottom side of the timing belt.

5. Inspect the crankshaft and camshaft sprockets for worn cogs (**Figure 43**), and damage or corrosion. Replace the sprockets if they are worn or damaged. Sprocket removal and installation are provided in Chapter Eight.

6. Install the flywheel cover (Chapter Eight). Install the manual starter (Chapter Ten).

7. Install the spark plugs and leads. Connect the cables to the battery.

Hose and Clamp Inspection

Inspect all fuel, and breather hoses and clamps at the intervals listed in **Table 1**.

Carefully squeeze all hoses to check their flexibility. Inspect the entire length of all fuel and breather hoses. Check for leakage and weathered, burned or cracked surfaces.

Replace fuel lines that are hard or brittle, are leaking, or have a spongy feel. Use only the recommended hose available from a Yamaha dealership. Other fuel hoses available at auto parts stores may not meet coast guard requirements.

Replace all fuel and breather hoses if defects are noted in any of them. The condition that damaged the affected hose is likely affecting the others.

Inspect spring-type clamps (**Figure 44**) for corrosion and damage. Remove and replace plastic tie clamps (**Figure 45**) if they are brittle.

Carefully tug on the fuel lines to ensure a tight fit at all connections. If a fitting is loose, check for loose plastic tie clamp or faulty spring-type clamps. Replace any faulty clamp before operating the engine.

Thermostat Inspection

Inspect or replace the thermostat at the intervals listed in **Table 1**. Thermostat removal, inspection and installation procedures are provided in Chapter Eight. To prevent overheating or oil dilution, replace faulty or damaged thermostat.

4

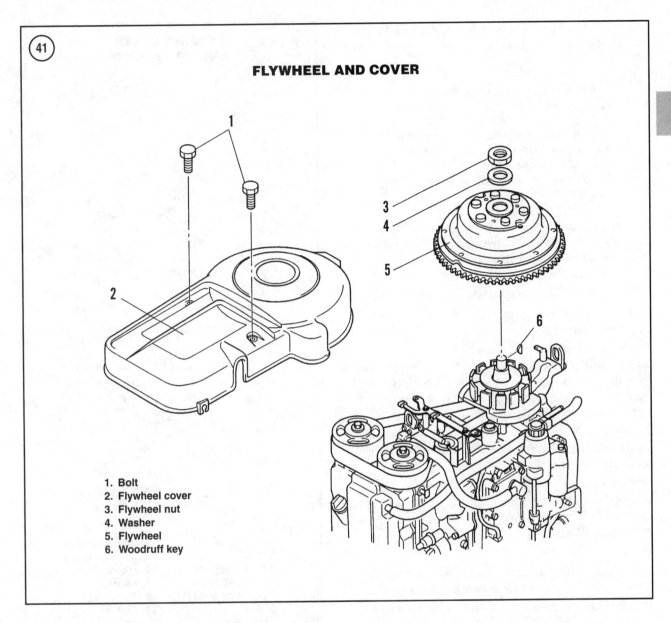

FLYWHEEL AND COVER

1. Bolt
2. Flywheel cover
3. Flywheel nut
4. Washer
5. Flywheel
6. Woodruff key

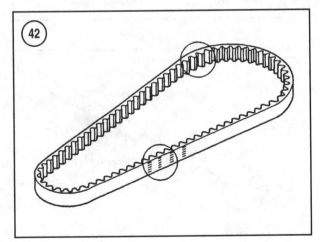

Gearcase Lubricant

CAUTION
Never use automotive gear lubricant in the gearcase. These types of lubricants are usually not suitable for marine applications. Using lubricants other than the recommended lubricants can lead to increased wear and corrosion of internal components.

Use Yamaha gearcase lubricant or a good grade SAE 90 marine gearcase lubricant that meets GL-4 specifications. Read the information on the container to ensure it meets this specification before using it in the outboard. **Table 2** lists the *approximate* gearcase lubricant capacity for the Yamaha four-stroke outboards.

CAUTION
To prevent gearcase damage due to an incorrect gearcase lubricant level, make sure that all correct gearcase oil level plugs are removed when checking and/or changing the gearcase lubricants. Both plugs must be removed when checking the lubricant level, draining the gearcase lubricant and filling the gearcase lubricant.

Check the gearcase lubricant level and condition at the intervals listed in **Table 1**. Some models have two oil level/vent plugs. Refer to Chapter Nine to identify the lubricant plugs.

Check the gearcase lubricant level as follows:

1. Position the engine upright for at least an hour before checking the lubricant.

2. Slowly remove the drain/fill plug (A, **Figure 46**) and allow a small sample (a teaspoon or less) of fluid to drain from the gearcase. Quickly replace the drain fill plug and tighten it securely. Refer to Chapter Three if water or a milky appearance was noted in the fluid sample.

3. Rub a small amount of the fluid sample between your finger and thumb. Refer to Chapter Three if the lubricant feels gritty or metal particles are present.

4. Remove the level/vent plug(s) (B, **Figure 46**). The lubricant level should be even with the bottom of the threaded level/vent plug hole.

5. Perform the following if a low lubricant level is indicated.

   a. Remove the lubricant drain/fill plug, then quickly install the lubricant pump hose into the opening.

   b. Add lubricant into the drain/fill plug opening (A, **Figure 46**) until fluid flows from the level/vent plug(s) (B, **Figure 46**).

   c. A leak is likely if over an ounce of lubricant is required to fill the gearcase. Pressure test the unit as described in Chapter Three.

   d. Install the level/vent plug(s), then tighten it securely.

   e. Remove the lubricant pump hose or tube, then quickly install the lubricant drain/fill plug.

6. Tighten the lubricant drain/fill and level/vent plugs to specification.

7. Allow the gearcase to remain undisturbed in a shaded area for 1 hour, then recheck the lubricant level. Top off the lubricant if necessary.

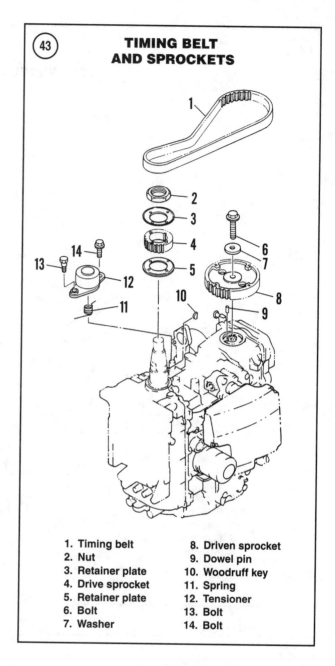

(43)

TIMING BELT AND SPROCKETS

1. Timing belt	8. Driven sprocket
2. Nut	9. Dowel pin
3. Retainer plate	10. Woodruff key
4. Drive sprocket	11. Spring
5. Retainer plate	12. Tensioner
6. Bolt	13. Bolt
7. Washer	14. Bolt

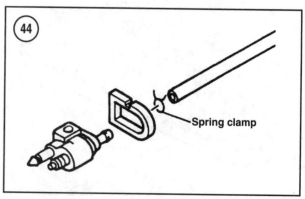

(44)

Spring clamp

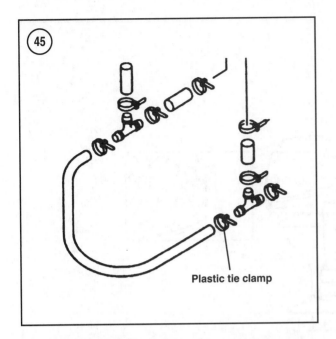

Plastic tie clamp

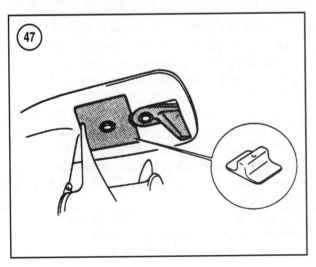

CAUTION
Inspect the sealing washers on all gearcase plugs. Replace missing or damaged sealing washers to prevent water or lubricant leakage.

NOTE
A small amount of very fine particles are usually present in the gear lubricant. These fine particles form during normal gearcase operation. Their presence does not necessarily indicate a problem. The presence of large particles, however, indicates a problem in the gearcase.

Changing the Gearcase Lubricant

Change the gearcase lubricant at the intervals listed in **Table 1**. **Table 2** lists the approximate gearcase lubricant capacity. Refer to the exploded views provided in Chapter Nine to locate the plugs.

Some models use two level/vent plugs. On these models, remove both plugs during the gearcase draining and filling procedure.

1. Remove the drain/fill plug from the gearcase (A, **Figure 46**). Remove the level/vent plug(s) (B, **Figure 46**).

2. Allow the gearcase to drain completely. Tilt the engine so that the drain/fill opening is at its lowest point to ensure the gearcase drains completely. After draining, place the engine in the upright or vertical position.

3. Use a pump-type dispenser or squeeze tube to *slowly* pump gearcase lubricant into the drain plug opening (**Figure 46**). Continue to fill the gearcase until lubricant flows out the level/vent plug(s) openings (**Figure 46**). Before removing the pump or tube from the drain/fill opening, install the level/vent plug(s) into the opening. Securely tighten the level plug(s).

4. Remove the pump from the drain/fill opening, then quickly install the drain/fill plug (**Figure 46**). Securely tighten the drain/fill plug.

5. Allow the engine to remain in the upright position for 1 hour in a shaded location. Check the gearcase lubricant level following the instructions provided in this section under *Checking the gearcase lubricant*.

Gearcase Anode Inspection

Sacrificial anodes (**Figure 47**, typical) are used on all models to lesson corrosion damage to exposed gearcase surfaces. The anode material is more corrosively active than the other exposed engine components. The anodes sacrifice themselves to protect the engine from corrosion damage.

4

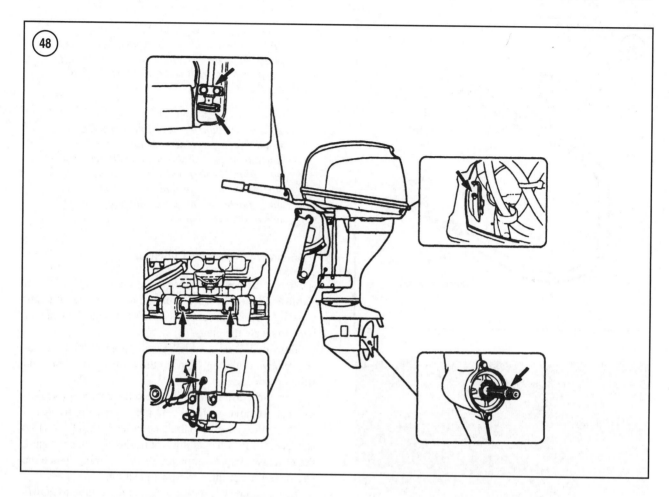

Clean and inspect the anodes at the intervals listed in **Table 1**. Inspect and clean the anodes more often if the engine is operated or stored in salt, brackish or polluted water. Use a stiff blush to clean deposits and other material from the anode. Replace the anode if it has lost 40% or more of its material. Never paint or cover the anode with a protective coating. This dramatically decreases its ability to protect the engine. Thoroughly clean the mounting area before installing a new anode. The anode must contact bare metal to ensure a proper connection.

Inspect the anode mounting area if corrosion is noted on engine components, but the anode is not eroding. It is likely that the anode is not making adequate contact with the mounting surface. Clean the area thoroughly if this condition is noted.

Water Pump and Impeller Inspection

Inspect the water pump impeller at the intervals listed in **Table 1** to help ensure reliable operation of the cooling system. Water pump inspection is provided in Chapter Nine.

Propeller Shaft

Lubricate and inspect the propeller shaft at the interval listed in **Table 1** to reduce wear on the propeller shaft and propeller components. Other benefits include reduced corrosion damage and a quick detection of a bent propeller shaft.

1. Remove the propeller as described in Chapter Nine.

2. Observe the propeller shaft for wobbling while spinning the propeller shaft. Replace the propeller shaft if it wobbles. Propeller shaft replacement is provided in Chapter Nine.

3. Using solvent and a shop towel, clean all grease and debris from the propeller shaft splines, propeller nut threads and tapered section.

4. Inspect the propeller nut, thrust washer and spacers for wear, cracks or damage. Replace all defective or worn components.

5. Apply a generous coat of good-quality water-resistant grease to the splines of the propeller shaft.

6. Install the propeller. See Chapter Nine.

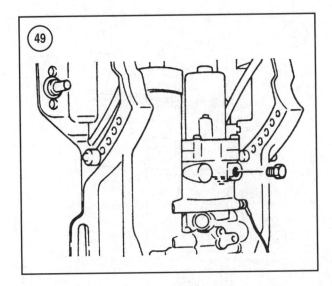

Swivel Tube and Tilt Tube Lubrication

Lubricate the pivot points of the swivel and tilt tubes at the intervals listed in **Table 1** to ensure smooth tilting and steering action. Use a grease pump to pump good quality water-resistant grease into all fittings on the swivel tube and tilt tube (**Figure 48**). Continue to pump until the old grease is expelled from between the pivot points.

CAUTION
The steering cable must be retracted before grease is injected into the fitting. The cable can become hydraulically locked if grease is injected with the cable extended. Refer to the cable manufacture's instructions for type of lubricant and frequency of lubrication.

Steering System Lubrication

Some steering cables are provided with a grease fitting. Regular lubrication of the steering cable and linkage dramatically increases their service life. Pump water-resistant grease into the grease fitting until a slight resistance is felt. Avoid overfilling the steering cable with grease. Apply grease to the sliding surfaces and pivot points of all steering linkage. Cycle the steering full port and full starboard several times to distribute the lubricant.

Trim System Fluid Level

WARNING
Always wear suitable eye protection, gloves and protective clothing when working around the engine. The fluid in the trim sys-tem may be under extreme pressure. Loosen all valves and reservoir plugs slowly, and allow any internal pressure to slowly sub-side.

Check the trim fluid level at the intervals specified in **Table 1**, or any time low fluid level is suspected.

Yamaha recommends using ATF (Dexron II) in all power trim systems.

Access to the fluid level check plug (**Figure 49**) is required to check the fluid level. The fluid level plug is located on the backside of the trim reservoir on all models. Secure the engine in the full tilt position to access the trim system fill plug. Use an overhead lift or wooden blocks to support the engine while checking and filling the reservoir. Do not rely solely on the tilt lock mechanism to support the engine. Two different types of system are used. On either type, the trim system fill cap (**Figure 49**) is located on the aft side of the pump portion of the trim system. The fluid in the reservoir may be under pressure. Always remove the reservoir plug slowly and allow the pressure to gradually subside.

1. Operate the trim/tilt system or open the manual relief valve, and move the engine to the full UP position. Securely tighten the manual relief valve, if loosened.

2. Secure the outboard motor in the UP position. Clean the area around the fill cap (**Figure 49**) using compressed air.

3. Slowly and carefully remove the fill cap from the trim system pump or reservoir.

4. Carefully clean the cap mounting surface. Keep debris from entering the fluid reservoir.

5. Note the level of the fluid. The fluid should just touch the bottom of the fill cap opening. Use a toothpick or piece of clean straw to gauge the depth of the fluid.

6. Add fluid until its level is even with the bottom of the fill cap opening (**Figure 49**). Install and securely tighten the fill cap.

7. Lower the engine and run the trim system to the full up and full down positions several times to purge air from the internal passages. Repeat Steps 1-5 if more than 2 oz. of fluid was required to correct the fluid level.

Starter Motor Maintenance

Maintenance to the electric starter motor involves cleaning external electrical terminals and applying good quality water-resistant grease to the starter drive (**Figure 50**). Apply only a light coat of grease to the pinion shaft of the starter motor. Excessive grease may attract dirt, and lead to a malfunction of the starter motor. Refer to Chapter

Seven if removal or disassembly of the starter motor is necessary to access the pinion shaft.

> *CAUTION*
> *Use only enough grease to lightly coat the electric contacts. Excessive grease may seep into some electrical components such as relays and cause the component to malfunction.*

Wiring and Terminals Inspection

Periodically inspect the main harness connector (**Figure 51**) for loose, corroded or damaged pins (**Figure 52**). Carefully scrape contamination from the contacts. Apply a light coat of good quality water-resistant grease to the main harness plug and terminals to seal out moisture and prevent corrosion. Inspect the entire length of all wires and the harness for worn, burnt, damaged or bare insulation. Repair or replace the wire harness as required.

Battery Inspection

The cranking battery requires more maintenance than any other component related to the engine. Unlike automobiles, boats may sit idle for weeks or more. Without proper maintenance, the battery loses its charge and begins to deteriorate. Marine engines are exposed to a great deal more moisture than automobiles resulting in more corrosion on the battery terminals. Clean the terminals and charge the battery at no more than 30 day intervals. Refer to Chapter Seven for complete battery testing, maintenance and charging instructions.

Throttle and Shift Linkage

Apply good quality all-purpose grease to all pivot points of the throttle (**Figure 53**) and shift linkage at the intervals listed in **Table 1**. This helps prevent corrosion and ensures smooth operation of the throttle and shift mechanisms. Refer to Chapter Five and Chapter Six to determine the location of the shift and throttle linkages. Only a small amount of grease is required. Use just enough to lubricate the connector or pivot point. Use penetrating corrosion prevention oil if difficult access prevents grease from being properly applied.

TUNE-UP

A complete tune up involves a series of adjustments, tests, inspections and parts replacement to return the engine to original factory specifications. Only a complete

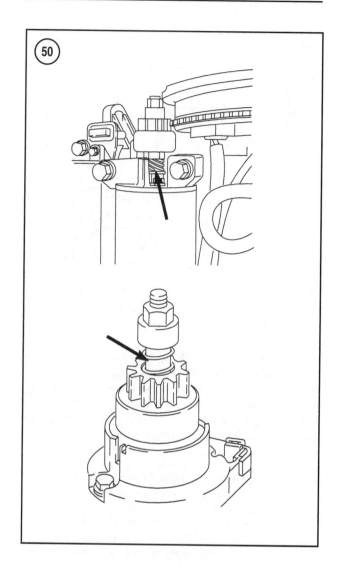

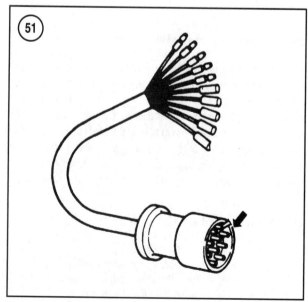

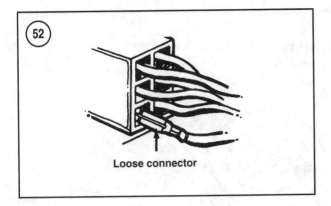

Loose connector

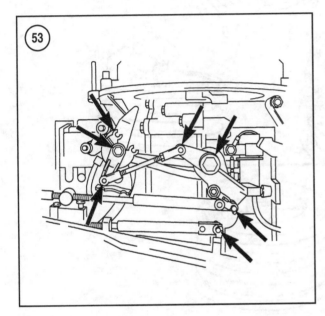

tune-up delivers the expected performance, economy and durability. Perform all operations in this order:

1. Compression test.
2. Spark plugs.
3. Valve adjustment.
4. Carburetor adjustment.
5. Checking the ignition timing.
6. Test running the outboard.

Compression Test

An engine with low or weak compression on one or more cylinders cannot be properly tuned. Perform a compression test before replacing any components or performing any adjustments. Correct the cause of low compression before proceeding with the tune-up. Compression testing is provided in Chapter Three.

Spark Plug Replacement

Spark plug replacement is the most important part of a complete tune-up. No other component on the engine can adversely effect the engine running characteristics more than a defective spark plug. Spark plugs are repeatedly subjected to very high heat, high pressure and exposure to the corrosive by-products of combustion.

All Yamaha four-stroke outboards use breakerless ignition systems. These systems produce higher energy than conventional breaker point systems. Benefits of these higher energy systems are longer spark plug life and less chance of spark plug fouling.

Replacement spark plugs must be of the correct size, reach and heat range to operate properly in the engine. Refer to the spark plug recommendations in **Table 5**.

All models covered in this manual use a conventional spark plug. Inspection of the spark plug can reveal much about the condition of the engine. Problems can be corrected before expensive engine damage occurs. Remove the spark plug(s) and compare them to the ones shown in **Figure 54**.

Correct any engine problems prior to installing new spark plugs.

Removal

On 80 and 100 hp models, the spark plugs are positioned deep inside the rocker arm cover. Removal of the cover is required to access them. Remove all five retaining bolts, then carefully lift the spark plug cover from the rocker arm cover. On 80 and 100 hp models, a long extension and thin-wall socket is required to remove or install the spark plugs. On all other models, the spark plugs are located on the rear port side of the cylinder head.

Mark the cylinder number on the spark plug leads before removing them from the spark plugs. Use compressed air to blow debris from around the spark plugs before removing them. If the plug is corroded at the threaded connection, apply penetrating oil to the threaded section and allow it to soak.

Sometimes the aluminum threads from the cylinder heads come out with the spark plug. This can be repaired without removing the cylinder head by installing a special threaded insert. Have a reputable marine repair shop perform this repair unless the necessary tools are available.

Clean the spark plug holes in the cylinder head with a thread chaser (**Figure 55**). These are available at most automotive parts stores. Thread the chaser by hand into each spark plug hole. Several passes may be required to remove all carbon or corrosion deposits from the threaded hole. Blow all debris from the holes with compressed air.

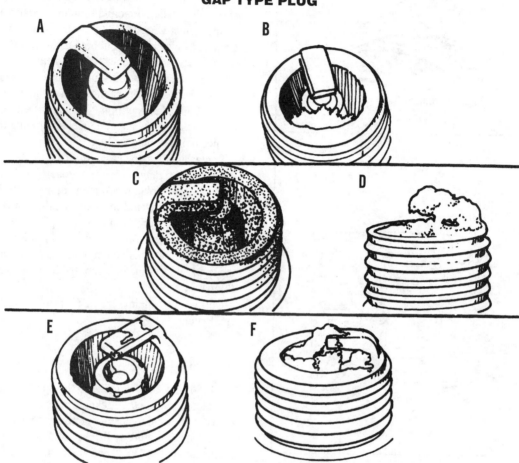

SPARK PLUG ANALYSIS
GAP TYPE PLUG

A. **Normal**—Light to tan gray color of insulator indicates correct heat range. Few deposits arepresent and the electrodes are not burned.

B. **Core bridging**—These defects are caused by excessive combustion chamber deposits striking and ahering to the firing end of the plg. In this case, they wedge or fuse betwen the electrode and core nose. They originate from the piston and cylinder head surfaces. Deposits are formed by one or more of the following:
  a. Excessive carbon in cylinder.
  b. Use of non-recommended oils.
  c. Immediate high-speed operation after prolonged trolling.

C. **Wet fouling**—Damp or wet, black carbon coating over entire firing end of plug. Forms sludge in some engines. Caused by one or more of the following:
  a. Spark plug heat range too cold.
  b. Prolonged trolling.
  c. Low-speed carburetor adjustment too rich.
  d. Induction manifold bleed-off passage obstructed.
  e. Worn or defective breaker points.

D. **Gap bridging**—Similar to core bridging, except the combustion particles are wedged or fused between the electrodes. Causes are the same.

E. **Overheating**—Badly worn electrodes and premature gap wear are indicative of this problem, along with a gray or white "blistered" appearance on the insulator. Caused by one or more of the following:
  a. Spark plug heat range too hot.
  b. Incorrect propeller usage, causing engine to lug.
  c. Worn or defective water pump
  d. Restricted water intake or restriction somewhere in the cooling system.

F. **Ash deposits or lead fouling**—Ash deposits are light brown to white in color and result from use of fuel or oil additives. Lead fouling produces a yellowish-brown discoloration and can be avoided by using unleaded fuels.

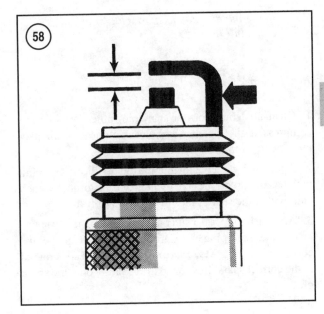

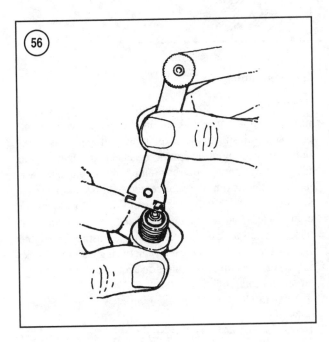

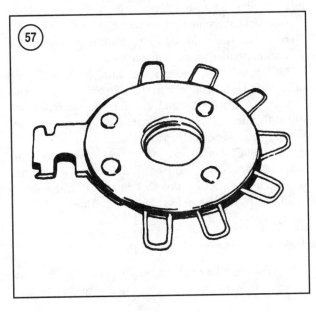

4

Inspection

Remove the plugs and compare them to the plugs shown in **Figure 54**. Spark plugs can give a clear indication of a problem in the engine sometimes before the symptoms occur. Additional inspection and testing may be required if abnormal spark plug conditions are noted. Refer to Chapter Three for troubleshooting and testing instructions.

Gap adjustment

Use a gap adjusting tool (**Figure 56**) to set the spark plug gap to the specification in **Table 5**. Never tap the plug against a hard object to close the gap. The ceramic insulator can crack and possibly break away. Gapping tools (**Figure 56**) are available at most automotive parts stores. They allow correction of the gap without damaging the plug.

1. Check the gap using a feeler or wire gauge (**Figure 57**) of the same thickness as the recommended gap. The gauge should pass between the electrodes (**Figure 58**) with a slight drag.

2. Open the gap and reset the gap if the gauge cannot be inserted with only a slight drag.

3. Inspect the gap for parallel electrode surfaces (**Figure 58**). Carefully bend the electrode until the surfaces are parallel and the gap is correct.

NOTE
Some spark plugs require the terminal end to be installed prior to installation. Thread

*the terminal onto the spark plug(s) as indicated in **Figure 59**.*

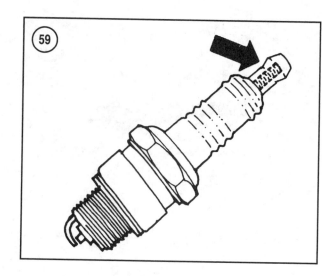

Installation

1. Clean all debris from the spark plug holes. Avoid using compressed air to clean the holes. Compressed air may blow debris into the cylinders.

2. Apply a light coat of engine oil to the spark plug threads and thread them in by hand. Use a torque wrench and tighten the spark plugs to 18 N•m (13 ft-lb.).

3. Apply a light coat of silicone lubricant to the inner surface of the spark plug cap. Carefully slide the cap over the correct spark plug. Make sure the spark plug lead is routed to the correct spark plug. Snap the cap fully onto the spark plug.

Valve Adjustment

Clearance between the valve train components increase as the components wear. Excessive clearance causes valve system noise and may increase wear on valve train components. Insufficient clearance can result in a rapid wear of certain valve train components, reduced power and rough engine operation. Perform valve adjustment at the intervals specified in **Table 1**. Valve adjustment is covered in Chapter Five.

Carburetor Adjustment

Proper carburetor adjustment is essential for the smoothest and most efficient running characteristics. Carburetor adjustment includes carburetor synchronization and idle speed adjustment. Some models also require pilot screw adjustment. To ensure correct operation, perform all applicable carburetor adjustments. Carburetor adjustment is covered in Chapter Five.

> *WARNING*
> *Remove the propeller before running an engine on a flush/test adapter. Disconnect all spark plug leads and disconnect the battery before removing or installing the propeller.*

> *CAUTION*
> *Never run the engine without first providing cooling water. Use either a test tank of flush/test adapter. Remove the propeller before running the engine.*

Ignition Timing

All Yamaha four-stroke outboards are equipped with ignition systems that provide automatic spark advancement. Although adjustment is not required, a proper tune-up requires that the ignition timing be checked. Operation at idle and full throttle requires running the engine in the water. Monitor the timing advancement while a qualified assistant operates the engine. It is possible to run smaller engines, less than 25 hp, at higher engine speeds in a test tank. Take all necessary precautions to ensure the engine is securely mounted to the test tank during testing. Checking the ignition timing requires an accurate shop tachometer and a timing light.

Refer to Chapter Three for ignition timing specifications.

1. Connect the shop tachometer to the engine following its manufacturer's instructions.

2. Connect the timing light to the No. 1 spark plug lead.

3. Start the engine and allow it to run at idle speed until it reaches normal operating temperature.

4. On 9.9 and 15 hp models, the timing pointer (**Figure 60**) is located at the upper port side of the power head. The timing reference marks are located on the circumference of the flywheel. On all models, the CDI unit controls the timing. There is no adjustment on timing.

5. A faulty CDI or engine control unit, or other ignition system component, is indicted if the timing is incorrect.

6. Test any suspect ignition system components following the instructions provided in Chapter Three.

Test Run

Perform a test run after a tune-up. Operate the engine on a flush/test device or in a test tank to ensure correct start-

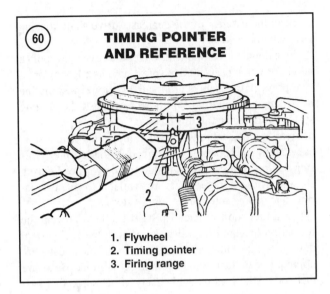

TIMING POINTER AND REFERENCE

1. Flywheel
2. Timing pointer
3. Firing range

ing and idle operation prior to running a water test. Connect a shop tachometer to the engine. Follow the manufacture instructions when attaching the tachometer to the engine. Check the idle speed while an assistant operates the boat. Refer to Chapter Five for instructions to adjust the idle speed.

Operate the boat at wide-open throttle. Using the trim system, if so equipped, position the motor at the optimum trim angle and note the maximum engine speed. Refer to Chapter Three to determine the recommended wide-open throttle speed range.

Check the propeller for damage or incorrect pitch if the measured engine speed is below or above the recommended engine speed range. Refer to Chapter Three if the correct propeller is installed, but the engine still fails to reach the recommended speed range. Check all fuel system, ignition system and timing adjustments.

Try a rapid acceleration and run the engine at various speed ranges. Refer to Chapter Three if rough operation is noted at any speed range, or if a hesitation or stall occurs during rapid acceleration.

SPECIAL MAINTENANCE REQUIREMENTS

This section provides special maintenance requirements for engines that have been submerged, stored long term, or are operating in salt or polluted water.

Submersion

If the engine completely submerged, three factors need to be considered. Was the engine running when the sub-

mersion occurred? Was the engine submerged in salt, brackish or polluted water? How long has the engine been retrieved from the water?

Complete disassembly and inspection of the power head is required if the engine was submerged while running. Internal engine damage, such as a bent connecting rod, is likely should this occur. Refer to Chapter Eight for power head repair instructions.

Many engine components can be damaged from submersion in salt, brackish or polluted water. The symptoms may not occur for some time after the submersion. Salt crystals form in many areas of the engine and promote intense corrosion in that area. The wire harness and its connections are usually damaged very quickly. It is difficult to remove all of the salt crystals from the harness connectors. Replace the wire harness and clean all electrical connections to ensure a reliable repair. The starter motor, relays and any switch on the engine will usually fail if not thoroughly cleaned of all salt residue.

Retrieve and service the engine as soon as possible after submersion. Vigorously wash the engine with freshwater after retrieval. Complete disassembly and inspection is required if sand, silt or other gritty material is noted in the engine cover. Refer to Chapter Eight for power head disassembly and assembly.

Service the engine and start it within two hours of retrieval. Clean the engine thoroughly and submerge it in a barrel or tank of clean freshwater if the engine cannot be serviced within this two-hour time frame. This is especially important if the engine was submerged in salt, brackish or polluted water. This protective submersion prevents exposure to air and decreases the potential for corrosion. This will not preserve the engine indefinitely. Service the engine within a few days after beginning protective submersion.

If an engine is not serviced soon after being retrieved from the water, it will have to be completely disassembled and all internal components will require inspection.

Perform the following steps as soon as the engine is retrieved from the water.

1. Remove the engine cover and *vigorously* wash all material from the engine using freshwater. Completely disassemble the engine and inspect the internal components if sand, silt or gritty material is present inside the engine cover.

2. Dry the exterior of the engine using compressed air. Remove the spark plugs and ground all spark plug leads. Remove the propeller as described in Chapter Nine.

3. Refer to Chapter Seven for fuel system service procedures. Drain all water and fuel from the fuel system. Remove any water from the carburetor cover. Replace all fuel filters on the engine.

4. Drain the engine oil. Position the engine with the spark plug openings facing down. Remove the rocker arm cover as described in Chapter Eight.

5. Slowly rotate the flywheel clockwise to force the water from the cylinder(s). Rotate the flywheel several times noting if the engine is turning freely. Completely disassemble and inspect the internal components if interference or rough rotation is noted.

6. Position the engine with the spark plug openings facing UP. Pour approximately 1 teaspoon of engine oil into each spark plug opening. Repeat Step 5 to distribute the oil in the cylinder.

7. Disconnect all electrical connections and inspect the terminals. Dry all exterior surfaces and wire connectors with compressed air. Remove, disassemble and inspect the starter motor as described in Chapter Seven.

8. Clean the rocker arm and rocker arm cover. Install the rocker arm cover as described in Chapter Eight.

9. Replace the oil filter, then fill the engine with fresh oil. Clean and install the spark plugs. Reconnect all wire harness and battery terminal connections.

10. Provide the engine with a fresh supply of fuel. Start the engine and run it at a low speed for a few minutes. Refer to Chapter Three (troubleshooting instructions) if the engine cannot be started. Stop the engine immediately and investigate if unusual noises are noted. Allow the engine to run at low speed for a minimum of 30 minutes to dry any residual water from the engine. Promptly investigate any unusual noises or unusual running conditions.

11. On manual start models, disassemble inspect then assemble the manual starter following the instructions provided in Chapter Ten.

12. Again change the engine oil and clean or replace the oil filter. Perform all maintenance items listed in **Table 1**.

Preparing the Engine for Storage

The objective when preparing the engine for long-term storage is to prevent any corrosion or deterioration during the storage period. This section provides the instructions to prepare your engine for storage. Recommissioning prepares the engine for operation after storage. Recommissioning instructions are provided in this chapter as well.

All major systems require some preparation before storage. If done correctly the engine should operate properly after recommissioning.

Perform any maintenance that becomes due during the storage period. Maintenance requirements are listed in **Table 1**.

Drain as much fuel from the fuel tank as possible. Clean or change all fuel filters on the engine prior to storage.

Clean the exterior of the gearcase, drive shaft housing and swivel brackets.

Wipe down the components under the cover and apply a good corrosion preventative spray such as CR66. Corrosive preventative sprays are available from most marine dealerships and marine supply stores. Flush the cooling system as described in this chapter.

Treat the internal power head components with a storage-sealing compound as described in this chapter. This step can prevent corrosion inside the power head during storage. These storage agents are available from most marine dealerships and marine supply stores.

Use a fuel additive such as Sta-Bil to help prevent the formation of gum or varnish deposits in the fuel system during storage. Other additives such as octane booster are not required under normal operating conditions. Be aware that some additives may adversely affect some fuel system components if mixed incorrectly. Deterioration of hoses, check valves and other non-metallic components may occur. Never mix these additives at a rate greater than specified on the label.

1. Remove the silencer cover as described in Chapter Six.

2. Run the engine at idle speed in a test tank or on a flush/test adapter until the engine reaches operating temperature.

3. Raise the engine speed to approximately 1500 rpm. Spray the storage-sealing compound into all carburetor openings. Try to spray the compound evenly into all carburetors on multiple carburetor engines. Spray in 5-10 second intervals. Continue to spray the compound into the engine until heavy smoking from the exhaust is noted. Stop the engine at this point.

4. Remove the engine from the test tank or remove the flush/test adapter. Remove each spark plug and spray the storage compound into each spark plug hole. Crank the engine over a few times to distribute the sealing compound.

5. Check the engine oil level and correct as required. Refer to Chapter Six to locate the carburetor bowl drain(s). Drain each carburetor float bowl. Disconnect the fuel hose from the fuel tank and route it to a container suitable for holding fuel. Slowly pump the primer bulb to move the residual fuel in the fuel hose to the float bowl for drainage. Install the drain plugs and securely tighten them. Disconnect the fuel hose from the engine. Treat any remaining fuel in the fuel tanks with fuel stabilizer.

6. Apply a light coat of engine oil to the spark plug threads and install them. Store the engine in the upright position.

7. Check the speedometer opening at the leading edge of the gearcase and other water drains on the gearcase for the presence of debris. They must be clear to ensure that water

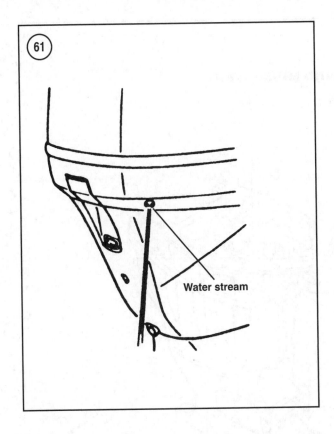

Water stream

4

engine reaches operating temperature. Check for proper operation of the cooling, electrical and warning systems, and correct them as required. Avoid continued operation if the engine is not operating properly. Refer to Chapter Three for troubleshooting and testing instructions if problems are noted.

Corrosion Prevention

Reducing corrosion damage increases the life and reliability of the engine. Corrosion damage can affect virtually every component of the engine.

Corrosion is far more prevalent if the engine is operated in salt or heavily polluted water. Serious damage to the engine will occur if steps are not taken to protect it. A simple and effective way to reduce corrosion in the power head cooling passages is to always flush the cooling system after running the engine. Refer to *After Each Use* in this chapter for instructions.

The use of a corrosion preventative spray on the external engine components can substantially reduce corrosion damage to engine wiring, terminals, exposed fasteners and other components. Regular use of corrosion preventative spray is highly recommended if the engine is operated in salt or polluted water. Corrosion preventative sprays are available from most marine dealerships or marine supply stores. Follow the instructions on the container for the proper use of these products.

is not trapped in the cooling system. Clean debris from them with a small piece of wire and compressed air.

8. Inspect the water stream fitting on the lower engine cover (**Figure 61**) for the presence of debris. Blow through the opening with compressed air to ensure it is clear. Remove stubborn debris with a small piece of stiff wire.

9. Disconnect the battery cables. Refer to Chapter Seven for battery storage instructions.

Recommissioning

When the time comes to use the outboard, a few items need attention. Perform all required maintenance. It is wise to service the water pump and replace the impeller as described in Chapter Nine. This vital component can deteriorate during extended storage.

Change the lubricants or correct the lubricant levels. Supply the engine with fresh fuel. Check for a flooding carburetor as described in Chapter Three. This problem is common after extended storage.

Install the battery, on models so equipped, as instructed in Chapter Seven. Supply cooling water and start the engine. Run the engine at low speed for the first few minutes. Avoid running it at wide-open throttle until the

Inspect all gearcase and power head anodes at more frequent intervals if the engine is operated in a corrosive environment. Special electronic equipment is available that uses current from the battery to balance or offset galvanic corrosion. The current draw from these systems is relatively low. Regular charging of the battery or operation of the engine easily recharges the battery. Consider installing this type of system if the boat is stored in the water for extended periods. These systems are available from most marine dealerships and marine supply stores.

Never connect the boat accessories to AC shore power. The potential for rapid corrosion of engine components exists under these circumstances. Disconnect the cables from the battery or remove the battery from the boat for charging.

Special isolators are available that allow charging of the battery or connections to shore power without promoting rapid corrosion. Contact a marine dealership or marine supply store for information on isolators.

Make sure all grounding wires (**Figure 62**) on the gearcase, midsection and power head are attached, and have a good connection at their terminal. Failure to maintain this ground connection prevents the sacrificial anodes from protecting the nongrounded components.

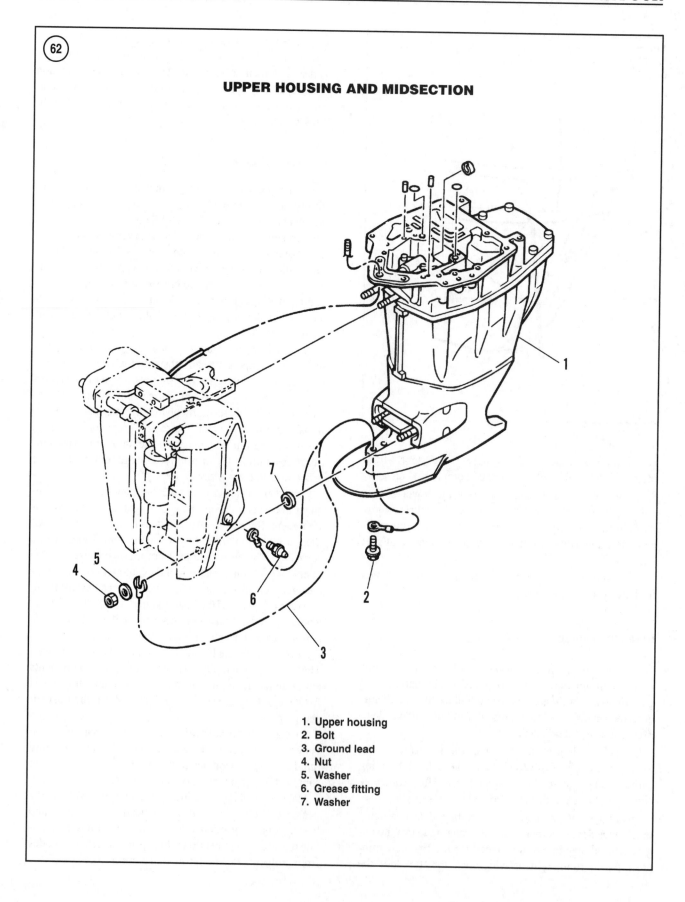

62

UPPER HOUSING AND MIDSECTION

1. Upper housing
2. Bolt
3. Ground lead
4. Nut
5. Washer
6. Grease fitting
7. Washer

Table 1 MAINTENANCE SCHEDULE

10 hours (break-in)	Inspect cowl latches and drain hole(s)
	Inspect/replace fuel filter
	Inspect/adjust throttle link rod
	Inspect/adjust start-in-gear protection
	Inspect/change engine oil
	Inspect/adjust valve clearance[1]
	Inspect engine for water leakage
	Inspect motor exterior
	Inspect for exhaust leakage
	Change lower unit gear oil
	Inspect battery every month
	Inspect/clean/change spark plug(s)
	Check connection of wiring harness
50 hours (3 months)	Inspect/replace fuel filter
	Inspect/change engine oil
	Replace engine oil filter
	Inspect/replace timing belt
	Check engine for exhaust leakage
	Inspect/clean cooling water passage(s)
	Inspect propeller for damage
	Inspect anode(s) for wear
	Inspect battery
	Inspect/clean/replace spark plug(s)
	Inspect and retighten all fasteners
100 hours (6 months)	Inspect fuel line(s)
	Inspect/replace fuel filter
	Inspect/adjust start-in-gear protection
	Inspect/change engine oil
	Replace engine oil filter
	Inspect/replace timing belt
	Inspect/adjust valve clearance[2]
	Inspect/replace thermostat[3]
	Inspect engine for exhaust leakage
	Inspect/clean cooling water passages
	Change lower unit gear oil
	Inspect water pump impeller
	Inspect lower unit for leakage
	Inspect propeller for damage
	Inspect anode(s) for wear
	Inspect battery
	Inspect/clean/replace spark plug(s)
	Inspect and retighten all fasteners
	Inspect and grease all grease points
200 hours (1 year)	Inspect cowl latches and drain hole(s)
	Inspect fuel line
	Inspect/adjust throttle cable(s)
	Inspect/adjust idle speed
	Inspect/adjust shift control cable
	Inspect spark timing
	Inspect/replace thermostat[4]
	Inspect lower unit for leakage
	Check/reconnect wiring harness
400 hours (2 year)	Inspect/adjust valve clearance[5]

1. Maintenance not required on F80 and F100 at this interval.
2. Maintenance is required only for F25, F40, F50 and T50 at this interval.
3. Maintenance is required only for F25 at this interval.
4. Maintenance is required only for F40, F50 and T50 at this interval.
5. Maintenance is suggested only for F80 and F100 at this interval.

4

Table 2 RECOMMENDED GEARCASE LUBRICANTS

Model	Oil type	SAE	API	Capacity
T9.9 (MH)(EH)(ER)	Hypoid	90	–	320 cm (10.82 oz)
F9.9 (MH)(EH)	Hypoid	90	–	185 cm (6.25 oz)
F15 (MH)(EH)	Hypoid	90	–	250 cm (8.45 oz)
F25 (MH)(EH)(TH)(ER) (TR)	Hypoid	90	–	320 cm (10.8 oz)
F40 (TR)(ER)(TH)(EH)	Hypoid	90	GL-4	430 cm (14.5 oz)
F50 (TR)(ER)(TH)(EH)	Hypoid	90	GL-4	430 cm (14.5 oz)
T50 (TR)	Hypoid	90	GL-4	610 cm (20.6 oz)
F80 and F100	Hypoid	90	GL-4	670 cm (22.6 oz)

Table 3 RECOMMENDED ENGINE SPEED

Idle speed	
F9.9	900-1000 rpm
T9.9	1100-1200 rpm
F15	900-1000 rpm
F25	875-975 rpm
F40-F50-FT50	700-800 rpm
F80-F100	850-950 rpm
Full-throttle speed	
F9.9-T9.9 and F15	4500-5500 rpm
F25-F100	5000-6000 rpm
Trolling range	
F9.9 and T9.9	800-900 rpm
Maximum horsepower output	
F9.9 and T9.9	5.9 kW (8 hp) @ 5000 rpm
F15	11 kW (15 hp) @ 5000 rpm
F25	18.4 kW (25 hp) @ 5500 rpm
F40	29.4 kW (40 hp) @ 5500 rpm
F50 and T50	36.8 kW (50 hp) @ 5500 rpm
F80	58.8 kW (80 hp) @ 5500 rpm
F100	73.6 kW (100 hp) @ 5500 rpm

Table 4 RECOMMENDED ENGINE OIL FOR FOUR-STROKE

Model	SAE	API	Capacity
F9.9 and T9.9	10W-30, 10W-40	SE, SF, SE-SF-CC	1.0 L (1.06 qt)
F15	10W-30, 10W-40	SE, SF, SG or SH	1.0 L (1.06 qt)[1]
			1.2 L (1.27 qt)[2]
F25	10W-30, 10W-40	SE, SF, SG, SH	1.7 L (1.80 qt)[1]
			1.9 L (2.01 qt)[2]
F40 and F50	10W-30, 10W-40	SE, SF, SG, SH	2.0 L (2.11 qt)[1]
			2.2 L (2.32 qt)[2]
T50	10W-30, 10W-40	SE, SF, SG, SH	2.0 L (2.11 qt)[1]
			2.2 L (2.32 qt)[2]
F80 and F100	10W-30, 10W-40	SE, SF, SG, SH	4.5 L (4.75 qt)[1]
			4.8 L (4.96 qt)[2]

1. Quantity without filter.
2. Quantity with filter.

Table 5 SPARK PLUG APPLICATION

Model	Ignition	Make	Type	Gap
F9.9	CDI	NGK	CR6HS	0.6-0.7 mm (0.024-0.028 in.)
F15	CDI	NGK	DPR6EA-9	0.9 mm (0.04 in.)
F25	CDI	NGK	DPR6EA-9	0.9 mm (0.04 in.)
F40-F50	CDI	NGK	DPR6EA-9	0.9 mm (0.035 in.)
F80-F100	CDI	NGK	LFR5A-11	1.1 mm (0.043 in.)

4

Table 6 GENERAL TORQUE SPECIFICATIONS

Nut	N•m	in.-lb.	ft.-lb.
8 mm	5.0	44	–
10 mm	8.0	71	–
12 mm	18	–	13
14 mm	36	–	26
17 mm	43	–	32

The torque specified in this chart is for standard fasteners with standard ISO pitch threads.
Special components or assemblies that require a special torque are covered in the applicable chapter in this book.

Table 7 RECOMMENDED LUBRICANTS AND SEALANTS

Item name	Part number
Lubricants	
Yamalube 4 Engine oil	ACC-11000-39-12
Hypoid (SAE 90) gear oil	Lub-Gearl-11-00 (11 oz. Tube)
	Lub-Gearl-01-GL (1 gal. Bottle)
All purpose grease	Lub-Greas-14-00
Sealants	
Yamabond 4	ACC-11001-30-00
Loctite	See local dealership
Gasket maker	907-90740-01-00

Chapter Five

Synchronization and Adjustment

To deliver the maximum efficiency and optimum performance, the ignition must be correctly timed and the throttle operation synchronized with the ignition timing. Always perform the synchronization and adjustment procedure after the fuel or ignition systems are serviced or adjusted.

This chapter is divided into sections that cover a particular model/ignition system for easy reference. Relevant specifications are provided in **Tables 1-13**, located at the end of this chapter.

FUEL SYSTEM ADJUSTMENT

This section provides adjustment procedures for fuel system components. Required adjustments vary by model, starting system serial number and year. Refer to *Engine Identification* in Chapter Three to determine the serial number and year. This section includes the following components.
1. Throttle position sensor.
2. Pilot screw.
3. Idle speed.
4. Dashpot.
5. Accelerator pump.
6. Choke valve.
7. Carburetor synchronization.

Throttle Position Sensor Adjustment

Throttle position sensor adjustment is only required on 80 and 100 hp models.
1. Disconnect both cables from the battery.
2. Locate the sensor (**Figure 1**) on the lower port side of the engine. Place the throttle in the idle position.
3. Loosen both sensor screws (**Figure 2**) only enough to allow rotation of the sensor body within the slots.
4. Rotate the sensor body (**Figure 2**) until the specified voltage is obtained, then securely tighten the sensor mounting screws.
5. Connect the cables to the battery.

Pilot Screw Adjustment

NOTE
An aluminum plug covers the pilot screw on 1998-on 50 hp and all 80 and 100 hp mod-

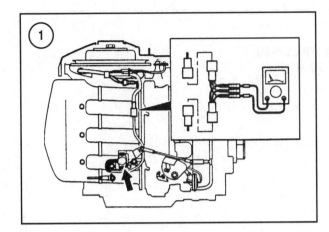

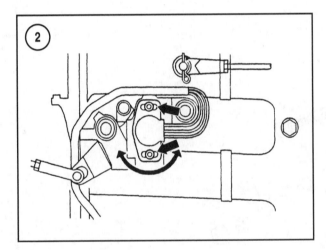

els. If the pilot circuit is restricted, remove the plug and turn the pilot screw clockwise until lightly seated, counting the turns required. Then remove the screw and clean the pilot circuit. When reinstalling the pilot screw, lightly seat the screw and turn it out the number of turns recorded during removal. Purchase a new plug from a Yamaha dealership and install it securely.

Pilot screw adjustment is required on 40 hp models (1999), 50 hp models (1995-1999) and 80-100 hp models (1999). Some 9.9 hp models (1999) use carburetors without exposed pilot adjustment screws. Adjustment is not required on these models.

40 hp (1999) and 50 hp models (1995-1999)

1. Use a scribe or small screwdriver to pry the rubber plug (15, **Figure 3**) from the pilot screw hole. Remove the plugs from all four carburetors.

2. Using a thin screwdriver, gently rotate the screw in until resistance is felt. Do not use excessive force when rotating the screw. Lightly seat the screw.
3. Back the screw out 1 3/4 to 2 3/4 turns.
4. Reinstall the rubber plugs into the pilot screw holes.

80 and 100 hp (1999) models

1. Use a scribe or small screwdriver to pry the rubber plug (7, **Figure 4**) from the pilot screw boss. Remove the plugs from all four carburetors.
2. Using a thin screwdriver, gently rotate the screw in until resistance is felt. Do not use excessive force when rotating the screw. Lightly seat the screw.
3. Back the screw out 1 1/2 to 2 1/2 turns.
4. Reinstall the rubber plugs into the pilot screw holes.

Idle Speed Adjustment

This section provides idle speed adjustment procedures for 9.9-50 hp models. On 80 and 100 hp models, the idle speed adjustments occur during carburetor synchronization Refer to *Carburetor Synchronization* in this chapter.
1. Install an accurate shop tachometer to the engine following the instructions provided with the tachometer. Start the engine and allow it to idle in neutral until it reaches operating temperature.
2. Locate the idle speed adjustment screw as follows:
   a. On 9.9 hp (1985-1995) and 15 hp models, the idle speed screw is located on the starboard side of the carburetor near the carburetor mounting boss (**Figure 5**).
   b. On 9.9 hp (1996-1999) models, the idle speed screw is located on the starboard rear side of the carburetor (**Figure 6**).
   c. On 25 hp models, the idle speed screw is located on the upper starboard side of the carburetor (**Figure 7**).
   d. On 40-50 hp models, the idle speed screw is located on the port side of the bottom carburetor (**Figure 8**).
3. Refer to **Table 13** to determine the correct idle speed. With the engine in neutral and the throttle closed, note the engine speed.
4. Using a screwdriver, slowly turn the idle speed screw until the engine speed reaches the middle of the neutral speed listed in **Table 12**.
5. Have an assistant shift the engine into forward gear. Allow the engine speed to stabilize, then note the idle speed in forward gear.
6. Adjust the idle speed in neutral to the higher end of the specification if the forward gear idle speed is too low. Ad-

③

**CARBURETOR ASSEMBLY
(40 AND 50 HP)**

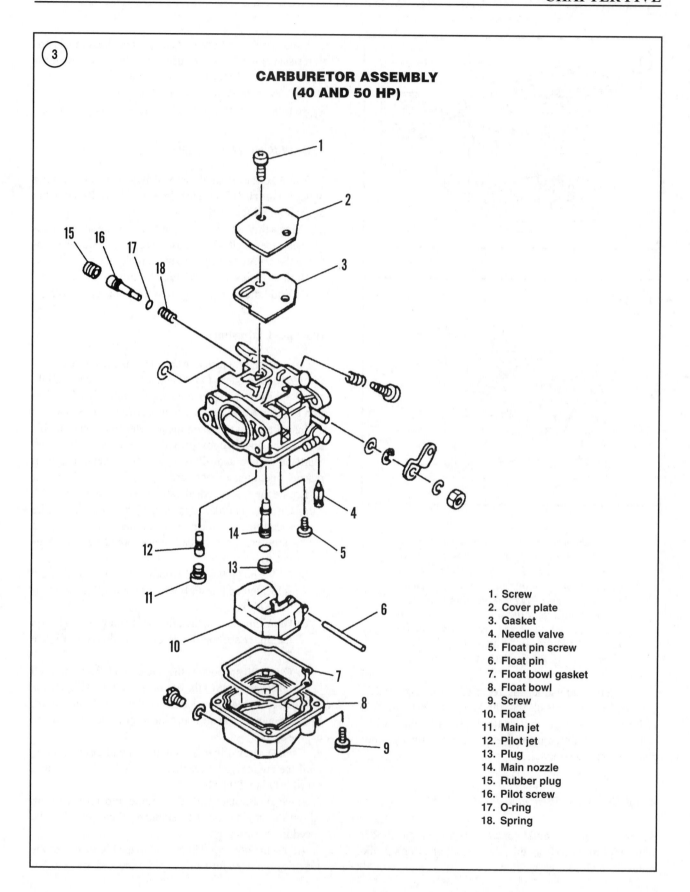

1. Screw
2. Cover plate
3. Gasket
4. Needle valve
5. Float pin screw
6. Float pin
7. Float bowl gasket
8. Float bowl
9. Screw
10. Float
11. Main jet
12. Pilot jet
13. Plug
14. Main nozzle
15. Rubber plug
16. Pilot screw
17. O-ring
18. Spring

5

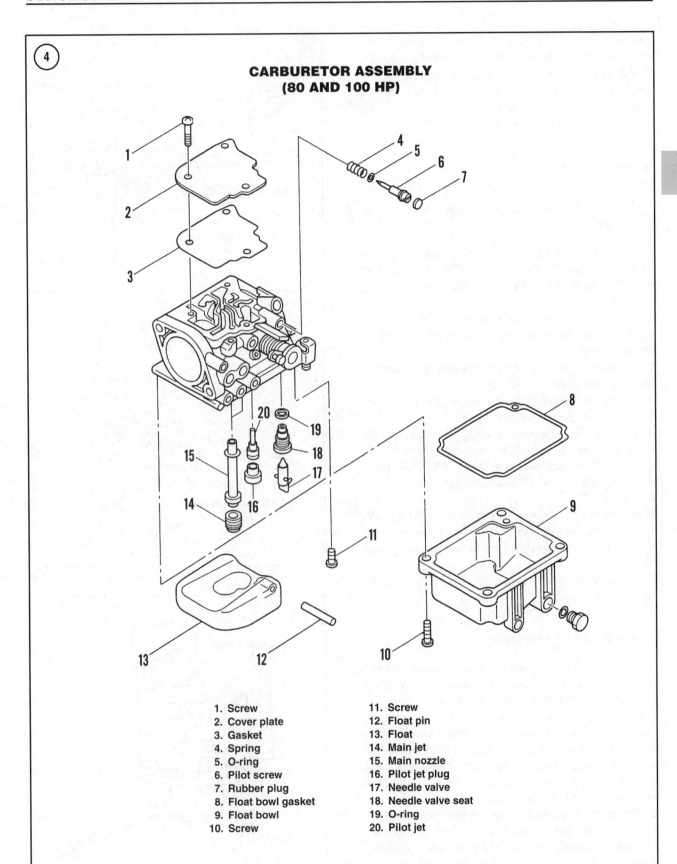

CARBURETOR ASSEMBLY
(80 AND 100 HP)

1. Screw
2. Cover plate
3. Gasket
4. Spring
5. O-ring
6. Pilot screw
7. Rubber plug
8. Float bowl gasket
9. Float bowl
10. Screw
11. Screw
12. Float pin
13. Float
14. Main jet
15. Main nozzle
16. Pilot jet plug
17. Needle valve
18. Needle valve seat
19. O-ring
20. Pilot jet

just the neutral gear idle speed to the lower end of the specification if the forward gear idle speed is too high.

7. Advance the engine speed for a few minutes, then return to idle. Check the idle speed after the speed stabilizes. Readjust the idle speed as required.

8. Remove the shop tachometer.

Dashpot Adjustment

NOTE
Adjust the carburetor prior to adjusting the dashpot.

This section provides dashpot adjustment procedures for 50 hp models. Dashpot adjustment is not required on 80 and 100 hp models. An accurate shop tachometer is required for this adjustment.

1. Connect an accurate shop tachometer to the No. 1 spark plug lead following the instructions provided with the tachometer.

2. Operate the engine until it reaches operating temperature. Shift the engine into neutral.

3. Locate the dashpot (**Figure 9**) on the lower starboard side toward the rear of the power head.

4. Observe the tachometer reading while pulling the plunger against the lever. Make sure the plunger is fully extended. The engine speed will reach 1650-1750 rpm if the adjustment is correct. Release the plunger after adjustment is correct.

5. If adjustment is required, loosen the jam nut (**Figure 9**) and rotate the dashpot body until the dashpot plunger just touches the lever. Securely tighten the jam nut, then repeat Step 4.

6. Close the throttle and stop the engine. Remove the shop tachometer.

Accelerator Pump Adjustment

Accelerator pump adjustment is not required on most models covered in this manual. The pump stroke length is automatically set during pump installation.

The accelerator pump linkage on 9.9 hp models may need minor adjustment after a carburetor repair.

1. Observe the linkage as the throttle is moved from idle to full throttle and back to idle. There should be a slight amount of free play in the linkage at idle and the linkage must not bind or hold the throttle open.

2. If there is excessive free play or binding, loosen the jam nut (**Figure 10**), then rotate the adjusting nut until adjustment is correct. Refer to Step 1 to check the adjustment.

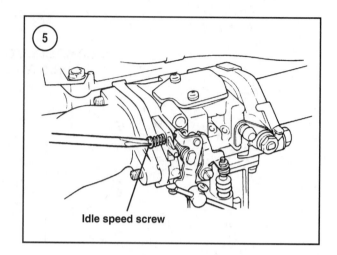

Idle speed screw

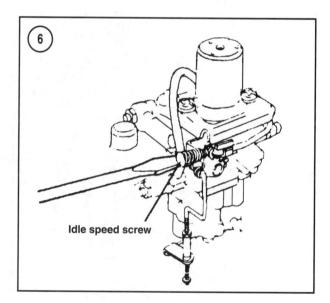

Idle speed screw

Idle speed screw

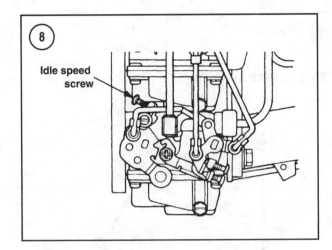

Idle speed screw

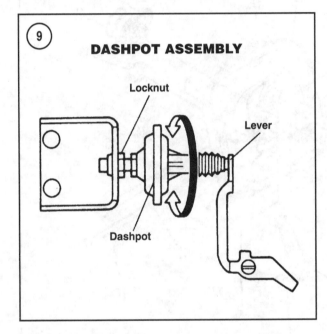

DASHPOT ASSEMBLY

Locknut

Lever

Dashpot

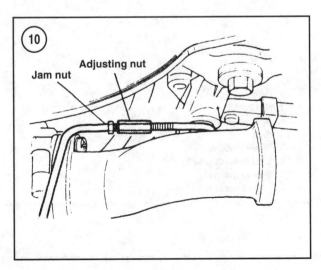

Jam nut

Adjusting nut

3. Make sure the adjusting nut engages the linkage a minimum of six threads. Hold the adjusting nut and securely tighten the jam nut.

4. Check for full accelerator pump travel without the linkage binding. Correct as required.

**Choke Valve Adjustment
(9.9 [1985-1995] and 15 hp models)**

1. Push the choke handle (5, **Figure 11**) inward to the choke off position.

2. Carefully pry the choke linkage from the choke lever (19, **Figure 11**). Gently rotate the lever counterclockwise to fully open the choke valve. Rotate the connector on the linkage until the connector aligns with the choke lever (19, **Figure 11**) with the choke knob pushed in.

3. Snap the linkage onto the connector. Observe the lever while pulling out the choke knob. The choke lever should just contact the stop lever. Push in the choke knob. The choke should return to the off position. Readjust as required.

Choke Valve Adjustment (50 hp models)

1. Loosen the adjusting screw for the choke linkage (1, **Figure 12**).

2. Measure the ambient air temperature. Move the linkage up or down to set the gap (2, **Figure 12**) for the given temperature.

   a. Set the gap at approximately 2.0 mm (0.080 in.) at 5° C (41° F).

   b. Set the gap at approximately 2.8 mm (0.110 in.) at 20° C (68° F).

   c. Set the gap at approximately 3.5 mm (0.137 in.) at 30° C (86° F).

   d. Set the gap at approximately 5.4 mm (0.212 in.) at 40° C (104° F).

3. Hold the linkage at the indicated gap and securely tighten the screw (1, **Figure 12**).

4. Back the adjustment screw (1, **Figure 13**) out until two threads protrude from the support. Push down on the choke linkage (2, **Figure 13**) until the choke lever on the No. 1 carburetor contacts the stop (3, **Figure 13**).

5. Hold lightly down on the choke linkage during screw adjustment. Turn the adjustment screw (1, **Figure 13**) in until it just contacts the lever (2, **Figure 13**).

6. Push down on the choke linkage (1, **Figure 14**). Measure the gap between the No. 4 carburetor choke lever (3, **Figure 14**) and the adjusting screw (2, **Figure 14**).

7. Turn the adjusting screw in or out to obtain the specified gap for the given ambient air temperature.

5

⑪

MANUAL STARTER ASSEMBLY

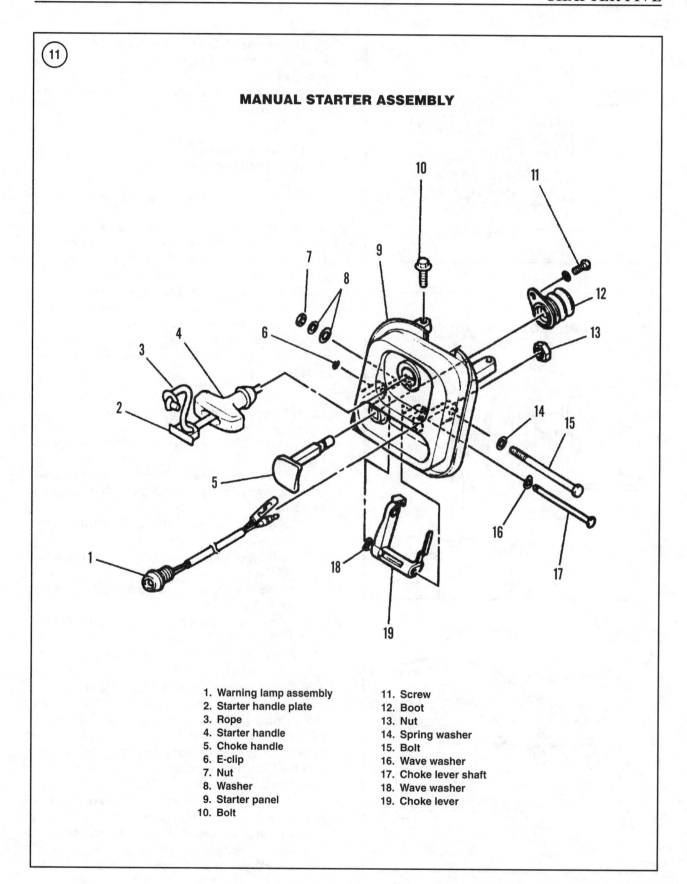

1. Warning lamp assembly
2. Starter handle plate
3. Rope
4. Starter handle
5. Choke handle
6. E-clip
7. Nut
8. Washer
9. Starter panel
10. Bolt
11. Screw
12. Boot
13. Nut
14. Spring washer
15. Bolt
16. Wave washer
17. Choke lever shaft
18. Wave washer
19. Choke lever

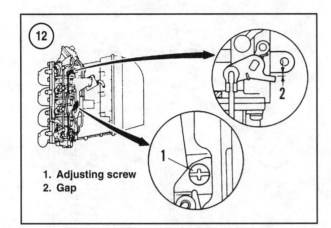

1. Adjusting screw
2. Gap

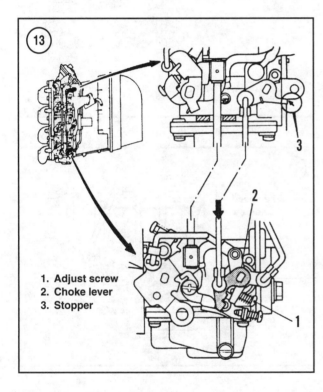

1. Adjust screw
2. Choke lever
3. Stopper

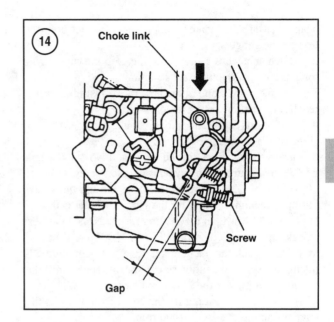

Choke link

Screw

Gap

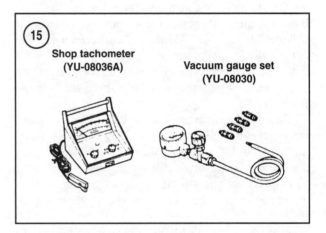

Shop tachometer
(YU-08036A)

Vacuum gauge set
(YU-08030)

a. Set the gap at approximately 3.0 mm (0.118 in.) at 10° C (50° F).

b. Set the gap at approximately 2.0 mm (0.080 in.) at 20° C (68° F).

c. Set the gap at approximately 1.0 mm (0.040 in.) at 25° C (77° F).

d. Set the gap at approximately 0.7 mm (0.027 in.) at 30° C (86° F).

CARBURETOR SYNCHRONIZATION

An accurate shop tachometer and carburetor synchronization gauges (**Figure 15**) are required for these adjust-ments. Purchase these tools from tool suppliers or at most automotive parts stores. Adapters included with the gauge set usually fit the plug openings in the intake runner. Remove the plugs from the intake runner, and compare the plug diameter and thread pitch with the adapters. Purchase the correct size adapters.

Synchronize the carburetors with the boat and motor in the water or with the motor in a test tank. Attempting to synchronize the carburetors using a flush/test device will result in poor performance when on the water.

40 and 50 hp Models

1. Remove all four synchronization port plugs (**Figure 16**) from the intake runners. Thread the adapters (**Figure 16**) into all four ports. Connect the gauge hoses onto the

adapters. Mark the intake runner number for each connection on the gauge set.

2. Attach an accurate shop tachometer to the engine following the manufacturer's instructions.

3. Start the engine and allow it to run at fast idle until it reaches normal operating temperature.

4. Shift into NEUTRAL and adjust the idle speed screw (**Figure 17**) to obtain 1000 rpm.

5. Observe the gauges for the No. 3 and No. 4 cylinders while slowly turning the synchronization screw (**Figure 18**) on the No. 3 carburetor. Continue turning the screw until the vacuum reading for the No. 3 cylinder is 0.4 in. Hg (1.3 kPa) less than the reading for the No. 4 cylinder. Check the idle speed and readjust to 1000 rpm, if necessary, then check the vacuum gauges again. Continue adjusting the synchronization screw and idle speed until the vacuum reading for the No. 3 cylinder is 0.4 in. Hg (1.3 kPa) less than the reading for the No. 4 cylinder with the engine running at exactly 1000 rpm.

6. Next, turn the synchronization screw on the No. 2 carburetor (**Figure 18**) until the vacuum reading for the No. 2 cylinder is 0.8 in. Hg (2.7 kPa) less than the reading for the No. 4 cylinder. Make sure the idle speed remains 1000 rpm. Continue adjusting the synchronization screw and idle speed until the vacuum and idle speed are as specified.

7. Turn the synchronization screw on the No. 1 carburetor (**Figure 18**) until the vacuum reading for the No. 1 cylinder is 1.2 in. Hg (4 kPa) less than the vacuum reading for the No. 4 cylinder. Make sure the idle speed remains at 1000 rpm. Continue adjusting the synchronization screw and idle speed until the vacuum and idle speed are as specified.

8. Advance the throttle to 2500 rpm, then throttle back to idle. Check the idle speed and vacuum readings and repeat the synchronization procedure if necessary.

9. Remove the synchronization gauges. Finish adjusting the idle speed as described in this chapter.

80 and 100 hp Models

1. Remove all four synchronization port plugs (**Figure 19**) from the intake runners. Thread the adapters (**Figure 19**) into all four ports. Connect the gauge to the adapters. Mark the intake runner number for each connection on the gauge set.

2. Attach an accurate shop tachometer to the engine following the manufacturer's instructions.

3. Start the engine and allow it to run at fast idle until it reaches normal operating temperature.

4. Shift into NEUTRAL and turn the idle speed screw (2, **Figure 19**) until the idle speed is 1000 rpm.

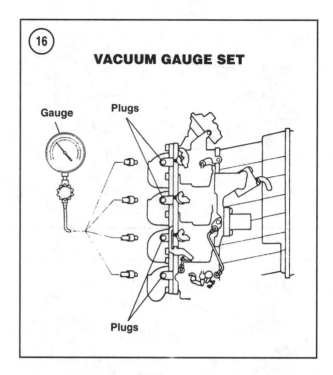

(16) **VACUUM GAUGE SET**

Gauge

Plugs

Plugs

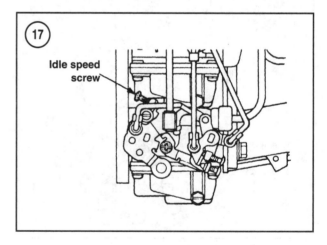

(17)

Idle speed screw

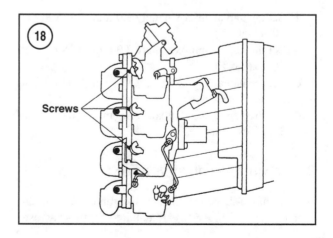

(18)

Screws

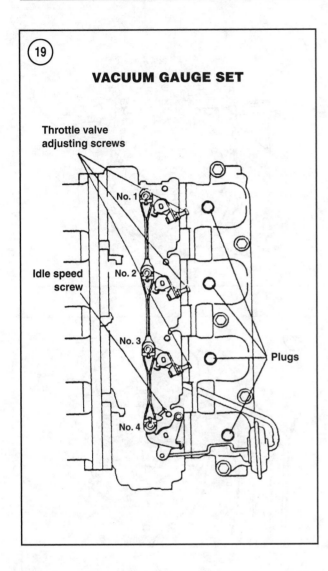

VACUUM GAUGE SET

Throttle valve
adjusting screws

No. 1

Idle speed
screw

No. 2

No. 3

Plugs

No. 4

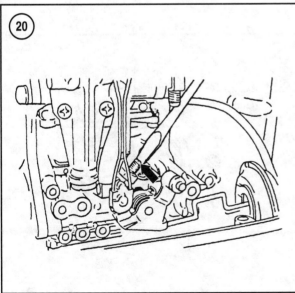

5. Adjust the synchronization screw (**Figure 20**) until the vacuum readings for the No. 3 and No. 4 cylinders are equal. Make sure the idle speed remains at 1000 rpm and readjust if necessary. Continue until the vacuum readings are equal at 1000 rpm.

6. Adjust the synchronization screw (**Figure 19**) on the No. 2 carburetor until the vacuum readings for cylinders No. 2 and No. 4 are equal. Make sure the idle speed remains at 1000 rpm. Readjust as necessary. Continue until the vacuum readings for cylinders 2-4 are equal at 1000 rpm.

7. Next, turn the synchronization screw on the no. 1 carburetor (**Figure 19**) until the vacuum reading for the No. 1 cylinder is equal with the other three cylinders. Make sure the idle speed remains at 1000 rpm. Continue until the vacuum is equal on all cylinders at 1000 rpm.

8. Advance the engine speed to 2500 rpm, then throttle back to idle. Check the vacuum gauges and idle speed and repeat the synchronization process if necessary.

9. Adjust the final idle speed as described in this chapter.

VALVE ADJUSTMENT

Adjust the valves while the engine is cold. A feeler gauge set is required to adjust the valves.

9.9 and 15 hp Models

1. Disconnect both cables from the battery, if so equipped. Remove the spark plugs and connect the spark plug leads to a suitable engine ground.

2. On manual start models, remove the manual starter as described in Chapter Ten.

3. On electric start models, remove the flywheel cover as described in Chapter Eight.

4. Remove the rocker arm cover as described in Chapter Eight

5. Position the No. 1 cylinder at TDC (top dead center) as follows:

   a. Rotate the flywheel clockwise until the timing pointer (**Figure 21**) aligns with the line next to the 0 mark.

   b. Check the camshaft sprocket timing marks. The No. 1 triangle mark on the camshaft sprocket should align with the triangle mark on the cylinder block (**Figure 22**). If the No. 1 triangle mark on the camshaft sprocket is not aligned with the triangle mark on the cylinder block, turn the flywheel one turn clockwise and align the timing pointer (**Figure 21**) with the 0 mark.

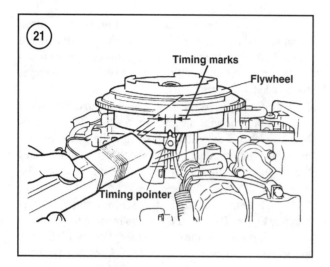

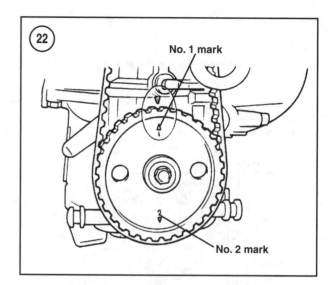

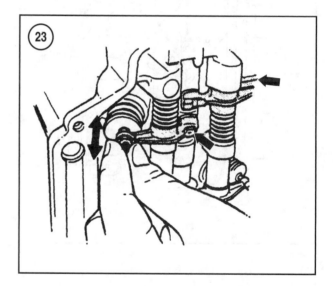

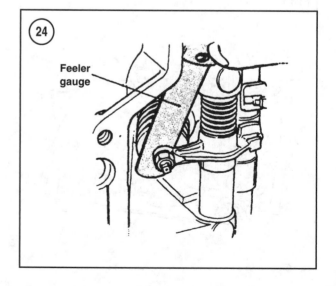

6. The No. 1 cylinder rocker arms are shown in **Figure 23**. Check the clearance between the valve stem and rocker arm using a flat feeler gauge (**Figure 24**). Measure the clearance for the intake and exhaust valves, and compare the clearance with the specification in **Table 13**.

7. If adjustment is necessary, loosen the rocker arm nut and turn the adjusting screw (**Figure 25**) as required. When the correct clearance is obtained, hold the adjusting screw securely and tighten the rocker arm nut to 14 N•m (10 ft.-lb.). Recheck the clearance after tightening the nut.

8. Position the No. 2 cylinder at TDC. Turn the flywheel clockwise one full turn clockwise and align the timing pointer (**Figure 22**) with the line adjacent to the 0 mark on the flywheel. Now the No. 2 triangle mark on the camshaft sprocket should be aligned with the triangle mark on the cylinder block (**Figure 22**). If not, turn the flywheel as necessary to align the marks.

9. Measure the clearance of the intake and exhaust valve for the No. 2 cylinder and compare the clearance with the specifications in **Table 13**.

10. If adjustment is required, loosen the rocker arm nut and turn the adjusting screw as required. Once the correct clearance is set, hold the adjusting screw and tighten the nut to 14 N•m (10 ft.-lb.). Check the clearance again after tightening the nut.

11. Install the rocker arm cover as described in Chapter Eight and the rewind starter as described in Chapter Ten.

25 hp Models

1. Disconnect both cables from the battery, if so equipped. Remove the spark plugs and connect the spark plug leads to a suitable engine ground.

2. On manual start models, remove the manual starter as described in Chapter Ten.

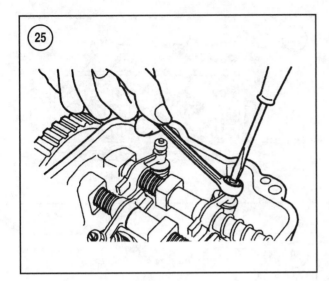

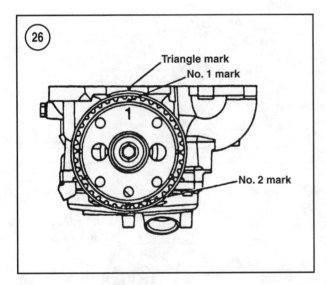

Triangle mark

No. 1 mark

1

No. 2 mark

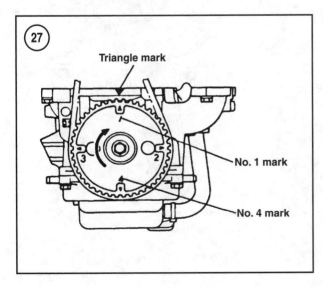

Triangle mark

No. 1 mark

No. 4 mark

3. On electric start models, remove the flywheel cover as described in Chapter Eight.

4. Remove the rocker arm cover following the instructions in Chapter Eight

5. Position the No. 1 piston at TDC. Rotate the flywheel clockwise until the triangle mark on the camshaft sprocket (**Figure 26**) aligns with the triangle mark on the cylinder block (1).

6. Using feeler gauges, check the clearance between the rocker arm and valve stem (**Figure 24**) for both valves for the No. 1 cylinder. Compare the clearance with the specifications in **Table 13**.

7. If adjustment is necessary, loosen the rocker arm nut and turn the adjusting screw (**Figure 25**) as required to set the correct clearance. Hold the adjusting screw securely and tighten the rocker arm nut to 14 N•m (10 ft.-lb.). Check the clearance again after tightening the nut.

8. Place the No. 2 cylinder at TDC. Turn the flywheel clockwise one full turn until the raised circle on the camshaft sprocket aligns with the triangle mark on the cylinder block (**Figure 26**).

9. Repeat Step 6 and Step 7 for the No. 2 cylinder valves.

10. Install the rocker arm cover (Chapter Eight). Install the flywheel cover (Chapter Eight) on electric start models. Install the rewind starter on models so equipped.

40 and 50 hp Models

1. Disconnect the battery cables from the battery and remove the spark plugs.

2. Remove the flywheel cover as described in Chapter Eight.

3. Remove the rocker arm cover as described in Chapter Eight.

4. Place the No. 1 piston at TDC. Rotate the flywheel clockwise until the timing pointer aligns with the 0 mark on the flywheel and the 1 triangle mark on the camshaft sprocket (**Figure 27**) align with the triangle mark on the cylinder block (1). If all marks do not align properly, remove the timing belt and correctly position all components. See Chapter Eight.

5. Using a feeler gauge, check the clearance between the rocker arm and valve stem (**Figure 28**) on the following valves (**Figure 29**):

   a. No. 1 intake and exhaust valves.

   b. No. 3 exhaust valve.

6. Compare the clearance with the specifications in **Table 13**.

7. If adjustment is required, loosen the rocker arm nut and turn the adjusting screw (**Figure 30**) as required to set the correct clearance. Hold the adjusting screw securely and

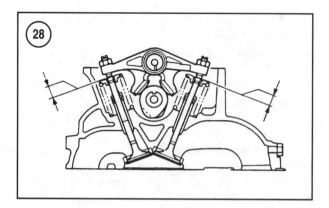

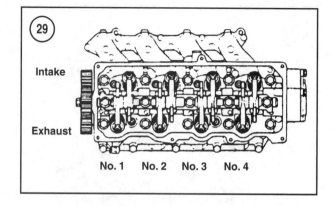

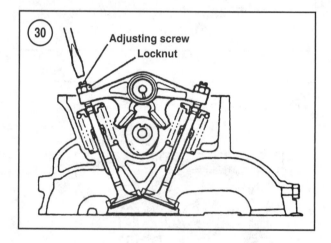

tighten the rocker arm nut to 14 N•m (10 ft.-lb.). Check the clearance again after tightening the nut.

8. Next, turn the flywheel clockwise one full turn and align the timing pointer with the 0 mark on the flywheel and the 4 mark and the triangle on the camshaft sprocket with the triangle on the cylinder block (**Figure 27**).

9. Repeat Step 5 on the following valves:

    a. No. 4 cylinder intake and exhaust valves.

    b. No. 2 cylinder exhaust valve.

    c. No. 3 cylinder intake valve.

10. If adjustment is required, loosen the rocker arm nut and turn the adjusting screw (**Figure 25**) as required to set the correct clearance. Hold the adjusting screw securely and tighten the rocker arm nut to 14 N•m (10 ft.-lb.). Check the clearance again after tightening the nut.

11. Install the flywheel cover and rocker arm cover as described in Chapter Eight.

80 and 100 hp Models

1. Disconnect the battery cables from the battery and remove the spark plugs.

2. Remove the flywheel cover and rocker arm cover as described in Chapter Eight.

3. Place the No. 1 piston at TDC. Rotate the flywheel clockwise until the marks on the camshaft sprockets (**Figure 31**) directly align. If the marks face opposite directions (**Figure 32**), the No. 4 cylinder is at TDC. Turn the flywheel one full turn clockwise and align the marks as specified.

4. Using a feeler gauge, check the clearance between the valve pad and camshaft lobe (**Figure 33**). With the No. 1 cylinder at TDC, check the clearance of the following valves (**Figure 34**):

    a. No. 1 cylinder—both intake and both exhaust valves.

    b. No. 2 cylinder—both intake valves.

    c. No. 3 cylinder—both exhaust valves.

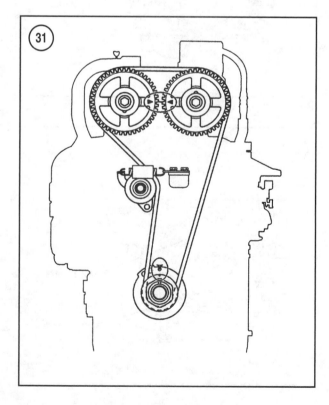

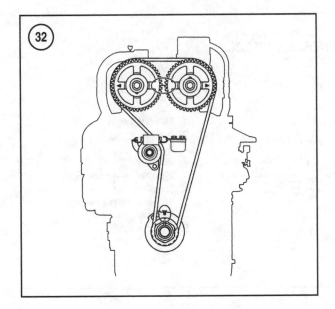

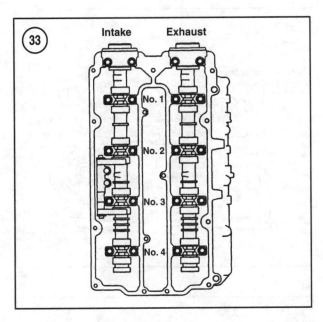

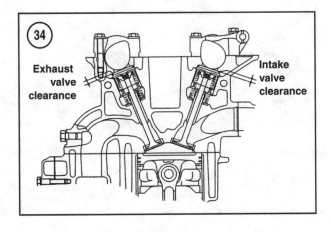

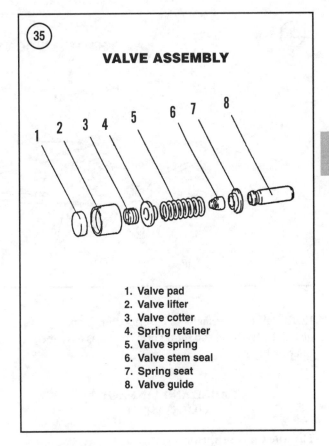

VALVE ASSEMBLY

1. Valve pad
2. Valve lifter
3. Valve cotter
4. Spring retainer
5. Valve spring
6. Valve stem seal
7. Spring seat
8. Valve guide

5. Place the No. 4 piston at TDC. Turn the flywheel one full turn clockwise so the camshaft sprocket marks face opposite directions (**Figure 32**).

6. With the No. 4 cylinder at TDC, check the clearance of the following valves using a feeler gauge (**Figure 33**):

   a. No. 3 cylinder—both intake valves

   b.. No. 4 cylinder—both intake and both exhaust valves.

   c. No. 2 cylinder—both exhaust valves.

7. Compare the valve clearance with the specification in **Table 13**. If adjustment is necessary, turn the flywheel one full turn clockwise to position the No. 1 piston at TDC.

8. Remove the camshaft and sprockets as described in Chapter Eight.

9. On the valve being adjusted, carefully lift the valve pad (**Figure 35**) from the lifter using a thin screwdriver.

10. Measure the pad thickness near the outer edge using a micrometer. Install a new valve pad of the thickness required to set the correct valve clearance. New valve pads are available from a Yamaha dealership. Install a thicker pad to decrease clearance and a thinner pad to increase clearance.

11. Repeat Step 10 for all valves that require adjustment.

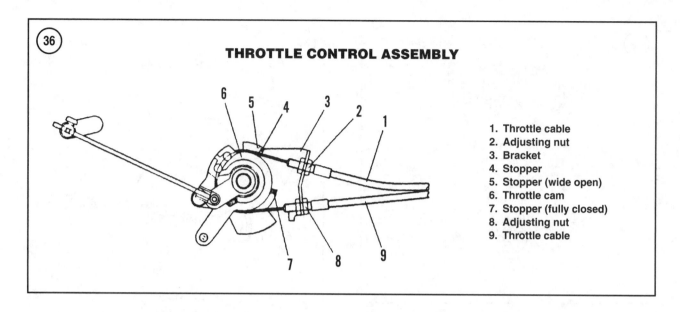

THROTTLE CONTROL ASSEMBLY

1. Throttle cable
2. Adjusting nut
3. Bracket
4. Stopper
5. Stopper (wide open)
6. Throttle cam
7. Stopper (fully closed)
8. Adjusting nut
9. Throttle cable

12. Install the camshafts as described in Chapter Eight. Install the flywheel and rocker arm covers as described in Chapter Eight.

CABLE AND LINKAGE ADJUSTMENT

Throttle Cable Adjustment (Remote Control Models)

1. Disconnect the cables from the battery, if so equipped.
2. Turn the tiller control throttle grip to the idle position.
3. Loosen the cable adjusting and locking nuts.
   a. On 9.9 and 15 hp models, set the throttle lever at the fully open position. Contact the stopper (4, **Figure 36**) on the bracket (3) with the wide-open stopper (5) on the throttle cam (6). Turn the adjusting nuts until slack in the cables are just removed, then securely tighten the adjusting nuts.
   b. On 25 hp models, loosen the screw (**Figure 37**). Turn the carburetor lever (**Figure 37**) clockwise to the wide-open position and hold it against the stopper (**Figure 38**). Next, hold the throttle lever (**Figure 37**) in the wide-open position and tighten the screw. Observe the carburetor throttle valve and operate the throttle control. Make sure the throttle valve opens and closes fully.
   c. On 40 and 50 hp models, loosen the locknut (**Figure 39**) and remove the clip (**Figure 39**). Disconnect the throttle cable (**Figure 39**) from the throttle control lever (**Figure 39**). Set the remote control lever in neutral position or throttle control grip to the fully closed position. Align the mark shown in **Figure 40**

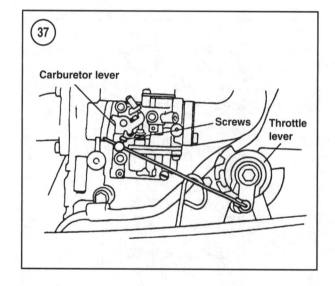

Carburetor lever

Screws   Throttle lever

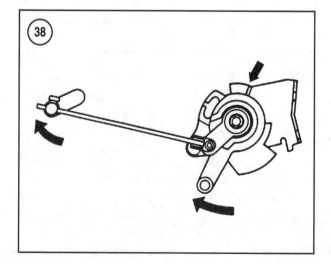

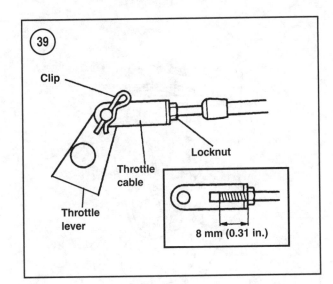

Clip

Locknut

Throttle cable

Throttle lever

8 mm (0.31 in.)

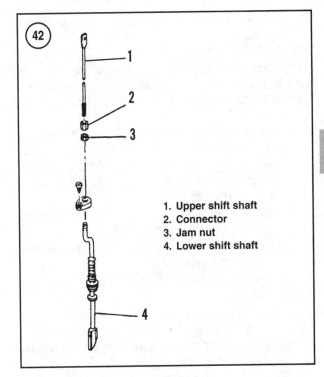

1. Upper shift shaft
2. Connector
3. Jam nut
4. Lower shift shaft

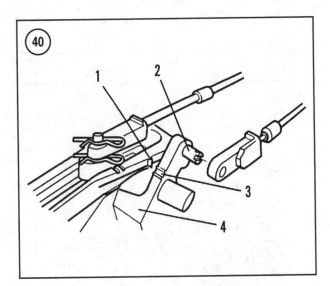

5

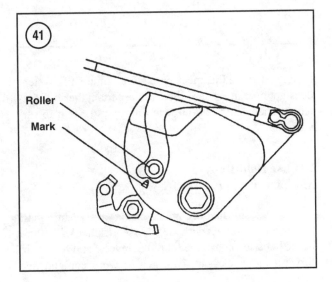

Roller

Mark

with the mark shown in 1, **Figure 40** on the shift bracket. Adjust the throttle cable joint position until its hole aligns with the set pin (2, **Figure 40**) on the throttle control lever (4, **Figure 40**). Install the clip and tighten the locknut.

d. On 80 and 100 hp models, rotate the throttle cable until the mark (2, **Figure 41**) on the throttle cam aligns with the throttle roller (1, **Figure 41**). Make sure the roller aligns with the cam as indicated in **Figure 41**.

4. Securely tighten all cable fasteners.

5. Turn the throttle grip to full throttle and back to idle several times. Check for free throttle movement, full throttle range and a consistent return to idle. Perform additional adjustments if binding, inconsistent idle return or lack of full range occurs.

Shift Cable/Linkage Adjustment (Tiller Control Models)

1. Disconnect the battery cables from the battery. Disconnect the spark plug leads and connect them to a good engine ground.

2A. On 9.9-25 hp models, loosen the jam nut (3, **Figure 42**) and remove the connector (2) from the lower shift shaft. Move the lower shift shaft up or down until the propeller spins freely in both directions. Without moving either shift shaft up or down, install the connector onto the lower shift shaft. Hold the connector and securely tighten the jam nut.

2B. On 40 and 50 hp models, incorrect shift operation is usually caused by misalignment of the upper and lower shift shaft splines during gearcase installation or bent or damaged linkage. Check shift cable adjustment as follows:

    a. Place the shift selector in the FORWARD gear position. Attempt to turn the propeller counterclockwise. If the shift cable is properly adjusted, the propeller will not turn counterclockwise while in FORWARD gear.

    b. Place the shift selector in NEUTRAL. The propeller should turn freely in both directions.

    c. Place the shift selector in REVERSE. The propeller should not turn clockwise.

3. Adjust the shift cable if the shift system does not function as described.

4. Connect the spark plug leads to the spark plugs and the battery cables to the battery..

5. Make sure the shift system operates properly before returning the boat to service.

Shift Cable Adjustment (Remote Control Models)

1. Disconnect the cables from the battery. Disconnect the spark plug leads and connect them to a good engine ground.

2. Place the remote control in the NEUTRAL position.

3. Disconnect the shift cable from the engine.

4. Push the shift linkage lightly toward REVERSE gear position. Do not push hard enough to engage reverse. Use just enough pressure to remove the slack from the linkage. Maintain the linkage in this position until the cable is attached.

5. Lightly push the end of the cable toward the barrel to remove the slack from the cable. Rotate the barrel until the cable attaches with the linkage positioned as described in Step 4.

6. Attach the shift cable to the shift linkage and barrel retainer. Secure all fasteners.

7. To check cable adjustment, shift from neutral to FORWARD, then to REVERSE while an assistant rotates the propeller in the appropriate direction.

    a. In forward, the propeller must not be able to rotate counterclockwise.

    b. In neutral, the propeller must be able to turn freely in both directions.

    c. In reverse, the propeller must not be able to rotate clockwise.

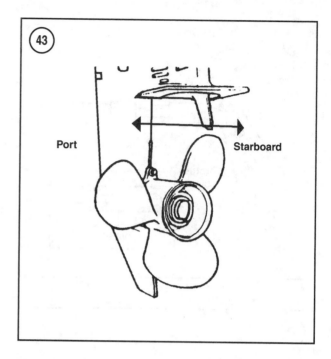

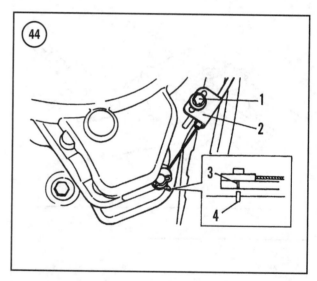

8. Repeat the adjustment procedure if the shift system does not operate as described. Make certain the shift system operates correctly prior to returning the unit to service.

Reverse Hold-Down Mechanism Adjustment

On 9.9-25 hp models, an extension on the shift shaft makes direct contact with the reverse lock hooks. Failure of the hook to engage the tilt pin in reverse and release in forward indicates bent, damaged or worn components.

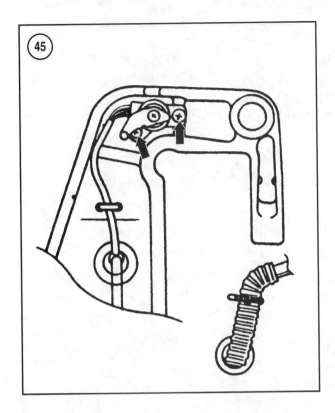

Replace the faulty component, then check for proper operation. On other models, adjust the mechanism as follows:

1. Shift the engine into REVERSE gear. Loosen the bolt and nut on the reverse lock-adjusting clamp. Move the adjusting clamp toward the mechanism until the reverse lock hooks fully engage the tilt pin. Securely tighten the bolt and nut.

2. Observe the reverse lock hooks and tilt pin while shifting the engine into NEUTRAL. If the hooks disengage the tilt pin, the adjustment is correct. Clearance between the hooks and pin must be sufficient to prevent unintentional engagement. Readjust the clamp to achieve the clearance. Make sure the hooks fully engage the pin when in REVERSE gear after adjustment.

3. Check for correct reverse hold-down operation using very low throttle settings. Readjust the mechanism if required.

Trim Tab Adjustment

1. Loosen the trim tab retaining bolt. On some models, the bolt is located just forward of the trim tab fin.

2. If the engine steers or pulls toward the port direction, pivot the trailing edge, or rear, of the trim tab slightly toward the port side (**Figure 43**). If the engine steers or pulls

toward the starboard direction, pivot the trailing edge of the trim tab slightly toward the starboard side (**Figure 43**).

3. Securely tighten the trim tab bolt.

4. Additional adjustment may be required to further reduce steering pull.

Neutral Start Mechanism Adjustment (9.9-25 hp Models)

1. Disconnect the spark plug leads. Shift the engine into NEUTRAL.

2. Loosen the jam nut (1, **Figure 44**) on the shift linkage.

3. Move the adjusting plate (2, **Figure 44**) until the point (3, **Figure 44**) on the wire connector aligns with the mark (4, **Figure 44**) in the flywheel cover.

4. Securely tighten the jam nut. Check for proper operation as follows:

    a. Shift the engine into FORWARD gear, then attempt to pull the manual starter. Adjustment is correct if the manual starter will not rotate.

    b. Shift the engine into REVERSE gear, then attempt to pull the manual starter. Adjustment is correct if the manual starter will not rotate.

    c. Shift the engine into NEUTRAL, then attempt to pull the manual starter. Adjustment is correct if the manual starter rotates.

5. Install the spark plugs and leads. Check for correct operation before returning the engine to service.

Trim Position Sender Adjustment

NOTE
Variations in gauge resistance, battery voltage, wire length and sender resistance may prevent the gauge from reaching the full up and down readings. Synchronize the sender to the full down position only.

On 40 and 50 hp models, adjust the sender as follows:

1. Observe the trim gauge reading while trimming the engine to the full down position. Adjustment is correct if the gauge indication reaches full down just as the engine reaches the full down position.

2. Adjust the sender as follows:

    a. Using the trim system, place the engine in the full up position. Engage the tilt lock lever, and use blocks or an overhead cable to secure the engine.

    b. Loosen both screws (**Figure 45**), then pivot the sender slightly clockwise or counterclockwise. Securely tighten the screws.

5

46

CLAMP BRACKET ASSEMBLY
(80 AND 100 HP)

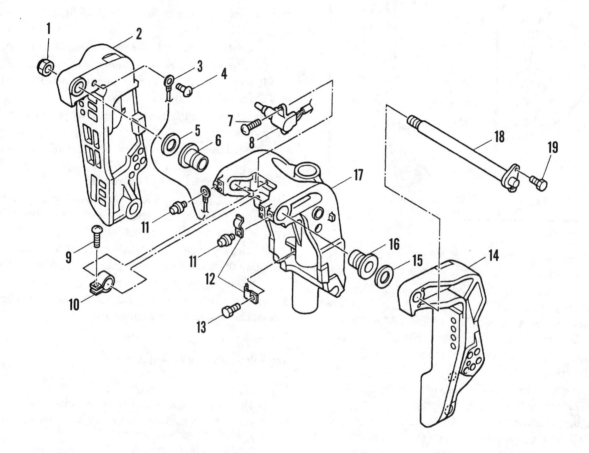

1. Self-locking nut
2. Clamp bracket
3. Ground lead
4. Screw
5. Washer
6. Bushing
7. Screw
8. Trim sender
9. Screw
10. Trim sender cam
11. Grease fitting
12. Clamp
13. Bolt
14. Clamp bracket
15. Washer
16. Bushing
17. Swivel bracket
18. Tube
19. Bolt

c. Remove the support, then disengage the tilt lock lever. Repeat Steps 2a-c until adjustment is correct. Several adjustments may be required.

3. On 80 and 100 hp models, adjust the sender as follows:

4. Observe the trim gauge reading while trimming the engine to the full down position. Adjustment is correct when the gauge indication reaches full down just as the engine reaches the full down position.

5. Adjust the sender as follows:

a. Using the trim system, place the engine in the full up position. Engage the tilt lock lever and use blocks or an overhead cable to secure the engine.

b. Loosen both screws (7, **Figure 46**), then move the sender slightly up or down. Tighten the screw securely.

c. Remove the support, then disengage the tilt lock lever. Repeat Steps 2a-c until adjustment is correct. Several adjustments may be required.

5

Table 1 TEST PROPELLERS

Engine	Part No.
T9.9	Yb-01627
F9.9	Yb-01619
F15	Yb-01619
F25	Yb-01621
F40-50	Yb-01611
F80-100	Yb-01620

Table 2 TUNE-UP SPECIFICATIONS (1985-1991 F9.9 AND T9.9 HP)

Ignition timing	Not adjustable
Spark plug type	CR6HS (NGK)
Spark plug gap	0.6-0.7 mm (0.024-0.028 in.)

Table 3 TUNE-UP SPECIFICATIONS (1992-1995 F9.9 AND T9.9 HP)

Ignition idle timing	4-6° BTDC
Full throttle timing	34-36° BTDC
Spark plug type	CR6HS (NGK)
Spark plug gap	0.6-0.7 mm (0.024-0.028 in.)

Table 4 TUNE-UP SPECIFICATIONS (1996-1997 F9.9 AND T9.9 HP)

Timing (full retard)	2-8° BTDC
Timing (full advance)	32-38° BTDC
Spark plug type	CR6HS (NGK)
Spark plug gap	0.6-0.7 mm (0.024-0.028 in.)

Table 5 TUNE-UP SPECIFICATIONS (1998-1999 F9.9 AND T9.9 HP)

Timing (full retard)	2-8° BTDC
Timing (full advance)	32-38° BTDC
Spark plug type	CR6HS (NGK)
Spark plug gap	0.6-0.7 mm (0.024-0.028 in.)

Table 6 TUNE-UP SPECIFICATIONS (1998-1999 F15 HP)

Ignition timing	2-33° BTDC
Spark plug type	DPR6EA-9 (NGK)
Spark plug gap	0.9 mm (0.04 in.)

Table 7 TUNE-UP SPECIFICATIONS (1998-1999 F25 HP)

Ignition timing	7-33° BTDC
Spark plug type	DPR6EA-9 (NGK)
Spark plug gap	0.9-1.0 mm (0.035-0.039 in.)

Table 8 TUNE-UP SPECIFICATIONS (1999 F40 HP-1995-1999 F50 HP)

Ignition firing order	Four cylinders	No. 1-3-4-2
Ignition timing	5-35° BTDC	
Spark plug type	DPR6EA-9 (NGK)	
Spark plug gap	0.9 mm (0.035 in.)	

Table 9 TUNE-UP SPECIFICATIONS (F80 AND F100 HP 1999)

Ignition firing order	Four cylinders	No. 1-3-4-2
Ignition timing	Full retard	5° ATDC
	Full advance	25° BTDC
Spark plug type	LFR5A-11 (NGK)	
Spark plug gap	1.1 mm (0.043 in.)	
Spark plug lead resistance*		
No. 1	4500-10,700 ohms	
No. 2	3300-8000 ohms	
No. 3	3700-8900 ohms	
No. 4	4300-10,200 ohms	
*At 20° C (68° F)		

Table 10 ENGINE SPECIFICATIONS

	Model				
	F9.9	T9.9	F15	F25	F40
Cylinders	2	2	2	2	4
Displacement					
Cubic centimeters	232	232	323	498	747
Cubic inches	14.2	14.2	19.7	30.4	45.6
Alternator output					
@ W.O.T.	6A	13A	10A	18A	15A
Induction system	OHC	OHC	OHC	OHC	OHC[1]
Lubrication	Wet sump	Wet sump	Wet sump	Wet sump	Wet sump
Ignition system	CDI	CDI	CDI	CDI Micro Computer	CDI Micro Computer[2]
Starting system	Manual/ or electric	Manual/ or electric	Manual/ or electric	Manual/ or electric	Manual/ or electric
Shaft length	15 in. or 20 in.	20 in. or 25 in.	15 in. or 20 in.	15 in. or 20 in.	15 in. or 20 in.
Gear ratio	13:38 (2.92)	13:38 (2.92)	13:27 (2.08)	13:27 (2.08)	13:27 (2.08)
Weight	42 kg (91 lb.)	45 kg (99 lb.)	45 kg (99 lb.)	62 kg (136 lb.)	82 kg (181 lb.)

1. Overhead camshaft
2. Capacitor discharge ignition

Table 11 ENGINE SPECIFICATIONS

	Model			
	F50	**T50**	**F80**	**F100**
Cylinders	4	4	4	4
Displacement				
Cubic centimeters	935	935	1596	1596
Cubic inches	57	57	97	97.4
Alternator output				
@ W.O.T.	10A	10A	20A	20A
Induction system	OHC	OHC[1]	DOHC	DOHC[2]
Lubrication	Wet sump	Wet sump	Wet sump	Wet sump
Ignition system	CDI Micro Computer	CDI Micro Computer	CDI Micro Computer	CDI Micro Computer[3]
Starting system	Electric	Electric	Electric	Electric
Shaft length	20 in.	20 in.	20 in. or 25 in.	20 in. or 25 in.
Gear ratio	13:24 (1.84)	12:28 (2.33)	13:30 (2.31)	13:30 (2.31)
Weight	106 kg (233 lb.)	110 kg (242 lb.)	162 kg (356 lb.)	162 kg (356 lb.)

1. Overhead camshaft
2. Dual overhead camshaft
3. Capacitor discharge ignition

Table 12 RECOMMENDED ENGINE SPEED

Idle speed	
F9.9	900-1000 rpm
T9.9	1100-1200 rpm
F15	900-1000 rpm
F25	875-975 rpm
F40-F50-FT50	700-800 rpm
F80-F100	850-950 rpm
Full-throttle speed	
F9.9-T9.9 and F15	4500-5500 rpm
F25-F100	5000-6000 rpm
Trolling range	
F9.9 and T9.9	800-900 rpm
Maximum horsepower output	
F9.9 and T9.9	5.9 kW (8 hp) @ 5000 rpm
F15	11 kW (15 hp) @ 5000 rpm
F25	18.4 kW (25 hp) @ 5500 rpm
F40	29.4 kW (40 hp) @ 5500 rpm
F50 and T50	36.8 kW (50 hp) @ 5500 rpm
F80	58.8 kW (80 hp) @ 5500 rpm
F100	73.6 kW (100 hp) @ 5500 rpm

Table 13 VALVE CLEARANCE (COLD)

Model F9.9	
Valve clearance	
Intake	0.15-0.20 mm (0.0059-0.0079 in.)
Exhaust	0.20-0.25 mm (0.0079-0.0098 in.)
Model F15	
Valve clearance	
Intake	0.15-0.25 mm (0.006-0.009 in.)
Exhaust	0.20-0.30 mm (0.008-0.012 in.)
Model F25	
Valve clearance	
Intake	0.15-0.25 mm (0.006-0.010 in.)
Exhaust	0.25-0.35 mm (0.010-0.014 in.)

(continued)

Table 13 VALVE CLEARANCE (COLD) (continued)

Model F40-F50	
Valve clearance	
Intake	0.15-0.25 mm (0.006-0.010 in.)
Exhaust	0.25-0.35 mm (0.010-0.014 in.)
Model F80-F100	
Valve clearance	
Intake	0.17-0.23 mm (0.007-0.009 in.)
Exhaust	0.31-0.37 mm (0.012-0.014 in.)

Chapter Six

Fuel System

Fuel system specifications are provided in **Table 1** located at the end of this chapter.

WARNING
Be careful when working with the fuel system. Never smoke around fuel of fuel vapor. Make sure that no flame or source of ignition is present in the work area. Flame or sparks can ignite fuel or vapor and cause a fire or explosion.

SERVICING THE FUEL SYSTEM

Always use gloves and eye protection when working on the fuel system. Take all necessary precautions against fire or explosion. Always disconnect the battery cables *before* servicing the outboard.

Pay close attention when removing and installing components, especially carburetors, to avoid installing them in the wrong location.

Catch fuel from disconnected hoses or fittings using a small container or clean shop towel. Use a clear container to be able to make a visual inspection of the fuel. Inspection of the drained fuel can indicate the cause of problems with the carburetor. If water or other contaminants are noted, clean and inspect all fuel system components, especially the fuel tank. Failure to thoroughly clean the system usually causes repeat problems.

Drain the fuel from the carburetor(s) using the float bowl drain plug (**Figure 1**). Refer to *Carburetor* in this chapter for diagrams that help locate the bowl drain screw. Position the carburetor over the container, then remove the drain screw.

Inspect all hoses for leakage or deterioration when servicing the fuel system. Damaged fuel hoses pose a safety hazard. Pieces of deteriorated or damaged hoses can break free and block fuel passages within the system. Refer to *Fuel Hoses* in this chapter.

On engines with multiple carburetors (**Figure 2**), repair *one* carburetor at a time. Some models have fuel and air jet sizes calibrated to the cylinder to which they supply fuel. Refer to *Carburetor* in this chapter for additional instructions.

Perform adjustments to all fuel system components during installation. Refer to Chapter Five for all adjustment procedures.

To avoid fuel or air leaks, replace all removed gaskets, seals or O-rings when a fuel system component is removed from the engine.

To ensure a safe and reliable repair, use only factory recommended replacement parts. Some commonly available seals or O-rings are not suitable for contact with fuel.

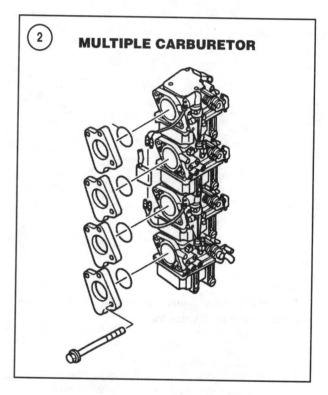

Carburetor Cleaning

The most important step in carburetor service is cleaning. Use only solvents suitable for carburetors. Some solvents can damage fuel system components. Aerosol carburetor cleaners are available at most automotive parts stores. They are effective in removing stubborn deposits. Do not use solvents that are not suitable for aluminum.

Remove all plastic or rubber components from the fuel pump, carburetor or filter assembly before cleaning with solvent. Gently scrape away gasket material using a gasket scraper. Use a stiff brush and solvent to remove deposits from the carburetor bowl. Never use a wire brush or delicate sealing surfaces can be damaged. Blow out all passages and orifices with compressed air (**Figure 3**). Use a piece of straw from a broom to clean out small passages. Never use stiff wire as the wire may enlarge the size of the passage and alter the carburetor calibration. Allow components to soak in the solvent for several hours if deposits are difficult to remove.

Be very careful and patient when removing fuel jets, and other threaded or pressed-in components. Clean the passage without removing the jet if it cannot be removed without being damaged. Carburetor fuel jets are easily damaged if a screwdriver slips in the slot.

A particle left in the carburetor can cause major problems with engine operation. Never compromise the cleaning process. Continue to clean until all deposits and debris are removed.

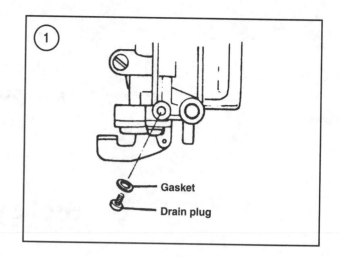

MULTIPLE CARBURETOR

Carburetor Inspection

Place all components on a clean surface as they are removed from the carburetor and cleaned. Arrange the components to resemble the provided illustrations. This saves

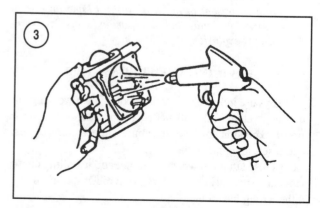

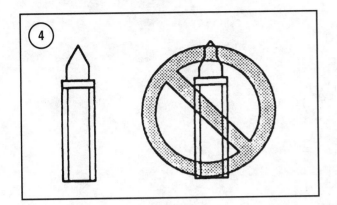

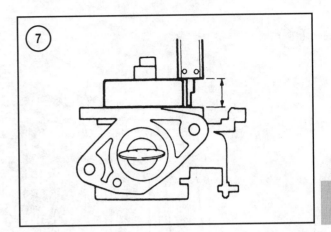

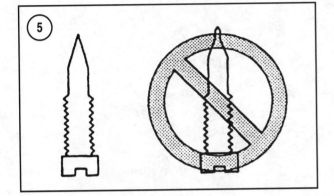

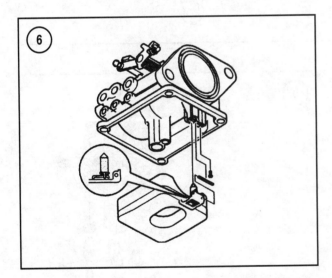

time and helps ensure the parts are installed in the correct locations.

Inspect the inlet needle for wear or deterioration (**Figure 4**). Replace the inlet needle unless its tip is perfectly cone shaped (**Figure 4**).

Inspect the inlet needle seat for grooved or damaged surfaces. All 9.9-50 hp models utilize a pressed-in needle seat. On these models, replace the carburetor if the seat is damaged. Carburetor flooding can occur if a worn or faulty inlet needle or seat is used.

Inspect the tip of the pilot screw, on models so equipped, for wear or damage (**Figure 5**). Damage to the tip usually occurs from improper seating of the screw during adjustment. In many instances, the seat for the tip is also damaged. Damage to the screw or seat usually causes rough idle or improper off-idle engine operation.

Inspect the float (**Figure 6**, typical) for wear or damage. Some floats are made of a translucent material that can show if fuel is inside the float.

Push a thumbnail gently against the material on non-translucent floats. The float is leaking or fuel saturated if fuel appears at the thumbnail contact area. Replace the float if it is visibly damaged, leaking or fuel saturated. Check the float for free movement on the float pin. Replace the float valve if it does not move freely.

Adjust the float level (**Figure 7**) before assembling the carburetor. Use an accurate ruler or a caliper with depth reading capability. Set the float *exactly* as specified to help ensure proper carburetor operation. Float level specifications and measuring points vary by models. Specific instructions are provided in the carburetor disassembly and assembly sections. Float level specifications are in **Table 1**.

Move the throttle lever (**Figure 8**) from the closed throttle to wide-open positions. Remove the throttle plate and repeat this step if binding or rough operation is noted. If the binding continues, the throttle shaft is bent. If free movement is noted with the plate removed, the throttle plate is misaligned or damaged. Replace the components necessary to provide free throttle movement. Apply a suitable threadlocking compound and stake all throttle plate retaining screws during assembly.

Fuel jets (**Figure 9**) meter the fuel flow through various passages in the carburetor. They, along with other components, allow the carburetor to deliver the precise amount

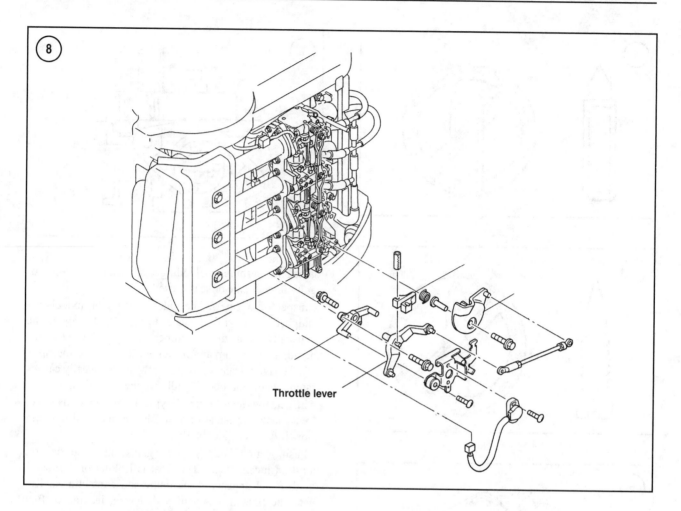

⑧

Throttle lever

of fuel needed for the engine. Fuel jet sizes vary by model and carburetor location on the engine. Fuel jets normally have a jet number stamped on the side or opening end. Make a drawing or note indicating the fuel jet number and location in the carburetor prior to removal. Make sure fuel jets and other carburetor components are reinstalled in the correct locations.

Purchase replacement fuel jets at a Yamaha dealership or carburetor specialty shop. For proper engine operation, replacement fuel jets must have the same size and shape of opening as the original fuel jets. Improper engine operation, increased exhaust emissions or potentially serious power head damage can result from using incorrect fuel jets.

Using the engine at a higher elevation (5000 ft. [1524 m] and greater) may require alternate fuel jets to achieve optimal engine operation. Contact a Yamaha dealership in the area for information on fuel jet changes.

Never install a damaged jet in the carburetor. The fuel or airflow characteristics may be altered. Altering the fuel and airflow can cause engine malfunction or potentially serious power head damage.

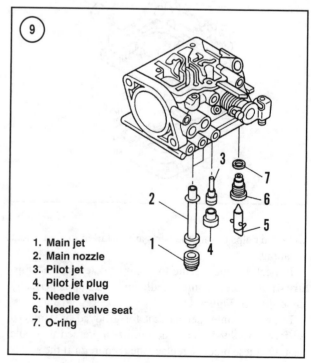

⑨

1. Main jet
2. Main nozzle
3. Pilot jet
4. Pilot jet plug
5. Needle valve
6. Needle valve seat
7. O-ring

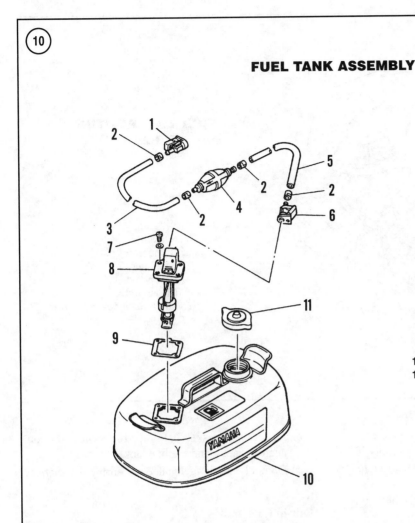

⑩

FUEL TANK ASSEMBLY

1. Fuel connector (engine end)
2. Clamp
3. Fuel hose
4. Primer bulb
5. Fuel hose
6. Connector
7. Screw
8. Fuel level gauge
9. Gasket
10. Tank
11. Cap

6

FUEL TANK

Two types of fuel tanks are used with Yamaha four-stroke outboards. They are portable fuel tanks (**Figure 10**) and built-in fuel tanks.

Most models use the portable fuel tank that came with the engine. Purchase any required parts for these fuel tanks from a local Yamaha dealership.

Several different companies manufacture portable fuel tanks. The engine may be equipped with any one of them. Types of components used, cleaning and repair instructions are similar for all brands of fuel tanks. Reputable marine repair shop or marine dealership carry parts needed for other brands of fuel tanks.

Proper long-term storage and fuel system inspection is much more important with built in fuel tanks. Long-term storage and fuel system inspection are covered in Chapter Four.

Portable Fuel Tank

Portable fuel tanks may require periodic cleaning and inspection. Inspect the remainder of the fuel system for contamination if water is found in the tank. The tank used may differ in appearance and component usage from the illustration (**Figure 10**).

Clean and inspect the tank as follows:

1. Remove the fuel tank cap (11, **Figure 10**) from the fuel tank. Carefully pour the fuel from the tank into a suitable container.

2. Remove the screws (7, **Figure 10**) that retain the gauge (8) to the fuel tank. Carefully lift the fuel gauge assembly (8, **Figure 10**) from the tank. Never force the assembly or damage may occur. Rotate or tilt the assembly as required for removal. Remove and discard the gasket (9, **Figure 10**) from between the connector/adapter and fuel tank.

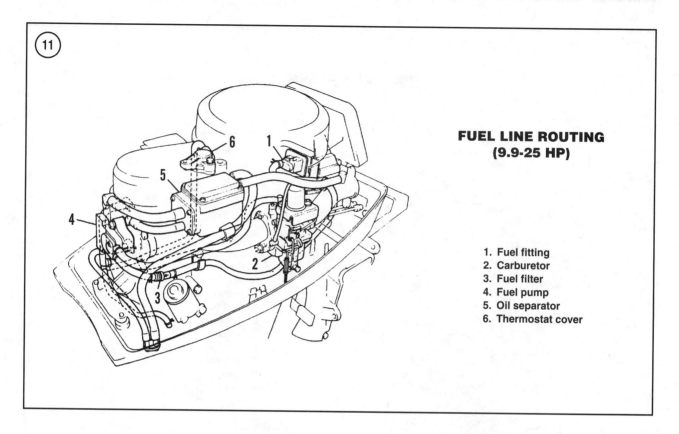

FUEL LINE ROUTING
(9.9-25 HP)

1. Fuel fitting
2. Carburetor
3. Fuel filter
4. Fuel pump
5. Oil separator
6. Thermostat cover

3. Check for free movement of the float arm on the fuel gauge assembly (8, **Figure 10**). Replace the assembly if binding cannot be corrected by bending the float arm into the correct position.

4. Replace the float if it is damaged or appears to be saturated with fuel.

5. Carefully pull the screen and pickup tube from the fuel gauge assembly (8, **Figure 10**). Clean the tube and screen using a suitable solvent. Dry them with compressed air. Inspect the screen for torn or damaged surfaces. Inspect the pickup tube for cracks or deterioration. Replace the screen and/or tube if defects are noted.

6. Remove the connectors (1 and 6, **Figure 10**) from the connector/adapter (8). Clean the fittings and all passages of the connector/adapter using a suitable solvent.

7. Add a small amount of solvent to the fuel tank. Block the gauge/pickup opening with a shop towel. Install the fuel tank cap (11, **Figure 10**). Shake the tank to distribute the solvent throughout the tank. Empty the solvent, then dry the tank dry with compressed air.

8. Inspect the internal and external tank surfaces. Repeat Step 7 if debris remains in the tank. Inspect the tank for cracked, damaged or softened surfaces. Replace the tank if any defects are noted or if there may be leakage.

9. Assembly is the reverse of disassembly.
    a. Clean the adapter-to-fuel tank gasket surface.

    b. Install a new gasket (9, **Figure 10**) between the connector/adapter and the fuel tank.
    c. Do not bend the fuel gauge rod during installation.

Built-in Fuel Tank

The only components that can be serviced without major disassembly of the boat are the fuel pickup, fuel fill, fuel level sender and antisiphon device. These components are available from most marine dealerships and marine supply stores. Removal and inspection instructions vary by the model and brand of fuel tank. Contact the tank manufacturer or boat manufacturer for specific instructions. Always replace any gasket or seal when removed or suspected of leaking. Correct suspected fuel leakages before filling the tank or operating the engine.

Fuel Hoses

Refer to **Figures 11-14** for fuel hose routing and connections.

Use only Yamaha replacement hoses or hoses that meet U.S. Coast Guard requirements for marine applications. Never install a fuel hose that is smaller in diameter than the original hose.

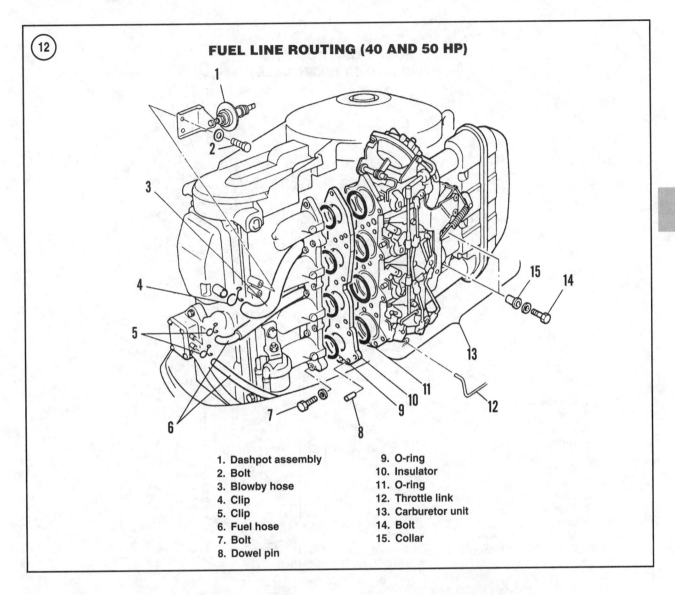

⑫   **FUEL LINE ROUTING (40 AND 50 HP)**

1. Dashpot assembly	9. O-ring
2. Bolt	10. Insulator
3. Blowby hose	11. O-ring
4. Clip	12. Throttle link
5. Clip	13. Carburetor unit
6. Fuel hose	14. Bolt
7. Bolt	15. Collar
8. Dowel pin	

Inspect all fuel hoses and replace hoses that are sticky, spongy, are hard and brittle, or cracked. Replace hoses that are split on the ends. Do not cut off the split end and reattach the hose. The hose usually splits again and leads to a potentially dangerous fuel leak. To avoid hose failure or interference with other components, never cut the replacement hose shorter or longer than the original. If one fuel hose on the engine requires replacement, others probably are in similar condition. Replace all fuel hoses on the engine to ensure a reliable repair.

Fuel Hose Connectors

Connectors used on fuel hoses are the quick connector type (**Figure 15**), spring type hose clamp (3, **Figure 14**) and plastic locking clamp (1, **Figure 14**). Never replace

hose clamps with a different type or size of hose clamp. Improper clamp size or type can result in fuel leakage or interference with other engine components. To prevent leakage and ensure a reliable repair, use Yamaha clamps on all hose connections.

Replace both ends of quick connector clamps if either side is leaking.

When replacing the quick connector on the fuel tank hose end, position the connector over a container suitable for holding fuel. Remove and discard the hose clamp. Pull the fuel hose from the connector. Slide the hose onto the new connector. Install a new hose clamp onto the hose and tighten it securely.

When replacing the connector at the engine end (4, **Figure 15**), remove the screw (3) or spring clip that retains the quick connector (4) to the lower engine cover. Pull the

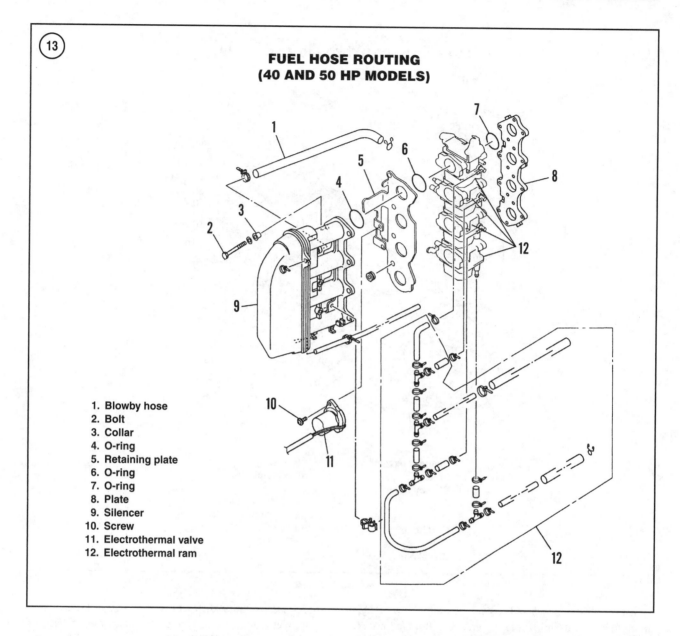

**FUEL HOSE ROUTING
(40 AND 50 HP MODELS)**

1. Blowby hose
2. Bolt
3. Collar
4. O-ring
5. Retaining plate
6. O-ring
7. O-ring
8. Plate
9. Silencer
10. Screw
11. Electrothermal valve
12. Electrothermal ram

connector and its grommet from the lower engine cover. Position the hose and connector over a container suitable for holding fuel. Remove the spring clamp (2), then carefully pull the connector (4) from the fuel hose. Drain the fuel from the hose. Carefully slide the hose over the fitting of the new connector. Install a new clamp over the hose and fitting. Securely tighten the clamp. Place the quick connector and grommet into position on the lower engine cover. Install the screw or clip onto the connector. Securely tighten the retaining screw.

Remove the spring clamps (**Figure 16**) by squeezing the ends together using pliers while carefully moving the clamp away from the fitting. Replace the clamp if it is corroded, bent, deformed, or if it has lost spring tension.

The plastic clamp (1, **Figure 14**) must be cut before it can be removed. Some plastic locking clamps are not suitable for the application and may fail. Use only the Yamaha part for hose clamps. After placing the clamp into position, pull the end through the clamp until the hose is securely fastened and does not rotate on the fitting. Avoid pulling the clamp too tight or the clamp may be damaged, and loosen or fail. Cut off excess length of the clamp.

Fuel Filter

An inline fuel filter (**Figure 17**) is used on 9.9-25 hp and 80-100 hp models. The 40-50 hp models use a ser-

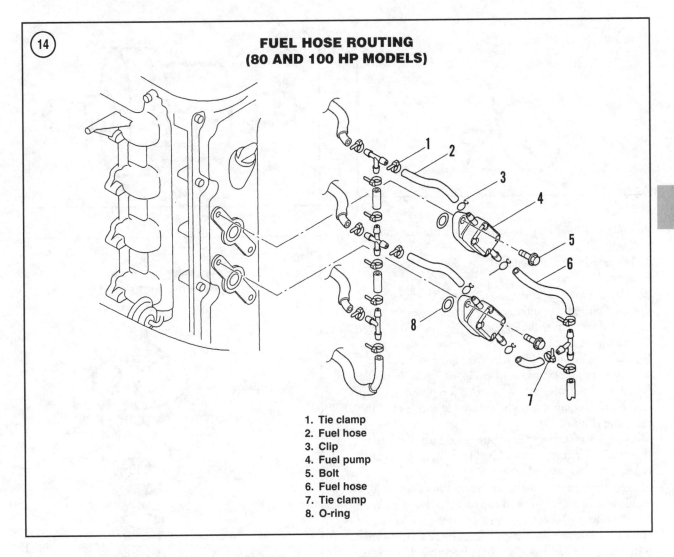

**FUEL HOSE ROUTING
(80 AND 100 HP MODELS)**

14

1. Tie clamp
2. Fuel hose
3. Clip
4. Fuel pump
5. Bolt
6. Fuel hose
7. Tie clamp
8. O-ring

6

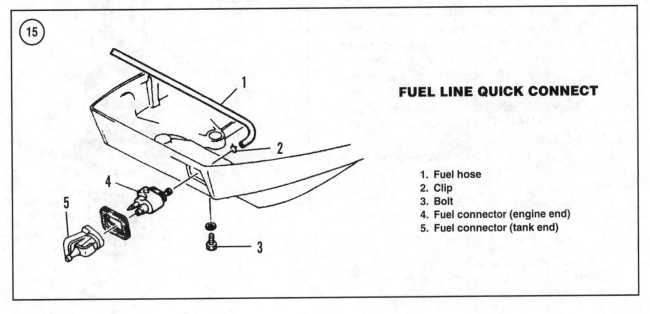

15

FUEL LINE QUICK CONNECT

1. Fuel hose
2. Clip
3. Bolt
4. Fuel connector (engine end)
5. Fuel connector (tank end)

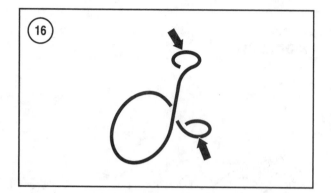

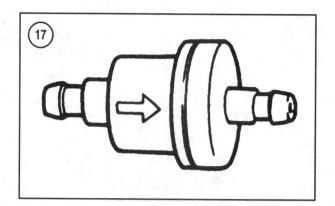

viceable fuel filter (**Figure 18**). Replace the fuel filter as follows:

1. Disconnect both cables from the battery, if so equipped.

2. Note the location and remove plastic locking clamps that may prevent the filter and connected hoses from being pulled away from the engine.

3. Place a suitable container or shop towel under the fuel filter to capture any spilled fuel.

4. Move spring clamps, if so equipped, away from the fuel hose fittings. Carefully remove the plastic locking clamps, if so equipped, from the hoses at each end of the fuel filter (**Figure 19**).

5. Use a blunt screwdriver to push each hose away from filter body. Drain any residual fuel from the disconnected hoses. Clean up any spilled fuel at once.

6. Note the arrow on the replacement filter (**Figure 17**) for all models except 40 and 50 hp models. Note the direction the filter (2, **Figure 20**) and the O-ring (3, **Figure 20**) are placed into the filter cup (4, **Figure 20**). Then carefully slide each fuel hose fully over its fitting. Make sure the arrow on the filter body faces toward the fuel pump(s).

7. Carefully slide the spring clamps, if so equipped, over their respective fittings on the filter. Install new plastic locking type clamps, if so equipped, over each hose and filter fitting. Make sure each clamp is securely tightened.

8. Place the filter into its original location in the lower engine cover. Install new plastic tie clamps to replace those removed in Step 2. Make sure the hoses and filter are routed away from moving components.

9. Observe the fuel filter and other fuel system components while pumping the primer bulb. Correct the cause of fuel leakage if detected.

10. Clean the terminals, then connect the cables to the battery, if so equipped.

WARNING
Fuel leakage can lead to a fire and explosion. Check for fuel leakage after any repair to the fuel system.

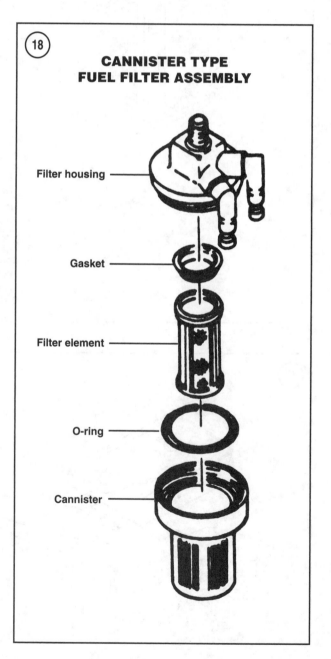

CANNISTER TYPE FUEL FILTER ASSEMBLY

Filter housing

Gasket

Filter element

O-ring

Cannister

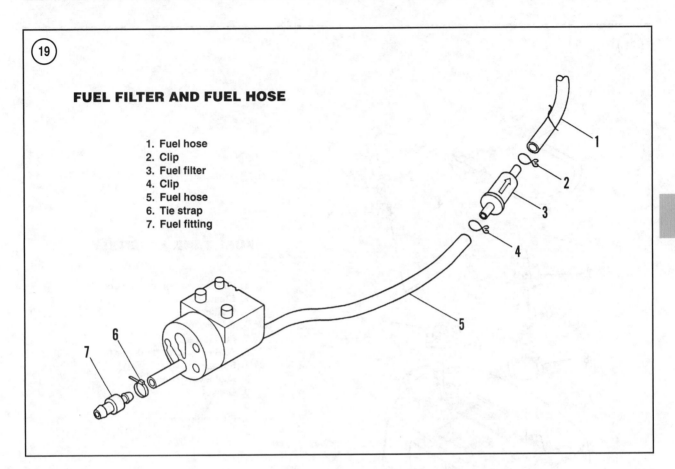

(19)

FUEL FILTER AND FUEL HOSE

1. Fuel hose
2. Clip
3. Fuel filter
4. Clip
5. Fuel hose
6. Tie strap
7. Fuel fitting

6

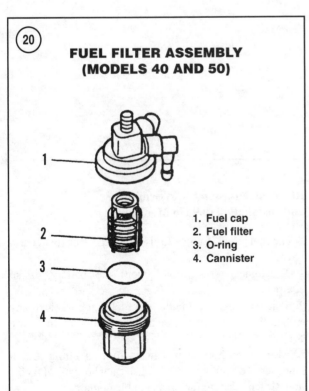

(20)

FUEL FILTER ASSEMBLY (MODELS 40 AND 50)

1. Fuel cap
2. Fuel filter
3. O-ring
4. Cannister

Primer Bulb Removal and Installation

The primer bulb (**Figure 21**) is located in the fuel hose that connects the fuel tank to the engine.

1. Disconnect the quick connector (1, **Figure 21**) from the engine. Drain any residual fuel into a suitable container. Remove and discard the fuel hose clamps (2, **Figure 21**).

2. Note the arrow on the primer bulb (4, **Figure 21**) and remove the primer bulb from the fuel hoses. Drain any fuel remaining from the primer bulb into a suitable container.

3. Squeeze the primer bulb until it is fully collapsed. Replace the bulb if it does not freely expand when released. Replace the bulb if it is weathered, has surface cracks or is hard to squeeze.

4. Inspect the fuel hoses (3 and 5, **Figure 21**) for a worn, damaged or weathered appearance, or for the presence of leakage. Replace both fuel hoses if defects are noted.

5. Installation is the reverse of removal. Note the direction of the arrow (**Figure 22**) while installing the new primer bulb. The arrow on the bulb must point toward the direction of fuel flow. The arrows must align with the di-

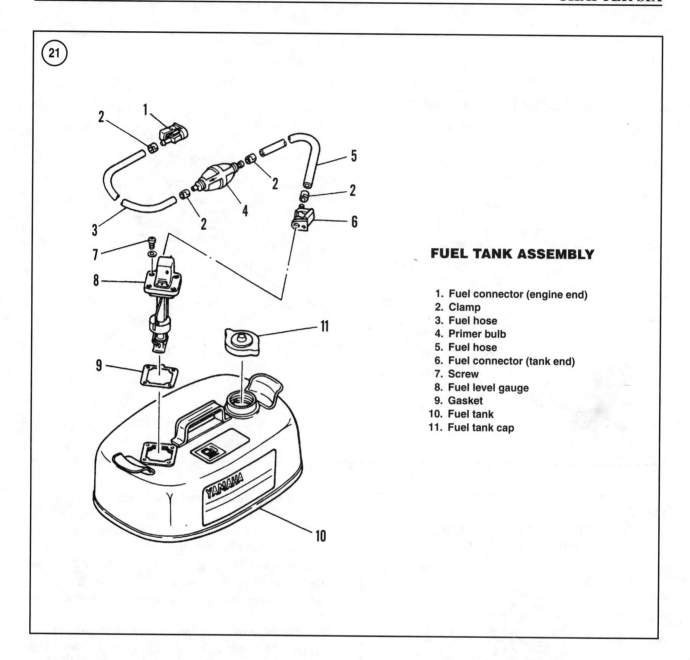

㉑

FUEL TANK ASSEMBLY

1. Fuel connector (engine end)
2. Clamp
3. Fuel hose
4. Primer bulb
5. Fuel hose
6. Fuel connector (tank end)
7. Screw
8. Fuel level gauge
9. Gasket
10. Fuel tank
11. Fuel tank cap

rection of fuel flow toward the engine. Carefully slide the fuel hoses onto the fittings of the primer bulb.

6. Install new fuel clamps at the primer bulb. Make sure that the fuel clamps fit tightly. Squeeze the primer bulb to check for fuel leakage.

Fuel Pump

The following sections describe fuel pump removal, disassembly, inspection, assembly and installation. If only removing the pump, follow the steps required to remove the pump, then reverse the removal steps for installation.

Removal, Disassembly, Assembly and Installation (9.9 Hp Models)

The fuel pump (**Figure 23**) is mounted to the rocker arm cover.

1. Disconnect both cables from the battery, if so equipped.
2. Place a shop towel under the fuel pump to catch any spilled fuel. Mark each hose and the fuel pump to ensure correct installation.
3. Move each hose clamp away from its fitting. Use a blunt screwdriver to carefully push each hose off of its fitting. Catch residual fuel in a suitable container.

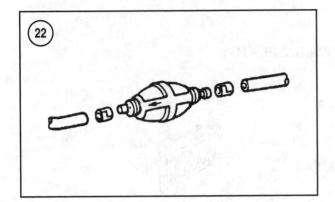

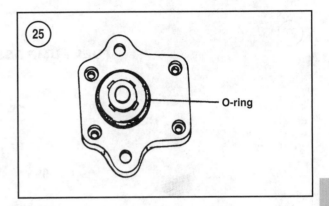

O-ring

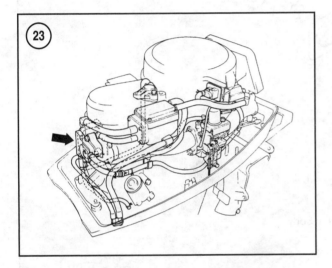

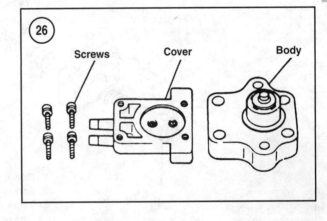

Screws   Cover   Body

6

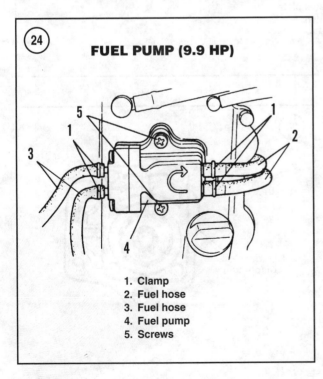

FUEL PUMP (9.9 HP)

1. Clamp
2. Fuel hose
3. Fuel hose
4. Fuel pump
5. Screws

4. Remove the screws (5, **Figure 24**) from the fuel pump. Pull the fuel pump away from the cylinder block and drain all fuel from the pump. Place the pump on a clean work surface. Remove the O-ring (**Figure 25**) from the mounting cover or cylinder block. Clean the mounting surfaces. Stuff a small shop towel into the opening to prevent contamination of the crankcase.

5. Remove the four screws (**Figure 26**) that retain the cover to the fuel pump body. Lift the cover (**Figure 26**) from the fuel pump body.

6. Push in on the plunger (1, **Figure 27**) and spring (2), and push in on the diaphragm and spring (6 and 5, **Figure 27**), while rotating the diaphragm (**Figure 28**) 90°. Carefully pull the diaphragm, plunger and spring from the mounting cover.

7. Remove the screws (7, **Figure 27**), then lift the check valve plate (8) and check valve (9) from the pump cover (10).

8. Inspect the diaphragm for deterioration or damage. Replace the diaphragm if any defects are noted.

9. Inspect the check valve for wear, cracks or damage. Replace the check valve if defects are noted.

10. Clean the fuel pump body, springs, plunger and both covers using a suitable solvent. Dry all surfaces using

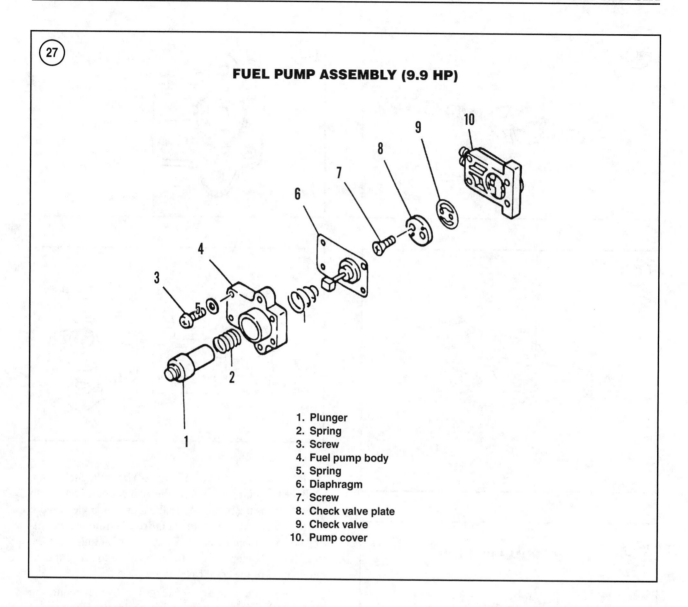

FUEL PUMP ASSEMBLY (9.9 HP)

1. Plunger
2. Spring
3. Screw
4. Fuel pump body
5. Spring
6. Diaphragm
7. Screw
8. Check valve plate
9. Check valve
10. Pump cover

compressed air. Direct the air through both fuel hose fittings to clear debris.

11. Inspect the fuel pump body and both covers for corrosion or damage. Replace defective components. Inspect both springs for corrosion or damage. Replace them if any defects are noted. Inspect the plunger for wear or corrosion. Replace the plunger if defects are noted.

12. Reverse the disassembly and removal procedure to assemble and install the fuel pump.

**Removal, Disassembly, Assembly
and Installation (15-100 Hp Models)**

The fuel pump(s) (**Figure 29**) is mounted to the rocker arm cover. Two pumps are used on 80 and 100 hp models (**Figure 30**).

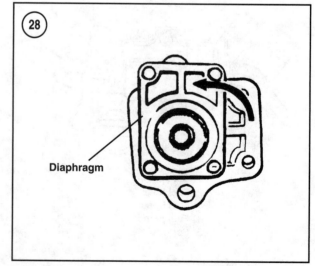

Diaphragm

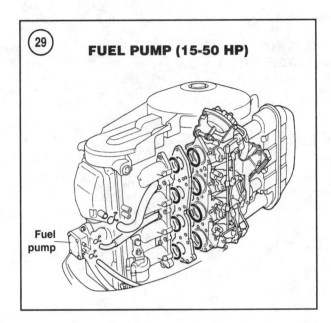

(29) **FUEL PUMP (15-50 HP)**

Fuel pump

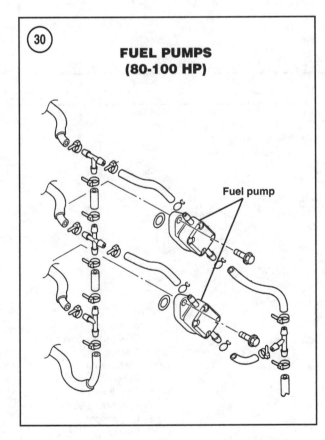

(30) **FUEL PUMPS (80-100 HP)**

Fuel pump

1. Disconnect both cables from the battery, if so equipped.

2. Place a shop towel under the fuel pump to catch spilled fuel. Mark each hose and the fuel pump to ensure correct installation.

3. Remove each hose clamp from its fitting. Use a blunt screwdriver to carefully push each hose off of its fitting. Catch residual fuel in a suitable container.

4. Remove both bolts (5, **Figure 31**) from the fuel pump (4). Pull the fuel pump away from the cylinder block and drain all fuel from the pump. Place the pump on a clean work surface. Remove the O-ring (7, **Figure 31**) from the pump or cylinder block. Replace the O-ring during installation. Clean the mounting surfaces. Stuff a small shop towel into the opening to prevent contamination of the crankcase.

5. Remove the four screws (1, **Figure 32**) that retain the outer cover (2) and mounting cover (10) to the fuel pump body (7). Remove the four nuts (14, **Figure 32**) from the recess in the mounting cover.

6. Lift the mounting cover (10, **Figure 32**) from the fuel pump body (7). Pull the O-ring from the mounting cover (**Figure 31**). Replace the O-ring during assembly. Lift the gasket (3, **Figure 32**) diaphragm (4) from the fuel pump body (7). Lift the fuel pump body (7, **Figure 32**) from the mounting cover (10). Remove the screw (5, **Figure 32**) and check valve (6) from both sides of the fuel pump body (7).

7. Push in on the plunger (13, **Figure 32**), while rotating the diaphragm (8) until the pin (12) aligns with the notch in the mounting cover (10). Pull the pin (12, **Figure 32**) from the diaphragm arm. Carefully pull the diaphragm, plunger and spring from the mounting cover.

8. Inspect both diaphragms for ripped, creased or stretched surfaces. Replace the diaphragms if any defects are noted.

9. Inspect the check valves for wear, cracks or damage. Replace the check valves if defects are noted.

10. Clean the fuel pump body, springs, plunger and both covers using a suitable solvent. Dry all surfaces using compressed air. Direct air through both fuel hose fittings to clear debris.

11. Inspect the fuel pump body and both covers for corrosion or damage. Replace defective components. Inspect both springs for corrosion or damage. Replace them if any defects are noted. Inspect the plunger for wear or corrosion. Replace the plunger if defects are noted.

12. Reverse the disassembly and removal procedure to assemble and install the fuel pump.

Silencer Cover, Carburetor(s) and Intake Manifold Removal and Installation

Have shop towels and a suitable container on hand to catch residual fuel as the fuel hose is removed.

If only the silencer cover and/or carburetors require removal, perform only the steps necessary to remove them

6

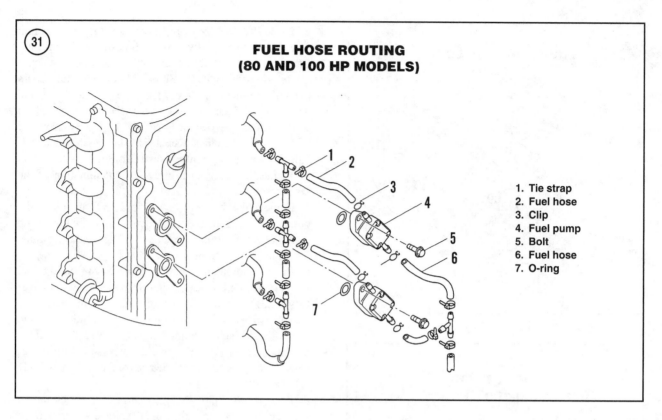

31

FUEL HOSE ROUTING
(80 AND 100 HP MODELS)

1. Tie strap
2. Fuel hose
3. Clip
4. Fuel pump
5. Bolt
6. Fuel hose
7. O-ring

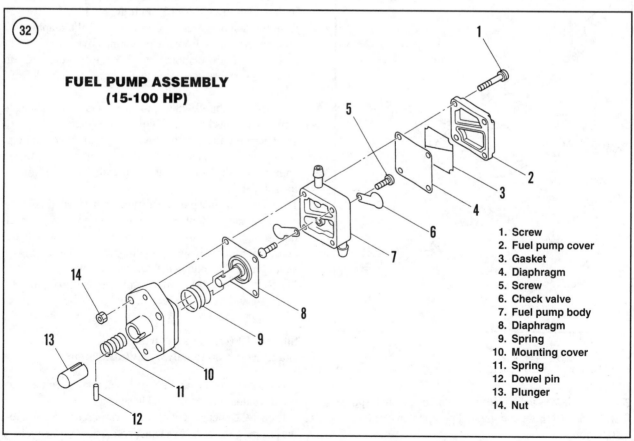

32

FUEL PUMP ASSEMBLY
(15-100 HP)

1. Screw
2. Fuel pump cover
3. Gasket
4. Diaphragm
5. Screw
6. Check valve
7. Fuel pump body
8. Diaphragm
9. Spring
10. Mounting cover
11. Spring
12. Dowel pin
13. Plunger
14. Nut

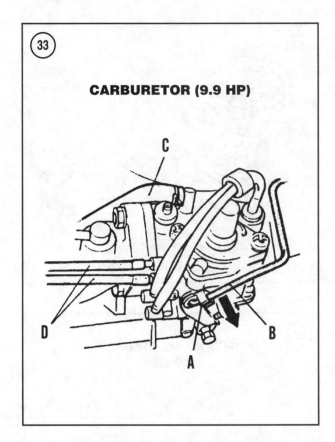

CARBURETOR (9.9 HP)

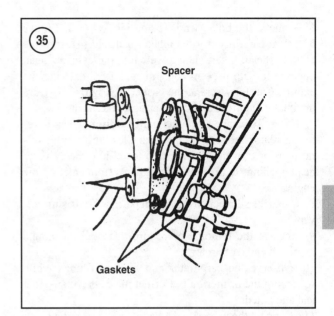

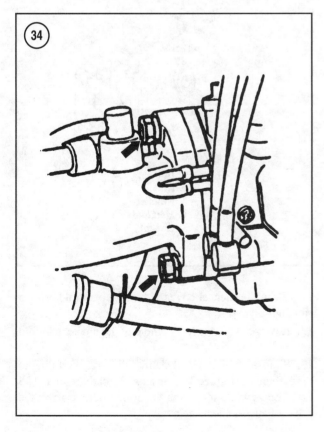

from the engine. Reverse the removal steps to reinstall the components.

9.9 hp models (1985-1991)

1. Disconnect both cables from the battery, if so equipped.

2. Slide the linkage retainer (A, **Figure 33**) forward and slide the throttle linkage (B) from the carburetor throttle lever.

3. Place a small container or shop towel under the fuel hose fitting and carefully pull the fuel hose (C, **Figure 33**) from the carburetor. Remove the two BVSV (bimetal vacuum switching valve) control hoses (D, **Figure 33**) from the carburetor.

> *CAUTION*
> *After removing the BVSV control hoses, cover them so no dust or dirt can enter the hoses.*

> *NOTE*
> *The bimetal vacuum switching valve (BVSV) senses engine temperature and activates an enrichment circuit during cold starting.*

4. Drain the fuel remaining in the hose into a suitable container. Clean up any spilled fuel at once.

5. Remove the two nuts (**Figure 34**) and two washers. Next remove the gaskets (**Figure 35**) and the spacer from the carburetor. Remove the screws (**Figure 36**), funnel and gasket.

6. Remove the bolts, washers and bracket (1-3, **Figure 37**), then carefully pry the intake manifold (4) from the cylinder head. Insert shop towels into the cylinder head opening to help prevent contaminants from entering the engine. Carefully scrape the gasket (5, **Figure 37**) from the intake manifold and cylinder head mating surfaces.

7. Carefully scrape all gasket material from the carburetor, insulator and intake manifold. Clean the mating surfaces using solvent. Stuff a shop towel into the cylinder head openings to prevent contaminants from entering the engine.

8. Clean the silencer cover and intake manifold using solvent.

9. Reverse the removal procedure to install the intake manifold and carburetor.

10. Observe the carburetor and all fuel fittings while squeezing the primer bulb. Correct the cause of any fuel leakage noted.

11. Connect the cables to the battery, if so equipped.

12. Perform all carburetor adjustments as described in Chapter Five.

9.9 hp models (1992-1999)

1. Disconnect both cables from the battery, if so equipped.

2. Carefully pry the throttle linkage from to the throttle lever. Do not damage the plastic connector.

3. Disconnect the electrothermal valve wires on the topside of the carburetor from the engine wire harness.

4. Place a small container or shop towels under the fuel hose fitting (C, **Figure 33**) and carefully pull the fuel hose from the carburetor. Drain the fuel remaining in the hose into a suitable container. Clean up any spilled fuel at once.

5. Remove the screws (7, **Figure 38**) and pull the funnel (9) and gasket (10) from the carburetor (5). Pull the screen (8, **Figure 38**) from the funnel (9).

6. Remove the nuts and washers (3, **Figure 38**) and pull the carburetor from the intake manifold.

7. Remove the gaskets and insulator (4, **Figure 38**) from the carburetor.

8. Remove the bolt (1, **Figure 37**), then pull the bracket (3)from the intake manifold (4). Remove the nuts and washers (2, **Figure 37**), and remove the intake manifold from the cylinder head.

9. Insert shop towels into the cylinder head openings to help prevent contaminants from entering the engine. Carefully scrape the gasket (5, **Figure 37**) from the intake manifold and cylinder head mating surfaces.

10. Carefully scrape all gasket material from the carburetor, insulator and intake manifold. Clean the mating surfaces using a suitable solvent.

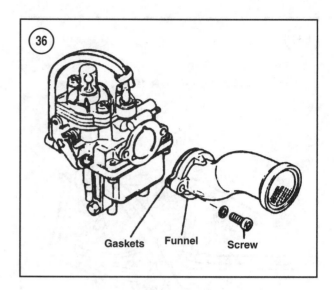

Gaskets   Funnel   Screw

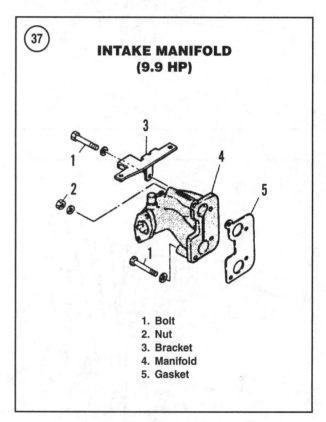

INTAKE MANIFOLD (9.9 HP)

1. Bolt
2. Nut
3. Bracket
4. Manifold
5. Gasket

11. Clean the silencer cover and intake manifold using a suitable solvent.

12. Reverse Steps 1-8 to assemble of the intake manifold and carburetor.

13. Slide the fuel hose and clamp fully onto the fitting to the carburetor (**Figure 33**). Observe the carburetor and all fuel fittings while squeezing the primer bulb. Correct the cause of any fuel leakage noted.

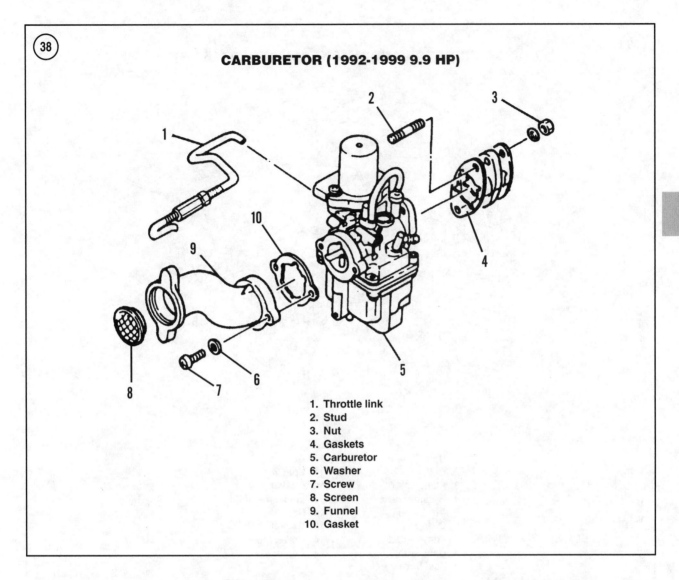

CARBURETOR (1992-1999 9.9 HP)

1. Throttle link
2. Stud
3. Nut
4. Gaskets
5. Carburetor
6. Washer
7. Screw
8. Screen
9. Funnel
10. Gasket

14. Connect the cables to the battery, if so equipped. Connect the electrothermal valve wires to the engine wire harness. Make sure the wires are routed away from moving components.

15. Perform all applicable carburetor adjustments as described in Chapter Five.

15 hp models

1. Disconnect both cables from the battery, if so equipped.

2. Remove the throttle rod (7, **Figure 39**) from the throttle cam. Remove the choke rod (17) from the carburetor.

3. Remove the two bolts (1, **Figure 39**) securing the carburetor to the intake manifold (13). Pull the plate (3, **Figure 39**), funnel (5) and O-ring (6) from the carburetor.

4. Place a small container or shop towels under the carburetor (9, **Figure 39**), then carefully pull the fuel hose from the carburetor. Drain the fuel remaining in the hose into a suitable container. Clean up any spilled fuel at once.

5. Remove the carburetor assembly (8, **Figure 39**) from the intake manifold (13). Remove the gasket (10) from the carburetor

6. Pull the spacer (11, **Figure 39**) and the gasket (12) from the intake manifold (13).

7. Remove the bolts and washers (14, **Figure 39**) securing the intake manifold (13) to the cylinder block (16).

8. Remove the intake manifold (13, **Figure 39**) and the intake manifold gasket (15).

9. Insert shop towels into the cylinder head openings to help prevent contaminants from entering the engine. Carefully scrape the gasket (15, **Figure 39**) from the intake manifold and cylinder head mating surfaces.

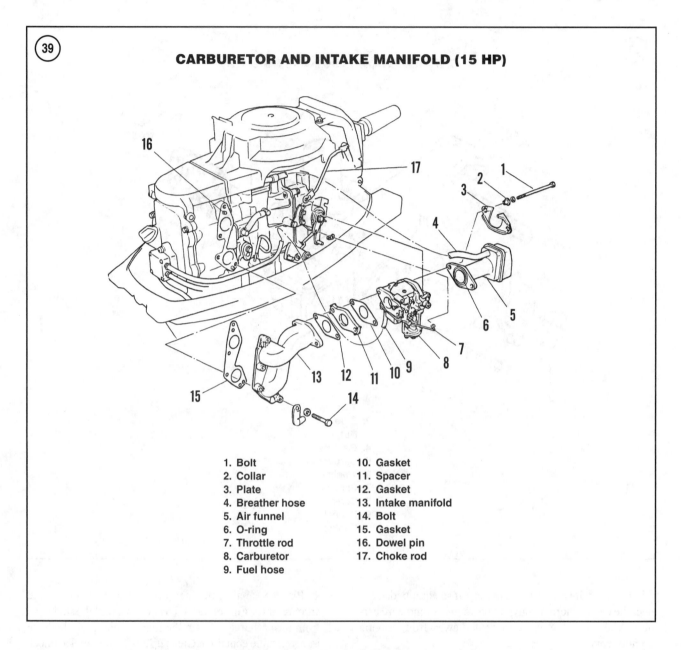

CARBURETOR AND INTAKE MANIFOLD (15 HP)

1. Bolt
2. Collar
3. Plate
4. Breather hose
5. Air funnel
6. O-ring
7. Throttle rod
8. Carburetor
9. Fuel hose
10. Gasket
11. Spacer
12. Gasket
13. Intake manifold
14. Bolt
15. Gasket
16. Dowel pin
17. Choke rod

10. Carefully scrape all gasket material from the carburetor, insulator and intake manifold mating surfaces. Clean the mating surfaces using a suitable solvent.

11. Clean the silencer cover and intake manifold using a suitable solvent.

12. Reverse Steps 1-11 to assemble the intake manifold and carburetor.

13. Slide the fuel hose and clamp fully onto the fitting on the carburetor (**Figure 39**). Observe the carburetor and all fuel fittings while squeezing the primer bulb. Correct the cause of fuel leakage.

14. Connect the cables to the battery, if so equipped. Connect the electrothermal valve wires to the engine wire harness. Make sure the wires are routed away from moving components.

15. Perform all applicable carburetor adjustments as described in Chapter Five.

25 hp models

1. Disconnect both cables from the battery, if so equipped.

2. Remove the breather hose (**Figure 40**) from the air funnel (1, **Figure 41**).

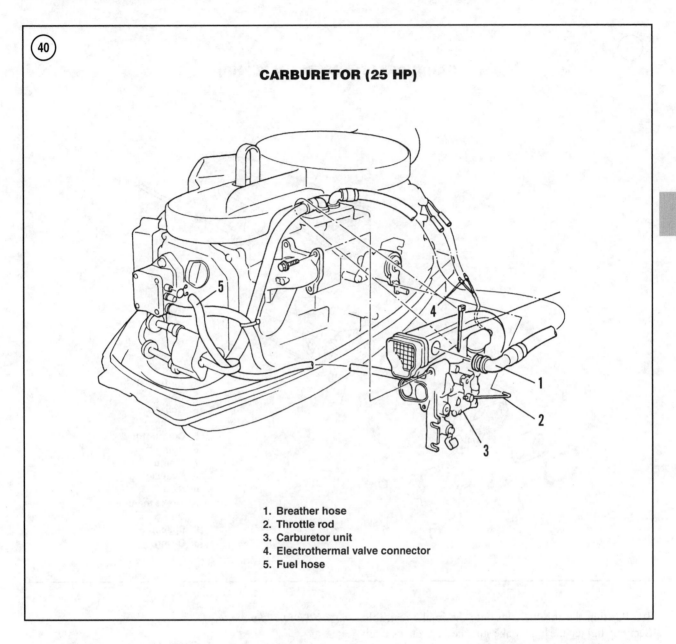

⑩

CARBURETOR (25 HP)

1. Breather hose
2. Throttle rod
3. Carburetor unit
4. Electrothermal valve connector
5. Fuel hose

6

3. Place a small container or shop towel under the fuel hose fitting (6, **Figure 40**). Cut the hose clamp, then carefully pull the fuel hose from the carburetor.

4. Drain the fuel remaining in the hose into a suitable container. Clean up any spilled fuel at once. Disconnect both yellow electrothermal valve wires (4, **Figure 40**) from the engine harness.

5. Remove both bolts and sleeves (2 and 3, **Figure 41**) from the air funnel (1). Then pull the throttle rod (2, **Figure 40**) away from the throttle cam. Pull the air funnel and O-ring (1 and 4, **Figure 41**) from the carburetor (5).

6. Pull the carburetor and spacer (5 and 12, **Figure 41**) from the intake manifold bracket (10). Remove the O-ring

(13, **Figure 41**) from the insulator. Remove the other O-ring (11, **Figure 41**) from the insulator or intake manifold bracket (10).

7. Remove the three bolts, then carefully pry the intake manifold (10, **Figure 41**) from the cylinder block. Insert shop towels into the block opening to help prevent contaminants from entering the engine. Pull the separator and O-ring (8 and 9, **Figure 41**) from the intake manifold bracket (10). Replace the O-rings during assembly.

8. Clean the silencer cover and intake manifold using a suitable solvent.

9. Reverse the removal procedure to install the intake manifold and carburetor.

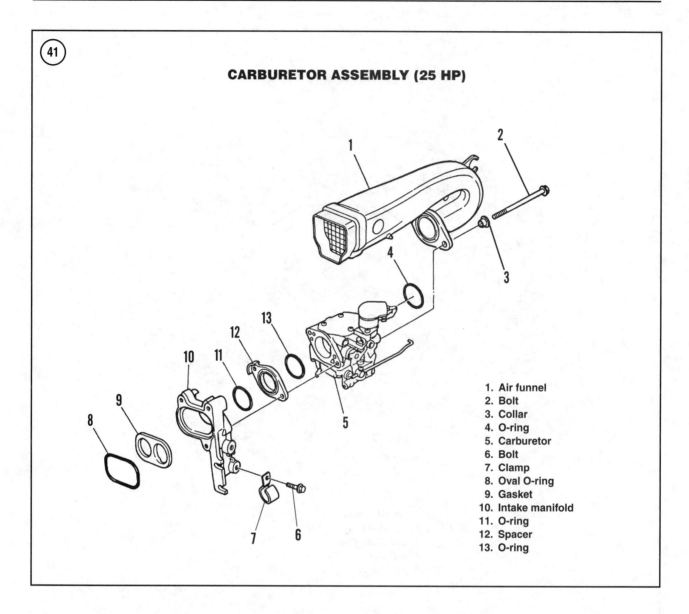

(41)

CARBURETOR ASSEMBLY (25 HP)

1. Air funnel
2. Bolt
3. Collar
4. O-ring
5. Carburetor
6. Bolt
7. Clamp
8. Oval O-ring
9. Gasket
10. Intake manifold
11. O-ring
12. Spacer
13. O-ring

10. Position the throttle cam onto the intake manifold. Securely tighten the bolt. Make sure the cam rotates freely after installation.

11. Slide the breather tube onto its fitting on the air funnel (1, **Figure 41**). Slide the fuel hose onto the carburetor fitting (5, **Figure 40**). Install a new hose clamp over the fitting. Make sure the hose clamp fits tightly.

12. Observe the carburetor and all fuel fittings while squeezing the primer bulb. Correct the cause of any fuel leakage. Connect both yellow wire terminals to the engine wire harness. Route the wires away from moving components.

13. Connect the cables to the battery, if so quipped.

14. Perform all applicable carburetor adjustments as described in Chapter Five.

40 and 50 hp models

CAUTION
Mark the location on each carburetor before removing them from the intake manifold. Improper fuel calibration, or problems with linkage and hose connections will occur if carburetors are installed in the wrong location.

1. Disconnect both cables from the battery, if so equipped.

2. Disconnect the electrothermal valve wires (4, **Figure 42**) from the engine wire harness.

3. Put a small container under the outlet fitting on the fuel pump. Remove the clamp, then carefully pull the fuel hose from the fitting. Drain all fuel from the disconnected hose.

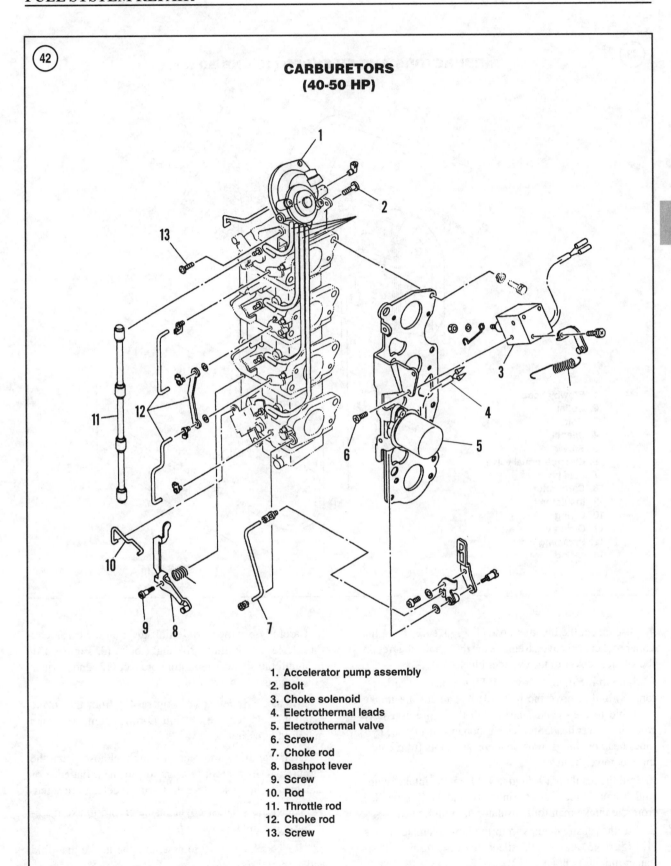

CARBUROTERS
(40-50 HP)

1. Accelerator pump assembly
2. Bolt
3. Choke solenoid
4. Electrothermal leads
5. Electrothermal valve
6. Screw
7. Choke rod
8. Dashpot lever
9. Screw
10. Rod
11. Throttle rod
12. Choke rod
13. Screw

6

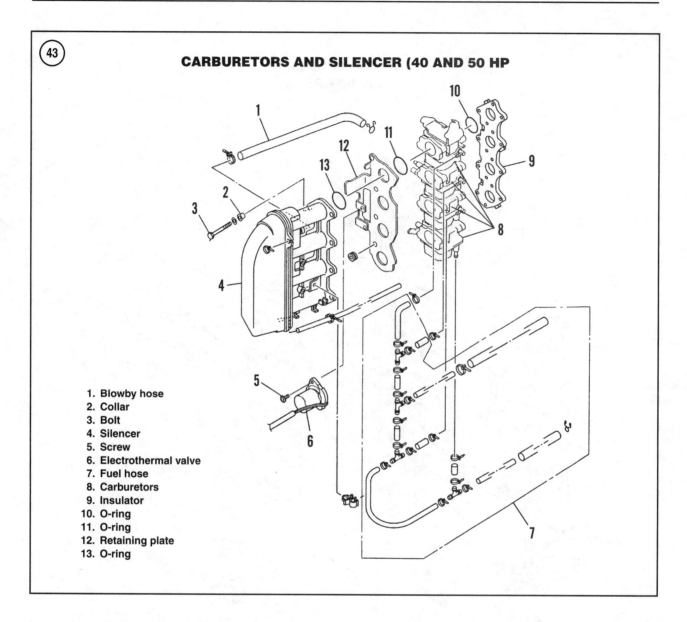

CARBURETORS AND SILENCER (40 AND 50 HP

1. Blowby hose
2. Collar
3. Bolt
4. Silencer
5. Screw
6. Electrothermal valve
7. Fuel hose
8. Carburetors
9. Insulator
10. O-ring
11. O-ring
12. Retaining plate
13. O-ring

4. Disconnect the breather hose (1, **Figure 43**) from the upper rocker arm cover. Remove the three bolts that retain the silencer cover to the cylinder block.

5. Support the silencer cover (4, **Figure 43**) and carburetors (8) and remove the bolts (3) that retain the intake manifold to the cylinder head. Pull the entire assembly from the power head. Stuff clean shop towels into the cylinder head openings to prevent contaminants from entering the power head.

6. Pull the insulator (9, **Figure 43**) from the intake manifold. Remove the eight O-rings (10 and 11, **Figure 43**) from the intake manifold, insulator or cylinder head.

7. Cut the plastic clamps from the large diameter hoses (1, **Figure 43**) and pull the silencer cover (4) from the silencer mounting bracket (12).

8. Carefully pry the throttle linkage from the carburetor throttle levers. Remove the eight bolts (3, **Figure 43**), then pull the silencer mounting bracket (12) and O-rings (13) from the carburetor (8).

9. Lift the carburetors (8, **Figure 43**) from the intake manifold, and remove all four O-rings from the intake manifold or carburetors.

10. Remove the clamps and pull the fuel hoses from the carburetors. Inspect all O-rings for pinched, flattened or damaged surfaces. Replace the O-ring if defects are noted.

11. Clean the silencer cover insulator and intake manifold using a suitable solvent.

12. Reverse Steps 1-10 to assemble the intake manifold and carburetor(s).

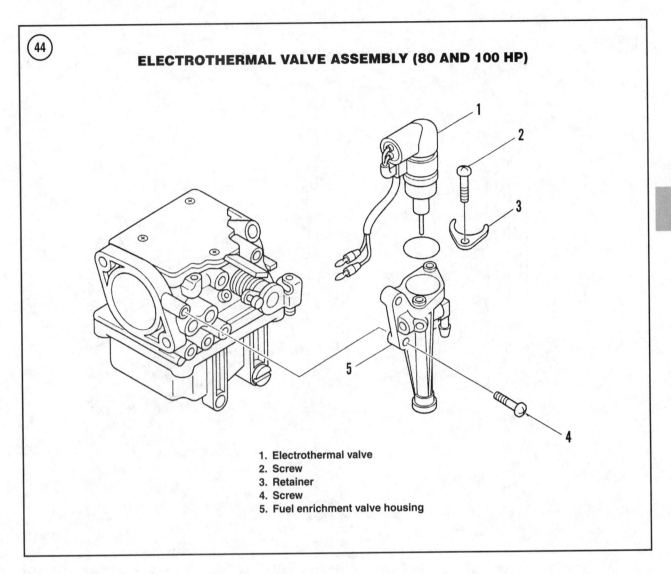

ELECTROTHERMAL VALVE ASSEMBLY (80 AND 100 HP)

1. Electrothermal valve
2. Screw
3. Retainer
4. Screw
5. Fuel enrichment valve housing

13. Reconnect the fuel hoses to the carburetors. Install new clamps as required. Carefully snap the throttle linkage onto the carburetor throttle levers. Apply a light coat of engine oil to the O-rings, then place them onto their locations on the intake manifold.

14. Observe the carburetor and all fuel fittings while squeezing the primer bulb. Correct the cause of any fuel leakage. Make sure all hoses are routed away from moving components.

15. Connect the cables to the battery, if so equipped. Perform all applicable carburetor adjustments as described in Chapter Five.

CAUTION
Mark the location on each carburetor before removing them from the intake manifold. Improper fuel calibration, or problems with the linkage or hose connections can oc-

cur when carburetors are installed in the wrong locations.

80 and 100 hp models

1. Disconnect both cables from the battery, if so equipped.

2. Disconnect both electrothermal valve wires (1, **Figure 44**) from the engine wire harness. Put a small container under the outlet fittings on each fuel pump (**Figure 45**). Remove the clamp (3, **Figure 45**) then carefully pull both outlet hoses (2) from their fittings. Drain all fuel from the disconnected hose.

3. Disconnect the throttle position sensor (**Figure 46**) from the engine wire harness. Remove the throttle control shaft (5, **Figure 46**) from the accelerator cam (3) and throttle control lever (11). Remove the bolts and pull the

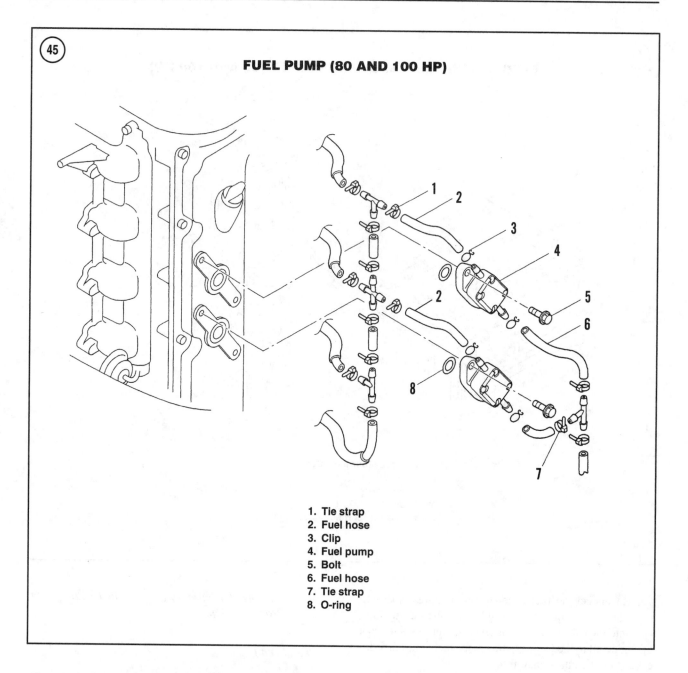

(45)

FUEL PUMP (80 AND 100 HP)

1. Tie strap
2. Fuel hose
3. Clip
4. Fuel pump
5. Bolt
6. Fuel hose
7. Tie strap
8. O-ring

throttle lever (11, **Figure 46**) and bracket (12) away from the carburetors. Remove the bolt (4, **Figure 46**) and pull the throttle cam (3) away from the intake manifold. Disconnect the accelerator pump linkage (3, **Figure 47**) from the bottom carburetor linkage.

4. Remove the three bolts (4, **Figure 48**) that retain the silencer cover (2) to the cylinder block. Support the silencer cover (2, **Figure 48**) and carburetors (6), and remove the five bolts (7) from the intake manifold. Disconnect the breather tube (1, **Figure 48**) from the silencer cover.

5. Pull the entire assembly from the power head. Stuff clean shop towels into the cylinder head openings to pre-

vent contaminants from entering the power head. Remove the gasket (8, **Figure 48**) from the cylinder head or intake manifold.

6. Remove the eight bolts (3, **Figure 48**) and lift the silencer cover from the intake assembly. Remove the four spacers (8, **Figure 47**) from the carburetors. Remove the O-rings (9, **Figure 47**) from the carburetors or spacers.

7. Remove the four spacers (12, **Figure 47**) from the intake manifold (1). Remove the eight O-rings (11 and 13, **Figure 47**) from the spacers (12) and the intake manifold (1).

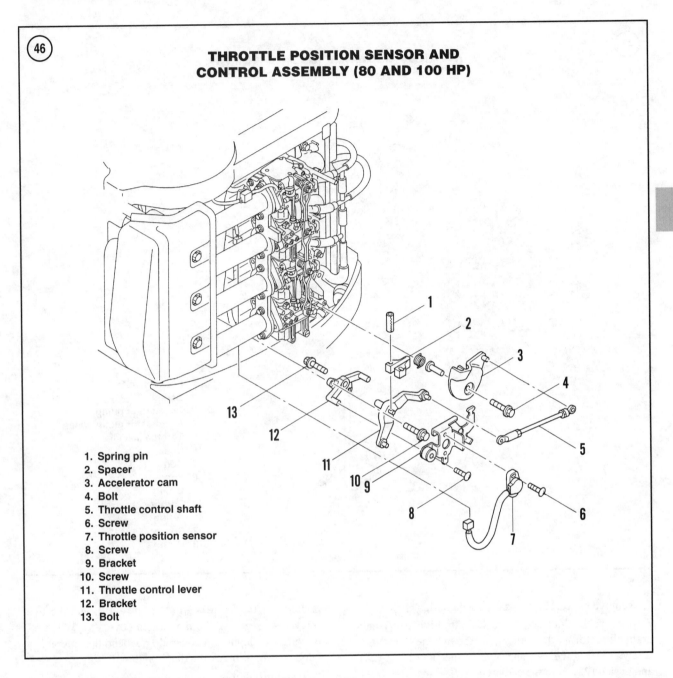

46

**THROTTLE POSITION SENSOR AND
CONTROL ASSEMBLY (80 AND 100 HP)**

1. Spring pin
2. Spacer
3. Accelerator cam
4. Bolt
5. Throttle control shaft
6. Screw
7. Throttle position sensor
8. Screw
9. Bracket
10. Screw
11. Throttle control lever
12. Bracket
13. Bolt

8. Carefully pull the throttle linkage lever (5, **Figure 47**) from the carburetor throttle levers. Disconnect the fuel hoses from the carburetors.

9. Inspect all O-rings for pinched, flattened or damaged surfaces. Replace the O-rings if defects are noted. Clean the silencer cover, insulators and intake manifold using a suitable solvent.

10. Reverse Steps 1-9 to assemble the intake manifold and carburetor(s).

11. Observe the carburetor and all fuel fittings while squeezing the primer bulb. Correct the cause of any fuel leakage. Make sure all hoses are routed away from moving components.

12. Connect the cables to the battery, if so equipped. Perform all applicable throttle position sensor and carburetor adjustments as described in Chapter Five.

**Carburetor Disassembly and Assembly
(1985-1991 9.9 Hp Models)**

Refer to **Figure 49** during this procedure.

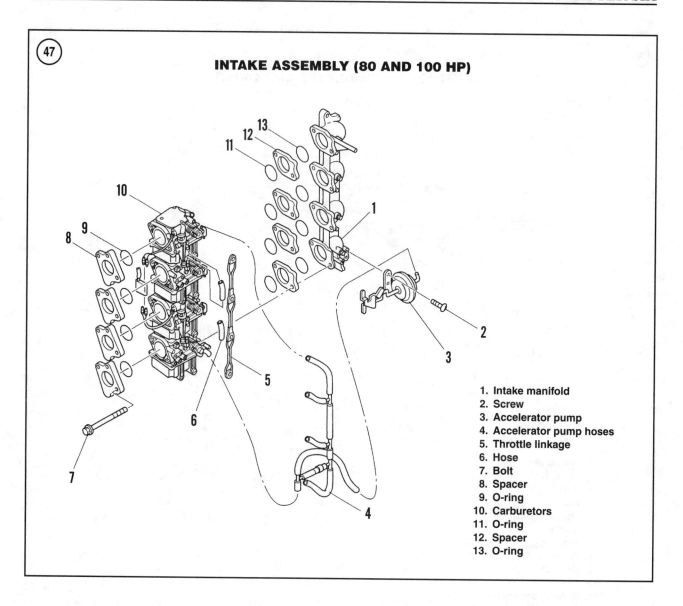

INTAKE ASSEMBLY (80 AND 100 HP)

1. Intake manifold
2. Screw
3. Accelerator pump
4. Accelerator pump hoses
5. Throttle linkage
6. Hose
7. Bolt
8. Spacer
9. O-ring
10. Carburetors
11. O-ring
12. Spacer
13. O-ring

1. Remove the carburetor as described in this chapter.

2. Remove the drain screw and seal (25, **Figure 49**), and drain all fuel from the carburetor. Remove the float bowl screws (23 **Figure 49**), and remove the float bowl (24) and gasket (22) from the carburetor.

3. Pull the starter tube (28, **Figure 49**) from the carburetor and lift the filter (27) from its opening. Remove the float pin (16, **Figure 49**), float (21) and needle valve (18) from the carburetor.

4. Remove the plug (20, **Figure 49**) and pilot jet (19) using needlenose pliers. Remove the main jet (29, **Figure 49**) and main nozzle (30). Remove the seal cap (12, **Figure 49**), pilot screw (13) and spring (14).

5. Disconnect the hose (9, **Figure 49**) from the bimetal vacuum switching valve (BVSV). Then remove the screw and plate (10, **Figure 49**) and remove the BVSV (11).

6. Remove the starter cap (1, **Figure 49**), and the two screws (4) securing the diaphragm cover (3). When removing the diaphragm cover, do not bend the emergency knob or tear, or break the diaphragm.

7. Carefully pull or lift the upper diaphragm (5, **Figure 49**), spacer (6), lower diaphragm (7) and starter plunger with the spring (8) from the bore of the carburetor.

8. Clean and inspect all carburetor components as described in this chapter.

9. Assembly is the reverse of disassembly, noting the following:

 a. Clean the filter before assembly. Use a petroleum based solvent for cleaning. Blow out all passages and jets with compressed air.

 b. Adjust the float level as described in this chapter.

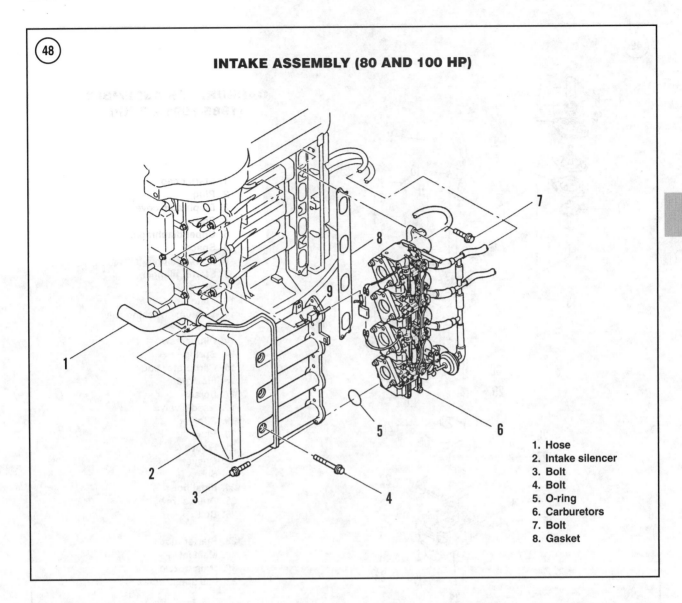

48

INTAKE ASSEMBLY (80 AND 100 HP)

6

1. Hose
2. Intake silencer
3. Bolt
4. Bolt
5. O-ring
6. Carburetors
7. Bolt
8. Gasket

c. Install new gaskets, seals and O-rings during assembly.

d. Push the main nozzle (1, **Figure 50**) fully into its opening. Position the nozzle so the cutaway of the nozzle faces the intake manifold. Align the slit in the main nozzle with the screw hole in the carburetor.

e. Turn the idle speed screw in until the throttle plate is slightly open.

10. Install the carburetor as described in this chapter.

**Carburetor Disassembly and Assembly
(1992-1999 9.9 Hp Models)**

Refer to **Figure 51** during this procedure.

1. Remove the carburetor as described in this chapter.

2. Remove the drain plug (26, **Figure 51**) and drain all fuel from the carburetor. Remove the screws and retainer (1 and 2, **Figure 51**), then lift the electrothermal valve (3, **Figure 51**) and O-ring (5) from the carburetor. Replace the O-ring if removed.

3. Remove the float bowl screws (20, **Figure 51**), then remove the float bowl (19) and gasket (17) from the carburetor. Remove the screws (24, **Figure 51**) and cover (25) from the float bowl. Remove the diaphragm and spring (21, **Figure 51**) from the float bowl.

4. Pull the float pin (11, **Figure 51**) from its mounting bosses. Lift the float (16, **Figure 51**) and inlet needle (13) from the carburetor. Use a suitable screwdriver to remove the main fuel jet (30, **Figure 51**). Remove the main nozzle retaining screw (12, **Figure 51**). Insert a screwdriver into

Carb for 9.9

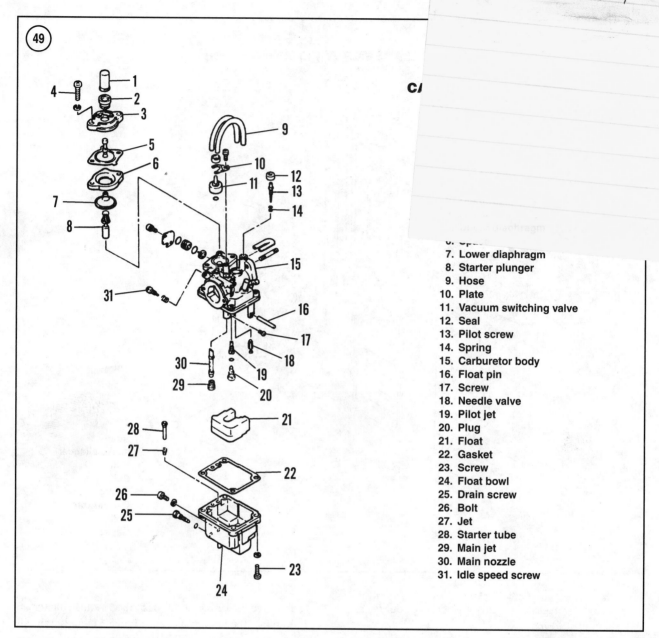

49

1
2
3
4
5
6
7
8
9
10
11
12
13
14
15
16
17
18
19
20
21
22
23
24
25
26
27
28
29
30
31

CA

6. Spa... diaphragm
7. Lower diaphragm
8. Starter plunger
9. Hose
10. Plate
11. Vacuum switching valve
12. Seal
13. Pilot screw
14. Spring
15. Carburetor body
16. Float pin
17. Screw
18. Needle valve
19. Pilot jet
20. Plug
21. Float
22. Gasket
23. Screw
24. Float bowl
25. Drain screw
26. Bolt
27. Jet
28. Starter tube
29. Main jet
30. Main nozzle
31. Idle speed screw

the throttle bore opening and push the main nozzle (31, **Figure 51**) down and out of the carburetor.

5. Remove the clamp (7, **Figure 51**), then pull the hose (6) from the carburetor. Remove the idle speed screw (8, **Figure 51**) and spring (9). Remove the clip (34, **Figure 51**), then pull the accelerator pump linkage (35) from the throttle linkage.

6. Clean and inspect the carburetor as described in this chapter.

7. Assembly is the reverse of disassembly, plus the following:

   a. Adjust the float level as described in this chapter.

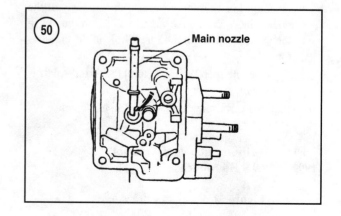

50

Main nozzle

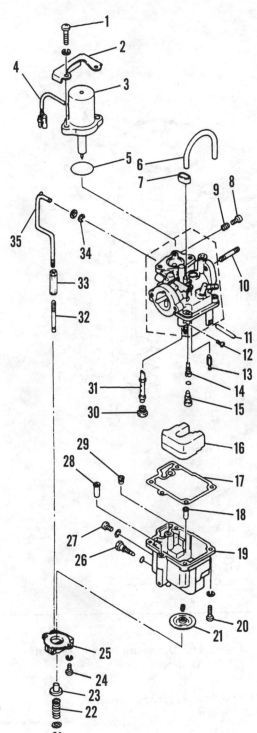

51

**CARBURETOR ASSEMBLY
(1992-1999 9.9 HP)**

1. Screw
2. Retainer
3. Electrothermal valve
4. Electrothermal valve leads
5. O-ring
6. Hose
7. Clamp
8. Idle speed screw
9. Spring
10. Stud
11. Pin
12. Screw
13. Needle valve
14. Pilot jet
15. Plug
16. Float
17. Gasket
18. Filter
19. Float bowl
20. Screw
21. Diaphragm
22. Spring
23. Seal
24. Screw
25. Cover
26. Drain Screw
27. Drain plug
28. Check valve
29. Cap
30. Main jet
31. Main nozzle
32. Rod
33. Coupler
34. Clip
35. Linkage

6

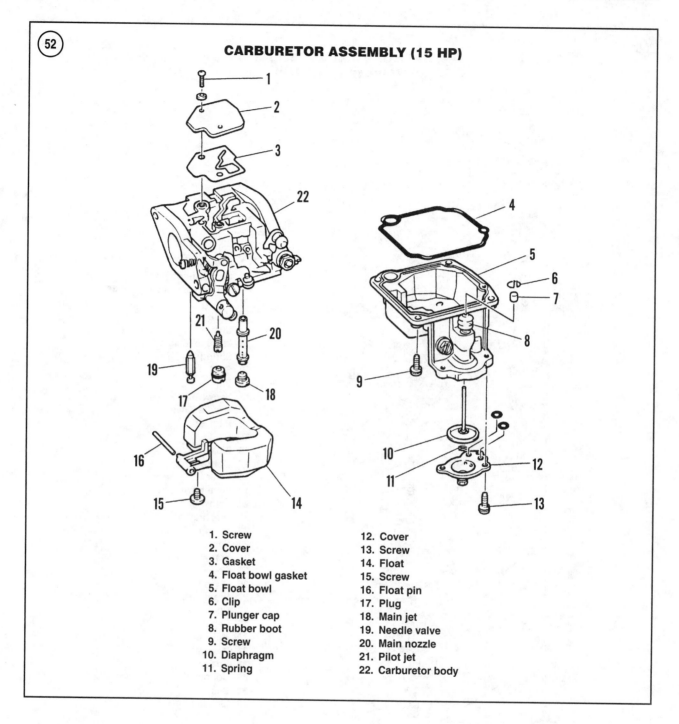

CARBURETOR ASSEMBLY (15 HP)

1. Screw
2. Cover
3. Gasket
4. Float bowl gasket
5. Float bowl
6. Clip
7. Plunger cap
8. Rubber boot
9. Screw
10. Diaphragm
11. Spring
12. Cover
13. Screw
14. Float
15. Screw
16. Float pin
17. Plug
18. Main jet
19. Needle valve
20. Main nozzle
21. Pilot jet
22. Carburetor body

b. Install new gaskets, seals and O-rings during assembly.

c. Push the main nozzle fully into its opening. Position the nozzle so the cutaway of the nozzle faces the intake manifold.

d. Turn the idle speed screw in until the throttle plate is slightly open.

8. Install the carburetor as described in this chapter.

Carburetor Disassembly and Assembly (15 Hp Models)

Refer to **Figure 52** during this procedure.

1. Remove the carburetor from the engine as described in this chapter.

2. Remove the four screws (9, **Figure 52**) and lift the float bowl (5) from the carburetor. Drain all fuel from the

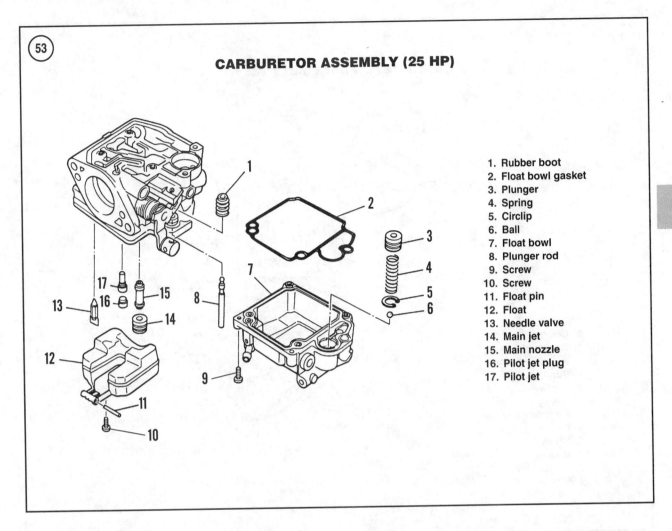

(53)

CARBURETOR ASSEMBLY (25 HP)

1. Rubber boot
2. Float bowl gasket
3. Plunger
4. Spring
5. Circlip
6. Ball
7. Float bowl
8. Plunger rod
9. Screw
10. Screw
11. Float pin
12. Float
13. Needle valve
14. Main jet
15. Main nozzle
16. Pilot jet plug
17. Pilot jet

6

carburetor. Remove the gasket (4, **Figure 52**) from the carburetor or float bowl. Replace the gasket during assembly.

3. Remove the clip (6, **Figure 52**), then remove the cap (7) and diaphragm from the bottom of the carburetor. Remove the three screws (13, **Figure 52**) and remove the diaphragm cover (12, **Figure 52**), spring (11) and diaphragm/rod (10) through the rubber boot (8).

4. Remove the screw (15, **Figure 52**), float (14), float pin (16) and inlet needle (19) from the carburetor.

5. Use a suitable screwdriver to remove the main fuel jet (18, **Figure 52**). Insert a screwdriver into the throttle bore opening and push the main nozzle (20, **Figure 52**) down and out of the carburetor.

6. Remove the plug (17, **Figure 52**) and pilot jet (21) from the carburetor. Pull the accelerator pump rod boot from the carburetor body.

7. Remove the screws (1, **Figure 52**), and cover (2) and gasket (3).

8. Clean and inspect all carburetor components as described under *Servicing the Fuel System*.

9. Assembly is the reverse of disassembly, plus the following:

    a. Make sure the inlet needle clip fits over the float tab.

    b. Install new gaskets, seals and O-rings during assembly.

    c. Make sure all screws and jets are securely tightened.

    d. Adjust the float level as described in this chapter.

10. Install the carburetor following the instructions in this chapter.

Carburetor Disassembly and Assembly (25 Hp Models)

Refer to **Figure 53** and **Figure 54** during this procedure.

1. Remove the carburetor from the engine as described in this chapter.

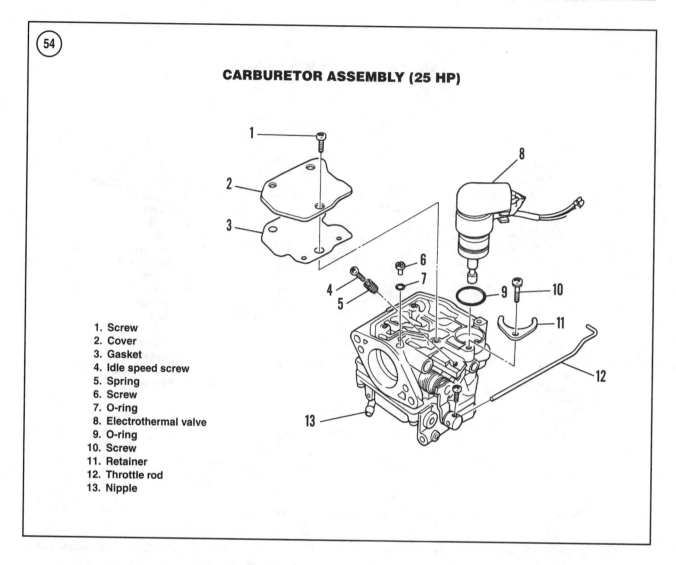

54

CARBURETOR ASSEMBLY (25 HP)

1. Screw
2. Cover
3. Gasket
4. Idle speed screw
5. Spring
6. Screw
7. O-ring
8. Electrothermal valve
9. O-ring
10. Screw
11. Retainer
12. Throttle rod
13. Nipple

2. When the fuel line is removed from the float bowl nipple (A, **Figure 54**) on the lower port side of the carburetor, the fuel will drain out. Plug the nipple until the carburetor is over a suitable container. Remove the drain plug from the opposite side of the float bowl, and drain the residual fuel from the carburetor. Remove the screws (9, **Figure 53**) and lift the float bowl (7) from the carburetor. Remove the gasket (2, **Figure 53**) from the carburetor or float bowl.

3. Pull the plunger and spring (3 and 4, **Figure 53**) from the float bowl. Remove screw (10, **Figure 53**), float (12), float pin (11) and inlet needle (13) from the carburetor.

4. Use a suitable screwdriver to remove the main fuel jet (14, **Figure 53**) from the carburetor. Insert a screwdriver into the throttle bore opening and push the main nozzle (15, **Figure 53**) down and out of the carburetor.

5. Carefully pry off the plug (16, **Figure 53**), then remove the pilot jet (17) from the carburetor. Pull the accelerator

pump rod (8) and boot (1, **Figure 53**) from the carburetor body.

6. Remove the screw (10, **Figure 54**), and electrothermal valve (8) and bracket (11). Remove the O-ring (9, **Figure 54**) from the electrothermal valve or carburetor.

7. Remove the three screws (1, **Figure 54**), cover (2) and gasket (3). Remove the pilot jet (6, **Figure 54**) and O-ring (7). Remove the throttle stop screw and spring (4 and 5, **Figure 54**).

8. Clean and inspect all carburetor as described in this chapter.

9. Assembly is the reverse of disassembly, while noting the following:

    a. Make sure the inlet needle clip fits over the float tab.

    b. Install new gaskets, seals and O-rings during assembly.

    c. Make sure all screws and jets are securely tightened.

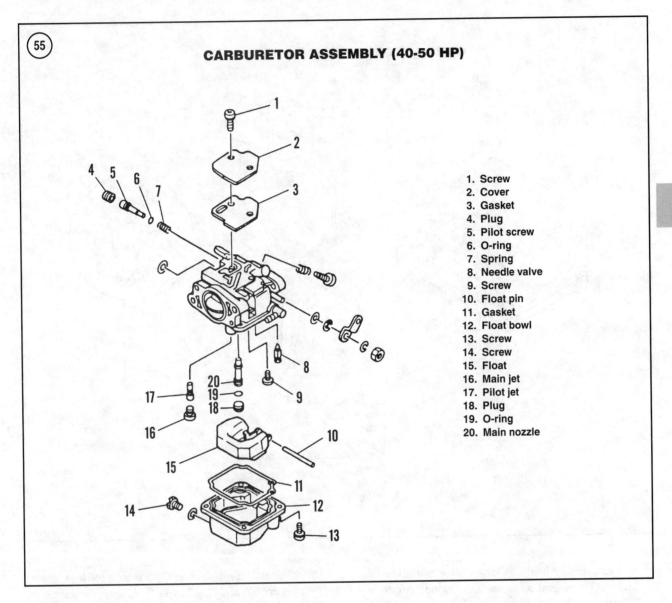

CARBURETOR ASSEMBLY (40-50 HP)

1. Screw
2. Cover
3. Gasket
4. Plug
5. Pilot screw
6. O-ring
7. Spring
8. Needle valve
9. Screw
10. Float pin
11. Gasket
12. Float bowl
13. Screw
14. Screw
15. Float
16. Main jet
17. Pilot jet
18. Plug
19. O-ring
20. Main nozzle

d. Adjust the float level as described in this chapter.

10. Install the carburetor as described in this chapter.

Carburetor Disassembly and Assembly (40 and 50 Hp Models)

Refer to **Figure 55** during this procedure.

1. Remove the carburetor from the engine following the instructions in this chapter.

2. Remove the drain plug and seal (14, **Figure 55**), and drain the fuel from the carburetor. Remove the screws (1, **Figure 55**), cover plate (2) and gasket/packing (3). Remove all four screws (13, **Figure 55**), then lift the float bowl (12) from the carburetor. Remove the gasket (11, **Figure 55**) from the carburetor or float bowl.

3. Remove the screw (9, **Figure 55**), float (15, **Figure 55**), float pin (10) and inlet needle (8).

4. Use a suitable screwdriver to remove the plug and O-ring (18 and 19, **Figure 55**). Insert a screwdriver into the throttle bore opening and push the main nozzle (20, **Figure 55**) down and out of the carburetor.

5. Use a suitable screwdriver to remove the main fuel jet (16, **Figure 55**) and pilot jet (17).

6. Use a suitable screwdriver to remove the plug (4, **Figure 55**), then remove the pilot screw (5), O-ring (6) and spring (7) from the carburetor.

7. Clean and inspect the carburetor as described in this chapter

8. Assembly is the reverse of disassembly, plus the following:

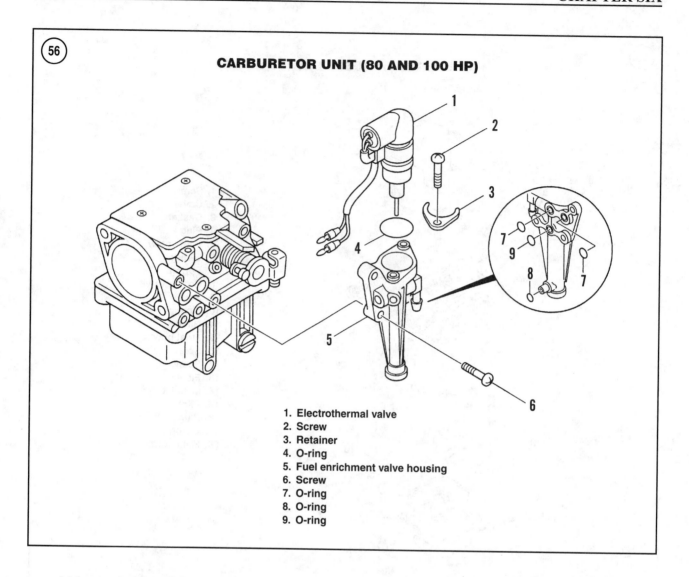

CARBURETOR UNIT (80 AND 100 HP)

56

1. Electrothermal valve
2. Screw
3. Retainer
4. O-ring
5. Fuel enrichment valve housing
6. Screw
7. O-ring
8. O-ring
9. O-ring

a. Make sure the inlet needle clip fits over the float tab.
b. Install new gaskets, seals and O-rings during assembly.
c. Make sure all screws and jets are securely tightened.
d. Adjust the float level as described in this chapter.

9. Install the carburetor following the instructions in this chapter.

Carburetor Disassembly and Assembly (80 and 100 Hp Models)

Refer to **Figure 56** and **Figure 57** during this procedure.

1. Remove the carburetor from the engine following the instructions in this chapter.

2. Remove the drain plug (10, **Figure 57**) and drain the fuel from the carburetor. Remove the three screws (1, **Fig-**ure 57), cover (2) and gasket (3). Remove the four screws (11, **Figure 57**) and float bowl (9). Remove the gasket (8, **Figure 57**) from the carburetor or float bowl.

3. Remove the screw (12, **Figure 57**), float (14), float pin (13) and inlet needle (15) from the carburetor. Use a large screwdriver to remove the inlet seat (16, **Figure 57**) and gasket (17).

4. Use a suitable screwdriver to remove the main fuel jet (18, **Figure 57**) from the carburetor. Insert a screwdriver into the throttle bore opening and push the main nozzle (19, **Figure 57**) down and out of the carburetor. Carefully pry the plug (20, **Figure 57**) from the carburetor and remove the pilot jet (21).

5. Remove the blind plug (7, **Figure 57**) using a suitable screwdriver, then remove the pilot screw (6), O-ring (5) and spring (4).

6. Remove the screw (2, **Figure 56**), then lift the electrothermal valve (1) and bracket (3) from the carbure-

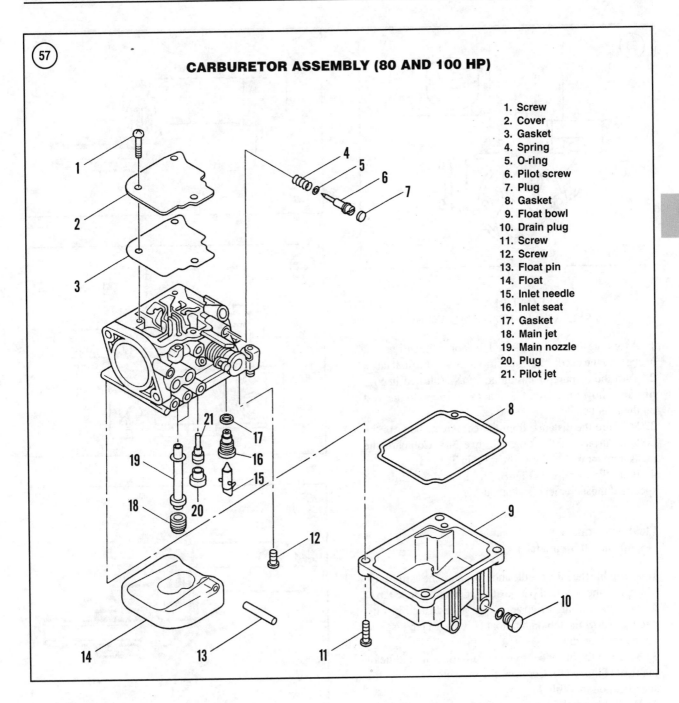

CARBURETOR ASSEMBLY (80 AND 100 HP)

1. Screw
2. Cover
3. Gasket
4. Spring
5. O-ring
6. Pilot screw
7. Plug
8. Gasket
9. Float bowl
10. Drain plug
11. Screw
12. Screw
13. Float pin
14. Float
15. Inlet needle
16. Inlet seat
17. Gasket
18. Main jet
19. Main nozzle
20. Plug
21. Pilot jet

tor. Remove the O-ring (4, **Figure 56**) from the electrothermal valve.

7. Remove the screws (6, **Figure 56**) and valve housing (5) from the side of the carburetor. Remove the four O-rings (7-9, **Figure 56**) from the carburetor or valve housing.

8. Clean and inspect the carburetor as described in this chapter.

9. Assembly is the reverse of disassembly, plus the following:

a. Make sure the inlet needle clip fits over the float tab.

b. Install new gaskets, seals and O-rings during assembly.

c. Make sure all screws and jets are securely tightened.

d. Adjust the float level as described in this chapter.

10. Install the carburetor following the instructions in this chapter.

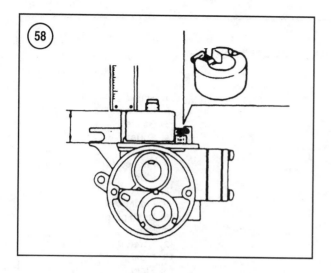

FLOAT LEVEL
(9.9, 25 AND 80-100 HP MODELS)

1. Assemble the inlet needle and float onto the carburetor. Make sure the needle clip is positioned over the float tab.

2. Turn the carburetor upside down as indicated in **Figure 58**. Allow the tab on the float (**Figure 59**) to just rest on the inlet needle.

3. Measure the distance from the carburetor body to the bottom surface of the float (**Figure 58**). Compare the measurement with the specification in **Table 1**.

4. Bend the metal tab (**Figure 58**) up or down until the specified measurement is attained.

Float Adjustment
(15, 40 and 50 hp models)

1. Assemble the inlet needle and float onto the carburetor. Make sure the needle clip is positioned over the float tab.

2. Turn the carburetor upside down as indicated in **Figure 60**. Allow the tab on the float (**Figure 61**) to just rest on the inlet needle.

3. Measure the distance from the carburetor to middle of the float (**Figure 60**). Compare the measurement with the specification in **Table 1**.

4. Bend the metal tab (**Figure 61**) up or down until the specified measurement is attained. On 15 hp models, the float tab cannot be bent. Replace the float if the float measurement is not correct.

Dashpot Removal and Installation
(40 and 50 Hp Models)

   The dashpot is mounted on the rear starboard side of the power head.

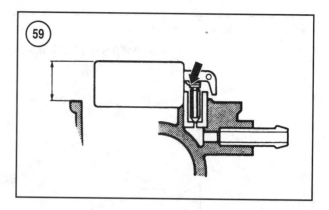

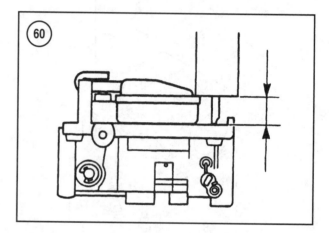

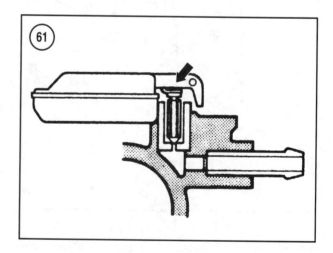

1. Disconnect both cables from the battery.

2. Remove the screws (**Figure 62**), and lift the dashpot and bracket from the intake manifold. Count the number of threads exposed on the adjustment bolt.

3. Loosen the jam nut (**Figure 63**) and thread the dashpot from the bracket. Thread the replacement dashpot onto the bracket until the same number of threads counted in Step 2 are exposed. Securely tighten the jam nut.

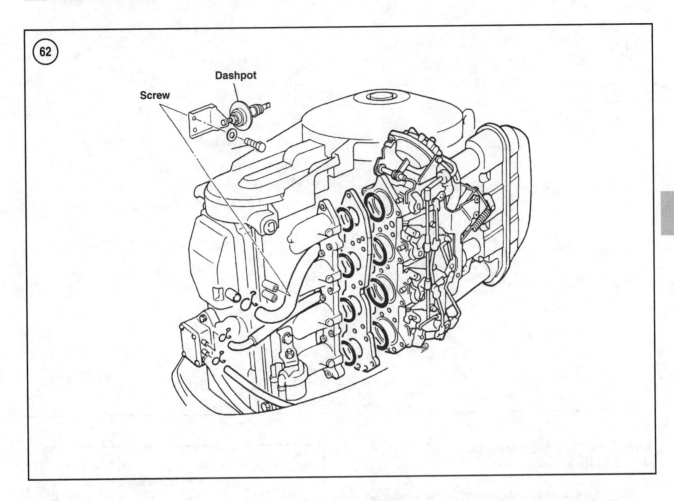

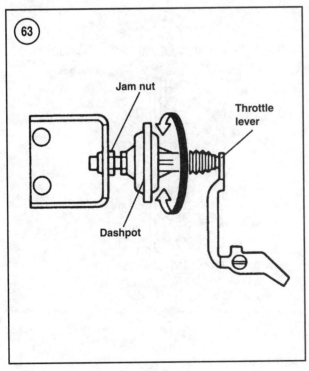

4. Install the dashpot and bracket in position on the intake manifold. Install the mounting screws (**Figure 62**). Securely tighten the screws.

5. Connect the cables to the battery, if so equipped. Adjust the dashpot (Chapter Five).

Dashpot Removal and Installation (80 and 100 Hp Models)

The dashpot is mounted to the lower rear port side of the power head (**Figure 64**).

1. Disconnect both cables from the battery.

2. Disconnect the dashpot linkage from the throttle lever. Remove the screws (**Figure 64**) and lift the dashpot from the intake manifold.

3. Connect the dashpot linkage to the throttle lever. Install the dashpot and bracket into position on the intake manifold. Install the mounting screws (**Figure 64**). Securely tighten the screws.

4. Connect the cables to the battery, if so equipped. Adjust the dashpot (Chapter Five).

6

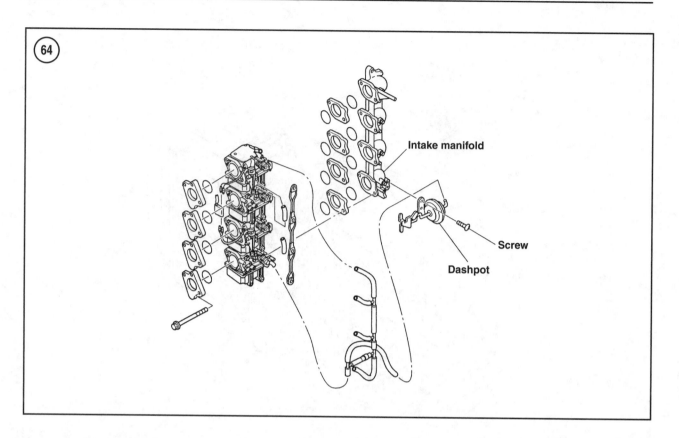

**Accelerator Pump Replacement
(40 and 50 Hp Models**

This section covers replacement of the accelerator pump (**Figure 65**) used on 40 and 50 hp models. Other models are equipped with a carburetor-mounted accelerator pump. Refer to *Carburetors* in this chapter.

1. Disconnect both cables from the battery.

2. Disconnect the pump linkage from the throttle lever on the top carburetor. Remove each hose (**Figure 65**) from the accelerator pump. Remove the mounting screws (**Figure 65**) and remove the accelerator pump from its mounting bracket.

3. Remove both screws (1, **Figure 66**), then lift the cover (2) and check valve (3) from the pump. Remove both screws (6, **Figure 66**) and pump body (4) from the diaphragm unit (5).

4. Clean all components with a mild solvent such as kerosene. Inspect the diaphragm unit for holes, wear or damage. Inspect the check valve for wear, cracks or damage. Replace any damaged components.

5. Assembly is the reverse of disassembly.

   a. Assemble the components as shown in **Figure 66**.

   b. Securely tighten all screws.

6. Install the accelerator pump onto its bracket. Connect the linkage to the throttle lever of the top carburetor. In-

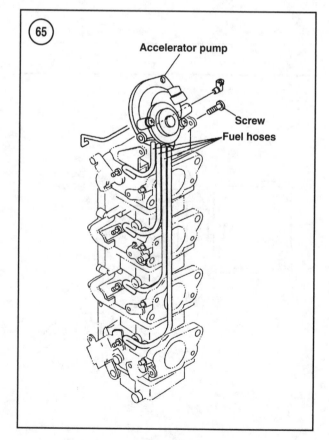

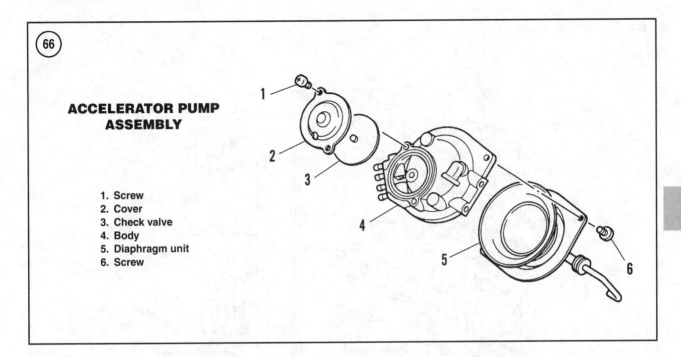

ACCELERATOR PUMP ASSEMBLY

1. Screw
2. Cover
3. Check valve
4. Body
5. Diaphragm unit
6. Screw

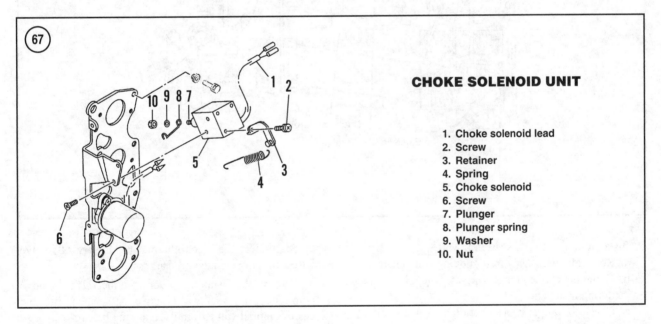

CHOKE SOLENOID UNIT

1. Choke solenoid lead
2. Screw
3. Retainer
4. Spring
5. Choke solenoid
6. Screw
7. Plunger
8. Plunger spring
9. Washer
10. Nut

stall the mounting screws (**Figure 65**). Securely tighten the screws. Connect all hoses to the proper fittings on the pump (**Figure 65**).

7. Connect the cables to the battery, if so equipped.

Choke Solenoid Removal and Installation

1. On 40 and 50 hp models, remove the silencer cover, carburetors and intake manifold as an assembly. Refer to *Silencer Cover, Carburetor(s) and Intake Manifold* in this chapter.

2. Disconnect the choke solenoid wires (1, **Figure 67**) from the engine wire harness.

3. Disconnect the spring (4, **Figure 67**) from the lever (3). Remove the mounting screws (6, **Figure 67**), then lift the solenoid (5) from the solenoid plunger (7).

4. Clean the solenoid plunger and plunger opening in the solenoid using a corrosion preventative spray such as WD 40.

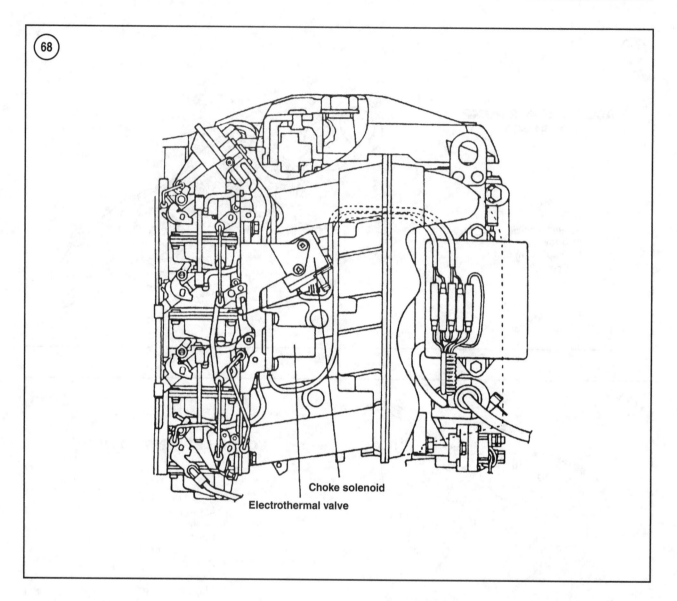

⑥⑧

Choke solenoid
Electrothermal valve

5. Installation is the reverse of removal.
  a. Route all wires away from moving components.
  b. Guide the choke plunger into the solenoid opening during installation.
  c. Check for proper choke operation after installation. Refer to Chapter Three for testing instructions.

Electrothermal Valve
Removal and Installation
(40 and 50 Hp Models)

This section provides electrothermal valve removal and installation on 40 and 50 hp models. Electrothermal valve removal and installation on other models is covered in the carburetor section.

1. Disconnect both cables from the battery.

2. Disconnect the electrothermal (1, **Figure 68**) valve wires from the engine wire harness.

3. Remove the insulation cover from the valve. Remove both mounting screws (**Figure 69**), then lift the electrothermal valve from its mounting bracket.

4. Installation is the reverse of removal.

  a. Mount the valve with the wires exiting the valve on the lower side.

  b. Securely tighten the mounting screws.

  c. Make sure all wires are routed away from moving components.

  d. Install the insulation cover to help ensure correct operation of the valve.

5. Clean the terminals, then connect the cables to the battery, if so equipped.

6

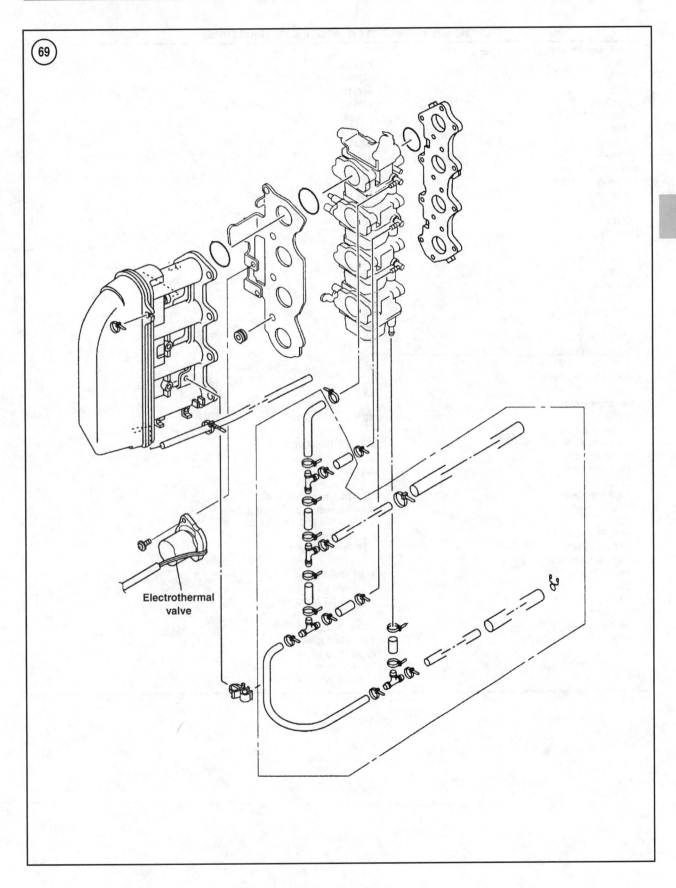

Electrothermal
valve

Table 1 CARBURETOR MODEL SPECIFICATIONS

Carburetor identification number	
F9.9	6G920
T9.9	6G820
F15	66M10
F25	65W01
F40 and F50	62Y01
T50	64J01
F80	67G10
F100	67F10
Main jet number	
F9.9 and T9.9	86
F15	104
F25-F80	112
F100	128
Main air jet	
F25	90
F80	115
F100	75
Pilot jet number	
F9.9 and T9.9	48
F15 and F80	45
F25	50
F40, F50, T50 and F100	42
Pilot air jet number	
F25, F80 and F100	85
Pilot outlet jet number	
F25	52
Mid-range jet number	
F100	40
Main nozzle size	
F9.9 and T9.9	2.2 mm (0.087 in.)
Valve seat size	
F9.9 and T9.9	1.2 mm (0.047 in.)
Float height	
F9.9 and T9.9	24.5-24.6 mm (0.96-1.04 in.)
F15	9.5-10.5 mm (0.37-0.41 in.)
F25	13.5-14.5 mm (0.53-0.57 in)
F40, F50 and T50	9.5-10.5 mm (0.37-0.41 in.)
F80 and F100	14.0 mm (0.55 in.)
Initial pilot screw setting	
F40, F50 and T50	1 3/4 -2 3/4 turns out
F80	2-3 turns out
F100	1 1/2 -2 1/2 turns out
Idle speed	
F9.9 and F15	900-1000 rpm
T9.9	1100-1200 rpm
F25	875-975 rpm
F40, F50 and T50	700-800 rpm
F80 and F100	850-950 rpm

Chapter Seven

Electrical and Ignition System

This chapter provides removal, repair and installation procedures for electrical system components.

Tables 1-15, located at the end of this chapter, provide ignition system specifications, electric starter motor specifications, battery requirements, and battery capacities.

Battery

Batteries used in marine applications are subjected to a lot more vibration and pounding than those used in automotive applications. Always use a battery that is designated for marine applications. Marine batteries have thicker cases and plates than typical automobile batteries.

Use a battery that meets or exceeds the cold cranking amperage requirements for the engine. Cold cranking amperage requirements are provided in **Table 14**. Some marine batteries lists *marine/deep cycle* on the label. Deep cycle batteries allow repeated discharge and charge cycles. These batteries are excellent for powering accessories such as trolling motors. Always charge deep cycle batteries at a low amperage rate. A deep cycle battery is not designed to be charged or discharged at a rapid rate. Rapid charging rates can significantly reduce the life of a deep cycle battery.

Deep cycle batteries can be used as the starting battery if they meet the cold cranking amperage requirements for the engine.

Loose or corroded battery cable connections cause many problems in marine applications. Use cable connectors that are securely crimped or molded to the cable. Avoid using temporary or emergency clamps for normal usage. They corrode and do not meet the coast guard requirements for terminal connections.

Use a cover on the positive (+) terminal post. Covers are available at marine dealerships. Use the around the post connector or the spade type clamp that attaches to the top of the post.

Make sure the battery is securely mounted in the boat to avoid an acid spill or arcing that can cause a fire. Mount the battery using a bracket mounted to the boat floor along with a support across the top of the battery (**Figure 1**) or using a battery case attached to the boat structure (**Figure 2**).

Mount the battery in a location that allows easy access for maintenance. Make sure the battery terminals cannot contact any component in the mounting area.

> *WARNING*
> *If mounting a battery in an aluminum boat, make sure the battery is securely mounted to eliminate the possibility of the battery contacting metal components. Electrical arcing can result in fire or explosion if a fuel source is present. Batteries produce explosive gasses that can ignite if arcing is present.*

> *WARNING*
> *Always wear gloves and protective eyewear when working with batteries. Batteries contain a corrosive and dangerous acid solution. Never smoke or allow any source of ignition to be near a battery. Batteries produce explosive gases that can ignite if an ignition source is present.*

Inspect the battery case for cracks, leakage, abrasion points and other damage if the battery is removed for charging. Replace the battery if any questionable conditions exist. During normal usage, a corrosive deposit forms on the top of the battery. The deposit may allow the battery to discharge at a rapid rate as current travels through the deposits from one post to the other.

Make sure the battery caps are properly installed. Remove the battery from the boat and carefully wash loose material from the top of the battery with clean water.

> *CAUTION*
> *Never allow the water and baking soda solution to enter the battery solution through the vent caps. The acid solution will become neutralized and cause permanent damage to the battery.*

Use a solution of warm water and baking soda along with a soft bristled brush to clean deposits from the battery (**Figure 3**). Wash the battery with clean water again and remove the baking soda solution from the battery case.

> *CAUTION*
> *Never overfill the battery. The electrolyte may expand with heat created during charging and overflow from the battery.*

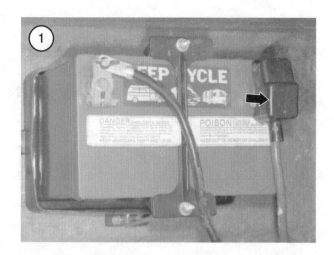

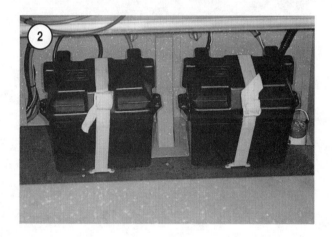

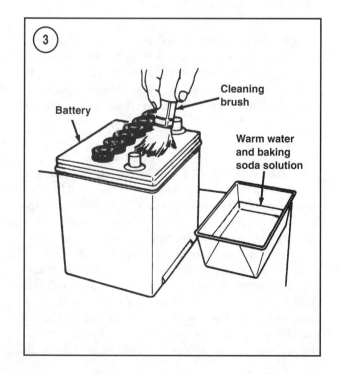

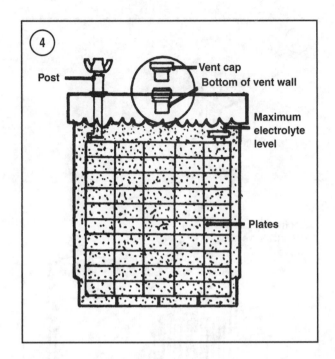

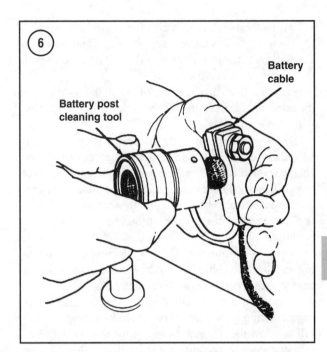

7

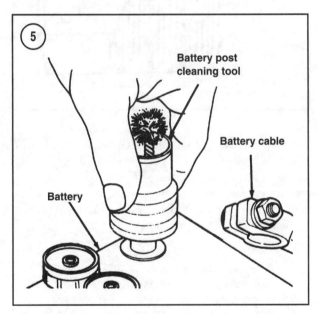

Electrolyte Level

Check the battery electrolyte level at regular intervals. Heavy use or use in warm climates increases the frequency that water needs to be added to the battery. Carefully remove the vent caps (**Figure 4**) and inspect the electrolyte level in each cell. The electrolyte level should be 3/16 in. (4.8 mm) above the plates and below the bottom of the vent well (**Figure 4**). Use distilled water to fill the cells to the proper level. Never use battery acid to cor-

rect the electrolyte level. The acid solution will be too strong, and lead to damaged or deteriorated plates.

Battery Terminals

Clean the battery terminals at regular intervals or anytime the terminal is removed. Use a battery-cleaning tool available at most automotive part stores to remove stubborn corrosion and deposits. Remove the terminal and clean the post as shown in **Figure 5**. Rotate the tool on the post until the post is clean. Avoid removing too much material from the post or the terminal may not attach securely to the post.

Use the other end of the tool to clean the cable end terminal. Clean flat spade type connectors and the attaching nuts with the wire brush end of the tool (**Figure 6**).

Apply a coating of petroleum gel or another corrosion preventative agent to the battery post and cable terminal. Tighten the fasteners securely. Avoid using excessive force when tightening the terminals. The battery and terminals can be damaged if excessive force is applied.

Battery Testing

NOTE
Inaccurate reading occurs if the specific gravity is checked immediately after adding water to the battery. To ensure accuracy, charge the battery at a high rate for 15-20 minutes.

Two methods are commonly used to test batteries. A load tester measures the battery voltage as it applies a load across the terminals. Follow the instruction provided with the load tester to test the battery.

Perform a *Cranking Voltage* following the instructions included in this section to check the battery condition without a load tester.

Use a hydrometer check the specific gravity of the battery electrolyte. This gives an accurate reading of the charge level of the battery. Using a hydrometer is the most practical method for checking battery condition. Hydrometers are available at most automotive part stores. Select one that has number graduation that spans 1.100-1.300 readings.

To use the hydrometer, insert the tip into the vent opening and use the rubber bulb to draw some of the solution from a single cell into the hydrometer (**Figure 7**). Read the specific gravity in all cells. If using a temperature compensating hydrometer, take several readings in each cell to allow the thermometer to adjust to the electrolyte temperature. Always return the electrolyte to the cell from which it was drawn. With the hydrometer vertical, determine the specific gravity by reading the number on the float that is even with the surface of the electrolyte (**Figure 8**). A specific gravity reading of 1.260 or higher indicates a fully charged battery. Always charge the battery if the specific gravity varies more than .050 from one cell to another.

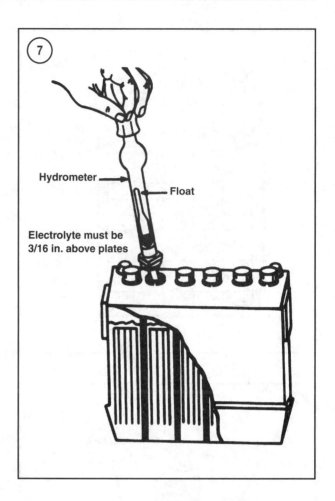

NOTE
Add 0.004 to the reading for every 10° above 25° C (80° F) if the hydrometer is not temperature compensating. Subtract 0.004 from the reading for every 10° below 25° C (80° F).

Cranking voltage test

Battery condition can be checked by measuring the voltage at the battery terminals while cranking the engine. Connect the positive meter test lead to the positive battery terminal. Connect the negative meter test lead to a suitable engine ground. Measure the voltage while cranking the engine (**Figure 9**). Fully charge the battery if the voltage drops below 9.6 volts while cranking. Repeat the cranking voltage test. Replace the battery if a low voltage reading persists.

Battery Storage

Batteries lose some of the charge during storage. The rate of discharge increases in a warm environment. Store the battery in a cool dry location to minimize the loss of charge. Check the specific gravity every 30 days during storage and charge the battery if required. Perform the maintenance on the battery case and terminals as described in this section. Refer to *Battery Charging* in this section for battery charging times.

WARNING
Batteries produce explosive hydrogen gas, especially during charging. Charge the battery in a well-ventilated area. Wear protective eyewear and gloves when working around batteries. Never smoke or allow any source of ignition in the area where batteries are stored or charged. Never allow any uninsulated components to contact the battery terminals, or arcing can occur and ignite the hydrogen gas.

Battery Charging

Always remove the battery from the boat when charging. Batteries produce explosive hydrogen gas. Because

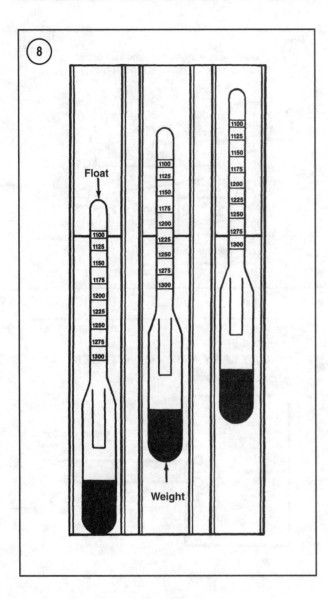

Float

Weight

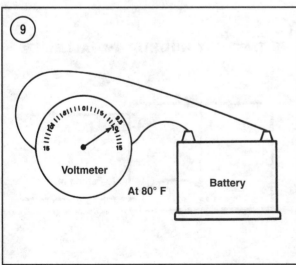

Voltmeter

At 80° F

Battery

most boats provide limited ventilation, the explosive gas may remain in the area for a long time. In addition to the hazards of explosion, the gas causes accelerated corrosion of components in the battery compartment. Removing the battery allows easier inspection of the case for damage and cleaning of the battery terminals.

> *WARNING*
> *Be extremely careful when connecting any wires to the battery terminals. Avoid making the last connection at the battery terminal. Explosive hydrogen gas in and around the battery may ignite and lead to an explosion.*

Make the connections to the battery *before* plugging the charger in or switching the charger on. This can prevent dangerous arcing at the terminals. Connect the battery charger cables to the proper terminals on the battery. Plug the charger into its power supply and select the 12-volt setting.

Charging the battery at a slow rate, or low amperage, results in a more efficient charge and helps prolong the life of the battery. With a severely discharged battery it may be necessary to charge the battery at a higher amperage rate for a few minutes before switching to the lower rate charge. A severely discharged battery may not allow the charging process to begin without first *boost* charging at the high rate.

Battery charging times vary by the battery capacity and the state of charge. Check the specific gravity often and stop the charging process when the battery is fully charged. Severely discharged batteries may require as long as 8 hours to recharge. Check the temperature of the electrolyte during the charging process. Discontinue the charging process if the electrolyte temperature reaches or exceeds 53° C (125° F).

Jump Starting

If the battery is severely discharged, it is possible to start the engine using another fully charged battery. However, jump starting can be dangerous is the proper procedure is not followed. Never attempt to jump start an engine if its battery is frozen. Always check the electrolyte level and add water to the cells if necessary before connecting the jumper cables. A significant risk of explosion exists if the electrolyte is at or below the top of the plates. Always use a good pair of jumper cables with clean connector clamps. Keep all clamps away from metallic or conductive material. Never allow the clamps to contact each other.

Follow Steps 1-6 to make jumper cable connections.

1. Connect the jumper cable to the positive (+) terminal of the discharged battery (1, **Figure 10**).

2. Connect the same jumper cable to the positive (+) terminal of the fully charged battery (2, **Figure 10**).

3. Connect the second jumper cable to the negative (−) terminal of the fully charged battery (3, **Figure 10**).

4. Connect the second jumper cable to a good engine ground such as the starter ground cable (4, **Figure 10**).

5. Make sure the cables and clamps will not become trapped or interfere with moving components.

6. Start the engine, then remove the cables in exactly the reverse of the connection order in Steps 1-4.

Wiring for 12- and 24-volt Electric Trolling Motors

Many fishing boats have an electric trolling motor that requires 24 volts to operate. Two or more batteries are necessary with the electric trolling motor. A series battery hookup (**Figure 11**) provides 24 volts for the trolling motor.

A series connection provides the approximate total of the two batteries (24 volts). The amperage provided is the approximate average of the two batteries.

Connect the trolling motor batteries in a parallel arrangement (**Figure 12**) when the trolling motor requires 12 volts to operate.

The voltage provided is the approximate average of the two batteries (12-volt). The amperage provided is the approximate total of the two batteries.

Follow these or the manufacture's instructions, for battery connection with special quick connect plugs at the trolling motor. Have one battery for the gasoline motor if possible. This prevents having a discharged battery from using the trolling motors and other electrical accessories, and being unable to start the gasoline engine.

STARTING SYSTEM

Starter Relay Removal and Installation

Two different starter relays are used on four-stroke models. All 9.9, 15, 40, 50, 80 and 100 hp models utilize a rubber-mounted starter relay (**Figure 13**). On 25 hp models, the relay (**Figure 14**) attaches to a metal mounting bracket.

Rubber-mounted starter relay

1. Disconnect both cables from the battery.

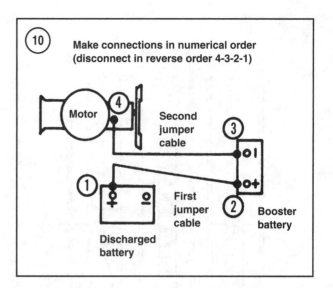

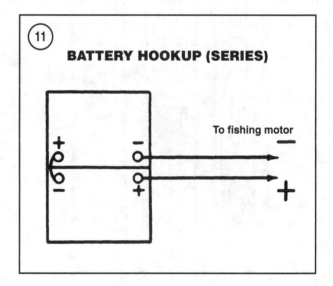

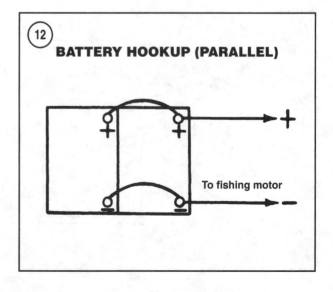

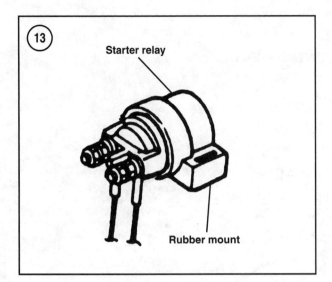

Starter relay

Rubber mount

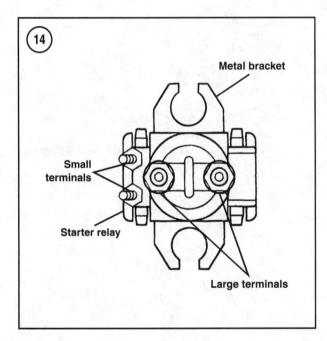

Metal bracket

Small terminals

Starter relay

Large terminals

6. Connect one large wire terminal over each large terminal of the relay. Securely tighten the terminal nuts. Make sure the wire terminals are not touching the other terminal or other components.

7. Connect one of the small diameter wires to the engine wire harness. Connect the other small diameter wire to the engine wire harness or engine ground. Make sure all wires are routed away from moving components.

8. Connect the cables to the battery. Check for proper starting system operation.

Bracket-mounted starter relay

1. Disconnect both cables from the battery.

2. Disconnect both large diameter wires (**Figure 14**) from the starter relay. Remove the small screws and disconnect both small wires from the starter relay.

3. Remove the mounting bolts, washers, spacers and grommets then lift the relay from the power head. Clean the relay mounting surfaces.

4. Install the relay, washers, spacers and grommets. Install the mounting bolts, then securely tighten them. If a relay ground wire is used, be sure to connect the ground wire to the mounting bolt.

5. Connect one large wire over each large terminal of the relay. Securely tighten the terminal nuts. Make sure the wire terminals are not touching the other terminal or any metal components.

6. Connect one of the smaller diameter wires to its terminal (**Figure 14**). Connect the other smaller diameter wire to its terminal. Make sure the wires do not touch each other or any metal components.

7. Make sure all wires are routed away from moving components.

8. Connect the cables to the battery. Check for proper starting system operation.

**Starter Solenoid Removal
(80 and 100 hp Models)**

1. Remove the electric starter motor as described in this chapter. Disconnect the short cable from the starter solenoid.

2. Remove both bolts (1, **Figure 15**), then lift the starter solenoid (9) from the electric starter motor housing (2).

3. Pull the shift lever (3, **Figure 15**) from the electric starter motor housing (2). Pull the lever spring (4, **Figure 15**) from the starter solenoid (9).

4. Remove both screws (5, **Figure 15**), then lift the dust seal (6), dust seal cover (7) and seal (8) from the starter solenoid (9).

2. Disconnect both large diameter wires from the starter relay. Disconnect the small diameter wires from engine wire harness or engine ground.

3. Carefully tug the starter relay from the rubber mount.

4. Inspect the mount for damage or deterioration. Remove the mount by carefully pulling it from the mounting bracket. Replace the mount by slipping the elongated openings over the mounting arms. Make sure the arms pass completely through the elongated openings and the hooked ends engage the openings.

5. Slide the replacement relay fully into its opening in the rubber mount. Make sure the lip on the opening fits over the outer edge of the relay.

7

⑮

STARTER MOTOR AND SOLENOID

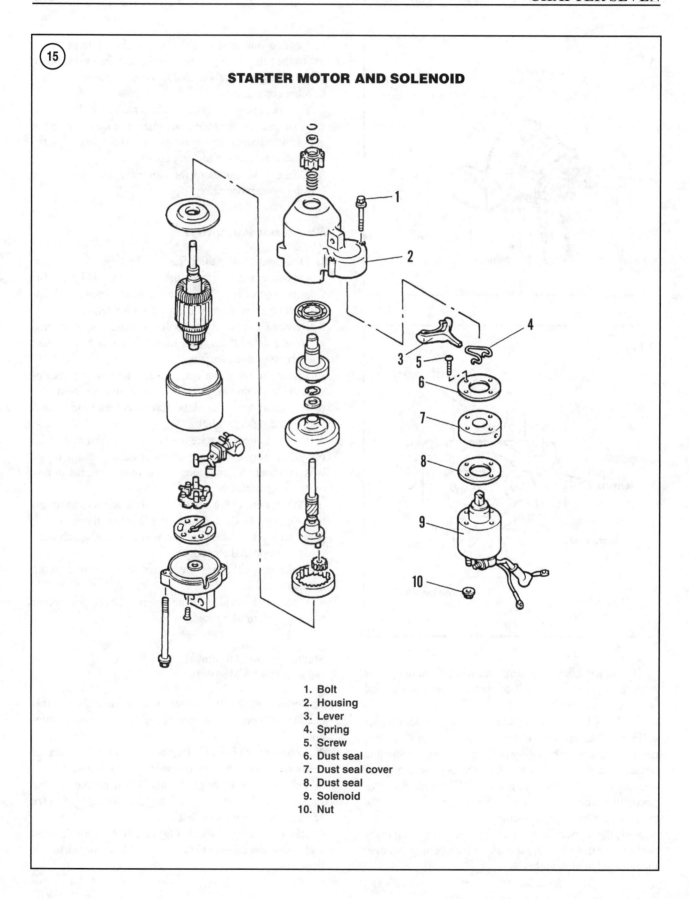

1. Bolt
2. Housing
3. Lever
4. Spring
5. Screw
6. Dust seal
7. Dust seal cover
8. Dust seal
9. Solenoid
10. Nut

5. Remove the nut (10, **Figure 15**) and remove the wire from the solenoid.

Starter Solenoid Test
(80 and 100 hp Models)

1. Remove the solenoid from the electric starter motor as described in this chapter.

2. Connect the positive ohmmeter lead to one of the large diameter terminals on the starter solenoid. Connect the negative lead to the other large diameter terminal. Note the meter reading. The correct result is no continuity.

3. Clamp the solenoid into a vise with soft jaws. Use a jumper wire to connect the black/white solenoid terminal to the positive terminal of the battery. Connect another jumper lead to the negative terminal of the battery.

4. Observe the meter reading while touching the jumper wire (negative terminal) to an unpainted surface of the solenoid housing. The correct test result is continuity.

5. Observe the solenoid shaft as the connections in Steps 3 and 4 are made. Rapid extension of the shaft as the connections are made indicated correct test results.

6. Replace the solenoid if it fails to operate as described.

Starter Solenoid
(80 and 100 hp Models)

1. Align the screw and spring holes in the two dust seals and the dust cover with their matching holes in the solenoid (9, **Figure 15**). Install both screws (5, **Figure 15**) and tighten them securely. Install both ends of the spring into the cover and solenoid as indicated in **Figure 15**.

2. Install the lever (3, **Figure 15**) into the electric starter motor housing (2). Make sure the lever engages the pinion shaft with the spring notch facing outward.

3. Make sure the rubber block is positioned in the starter relay opening. Carefully insert the relay into the electric starter motor housing. Make sure the spring (4, **Figure 15**) contacts the notch and the tip of the lever (3) passes through the opening in the solenoid shaft.

4. Hold the solenoid in position and install the bolts (1, **Figure 15**). Tighten the bolts evenly. Connect the short cable attached to the electric starter motor to the starter solenoid terminal. Install the washers and securely tighten the terminal nut.

5. Install the starter motor as described in this chapter.

Ignition Switch
Removal and Installation

Follow Steps 1-8 if the switch is mounted in the remote control. Follow Steps 3-5 if the switch is mounted in the dash.

1. Disconnect both battery cables from the battery terminals. Refer to Chapter Twelve and remove the remote control.

2. Disassemble the remote control to the point where the ignition key switch leads and retainer (**Figure 16**) are accessible.

3. Make sure both cables are disconnected from the battery. Disconnect ignition switch wires from the remote control wire harness.

4. Install the ignition key into the switch, then mark the *up* side of the switch and ignition key. Remove the ignition key. Note the Yamaha mark relative to the *up* mark.

5. Use the Yamaha marking on the ignition key to identify the *up* side of the replacement ignition key switch. Install the replacement ignition switch and securely tighten the retaining nut.

6. Attach the switch wires to the wire harness connector. Make sure the switch wire connectors are fully engage the wire harness connectors.

7. Refer to Chapter Twelve and assemble the remote control. Install the control.

8. Connect the battery cables to the battery.

STARTER MOTOR

Removal and Installation
(9.9 hp Models)

1. Disconnect both battery cables from the battery. Remove all spark plugs and connect the spark plug leads to a suitable engine ground.

2. Remove the flywheel cover (**Figure 17**, typical) following the instructions in Chapter Eight. This is necessary to ensure all starter mounting bolts and nuts are accessible.

3. Remove the nut and remove the large diameter wire (1, **Figure 18**) from the starter motor.

4. Support the electric starter motor (2, **Figure 18**) and remove the starter mounting bolts (3). Lift the electric starter from the power head.

5. Installation is the reverse of removal.

   a. Position the large wire terminal away from other components. To prevent damage to the insulator, do not over tighten the wire terminal nut.

   b. Install the insulating boots over the large diameter wire terminals.

7

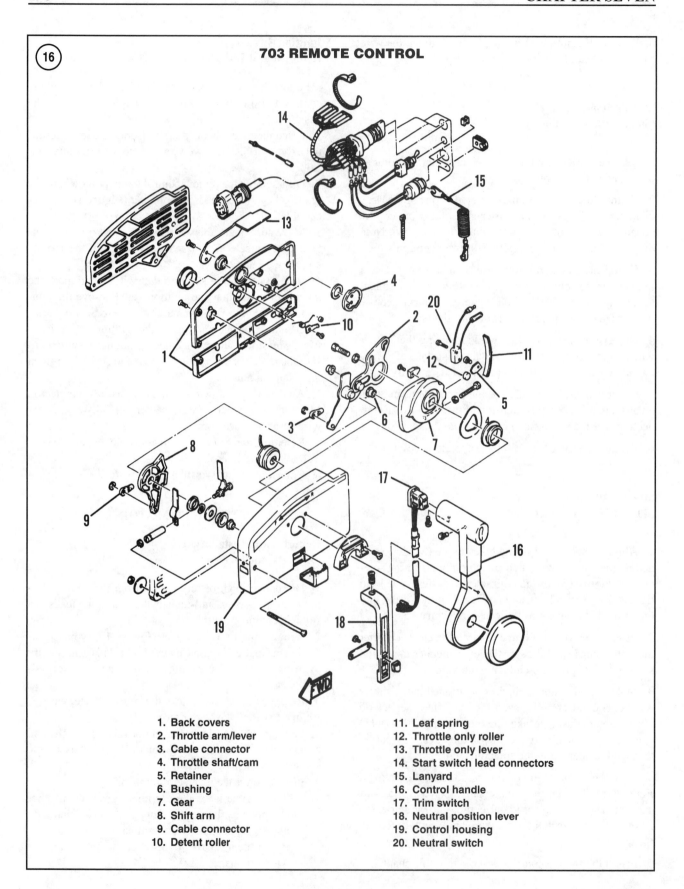

703 REMOTE CONTROL

1. Back covers
2. Throttle arm/lever
3. Cable connector
4. Throttle shaft/cam
5. Retainer
6. Bushing
7. Gear
8. Shift arm
9. Cable connector
10. Detent roller
11. Leaf spring
12. Throttle only roller
13. Throttle only lever
14. Start switch lead connectors
15. Lanyard
16. Control handle
17. Trim switch
18. Neutral position lever
19. Control housing
20. Neutral switch

(17)

Bolt

Flywheel cover

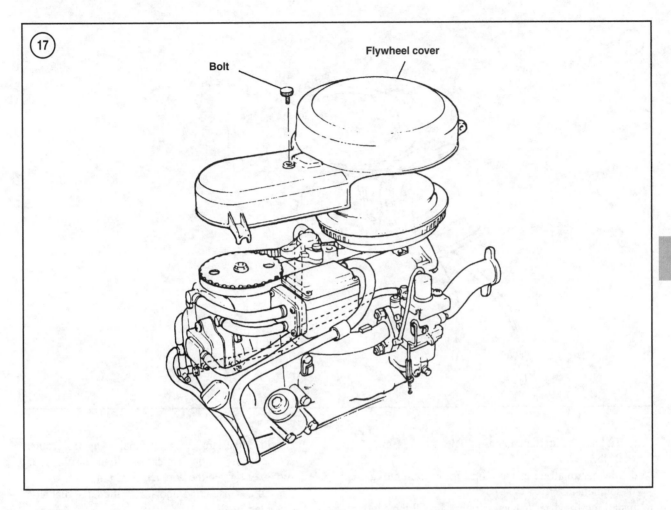

7

(18)

3

STARTER MOTOR (9.9 HP)

1. Positive lead
2. Starter motor
3. Mounting bolts

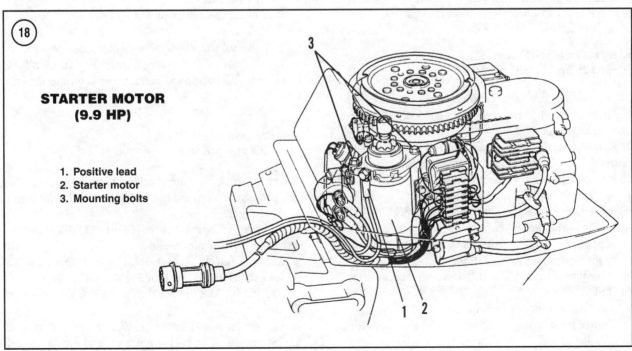

1 2

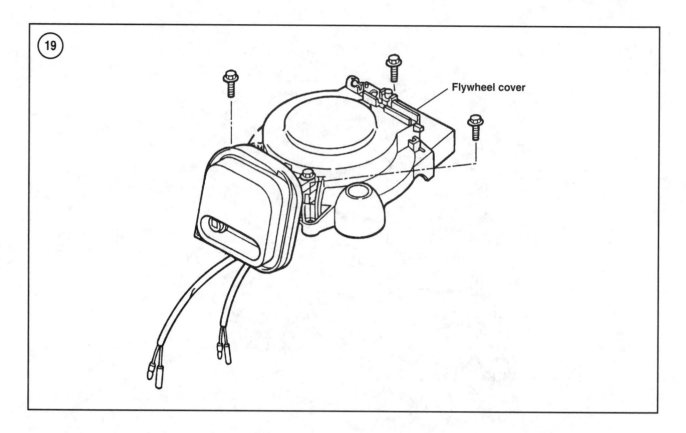

c. Tighten the starter mounting bolts to 32 N•m (23 ft.-lb.).

d. Make sure all wires are routed away from moving components.

6. Install the flywheel (Chapter Eight). Install the spark plug and leads. Connect the cables to the battery.

**Removal and Installation
(15 and 25 hp Models)**

1. Disconnect both battery cables from the battery. Remove the spark plugs and connect the spark plug leads to a suitable engine ground.

2. Remove the flywheel cover (**Figure 19**) following the instructions in Chapter Eight. This is necessary to ensure all starter mounting bolts and nuts are accessible.

3. Slip the insulating boot (**Figure 20**) from the wire terminal then remove the terminal nut. Disconnect the large wire from the starter motor.

4. Support the electric starter motor (**Figure 20**) and remove three mounting bolts. Lift the electric starter motor from the power head. Clean the starter mounting surface and bolt holes.

5. Installation is the reverse of removal.

a. Attach the large ground wire to the front mounting bolt.

b. Position the large wire terminal away from other components. To prevent damage to the insulator, do not over tighten the wire terminal nut.

c. Install the insulating boots over the large diameter wire terminals.

d. Tighten the starter mounting bolts to 32 N•m (23 ft.-lb.).

e. Route all wires away from moving components.

6. Install the flywheel cover (Chapter Eight). Install the spark plugs and leads and connect the cables to the battery.

**Removal and Installation
(40 and 50 hp Models)**

1. Disconnect both battery cables from the battery. Remove the spark plugs and connect the spark plug leads to a suitable engine ground.

2. Remove the flywheel cover (**Figure 21**) following the instructions in Chapter Eight.

3. Locate the electric starter motor on the front side of the power head (**Figure 22**). Remove the nut (5, **Figure 23**) and washer (4), and remove the cable (3) from the starter motor.

4. Support the starter motor (2, **Figure 23**), and remove the two mounting bolts (1) from the top of the starter and

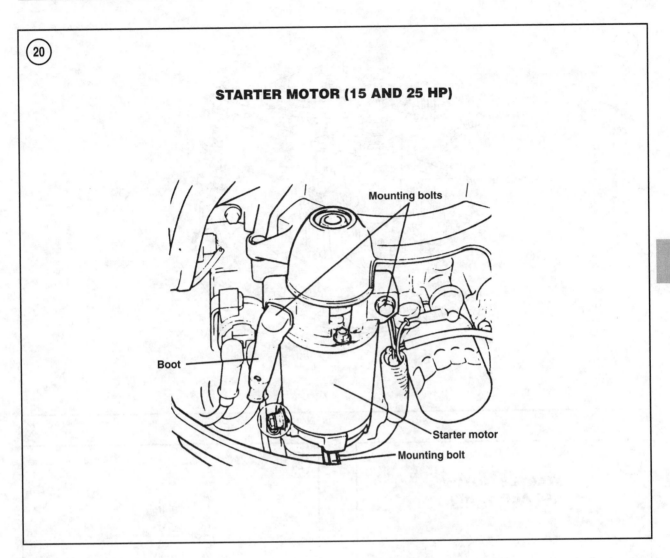

(20)

STARTER MOTOR (15 AND 25 HP)

Mounting bolts

Boot

Starter motor

Mounting bolt

7

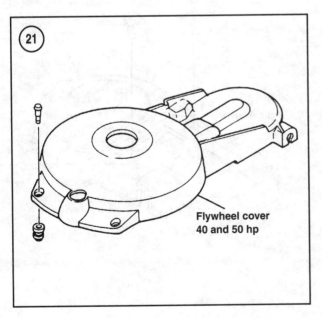

(21)

Flywheel cover
40 and 50 hp

one bolt (6) from the bottom of starter. Lift the electric starter from the power head.

5. Installation is the reverse of removal.

    a. Position the positive cable away from other components. To prevent damage to the insulator, do not over tighten the terminal nut.

    b. Tighten the starter mounting bolts to 30 N•m (22 ft.-lb.).

    c. Route all wires away from moving components.

6. Install the spark plugs and leads, and connect the cables to the battery.

**Removal and Installation
(80 and 100 hp Models)**

1. Disconnect both battery cables from the battery. Remove the spark plugs and connect the spark plug leads to a suitable engine ground.

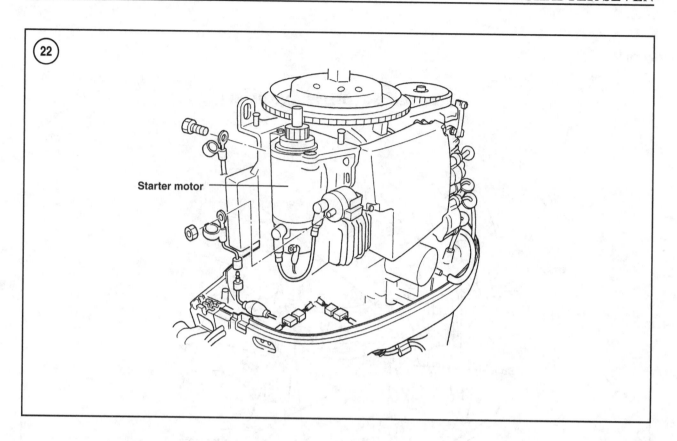

Starter motor

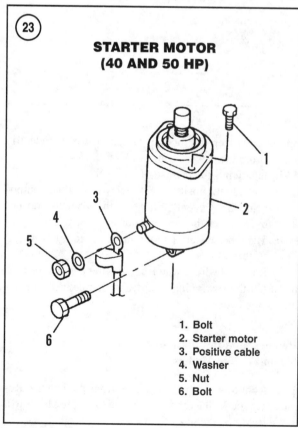

**STARTER MOTOR
(40 AND 50 HP)**

1. Bolt
2. Starter motor
3. Positive cable
4. Washer
5. Nut
6. Bolt

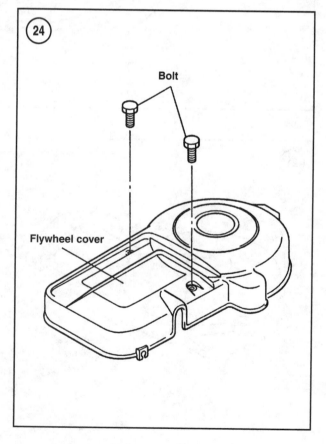

Bolt

Flywheel cover

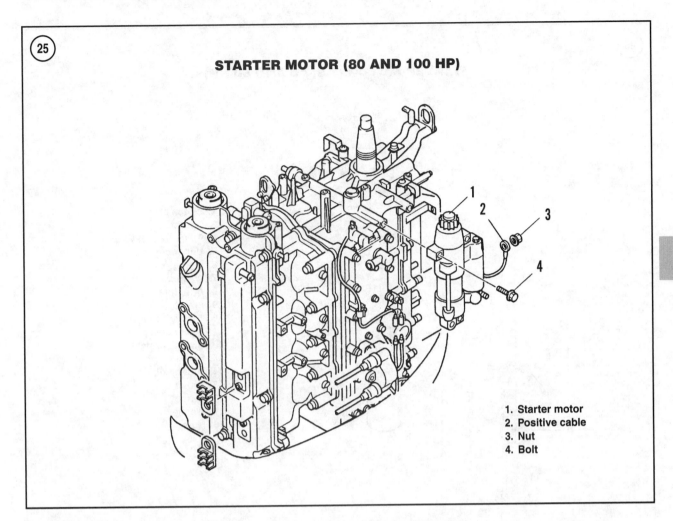

(25)

STARTER MOTOR (80 AND 100 HP)

1. Starter motor
2. Positive cable
3. Nut
4. Bolt

7

2. Remove the flywheel cover (**Figure 24**) following the instructions in Chapter Eight.

3. Slip the insulating boot from the wire terminal and re-move the terminal nut (3, **Figure 25**) and remove the large wire terminal (2) from the starter motor (1).

4. Support the electric starter motor, and remove the three mounting bolts (4, **Figure 25**). Lift the electric starter mo-tor from the power head. Clean the electric starter mount-ing surface and bolt holes.

5. Installation is the reverse of removal.

   a. Connect the large ground wire to the front mounting bolt.

   b. Position the large wire other components. To pre-vent damage to the insulator, do not over tighten the wire terminal nut.

   c. Tighten the starter mounting bolts to 30 N•m (22 ft.-lb.).

   d. Route all wires away from moving components.

6. Install the spark plugs and leads and connect the cables to the battery.

Starter Motor Disassembly and Assembly

9.9, 40 and 50 hp models

Refer to **Figure 26** during this procedure.

1. Note the match marks on the starter frame and covers (**Figure 27**). Use the marks during assembly to correctly position the components.

2. Secure the starter motor in a vice with soft jaws. Do not overtighten the vice.

3. Push the pinion stopper (2, **Figure 26**) toward the starter pinion (4) to expose the locking clip (1). Use a screwdriver to carefully pry the locking clip (1) from the armature shaft. Pull the pinion stopper and spring (2 and 3, **Figure 26**) from the armature shaft. Rotate the starter pinion counterclockwise and remove it from the armature shaft.

4. Remove both throughbolts (10, **Figure 26**), then tap the lower cover (11) from the frame (9). Pull the lower cover and O-ring (11 and 16, **Figure 26**) from the starter.

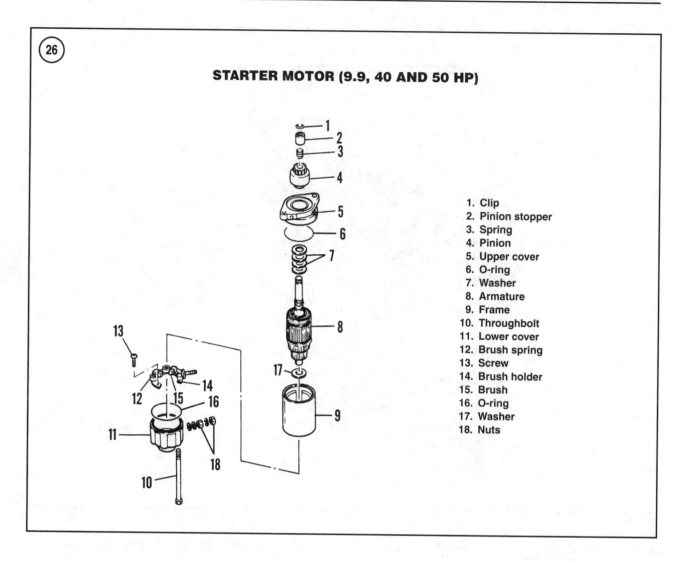

STARTER MOTOR (9.9, 40 AND 50 HP)

1. Clip
2. Pinion stopper
3. Spring
4. Pinion
5. Upper cover
6. O-ring
7. Washer
8. Armature
9. Frame
10. Throughbolt
11. Lower cover
12. Brush spring
13. Screw
14. Brush holder
15. Brush
16. O-ring
17. Washer
18. Nuts

Pull the washer (17, **Figure 26**) from the rear (lower) cover or armature shaft.

5. Tap on the lower end of the armature shaft, not the commutator surface, with a plastic mallet to free the upper cover (5, **Figure 26**) from the frame (9).

6. Pull the upper cover (5, **Figure 26**), O-ring (6) and washers (7, 18 and 19) from the frame assembly (9). Pull the armature (8, **Figure 26**) from the frame assembly.

7. Remove the terminal nuts (A, **Figure 26**) and all insulating washers from the terminal.

8. Remove the screws (13, **Figure 26**) and lift the brush plate (14) from the lower cover (11).

9. Clean the upper cover, lower cover, armature and frame assembly using a quick drying solvent such as Brake Kleen or denatured alcohol.

10. Inspect all components for worn, damaged or shorted components following the instructions under *Inspection* in this chapter.

11. Place the brush plate (14, **Figure 26**) into the lower cover (11) with the terminal inserted through its opening. Install the screws (13, **Figure 26**) through the brush plate (14). Securely tighten the screws.

12. Place the insulating washers onto the terminal and install the terminal nut (A, **Figure 26**). To prevent damage to the insulating washers, do not over tighten the nut.

13. Place the washers (7, 18 and 19, **Figure 26**) over the upper end of the armature shaft (8). Apply a light coat of water-resistant grease to the bearing surface in the upper cover (5, **Figure 26**). Slide the armature into the upper cover. Place a new O-ring (6, **Figure 26**) onto the step on the upper cover (5).

14. Slide the frame assembly (9, **Figure 26**) over the armature (8) and mate the frame assembly with the upper cover (5).

15. Apply a drop or two of engine oil to the bushing in the lower cover. Do not allow any oil to contact the brushes or commutator.

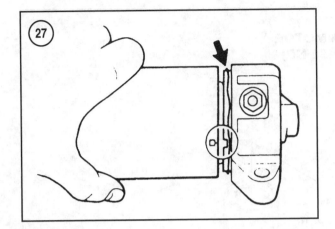

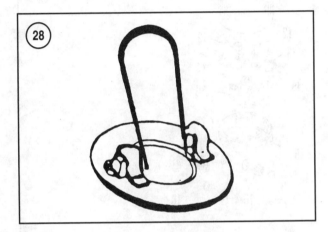

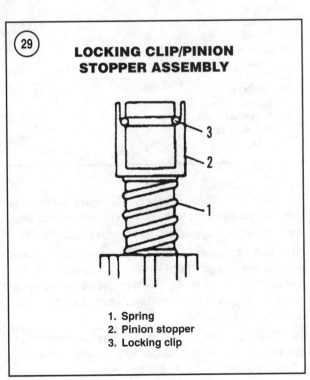

LOCKING CLIP/PINION STOPPER ASSEMBLY

1. Spring
2. Pinion stopper
3. Locking clip

16. Make sure both brushes and springs are placed in their openings in the brush plate. Fashion a brush holder from a bent piece of stiff wire (**Figure 28**). Place the ends of the wire in contact with the brushes as shown.

17. Place the washer (17, **Figure 26**) over the lower armature shaft. Install a new O-ring (16, **Figure 26**) onto its step in the lower cover. Carefully position the lower cover onto the frame assembly. Make sure the brushes do not hang on the commutator. After the armature shaft enters the bushing in the lower cover, pull the brush holder from the lower cover.

18. Align the match marks (**Figure 27**). Make sure both O-rings (6 and 16, **Figure 26**) remain in position, then install both throughbolts (10). Tighten the bolts to 8 N•m (70 in.-lb.).

19. Apply a light coat of water-resistant grease to the armature shaft, then thread the starter pinion onto the armature shaft. Place the spring and pinion stopper (3 and 2, **Figure 26**) over the armature shaft as indicated.

20. Push the pinion stopper toward the starter and position the locking clip (1, **Figure 26**) into the armature shaft groove. Release the pinion stopper and inspect the locking clip. The clip must be positioned in the groove with the pinion stopper fully over the clip as indicated in **Figure 29**. Use pliers to reshape the locking clip if it was distorted during installation.

15 and 25 hp models

Refer to **Figure 30** during this procedure.

1. Note the match marks on the starter frame and covers. During assembly, use the marks to correctly position the components.

2. Secure the starter motor in a vice with soft jaws. Do not overtighten the vice.

3. Remove the cap (1, **Figure 30**) and push the pinion stopper toward the starter pinion to expose the locking clip. Carefully pry the locking clip (2) from the armature shaft. Pull the pinion stopper and spring (3 and 4, **Figure 30**) from the armature shaft. Rotate the starter pinion counterclockwise to remove it from the armature shaft.

4. Remove both throughbolts (8, **Figure 30**), then tap the lower cover (15) from the frame (11).

5. Tap on the lower end of the armature shaft, not the commutator surface with a plastic mallet to free the front upper cover (9, **Figure 30**) from the frame (11).

6. Pull the upper cover (9, **Figure 30**) and washer (7) from the frame assembly (11). Pull the armature (10, **Figure 30**) from the frame assembly.

7. Remove the terminal nuts (16, **Figure 30**) and insulating washers (17) from the terminal.

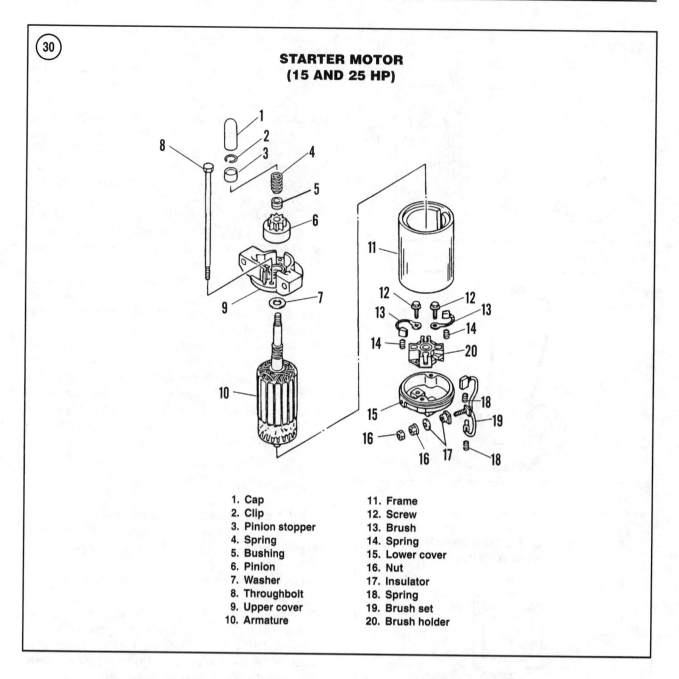

**STARTER MOTOR
(15 AND 25 HP)**

1. Cap
2. Clip
3. Pinion stopper
4. Spring
5. Bushing
6. Pinion
7. Washer
8. Throughbolt
9. Upper cover
10. Armature
11. Frame
12. Screw
13. Brush
14. Spring
15. Lower cover
16. Nut
17. Insulator
18. Spring
19. Brush set
20. Brush holder

8. Remove the screws (12, **Figure 30**) and brush plate (20) from the lower cover (15).

9. Clean the upper cover, lower cover, and armature and frame assembly using a quick drying solvent such as Brake Kleen or denatured alcohol.

10. Inspect all components following the instructions under *Inspection* in this chapter.

11. Place the brush plate (20, **Figure 30**) into the lower cover (15) with the terminal inserted through its opening. Install the screws (12, **Figure 30**) through the brush plate (20). Securely tighten the screws.

12. Place the insulating washers (17, **Figure 30**) onto the terminal and install the terminal nut (16). To prevent damage to the insulating washers, do not over tighten the nut.

13. Place the washer (7, **Figure 30**) over the upper end of the armature shaft (10). Apply a light coat of water-resistant grease to the bearing surface in the upper cover (9, **Figure 30**). Slide the armature into the upper cover.

14. Slide the frame assembly (11, **Figure 30**) over the armature (10) and mate the frame with the upper cover (9). Align the marks on the frame and cover.

15. Apply a drop or two of engine oil to the bushing the lower cover. Do not allow any oil to contact the brushes or commutator.

16. Make sure both brushes and springs are placed in their openings in the brush plate. Carefully position the lower cover onto the frame assembly. Make sure the brushes do not hang on the commutator. After the armature shaft enters the bushing in the lower cover, rotate the armature to make sure the brushes are in the correct position in the lower cover.

17. Align the match marks on the frame and cover. Install both throughbolts (8). Tighten the bolts to 8 N•m (70 in.-lb.).

18. Apply a light coat of water-resistant grease to the armature shaft and thread the starter pinion onto the armature shaft. Place the spring and pinion stopper (4 and 3, **Figure 30**) over the armature shaft as indicated.

19. Push the pinion stopper toward the starter and position the locking clip (2, **Figure 30**) into the armature shaft groove. Release the pinion stopper and inspect the locking clip. The clip must be positioned in the groove with the pinion stopper fully over the clip as indicated in **Figure 30**. Use pliers to reshape the locking clip if it was distorted during installation.

80 and 100 hp models

Refer to **Figure 31** during this procedure.

1. Remove the starter solenoid (12, **Figure 31**) as described in this chapter.

2. Note the match marks on the starter frame and covers (**Figure 32**). If the marks are not visible, make the marks now to ensure correct assembly.

3. Secure the electric starter motor in a vice with soft jaws. Do not overtighten the vice. Pry the starter pinion gear (3, **Figure 31**) downward. Tap the edge of the pinion stopper (2, **Figure 31**) down with a small hammer until the locking clip (1) is exposed. Carefully pry the locking clip from the pinion stopper.

4. Rotate the starter pinion counterclockwise to remove it from the clutch shaft (20, **Figure 31**). Pull the spring (4, **Figure 31**) from the shaft.

5. Remove both screws (32, **Figure 31**) from the lower cover (30). Remove both throughbolts (32, **Figure 31**), then carefully tap the lower cover (30) off the frame (25).

6. Use a small punch to tap, from the slotted side, the plate (28, **Figure 31**) from its groove on the lower end of the armature (24). Pull the brush holder plate (27, **Figure 31**) from the commutator portion of the armature (24). Remove the brush assembly (26) from the brush holder.

7. Pull the yoke and armature (25 and 24, **Figure 31**) from the starter housing (6). Mark the armature side, then remove the center bracket plate (23, **Figure 31**) from the

yoke (25). Remove the outer ring gear (14, **Figure 31**) and pull the planetary gear (15) from the pinion shaft (16).

8. Remove the pinion shaft from the clutch assembly (20, **Figure 31**) by carefully prying the E-clip (19, **Figure 31**) from the pinion shaft (16). Lift the washer and cover (18 and 17, **Figure 31**) from the pinion shaft. Remove the bearing (22, **Figure 31**) from the clutch assembly (20).

9. Clean all components using a mild solvent. Dry all components with compressed air.

10. Inspect all parts following the instructions under *Inspection* in this chapter.

11. Lubricate the entire pinion shaft (16, **Figure 31**) with a light coat of water-resistant grease.

12. Reverse Steps 1-8 to assemble the motor.

13. Make sure all bushes and springs are in position before installing the brush plate (26, **Figure 31**). Hold the brushes fully retracted into their opening in the brush plate holder and slide the brush plate over the commutator end of the armature (24, **Figure 31**). Release the brushes only after the brush plate is in position.

Starter Motor Inspection

1. Inspect the pinion for chipped, cracked or worn teeth (**Figure 33**). Replace the pinion if any of these conditions are noted. Inspect the helical splines at the pinion end of the armature. Replace the armature if corroded, damaged or worn.

2. Repeatedly thread the pinion drive onto and off of the armature shaft. Replace the pinion drive and/or armature if the pinion drive will not turn smoothly on the shaft.

3. Carefully secure the armature in a vise with soft jaws. Tighten the vise only enough to secure the armature. Carefully polish the commutator (**Figure 34**) using 600 grit carburundum cloth. Polish the area only enough to clean the commutator. Rotate the armature to polish the commutator evenly.

4. Connect the negative ohmmeter lead to one of the commutator segments and the positive test lead to the laminated section of the armature (**Figure 35**). The correct reading is no continuity.

5. Connect the negative ohmmeter lead to one of the commutator segments and the positive meter lead to the armature shaft (**Figure 35**). The correct reading is no continuity.

6. Connect the negative ohmmeter lead to one of the commutator segments and the positive lead to each of the remaining commutator segments (**Figure 36**). Note the meter reading for each contact. The correct readings are continuity. Replace the armature if any incorrect meter readings are noted.

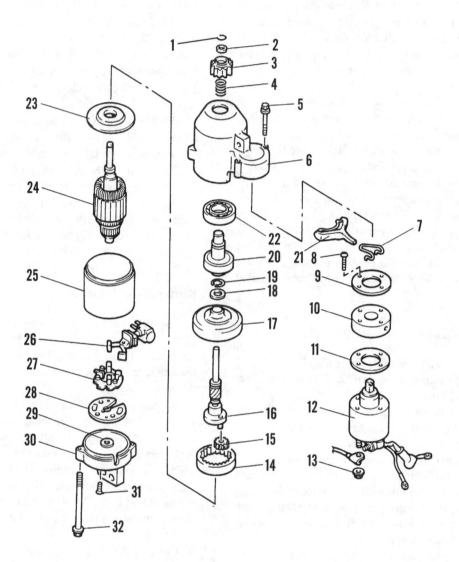

STARTER MOTOR (80 AND 100 HP)

1. Clip
2. Pinion stopper
3. Pinion gear
4. Spring
5. Bolt
6. Upper cover
7. Spring
8. Screw
9. Dust seal
10. Dust seal cover
11. Dust seal
12. Solenoid
13. Nut
14. Outer ring gear
15. Planetary gear
16. Pinion shaft
17. Center bracket
18. Thrust washer
19. E-ring
20. Clutch assembly
21. Lever
22. Bearing
23. Center bracket plate
24. Armature
25. Frame
26. Brushes
27. Brush holder
28. Plate
29. Thrust washer
30. Lower cover
31. Screw
32. Throughbolt

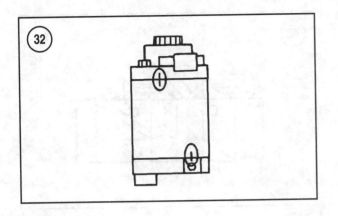

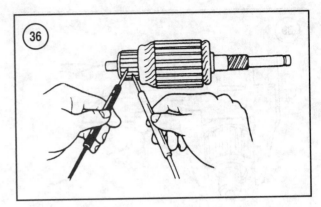

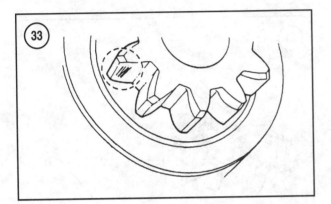

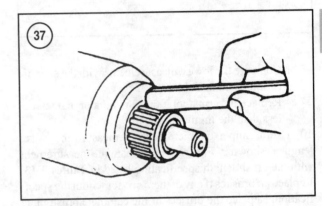

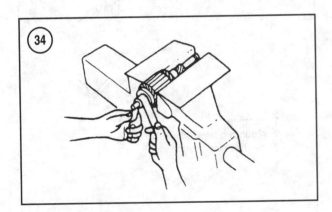

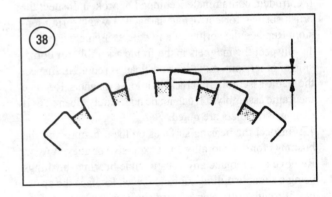

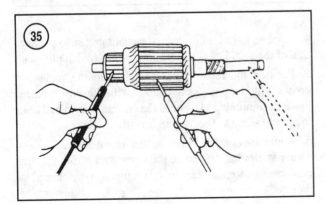

7. Use a small file (**Figure 37**) to remove the metal and mica particles from the undercut area between the commutator contacts.

8. Blow away particles with compressed air and use a depth micrometer to measure the depth of the undercut (**Figure 38**). Compare the measurement with the specification listed in **Tables 9-13**. Replace the armature if the undercut is less than the minimum depth specification.

9. Perform this step on 9.9 hp, 40 and 50 hp, 80 and 100 hp models only.

a. Measure the diameter of the armature (**Figure 39**) at several locations along the length of the commutator.

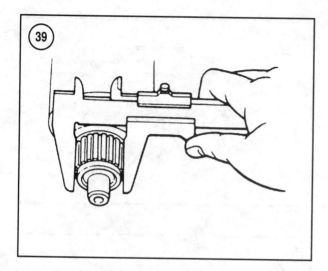

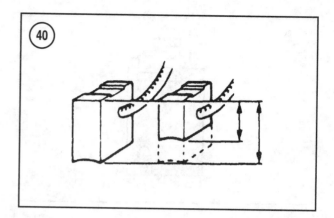

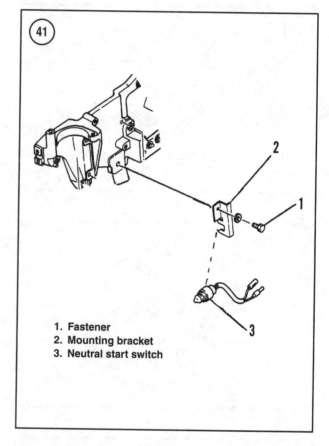

1. Fastener
2. Mounting bracket
3. Neutral start switch

b. Compare the lowest measurements with the specification listed in **Tables 9-13**.

c. Replace the armature if the commutator diameter is less than the minimum specification.

10. Use a caliper or micrometer to measure the brush length as shown in **Figure 40**. Compare the measurement with the brush length specification listed in **Tables 9-13**. Replace all brushes if any of them are not within the specification. Replace the brushes or the complete brush plate if corroded, contaminated, chipped or broken. Inspect the brush springs for corrosion, damage or weak spring tension. Replace the springs if any defects are noted.

11. Inspect the magnets in the frame assembly for corrosion or other contamination and clean as required. Inspect the frame assembly for cracked or loose magnets. Replace the frame assembly if it cannot be adequately cleaned or if damaged magnets are noted.

12. Inspect the bearing surfaces on the armature and the bushings for discoloration, and excessive or uneven wear. Remove and replace any questionable bearings/bushings using a suitable pulling tool and driver. Replace the armature if rough or uneven bearing surfaces are present.

Neutral Start Switch
Removal and Installation

A neutral start switch (**Figure 41**) is utilized on all electric start tiller control models.

1. Disconnect both cables from the battery. Shift the engine into NEUTRAL.

2. Disconnect the neutral start switch (**Figure 41**) wires.

3. Remove both switch mounting screws, and remove the switch and mounting plate from the mounting boss. Clean the switch mounting surface and the cam portion of the shift linkage.

4. Apply a light coat of water-resistant grease to the portion of the shift linkage that contacts the switch plunger.

5. Position the replacement switch onto the mounting bosses with the plunger in contact with the shift linkage. Place the mounting plate onto the switch, then install both mounting screws. Securely tighten the screws.

6. Route the switch wires to the engine wire harness and/or starter button. Route the wires away from moving components. Retain the wires with plastic type clamps as required.

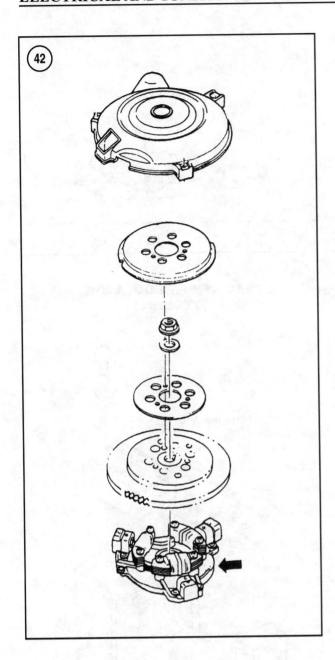

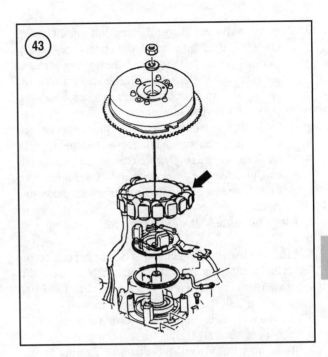

7

7. Connect the cables to the battery. Check for proper operation of the neutral start switch following the instructions in Chapter Three.

CHARGING SYSTEM

CAUTION
It may be necessary to use an impact driver to remove the battery charge/lighting and ignition charge coil mounting screws. Work carefully and avoid using excessive force. The cylinder block can be damaged if excessive force is used.

NOTE
The battery charge coil and ignition charge coil appear almost identical on some models. Use the wire colors and illustrations to identify the proper component.

Battery Charge/Lighting Coil
Removal and Installation

To access the battery charge or lighting coils, the recoil starter assembly must be removed on some models. Flywheel removal is required on all models. Refer to Chapter Eight for flywheel removal and installation. Before component removal, make a drawing or take a photograph of the wire routing. This will help ensure proper routing during assembly.

On 9.9 and 15 hp models, the battery charge/lighting coil is fastened to a mounting base alongside the ignition charge coils (**Figure 42**). Refer to the wiring diagrams located at the end of the manual to identify the wire colors for the battery charge/lighting coil. Note the size and location of any plastic tie clamps.

The battery/lighting coil and ignition charge coil are integrated into a single stator assembly on 25-100 hp models (**Figure 43**).

1. Disconnect both cables from the battery. Remove the spark plugs, then connect the spark plug leads to a suitable engine ground. Remove the recoil starter, if equipped, as instructed in Chapter Ten.
2. Remove the flywheel as described in Chapter Eight.

3. Remove the battery charge/lighting coil as follows:

   a. On 9.9 and 15 hp models, disconnect the battery charge/lighting coil wires from the lighting harness, rectifier or rectifier/regulator. Remove all four retaining screws, then lift the battery charge/lighting coils from the cylinder block.

   c. On 25-100 hp models, disconnect the battery charge coil from the harness leading to the rectifier regulator. Remove the single wire clamp located near the coil, then remove the mounting screws (**Figure 44**). Lift the battery charging coil from its mounting plate.

4. Clean the battery charge/lighting coil mounting surface.

5. Place the battery charge/lighting coil(s) in position on the cylinder block or mounting bracket. Make sure the wires are routed as noted prior to removal. On 80 and 100 hp models, install the single clamp over the coil harness. Secure the wire and clamp with the clamp screw.

6. Install and securely tighten the mounting screws.

7. Route the wires to the lighting harness, rectifier or rectifier/regulator. Route the wires away from moving components, especially the flywheel. Retain the wires with plastic type clamps as required.

8. Connect the coil wires to the lighting harness, rectifier or rectifier/regulator. Refer to the wiring diagrams located at the end of the manual.

9. Install the flywheel following the instructions in Chapter Eight.

10. Install the spark plugs and leads and connect the cables to the battery.

Rectifier or Rectifier/Regulator Removal and Installation

   Refer to **Figure 45**.

1. Disconnect both battery cables from the battery.

2. Use the wiring diagrams located at the back of the manual to identify the wire used for the rectifier/regulator.

3. Remove the retaining clamp after the rectifier/regulator mounting bolts are removed.

4. Disconnect the wires leading to the rectifier or rectifier/regulator. Remove the screw and ground wire from the mounting plate, if so equipped.

5. Remove the screw(s) that retain the rectifier or rectifier/regulator to the mounting plate. Carefully route the disconnected wires away from other components, and lift the rectifier or rectifier/regulator from the engine.

6. Clean all the mounting surfaces thoroughly.

7. Carefully route the rectifier or rectifier/regulator unit wires, and position the unit on the power head. Install the mounting screws and securely tighten. Make sure the

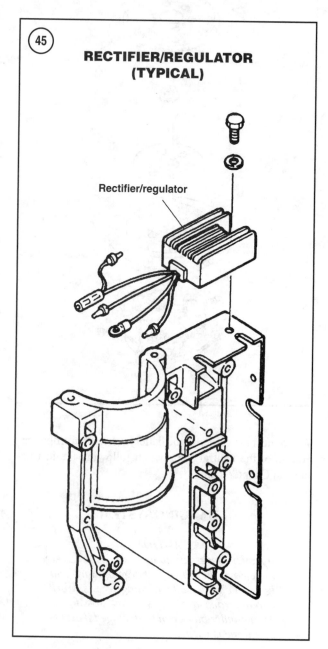

RECTIFIER/REGULATOR (TYPICAL)

Rectifier/regulator

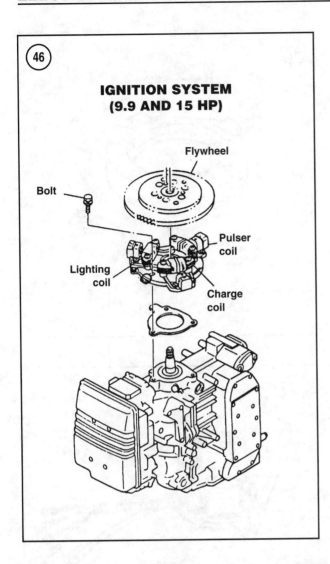

(46)

**IGNITION SYSTEM
(9.9 AND 15 HP)**

Flywheel

Bolt

Pulser coil

Lighting coil

Charge coil

7

ground wire terminal is positioned below the mounting plate screw, on models so equipped.

8. Connect all wire harness and/or battery charge/lighting coil wires to the rectifier or rectifier/regulator.

9. Install the spark plugs and spark plug leads and connect the cables to the battery. Check for proper charging and ignition system operation immediately after starting the engine.

IGNITION SYSTEM

Ignition Charge Coil
Removal and Installation

NOTE
The battery charge coil and ignition charge coil appear almost identical on some models. Use the wire colors and illustrations to identify the proper component.

9.9 hp (1985-1991) and 15 hp models

1. Disconnect both cables from the battery. Remove the spark plugs and connect the spark plug leads to a suitable engine ground.

2. Remove the flywheel following the instructions in Chapter Eight.

3. Refer to the wiring diagrams located at the end of the manual to identify the wire color used for the ignition charge coil (**Figure 46**).

4. Remove the screw from the clamp holding the wire bundle to access the wire connectors. Disconnect both ignition charge coil wires from the engine control unit harness.

5. Remove the mounting screws and ignition charge coil from the power head.

6. Clean the ignition charge coil mounting surface.

7. Place the ignition charging coil in position on the cylinder block or mounting bracket. Route the wires as noted prior to removal. Install and tighten the mounting screws to 18 N•m (13 ft.-lb.).

8. Connect the ignition charging coil wires to the engine control unit harness. Route the wires away from moving components, especially the flywheel. Bundle the wires together and retain them with a clamp and screw.

9. Install the flywheel (Chapter Eight).

10. Install the spark plugs and leads, and connect the cables to the battery.

9.9 hp (1992-1999) and 25-100 hp models

On these models, the ignition charge coil, battery charge/lighting and power source coil, if so equipped, are combined into a single component (**Figure 47**). Note the size and location of any plastic locking tie clamps, or metal clamp and screw, that must be removed and replace them during assembly.

1. Disconnect both cables from the battery. Remove the spark plugs and connect the spark plug leads to a suitable engine ground.

2. Remove the flywheel as described in Chapter Eight.

3. Refer to the wiring diagrams located at the end of the manual to identify the wires connected to the stator.

4. Note all wire routing and connection points, then disconnect all applicable wires from the CDI or engine control unit, rectifier/regulator and electrothermal valve.

5. Mark the alignment of the coil wire position relative to the power head on the power head. This is important to ensure correct wire routing and phasing of the ignition charging cycles.

6. Remove the mounting screws (**Figure 47**) and stator from the power head. Clean the stator coil mounting surface.

7. Place the stator in position on the power head. Align the stator with its mounting holes and position its wires as noted in Step 6. Apply Loctite 222 to the threads, then install the mounting screws (**Figure 47**). Evenly tighten the screws to 5 N•m (44 in.-lb.).

8. Route the wires away from moving components. Retain the wires with plastic clamps as required.

9. Install the flywheel (Chapter Eight).

10. Install the spark plugs and leads, and connect the cables to the battery.

Power Source Coil

The power source coil is integrated into the combination battery/ignition charge coil. Replace the entire component if any portion of the assembly fails. Refer to *Ignition Charge Coil* in this chapter for removal and installation.

Pulser Coil Removal and Installation

9.9 hp models

1. Disconnect both cables from the battery, if so equipped. Remove the spark plugs and connect the spark plug leads to a suitable engine ground.

2. On electric start models, remove the flywheel cover and flywheel following the instructions in Chapter Eight. On manual start models, remove the manual starter following the instructions in Chapter Ten.

3. Disconnect the white/red and black pulser coil wires from the CDI unit harness.

4. Remove both pulser coil mounting screws (**Figure 48**) and remove the pulser coil from the engine.

5. Clean the mounting base and screw holes.

6. Place the pulser coil onto the engine. Install both washers and screws, but do not tighten the screws at this time.

7. Connect the pulser coil wires to the CDI unit wire harness. Route all wires away from moving components, especially the flywheel. Retain the wires with plastic clamps as required.

8. On electric start models, install the flywheel and flywheel cover (Chapter Eight). On manual start models, install the manual starter (Chapter Ten).

9. Install the spark plugs and leads, and connect the cables to the battery, if so equipped.

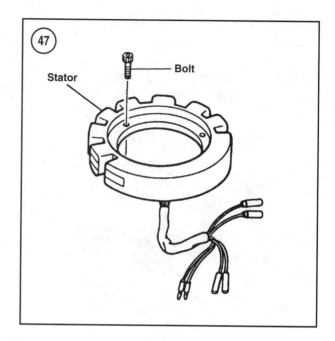

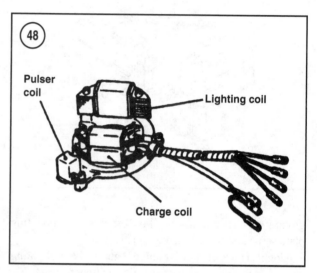

15 hp models

1. Disconnect both cables from the battery, if so equipped. Remove the spark plugs and connect the spark plug leads to a suitable engine ground.

2. On electric start models, remove the flywheel cover and flywheel following the instructions in Chapter Eight. On manual start models, remove the manual starter following the instructions in Chapter Ten.

3. Disconnect the white/red and black pulser coil wires from the CDI unit harness.

4. Remove mounting screws and the pulser coil (5, **Figure 49**) from the engine.

5. Clean the mounting base and screw holes.

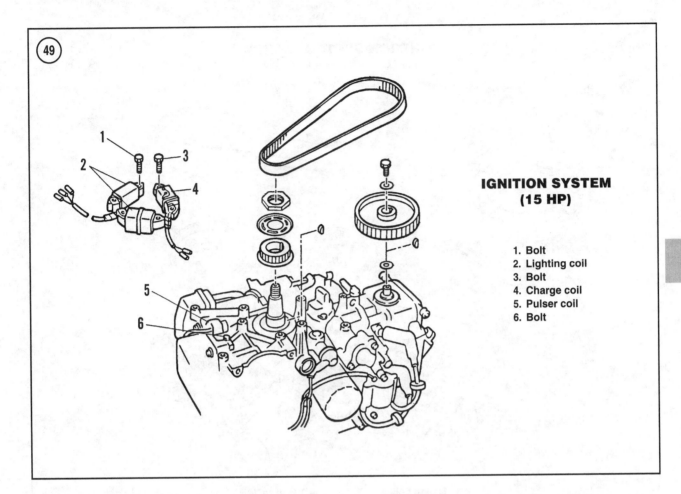

**IGNITION SYSTEM
(15 HP)**

1. Bolt
2. Lighting coil
3. Bolt
4. Charge coil
5. Pulser coil
6. Bolt

7

6. Place the pulser coil onto the engine. Install both washers and screws, but do not tighten the screws at this time.

7. Connect the pulser coil wires to the CDI unit wire harness. Route all wires away from moving components, especially the flywheel. Retain the wires with plastic clamps as required.

8. On electric start models, install the flywheel and flywheel cover (Chapter Eight). On manual start models, install the manual starter (Chapter Ten).

9. Install the spark plugs and leads, and connect the cables to the battery, if so equipped.

25 hp models

1. Disconnect both cables from the battery, if so equipped. Remove the spark plugs and connect the spark plug leads to a suitable engine ground.

2. On electric start models, remove the flywheel cover and flywheel following the instructions in Chapter Eight. On manual start models, remove the manual starter following the instructions in Chapter Ten.

3. Disconnect the white/red and black pulser coil wires from the CDI unit harness.

4. Remove the mounting screws and pulser coil (5, **Figure 50**) from the engine.

5. Clean the mounting base and screw holes.

6. Place the pulser coil onto the engine. Install both washers and screws, but do not tighten the screws at this time.

7. Connect the pulser coil wires to the CDI unit wire harness. Route all wires away from moving components, especially the flywheel. Retain the wires with plastic clamps as required.

8. On electric start models, install the flywheel and flywheel cover (Chapter Eight). On manual start models, install the manual starter (Chapter Ten).

9. Install the spark plugs and leads, and connect the cables to the battery, if so equipped.

40 and 50 hp models

The pulser coil (7, **Figure 51**) is mounted on the stator base (4, **Figure 51**) on the upper port side of the power head near the flywheel.

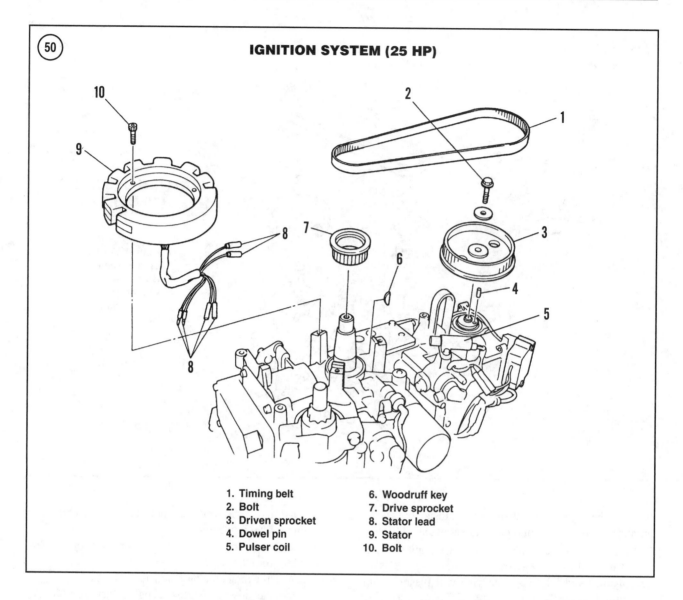

IGNITION SYSTEM (25 HP)

50

1. Timing belt	6. Woodruff key
2. Bolt	7. Drive sprocket
3. Driven sprocket	8. Stator lead
4. Dowel pin	9. Stator
5. Pulser coil	10. Bolt

1. Disconnect both cables from the battery, if so equipped. Remove the spark plugs and connect the spark plug leads to a suitable engine ground.

2. On electric start models, remove the flywheel cover and flywheel following the instructions in Chapter Eight. On manual start models, remove the manual starter following the instructions Chapter Ten.

3. Disconnect the pulser coil harness from the engine wire harness.

4. Remove both mounting bolts (8, **Figure 51**) and washers, then lift the pulser coil (7) from its mounting boss (4). Clean the pulser coil mounting boss and bolt holes.

5. Place the pulser coil onto its mounting boss (4). Install the washers and mounting bolts (8, **Figure 51**). Tighten the bolts to 4 N•m (36 in.-lb.).

6. Connect the pulser coil wire harness to its engine wire harness connector. Route all wires away from moving components, especially the flywheel. Retain the wires with plastic clamps or metal clamps as required.

7. On electric start models, install the flywheel and flywheel cover (Chapter Eight). On manual start models, install the manual starter (Chapter Ten).

8. Install the spark plugs and leads, and connect the cables to the battery.

Pickup Coil Removal and Installation (80 and 100 hp models)

1. Disconnect both cables from the battery. Remove the spark plugs and connect the spark plug leads to a suitable engine ground.

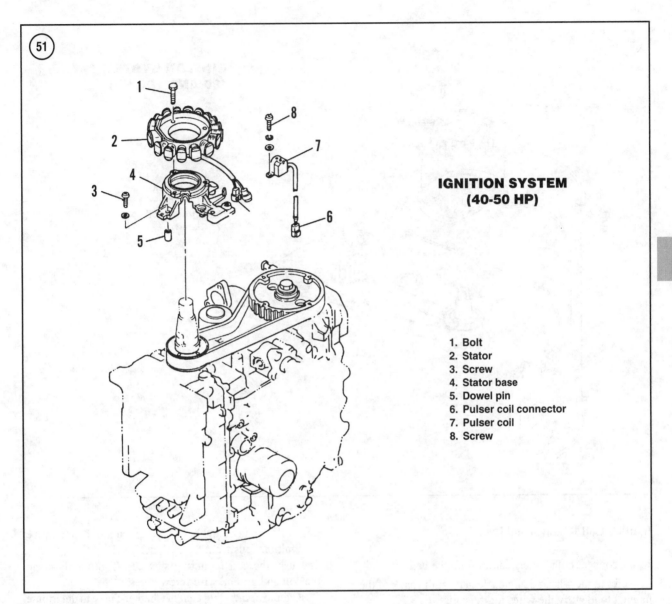

**IGNITION SYSTEM
(40-50 HP)**

1. Bolt
2. Stator
3. Screw
4. Stator base
5. Dowel pin
6. Pulser coil connector
7. Pulser coil
8. Screw

2. Remove the flywheel cover and flywheel following the instructions in Chapter Eight.

3. Remove the battery charge coil following the instructions provided in this chapter.

4. Disconnect the pulser coil harness from the engine wire harness. Remove the screw (8, **Figure 52**) and lift the clamp (7) from the stator base (4).

5. Mark the stator coil (2, **Figure 52**) relative to the power head. This is necessary to ensure correct wire routing and phasing of the coil after installation.

6. Remove the three bolts (1, **Figure 52**) and remove the stator assembly (2).

7. Remove the four screws (3, **Figure 52**) and remove the pickup coil (4) from the power head.

8. Make sure the pickup coil (4, **Figure 52**) is positioned correctly, then install bolts (3) and tighten them to 8 N•m (70 in.-lb.).

9. Position the mark on the stator (2, **Figure 52**) correctly and install the three bolts (1). Torque the bolts to 8 N•m (70 in.-lb.).

10. Install the clamp (7, **Figure 52**) and a screw (8).

11. Connect the harness connector (5, **Figure 52**) to the engine harness.

12. Route all wires away from moving components, especially the flywheel.

13. Install the flywheel and flywheel cover following the instructions in Chapter Eight.

14. Install the spark plugs and leads, and connect the cables to the battery.

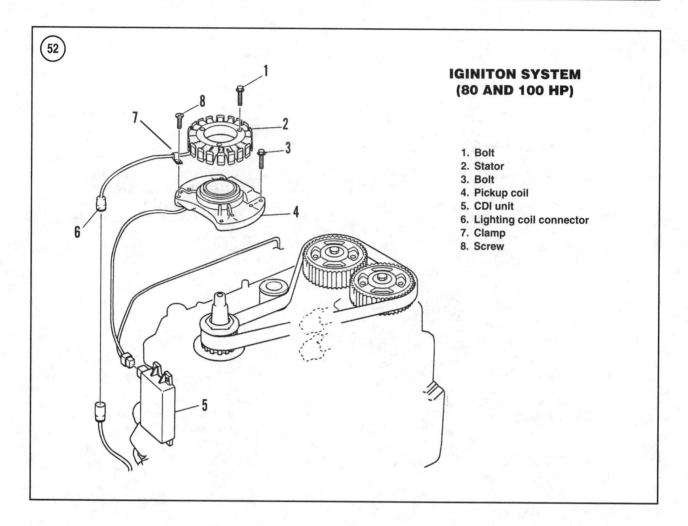

(52)

**IGINITON SYSTEM
(80 AND 100 HP)**

1. Bolt
2. Stator
3. Bolt
4. Pickup coil
5. CDI unit
6. Lighting coil connector
7. Clamp
8. Screw

Ignition Coil Removal and Installation

1. Disconnect both battery cables from the battery.

2. Refer to the wiring diagrams located at the back of the manual to identify the wires for the coil.

3A. On 9.9 and 15 hp models, cut the clamp from the wire bundle, then disconnect the coil wire terminals. Remove the mounting bolts and remove the coil (**Figure 53**) from the engine.

3B. On 25 hp models, disconnect the orange and black/white coil wires from the engine wire harness. Remove both mounting bolts (**Figure 54**) and lift the coil from the rocker arm cover.

3C. On 40 and 50 hp models, disconnect the coil primary wire (2, **Figure 55**) from the engine wire harness. Remove the mounting screw and the ground wire bolt (4, **Figure 55**) and remove the coil from the cylinder head.

3D. On 80 and 100 hp models, disconnect the primary wires (4, **Figure 56**) from the engine harness. Remove the bolt (3, **Figure 56**) securing the ground wires to the igni-

tion coils. Remove the bolts (2, **Figure 56**), then remove the ignition coils from the cylinder head.

4. Clean the coil mounting surfaces. Thoroughly clean the coil and ground wire screw holes.

5. Refer to *Spark Plug Cap* in Chapter Three to determine if cap or wire removal is required. Remove the cap or wire as described in Chapter Three.

6. Installation is the reverse of disassembly:
   a. Connect all coil ground wires to the common terminal or harness connection.
   b. Install the spark plug cap as described in Chapter Three.
   c. Tighten the ignition coil mounting bolts to 7 N•m (63 in.-lb.).
   d. Route all wires away from moving components. Retain the wires with plastic clamps or metal clamps as required.
   e. On 50-100 hp models, install all coil ground wires to the ground terminal. Securely tighten the ground screw.

7. Connect the cables to the battery, if so equipped.

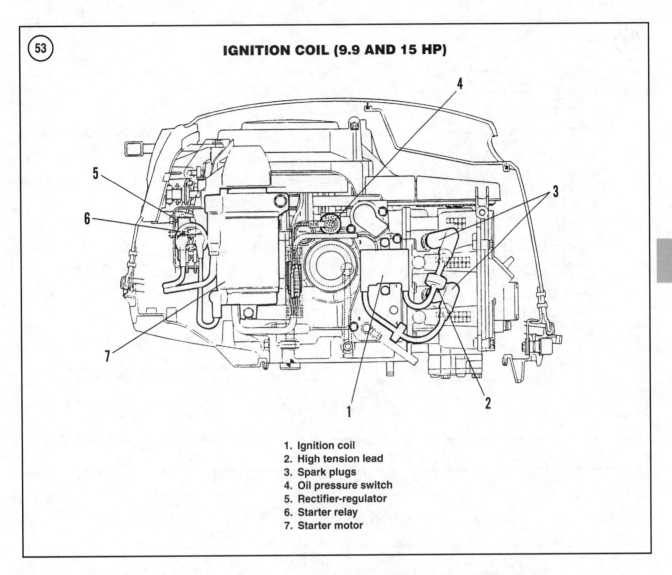

IGNITION COIL (9.9 AND 15 HP)

1. Ignition coil
2. High tension lead
3. Spark plugs
4. Oil pressure switch
5. Rectifier-regulator
6. Starter relay
7. Starter motor

7

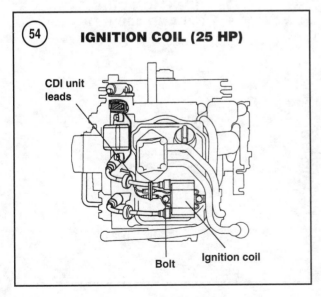

IGNITION COIL (25 HP)

CDI unit leads

Bolt

Ignition coil

CDI Unit Removal and Installation

1. Disconnect both cables from the battery, if so equipped.

2. Mark all wire attaching points and routing to ensure proper installation.

3A. On 9.9 hp models, the CDI is mounted above the ignition coil on the port side of the engine. Unplug all leads to the CDI and remove the bolts securing it to the block bracket. All leads are colored coded and have male or female connectors to help identify them.

3B. On 15 hp models, the CDI unit mounts on the back of the engine on the rocker arm cover. Release the two clamps and unplug all the leads from the CDI unit. Remove the bolt securing the ground wire to the CDI unit. Remove the four mounting bolts, then lift the engine control unit from its mounting plate.

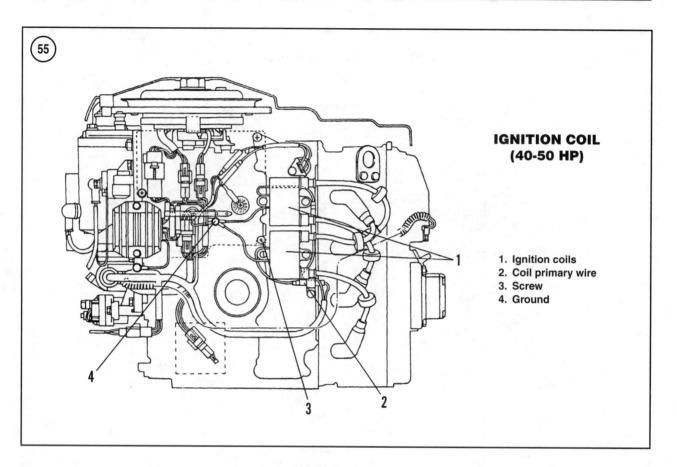

IGNITION COIL
(40-50 HP)

1. Ignition coils
2. Coil primary wire
3. Screw
4. Ground

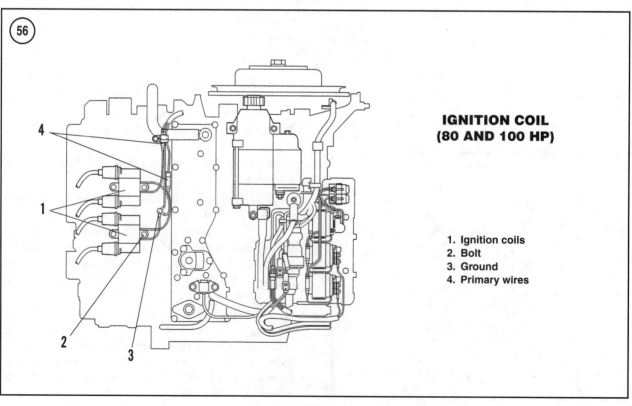

IGNITION COIL
(80 AND 100 HP)

1. Ignition coils
2. Bolt
3. Ground
4. Primary wires

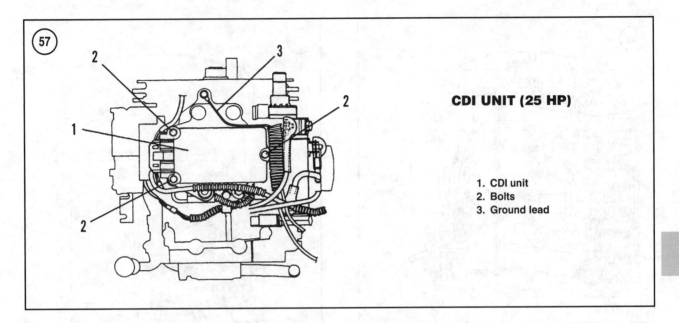

CDI UNIT (25 HP)

1. CDI unit
2. Bolts
3. Ground lead

7

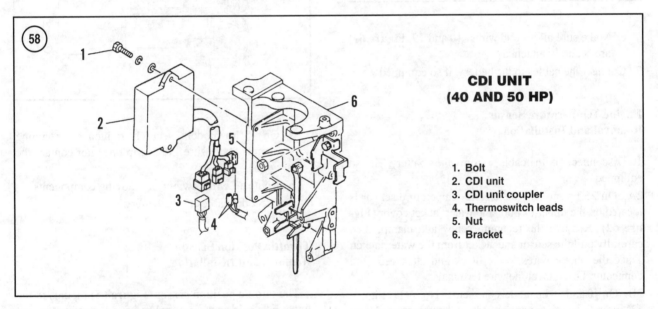

**CDI UNIT
(40 AND 50 HP)**

1. Bolt
2. CDI unit
3. CDI unit coupler
4. Thermoswitch leads
5. Nut
6. Bracket

3C. On 25 hp models, the CDI unit (1, **Figure 57**) mounts on the front of the engine. Remove the three bolts (2) securing the CDI unit. Remove the bolt (4, **Figure 57**) that secures the ground wire (3). Unplug all leads from CDI unit and remove the unit.

3D. On 40 and 50 hp models, the CDI unit (2, **Figure 58**) mounts on the starboard front (**Figure 59**) side of the power head. Unplug all leads (3 and 4, **Figure 58**) from the CDI (2), remove the two bolts (1) and remove the CDI unit.

3E. On 80 and 100 hp models, the CDI unit (**Figure 60**) mounts on the front starboard side of the power head. Remove the four mounting bolts (17, **Figure 61**), then pull the CDI unit (16) from behind the cover (6). Push in on the tabs and disconnect the harness connectors (12) from the control unit (16, **Figure 61**).

4. Inspect and clean all terminals the wire harness and CDI unit connectors.

5. Clean the CDI unit and the bolt holes.

6. Installation is the reverse of removal, noting the following:

    a. Tighten all mounting screws to 8 N•m (70 in.-lb.).

    b. Make sure all wire terminals and connectors are securely attached to the CDI, engine control unit and the wire harness.

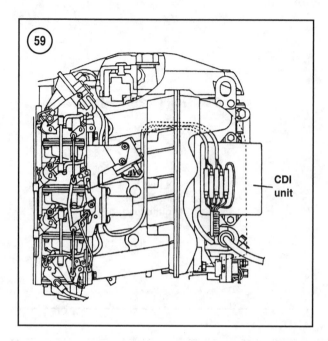

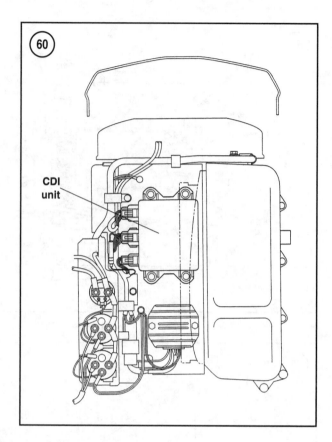

c. Make sure all ground wires (10 and 19, **Figure 61**) are securely attached.

7. Connect the cables to the battery, if so equipped.

Engine Temperature Sensor
Removal and Installation

1. Disconnect both cables from the battery, if so equipped.

2A. On 25 hp models, the engine temperature sensor is located on the upper or port side water jacket cover (**Figure 62**). Remove the retaining screw and clamp, then carefully pull the sensor and jacket from the water jacket. Trace the sensor wires to the black and tan/green wire connector. Disconnect the wire terminals.

2B. On 40 and 50 hp models, the sensor No. 1 (11, **Figure 63**) mounts on the upper port side of the power head next to the ignition coils and sensor No. 2 (1, **Figure 63**) mounts on the rocker arm cover. Disconnect the sensor wire from the engine wire harness connector. Remove the sensor from the block.

2C. On 80 and 100 hp models, the engine temperature sensor mounts (4, **Figure 64**) on the lower starboard side of the power head. Pinch the sides of the connector and pull it from the sensor. Remove both mounting bolts and pull the sensor (4, **Figure 64**) from its opening.

3. Clean the sensor opening using solvent. Dry the opening with compressed air.

4. Installation is the reverse of removal, noting the following:

a. On 25 hp models, securely tighten the retaining clamp. Make sure the clamp does not contact the wires.

b. Route all wires away from moving components.

5. Connect the cables to the battery.

Throttle Position Sensor
Removal and Installation

The throttle position sensor (**Figure 65**) mounts to the lower port side of the power head and is operated by the throttle linkage.

1. Disconnect both cables from the battery. Place the remote control in the idle position.

2. Disconnect the throttle position sensor from the engine wire harness. Cut the plastic clamp to free the throttle position sensor harness.

3. Remove the mounting screws (2, **Figure 65**). Carefully pull the throttle position sensor away from the coupler.

4. Position the replacement throttle position sensor in place with the wires facing toward the front of the engine (**Figure 65**). Rotate the throttle position sensor until the pin in its shaft aligns with the slot in the coupler.

⑥¹

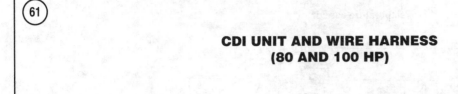

**CDI UNIT AND WIRE HARNESS
(80 AND 100 HP)**

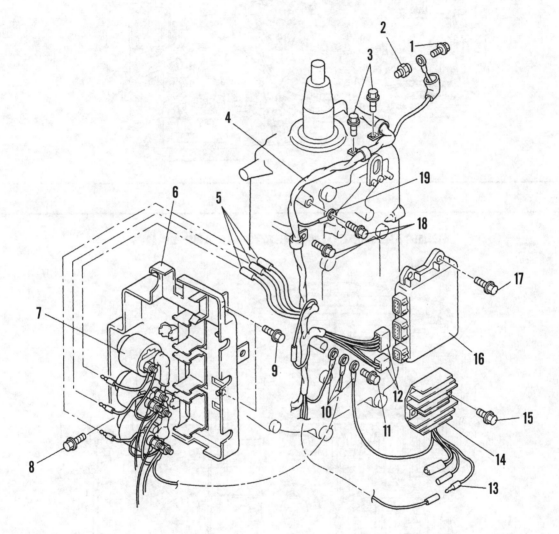

7

1. Bolt	11. Bolt
2. Oil pressure switch	12. CDI connectors
3. Bolts	13. Rectifier/regulator connector
4. Wire harness	14. Rectifier/regulator
5. Relay connectors	15. Bolt
6. Cover assembly	16. CDI unit
7. Relay	17. Bolt
8. Bolt	18. Bolt
9. Bolt	19. Ground lead
10. Ground leads	

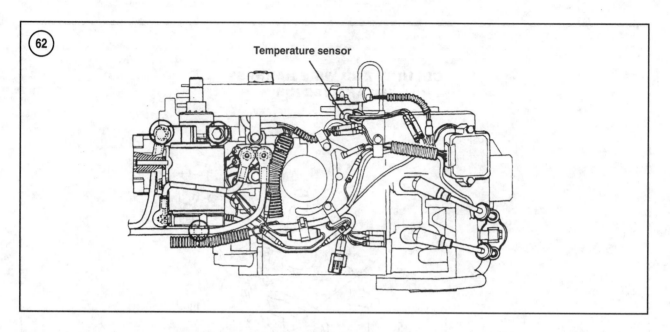

Temperature sensor

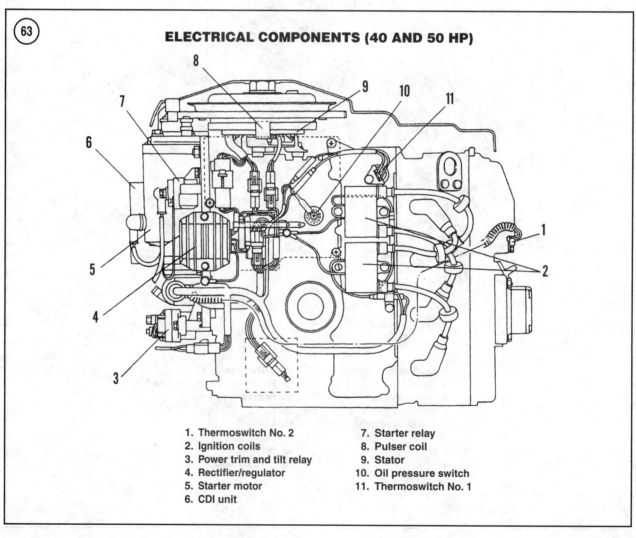

ELECTRICAL COMPONENTS (40 AND 50 HP)

1. Thermoswitch No. 2   7. Starter relay
2. Ignition coils   8. Pulser coil
3. Power trim and tilt relay 9. Stator
4. Rectifier/regulator   10. Oil pressure switch
5. Starter motor   11. Thermoswitch No. 1
6. CDI unit

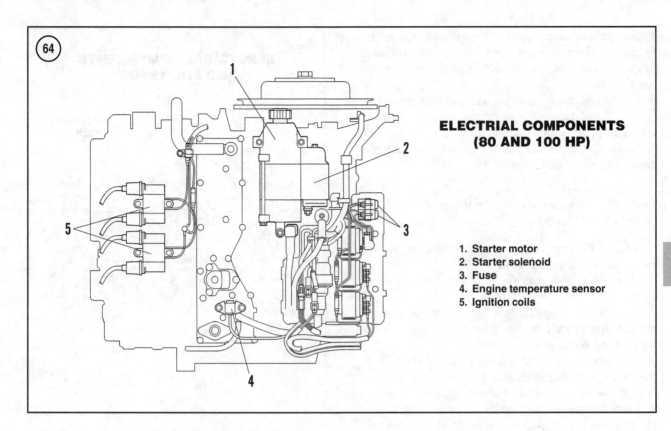

**ELECTRIAL COMPONENTS
(80 AND 100 HP)**

1. Starter motor
2. Starter solenoid
3. Fuse
4. Engine temperature sensor
5. Ignition coils

7

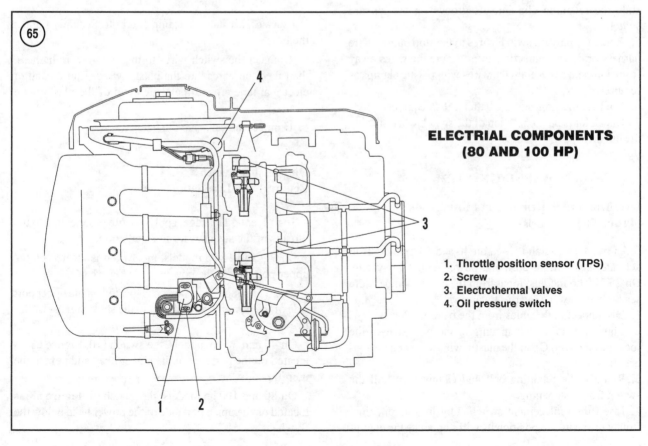

**ELECTRIAL COMPONENTS
(80 AND 100 HP)**

1. Throttle position sensor (TPS)
2. Screw
3. Electrothermal valves
4. Oil pressure switch

5. Install the mounting screws (2, **Figure 65**). Rotate the throttle position sensor clockwise until it reaches the limit of its adjusting slot, then securely tighten the mounting screws.

6. Connect the throttle position sensor to the engine wire harness. Route the wires away from moving components. Install the plastic clamp to retain the wire harnesses.

7. Connect the cables to the battery. Adjust the throttle position sensor as described in Chapter Five.

Lanyard Switch Removal and Installation (Tiller Control Models)

Refer to Chapter Twelve to remove and install the switch on remote control models.

1. Disconnect both cables from the battery, if so equipped.

2. Refer to the wiring diagrams located at the back of the manual, then identify the lanyard switch wires. Note the wire routing and disconnect the wires.

3. Carefully pry up on the retaining clip and slip it from the switch. Pull the switch from the lower engine cover. Wipe the switch opening in the lower engine cover clean.

4. Route the wire through the opening and install the replacement switch. Make sure the *run* mark faces up and slide the retaining clip into its groove on the lanyard switch.

5. Route the lanyard switch wires to the stop button, wire harness or other connection point. Route the wires away from components. Retain the wires with plastic clamps as required.

6. Connect the cables to the battery, if so equipped.

7. Check for proper operation of the switch when starting the engine.

WARNING SYSTEM

Overheat Switch Removal and Installation (40 and 50 hp Models)

An overheat switch is used on 40 and 50 hp models to activate the warning horn and power reduction system. On 25-100 hp models, input from the engine temperature sensor activates the overheat warning.

1. Disconnect both cables from the battery.

2. The overheat switch mounts to the port side of the rocker arm cover. Open the plastic wire wrap and disconnect both wires.

3. Remove the retaining bolt and clamp, then pull the switch from its opening.

4. Insert the replacement switch fully into its opening. Rotate the switch to position its wires opposite the clamp-

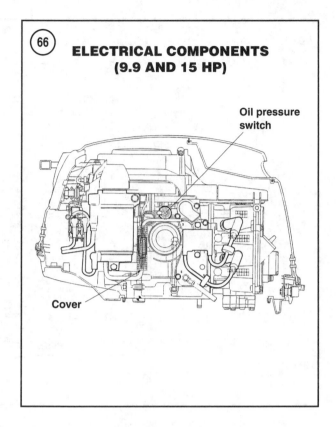

66 **ELECTRICAL COMPONENTS (9.9 AND 15 HP)**

Oil pressure switch

Cover

ing surfaces. Install the clamp and bolt. Securely tighten the bolt.

5. Connect the switch wires to the engine wire harness, then feed the wires into the plastic wrap. Run a band of electrical tape around the switch end of the plastic wire wrap.

6. Connect the cables to the battery.

Oil Pressure Switch Removal and Installation

To prevent oil leakage, apply Loctite pipe sealant to the threads of the switch prior to installation.

On 9.9 and 15 hp models, the switch is located on the upper port side of the power head (**Figure 66**).

On 25 hp models, the switch is located on the upper port side of the power head and next to the starter relay (1, **Figure 67**).

On 40 and 50 hp models, the switch (10, **Figure 63**) is located on the port side of the power head and next to the ignition coils.

On 80 and 100 hp models, the switch (4, **Figure 65**) is located on the upper port side of the power head below the flywheel.

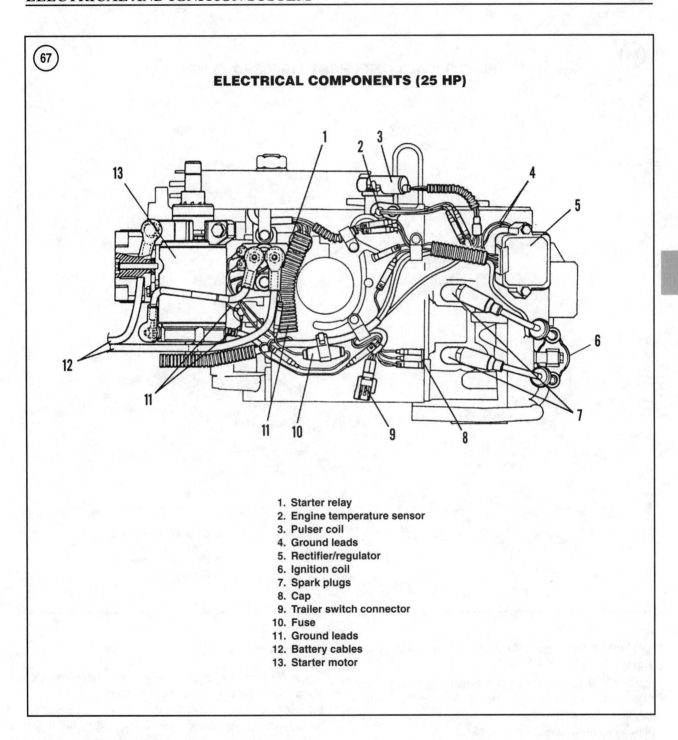

ELECTRICAL COMPONENTS (25 HP)

1. Starter relay
2. Engine temperature sensor
3. Pulser coil
4. Ground leads
5. Rectifier/regulator
6. Ignition coil
7. Spark plugs
8. Cap
9. Trailer switch connector
10. Fuse
11. Ground leads
12. Battery cables
13. Starter motor

1. Disconnect both cables from the battery, if so equipped.

2. On all models except 40 and 50 hp, carefully pull the protective boot from the oil pressure switch. Slide the boot down the switch wire.

3. On 40-50 hp models, pull the wire connector from the switch. On other models, remove the terminal nut and disconnect the wire from the wire terminal.

4. Use a deep socket to remove the oil pressure switch from the power head. Clean all remnants of sealant from the threads of the switch. Carefully wipe all remnants of sealant from the switch opening in the power head. Do not allow any particles into the opening.

5. Apply a light coat of Loctite pipe sealant to the upper 2/3 of the threads of the switch. Do not allow any sealant near the opening in the switch.

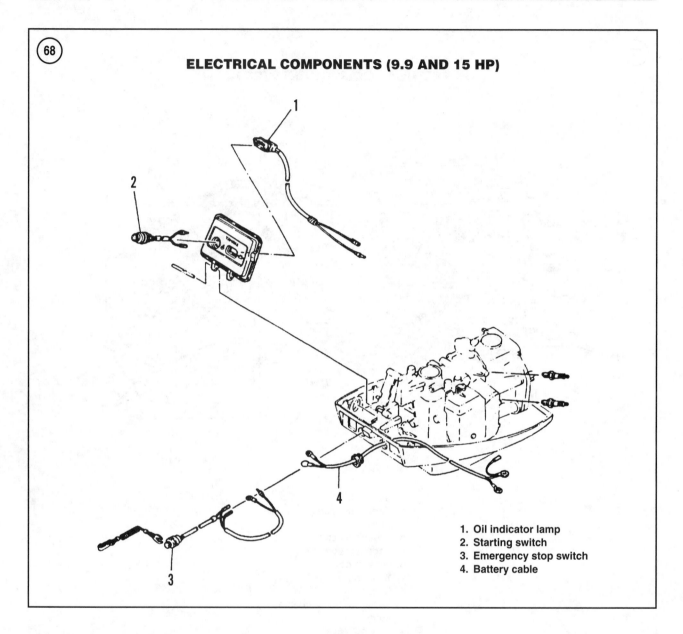

ELECTRICAL COMPONENTS (9.9 AND 15 HP)

1. Oil indicator lamp
2. Starting switch
3. Emergency stop switch
4. Battery cable

6. Thread the oil pressure switch into the power head. Tighten the switch to 8 N•m (70 in.-lb.).

7. On 40-50 hp models, push the switch wire onto the switch. The terminal must fit tightly. Remove the terminal, then squeeze it to tighten its fit. Secure the wire with plastic clamps to prevent it from loosening.

8. On other models, place the switch wire onto the switch. Install and securely tighten the terminal nut. Carefully slide the protective boot fully over the switch.

9. Route all wires away from moving components. Secure the wires with plastic clamps if required.

10. Connect the cables to the battery, if so equipped.

Oil Pressure Light

The oil pressure light (1, **Figure 68**) mounts to the lower engine cover or the manual starter bracket. Refer to the wiring diagrams located at the back of the manual to identify the colors of the wires connected to the light. Note the wire routing and disconnect the wires. Remove the retaining nut or clip, and pull the light from its opening. Wipe the opening clean, then install the replacement light. Install the retaining nut or clip. Securely tighten the nut. Connect the wires to the wire harness. Route all wires away from moving components. Retain the wires with plastic clamps if required.

Table 1 IGNITION SYSTEM SPECIFICATIONS (1985-1991 F9.9 AND T9.9)

Ignition timing	Not adjustable
Pulser coil resistance	173-211 ohms at 20° C (68° F)
Charge coil resistance	569-695 ohms at 20° C (68° F)
Ignition coil resistance	
Primary winding	0.085-0.115 ohm at 20° C (68° F)
Secondary winding	2890-3910 ohms at 20° C (68° F)
Lighting coil resistance	0.25-0.30 ohm at 20° C (68° F)
Spark plug type	CR6HS (NGK)
Spark plug gap	0.6-0.7 mm (0.024-0.028 in.)

Table 2 IGNITION SYSTEM SPECIFICATIONS (1992-1995 F9.9 AND T9.9)

Ignition idle timing	4-6° BTDC
Full throttle timing	34-36° BTDC
Charge coil resistance*	280-420 ohms (brown-blue)
Pulser coil resistance*	168-152 ohms (white/red-black)
Ignition coil resistance*	
Primary wire	0.074-0.110 ohm
Secondary wire	3280-4920 ohms)
Spark plug type	CR6HS (NGK)
Spark plug gap	0.6-0.7 mm (0.024-0.028 in.)

*At 20° C (68° F)

Table 3 IGNITION SYSTEM SPECIFICATIONS (1996-1997 F9.9 AND T9.9)

Timing (full retard)	2-8° BTDC
Timing (full advance)	32-38° BTDC
CDI voltage output	
Cranking speed	150 volts
1500 rpm	210 volts
Charge coil output	
Cranking speed	160 volts
1500 rpm	230 volts
Pulser coil output	
Cranking speed	7 volts
1500 rpm	10 volts
Spark plug type	CR6HS (NGK)
Spark plug gap	0.6-0.7 mm (0.024-0.028 in.)

Table 4 IGNITION SYSTEM SPECIFICATIONS (1998-1999 F9.9 AND T9.9)

Timing (full retard)	2-8° BTDC
Timing (full advance)	32-38° BTDC
CDI voltage output	
Cranking speed	90 volts
1500 rpm	205 volts
3500 rpm	195 volts
Charge coil output	
Cranking speed	150 volts
1500 rpm	220 volts
3500 rpm	210 volts
Pulser coil output	
Cranking speed	2.5 volts
1500 rpm	7.5 volts
3500 rpm	12.0 volts
Spark plug type	CR6HS (NGK)
Spark plug gap	0.6-0.7 mm (0.024-0.028 in.)

7

Table 5 IGNITION SYSTEM SPECIFICATIONS (F15)

Ignition timing	2-33° BTDC	
Charge coil output		
500 rpm	130 volts	Brown-blue
500 rpm	135 volts	
1500 rpm	180 volts	
3500 rpm	180 volts	
Pulser coil output		
500 rpm	4.0 volts	White/green-black
500 rpm	3.5 volts	
1500 rpm	11.0 volts	
3500 rpm	23.0 volts	
CDI unit output		
500 rpm	120 volts	Orange-black
500 rpm	115 volts	
1500 rpm	160 volts	
3500 rpm	160 volts	
Spark plug type	DPR6EA-9 (NGK)	
Spark plug gap	0.9 mm (0.04 in.)	

Table 6 IGNITION SYSTEM SPECIFICATIONS (F25)

Ignition timing	7-33° BTDC	
Charge coil output		
500 rpm	210 volts	Green/white-white/green
500 rpm	240 volts	
1500 rpm	210 volts	
3500 rpm	210 volts	
Pulser coil output		
500 rpm	90 volts	Red-white
500 rpm	90 volts	
1500 rpm	210 volts	
3500 rpm	240 volts	
CDI unit output		
500 rpm	180 volts	Black/white-orange
500 rpm	200 volts	
1500 rpm	190 volts	
3500 rpm	190 volts	
Charge coil resistance	660-710 ohms	
White/green-green/white		
Pulser coil resistance	300-350 ohms	
Ignition coil resistance		
Primary winding	0.08-0.70 ohm	
Secondary winding	3500-4700 ohms	
Spark plug type	DPR6EA-9 (NGK)	
Spark plug gap	0.9-1.0 mm (0.035-0.039 in.)	

Table 7 IGNITION SYSTEM SPECIFICATIONS (F40 AND F50)

Ignition firing order	No.1-3-4-2	
Ignition timing	5-35° BTDC	
Charge coil output		
400 rpm	140 volts	Brown-blue
1500 rpm	150 volts	
3500 rpm	135 volts	
Pulser coil output		
400 rpm	7.0 volts	White/black-white/red
1500 rpm	14.0 volts	
3500 rpm	20.0 volts	

(continued)

Table 7 IGNITION SYSTEM SPECIFICATIONS (F40 AND F50) (continued)

CDI output		
400 rpm	105 volts	Black/orange-black
Black/white-black		
1500 rpm	110 volts	
3500 rpm	100 volts	
Charge coil resistance*	272-408 ohms	Brown-blue
Pulser coil resistance*	340-510 ohms	White/black-white/red
Ignition coil resistance*		
Primary windings	0.078-0.106 ohm	
Secondary windings	3500-4700 ohms	
Spark plug type	DPR6EA-9 (NGK)	
Spark plug gap	0.9 mm (0.035 in.)	
*At 20° C (68° F)		

Table 8 IGNITION SYSTEM SPECIFICATIONS (F80 AND F100)

Ignition firing order	No.1-3-4-2	
Ignition timing	Full retard	5° ATDC
	Full advance	25° BTDC
Pick-up coil output		
400 rpm	4.5 volts	White/black-black
		White/red-black
1500 rpm	10.0 volts	
3500 rpm	16.0 volts	
CDI unit output		
400 rpm	107 volts	Black/white-black
		Black/orange-black
1500 rpm	110 volts	
3500 rpm	111 volts	
Pickup coil resistance*	445-545 ohms	White/black-black
		White/red-black
Ignition coil resistance*		
Primary winding	0.078-0.106 ohm	
Secondary winding	3500-4700 ohms	
Spark plug type	LFR5A-11 (NGK)	
Spark plug gap	1.1 mm (0.043 in.)	
Spark plug lead resistance		
No.1	4500-10,700 ohms	
No.2	3300-8000 ohms	
No.3	3700-8900 ohms	
No.4	4300-10,200 ohms	
*At 20° C (68° F)		

Table 9 STARTER MOTOR SPECIFICATIONS (1985-1999 9.9 HP)

Rating	30 cranking seconds
Output	0.6 kW
Brush length	9.0-12.5 mm (0.35-0.49 in.)
Wear limit	9 mm (0.35 in.)
Commutator	
Diameter	29.0-30.0 mm (1.14-1.18 in.)
Wear limit	29.0 mm (1.14 in.)
Under cut	0.2-0.8 mm (0.01-0.03 in.)
Wear limit	0.2 mm (0.01 in.)
Fuse	12 volt-20 amp

7

Table 10 STARTER MOTOR SPECIFICATIONS (1998-1999 15 AND 25 HP)

Type	Bendix
Rating	30 cranking seconds
Output	1.1 kW (12 v)
Brush length	12.6 mm (0.5 in.)
Wear limit	6.4 mm (0.25 in.)
Commutator	
Diameter	Not available
Wear limit	Not available
Under cut	2 mm (0.08 in.)
Wear limit	0.8 mm (0.03 in.)
Fuse	12 volt-20 amp

Table 11 STARTER MOTOR SPECIFICATIONS (1995-1998 50 HP)

Starter motor	
Output	1.1 kW (12 v)
Brush length	16.0 mm (0.63 in.)
Wear limit	12.0 mm (0.47 in.)
Commutator	
Diameter	33.0 mm (1.30 in.)
Wear limit	31.0 mm (1.22 in.)
Undercut	0.8 mm (0.03 in.)
Wear limit	0.2 mm (0.01 in.)
Fuse	12 volt-20 amp
Neutral switch	
Position on	18.5-19.5 mm (0.73-0.77 in.)
Position off	19.5-20.5 mm (0.77-0.81 in.)

Table 12 STARTER MOTOR SPECIFICATIONS (1999 40 AND 50 HP)

Manufacture	Hitachi
Model	S114-323C
Output	1.1 kW (12v)
Brush length	16.0 mm (0.63 in.)
Wear limit	12.0 mm (0.47 in.)
Commutator	
Diameter	33.0 mm (1.30 in.)
Wear limit	31.0 mm (1.22 in.)
Undercut	0.8 mm (0.03 in.)
Wear limit	0.2 mm (0.01 in.)
Fuse	12 volt-20 amp

Table 13 STARTER MOTOR SPECIFICATIONS (80 AND 100 HP)

Type	Sliding gear
Manufacturer	Hitachi
Model	S114-828
Weight	3.5 kW (7.7 lb.)
Output	1.4 kW (12 v)
Reduction gear ratio	7.85 (102:13)
Brush length	15.5 mm (0.61 in.)
Wear limit	9.5 mm (0.37)
Commutator	
Diameter	29.0 mm (1.14 in.)
Wear limit	28.0 mm (1.10 in.)
Undercut	0.5 mm (0.02 in.)
Wear limit	0.2 mm (0.01 in.)
Fuse	12 volt-20 amp

Table 14 BATTERY CAPACITY (HOURS OF USE)

Amperage draw	Hours of usage with 80 amp-hour battery	Hours of usage with 105 amp-hour battery	Recharge time (approximate)
5 amps	13.5 hours	15.8 hours	16 hours
15 amps	3.5 hours	4.2 hours	13 hours
25 amps	1.8 hours	2.4 hours	12 hours

7

Chapter Eight

Power Head

This chapter covers power head removal, installation, disassembly, assembly, cleaning and inspection for all models.

The components shown in the accompanying illustrations are generally from the most common models. While it is possible that the components shown may not be identical to those being service, the step-by-step instructions cover every model in this manual.

Tables 1-5 provide torque specifications for most power head fasteners. **Tables 6-15** provide tolerances and dimensions for the cylinder head and cylinder block components. **Tables 1-15** are located at the end of this chapter.

FLYWHEEL REMOVAL AND INSTALLATION

Securely mount the engine to the boat or workbench before removing the flywheel. When removing both the flywheel and power head, remove the flywheel before loosening the power head mounting fasteners.

Flywheel removal requires a spanner wrench, or strap wrench and puller. The Yamaha part number for these tools is listed in the removal and installation procedure.

WARNING
Wear safety glasses when removing or installing the flywheel or other engine components. Never use a hammer or other tools without wearing safety glasses.

CAUTION
Use only the appropriate tools to remove the flywheel. Never strike the flywheel with a hard object. The flywheel magnets may break and result in poor ignition system performance or potential damage to other engine components.

9.9 hp Models

1. Disconnect both cables from the battery, if so equipped. Remove the spark plugs and connect the spark plug leads to a suitable engine ground.
2. On manual start models, remove the manual starter following the instructions in Chapter Ten.
3. On electric start models, remove the mounting bolt (**Figure 1**) and pull the pin from the flywheel cover. Lift the flywheel cover (**Figure 1**) from the power head.

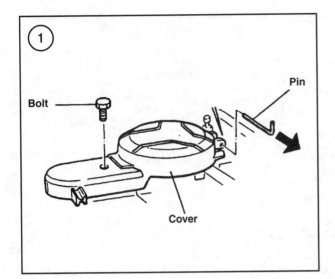

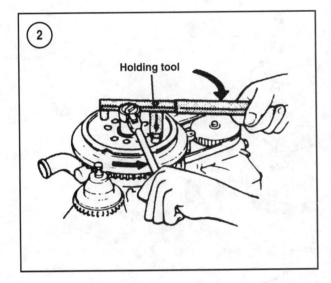

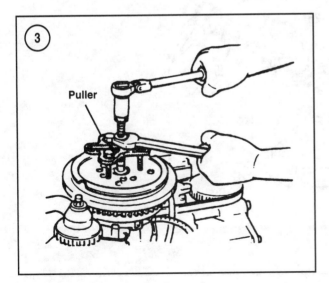

4. Attach the flywheel holding tool (Yamaha part No.YB-6139) to the holes in the flywheel (**Figure 2**). Use a breaker bar and socket to loosen the flywheel nut until its top surface is flush with the upper threaded end of the crankshaft.

5. Thread the three bolts of the puller (**Figure 3**) (Yamaha part No.YB-6117) through the puller plate and into the flywheel (1). Make sure the puller center bolt contacts the crankshaft and make sure the surfaces of the puller and flywheel are parallel before tightening the puller bolt .

6. Secure the puller with a pry bar while tightening the puller bolt. Tighten the center bolt until the flywheel is free of the crankshaft. Remove the flywheel nut and washer (1, **Figure 4**) and lift the flywheel (2) from the crankshaft (22). Wipe the flywheel and crankshaft tapered surfaces clean.

7. Pull the Woodruff key (26, **Figure 4**) from its slot in the crankshaft or flywheel. Inspect the key for wear or damage. Replace the key if bent, worn or damaged.

8. Remove all metal filings from the flywheel magnets. Inspect the magnets and flywheel surfaces for cracks or corrosion. Clean corroded surfaces with fine sandpaper. Replace the flywheel if deep pitting, cracks or damaged magnets are noted.

9. Place the Woodruff key (26, **Figure 4**) into the crankshaft slot with the rounded side facing in. Place the flywheel (2, **Figure 4**) over the end of the crankshaft (22) and align the flywheel key slot with the flywheel key. Lower the flywheel onto the crankshaft taper. Make sure the key enters the slot.

10. Place the washer over the crankshaft and thread the flywheel nut (1, **Figure 4**) onto the crankshaft.

11. Attach the flywheel holding tool (**Figure 2**) to the flywheel. Tighten the flywheel nut to the specification in **Table 1**.

12. On manual start models, install the manual starter following the instructions in Chapter Ten.

13. On electric start models, place the flywheel cover (2, **Figure 1**) onto the mounting bosses. Align the holes, then slide the pin (**Figure 1**) through the flywheel cover. Install the mounting bolt and securely tighten it. Check for adequate clearance between the belt, flywheel and cover.

14. Install the spark plugs and leads and connect the cables to the battery, if so equipped.

15 hp Models

1. Disconnect both cables from the battery, if so equipped. Remove the spark plugs, then connect the spark plug leads to a suitable engine ground.

2. On manual start models, remove the manual starter following the instructions in Chapter Ten.

8

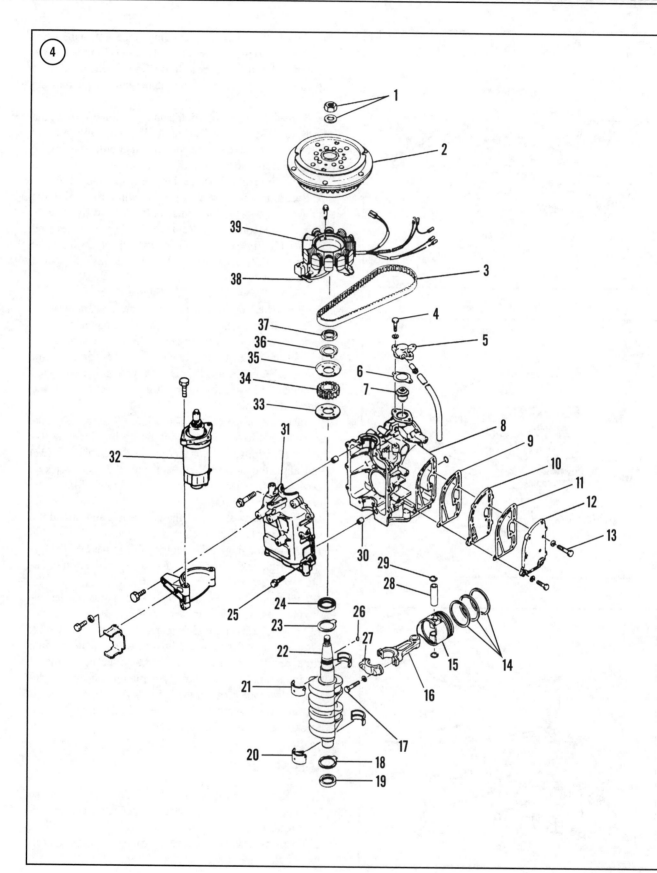

POWER HEAD ASSEMBLY
(9.9 HP)

1. Flywheel nut and washer
2. Flywheel
3. Timing belt
4. Bolt
5. Thermostat cover
6. Gasket
7. Thermostat
8. Cylinder block
9. Gasket
10. Exhaust plate
11. Gasket
12. Exhaust cover
13. Bolt
14. Piston rings
15. Piston
16. Connecting rod
17. Bolt
18. Thrust washer
19. Crankshaft seal
20. Main bearing
21. Main bearing
22. Crankshaft
23. Thrust washer
24. Crankshaft seal
25. Bolt
26. Woodruff key
27. Connecting rod cap
28. Piston pin
29. Piston pin keeper
30. Dowel pin
31. Crankcase
32. Starter motor
33. Washer
34. Drive sprocket
35. Washer
36. Lockwasher
37. Nut
38. Stator bracket
39. Stator

3. On electric start models, unplug the low-oil-pressure warning indicator leads (8, **Figure 5**) and starter switch leads (7), if equipped, from the engine wiring harness. Remove the mounting bolts (10, **Figure 5**) from the flywheel cover (1). Lift the flywheel cover (1, **Figure 5**) and driven sprockets cover (2) from the power head.

4. Attach the flywheel, holding tool (Yamaha part No.YB-6139) to the flywheel (**Figure 2**). Use a breaker bar and socket to loosen the flywheel nut until its top surface is flush with the upper threaded end of the crankshaft.

5. Thread the three bolts of the puller (Yamaha part No.YB-6117) through the puller plate and into the flywheel (**Figure 3**). Make sure the puller center bolt is in direct contact with the crankshaft and make sure the surfaces of the puller and flywheel are parallel before tightening the center bolt.

6. Secure the puller with a pry bar while tightening the puller bolt. Tighten the center bolt until the flywheel is free of the crankshaft. Remove the flywheel nut and washer (3 and 4, **Figure 5**), then lift the flywheel (5) from the crankshaft. Wipe all debris from the flywheel and crankshaft surfaces.

7. Pull the Woodruff key (6, **Figure 5**) from its slot in the crankshaft or flywheel. Inspect the key for wear or damage. Replace the key if bent, worn or damaged.

8. Remove all metal filings from the flywheel magnets. Inspect the magnets and flywheel surfaces for cracks or corrosion. Clean corrosion with fine sandpaper. Replace the flywheel if deep pitting, cracks or damaged magnets are noted.

9. Place the key (6, **Figure 5**) into the crankshaft slot with the rounded side facing in. Place the flywheel (5, **Figure 5**) over the end of the crankshaft and align the key slot with the key. Lower the flywheel onto the crankshaft taper. Make sure the key enters the slot.

10. Place the washer (4, **Figure 5**) over the crankshaft and apply a very light coat of engine oil to the crankshaft threads. Thread the flywheel nut (3, **Figure 5**) onto the crankshaft.

11. Attach the flywheel holding tool (**Figure 2**) to the flywheel. Tighten the flywheel nut to the specification in **Table 2**.

12. On manual start models, install the manual starter following the instructions in Chapter Ten.

13. On electric start models, place the flywheel cover (1, **Figure 5**) onto the power head. Install the flywheel cover bolts (10, **Figure 5**) and securely tighten the bolts. Check for adequate clearance between the belt, flywheel and cover. Plug the harnesses (8 and 7, **Figure 5**) back into the engine harness.

14. Install the spark plugs and leads and connect the cables to the battery, if so equipped.

8

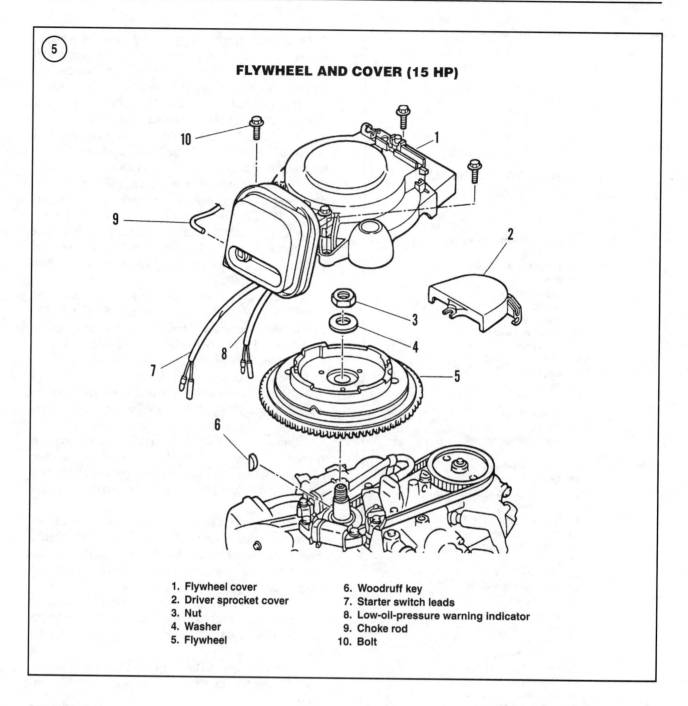

FLYWHEEL AND COVER (15 HP)

1. Flywheel cover
2. Driver sprocket cover
3. Nut
4. Washer
5. Flywheel
6. Woodruff key
7. Starter switch leads
8. Low-oil-pressure warning indicator
9. Choke rod
10. Bolt

25 hp Models

1. Disconnect both cables from the battery, if so equipped. Remove the spark plugs and connect the spark plug leads to a suitable engine ground.

2. On manual start models, remove the manual starter following the instructions in Chapter Ten.

3. On electric start models, disconnect the oil warning light wires (10, **Figure 6**) from the engine wire harness.

Remove the mounting bolts (1, **Figure 6**) and flywheel cover (2) from the power head.

4. Attach the flywheel holding tool (Yamaha part No.YB-6139) to the flywheel (**Figure 2**). Use a breaker bar and socket to loosen the flywheel nut until its top surface is flush with the upper threaded end of the crankshaft.

5. Thread the three bolts of the puller (Yamaha part No.YB-6117) through the puller plate and into the flywheel as indicated (**Figure 3**). Make sure the puller center bolt is in direct contact with the crankshaft and make sure

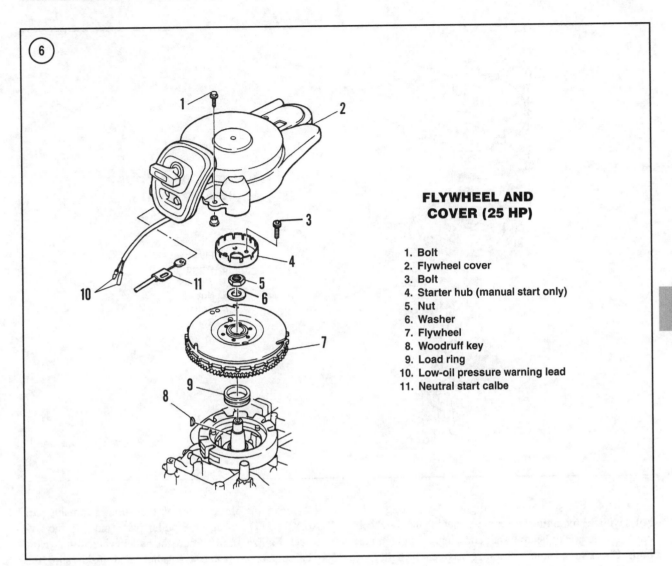

⑥

**FLYWHEEL AND
COVER (25 HP)**

1. Bolt
2. Flywheel cover
3. Bolt
4. Starter hub (manual start only)
5. Nut
6. Washer
7. Flywheel
8. Woodruff key
9. Load ring
10. Low-oil pressure warning lead
11. Neutral start calbe

8

the surfaces of the puller and flywheel are parallel before tightening the puller bolt.

6. Secure the puller with a pry bar while tightening the puller bolt. Tighten the center bolt until the flywheel is free of the crankshaft. Remove the flywheel nut and washer (5 and 6, **Figure 6**), then lift the flywheel (7) from the crankshaft. Remove the load ring (9, **Figure 6**) from the flywheel or crankshaft. Discard the load ring. Wipe all debris from the flywheel and crankshaft.

7. Pull the flywheel drive key (8, **Figure 6**) from its slot in the crankshaft or flywheel. Inspect the key for wear or damage. Replace the key if bent, worn or damaged.

8. Remove all metal filings from the flywheel magnets. Inspect the magnets and flywheel for cracks or corrosion. Clean corrosion with fine sandpaper. Replace the flywheel if deep pitting, cracks or damaged magnets are noted.

9. Place the Woodruff key (8, **Figure 6**) into the crankshaft slot with the rounded side facing in. Install a new load ring (9, **Figure 6**) over the crankshaft and rest it against the shoulder on the crankshaft. Place the flywheel (7, **Figure 6**) over the end of the crankshaft and align the key slot with the key. Lower the flywheel onto the crankshaft taper. Make sure the key enters the slot.

10. Place the washer (6, **Figure 6**) over the crankshaft and apply a very light coat of engine oil to the crankshaft threads. Thread the flywheel nut (5, **Figure 6**) onto the crankshaft.

11. Attach the flywheel holding tool (**Figure 2**) to the flywheel. Tighten the flywheel nut to the specification in **Table 3**.

12. On manual start models, install the manual starter following the instructions in Chapter Ten.

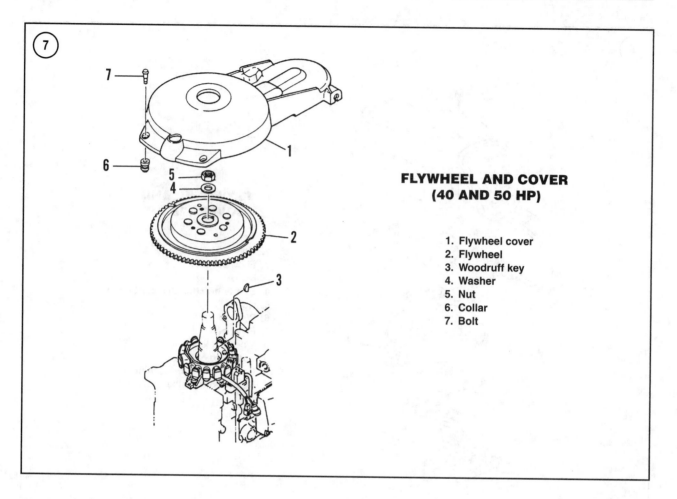

**FLYWHEEL AND COVER
(40 AND 50 HP)**

1. Flywheel cover
2. Flywheel
3. Woodruff key
4. Washer
5. Nut
6. Collar
7. Bolt

13. On electric start models, align the mounting bolt holes with the mounting bosses when placing the flywheel cover on the power head. Install and securely tighten the bolts. Check for adequate clearance between the belt, flywheel and cover. Connect the oil pressure warning light wires.

14. Install the spark plugs and leads, and connect the cables to the battery, if so equipped.

40 and 50 hp Models

1. Disconnect both cables from the battery. Remove the spark plugs and connect the spark plug leads to a suitable engine ground.

2. Remove both mounting bolts (7, **Figure 7**) from their mounting post. Lift the flywheel cover (1) from the power head. Remove the grommets (6, **Figure 7**) from the flywheel cover.

3. Attach the flywheel holding tool (Yamaha part No.YB-6139) to the flywheel (**Figure 2**). Use a breaker bar and socket to loosen the flywheel nut until its top surface is flush with the upper threaded end of the crankshaft.

4. Thread the three bolts of the puller (Yamaha part No.YB-6117) through the puller plate and into the flywheel (**Figure 3**). Make sure the puller center bolt is in direct contact with the crankshaft and make sure the surfaces of the puller and flywheel are parallel before tightening the puller bolt.

5. Secure the puller with a pry bar while tightening the puller bolt. Tighten the center bolt until the flywheel is free of the crankshaft. Remove the flywheel nut and washer (5 and 4, **Figure 7**), then lift the flywheel (2) from the crankshaft.

6. Wipe all debris from the flywheel and crankshaft.

7. Pull the Woodruff key (3, **Figure 7**) from its slot in the crankshaft or flywheel. Inspect the key for wear or damage. Replace the key if bent, worn or damaged.

8. Remove all metal filings from the flywheel magnets. Inspect the magnets and flywheel for cracks or corrosion. Clean corrosion with fine sandpaper. Replace the flywheel if deep pitting, cracks or damaged magnets are noted.

9. Place the key (3, **Figure 7**) into the crankshaft slot with the rounded side facing in. Place the flywheel over the end

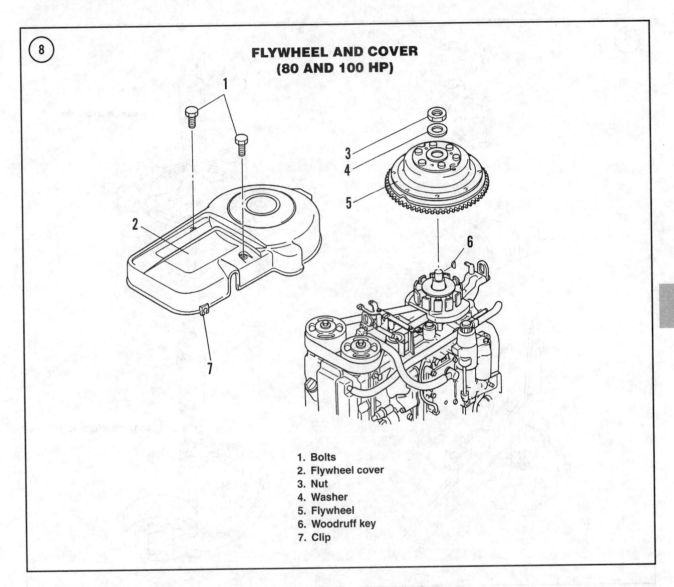

**FLYWHEEL AND COVER
(80 AND 100 HP)**

8

1. Bolts
2. Flywheel cover
3. Nut
4. Washer
5. Flywheel
6. Woodruff key
7. Clip

of the crankshaft and align the flywheel key slot with the key. Lower the onto the crankshaft taper. Make sure the key enters the slot.

10. Place the washer (4, **Figure 7**) over the crankshaft and apply a very light coat of engine oil to the crankshaft threads. Thread the flywheel nut (5, **Figure 7**) onto the crankshaft.

11. Attach the flywheel holding tool (**Figure 2**) to the flywheel. Tighten the flywheel nut to the specification in **Table 4**.

12. Place both grommets (6, **Figure 7**) into the mounting bolt openings. Align the mounting bolts holes with the mounting bosses when placing the flywheel cover on the power head. Install and securely tighten both mounting bolts (7, **Figure 7**). Check for adequate clearance between the belt, flywheel and cover.

13. Install the spark plugs and leads, and connect the cables to the battery.

80 and 100 hp Models

1. Disconnect both cables from the battery. Remove the spark plugs and connect the spark plug leads to a suitable engine ground.

2. Remove both mounting bolts (1, **Figure 8**), then carefully pull both slots (7) at the rear of the cover from their mounting post. Lift the flywheel cover (2, **Figure 8**) from the power head.

3. Attach the flywheel holding tool (Yamaha part No.YB-6139) to the flywheel (**Figure 2**). Use a breaker bar and socket to loosen the flywheel nut until its top surface is flush with the upper threaded end of the crankshaft.

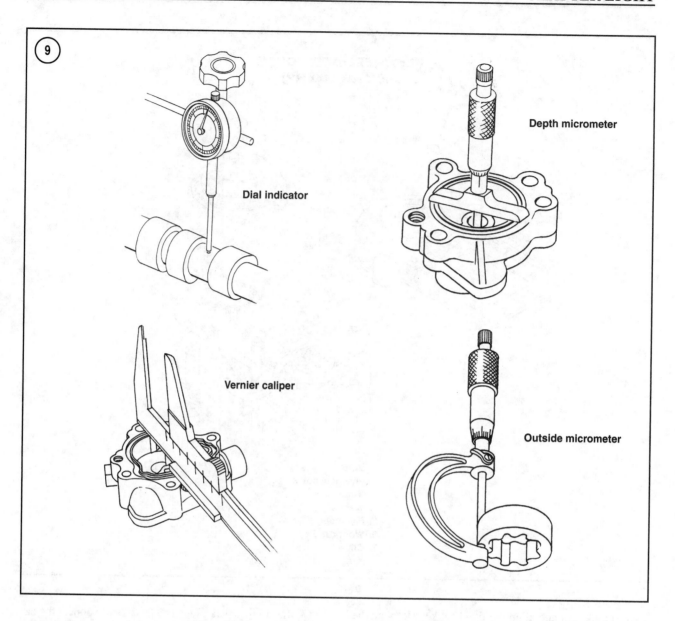

Dial indicator

Depth micrometer

Vernier caliper

Outside micrometer

4. Thread the three bolts of the puller (Yamaha part No.YB-6117) through the puller plate and into the flywheel as indicated (**Figure 3**). Make sure the puller center bolt is in direct contact with the crankshaft and make sure the surfaces of the puller and flywheel are parallel before tightening the puller bolt.

5. Secure the puller with a pry bar while tightening the puller bolt. Tighten the center bolt until the flywheel is free of the crankshaft. Remove the flywheel nut and washer (3 and 4, **Figure 8**), then lift the flywheel (5) from the crankshaft. Wipe all debris from the flywheel and crankshaft.

6. Pull the Woodruff key (6, **Figure 8**) from its slot in the crankshaft or flywheel. Inspect the key for wear or damage. Replace the key if bent, worn or damaged.

7. Remove all metal filings from the flywheel magnets. Inspect the magnets and flywheel for cracks or corrosion. Clean corrosion with fine sandpaper. Replace the flywheel if deep pitting, cracks or damaged magnets are noted.

8. Place the key (6) into the crankshaft slot with the rounded side facing in. Place the flywheel (5, **Figure 8**) over the end of the crankshaft and align the key slot with the key. Lower the flywheel onto the crankshaft taper. Make sure the key enters the slot.

9. Place the washer (4, **Figure 8**) over the crankshaft and apply a very light coat of engine oil to the crankshaft threads. Thread the flywheel nut (3, **Figure 8**) onto the crankshaft.

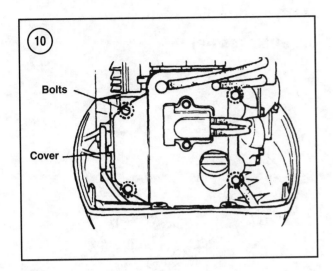

⑩

Bolts

Cover

10. Attach the flywheel holding tool (**Figure 2**) to the flywheel. Tighten the flywheel nut to the specification in **Table 5**.

11. Align the mounting bolts holes with the mounting bosses when placing the flywheel cover on the power head. Install and securely tighten both mounting bolts (1, **Figure 8**). Snap both slots at the rear of the cover over the mounting posts. Check for adequate clearance between the belt, flywheel and cover.

12. Install the spark plugs and leads and connect the cables to the battery.

CYLINDER HEAD

This section provides removal and installation procedures for the rocker arm cover, timing belt, camshaft pulley(s) and cylinder head. Cylinder head disassembly, inspection and assembly procedures are also covered.

Cylinder head repair involves precision measurement, machining operations and equipment (**Figure 9**). Have cylinder head machine work performed at a reputable machine shop if this equipment is unavailable.

Rocker Arm Cover Removal

1. Disconnect both cables from the battery, if so equipped. Remove the spark plug(s) then connect the spark plug lead(s) to a suitable engine ground.

2. On 9.9-100 hp models, remove the fuel pump as described in Chapter Six.

3. On 9.9-100 hp models, remove the flywheel cover as described in this chapter.

4A. On 9.9 and 15 hp models, remove the four mounting bolts (**Figure 10**) and lift the cover from the cylinder head.

4B. On 25 hp models, remove the five mounting bolts (9, **Figure 11**), then lift the cover (10) from the cylinder head (1).

4C. On 40 and 50 hp models, pull the breather hose (3, **Figure 12**) from the cover. Note the mounting location of the hose clamp, then remove the seven mounting bolts (1, **Figure 12**). Lift the cover (2, **Figure 12**) from the cylinder head.

4D. On 80 and 100 hp models, remove the five bolts (2, **Figure 13**) and lift the spark plug cover (1) from the rocker arm cover (2, **Figure 14**). Remove the clip (5) and pull the breather hose (6, **Figure 14**) from the cover (2). Remove the 14 bolts (3, **Figure 14**), then pull the rocker arm cover (2) from the cylinder head.

5. Remove and discard the rubber gasket (4, **Figure 14**) from the rocker arm cover. Remove the eight screws (8, **Figure 14**) from breather cover (7). Using a suitable solvent, thoroughly clean the cover and deflector plate.

Rocker Arm Cover Installation

Refer to **Figures 10-14** as necessary during this procedure.

1. On 80-100 hp models, place the breather cover plate onto the cylinder cover. Install and securely tighten the breather plate screws.

2. On 9.9-100 hp models, place a new gasket, O-ring or seal on the rocker arm cover. Place the cover onto the cylinder head and install the cover mounting bolts hand tight.

3. On 80 and 100 hp models, apply Yamabond No. 4 sealer to the surfaces of the seal and the areas around the upper camshaft retainers.

4. Tighten all cover mounting bolts to the specification in **Tables 1-5**. Refer to the following to determine the torque sequence.

   a. On 9.9 and 15 hp models, refer to **Figure 15**.

   b. On 25 hp models, refer to **Figure 16**.

   c. On 40-50 hp models, refer to **Figure 17**.

   d. On 80 and 100 hp models, tighten the bolts in a crossing pattern working from the center outward.

5. Install the fuel pump following the instructions in Chapter Six. Install the flywheel cover following the instructions in this chapter.

6. On 50-100 hp models, slip the breather hose over its' fitting on the cover.

7. Install the spark plug(s) and lead(s), and connect the cables to the battery, if so equipped.

8

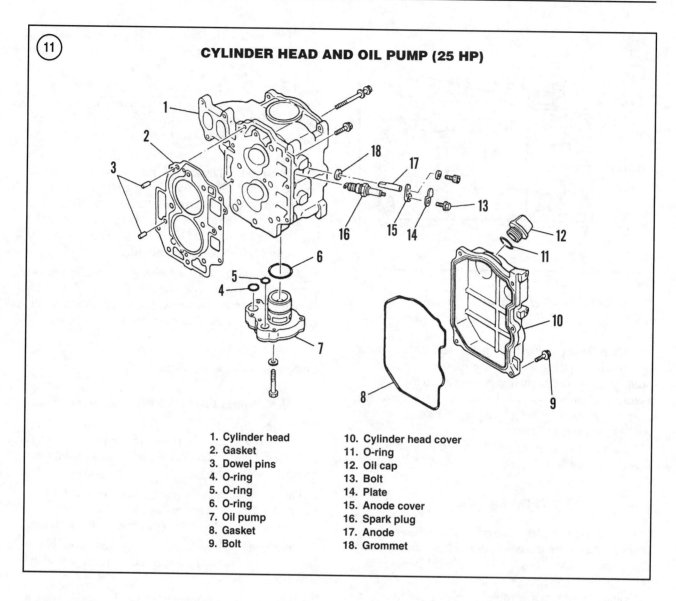

CYLINDER HEAD AND OIL PUMP (25 HP)

1. Cylinder head
2. Gasket
3. Dowel pins
4. O-ring
5. O-ring
6. O-ring
7. Oil pump
8. Gasket
9. Bolt
10. Cylinder head cover
11. O-ring
12. Oil cap
13. Bolt
14. Plate
15. Anode cover
16. Spark plug
17. Anode
18. Grommet

Timing Belt

This section covers removal and installation of the timing belt. Refer to **Figures 18-22** as appropriate during the removal and installation process.

> *CAUTION*
> *Do not turn the crankshaft or camshaft while the timing belt is removed or the pistons and valves can be damaged.*

Removal

1. Disconnect both cables from the battery, if so equipped. Remove the spark plugs and connect the spark plug leads to a suitable engine ground.

2. On manual start models, remove the manual starter following the instructions in Chapter Ten.

3. On electric start models, remove the flywheel cover following the instructions in this chapter.

4. Place the flywheel in the TDC (top dead center) position for the No. 1 cylinder as described under *Valve Adjustment* in Chapter Five.

5A. On 9.9-25 hp models, carefully push up on the belt until it slips off of the camshaft pulley.

5B. On 40 and 50 hp models, loosen the pivot bolt (9, **Figure 21**) and adjusting bolt (10) to relieve the belt tensioner (8). Push up on the belt until it slips off of the camshaft pulley.

5C. On 80 and 100 hp models, loosen the bolt (11, **Figure 22**) and remove the spring (12) from the tensioner (10).

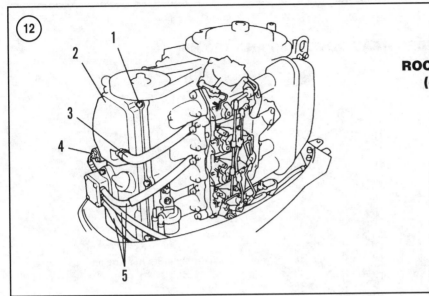

**ROCKER ARM COVER
(40 AND 50 HP)**

1. Bolt
2. Rocker arm cover
3. Blowby hose
4. Thermo switch
5. Fuel hoses

8

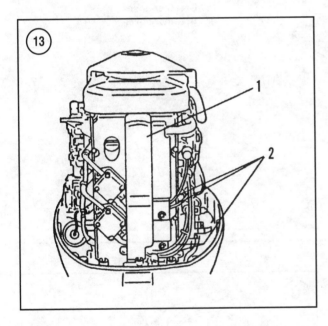

Push up on the timing belt until it slips off of the camshaft pulleys.

6. Do not rotate the flywheel or camshaft pulley(s) unless the cylinder head is first removed.

Installation (9.9-25 hp models)

> **CAUTION**
> *Always install the timing belt with the numbers right-side up. The timing belt may slip from the pulleys if the belt is installed with the letters upside down. Serious power head*

damage is likely if the belt slips off while the engine is running.

1. Align the flywheel and camshaft sprocket timing marks at TDC for the No. 1 cylinder as described under *Valve Adjustment* in Chapter Five.

2. Place the timing belt over the crankshaft and camshaft sprockets with the numbers or letters facing upward. Make sure the belt correctly engages the teeth on the sprockets.

3. Inspect the timing marks on the camshaft sprocket and the flywheel for correct alignment. If misaligned, correct it before rotating the flywheel or camshaft pulley.

4. On manual start models, install the manual starter (Chapter Ten).

5. On electric start models, install the flywheel cover (this chapter).

6. Install the spark plugs and leads, and connect the cables to the battery, if so equipped.

Installation (40-100 hp models)

1. Align the flywheel and camshaft sprocket timing marks at TDC (top dead center) for the No. 1 cylinder as described in Chapter Five.

2. Position the timing belt with its numbers or letters facing upward and install the belt over the crankshaft sprocket.

3. Take up the slack on the port side (opposite the tensioner) while wrapping the timing belt around the camshaft sprocket(s). Do not rotate the camshaft sprockets.

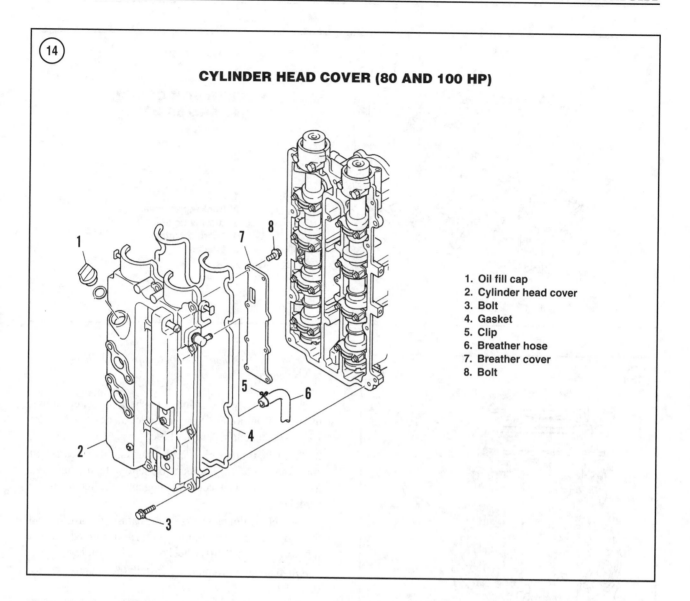

CYLINDER HEAD COVER (80 AND 100 HP)

1. Oil fill cap
2. Cylinder head cover
3. Bolt
4. Gasket
5. Clip
6. Breather hose
7. Breather cover
8. Bolt

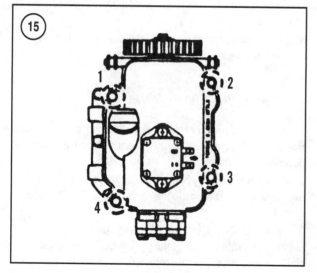

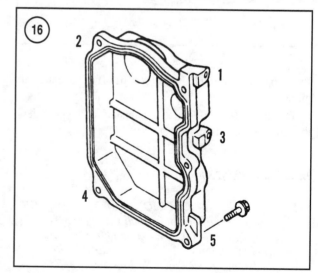

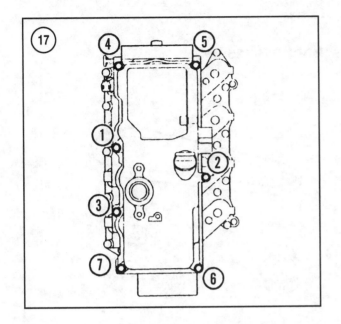

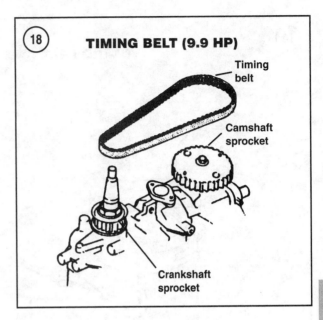

TIMING BELT (9.9 HP)

Timing belt

Camshaft sprocket

Crankshaft sprocket

8

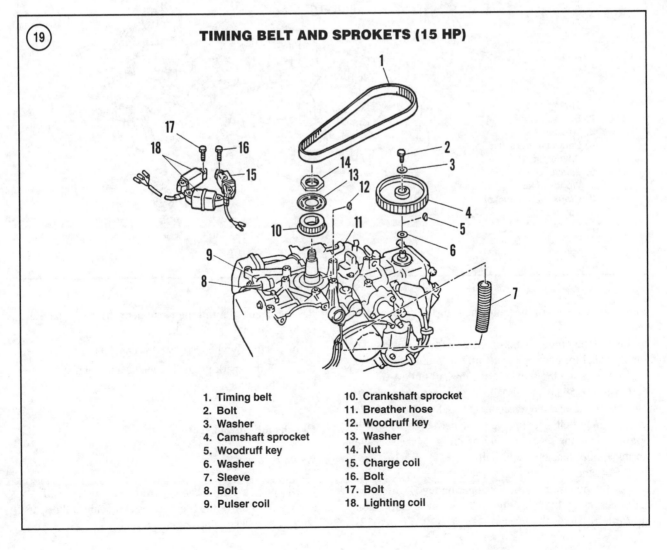

TIMING BELT AND SPROKETS (15 HP)

1. Timing belt
2. Bolt
3. Washer
4. Camshaft sprocket
5. Woodruff key
6. Washer
7. Sleeve
8. Bolt
9. Pulser coil
10. Crankshaft sprocket
11. Breather hose
12. Woodruff key
13. Washer
14. Nut
15. Charge coil
16. Bolt
17. Bolt
18. Lighting coil

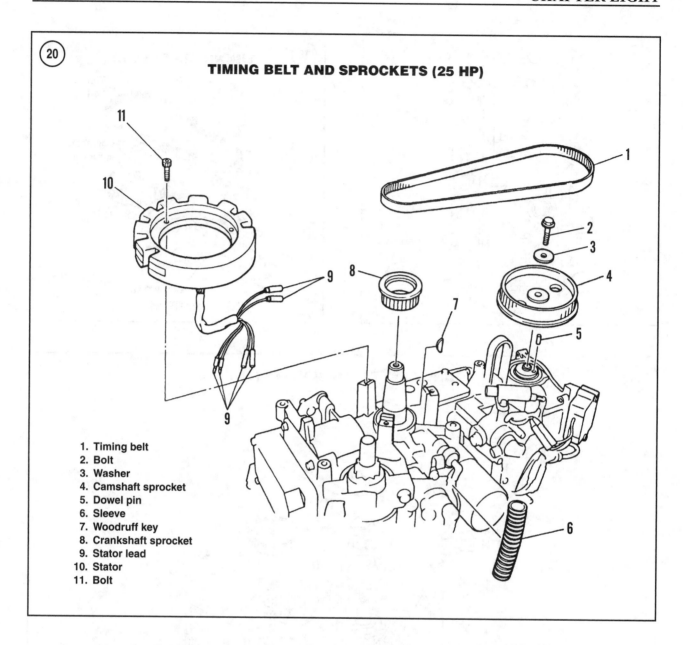

(20)

TIMING BELT AND SPROCKETS (25 HP)

1. Timing belt
2. Bolt
3. Washer
4. Camshaft sprocket
5. Dowel pin
6. Sleeve
7. Woodruff key
8. Crankshaft sprocket
9. Stator lead
10. Stator
11. Bolt

Make sure the cogs of the timing belt engage the sprocket teeth.

4. Inspect the timing marks on the camshaft sprocket and the flywheel for correct alignment. If misaligned, correct it before rotating the flywheel or camshaft pulley.

5. On 40 and 50 hp models, allow the tensioner spring (7, **Figure 21**) to load the tensioner (8) against the backside of the timing belt. Tighten the tensioner bolts (9 and 10, **Figure 21**) to the specification in **Table 4**. Make sure the spring applies tension on the belt.

6. On 80 and 100 hp models, route the backside of the belt to the port side of the tensioner pulley. Tighten the tensioner pulley bolt (11, **Figure 22**) to the specification in **Table 5**. Hook the tensioner spring (12, **Figure 22**)

through its opening in the tensioner (10). Make sure the spring applies tension on the belt.

7. Install the flywheel cover (this chapter).

8. Install the spark plugs and leads, and connect the cables to the battery.

Crankshaft Sprocket Removal

9.9 hp models

1. Disconnect both cables from the battery, if so equipped. Remove the spark plugs and connect the spark plug leads to a suitable engine ground.

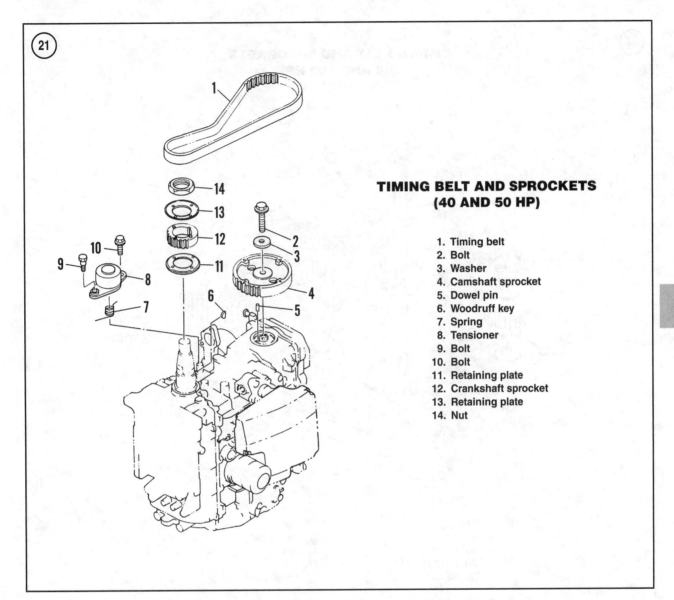

(21)

TIMING BELT AND SPROCKETS (40 AND 50 HP)

1. Timing belt
2. Bolt
3. Washer
4. Camshaft sprocket
5. Dowel pin
6. Woodruff key
7. Spring
8. Tensioner
9. Bolt
10. Bolt
11. Retaining plate
12. Crankshaft sprocket
13. Retaining plate
14. Nut

8

2. Remove the flywheel (**Figure 23**) and timing belt following the instructions in this chapter.

3. Refer to Chapter Four and fully loosen all valve adjusting screws.

4. Shift the engine into REVERSE gear and block the propeller from rotating counterclockwise using a block of wood.

5. Bend the locking tab washer (2, **Figure 24**) away from the nut (1). Use a deep socket to remove the nut (1, **Figure 24**) from the crankshaft.

6. Lift the locking tab washer and plate (2 and 3, **Figure 24**), then the crankshaft sprocket (4), from the crankshaft. Tap the sprocket with a rubber mallet if it will not lift freely from the crankshaft. Remove the lower plate (5, **Figure 24**) from the crankshaft.

7. Inspect the sprocket, plates and locking tab washer for wear or damage. Replace defective components.

8. Pull the drive key from the crankshaft. Inspect the key for damage. Replace the key if necessary.

15 hp models

1. Disconnect both cables from the battery, if so equipped. Remove the spark plugs and connect the spark plug leads to a suitable engine ground.

2. Remove the flywheel and timing belt following the instructions in this chapter.

3. Refer to Chapter Four and loosen all valve adjusting screws.

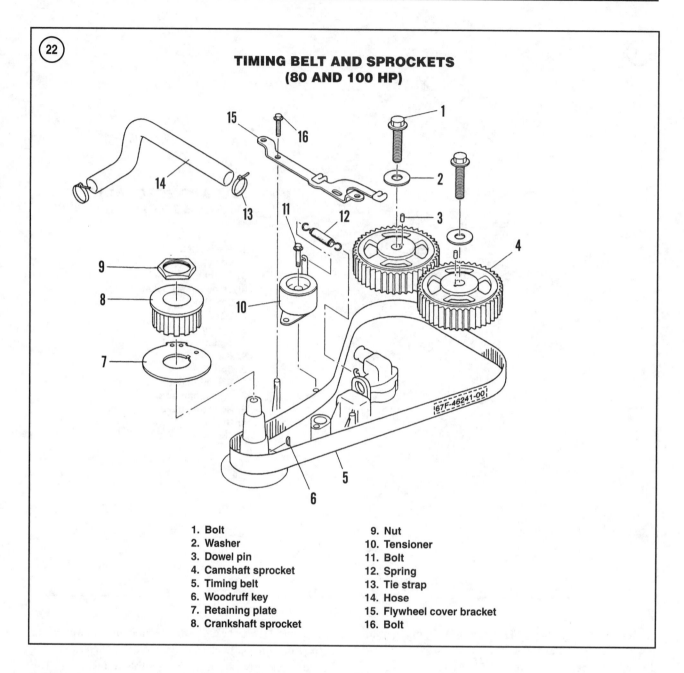

(22)

TIMING BELT AND SPROCKETS
(80 AND 100 HP)

1. Bolt
2. Washer
3. Dowel pin
4. Camshaft sprocket
5. Timing belt
6. Woodruff key
7. Retaining plate
8. Crankshaft sprocket
9. Nut
10. Tensioner
11. Bolt
12. Spring
13. Tie strap
14. Hose
15. Flywheel cover bracket
16. Bolt

4. Shift the engine into REVERSE gear then prevent the propeller from rotating counterclockwise using a block of wood.

5. Use a deep socket to loosen and remove the nut (14, **Figure 19**) from the crankshaft.

6. Lift the plate (13, **Figure 19**) and crankshaft sprocket (10) from the crankshaft. Tap the sprocket with a rubber mallet if it will not lift freely from the crankshaft.

7. Inspect the sprocket and plate for wear or damage. Replace both components if defects are noted.

8. Pull the Woodruff key (12, **Figure 19**) from the crankshaft. Inspect the key for damage.

25 models

1. Disconnect both cables from the battery. Remove the spark plugs and connect the spark plug leads to a suitable engine ground.

2. Remove the flywheel and timing belt as described in this chapter.

3. Lift the crankshaft sprocket (8, **Figure 20**) from the crankshaft. Tap the sprocket with a rubber mallet if it will not freely lift from the crankshaft. Inspect the sprocket for wear, cracks or damage. Replace the sprocket if any defects are noted.

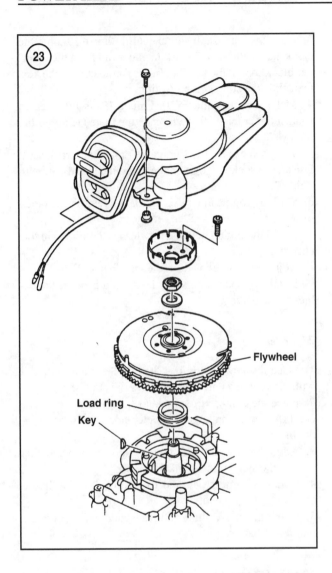

Flywheel

Load ring

Key

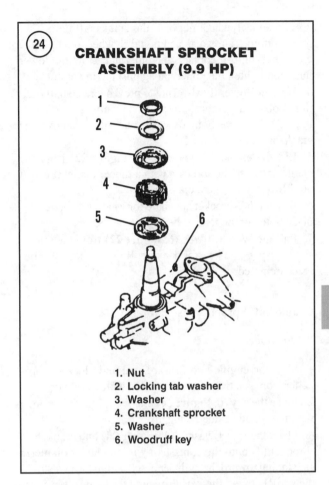

CRANKSHAFT SPROCKET ASSEMBLY (9.9 HP)

1. Nut
2. Locking tab washer
3. Washer
4. Crankshaft sprocket
5. Washer
6. Woodruff key

4. Remove the Woodruff key (7, **Figure 20**) from the crankshaft. Inspect the key for damage. Replace the key if defects are noted.

40 and 50 hp models

1. Disconnect both cables from the battery. Remove the spark plugs and connect the spark plug lead to a suitable engine ground.

2. Remove the flywheel and timing belt as described in this chapter.

3. Fully loosen all valve adjusting screws to help prevent damage should the flywheel rotate.

4. Thread a flywheel nut onto the crankshaft until it almost bottoms. Thread an additional flywheel nut onto the crankshaft until it contacts the other nut. Hold the lower nut and tighten the upper nut against the lower nut.

5. Hold the lower flywheel nut to prevent crankshaft rotation. Loosen the crankshaft sprocket nut (14, **Figure 21**). Remove both flywheel nuts, then remove the crankshaft sprocket nut.

6. Lift the plate (13, **Figure 21**) and the crankshaft sprocket (12) from the crankshaft. Tap the sprocket with a rubber mallet if it will not lift freely from the crankshaft. Lift the lower plate (11, **Figure 21**) from the crankshaft.

7. Inspect the sprocket and plate for wear or damage. Replace both components if defects are noted.

8. Pull the Woodruff key (6, **Figure 21**) from the crankshaft. Inspect the key for damage. Replace the key if defects are noted.

80 and 100 hp models

1. Disconnect both cables from the battery. Remove the spark plugs and connect the spark plug leads to a suitable engine ground.

2. Remove the flywheel and timing belt as described in this chapter.

3. Thread a flywheel nut onto the crankshaft until it almost bottoms. Thread an additional flywheel nut onto the crankshaft until it contacts the other nut. Hold the lower nut, then tighten the upper nut against the lower nut.

4. Hold the lower flywheel nut to prevent crankshaft rotation. Loosen the crankshaft sprocket retaining nut (9, **Figure 22**). Remove both flywheel nuts, then remove the crankshaft pulley nut.

5. Lift the crankshaft sprocket (8, **Figure 22**) from the crankshaft. Tap the sprocket with a rubber mallet if it will not lift freely from the crankshaft.

6. Inspect the sprocket and plate for wear or damage. Replace both components if defects are noted.

7. Pull the Woodruff key (6, **Figure 22**) from the crankshaft. Inspect the key for damage. Replace the key if defects are noted.

Crankshaft Sprocket Installation

9.9 hp models

1. Shift the engine into forward gear and block the propeller from rotating clockwise using a block of wood.

2. Place the key (6, **Figure 24**) into the crankshaft groove with the rounded side facing in.

3. Place the lower washer (5, **Figure 24**) and crankshaft sprocket (4) onto the crankshaft with the larger diameter side facing toward the cylinder block. Align the key slot in the sprocket with the key, then slide the sprocket in position.

4. Fully seat the sprocket against the crankshaft, then place the upper washer (3, **Figure 24**) and lockwasher (2) onto the sprocket with the edge curled away from the cylinder block.

5. Thread the nut (1, **Figure 24**) onto the crankshaft. Use a deep socket to tighten the nut to the specification in **Table 1**.

6. Shift the engine into NEUTRAL and remove the block of wood from the propeller.

7. Install the timing belt and flywheel as described in this chapter.

8. Adjust the valves as described in Chapter Four.

9. Install the spark plugs and leads, and connect the cables to the battery.

15 hp models

1. Shift the engine into FORWARD gear, then block the propeller from rotating clockwise using a block of wood.

2. Place the key (12, **Figure 19**) into the crankshaft groove with the rounded side facing in.

3. Place the crankshaft sprocket (10, **Figure 19**) onto the crankshaft with the UP mark facing away from the cylinder block. Align the key slot in the sprocket with the key, then slide the sprocket in position.

4. Make sure the pulley (10, **Figure 19**) is fully seated against the crankshaft, then place the plate (13) onto the pulley.

5. Thread the nut (14, **Figure 19**) onto the crankshaft. Use a deep socket to tighten the nut to the specification in **Table 2**.

6. Shift the engine into NEUTRAL and remove the block of wood from the propeller.

7. Install the timing belt and flywheel as described in this chapter.

8. Adjust the valves as described in Chapter Four.

9. Install the spark plugs and leads, and connect the cables to the battery.

25 models

1. Place the key (7, **Figure 20**) into the crankshaft slot with the rounded end facing toward the crankshaft.

2. Place the crankshaft sprocket (8, **Figure 20**) onto the crankshaft with the larger diameter side facing the cylinder block.

3. Align the key slot with the key and seat the sprocket against the step on the crankshaft.

4. Install the timing belt and flywheel following the instructions in this chapter.

5. Install the spark plugs and leads, and connect the cables to the battery.

40 and 50 hp models

1. Place the lower plate (11, **Figure 21**) over the crankshaft with the curled edge facing toward the cylinder block.

2. Place the key (6, **Figure 21**) into the crankshaft groove with the rounded side facing in.

3. Place the crankshaft sprocket (12, **Figure 21**) over the crankshaft. Align the key slot in the sprocket with the key and slide the sprocket in position. Align the protrusions on the bottom of the sprocket with the openings in the lower plate (11), then seat the sprocket and plate against the crankshaft.

4. Place the upper plate (13, **Figure 21**) onto the sprocket with the edge curled away from the cylinder block. Align the protrusions on the top of the sprocket with the openings in the upper plate. Thread the crankshaft sprocket nut (14, **Figure 21**) onto the crankshaft until it just contacts the plate.

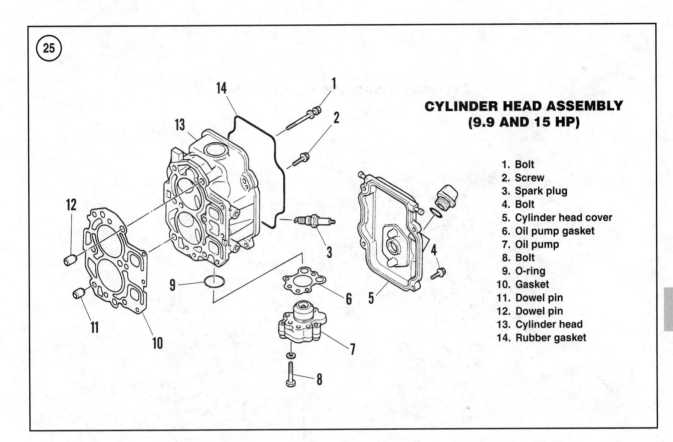

**CYLINDER HEAD ASSEMBLY
(9.9 AND 15 HP)**

1. Bolt
2. Screw
3. Spark plug
4. Bolt
5. Cylinder head cover
6. Oil pump gasket
7. Oil pump
8. Bolt
9. O-ring
10. Gasket
11. Dowel pin
12. Dowel pin
13. Cylinder head
14. Rubber gasket

8

5. Thread a flywheel nut onto the crankshaft until it almost bottoms. Thread an additional flywheel nut onto the crankshaft until it contacts the other nut. Hold the lower nut, then tighten the upper nut against the lower nut.

6. Hold the lower flywheel nut to prevent crankshaft rotation. Tighten the crankshaft sprocket, retaining nut (14, **Figure 21**) to the specification in **Table 4**. Remove both flywheel nuts.

7. Install the timing belt and flywheel as described in this chapter.

8. Adjust the valves following the instructions in Chapter Four.

9. Install the spark plugs and leads, and connect the cables to the battery.

80 and 100 hp models

1. Place the key (6, **Figure 22**) into the crankshaft groove with the rounded side facing in.

2. Place the crankshaft sprocket (8, **Figure 22**) over the crankshaft with the larger diameter side facing up. Align the key slot in the sprocket with the key and slide the sprocket into position.

3. Thread the crankshaft sprocket nut (9, **Figure 22**) onto the crankshaft until it just contacts the plate.

4. Thread a flywheel nut onto the crankshaft until it almost bottoms. Thread an additional flywheel nut onto the crankshaft until it contacts the other nut. Hold the lower nut, then tighten the upper nut against the lower nut.

5. Hold the lower flywheel nut to prevent crankshaft rotation. Tighten the crankshaft sprocket retaining nut (9, **Figure 22**) to the specification in **Table 5**. Remove both flywheel nuts.

6. Install the timing belt and flywheel following the instructions in this chapter.

7. Install the spark plugs and leads, and connect the cables to the battery.

CYLINDER HEAD

Removal (All Models)

Refer to **Figures 25-32** as required during the cylinder head removal procedure.

CAUTION
Loosen the head bolts in the opposite order of the tightening sequence to reduce the chance of a warped cylinder head.

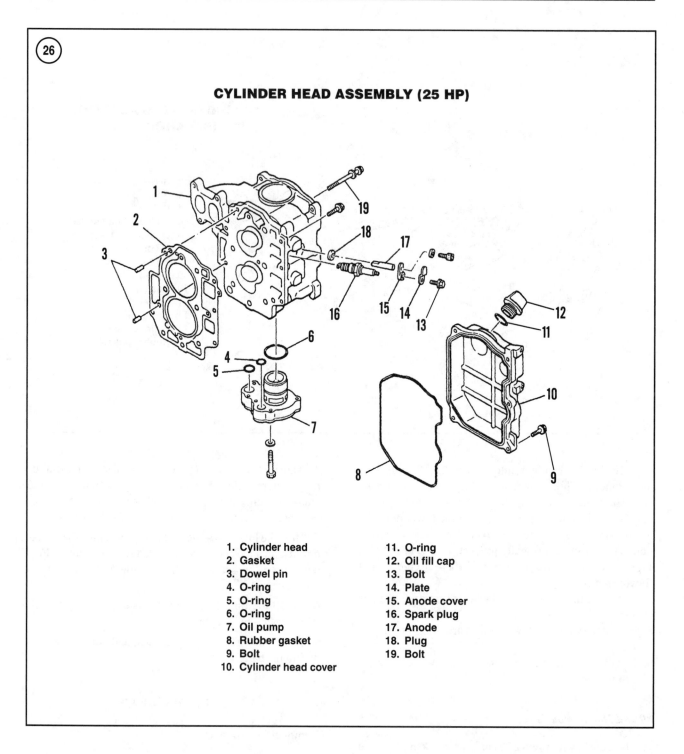

CYLINDER HEAD ASSEMBLY (25 HP)

1. Cylinder head
2. Gasket
3. Dowel pin
4. O-ring
5. O-ring
6. O-ring
7. Oil pump
8. Rubber gasket
9. Bolt
10. Cylinder head cover
11. O-ring
12. Oil fill cap
13. Bolt
14. Plate
15. Anode cover
16. Spark plug
17. Anode
18. Plug
19. Bolt

1. Remove the carburetors and intake manifold as described in Chapter Six.

2. Remove the timing belt and rocker arm cover as described in this chapter.

3. On 80 and 100 hp models, camshaft removal is required to access the cylinder head bolts. Remove the camshafts as follows:

a. Engage the lugs of the flywheel-holding tool (Yamaha part No.YB-6139) with the camshaft sprockets (**Figure 29**) to prevent camshaft rotation.

b. Remove the bolts and washers (1 and 2, **Figure 30**), and remove the sprockets (4) from the camshafts.

c. Mark the location and up side of each camshaft bearing cap (**Figure 31**). Remove both camshaft

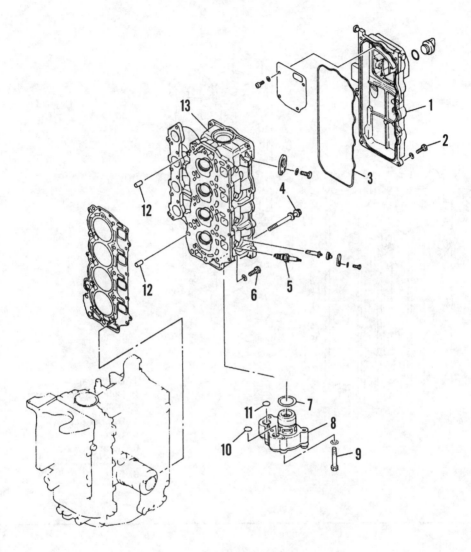

**CYLINDER HEAD ASSEMBLY
(40 AND 50 HP)**

8

1. Cylinder head cover
2. Bolt
3. Rubber gasket
4. Bolt
5. Spark plug
6. Bolt
7. O-ring
8. Oil pump
9. Bolt
10. O-ring
11. O-ring
12. Dowel pin
13. Cylinder head

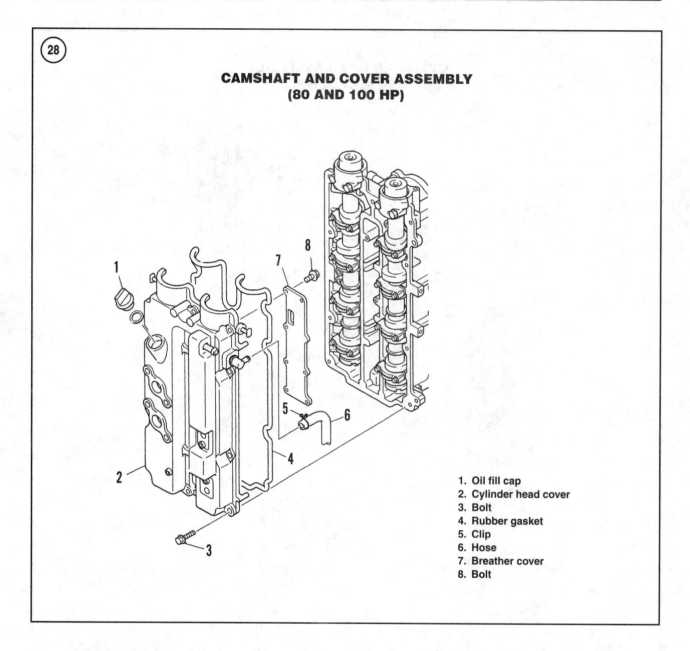

28

CAMSHAFT AND COVER ASSEMBLY
(80 AND 100 HP)

1. Oil fill cap
2. Cylinder head cover
3. Bolt
4. Rubber gasket
5. Clip
6. Hose
7. Breather cover
8. Bolt

seals (10, **Figure 31**) from the top of the camshafts (6). Loosen the camshaft cap bolts 1/4 turn at a time.

d. Support the camshafts and remove each camshaft bearing cap.

e. Mark the location (port or starboard) of each camshaft and pull each camshaft (6, **Figure 31**) from the cylinder head.

4. Loosen the cylinder head bolts 1/4 turn at a time following a crossing pattern

5. Remove the cylinder head bolts. Pull the cylinder head away from the cylinder block and place it on a clean work surface.

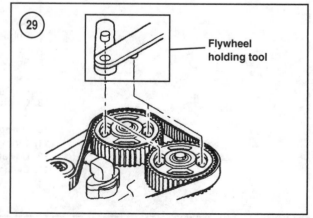

29

Flywheel
holding tool

**CAMSHAFT AND CRANKSHAFT SPROCKETS
(80 AND 100 HP)**

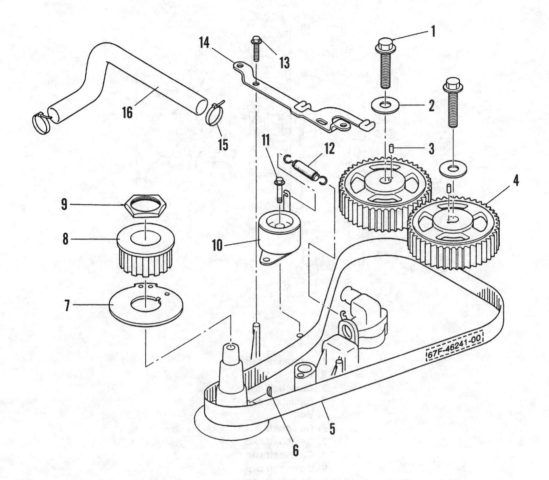

1. Bolt
2. Washer
3. Dowel pin
4. Camshaft sprocket
5. Timing belt
6. Woodruff key
7. Plate
8. Crankshaft sprocket
9. Nut
10. Tensioner
11. Bolt
12. Spring
13. Bolt
14. Flywheel cover bracket
15. Tie wrap
16. Hose

8

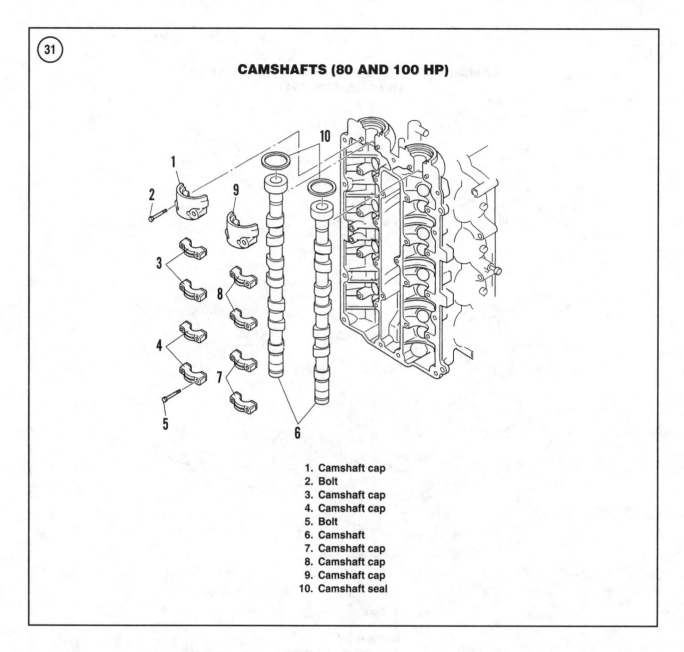

(31)

CAMSHAFTS (80 AND 100 HP)

1. Camshaft cap
2. Bolt
3. Camshaft cap
4. Camshaft cap
5. Bolt
6. Camshaft
7. Camshaft cap
8. Camshaft cap
9. Camshaft cap
10. Camshaft seal

6. Carefully scrape all head gasket material and carbon from the cylinder block and cylinder head (**Figure 33**). Do not gouge or scratch the surfaces. All gasket surfaces must be absolutely clean.

7. Inspect the cylinder head for warpage as described under *Inspection* in this chapter.

Installation (9.9-50 hp models)

CAUTION
On 9.9-50 hp models, the valve adjusting nuts must be fully loosened prior to installing the cylinder head.

Refer to **Figures 25-27** as required during this procedure.

1. Position the flywheel so the No. 1 cylinder is at TDC as described under *Valve Adjustment* in Chapter Five.

2. Make sure all aligning pins are positioned in the cylinder head or cylinder block. Make sure that all gasket surfaces are absolutely clean and free of defects.

3. Place a new head gasket onto the cylinder head or cylinder block. Make sure the gasket openings match the openings in the cylinder head and cylinder block.

4. Align the pins with the openings and seat the cylinder head on the cylinder block.

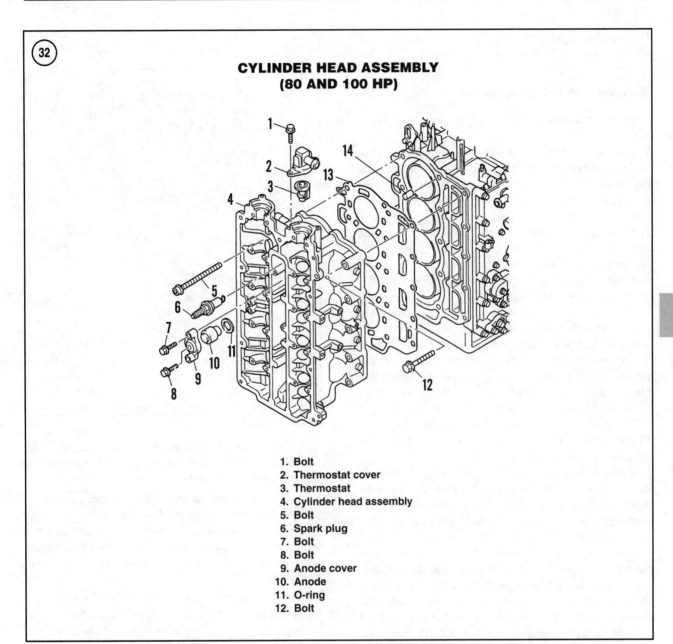

**CYLINDER HEAD ASSEMBLY
(80 AND 100 HP)**

1. Bolt
2. Thermostat cover
3. Thermostat
4. Cylinder head assembly
5. Bolt
6. Spark plug
7. Bolt
8. Bolt
9. Anode cover
10. Anode
11. O-ring
12. Bolt

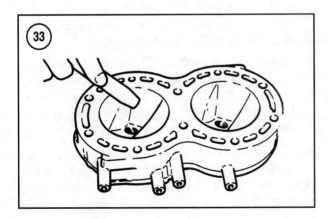

5. Apply a light coat of engine oil to the threads and underside of the head of each mounting bolt. Thread all bolts into the cylinder block by hand.

6. Tighten the cylinder head bolts to half of the specification in **Tables 1-5** following a crossing sequence.

7. Tighten the head mounting bolts a second time following a crossing sequence to the full specification in **Table 1-5**.

8. Install the timing belt as described in this chapter.

9. Adjust the valves as described in Chapter Five.

10. Install the rocker arm cover following the instructions in this chapter.

11. Install the intake manifold and carburetors following the instructions in Chapter Six.

Installation (80 and 100 hp models)

Refer to **Figures 28-32** as needed during this procedure.

1. Position the crankshaft at the TDC for the No. 1 cylinder as described under *Valve Adjustment* in Chapter Five. Rotate the flywheel 90° clockwise. This helps prevent damage to valves and/or pistons during camshaft installation.

2. Make sure all gasket surfaces are absolutely clean and free of defects. Install a new head gasket (13, **Figure 32**) on the cylinder head. Align the openings in the gasket with the openings in the cylinder head. All four pistons must be down in their bores.

3. Seat the cylinder head against the cylinder block and gasket. Hold the cylinder head in position and thread the bolts into the block. Do not tighten the bolts at this time.

4. Tighten the cylinder head bolts following a circular pattern starting at the center to half the specification in **Table 5**. Tighten all cylinder head bolts a second time in sequence to the full specification in **Table 5**.

5. Using a T55 internal Torx adapter, tighten each of the 10 mm bolts (5, **Figure 32**) an additional 90° following the same circular pattern.

6. Apply molybdenum disulfide grease to each camshaft lobe. Identify the exhaust cam by locating its tang or the pink mark. Install the exhaust cam into its cradle on the starboard side on the cylinder head with the threaded opening and locating pin hole positioned on the topside.

7. Apply engine oil to the camshaft contact surfaces, then place the camshaft cap (1, **Figure 31**) onto the camshaft and cylinder head. Make sure the up side of each cap is facing up. Stamped numbers on the caps usually face down. Thread the bolts for each cap into the cylinder head until finger-tight. Tighten the bolts gradually until the caps just contact the cylinder head.

8. Install the intake camshaft into its cradle on the port side of the cylinder head with the threaded opening and hole for the pin positioned on the topside. Apply engine oil to the camshaft contact surfaces, then place the camshaft cap (9, **Figure 31**) onto the camshaft and cylinder head. Make sure the up side of each cap is facing up. Stamped numbers on the caps usually face down. Thread the bolts for each cap into the cylinder head until finger-tight. Tighten the bolts gradually until the caps just contact the cylinder head.

9. Tighten all camshaft cap bolts to half the specification in **Table 5** under camshaft retainer. Tighten the bolts a second time to the full specification in **Table 5**.

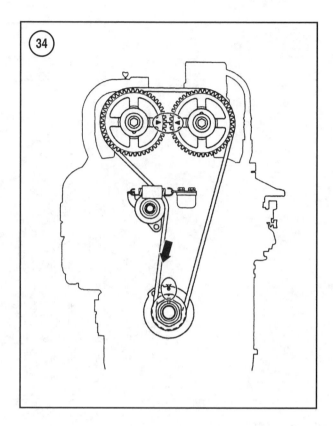

10. Place each seal (10, **Figure 31**) over the top of the camshafts with the seal lip facing inward. Push each seal in until it bottoms in the bore.

11. Place the pin into its opening in the intake camshaft. Guide the pin into the bottom of the port side sprocket and lower the sprocket onto the camshaft. Install and hand tighten the bolts (1 and 2, **Figure 30**). Rotate the sprocket until the timing mark (**Figure 34**) faces toward the starboard side.

12. Place the pin into the exhaust camshaft. Rotate the exhaust camshaft until the sprocket can be installed with the timing marks aligned. Guide the pin into the sprocket and lower the sprocket onto the camshaft. Make sure the timing marks perfectly align (**Figure 34**).

13. Rotate the flywheel 90° counterclockwise until it just reaches TDC for the No. 1 cylinder.

14. Install the timing belt as described in this chapter.

15. Attach the flywheel holding tool (Yamaha part No.YB-6139) to the camshaft sprocket (**Figure 29**) to prevent camshaft rotation. Tighten each camshaft sprocket bolt (1, **Figure 30**) to the specification in **Table 5**.

16. Adjust the valves (Chapter Five).

17. Install the rocker arm cover following the instructions in this chapter. Install the flywheel cover following the instructions in this chapter.

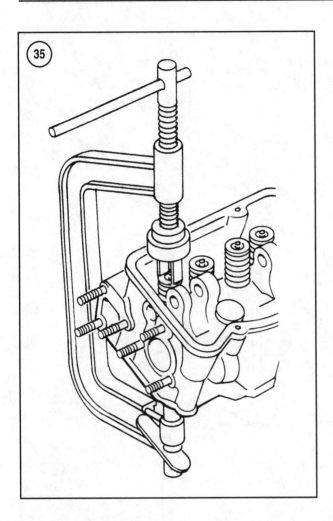

Cylinder Head Disassembly

A valve spring compressor (**Figure 35**) is required for cylinder head disassembly on 9.9-100 hp models. Note the location and orientation of each component prior to removal from the cylinder head.

9.9 and 15 hp models

Refer to **Figure 36** during this procedure.
1. Remove the oil pump as described in this chapter.
2. Refer to *Valve Adjustment* in Chapter Five and fully loosen each valve adjusting screw (1, **Figure 36**).
3. Gently shake the cylinder head to slide the rocker arm shafts (12, **Figure 36**) from their bores.
4. Remove each rocker arm shaft and collar from the cylinder head.
5. Attach the valve spring compressor tool (Yamaha part No.YM-1253) to the valve and spring cap as indicated (**Figure 37**). Tighten the clamp just enough to remove the keepers (1, **Figure 37**) from the valve stem.

6. Slowly loosen the clamp and remove the spring cap, spring and spring base (5, 6, and 8, **Figure 36**) from the cylinder head. Repeat Steps 6 and 7 for the remaining valves.
7. Hold the flywheel from turning using the flywheel holding tool (part No. YB-6139). Remove the bolt and lift the camshaft sprocket (4, **Figure 38**), washer (6) and drive key (5) from the camshaft.
8. Slip the camshaft from the bottom of the cylinder head. Carefully pry the seal (16, **Figure 36**) from the camshaft bore.

25-50 hp models

Mark all components prior to removing them from the cylinder head. Refer to **Figure 39** and **Figure 40** during this procedure.
1. Remove the oil pump following the instructions in this section. Place the cylinder head on a clean workbench with the piston side down.
2. Refer to *Valve Adjustment* in Chapter Five and fully loosen each valve adjusting screw.
3. Evenly loosen the rocker arm retainer bolts, then pull the rocker arm shaft straight up and away from the cylinder head. Remove each rocker arm and retainer from the rocker arm shaft.
4. Attach the valve spring compressor (Yamaha part No.YM-1253) to the valve and spring cap (**Figure 41**). Tighten the clamp just enough to remove the keepers from the valve stem.
5. Slowly loosen the clamp, then remove the spring cap, spring and spring seat from the cylinder head. Repeat Steps 6 and 7 for the remaining valves.
6. Attach the flywheel holding tool (Yamaha part No.YB-6139) to the camshaft sprocket (**Figure 42**) to prevent camshaft rotation. Remove the bolt (2, **Figure 40**) and washer (3), then lift the camshaft sprocket (4) and pin (5) from the camshaft.
7. Slip the camshaft from the bottom of the cylinder head. Carefully pry the camshaft (16, **Figure 39** and 1, **Figure 40**) from the camshaft bore.

80 and 100 hp models

> *CAUTION*
> *Arrange the valve lifter and valve pads on a clean work surface as they are removed from the cylinder head. Mark the work surface next to the lifter and pads indicating the cylinder head location for each component. This saves a great deal of time during valve adjustment.*

8

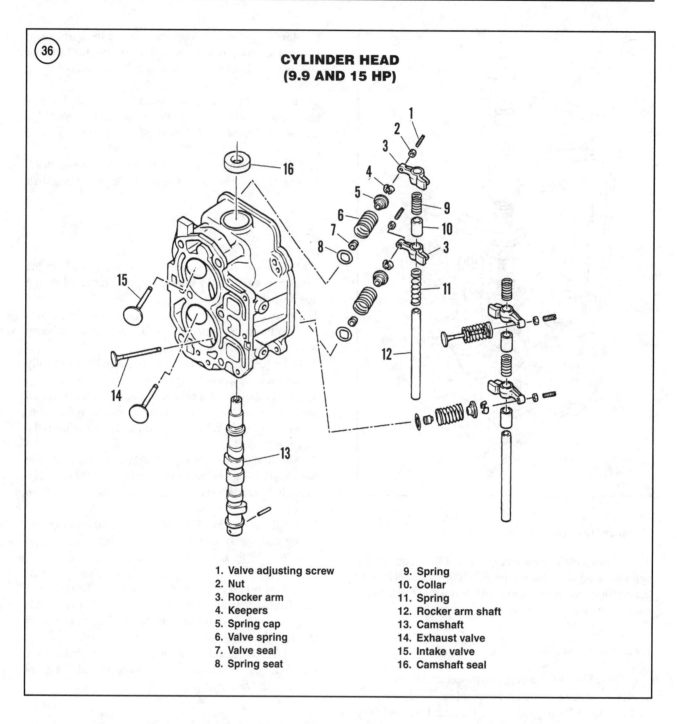

36

**CYLINDER HEAD
(9.9 AND 15 HP)**

1. Valve adjusting screw
2. Nut
3. Rocker arm
4. Keepers
5. Spring cap
6. Valve spring
7. Valve seal
8. Spring seat
9. Spring
10. Collar
11. Spring
12. Rocker arm shaft
13. Camshaft
14. Exhaust valve
15. Intake valve
16. Camshaft seal

Refer to **Figure 43** during this procedure.

1. Use pliers to carefully pull each lifter and valve pad (9 and 10, **Figure 43**) from the cylinder head.

2. Attach the valve spring compressor (Yamaha part No. YM-1253) to the valve and spring cap (**Figure 41**). Tighten the clamp just enough to remove the keepers (1, **Figure 41**) from the valve stem.

3. Slowly loosen the clamp, then remove the spring cap, spring and spring seat from the cylinder head. Repeat

Steps 2 and 3 for the remaining valves on the cylinder head.

OIL PUMP

This section provides oil pump removal, disassembly, assembly and installation procedures for the oil pump used on 9.9-50 hp models. Refer to *Cylinder Block* in this

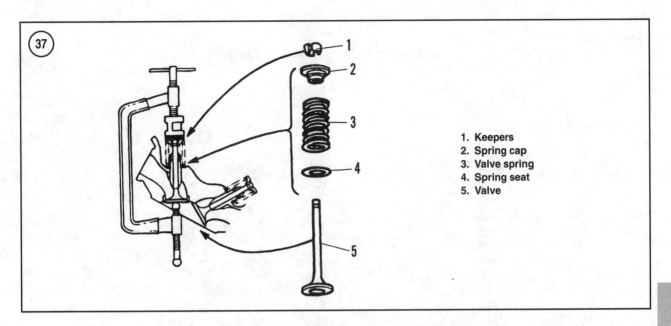

37

1. Keepers
2. Spring cap
3. Valve spring
4. Spring seat
5. Valve

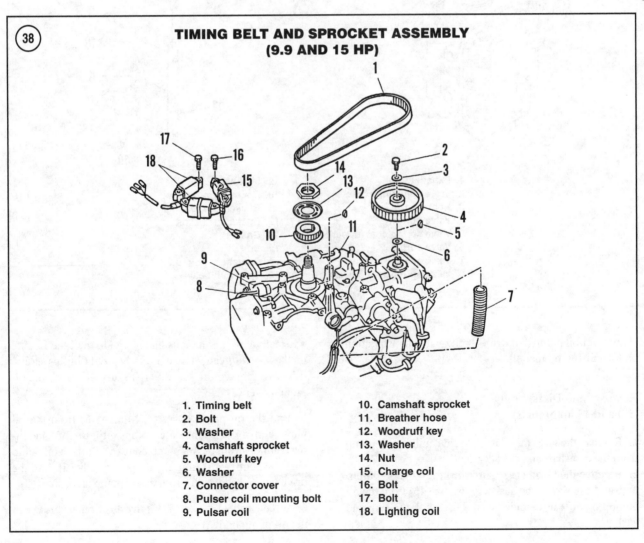

38

TIMING BELT AND SPROCKET ASSEMBLY
(9.9 AND 15 HP)

1. Timing belt	10. Camshaft sprocket
2. Bolt	11. Breather hose
3. Washer	12. Woodruff key
4. Camshaft sprocket	13. Washer
5. Woodruff key	14. Nut
6. Washer	15. Charge coil
7. Connector cover	16. Bolt
8. Pulser coil mounting bolt	17. Bolt
9. Pulsar coil	18. Lighting coil

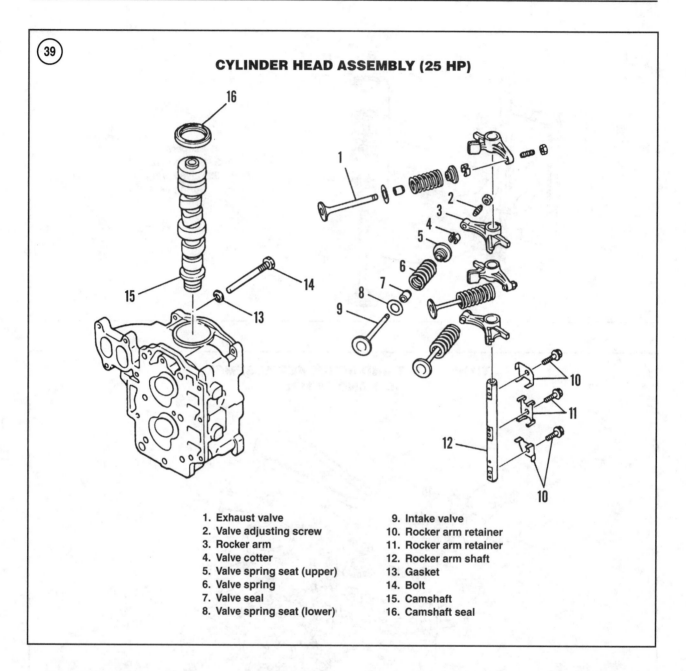

(39) **CYLINDER HEAD ASSEMBLY (25 HP)**

1. Exhaust valve
2. Valve adjusting screw
3. Rocker arm
4. Valve cotter
5. Valve spring seat (upper)
6. Valve spring
7. Valve seal
8. Valve spring seat (lower)
9. Intake valve
10. Rocker arm retainer
11. Rocker arm retainer
12. Rocker arm shaft
13. Gasket
14. Bolt
15. Camshaft
16. Camshaft seal

chapter for oil pump (**Figure 44**) removal and installation on 80 and 100 hp models.

**Removal and Disassembly
(9.9 and 15 hp Models)**

1. Remove the three oil pump bolts, and pull the oil pump from the camshaft and cylinder head.
2. Remove the O-ring (9, **Figure 45**) from the oil pump.
3. Carefully scrape the gasket (6, **Figure 45**) from the oil pump body (7) or cylinder head. Discard the O-ring and gasket.

4. Heat the oil pump housing enough to melt the Loctite on the screw threads. Use a properly sized Phillips screwdriver to remove the screws (1, **Figure 46**) from the oil pump cover (2).

5. Pull the oil pump cover (2, **Figure 46**) from the oil pump body (6). Lift the outer rotor (3, **Figure 46**) and inner rotor (4) from the oil pump body (6). Pull the oil pump shaft (8, **Figure 46**) from the oil pump body (6). Pull the drive pin (5, **Figure 46**) from the oil pump drive shaft (8).

6. Lift the rubber gasket (7, **Figure 46**) from its groove in the oil pump body (6).

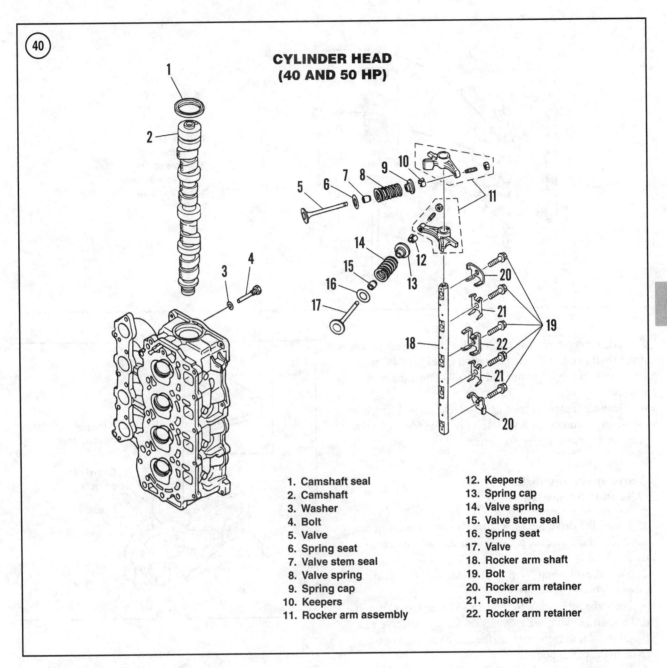

**CYLINDER HEAD
(40 AND 50 HP)**

1. Camshaft seal
2. Camshaft
3. Washer
4. Bolt
5. Valve
6. Spring seat
7. Valve stem seal
8. Valve spring
9. Spring cap
10. Keepers
11. Rocker arm assembly
12. Keepers
13. Spring cap
14. Valve spring
15. Valve stem seal
16. Spring seat
17. Valve
18. Rocker arm shaft
19. Bolt
20. Rocker arm retainer
21. Tensioner
22. Rocker arm retainer

7. Discard the rubber gasket. Clean all components using a suitable solvent. Inspect all oil pump components and measure them for excessive wear as described under *Inspection*.

**Removal and Disassembly
(25-50 hp Models)**

1. Remove the four oil pump mounting bolts (9, **Figure 47**), then pull the oil pump (8) from the camshaft and cylinder head.

2. Pull the O-ring (7, **Figure 47**) from the oil pump body (8). Remove and discard the O-ring.

3. Heat the oil pump housing enough to melt the Loctite on the screw threads. Use a Phillips screwdriver to remove the screws (1, **Figure 48**) from the oil pump cover (2).

4. Pull the oil pump cover (2, **Figure 48**) from the oil pump body (8). Lift the outer rotor (4, **Figure 48**) and inner rotor (5) from the oil pump body. Pull the oil pump shaft (7, **Figure 48**) from the oil pump body (8).

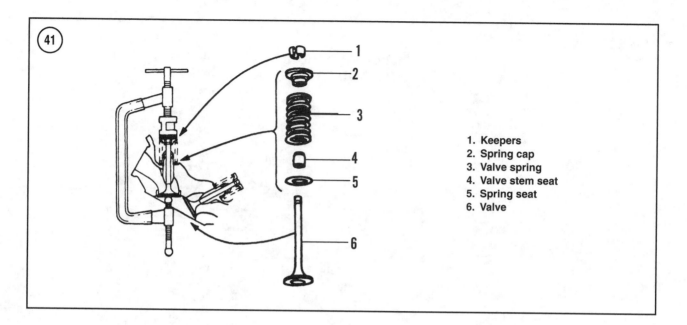

1. Keepers
2. Spring cap
3. Valve spring
4. Valve stem seat
5. Spring seat
6. Valve

5. Pull the drive pin (6, **Figure 48**) from the oil pump drive shaft (7). Lift the rubber gasket (3, **Figure 48**) from its groove in the oil pump body (8). Discard the rubber gasket.

6. Clean all components using a suitable solvent. Inspect all oil pump components and measure them for excessive wear as described under *Inspection*.

**Assembly and Installation
(9.9 and 15 hp models)**

1. Install the drive pin (5, **Figure 46**) into the oil pump shaft (8). Make sure the pin protrudes the same amount on each side of the shaft.

2. Slide the oil pump drive shaft slotted side first into the oil pump body (6, **Figure 46**).

3. Place the inner rotor (4, **Figure 46**) over the oil pump drive shaft (8) with the slotted side facing the drive pin. Align the slot in the rotor with the drive pin, then seat the rotor in the pump body.

4. Insert the outer rotor (3, **Figure 46**) into the oil pump opening. Rotate the rotor until it aligns with the inner rotor and drops into place.

5. Push down on both rotors until they are firmly seated in the body.

6. Fill the oil pump cavity with engine oil. Install a new rubber gasket (7, **Figure 46**) into the groove in the oil pump body (6).

7. Place the cover (2, **Figure 46**) onto the oil pump body. Apply Loctite 222 to the threads and install both screws (1, **Figure 46**). Tighten the cover screws to 4.0 N•m (35.5 in.-lb.).

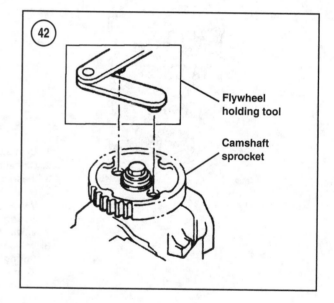

Flywheel holding tool

Camshaft sprocket

8. Install a new gasket (6, **Figure 45**) on the oil pump body. Lubricate the new O-ring (9, **Figure 45**) with engine oil, then slide it over the pump body. Seat the O-ring in the groove.

9. Carefully slide the oil pump into the opening on the bottom of cylinder head. Rotate the pump body until the slot in the oil pump drive shaft aligns with the drive pin in the camshaft.

10. Rotate the oil pump body until its mounting holes align with the threaded holes in the cylinder head.

11. Align the gasket and install the four mounting bolts. Tighten the oil pump mounting bolts to 10 N•m (88 in.-lb.).

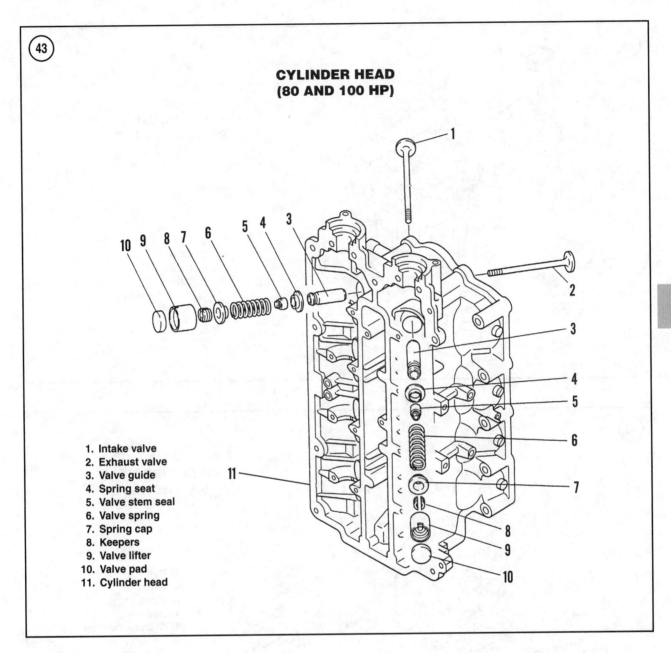

**CYLINDER HEAD
(80 AND 100 HP)**

1. Intake valve
2. Exhaust valve
3. Valve guide
4. Spring seat
5. Valve stem seal
6. Valve spring
7. Spring cap
8. Keepers
9. Valve lifter
10. Valve pad
11. Cylinder head

8

Assembly and Installation
(25-50 hp Models)

1. Install the drive pin (6, **Figure 48**) into the oil pump shaft (7). Make sure the pin protrudes the same amount on each side of the shaft.

2. Slide the oil pump drive shaft slotted side first into the oil pump body (8, **Figure 48**).

3. Place the inner rotor (5, **Figure 48**) over the oil pump drive shaft (7) with the slotted side facing the drive pin. Align the slot in the rotor with the drive pin and seat the rotor in the pump body.

4. Insert the outer rotor (4, **Figure 48**) into the oil pump opening. Rotate the rotor until it aligns with the inner rotor and drops into place.

5. Push down on both rotors until they are firmly seated in the body.

6. Fill the oil pump cavity with engine oil. Install a new rubber gasket (3, **Figure 48**) into its groove on the oil pump body (8).

7. Place the cover (2, **Figure 48**) onto the oil pump body. Apply Loctite 222 to the threads, then install both screws (1, **Figure 48**). Tighten the cover screws to 4.0 N•m (35.5 in.-lb.).

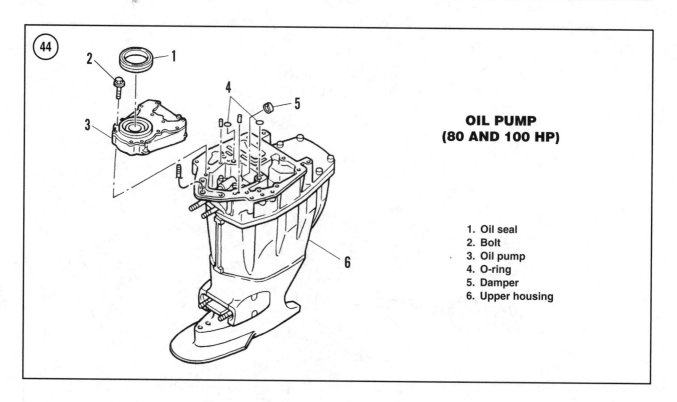

**OIL PUMP
(80 AND 100 HP)**

1. Oil seal
2. Bolt
3. Oil pump
4. O-ring
5. Damper
6. Upper housing

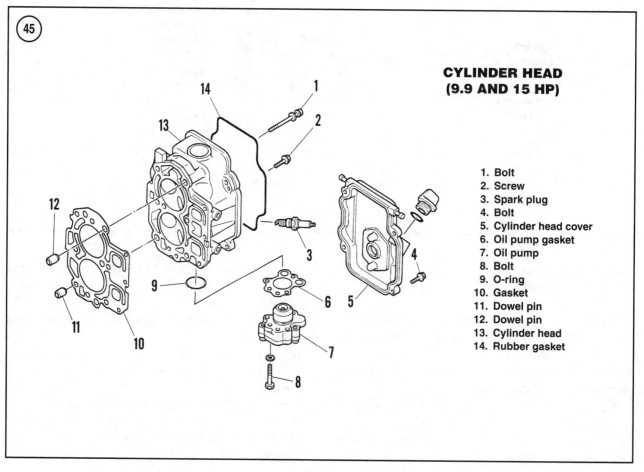

**CYLINDER HEAD
(9.9 AND 15 HP)**

1. Bolt
2. Screw
3. Spark plug
4. Bolt
5. Cylinder head cover
6. Oil pump gasket
7. Oil pump
8. Bolt
9. O-ring
10. Gasket
11. Dowel pin
12. Dowel pin
13. Cylinder head
14. Rubber gasket

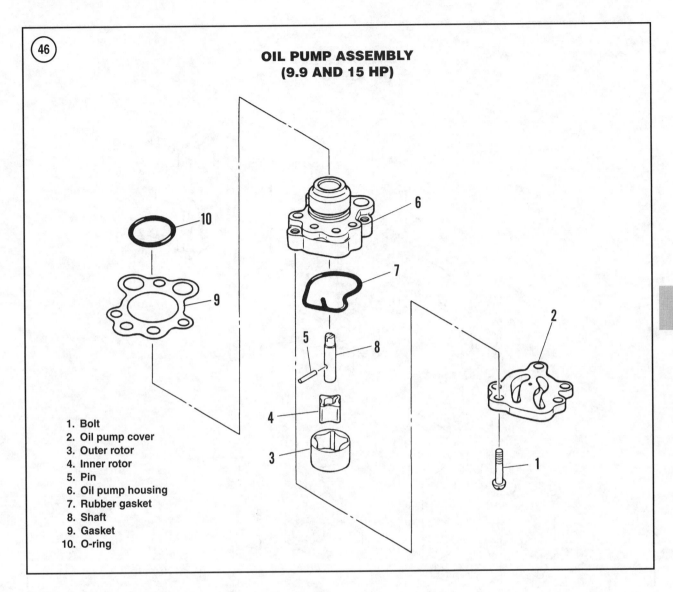

**OIL PUMP ASSEMBLY
(9.9 AND 15 HP)**

46

1. Bolt
2. Oil pump cover
3. Outer rotor
4. Inner rotor
5. Pin
6. Oil pump housing
7. Rubber gasket
8. Shaft
9. Gasket
10. O-ring

8. Lubricate the three new O-rings with engine oil and place them into the grooves in the pump body.

9. Carefully slide the oil pump into the bottom of cylinder head. Rotate the pump body until the slot in the oil pump drive shaft aligns with the drive pin in the camshaft.

10. Pull the pump away from the cylinder head just enough to inspect both small O-rings. Reposition the O-rings if they are out of position. Install the oil pump mountings bolts (9, **Figure 47**) and tighten them to 10 N•m (88 in.-lb.).

INSPECTION

This section provides instructions to inspect and measure all components of the cylinder head. Many of the measurements in this section require the use of precision measuring instruments. Have the components measured at a reputable machine shop if these instruments are not available.

Cylinder Head

1. Scrape all carbon deposits from the combustion chamber with a blunt scraper (**Figure 49**). Avoid scraping aluminum material from the cylinder head.

2. Pull the valve stem seals from the spring side of the valve guides.

3. Remove the anode, thermostats and sensors following the instructions in this manual.

4. Thoroughly clean all grease or corrosion from the cylinder head using a solvent suitable for aluminum material.

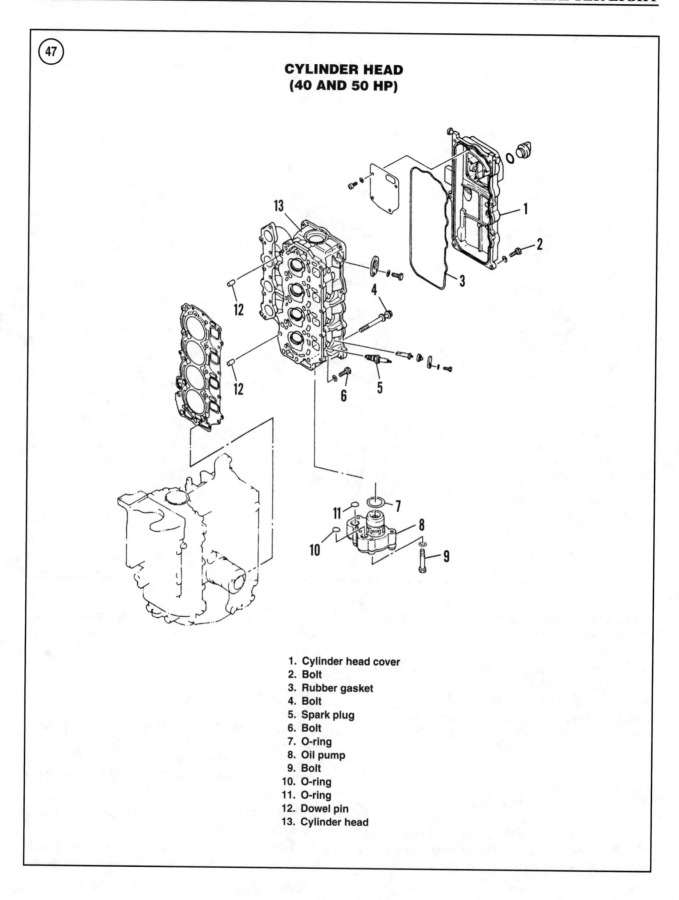

47

**CYLINDER HEAD
(40 AND 50 HP)**

1. Cylinder head cover
2. Bolt
3. Rubber gasket
4. Bolt
5. Spark plug
6. Bolt
7. O-ring
8. Oil pump
9. Bolt
10. O-ring
11. O-ring
12. Dowel pin
13. Cylinder head

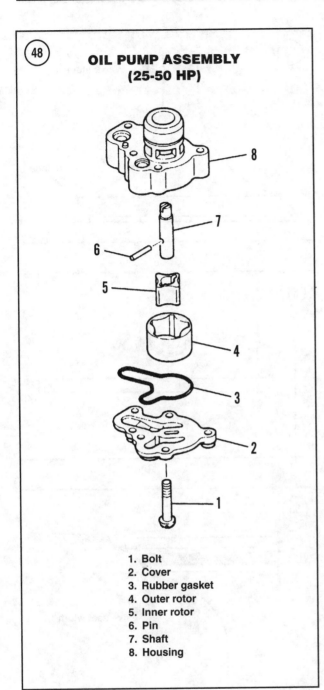

48 OIL PUMP ASSEMBLY
(25-50 HP)

8

7

6

5

4

3

2

1

1. Bolt
2. Cover
3. Rubber gasket
4. Outer rotor
5. Inner rotor
6. Pin
7. Shaft
8. Housing

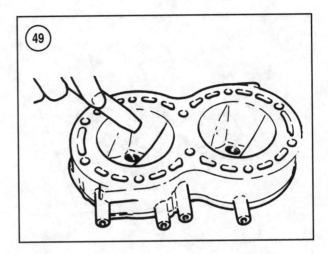

49

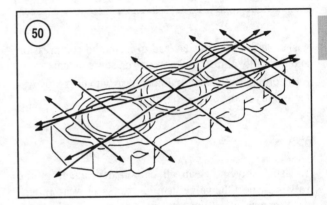

50

8

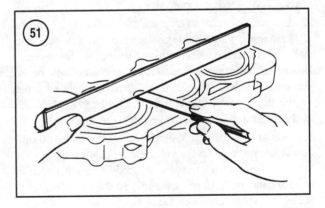

51

5. Check for surface warpage by placing a straightedge at various points (**Figure 50**) on the cylinder head mating surface. Hold the straightedge firmly against the head, then use a feeler gauge to check the gap at various points along the straightedge (**Figure 51**). Compare the thickness of the feeler gauge that can be passed under the straightedge with the warpage limit in **Table 6**.

6. Minor warpage can be repaired by placing a sheet of 400-600 grit wet sandpaper on a surface plate. Use slight

downward pressure and move the cylinder head in a figure eight motion as indicated in **Figure 52**. Stop periodically and check the amount of warpage. Rotate the head several times to avoid removing too much material from one side. Remove only the material necessary to remove the excess warpage.

7. Have this operation performed at a machine shop if a surfacing plate is unavailable. Replace the cylinder head if warpage is excessive. Do not cut down or machine the

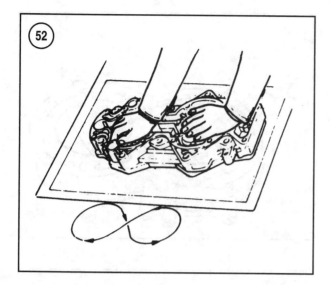

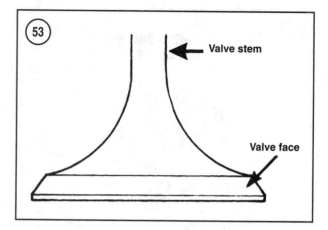

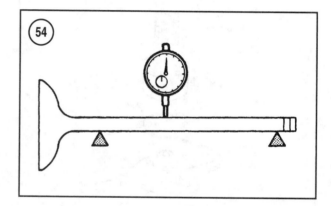

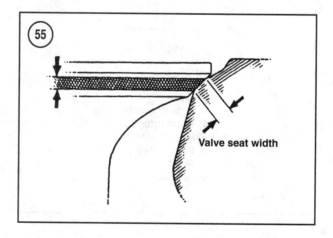

gasket surface as this can lead to increased compression and difficulty adjusting the valves on some models.

8. Thoroughly clean the cylinder head with hot soapy water and dry with compressed air.

Valves

1. Using solvent, clean all carbon deposits from the valves. Inspect the valve stem for excessive wear, roughness, cracks, corrosion or other damage. Replace the valve if corroded or damaged.

2. Use a micrometer to measure each valve stem (**Figure 53**) along the valve guide contact area. Rotate the valve 90° and repeat the measurements. Record the highest and lowest measurements. Repeat these measurements for the remaining valves. Compare the measurements with the valve stem specifications listed in **Table 8**. Replace the valve if its stem diameter is less than the specification.

3. Mount the valve on V-blocks and position the tip of a dial indicator against the valve stem as indicated in **Figure 54**. Observe the amount of needle movement while rotating the valve. Replace the valve if the stem runout exceeds the specification in **Table 8**.

4. Inspect the valve face for cracks, corrosion or pits.

5. Using a vernier caliper, measure the width of the valve seat (**Figure 55**). Compare the measurement with the specification listed in **Table 8**.

6. Have the valve and valve seat reconditioned at a machine shop if the valve seat is worn or if incorrect valve seat width is indicated. Cut the valve seat surface to a 45° angle. Cut the first angle (combustion chamber side of the seat) to 15°. Cut the third angle (intake side of the seat) to 60°.

7. Inspect the valve guide bore for cracks, discoloration or damage. Have the valve guides replaced at a machine shop if damage is noted.

8. Measurement of the valve guide requires a special precision measuring instrument (**Figure 56**). Have these measurements performed at a machine shop if this precision measuring instrument is unavailable.

9. Measure the inside diameter of the valve guide along the entire length of the bore (**Figure 56**). Rotate the gauge

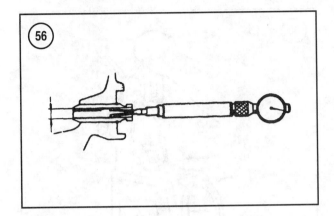

56

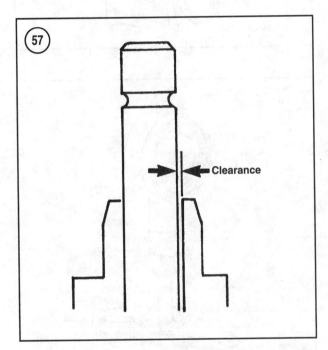

57

Clearance

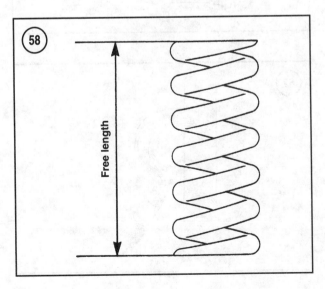

58

Free length

90° and repeat the measurement. Record the highest and lowest measurement. Repeat the measurement for the remaining valve guides. Compare the measurements with the specification in **Table 8**. Replace the valve guides if the lowest reading is below the standard diameter or the highest reading is above the maximum diameter.

10. Subtract the highest valve stem measurement from the lowest valve guide measurement to determine the lowest valve stem clearance (**Figure 57**).

11. Subtract the lowest valve stem diameter from the largest valve guide clearance to determine the highest valve stem clearance.

12. Compare the results with the specification in **Table 8**. Repeat the valve and valve seat measurements before failing either component. A worn valve stem or valve guide is likely if excessive clearance is noted. A damaged or improperly installed valve guide is likely if the stem clearance is too low.

> *CAUTION*
> *Improper valve guide installation can lead to poor valve sealing, increased valve wear and potential failure. Make sure that the replacement valve guides are installed to the proper depth on 80 and 100 hp models. Valve guide depth specifications for these models are in **Table 8**.*

13. Inspect each valve spring for excessive wear, cracks or other damage. Never switch the intake and exhaust valves as their spring tension may differ. Damage to the valve and other components can occur if the valve springs are installed at the incorrect valve.

14. On all models, except 9.9 hp, measure the free length of each spring (**Figure 58**). Compare the measurement with the specification in **Table 13**. Replace the spring if the free length is incorrect.

15. Using a carpenter's square, measure the valve spring tilt as indicated in **Figure 59**. Compare the out-of-square measurement with the specification in **Table 14**.

16. 9.9 hp models require measurement of spring pressure to determine its condition. This measurement requires a special spring tester (**Figure 60**). Have the spring tested at a machine shop. Spring pressure specifications are provided in **Table 13**.

Rocker Arm and Shaft

A rocker arm and shaft arrangement is used only on 9.9-50 hp models.

1. Inspect each rocker arm for excessive wear, corrosion, discoloration or roughness.

8

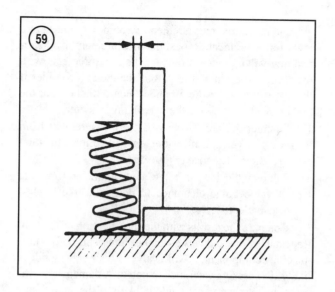

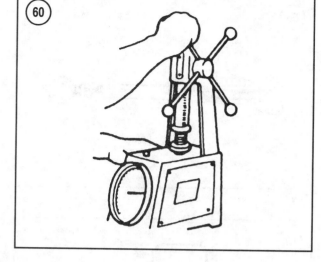

2. Using an inside micrometer, measure the inside diameter of each rocker arm (**Figure 61**). Compare the measurement with the specification in **Table 14**.

3. Inspect each rocker arm shaft(s) for wear, corrosion or discoloration.

4. Using an outside micrometer, measure the shaft diameter at the areas that contact the rocker arms (**Figure 62**).

5. Compare the measurements with the specification in **Table 14**.

Camshaft and Lifters

1. Inspect the camshaft (**Figure 63**) for excessive wear, cracks or corrosion.

2. On 80 and 100 hp models, inspect the lifters and valve pads (**Figure 64**) for wear or damage.

3. Measure each camshaft lobe as indicated in **Figure 65**. Compare the lobe height measurement with the specification in **Table 7**.

4. Measure each lobe width at a point 90° from the lobe length measuring points. Compare the lobe width with the specification in **Table 7**.

5. Measure the camshaft bearing journals (**Figure 66**). Compare the measurements with the specifications in **Table 7**.

6. On 9.9 hp models, place the camshaft on V-blocks located under the top and bottom journals. Securely mount a dial indicator so the plunger directly contacts one of the middle camshaft journals (**Figure 67**). Observe the dial indicator while slowly rotating the camshaft. Repeat the measurement on all journals between the top and bottom journals. The amount of needle movement on the dial indicator indicates the camshaft runout. Compare the runout with the specification in **Table 7**. Replace the camshaft if

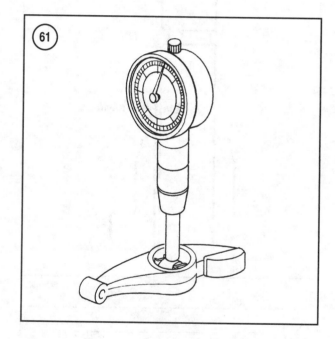

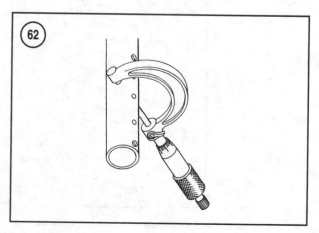

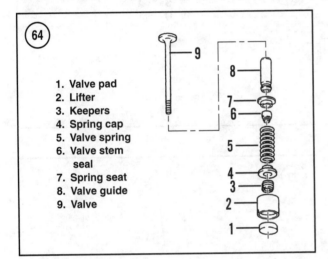

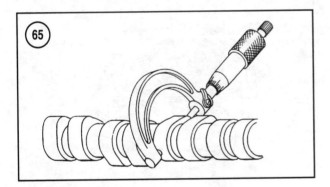

1. Valve pad
2. Lifter
3. Keepers
4. Spring cap
5. Valve spring
6. Valve stem seal
7. Spring seat
8. Valve guide
9. Valve

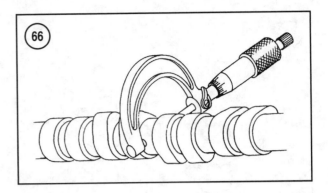

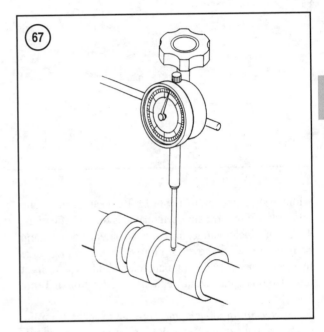

8

the amount of camshaft runout on any journal exceeds the specification.

7. On 80 and 100 hp models, install all camshaft caps, without the camshafts, at their respective locations on the cylinder head. Tighten the caps to the specification in **Table 5**. Measure the diameter of each camshaft bore in the cylinder head. Record the measurements. Compare these measurements with the specification in **Table 7**. Replace

the cylinder head if the bore diameter exceeds the specification.

Oil Pump

The oil pump used on 80 and 100 hp models is not serviceable. If oil pressure is insufficient, first inspect the oil pressure relief valve and main bearings. If the pressure relief valve and main bearings are in acceptable condition, replace the oil pump. Refer to **Figure 68** during the inspection process

1. Clean all oil pump components using solvent, then dry them using compressed air.

2. Place the inner and outer rotor into the oil pump body.

3. Using a feeler gauge, measure the clearance between the inner and outer rotor at the point indicated in **Figure 69**. Select the feeler gauge that passes between the rotors with a slight drag. Compare the feeler gauge thickness

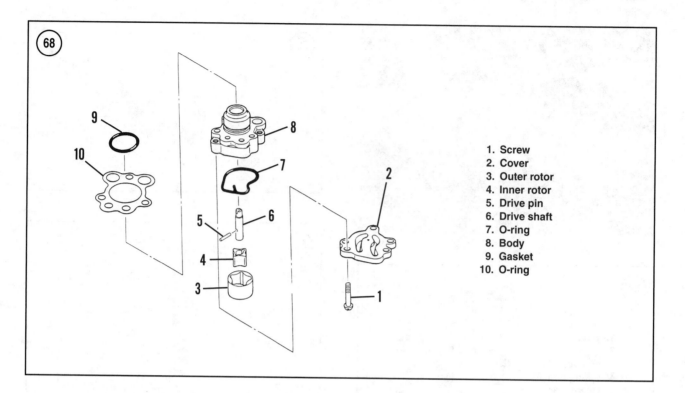

(68)

1. Screw
2. Cover
3. Outer rotor
4. Inner rotor
5. Drive pin
6. Drive shaft
7. O-ring
8. Body
9. Gasket
10. O-ring

with the specification in **Table 15**. Replace the inner and outer rotor if the measurement exceeds the specification.

4. Using a feeler gauge, measure the outer rotor-to-pump body clearance as shown in **Figure 70**. Select the gauge that passes between the rotor and pump body with a slight drag. Compare the clearance to the specification in **Table 15**.

5. On 9.9-50 hp models, measure the distance from the pump-mating surface to the outer rotor using a depth micrometer as shown in **Figure 71**. If the rotor depth is excessive (**Table 15**), inspect the outer rotor for excessive wear (**Figure 72**) or damage. No rotor thickness specification is available. Replace the outer rotor if it appears worn or damaged and measure the outer rotor depth again to verify the repair. If the rotor is in acceptable condition, replace the pump body and measure the rotor depth again.

Cylinder Head Assembly

Coat all bearing or sliding surfaces with engine oil during assembly. Apply molybdenum disulfide lubricant (moly lube) to the camshaft lobes prior to installation. Install any anodes, thermostats, sensors or brackets prior to installing the cylinder head.

9.9 and 15 hp models

Refer to **Figure 73** during this procedure.

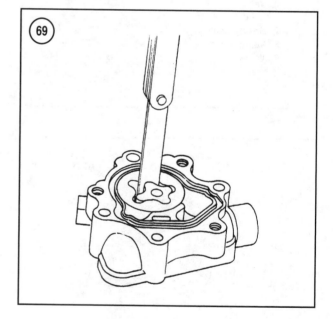

(69)

1. Press the new valve stem seal (4, **Figure 74**) onto the exposed end of the valve guide by hand. Install the No. 1 intake valve into the valve guide and seat it against the valve seat.

2. Place the valve spring (8, **Figure 73**) and valve spring (6) over the valve stem (15). Seat them against the cylinder head. Place the spring cap (5, **Figure 73**) onto the valve spring (6) with the keeper (4) recess facing out.

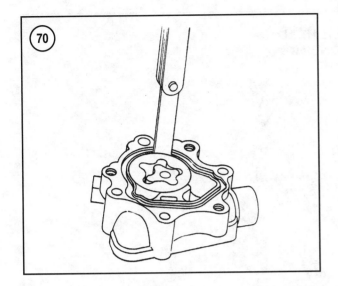

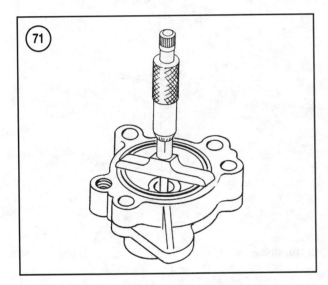

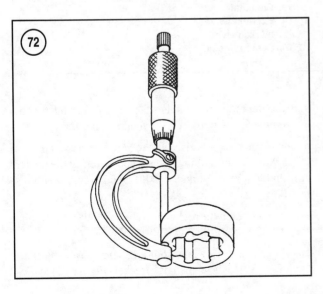

3. Attach the valve spring compressor (Yamaha part No.YM-1253) to the valve and spring cap (**Figure 74**). Tighten the clamp just enough to expose the grooved allow installation of the valve keepers (**Figure 74**).

4. Slowly loosen the valve spring compressor and inspect the spring cap and stem for proper seating of the keepers. Repeat Steps 1-4 for the remaining valves.

5. Position the new seal (16, **Figure 73**) into the opening at the top of the cylinder head with the lip side facing in or down. Use an appropriately sized socket to drive the seal into the bore until flush with the cylinder head surface.

6. Lubricate the camshaft bearing surfaces with engine oil, then slide the camshaft into its bore with the threaded opening facing the top of the cylinder head.

7. Place the rocker arms, springs and spacers in the cylinder head. Apply engine oil to the rocker arm shafts, then slide them through the cylinder head bores, springs, spacers and rocker arms.

8. Place the drive key into its groove in the camshaft. Place the washer over the camshaft and seat it against the seal. Align the drive key grooves and install the camshaft pulley onto the camshaft. Thread the retaining bolt and washer through the pulley and into the camshaft.

9. Attach the flywheel holding tool (Yamaha part No.YB-6139) to the camshaft sprocket (**Figure 75**) to prevent camshaft rotation. Tighten the camshaft sprocket bolt to the specification in **Table 1**.

10. Install the oil pump following the instructions in this section.

11. Adjust the valves as described in Chapter Five.

25-50 hp models

Refer to **Figure 76** (25 hp models) or **Figure 77** (40 and 50 hp models) as necessary during this procedure.

1. Press the new valve stem seal onto the valve guide by hand. Install the No. 1 intake valve into the valve guide and seat it against the valve seat.

2. Place the valve spring seat and valve spring over the valve stem. Make sure the wider spring spacing is positioned toward the rocker arm side. Seat the spring and base against the cylinder head. Place the upper valve spring seat onto the valve spring with the valve keeper recess facing out.

3. Attach the valve spring compressor (Yamaha part No.YM-1253) to the valve and spring cap (**Figure 78**). Tighten the clamp just enough to allow installation of the valve keepers and install the keepers.

4. Slowly loosen the compressor and inspect the spring cap and stem for proper seating of the keepers. Repeat Steps 1-4 for the remaining valves.

8

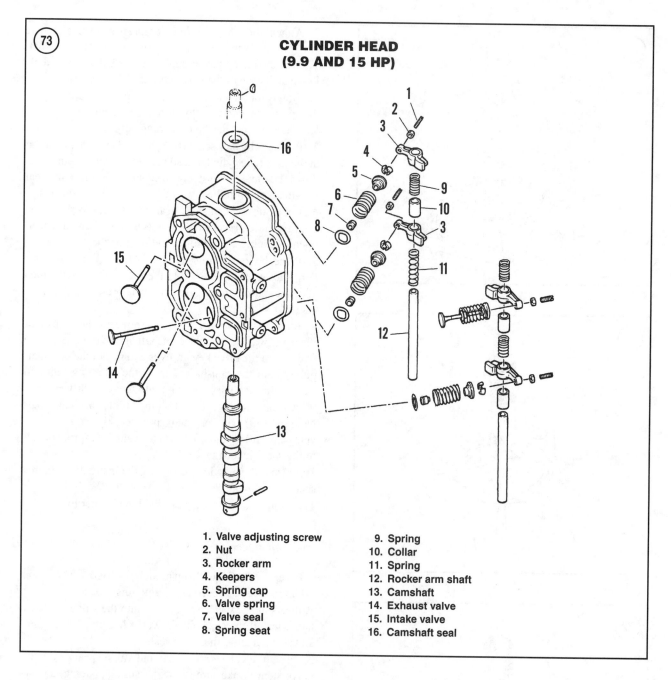

**CYLINDER HEAD
(9.9 AND 15 HP)**

1. Valve adjusting screw
2. Nut
3. Rocker arm
4. Keepers
5. Spring cap
6. Valve spring
7. Valve seal
8. Spring seat
9. Spring
10. Collar
11. Spring
12. Rocker arm shaft
13. Camshaft
14. Exhaust valve
15. Intake valve
16. Camshaft seal

5. Position the new camshaft seal (16, **Figure 76** or 1, **Figure 77**) into the opening at the top of the cylinder head with the lip side facing inward. Use an appropriately sized driver to drive the seal into the bore until it is flush with the cylinder head surface.

6. Lubricate the camshaft bearing surfaces with engine oil, then slide the camshaft into its bore with the threaded opening facing the top of the cylinder head.

7. Lubricate the rocker arm shaft with engine oil, then slide the rocker arms over the shaft. Separate the rocker arms enough to place the retainers against the shaft. Make sure the flat mounting notches face away from the retainers and the arrow marks on the retainers face up.

8. Align the rocker arms with the valve stems and the retainer with the mounting bosses when lowering the rocker arm shaft onto the cylinder head. Thread the retainer bolts into the cylinder head.

9. Evenly tighten the rocker arm shaft retainer bolts to the specification in **Table 3** or **Table 4**.

10. Attach the flywheel holding tool (Yamaha part No. YB-6139) to the camshaft sprocket (**Figure 79**) to pre-

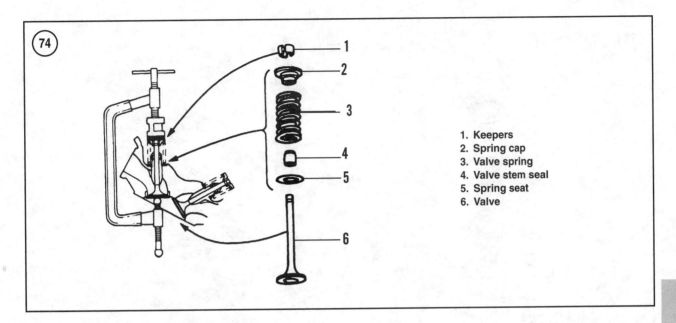

1. Keepers
2. Spring cap
3. Valve spring
4. Valve stem seal
5. Spring seat
6. Valve

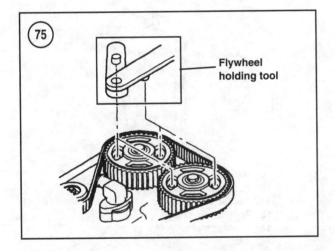

Flywheel
holding tool

vent camshaft rotation. Tighten the camshaft sprocket bolt to the specification in **Table 3** and **Table 4**.

11. Install the oil pump as described in this chapter.

12. Adjust the valves as described in Chapter Five.

80 and 100 hp models

Refer to **Figure 79** during this procedure.

1. Press the new valve stem seal (5, **Figure 79**) onto the valve guide by hand. Install the No. 1 intake valve (1, **Figure 79**) into the valve guide and seat it against the valve seat.

2. Place the valve spring seat (4, **Figure 79**) over the valve spring (6) with the larger diameter side facing the cylinder head. Slide the valve spring (6, **Figure 79**) over the valve stem and seat the spring and base against the

head. Place the upper valve spring seat (7, **Figure 79**) onto the valve spring (6) with the valve keeper (8) recess facing outward.

3. Attach the valve spring compressor (Yamaha part No.YM1253) to the valve and spring cap (**Figure 78**). Tighten the clamp just enough to allow installation of the keepers (8, **Figure 79**). Install both keepers as indicated in **Figure 79**.

4. Slowly loosen the clamp, then inspect the spring cap and stem for proper seating of the keepers. Repeat Steps 1-4 for the remaining valves.

5. Place the valve pad (10, **Figure 79**) into its opening in the lifter (9). Lubricate the lifter with engine oil and slide it over its respective valve stem. Carefully push the lifter and pad into the bore until the backside of the pad just contacts the valve stem. Repeat this step for the remaining pads and lifters.

CAUTION
Install the valve lifter and pads into the same location from which removed. This saves a great deal of time during valve adjustment.

Power Head Removal

Inspect the engine to locate the fuel supply hose, throttle and shift cables, battery cables, and trim system connections. Most hoses and wires must be removed for complete power head disassembly. Many of the hoses and wires are more accessible after the power head is removed. Disconnect only the hoses, wires and linkage re-

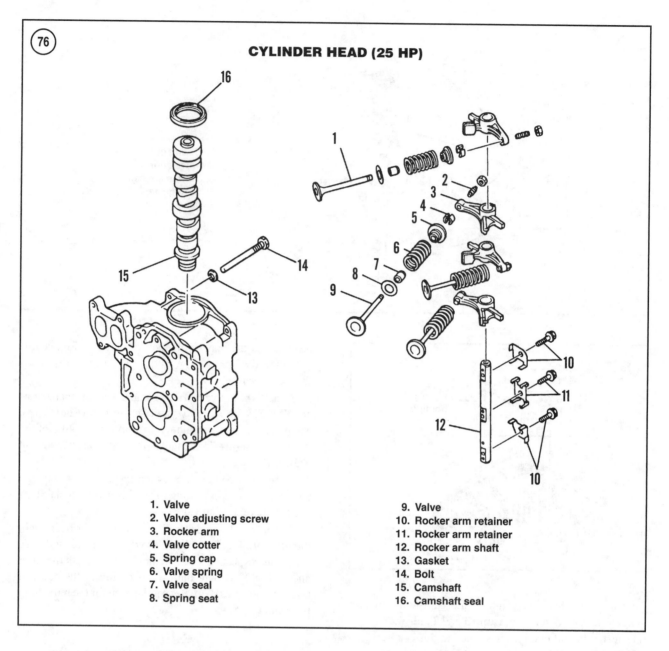

CYLINDER HEAD (25 HP)

1. Valve
2. Valve adjusting screw
3. Rocker arm
4. Valve cotter
5. Spring cap
6. Valve spring
7. Valve seal
8. Spring seat
9. Valve
10. Rocker arm retainer
11. Rocker arm retainer
12. Rocker arm shaft
13. Gasket
14. Bolt
15. Camshaft
16. Camshaft seal

quired for power head removal. Disconnect the remaining hoses and wires after removal.

Diagrams of the fuel and electrical systems are provided in this manual. To ease installation and help ensure correct connections, *always* take pictures or make a drawing of all wire and hose connections before beginning the removal process.

Secure the proper lifting equipment (**Figure 80**) before attempting to remove the power head. It is relatively easy to manually lift a 15 hp and smaller engine with some assistance. Larger engines require an overhead hoist.

Lifting hooks are provided on 25-100 hp models. On 80 and 100 hp models, there is a lifting eye on the front of the power head and one just behind the flywheel.

WARNING
The power head may abruptly separate from the midsection during removal. Avoid using excessive lifting force. Carefully pry the power head loose from the midsection before lifting.

CAUTION
Be careful when lifting the power head from the midsection. Corrosion may form at the

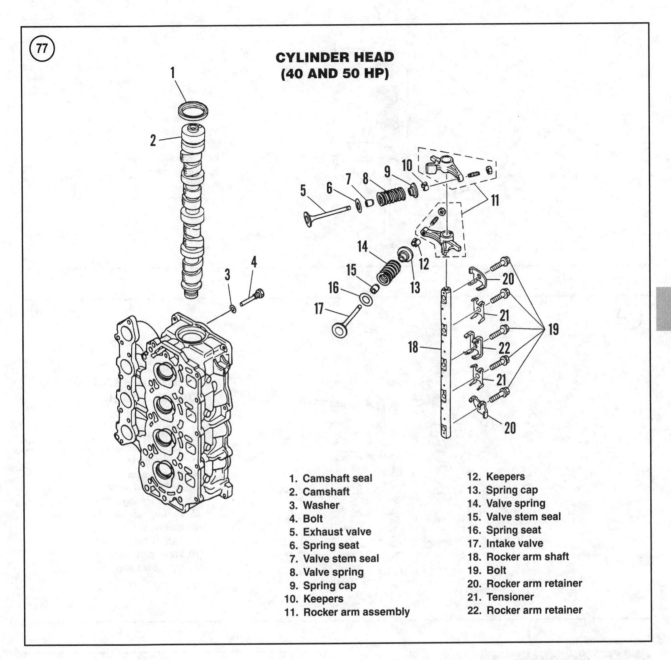

**CYLINDER HEAD
(40 AND 50 HP)**

1. Camshaft seal
2. Camshaft
3. Washer
4. Bolt
5. Exhaust valve
6. Spring seat
7. Valve stem seal
8. Valve spring
9. Spring cap
10. Keepers
11. Rocker arm assembly
12. Keepers
13. Spring cap
14. Valve spring
15. Valve stem seal
16. Spring seat
17. Intake valve
18. Rocker arm shaft
19. Bolt
20. Rocker arm retainer
21. Tensioner
22. Rocker arm retainer

8

power head and midsection mating surfaces, and prevent easy removal. To help prevent damage to the mating surfaces, avoid using any sharp objects to pry the components apart.

9.9 and 15 hp Models

1. Drain the engine as described in Chapter Four.
2. Remove the dipstick (**Figure 81**). Remove the bolts and nuts, then lift the covers from the port and starboard side of the drive shaft housing.

3. On remote control models, perform the following:
   a. Disconnect the throttle and shift cables.
   b. Disconnect the battery cables from the battery, then from the engine.
   c. Disconnect the remote control harness from the engine harness.
4. On tiller control models, perform the following:
   a. Disconnect the throttle cables from the throttle lever.
   b. Disconnect the battery cables, if so equipped, from the battery, then from the engine.

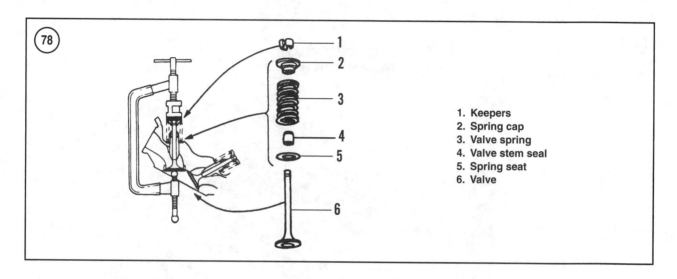

(78)

1. Keepers
2. Spring cap
3. Valve spring
4. Valve stem seal
5. Spring seat
6. Valve

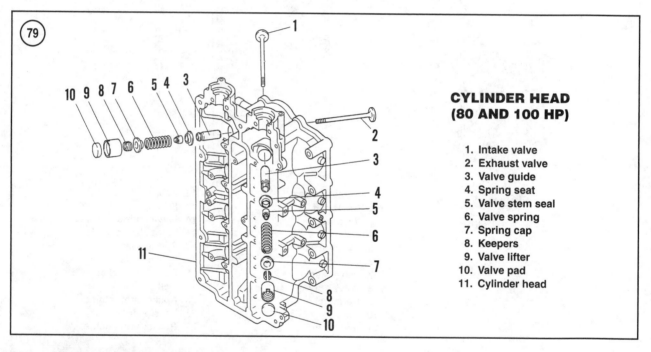

(79)

CYLINDER HEAD (80 AND 100 HP)

1. Intake valve
2. Exhaust valve
3. Valve guide
4. Spring seat
5. Valve stem seal
6. Valve spring
7. Spring cap
8. Keepers
9. Valve lifter
10. Valve pad
11. Cylinder head

(80)

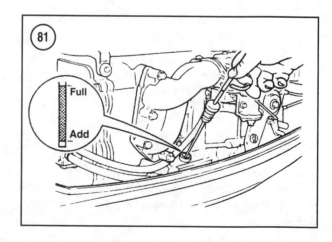

(81)

Full

Add

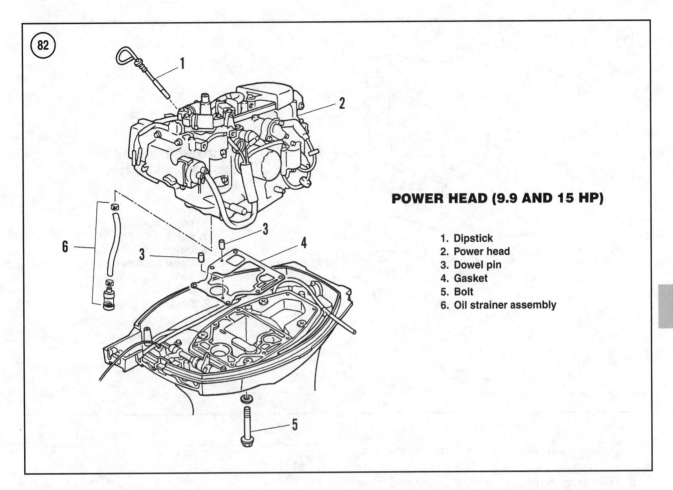

POWER HEAD (9.9 AND 15 HP)

1. Dipstick
2. Power head
3. Dowel pin
4. Gasket
5. Bolt
6. Oil strainer assembly

8

c. Disconnect the stop button wires from the engine wire harness.

d. Disconnect the oil pressure warning light from the engine wire harness.

e. Disconnect the choke linkage.

f. Disconnect the neutral start switch and starter switch leads on electric start models.

5. Remove the gearcase following the instructions in Chapter Nine.

6. Disconnect the fuel supply hose.

7. On manual start models, remove the manual starter and disconnect the neutral start mechanism following the instructions in Chapter Ten.

8. On electric start models, remove the flywheel cover following the instructions in this chapter.

9. Remove the six engine mounting bolts (5, **Figure 82**), then lift the power head from midsection. Place the power head on a suitable work surface.

10. Lift the power head gasket (4, **Figure 82**) from the midsection or the bottom of the power head.

11. Place clean shop towels in the midsection openings and keep contaminants from entering the oil pan. Care-

fully scrape all gasket material from the power head mounting surfaces.

12. Inspect the power head mating surfaces for pits or damage. Replace damaged or defective components. Oil and/or water leakage is likely if these surfaces are damaged.

25-50 hp models

1. Remove the cover from the port and starboard sides of the drive shaft housing.

2. Drain the engine following the instructions in Chapter Four.

3. Remove the dipstick (**Figure 81**).

4. On remote control models, perform the following:

a. Disconnect the throttle and shift cables.

b. Disconnect the battery cables from the battery, then from the engine.

c. Disconnect the remote control harness from the engine harness.

5. On tiller control models, perform the following:

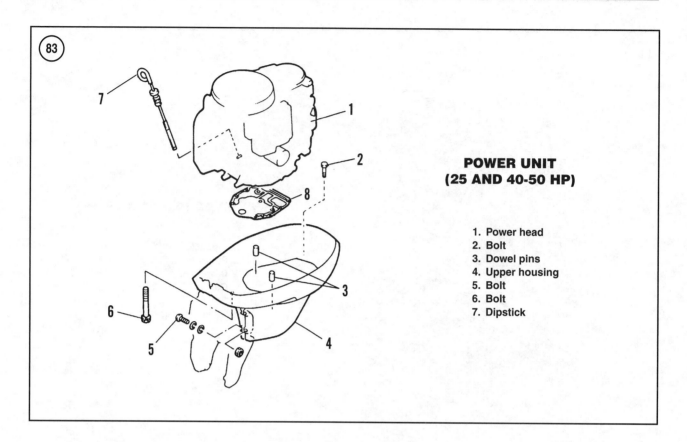

**POWER UNIT
(25 AND 40-50 HP)**

1. Power head
2. Bolt
3. Dowel pins
4. Upper housing
5. Bolt
6. Bolt
7. Dipstick

a. Disconnect the throttle cables from the throttle lever.

b. Disconnect the battery cables, if so equipped, from the battery, then from the engine.

c. Disconnect the stop button wires from the engine wire harness.

d. Disconnect the warning horn wires from the engine wire harness.

e. Disconnect the neutral start switch and starter switch leads on electric start models.

6. Remove the gearcase following the instructions in Chapter Nine.

7. Disconnect the fuel supply hose.

8. On manual start models, remove the manual starter and disconnect the neutral start mechanism following the instructions in Chapter Ten.

9. On electric start models, remove the flywheel cover following the instructions in this chapter.

10. Remove the eight engine mounting bolts (6, **Figure 83**). Using a suitable tool, pry the power head loose from the midsection.

11. Attach an overhead hoist to the lifting hook. Use a block of wood to keep the power head and midsection mating surfaces parallel and slowly lift the power head from the midsection.

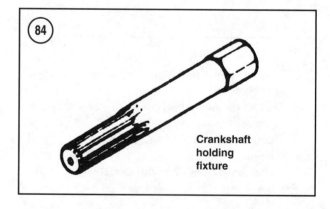

Crankshaft
holding
fixture

12. Remove the power head gasket (8, **Figure 83**) from the midsection or the bottom of the power head.

13. Mount the power head to a holding fixture (Yamaha part No. YW-6355) (**Figure 84**) or a sturdy work surface.

14. Place clean shop towels in the midsection openings and keep contaminants from entering the oil pan. Carefully scrape all gasket material from the power head mounting surfaces.

15. Inspect the power head mating surfaces for pits or damage. Replace damaged or defective components. Oil and/or water leakage is likely if these surfaces are damaged.

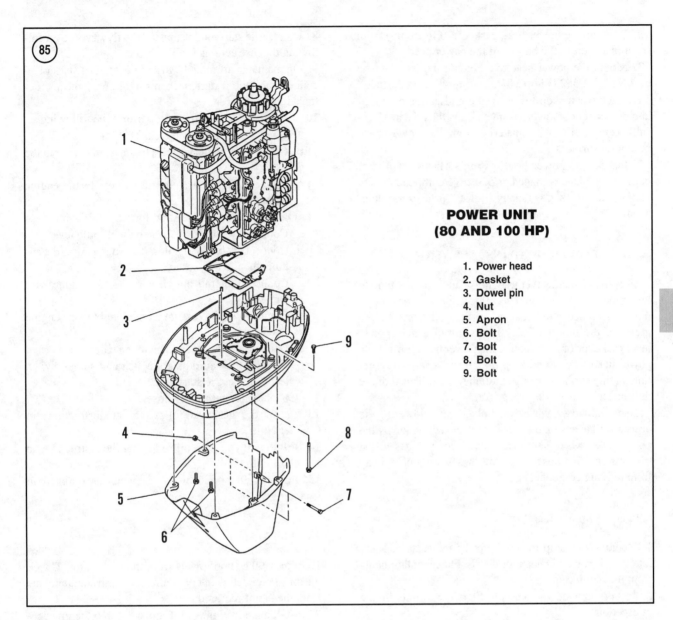

**POWER UNIT
(80 AND 100 HP)**

1. Power head
2. Gasket
3. Dowel pin
4. Nut
5. Apron
6. Bolt
7. Bolt
8. Bolt
9. Bolt

8

80 and 100 hp Models

1. Remove the five bolts shown in 9, **Figure 85**, the two bolts shown in 6, **Figure 85**, and two bolts and nuts shown in 7 and 4, **Figure 85**. Pull the apron (5) from the port and starboard sides of the drive shaft housing. Remove the six bolts (8, **Figure 85**) from the power head.

2. Drain the engine following the instructions in Chapter Four.

3. Remove the dipstick (**Figure 81**).

4. Disconnect both cables from the battery, then disconnect the battery cables from the engine.

5. Disconnect the throttle and shift cables. Disconnect the remote control harness from the engine harness.

6. Remove the gearcase following the instructions in Chapter Nine.

7. Disconnect the fuel supply hose.

8. Remove the flywheel cover following the instructions in this chapter.

9. Attach the combination flywheel removal/lifting tool (Yamaha part No.YB-6117) to the flywheel using the included bolts. Do not remove the flywheel nut. Thread the lifting hook fully into the tool.

10. Pry the power head loose from the midsection.

11. Attach an overhead hoist to the lifting hook. Use a block of wood to keep the power head and midsection mating surfaces parallel, and slowly lift the power head from the midsection (**Figure 85**).

12. Remove the power head gasket (2, **Figure 85**) from the midsection or the bottom of the power head.

13. Mount the power head to a holding fixture, Yamaha part No.YB-6552 (**Figure 84**), or a sturdy work surface.

14. Place clean shop towels in the midsection openings and prevent contaminants from entering the oil pan. Carefully scrape all gasket material from the power head mounting surfaces.

15. Inspect the power head mating surfaces for pits or damage. Replace damaged or defective components. Oil and/or water leakage is likely if these surfaces are damaged.

POWER HEAD INSTALLATION

Use an adequate overhead hoist and an assistant to lower the power head onto the midsection. Correct potential interference with linkage, wiring and hoses before lowering the power head. Always install a new power head gasket prior to mounting the power head. Lower the power head slowly and keep the power head-to-midsection mating surfaces parallel until they mate. This reduces the chance of damaging the gasket.

Inspect all hoses, wiring and linkage while lowering the power head to ensure they are not pinched or bound by the power head. Make sure that all wire connections to the trim system, fuel hoses and water hoses are routed away from moving components.

9.9 and 15 hp Models

1. Remove the shop towels from the midsection. Look into the oil pan and check for debris. Flush contaminants from the pan if required.

2. Install both dowel pins (3, **Figure 82**) into in the midsection.

3. Install the power head gasket and plate. Install the power head gasket (4, **Figure 82**) onto the midsection. Make sure the dipstick and pickup tube (1, **Figure 82**) openings in the gasket match the openings in the midsection.

4. Align the oil pickup tube (6, **Figure 82**) with its opening in the gasket and slowly lower the power head onto the midsection.

5. Seat the power head against the midsection.

6. Install the six mounting bolts and washers (5, **Figure 82**) into the power head. Tighten the bolts in a crossing pattern to the specification in **Table 1**.

7. Install the covers on the port and starboard sides of the drive shaft housing. Securely tighten the cover bolts. Install the oil dipstick (1, **Figure 82**).

8. On electric start models, install the flywheel cover following the instructions in this chapter.

9. On manual start models, install the manual starter and connect the neutral start mechanism following the instructions in Chapter Ten.

10. On remote control models, perform the following:
   a. Connect the throttle and shift cables.
   b. Connect the battery cables to the engine, then to the battery.
   c. Connect the remote control harness to the engine harness.

11. On tiller control models, perform the following:
   a. Connect the throttle cables to the throttle lever.
   b. Connect the battery cables, if so equipped, to the engine, then to the battery.
   c. Connect the stop button wires to the engine wire harness.
   d. Connect the oil pressure warning light to the engine wire harness.
   e. Connect the choke linkage to the carburetor.
   f. Connect the neutral start switch and starter switch leads on electric start models.

12. Connect the fuel supply hose.

13. Install the gearcase following the instructions in Chapter Nine.

14. Fill the oil pan with oil following the instructions in Chapter Four.

15. Perform all applicable adjustments as outlined in Chapter Five.

25-50 hp Models

1. Remove the shop towels from the midsection. Check the oil pan for debris or contaminants. Flush contaminants from the pan if required.

2. Install the dowel pins (3, **Figure 83**) into their respective holes in the midsection.

3. Place the power head gasket (8, **Figure 83**) onto the midsection. Align the pins (3, **Figure 83**) with the holes in the gasket.

4. Use an overhead hoist to lift the power head from the work surface. Keep the power head mounting surface parallel to the midsection and lower the power head onto the midsection.

5. Seat the power head against the midsection.

6. Install the eight mounting bolts (6, **Figure 83**) into the power head. Tighten the bolts in a crossing pattern to the specification in **Table 3** and **Table 4**.

7. Install the covers on the port and starboard sides of the drive shaft housing. Securely tighten the cover bolts. Install the dipstick (7, **Figure 83**).

8. On electric start models, install the flywheel cover following the instructions in this chapter.

9. On manual start models, install the manual starter and connect the neutral start mechanism following the instructions in Chapter Ten.

10. On remote control models, perform the following:

    a. Connect the throttle and shift cables.

    b. Connect the battery cables to the engine, then to the battery.

    c. Connect the remote control harness to the engine harness.

11. On tiller control models, perform the following:

    a. Connect the throttle cables to the throttle lever.

    b. Connect the battery cables, if so equipped, to the engine, then to the battery.

    c. Connect the stop button wires to the engine wire harness.

    d. Connect the warning horn wires to the engine wire harness.

    e. Connect the neutral start switch and starter switch leads on electric start models.

12. Connect the fuel supply hose.

13. Install the gearcase following the instructions in Chapter Nine.

14. Fill the oil pan with oil following the instructions in Chapter Four.

15. Perform all applicable adjustments following the instructions in Chapter Five.

80 and 100 hp Models

1. Remove the shop towels from the midsection. Check the oil pan for debris or contaminants. Flush contaminants from the pan if required.

2. Install the dowel pins into the holes in the midsection.

3. Attach the combination flywheel removal tool/lifting hook (Yamaha part No. YB-6117) to the flywheel with the included bolts. Do not remove the flywheel nut. Install the lifting hook fully into the threaded opening.

4. Place the power head gasket (2, **Figure 85**) onto the midsection. Align the pins (3, **Figure 85**) with their holes in the gasket.

5. Use an overhead hoist to lift the power head from the work surface. Keep the power head mounting surface parallel to the midsection mating surface and lower the power head onto the midsection.

6. Seat the power head against the midsection.

7. Install the six mounting bolts (8, **Figure 85**) into the power head. Tighten the bolts in a crossing pattern to the specification in **Table 5**.

8. Install the covers on the port and starboard sides of the drive shaft housing. Securely tighten the bolts and nuts (7 and 4, **Figure 85**). Install the oil dipstick.

9. Install the flywheel cover following the instructions in this chapter.

10. Connect the throttle and shift cables to the power head.

11. Connect the remote control harness to the engine harness.

12. Connect the battery cables to the engine, then to the battery.

13. Connect the fuel supply hose.

14. Install the gearcase following the instructions in Chapter Nine.

15. Fill the oil pan with oil following the instructions in Chapter Four.

16. Perform all applicable adjustments following the instructions in Chapter Five.

Thermostat and Water Pressure Relief Valve

A water pressure relief valve is used only on 80 and 100 hp models. Thermostats are used on all models.

On 9.9 hp models, the thermostat (7, **Figure 86**) is located beneath a cover on the top and rear side of the cylinder block.

On 15 hp models, the thermostat is located beneath a cover on the port side exhaust cover (**Figure 87**).

On 25 hp models, the thermostat is located beneath a cover on the port side exhaust cover (**Figure 88**).

On 40 and 50 hp models, the thermostat is located beneath a cover on the port side exhaust cover (**Figure 89**).

On 80 and 100 hp models, the thermostat is located beneath a cover on the topside of the cylinder head (**Figure 90**). The water pressure relief valve is located beneath a cover on the lower side of the starboard exhaust water cover (**Figure 91**).

Thermostat removal

1. Disconnect the cables from the battery, if so equipped.

2. Remove the two bolts from the thermostat cover.

3. Remove the thermostat cover from the power head. Carefully tap the cover loose with a rubber mallet if it does not easily pull free.

4. Use needlenose pliers to pull the thermostat from the opening.

5. Carefully scrape all gasket material from the thermostat cover and power head.

6. Test the thermostat following the instructions in Chapter Three.

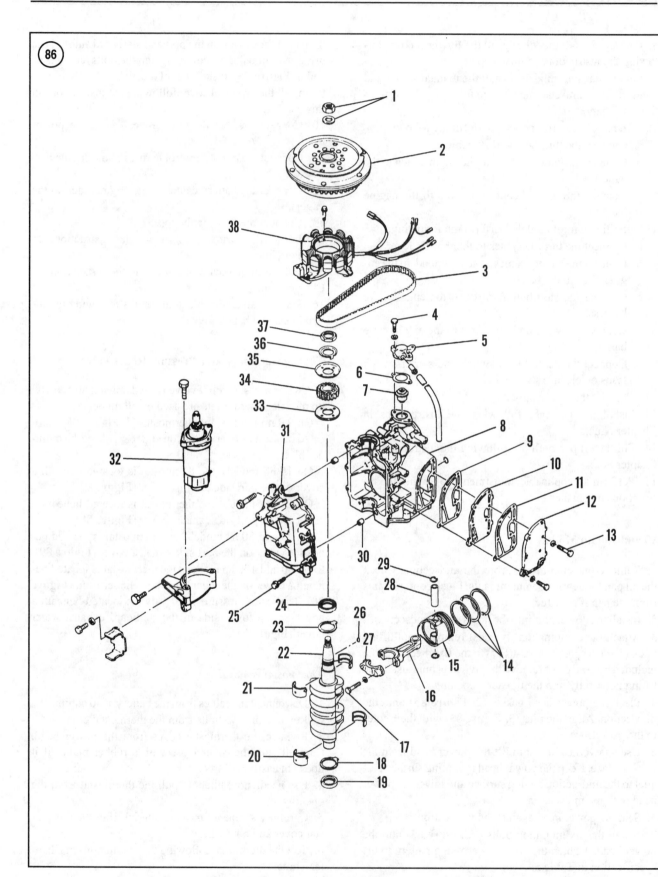

POWER HEAD ASSEMBLY (9.9 HP)

1. Flywheel nut and washer
2. Flywheel
3. Timing belt
4. Bolt
5. Thermostat cover
6. Gasket
7. Thermostat
8. Cylinder block
9. Gasket
10. Inner exhaust plate
11. Gasket
12. Exhaust cover
13. Bolt
14. Rings
15. Piston
16. Connecting rod
17. Bolt
18. Lower thrust washer
19. Lower crankshaft seal
20. Main bearing
21. Main bearing
22. Crankshaft
23. Upper thrust washer
24. Upper crankshaft seal
25. Bolt
26. Woodruff key
27. Connecting rod cap
28. Piston pin
29. Piston pin retainer
30. Dowel pin
31. Crankcase
32. Starter motor
33. Washer
34. Crankshaft sprocket
35. Washer
36. Locking tab washer
37. Nut
38. Stator

Thermostat installation

1. Install the thermostat into the engine with the spring side facing in. Seat the thermostat in the opening.
2. Place a new gasket on the thermostat cover. Slip the bolts through the holes to help retain the gasket.
3. Apply a light coat of water-resistant grease to the bolt threads, then install the cover over the thermostat opening.
4. Inspect the gasket for correct alignment, then install the bolts. Tighten both bolts evenly to the specification in **Tables 1-5**.
5. Make sure any hoses attached to the cover are routed away from moving components.
6. Connect the cables to the battery, if so equipped.

Water pressure relief valve removal (80 and 100 hp)

8

1. Disconnect the cables from the battery.
2. Remove the water pressure relief valve cover (10, **Figure 91**) from the lower side of the exhaust/water jacket cover (7).
3. Pull the spring (14, **Figure 91**) and valve (15) from the opening. Carefully pull the grommet (16, **Figure 91**) from the exhaust/water cover (7).
4. Carefully scrape all gasket material (17, **Figure 91**) from the cover and exhaust/water cover. Clean all corrosion, scale or other contaminants from the cover, valve, spring, seat and the opening.
5. Inspect the valve (15, **Figure 91**) and seat (16) for wear, broken or missing sections. Inspect the spring (14, **Figure 91**) for corrosion or breakage.

Water pressure control valve installation

1. Install the seat (16, **Figure 91**) into the opening in the exhaust/water jacket cover. Make sure the groove on the seat engages and locks into the opening.
2. Install one of the X-shaped ends of the valve (15, **Figure 91**) into the seat opening. Place the spring (14, **Figure 91**) over the other X-shaped end.
3. Install a new gasket (17, **Figure 91**) onto the cover (10). Slide the bolts (11, **Figure 91**) into the cover to hold the gasket in place.
4. Align the recess for the spring in the cover with the spring (14, **Figure 91**) and push the water pressure relief valve cover onto the exhaust/water jacket cover.
5. Inspect the gasket for correct alignment, then install the mounting bolts into the exhaust/water jacket cover. Tighten the bolts to the specification in **Table 5**. Install the bolt and clamp (12 and 13, **Figure 91**) to secure the cover.

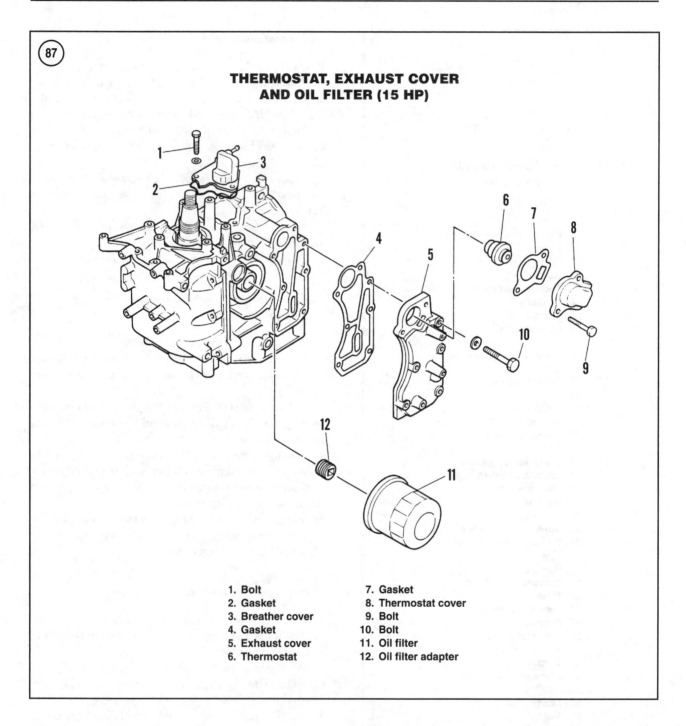

87

THERMOSTAT, EXHAUST COVER AND OIL FILTER (15 HP)

1. Bolt
2. Gasket
3. Breather cover
4. Gasket
5. Exhaust cover
6. Thermostat
7. Gasket
8. Thermostat cover
9. Bolt
10. Bolt
11. Oil filter
12. Oil filter adapter

6. Connect the cables to the battery.

Exhaust/Water Jacket Cover
Removal and Installation (All Models)

On 9.9 hp models, the combination water jacket and exhaust cover is mounted on the port side of the cylinder block (**Figure 86**).

On 15 hp models, the combination water jacket and exhaust cover is mounted on the port side of the cylinder block (**Figure 87**).

On 25 hp models, the combination exhaust cover and water jacket cover is mounted on the port side of the cylinder block (**Figure 88**).

On 40 and 50 hp models, the combination exhaust cover and water jacket cover is mounted on the port side of the cylinder block (**Figure 89**).

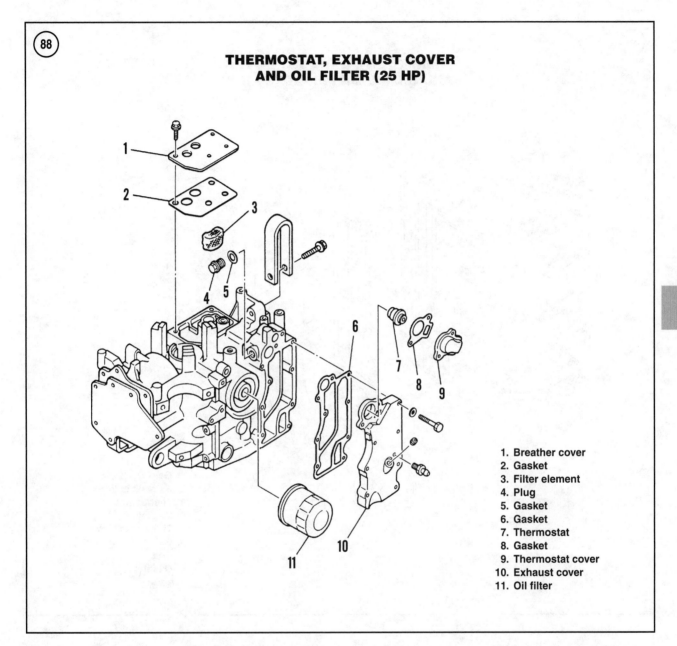

(88)

**THERMOSTAT, EXHAUST COVER
AND OIL FILTER (25 HP)**

1. Breather cover
2. Gasket
3. Filter element
4. Plug
5. Gasket
6. Gasket
7. Thermostat
8. Gasket
9. Thermostat cover
10. Exhaust cover
11. Oil filter

8

On 80 and 100 hp models, the combination exhaust cover and water jacket cover is mounted on the starboard side of the cylinder block (**Figure 91**).

1. Disconnect the cables from the battery, if so equipped.

2. On 25-100 hp models, disconnect the engine temperature sensor from the engine wire harness.

3. On models with a cover mounted thermostat, remove the thermostat following the instructions in this section.

4. On 80 and 100 hp models, remove the water pressure relief valve following the instructions in this section.

5. Note the tightening sequence numbers (**Figure 91**) cast into the cover. Gradually loosen the cover retain-

ing bolts 1/4 turn at a time in the reverse order of the tightening sequence. Continue until the bolts spin freely.

6. Note the location for each bolt, then remove them from the cover.

7. Carefully pry the water jacket and exhaust cover loose at the pry points at the top and bottom of the cover (**Figure 92**). Lift the cover(s) from the cylinder block.

8. Carefully scrape all carbon and gasket material from the cover mating surfaces and exhaust passages. Clean all corrosion, scale or other contamination from the water passages.

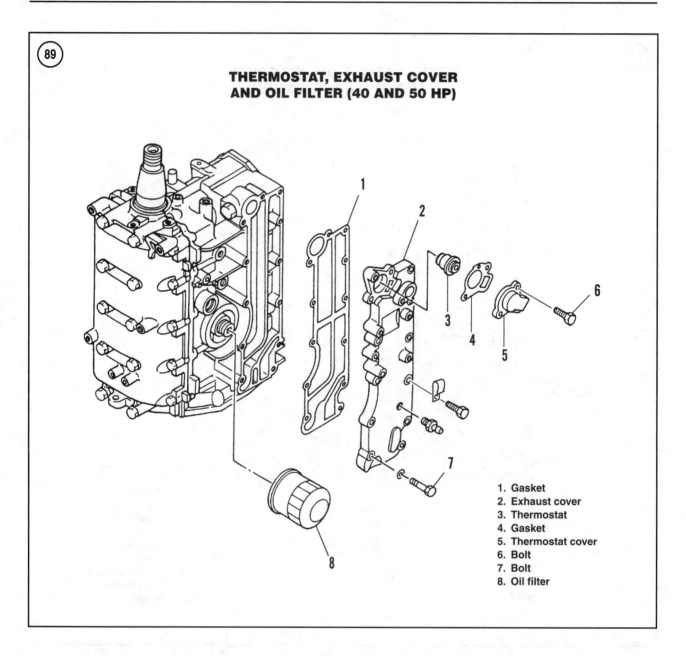

(89)

**THERMOSTAT, EXHAUST COVER
AND OIL FILTER (40 AND 50 HP)**

1. Gasket
2. Exhaust cover
3. Thermostat
4. Gasket
5. Thermostat cover
6. Bolt
7. Bolt
8. Oil filter

9. Inspect the cover(s) for holes or signs of leakage, and distorted or damaged surfaces. Replace the cover(s) if any defects are noted.

10. Use a thread chaser to clean all corrosion or contamination from the holes for the cover bolts. Inspect the holes for damaged threads. Install a thread insert if the chaser does not clean up damaged threads.

**Exhaust/Water Jacket Cover
Installation (All Models)**

1. Place the cover(s) and new gasket(s) onto the cylinder block.

2. Apply a light coat of water-resistant grease to the threads, then install the bolts until finger-tight. Inspect the gasket and plate for proper alignment.

3. Tighten the bolts in the sequence cast into the cover to half the tightening torque in **Tables 1-5**. Tighten the bolts a second time in sequence to the full torque specification.

4. On 25-100 hp models, connect the engine wire harness to the engine temperature sensor. Route all wires away from moving components.

5. Install the thermostat following the instructions in this section.

6. On 80 and 100 hp models, install the water pressure relief valve as described in this chapter.

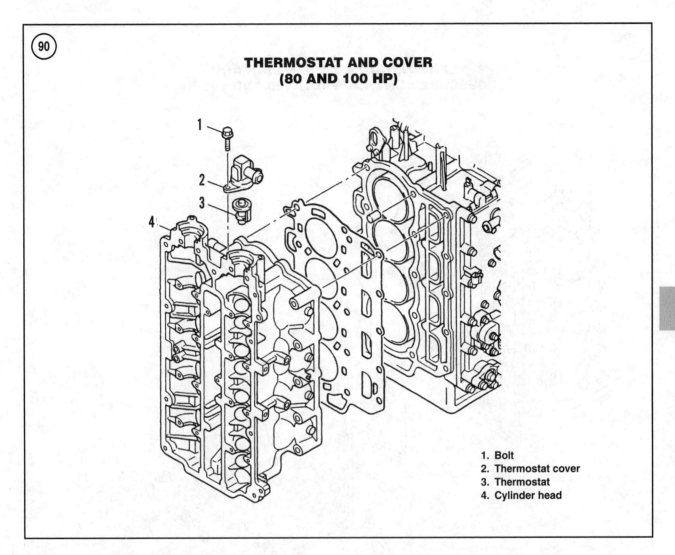

(90)

**THERMOSTAT AND COVER
(80 AND 100 HP)**

1

2

3

4

1. Bolt
2. Thermostat cover
3. Thermostat
4. Cylinder head

8

7. Connect the cables to the battery.

8. Start the engine and inspect the cover for water or exhaust leakage.

Cylinder Block Disassembly and Assembly

Always make notes, drawings and photographs of all external power head components *before* beginning disassembly.

Correct hose and wire routing is important for proper engine operation. An incorrectly routed hose or wire may interfere with linkage movement and interfere with throttle control.

If possible, remove components that share common wires or hoses in a cluster. This will reduce the time needed to disassemble and assemble the power head. This also reduces the chance of improper connections during assembly.

Use muffin tins or egg cartons to organize the fasteners as they are removed. Tag or mark all fasteners to ensure they are installed in the correct location on assembly.

Refer to the instructions for the selected model.

Disassembly (9.9-100 hp Models)

Refer to **Figures 93-98** as required during this procedure.

1. Remove the cylinder head following the instructions under *Cylinder Head* in this chapter.

2. Remove the crankshaft sprocket following the instructions under *Cylinder Head* in this chapter.

3. Remove all electrical components as described in Chapter Seven.

4. Remove any remaining fuel system components as described in Chapter Six.

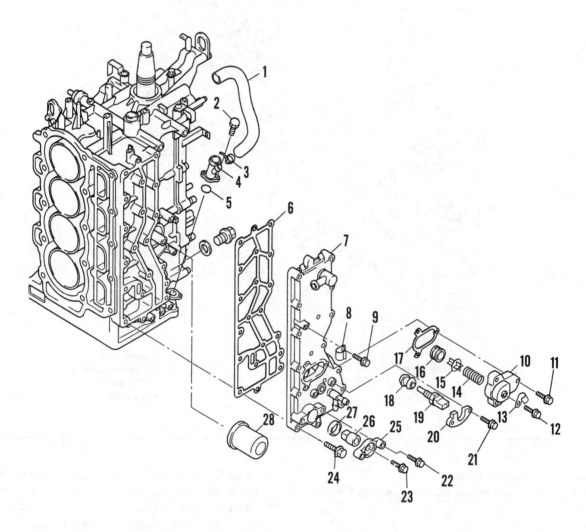

**EXHAUST COVER, OIL FILTER AND
PRESSURE CONTROL VALVE (80 AND 100 HP)**

1. Breather hose
2. Bolt
3. Tie wrap
4. Breather hose fitting
5. O-ring
6. Gasket
7. Exhaust cover
8. Retainer
9. Bolt
10. Pressure relief valve cover
11. Bolt
12. Bolt
13. Retainer
14. Spring
15. Pressure relier valve
16. Seat
17. Gasket
18. Grommet
19. Engine temperature sensor
20. Retainer
21. Bolt
22. Bolt
23. Bolt
24. Bolt
25. Anode cover
26. Anode
27. O-ring
28. Oil filter

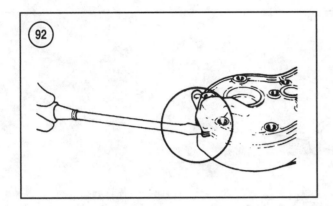

5. Remove the exhaust/water jacket covers and thermostat as described in this chapter.

6. Remove the oil filter or screen following the instructions in Chapter Four.

7. On 25 hp models, remove the balance piston as follows:

   a. Remove the bolts, grommet (6, **Figure 95**) and bracket (7), and remove the cover and O-ring (5 and 4) from the cylinder block (3).

   b. Use a breaker bar and socket to remove the balance piston retaining nut and pull the piston (1, **Figure 95**) from its connecting rod.

8. On 9.9 hp, 15 hp and 25 hp models, remove the breather housing or cover from the cylinder block. Refer to Chapter Six for disassembly of the air funnel and breather hose. Thoroughly clean the housing or element with a solvent.

9. Locate the torque sequence numbers cast into the crankcase cover. Loosen the crankcase cover bolts 1/4 turn at a time in the reverse order of the tightening sequence until all bolts turn freely. Note the location of each bolt, then pull them from the crankcase cover.

10. Locate the pry points at the top and bottom corners of the cover. Carefully pry the cover from the crankcase. Check for additional bolts if the cover is difficult to remove.

11. Note the seal lip direction, then remove the crankshaft seals from the top (1, **Figure 94**) and bottom (6) ends of the crankshaft.

12. Remove the main bearing inserts from the crankshaft or crankcase cover. Arrange the bearings in the order of removal.

13. Remove one piston and rod assembly at a time. Mark the cylinder number on the side of the connecting rod and rod cap prior to removal. This helps ensure the rod cap (**Figure 96**) is installed to the same connecting rod and in the same orientation upon assembly. Remove the piston and connecting rod as follows:

   a. Using white paint, highlight the UP mark on each piston dome. Verify the cylinder mark on the side of each connecting rod and cap.

   b. Evenly loosen the connecting rod bolts 1/4 turn at a time until they spin freely. Lightly tap the rod cap to free it from the crankshaft and connecting rod.

   c. Remove the rod cap from the crankshaft and connecting rod. Remove the bearing (7, **Figure 98**) from the connecting rod or crankshaft.

   d. Scrape the carbon ridge from the top of the cylinder bore with a small knife. Work carefully to avoid scratching the cylinder wall. Use a wooden dowel to push the piston and rod from the cylinder head end of the bore (**Figure 99**).

   e. Align the tab on the backside of the bearing with the notch and install the bearings (11 and 17, **Figure 96**) into the connecting rod and rod cap. Align the mark made prior to removal (**Figure 96**) and install the cap on the rod. Install the rod bolts (10, **Figure 98**) to retain the components.

14. Use a ring expander to remove both upper compression rings from the piston (**Figure 100**). Carefully pull the oil control ring from the piston. Work carefully to prevent damage to the piston.

15. Carefully pull the crankshaft from the cylinder block. Remove the main bearing from the cylinder block. Arrange the insert bearings in the order of removal.

   a. On 9.9 hp models, mark the topside and location of the thrust spacers, then remove them (18 and 23, **Figure 93**) from the crankshaft.

   b. On 25 hp models, mark the topside of the balance piston connecting rod, then lift it (2, **Figure 96**) from the crankshaft (4).

16. Remove the oil filter adapter. Remove the oil filter housing on engines not equipped with a spin-on oil filter.

17. Do not remove the connecting rod from the piston on 80 and 100 hp models. Replace the piston and rod as an assembly if either the connecting rod or piston is defective or excessively worn. Refer to *Inspection* in this chapter.

18. Disassemble the connecting rod and piston on 9.9-50 hp models as follows:

   a. Mark the topside of the piston and connecting rod (**Figure 96**).

   b. Use a pick or scribe to pry the lock rings (**Figure 101**) from the grooves in the piston pin bore.

   c. Use a deep socket or section of tubing as a piston pin removal and installation tool. The tool must be slightly smaller in diameter than the piston pin.

   d. Support the connecting rod, then carefully push the piston pin from the piston and connecting rod.

8

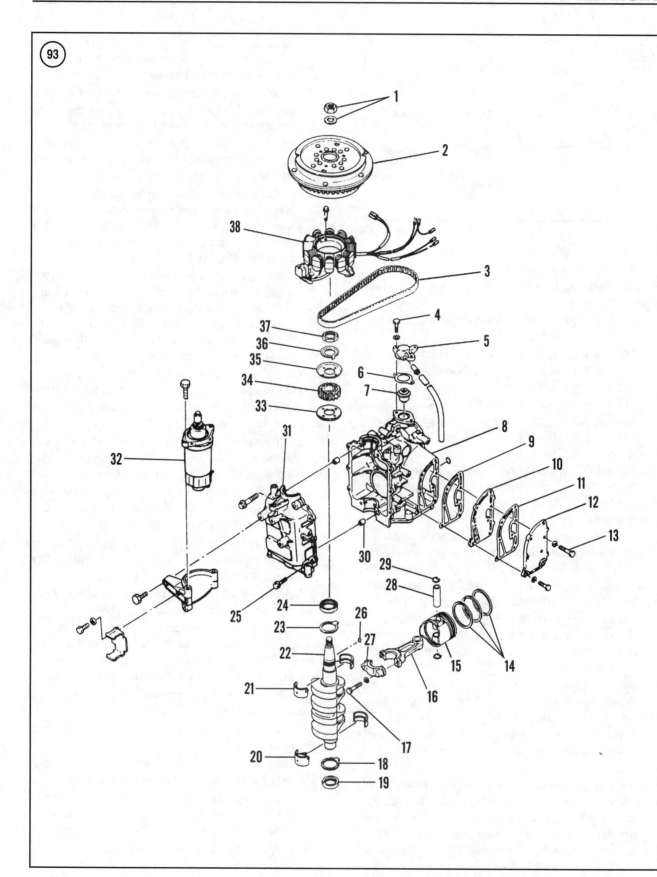

POWER HEAD ASSEMBLY
(9.9 HP)

1. Flywheel nut and washer
2. Flywheel
3. Timing belt
4. Bolt
5. Thermostat cover
6. Gasket
7. Thermostat
8. Cylinder block
9. Gasket
10. Exhaust plate
11. Gasket
12. Exhaust cover
13. Bolt
14. Rings
15. Piston
16. Connecting rod
17. Bolt
18. Thrust washer
19. Crankshaft seal
20. Main bearing
21. Main bearing
22. Crankshaft
23. Thrust washer
24. Crankshaft seal
25. Bolt
26. Woodruff key
27. Connecting rod cap
28. Piston pin
29. Pin retainer
30. Dowel pin
31. Crankcase
32. Starter motor
33. Washer
34. Drive gear
35. Washer
36. Lock washer
37. Nut
38. Stator

e. Clean the piston ring grooves using a piece of broken ring (**Figure 102**). Use only the ring originally installed on the piston.

19. Thoroughly clean the cylinder block with hot soapy water. Clean other components using clean solvent. Clean carbon from the piston dome with a stiff, non-metallic parts cleaning brush and solvent. Dry all components with compressed air. Apply a light coat of oil to the piston, piston pin, cylinder bore, bearings, connecting rod and crankshaft to prevent corrosion.

20. Inspect and measure all components following the instructions provided under *Inspection* in this chapter.

21. Note the color code on the side of each bearing insert (**Figure 103**). Order replacement bearings for the crankshaft and connecting rods noting the following:

   a. Note the cylinder number for each pair of connecting rod bearings.

   b. Note the main bearing number and its location (cylinder block side or crankcase cover side) for each crankshaft main bearing.

   c. Refer to *Bearing Selection* in this chapter.

Assembly (9.9-100 hp models)

Refer to **Figures 93-98** as required during this procedure.

1. Determine the main bearing clearance as follows:

   a. Clean all oil from the main bearings and their mounting locations prior to installing the bearings. Align the tab with the notch and insert the new crankshaft main bearings into the cylinder block. Make sure the bearing with the correct color code is installed. On 80 and 100 hp models, make sure the thrust bearing is installed at the third location.

   b. Align the tab with the notch and insert the new main bearings into the crankcase cover. Note the flywheel side of the crankshaft and cylinder block, then carefully place the crankshaft into the cylinder block. Make sure the main bearing surfaces of the crankshaft rest on the bearings.

   c. Place a section of Plastigage across each main bearing journal (**Figure 104**). Install the crankcase cover onto the cylinder block and crankcase. Install the crankcase bolts. Do not rotate the crankshaft.

   d. Tighten the crankcase cover to half the specification in **Tables 1-5** following the sequence cast into the cover. Tighten the bolts in sequence a second time to the full specification in **Tables 1-5**. Loosen the crankcase bolts 1/4 turn at a time in the reverse order of the tightening sequence. Remove the bolts,

8

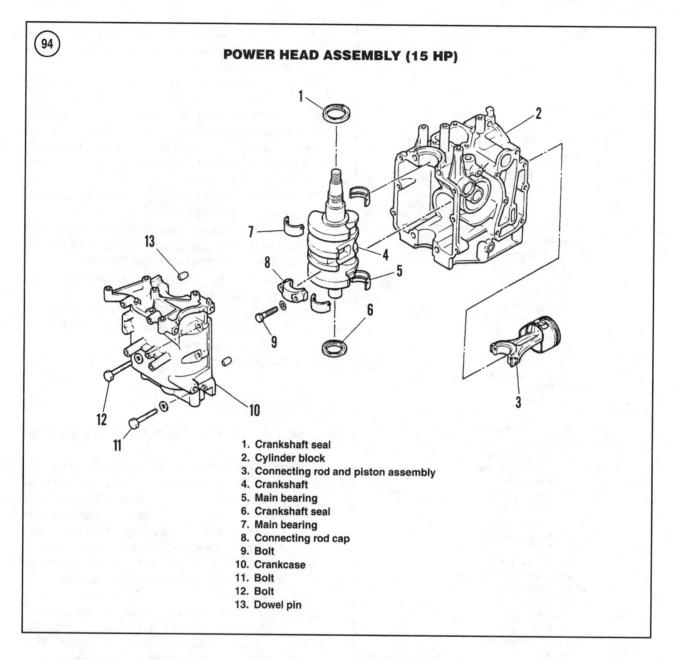

POWER HEAD ASSEMBLY (15 HP)

1. Crankshaft seal
2. Cylinder block
3. Connecting rod and piston assembly
4. Crankshaft
5. Main bearing
6. Crankshaft seal
7. Main bearing
8. Connecting rod cap
9. Bolt
10. Crankcase
11. Bolt
12. Bolt
13. Dowel pin

and lift the cover from the cylinder block and the crankshaft.

e. Measure the main bearing clearance at each location by comparing the width of the flattened Plastigage with the mark on the Plastigage envelope. Compare the main bearing clearance with the main bearing oil clearance specification in **Table 9**. Refer to *Bearing Selection* in this chapter if the clearance is incorrect.

f. Pull the crankshaft from the cylinder block and clean the Plastigage from the crankshaft and/or bearing.

2. Install the crankshaft as follows:

a. Apply engine oil to the main bearings and crankshaft main bearing journals.

b. On 9.9 hp models, place the thrust spacers onto the top and bottom ends of the crankshaft. Make sure the grooved sides face the crankshaft. Coat the spacers with engine oil. Guide the tabs on the spacers into the grooves in the cylinder block as the crankshaft is lowered into position.

c. On 25 hp models, lubricate the crankshaft engine oil, then slip the balance piston connecting rod onto the crankshaft. Make sure the UP mark faces the fly-

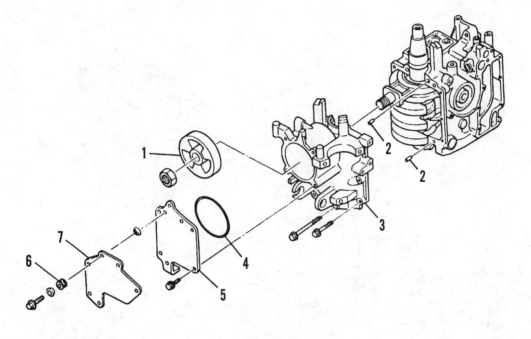

CYLINDER BLOCK AND BALANCER PISTION (25 HP)

1. Balancer piston
2. Dowel pin
3. Crankcase
4. O-ring
5. Cover
6. Grommet
7. Bracket

8

wheel side and the big end fits onto its crankshaft bearing surface.

d. Guide the balance piston connecting rod on 25 hp models into its opening as the crankshaft is lowered into the cylinder block.

e. Lower the crankshaft into the cylinder block. Make sure the crankshaft fully seats against the main bearings.

f. Slowly rotate the crankshaft to check for free movement. If binding or rough movement is detected, remove the crankshaft and check for proper bearing seating and installation.

3. Apply engine oil to the upper and lower seals, then carefully slide them onto the crankshaft with the lip side facing toward the crankcase. Make sure the seal fully seats in the groove in the cylinder block.

4. On 9.9-50 hp models only, assemble the piston and rod assembly as follows:

a. Align the piston pin bores in the piston and connecting rod. On 9.9 models (1985-1991), the 6G800 mark must face up. On 9.9 hp models (1992-1999), the XXX mark must face up. On 15-50 hp models, the Y mark on the connecting rod must face the same direction as the UP mark on the piston dome.

b. Lubricate the piston pin bores with engine oil, then push the piston pin into the piston and connecting rod.

c. Using needlenose pliers, install new C rings into the groove on each side of the piston pin bore (**Figure 105**). Make sure the lock rings span the notched part of the groove and are firmly seated in the grooves.

CYLINDER BLOCK ASSEMBLY (25 HP)

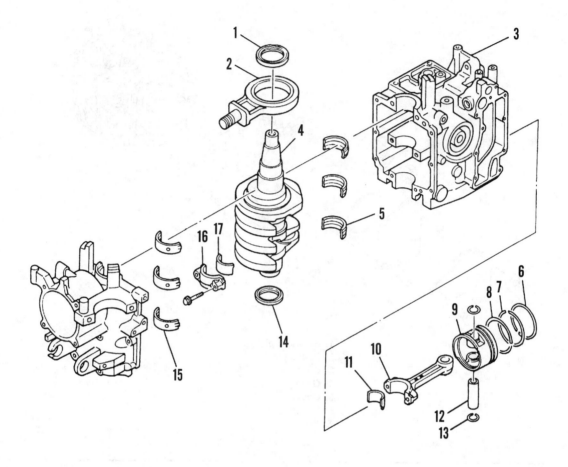

1. Crankshaft seal
2. Balancer rod
3. Cylinder block
4. Crankshaft
5. Main bearing
6. Top piston ring
7. Second piston ring
8. Oil ring
9. Piston
10. Connecting rod
11. Connecting rod bearing
12. Piston pin
13. Piston pin clip
14. Crankshaft seal
15. Main bearing
16. Connecting rod cap
17. Connecting rod bearing

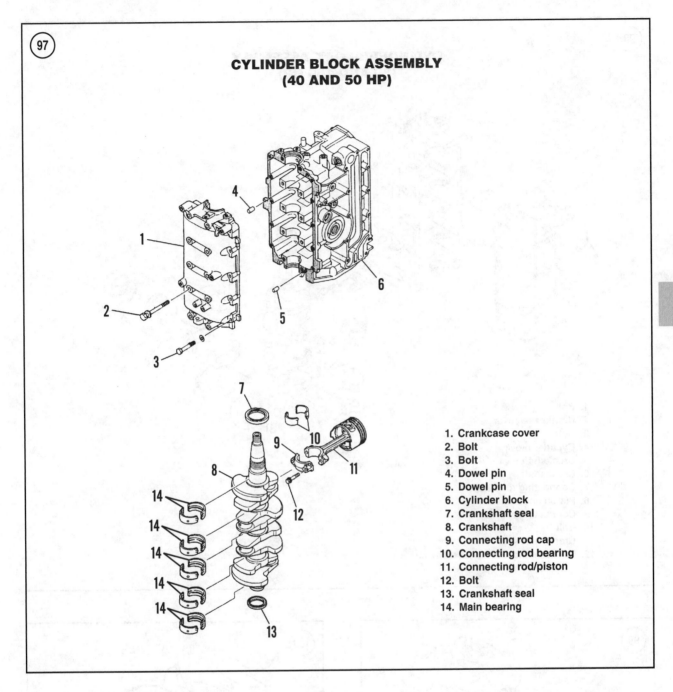

97

**CYLINDER BLOCK ASSEMBLY
(40 AND 50 HP)**

1. Crankcase cover
2. Bolt
3. Bolt
4. Dowel pin
5. Dowel pin
6. Cylinder block
7. Crankshaft seal
8. Crankshaft
9. Connecting rod cap
10. Connecting rod bearing
11. Connecting rod/piston
12. Bolt
13. Crankshaft seal
14. Main bearing

8

Pivot the piston on the piston pin. The piston should pivot smoothly on the connecting rod without any noticeable play.

5A. On 9.9 hp (1985-1991) and 15 hp models, identify the topside of both compression rings (**Figure 106**) by the N marks near the end gap. This mark must face UP after assembly. Install the new rails and expander ring (**Figure 107**) of the oil ring onto the lower ring groove. Use a ring expander to open the new rings just enough to pass over the piston.

5B. On 9.9 hp models (1992-1999), identify the top and second rings by the shape of the end gaps (**Figure 108**). The open end of the gap must face the top of the piston after installation. Use a ring expander to open the new rings just enough to pass over the piston. Release the rings into the groove on the piston (**Figure 100**). Rotate the top and second rings until they align with the locating pins in the ring groove (**Figure 109**). Install the new rails and expanders of the oil ring into the lower ring groove as indicated in **Figure 107**.

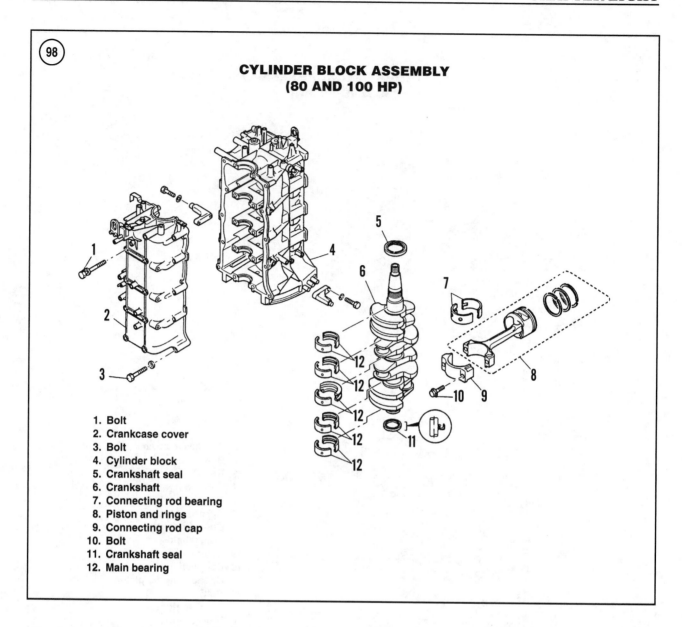

**CYLINDER BLOCK ASSEMBLY
(80 AND 100 HP)**

1. Bolt
2. Crankcase cover
3. Bolt
4. Cylinder block
5. Crankshaft seal
6. Crankshaft
7. Connecting rod bearing
8. Piston and rings
9. Connecting rod cap
10. Bolt
11. Crankshaft seal
12. Main bearing

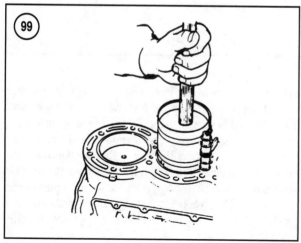

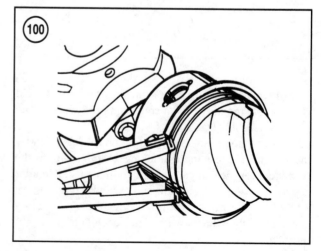

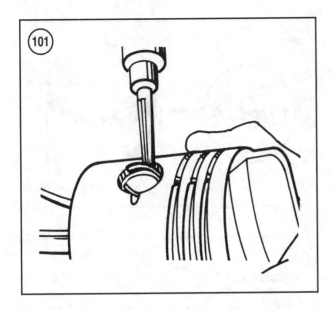

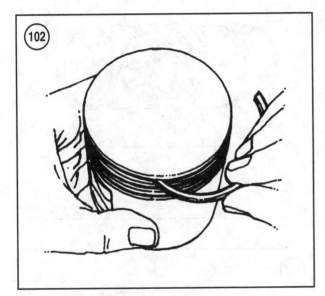

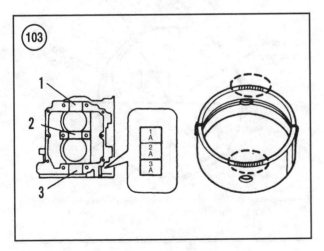

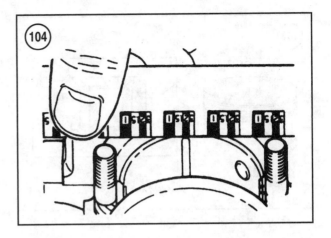

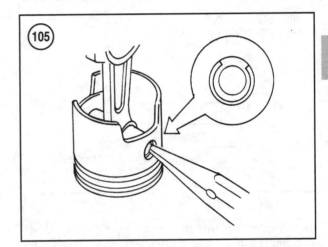

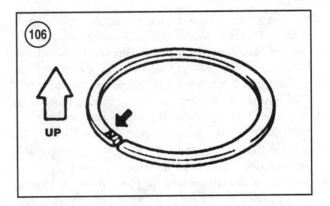

5C. On 25-100 hp models, the first compression ring (5, **Figure 110**) is thinner than the second compression ring (4). Identify the topside of each ring by the T mark near the end gap. The mark must face the top of the piston after installation. Use a ring expander to open the new rings just enough to pass over the piston. Release the rings into the groove on the piston. On 25 and 50 hp models, identify the upper oil ring rail (3, **Figure 110**) by the notch at the end

8

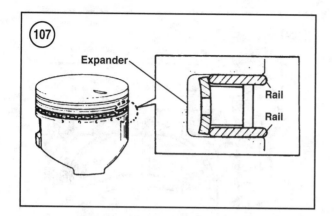

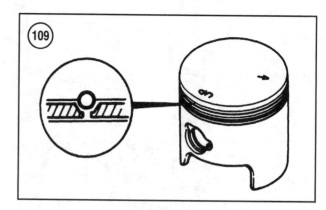

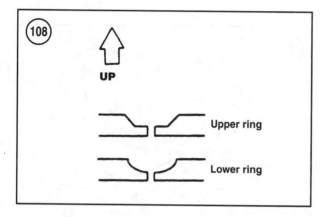

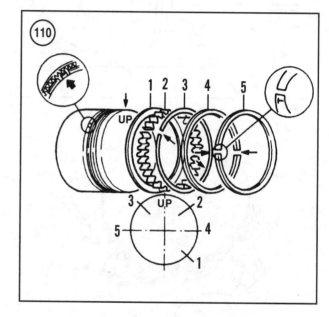

gap. Place both oil ring rails and the expander into the bottom ring groove. Make sure the expander separates the rails.

6A. On 9.9 hp models, align the compression ring gaps (**Figure 111**) with the locating pins in the ring grooves (**Figure 111**). Align the gap in the upper oil ring rail approximately 30° from the starboard side of the UP mark on the piston dome. Align the lower oil ring rail expander 180° from the top oil ring rail. Align the gap in the oil ring expander with the starboard side of the piston midway between the upper and lower rail gaps (**Figure 111**).

6B. On 15 hp models, align the end gap on the top compression ring with a point approximately 50° toward the port side of the UP mark on the piston dome (1, **Figure 112**). Position the end gap on the second compression ring (2, **Figure 112**) approximately 50° toward the starboard side of the UP mark on the piston dome. Align the gap of the upper oil ring rail (3, **Figure 112**) with the port side of the piston. Align the gap of the bottom oil rail ring (4, **Figure 112**) with the starboard side of the piston. Align the gap on the rail expander (5, **Figure 112**) with the bottom side of the piston.

6C. On 25-50 hp models, position the gap of the top compression ring (5, **Figure 110**) approximately 90° from the

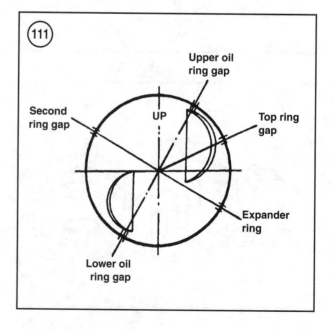

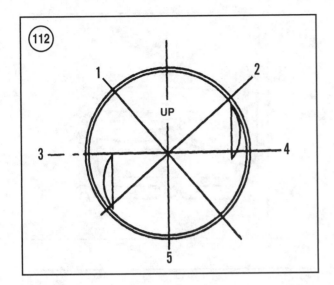

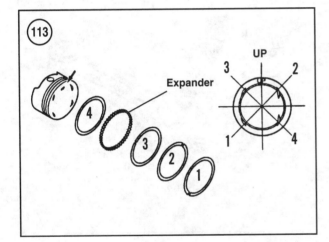

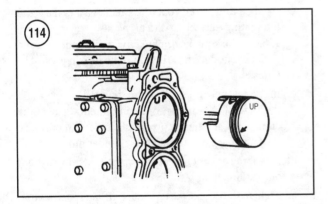

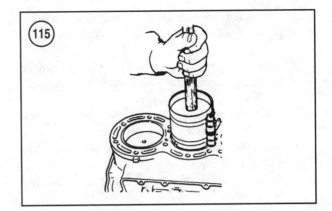

of the lower oil ring rail (1) with the starboard side of the piston. Position the gap in the oil ring expander (2, **Figure 110**) to approximately 45° on the starboard side of the UP mark on the piston dome.

6D. On 80-100 hp models, position the gap of the second compression ring (2, **Figure 113**) approximately 45° toward the starboard side from the UP mark. Align the gap of the top compression ring (1, **Figure 113**) with a point on the opposite side of the piston 180° from the gap of the second compression ring. Align the gap of the upper oil ring rail (3, **Figure 113**) with a point approximately 45° to the port side of the UP mark on the piston dome. Align the gap on the lower oil ring rail (4, **Figure 113**) to a point on the opposite side of the piston 180° from the upper oil ring rail.

7. Wipe a white shop towel through the cylinders to check for cleanliness. Repeat the cleaning process until the towel remains white after wiping the bores. Apply a coat of engine oil to the pistons, rings and cylinder walls in preparation for piston installation.

8. Install the piston and rods as follows:

   a. Slide a ring compressor (Yamaha part No. YU-33294) over the No. 1 piston and rings. Tighten the compressor enough to fully compress the rings, yet allow the piston to slide through the compressor.

   b. Have an assistant hold the crankshaft in the cylinder block during piston installation. Carefully rotate the crankshaft until the No. 1 crankpin is at the bottom of its stroke.

   c. Install the No. 1 piston into the cylinder block from the cylinder head side. Make sure the UP marks on the piston and rod face toward the flywheel side of the crankshaft (**Figure 114**). Guide the connecting rod into the bore toward the crankshaft.

   d. Hold the ring compressor firmly against the cylinder block (**Figure 115**) and gently drive the piston into the bore until the piston dome is slightly below the cylinder head mating surface. If any resistance

port side of the UP mark on the piston dome. Position the gap of the second compression ring (4, **Figure 110**) approximately 90° toward the starboard side of the UP mark on the piston dome. Align the gap in the upper oil ring rail (3) with the locating pin in the ring groove. Align the gap

is detected, stop and check for adequate ring compression (**Figure 116**) and/or improper ring alignment.

e. Align the tab on the connecting rod bearing with the notch in the connecting rod (**Figure 117**) and install the bearings into the connecting rod and rod cap. Pull the connecting rod toward the crankshaft until the bearing seats against the crankpin.

f. Align the mark on the connecting rod and rod cap and install the cap on the rod. Make sure the sides of the rod and cap align, and install the original rod bolts into the cap and connecting rod. Do not tighten the bolts at this time.

g. Repeat these steps for the remaining pistons and connecting rods.

9. Check the connecting rod bearing clearance as follows:

a. Remove the rod cap for the No. 1 cylinder. Make sure the bearings are properly seated in the rod cap and connecting rod.

b. Place a section of Plastigage on the crankpin along the length of the crankshaft. Install the rod cap and bolts. Make sure the rod cap is properly aligned with the connecting rod and install the original rod bolts. Tighten the rod bolts in two steps to the specification in **Tables 1-5**. Do not rotate the crankshaft.

c. Remove the bolts and rod cap. Measure the connecting rod oil clearance by comparing the width of the flattened Plastigage with the mark on the Plastigage envelope. Compare the clearance with the connecting rod oil clearance specification in **Table 12**.

d. Refer to *Bearing Selection* in this chapter if the clearance is incorrect. The crankshaft is excessively worn or the connecting rod is damaged if the correct bearings are installed but the clearance is excessive. Improper installation or incorrect bearing selection is likely if clearance is insufficient. Replace worn, incorrect or damaged components, then measure the clearance again.

e. Apply engine oil to the crankshaft and bearings, then install the rod cap. Install new connecting rod bolts. Check for proper rod cap alignment. Tighten the connecting rod bolts in two steps to the specification in **Tables 1-5**. On 80 and 100 hp models, tighten the bolts an additional 90° after the initial torque specification in **Table 5**.

f. Repeat these steps for the remaining cylinders.

10. Install the crankcase cover as follows:

a. Clean the crankcase cover and cylinder block mating surfaces.

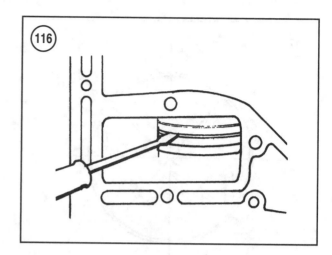

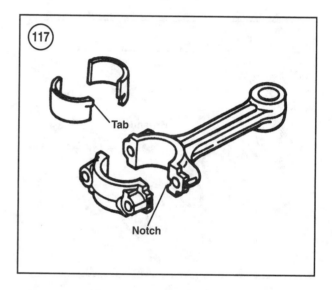

b. Apply a light, even coat of Yamaha gasket maker to the mating surface of the crankcase cover (**Figure 118**). Make sure the sealant covers the entire mating surface, but does not flow into the bearings or boltholes.

c. Inspect the crankshaft main bearing inserts and thrust washer tab for proper alignment. Inspect the crankshaft seals for correct placement, then place the crankcase cover onto the cylinder block.

d. Install the cover bolts. Tighten the bolts finger-tight only at this time.

e. Tighten the crankcase cover to half the specification in **Tables 1-5** following the sequence cast into the cover. Tighten the bolts in sequence a second time to the full specification in **Tables 1-5**. On 80 and 100 hp models, tighten the crankcase cover bolts an additional 60° after the torque specification is attained (**Table 5**).

f. Rotate the crankshaft and check for smooth rotation. If binding is noted, disassemble the cylinder block and check for incorrect installation.

11. On 25 hp models, install the balance piston and cover as follows:

   a. Apply a coat of engine oil to the balance piston bore and balance piston.

   b. Place the balance piston (1, **Figure 95**) into the bore and over the threaded end of the connecting rod. Thread the balance piston nut (**Figure 95**) onto the connecting rod (2, **Figure 96**) until it contacts the piston (1, **Figure 95**).

   c. Have an assistant support the cylinder block and tighten the balance piston nut to the specification in **Table 3**.

   d. Install a new O-ring (4, **Figure 95**) into the cover or cylinder block, then place the cover over the balance piston opening. Install the cover bolts and tighten them to the specification in **Table 3**.

12. Install the oil filter adapter on models with a spin-on filter into the cylinder block. Tighten the adapter to the specification in **Tables 1-5**.

13. On 9.9 hp (1985-1991), 15 hp and 25 hp models, install the breather housing or cover onto the cylinder block. Refer to Chapter six.

14. On the 9.9 hp models that have a serviceable oil filter, install the filter housing to the cylinder block. Tighten the housing retaining bolts to the specification in **Table 1**.

15. Install the oil filter as described in Chapter Four.

16. Install the exhaust/water jacket cover and thermostat. On 80 and 100 hp models, install the water pressure relief valve. Follow the instructions in this chapter.

17. Install the crankshaft sprocket following the instructions under *Cylinder Head Repair* in this chapter.

18. Install all electrical and ignition system components following the instructions in Chapter Seven.

19. Install the cylinder head, timing belt and flywheel following the instructions in this chapter.

20. Install the fuel system components following the instructions in Chapter Six.

Inspection and Measurement

Measurement of the cylinder block components requires precision measuring equipment and experience in its use.

All components must be clean and dry before measuring. Keep the components at room temperature for several hours before measuring them.

Cylinder block inspection

Inspect the cylinder bores for cracks or deep grooves. Deep grooves or cracks in the cylinder bores cannot be repaired by boring and installing oversize pistons. Replace the cylinder block or have a sleeve installed if a cracked or deeply scratched cylinder bore is found. Contact a marine dealership or machine shop to locate a source for block sleeving.

Inspect the mounting surfaces for the power head, exhaust/water jacket cover and crankcase cover for cracks or damage. Replace the cylinder block if cracks, deep scratches or gouging is noted

White powder-like deposits in the combustion chamber usually indicate that water is entering the combustion chamber. Inspect the cylinder walls and cylinder head thoroughly for cracks if this type of deposit is noted. Inspect the head gasket and mating surfaces for discolored areas. Discolored or corroded sealing surfaces indicate a likely source of leakage. Replace any defective or questionable components.

Inspect all boltholes for cracks, corrosion or damaged threads. Use a thread tap to clean the threads. Pay particular attention to the cylinder head bolt holes. Installing a thread insert can often repair damaged threads.

Clean and inspect all bolts, nuts and washers. Replace any bolts or nuts with damaged threads or a stretched appearance. Replace damaged washers.

Inspect the alignment pins and holes for bent pins or damaged openings. Replace damaged pins or components with damaged pin holes.

> *NOTE*
> *The cylinder block and crankcase cover are a matched assembly. Replace the entire assembly if either part requires replacement.*

8

1. Have the cylinder bore lightly honed at a marine repair shop or machine shop before taking any measurements.

2. Use a dial type (**Figure 119**) or spring type (**Figure 120**) cylinder bore gauge to measure the telescoping bore.

   a. On 9.9-50 hp models, measure the cylinder bore diameter at depths of 20 mm (0.8 in.), 40 mm (1.6 in.) and 60 mm (2.4 in.) from the cylinder head mating surface.

   b. On 80 and 100 hp models, measure the cylinder bore diameter at depths of 20 mm (0.8 in.), 70 mm (2.8 in.) and 120 mm (4.7 in.) from the cylinder head mating surface.

3. Take the measurements at 90° (**Figure 121**) apart at all three depths. Record the six measurements.

4. Compare the measurements with the specifications in **Table 6**. A previous repair to the power head may have required boring and the installation of an oversize piston. A second oversize piston is available for all models. Measure the pistons to determine if oversize components have been installed. Use the standard piston and bore specifications in **Table 10**.

5. Have the cylinder bored to the next oversize diameter and install oversize pistons if excessive bore size is indicated. Replace the cylinder block or have a sleeve installed if the measured bore diameter exceeds the specification in **Table 6**. Contact a marine dealership or machine shop for cylinder boring or sleeving.

6. Subtract the smallest diameter at the bottom of the bore from the largest measurement at the top to determine the cylinder taper. Compare the result with the maximum cylinder taper specification in **Table 6**.

7. Subtract the smallest cylinder bore diameter at a given depth with the diameter at the same depth 90° apart to determine the out-of-round measurement. Compare the result with the maximum out-of-round specification in **Table 6**. Have the cylinder bored and install an oversize piston if the taper or out of round measurements exceed the specification. Replace the cylinder block or have a sleeve installed if oversize pistons are not available in the required size.

8. Repeat the cylinder bore measurements for all cylinders. Record the measurements for each cylinder.

Piston and ring inspection

1. Inspect the piston for erosion at the edge of the dome, cracks near the ring grooves, and cracks or missing portions of the piston dome (**Figure 122**). Inspect for erosion in the ring groove, and scoring or scuffing on the piston skirt.

2. Inspect the piston pin for a worn, discolored or scrubbed appearance. Inspect the lock ring groove for

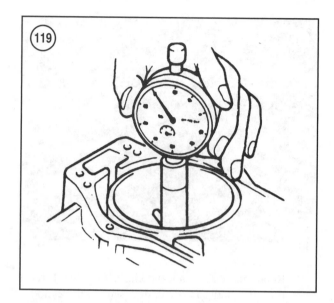

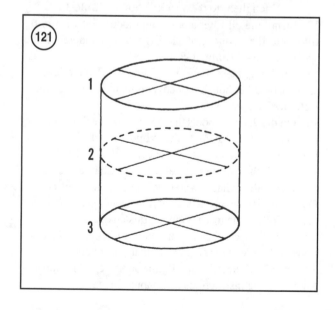

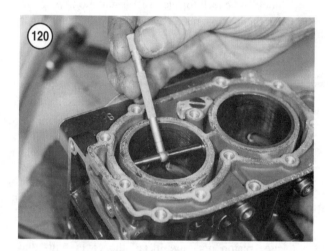

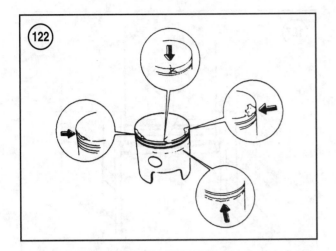

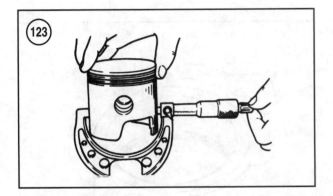

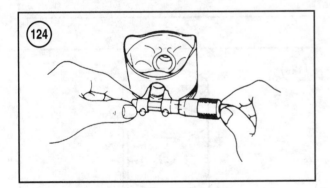

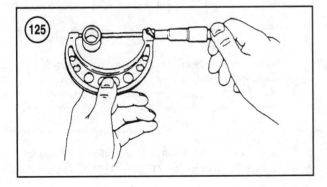

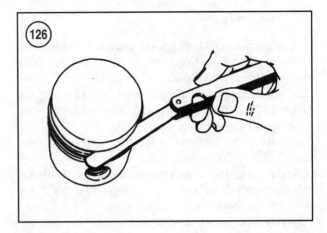

damage or erosion. Replace the piston if any of these defects are noted.

3. Replace the rings anytime the piston is removed from the cylinder. Low compression, high oil consumption and other problems may occur if used rings are installed.

4. Refer to **Table 10** to determine the measuring point on the piston. Using an outside micrometer, measure the diameter of the piston at a point 90° from the piston pin bore at the specified distance from the bottom of the skirt (**Figure 123**).

5. Compare the measurement to the specification in **Table 10**. Replace the piston if the measurement is below the specification. Measure the diameter of the remaining pistons.

6. Perform this measurement on 9.9-50 hp models. Using an inside micrometer, measure the piston pin bore diameter at both openings (**Figure 124**). Repeat this measurement for the remaining pistons. Replace any piston with an excessive pin bore diameter.

7. Measure the piston pin diameter (**Figure 125**) at the piston and rod contact areas. Compare the measurement with the specification in **Table 12**. Repeat this measurement for the remaining cylinders and record the diameters.

Piston ring side clearance

1. Temporarily install the new rings onto the piston following the instructions in this chapter.

2. Using feeler gauges, measure the piston ring side clearance as shown in **Figure 126**.

3. Select the feeler gauge that passes between the ring and the ring groove with a light drag. Compare the thickness of the feeler gauge with the specification in **Table 11**. Replace the piston if the clearance is not as specified.

Piston ring end gap

1. Using a piston without rings (**Figure 127**), push a new piston ring into the cylinder bore to 20 mm (0.8 in.) from the top of the cylinder block surface.
2. Using feeler gauges, measure the width of the ring gap (**Figure 128**). Select the feeler gauge that passes through the gap with a slight drag.
3. Compare the thickness of the feeler gauge with the specification in **Table 11**.
4. If the end gap is exceeds the specification in **Table 11**, measure the cylinder bore diameter again to verify that it is within the specification. If the cylinder bore is not excessively worn, insert another new piston ring into the cylinder and check its end gap. Continue until the correct end gap is obtained. Repeat this procedure for all rings and cylinders. Tag the rings to identify which cylinder they were fitted to.

Piston-to-cylinder bore clearance

1. Subtract the piston diameter from the largest cylinder bore diameter for the given cylinder. The result is the largest clearance (**Figure 129**).
2. Subtract the piston diameter from the smallest cylinder bore diameter for the given cylinder. The result is the smallest clearance. Compare the largest and smallest clearance with the specification in **Table 6** and **Table 10**.
3. If the piston clearance is excessive, either the cylinder or piston is excessively worn.

Connecting rod

Inspect the connecting rod(s) for bending, twisting, discoloration, excessive wear or damage. Replace the connecting rod if any defects are noted.

Crankshaft

1. Inspect the crankshaft bearing journals for cracks, corrosion, etching, bluing or discoloration.
2. Also check for rough or irregular surfaces, or transferred bearing material.
3. Replace the crankshaft if any of these defects are noted.
4. Grinding the crankshaft and installing undersize bearings is not recommended. Grinding or machining of the crankshaft can result in power head failure.

NOTE
Some minor surface corrosion, glaze-like deposits or minor scratches can be cleaned

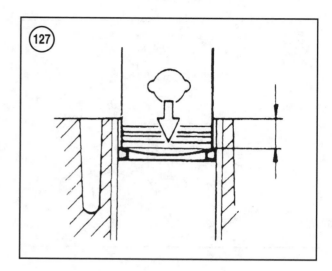

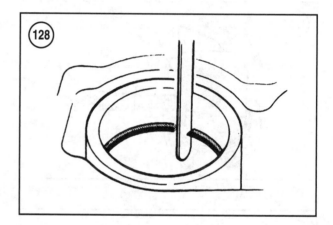

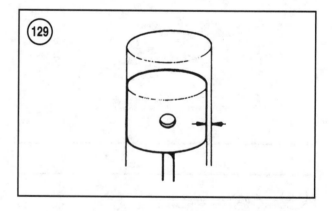

using crocus cloth or 320 grit carburundum. Polish the surfaces enough to remove the deposits. Excessive polishing can remove a considerable amount of material from the crankshaft.

5. Measure the crankpin journals on 50-100 hp models using an outside micrometer (**Figure 130**). Compare the

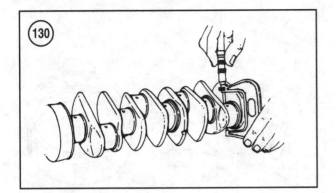

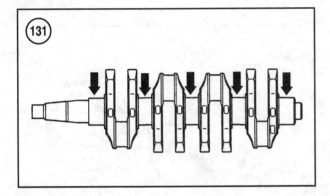

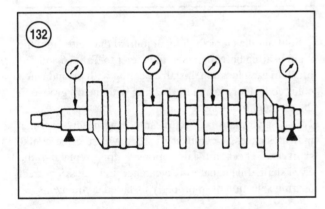

measurements with the specification in **Table 9**. Replace the crankshaft if the crankpin diameter is less than the specification. Record all diameters for use during bearing selection.

6. On 80 and 100 hp models, measure the main bearing journal diameters (**Figure 131**). Record the journal diameters for use in bearing selection. Compare the main bearing journal diameter with the specification in **Table 9**. Replace the crankshaft if any main bearing journal diameter is below the specification.

7. Thrust spacers inspection is required on 9.9 hp models. Inspect the thrust spacer for wear, discoloration or roughness. Replace the thrust spacer if necessary.

8. A V-block or balance wheel, and dial indicator is required to check crankshaft runout.

9. Support the crankshaft on the top and bottom main bearing journals with a V-block or a balance wheel. Position a dial indicator at one of the remaining main bearing journals (**Figure 132**) or other parallel bearing surface.

10. Observe the dial indicator while slowly rotating the crankshaft. Repeat the measurement with the indicator at each main bearing journal.

11. Compare the crankshaft runout with the specification in **Table 9**. Replace the crankshaft if any of the measurements exceed the specification.

Balance piston and balance piston bore

1. These measurements are required on 25 hp models only. Measure the balance piston outer diameter using an outside micrometer.

2. Compare the balance piston diameter with the specification in **Table 10**. Replace the balance piston if the diameter is below the specification.

3. Measure the balance piston bore in the crankcase cover using an inside micrometer.

4. Compare the bore diameter with the specification in **Table 6**. Replace the cylinder block assembly if the bore diameter exceeds the specification.

BEARING SELECTION

Bearing selection is required when replacing the crankshaft, connecting rod or cylinder block on 9.9-90 hp models.

Main Bearing Selection (9.9 and 15 hp models)

Select main bearings by reading the bearing codes on the upper and lower sides of the crankcase cover (**Figure 133**). The upper A, B or C marks are the bearing code for the upper main bearings. The lower A, B, or C marks are the bearing code for the lower main bearings. Refer to the marks, then refer to **Table 9**. In each location, install the bearing with the color code listed. Excessive main bearing clearance with a new bearing indicates excessive crankshaft wear.

Main Bearing Selection (25-50 hp models)

Select the main bearings by referring to the main bearing codes on the lower port side of the crankcase cover. See **Figure 134** (25 hp) or **Figure 135** (40 and 50 hp). The

8

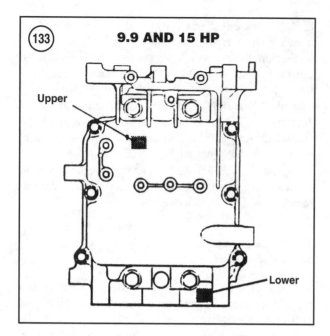

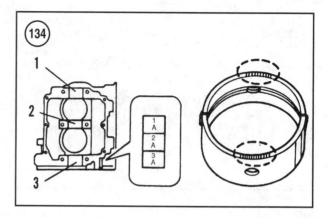

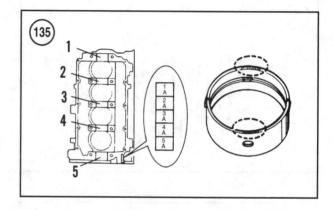

bearing codes are arranged to correspond to the main bearing location in the engine. The upper code represents the upper main bearing; the second code represents the No. 2 main bearing and so forth. Refer to the bearing codes, then refer to **Table 9** to select the correct bearing color code (B, **Figure 135**). If the bearing clearance is excessive with the correct bearing installed, the crankshaft journal is excessively worn.

Main Bearing Selection (80 and 100 hp models)

Select the main bearing by referring to the codes stamped into the crankshaft and cylinder block (**Figure 136**), and using the crankshaft measurements.

Determine the crankshaft main journal diameter by reading the code for the No. 1 journal (**Figure 136**). Multiply the number stamped into the crankshaft by 0.001. Add the results to the base measurement of 47.9. Record the results as the *crankshaft main diameter*. Perform the calculation for the remaining four main bearing surfaces. Record all results.

Determine the main bearing bore diameter by reading the codes stamped on the starboard side of the cylinder block (**Figure 136**). Read the code for the No. 1 main bearing bore. Multiply this number by 0.001. Add the results to a base measurement of 54.0. Record the results as the *main bearing bore* diameter. Perform the calculations for the remaining four main bearing bores. Record all results.

Subtract the crankshaft main journal diameter from the main bearing bore diameter, then refer to **Table 6** and **Table 9**. In each location, install a bearing with the indicated color code. Only install the bearing with the oil groove in the cylinder block side.

Excessive main bearing clearance with new bearings indicates excessive crankshaft wear. Measure the crankshaft and check all calculations before replacing the crankshaft. Inadequate oil clearance indicates incorrect bearing selection or improperly installed components.

Connecting Rod Bearing Selection (9.9-50 hp models)

On 9.9-50 models, bearing selection is determined by the oil clearance measurement. Excessive oil clearance with new bearings installed indicates excessive crankshaft wear.

Connecting Rod Bearing Selection (80 and 100 hp models)

Select the crankpin bearings by measuring the bearing clearance using Plastigage as described in this chapter.

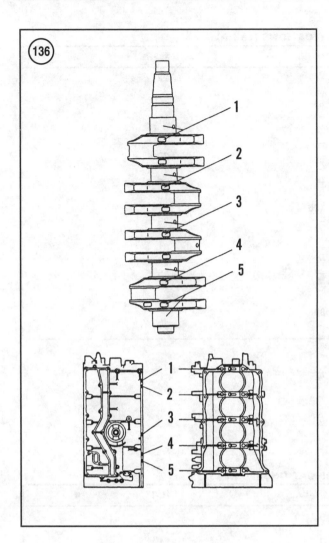

First, install new crankpin bearings with a yellow color code. Then check the clearance using Plastigage. Repeat the procedure on all crankpin journals, then refer to **Table 9** to select the color code that corresponds to the clearance measured with the yellow bearings installed.

Engine Break-In

Perform the break-in procedure anytime internal engine components are replaced. During the first few hours of operation, many of the components of the power head must not be under a full load until fully seated. Failure to properly break-in the engine can result in power head failure, decreased performance and increased oil consumption.

Full break-in is achieved in approximately 10 hours of running time. Expect increased oil consumption during this period. Check the oil frequently during break-in. Refer to Chapter Four. Check the tightness of all external fasteners during the break-in period.

Break-in the engine as follows:

During the first hour of operation, do not exceed 3500 rpm or half throttle. Do not run over a few minutes at a given throttle setting.

During the second hour of operation, apply full throttle for a period of one minute at two minute intervals. Otherwise, run the engine at 3/4 throttle, or 4500 rpm or less during the second hour.

During the next eight hours, operate the engine at full throttle for a maximum of 5 minutes at a time. Otherwise, run the engine at any throttle setting below wide open.

8

Table 1 TORQUE SPECIFICATIONS (9.9 HP)

Fastener	N•m	in.-lb.	ft.-lb.
Cylinder head bolt			
First torque	15	–	11
Second torque	30	–	22
Connecting rod bolt			
First torque	6	53	–
Second torque	12	106	–
Crankcase bolt			
First torque	15	–	11
Second torque	30	–	22
Oil element assembly	8	71	–
Exhaust cover bolt	12	106	–
Rocker arm adjusting screw	8	71	–
Drive sprocket	23	–	17
Driven sprocket	13	115	–
Flywheel nut	100	–	74
Spark plug	13	115	–
Power head mounting bolt	21	–	15

Table 2 TORQUE SPECIFICATIONS (15 HP)

Fastener	N•m	in.-lb.	ft.-lb.
Cylinder head bolt	30	–	22
Connecting rod bolt			
First torque	10	88	–
Second torque	22	–	16
Crankcase bolt			
First torque	15	–	11
Second torque	30	–	22
Oil filter	18	–	13
Oil filter plug	40	–	29
Valve adjusting screw	14	–	10
Exhaust cover	12	106	–
Drive sprocket	40	–	29
Driven sprocket	13	115	–
Flywheel nut	110	–	81
Spark plug	18	–	13
Power head mounting bolt	21	–	15
Cylinder head cover bolt	8.0	71	–
Oil pump cover bolt	4.0	35	–
Carburetor nut	10	88	–
Starter motor bolt	29	–	21

Table 3 TORQUE SPECIFICATIONS (25 HP)

Fastener	N•m	in.-lb.	ft.-lb.
Cylinder head bolt			
First torque	23	–	17
Second torque	46	–	34
Cylinder head cover bolt			
First torque	6	53	–
Second torque	12	106	–
Connecting rod bolt			
First torque	6	53	–
Second torque	16	–	12
Crankcase bolt			
First torque	15	–	11
Second torque	30	–	22
Exhaust cover			
First torque	6	53	–
Second torque	12	106	–
Rocker arm shaft	18	–	13
Tappet adjusting screw	13	–	10
Drive sprocket	140	–	103
Driven sprocket	38	–	28
Flywheel nut	157	–	116
Oil filter cartridge	40	–	29
Power head mounting	21	–	15
Recoil starter roller	8	71	–
Sheave drum	15	–	11
Carburetor nut	8	71	–
Balancer piston	157	–	116

Table 4 TORQUE SPECIFICATIONS (40-50 HP)

Fastener	N•m	in.-lb.	ft.-lb.
Cylinder head bolt			
First torque	23	–	17
Second torque	47	–	34
Connecting rod			
First torque	6	53	–
Second torque	17	–	12.5
Crankcase			
First torque	6	53	–
Second torque	12	106	–
Power head mounting bolt	21	–	15
Flywheel nut	160	–	116
Carburetor	8	71	–
Oil filter	18	–	13
Oil filter plug	39	–	29
Spark plug	18	–	13
Timing belt tensioner	8	71	–
	25	–	18
Drive sprocket	140	–	101
Driven sprocket	38	–	27
Rocker shaft	18	–	13
Tappet adjusting screw	14	–	10
Exhaust cover			
First torque	6	53	–
Second torque	12	106	–

Table 5 TORQUE SPECIFICATIONS (80 and 100 HP)

Fastener	N•m	in.-lb.	ft.-lb.
Cylinder head bolt			
First torque	14	–	10
Second torque	28	–	20
Cylinder head bolt			
First torque	15	–	11
Second torque	33	–	24
Third torque	Additional 90°		
Cylinder head cover	8	70.1	–
Connecting rod			
First torque	8	70.1	–
Second torque	Additional 90°		
Crankcase bolt			
First torque	14	–	10
Second torque	28	–	20
Crankcase journal			
First torque	19	–	14
Second torque	Additional 60°		
Camshaft cap			
First torque	8	71	–
Second torque	17	–	12
Camshaft sprocket	60	–	43
CDI cover	4	34.8	–
Crankshaft sprocket	265	–	195
Outer exhaust cover			
First torque	6	53	–
Second torque	12	106	–
Flywheel nut	190	–	140
Fuel pump bracket	17	–	12
Oil filter	18	–	13

(continued)

8

Table 5 TORQUE SPECIFICATIONS (80 and 100 HP) (continued)

Fastener	N•m	in.-lb.	ft.-lb.
Oil filter plug	50	–	36
Spark plug	25	–	18
Spark plug cover	4	35	–
Timing belt tensioner	40	–	29
Timing plate	4	35	–

Table 6 CYLINDER HEAD AND CYLINDER BLOCK SPECIFICATIONS

Model	Bore size mm (in.)	Taper limit mm (in.)	Out-of-round limit mm (in.)
9.9	59.00-59.02 (2.323-2.324)	0.08 (0.003)	0.05 (0.002)
15	59.00-59.02 (2.323-2.324)	0.08 (0.003)	0.05 (0.002)
25	65.00-65.015 (2.5590-2.5596)	0.08 (0.003)	0.08 (0.003)
25 Balancer cyl.	95.018 (3.7409)		
40-50	63.000-63.015 (2.4803-2.4809)	0.08 (0.003)	0.08 (0.003)
80-100	79.000-79.020 (3.110-3.111)	0.08 (0.003)	0.08 (0.003)

All models cylinder head has a 0.1 mm (0.004 in.) warp limit.

Table 7 CAMSHAFT DIMENSIONS

Intake lobe height	
F9.9	24.541-24.641 mm (0.966-0.970 in.)
F15	23.895-23.995 mm (0.9407-0.9447 in.)
F25	30.884-30.984 mm (1.2159-1.2198 in.)
F40-F50	30.89-30.99 mm (1.2161-1.2200 in.)
F80-F100	37.22-37.38 mm (1.465-1.472 in.)
Intake lobe width	
F9.9	20.137-20.237 mm (0.793-0.797 in.)
F15	19.950-20.050 mm (0.7854-0.7894 in.)
F25	25.95-26.05 mm (1.022-1.025 in.)
F40-F50	25.95-26.05 mm (1.0217-1.0256 in.)
F80-F100	29.92-30.08 mm (1.178-1.184 in.)
Exhaust lobe height	
F9.9	24.578-24.678 mm (0.968-0.972 in.)
F15	23.917-24.017 mm (0.9416-0.9456 in.)
F25	30.884-30.984 mm (1.2159-1.2198 in.)
F40-F50	30.82-30.92 mm (1.2135-1.2175 in.)
F80-F100	36.90-37.06 mm (1.453-1.459 in.)
Exhaust lobe width	
F9.9	20.178-20.278 mm (0.794-0.798 in.)
F15	19.950-20.050 mm (0.7854-0.7894 in.)
F25	25.95-26.05 mm (1.022-1.025 in.)
F40-F50	25.95-26.05 mm (1.0217-1.0256 in.)
F80-F100	29.92-30.08 mm (1.178-1.184 in.)
Journal diameter	
F9.9	15.973-15.984 mm (0.6289-0.6293 in.)
F15	17.975-17.991 mm (0.7077-0.7088 in.)
F25	36.925-36.945 mm (1.4537-1.4545 in.)
F40-F50	
No. 1	36.925-36.945 mm (1.4537-1.4545 in.)
No. 2-3-4	36.935-36.955 mm (1.4541-1.4549 in.)
F80-F100	24.96-24.98 mm (0.9827-0.9835 in.)
Minimum runout	
F15-F100	0.1 mm (0.004 in.)

Table 8 VALVE, VALVE SEAT, AND VALVE GUIDE DIMENSIONS

F9.9
  Valve clearance (cold)
    Intake   0.15-0.20 mm (0.0059-0.0079 in.)
    Exhaust   0.20-0.25 mm (0.0079-0.0098 in.)
  Valve
    Head diameter
      Intake   25.9-26.1 mm (1.020-1.028 in.)
      Exhaust   21.9-22.1 mm (0.862-0.870 in.)
    Face width
      Intake and exhaust   1.98-3.11 mm (0.078-0.122 in.)
    Seat width
      Intake and exhaust   0.6-0.8 mm (0.024-0.031 in.)
    Margin thickness
      Intake and exhaust   0.5-0.9 mm (0.020-0.035 in.)
    Stem diameter
      Intake   5.475-5.490 mm (0.2156-0.2161 in.)
      Exhaust   5.460-5.475 mm (0.2150-0.2156 in.)
    Guide inside diameter
      Intake and exhaust   5.500-5.512 mm (0.2165-0.2170 in.)
    Stem-to-guide clearance
      Intake   0.010-0.037 mm (0.0004-0.0015 in.)
      Exhaust   0.025-0.052 mm (0.0010-0.0020 in.)
      Runout limit   0.016 mm (0.0006 in.)
F15
  Valve clearance (cold)
    Intake   0.15-0.25 mm (0.006-0.009 in.)
    Exhaust   0.20-0.30 mm (0.008-0.012 in.)
  Valve
    Head diameter
      Intake   27.9-28.1 mm (1.10-1.11 in.)
      Exhaust   21.9-22.1 mm (0.862-0.870 in.)
    Face width
      Intake and exhaust   2.0-3.1 mm (0.078-0.122 in.)
    Seat width
      Intake and exhaust   0.6-0.8 mm (0.024-0.031 in.)
    Margin thickness
      Intake and exhaust   0.5-0.9 mm (0.020-0.035 in.)
    Stem diameter
      Intake   5.475-5.490 mm (0.2156-0.2161 in.)
      Exhaust   5.460-5.475 mm (0.2150-0.2156 in.)
    Guide inside diameter
      Intake and exhaust   5.500-5.512 mm (0.2165-0.2170 in.)
    Stem-to-guide clearance
      Intake   0.010-0.037 mm (0.0004-0.0015 in.)
      Exhaust   0.025-0.052 mm (0.0010-0.0020 in.)
      Runout limit   0.016 mm (0.0006 in.)
F25
  Valve clearance (cold)
    Intake   0.15-0.25 mm (0.006-0.010 in.)
    Exhaust   0.25-0.35 mm (0.010-0.014 in.)
  Valve
    Head diameter
      Intake   31.9-32.1 mm (1.255-1.263 in.)
      Exhaust   25.9-26.1 mm (1.020-1.027 in.)
    Face width
      Intake and exhaust   2.4-2.8 mm (0.095-0.110 in.)
    Seat width
      Intake and exhaust   0.9-1.1 mm (0.035-0.043 in.)
    Margin thickness
      Intake and exhaust   0.6-1.1 mm (0.025-0.043 in.)

(continued)

8

Table 8 VALVE, VALVE SEAT, AND VALVE GUIDE DIMENSIONS (continued)

F25
- Valve
  - Stem diameter
    - Intake .... 5.475-5.490 mm (0.2156-0.2161 in.)
    - Exhaust .... 5.460-5.475 mm (0.2150-0.2156 in.)
  - Guide inside diameter
    - Intake and exhaust .... 5.500-5.512 mm (0.2165-0.2170 in.)
  - Stem-to-guide clearance
    - Intake .... 0.010-0.037 mm (0.0004-0.0015 in.)
    - Exhaust .... 0.025-0.052 mm (0.0010-0.0020 in.)
    - Runout limit .... 0.016 mm (0.0006 in.)

F40-F50
- Valve clearance (cold)
  - Intake .... 0.15-0.25 mm (0.006-0.010 in.)
  - Exhaust .... 0.25-0.35 mm (0.010-0.014 in.)
- Valve
  - Head diameter
    - Intake .... 29.9-30.1 mm (1.177-1.185 in.)
    - Exhaust .... 25.9-26.1 mm (1.020-1.027 in.)
  - Face width
    - Intake .... 3.25-3.82 mm (0.128-0.150 in.)
    - Exhaust .... 3.54-4.10 mm (0.139-0.161 in.)
  - Seat width
    - Intake .... 1.03-1.38 mm (0.041-0.054 in.)
    - Exhaust .... 0.67-1.17 mm (0.026-0.046 in.)
  - Margin thickness
    - Intake and exhaust .... 0.6-1.1 mm (0.025-0.043 in.)
  - Stem diameter
    - Intake .... 5.475-5.490 mm (0.2156-0.2161 in.)
    - Exhaust .... 5.460-5.475 mm (0.2150-0.2156 in.)
  - Guide inside diameter
    - Intake and exhaust .... 5.500-5.512 mm (0.2165-0.2170 in.)
  - Stem-to-guide clearance
    - Intake .... 0.015-0.040 mm (0.0006-0.0016 in.)
    - Exhaust .... 0.030-0.055 mm (0.0012-0.0022 in.)
    - Runout limit .... 0.016 mm (0.0006 in.)

F80-F100
- Valve clearance (cold)
  - Intake .... 0.17-0.23 mm (0.007-0.009 in.)
  - Exhaust .... 0.31-0.37 mm (0.012-0.014 in.)
- Valve
  - Head diameter
    - Intake .... 29.00-29.20 mm (1.142-1.150 in.)
    - Exhaust .... 24.00-24.20 mm (0.945-0.953 in.)
  - Face width
    - Intake .... 2.00-2.43 mm (0.079-0.096 in.)
    - Exhaust .... 2.28-2.71 mm (0.090-0.107 in.)
  - Seat width
    - Intake .... 1.58-1.94 mm (0.062-0.076 in.)
    - Exhaust .... 1.80-2.02 mm (0.071-0.080 in.)
  - Margin thickness
    - Intake .... 0.45-0.65 mm (0.018-0.026 in.)
    - Exhaust .... 0.65-0.85 mm (0.026-0.033 in.)
  - Stem diameter
    - Intake .... 5.975-5.990 mm (0.2352-0.2358 in.)
    - Exhaust .... 5.960-5.975 mm (0.2346-0.2352 in.)
  - Guide inside diameter
    - Intake and exhaust .... 6.005-6.018 mm (0.2364-0.2369 in.)
  - Stem-to-guide clearance
    - Intake .... 0.015-0.043 mm (0.0006-0.0017 in.)
    - Exhaust .... 0.030-0.058 mm (0.0012-0.0023 in.)
    - Runout limit .... 0.03 mm (0.001 in.)

Table 9 CRANKSHAFT AND CONNECTING ROD SPECIFICATONS

F9.9 and T9.9	
Crank width	123.7-123.9 mm (4.87 –4.88 in.)
Runout limit	0.05 mm (0.002 in.)
Main bearing clearance	0.000-0.027 mm (0.000-0.0011 in,)
Crankcase bearing color code	A-blue, B-black, C-brown
F15	
Crank width	126.7-126.9 mm (4.99-5.00 in.)
Radial clearance	0.05 mm (0.002 in.)
Connecting rod side clearance (big end)	0.05-0.22 mm (0.002-0.009 in)
Crankcase bearing color code	A-blue, B-black, C-brown
Crankshaft journal clearance	0.012-0.045 mm (0.0005-0.0018 in.)
Runout limit	0.03 mm (0.0012 in.)
F25	
Crankshaft journal outside diameter	42.984-43.000 mm (1.692-1.693 in.)
Main journal clearance	0.012-0.044 mm (0.0005-0.0017 in.)
Connecting rod side clearance (big end)	0.05-0.22 mm (0.002-0.009 in.)
Crankpin journal clearance	0.020-0.052 mm (0.0008-0.0020 in.)
Crankcase bearing color code	A-blue, B-black, C-brown
Runout limit	0.03 mm (0.0012 in.)
F40, F50 and T50	
Crankshaft journal diameter	42.984-43.000 mm (1.6923-1.6929 in.)
Crankpin diameter	32.984-33.000 mm (1.2986-1.2992 in.)
Runout limit	0.03 mm (0.001 in.)
Crankcase main journal inside diameter	46.000-46-024 mm (1.8110-1.8120 in.)
Crankcase oil journal clearance	0.012-0.044 mm (0.0005-0.0017 in.)
Crankcase journal bearing thickness	(Blue) 1.498-1.502 mm (0.0590-0.0591 in.)
	(Black) 1.494-1.498 mm (0.0588-0.0590 in.)
	(Brown) 1.490-1.494 mm (0.0587-0.0588 in.)
F80 and F100	
Journal diameter	47.985-48.000 mm (1.8892-1.8898 in.)
Minimum diameter	47.972 mm (1.8887 in.)
Crankpin diameter	43.982-44.000 mm (1.7316-1.7323 in.)
Minimum diameter	43.971 mm (1.7311 in.)
Runout limit	0.03 mm (0.001 in.)
Crankcase main journal inside diameter	54.023-54.042 mm (2.1269-2.1276 in.)
Journal oil clearance	0.024-0.044 mm (0.0009-0.0017 in.)
Upper crankcase main	(Green) 2.992-2.999 mm (0.1178-0.1181 in.)
journal bearing thickness	(Blue) 2.999-3.006 mm (0.1181-0.1183 in.)
	(Red) 3.006-3.013 mm (0.1183-0.1186 in.)
Lower crankcase main	(Yellow) 3.010-3.017 mm (0.1185-0.1188 in.)
journal bearing thickness	(Green) 3.017-3.024 mm (0.1188-0.1191 in.)
	(Blue) 3.024-3.031 mm (0.1191-0.1193 in.)
	(Red) 3.031-3.038 mm (0.1193-0.1196 in.)
No. 3 main journal bearing thickness	(Green) 2.992-2.999 mm (0.1178-0.1181 in.)
	(Blue) 2.999-3.006 mm (0.1181-0.1183 in.)
	(Red) 3.006-3.013 mm (0.1183-0.1186 in.)

8

Table 10 STANDARD PISTON DIAMETER

Model	Piston diameter
F9.9 and F15	58.950-58.965 mm (2.3209-2.3215 in.)
F25	64.950-64.965 mm (2.5570-2.5573 in.)
F25 balancer piston	94.893 mm (3.7360 in.)
F40 and F50	62.950-62.965 mm (2.4783-2.4789 in.)
F80 and F100	78.928-78.949 mm (3.1074-3.1082 in.)

Table 11 PISTON RING SPICIFICATIONS

Model F9.9	
Top ring-barrel face	
End gap	0.15-0.30 mm (0.006-0.012 in.)
Side clearance	0.04-0.08 mm (0.002-0.003 in.)
Second ring-taper face	
End gap	0.15-0.30 mm (0.006-0.012 in.)
Side clearance	0.03-0.07 mm (0.001-0.003 in.)
Oil ring	
End gap	0.20-0.70 mm (0.008-0.028 in.)
Model F15	
Top ring-barrel face	
End gap	0.15-0.30 mm (0.006-0.012 in.)
Side clearance	0.013-0.035 mm (0.0005-0.0013 in.)
Second ring-taper face	
End gap	0.30-0.50 mm (0.012-0.020 in.)
Side clearance	0.02-0.04 mm (0.001-0.002 in.)
Oil ring	
End gap	0.2-0.7 mm (0.008-0.028 in.)
Model F25, F40, and F50	
Top ring-barrel face	
End gap	0.15-0.30 mm (0.006-0.012 in.)
Side clearance	0.04-0.08 mm (0.002-0.003 in.)
Second ring-taper face	
End gap	0.30-0.50 mm (0.012-0.020 in.)
Side clearance	0.03-0.07 mm (0.001-0.003 in.)
Oil ring	
End gap	0.20-0.70 mm (0.008-0.028 in.)
Model F80 and F100	
Top ring-barrel face	
End gap	0.15-0.30 mm (0.006-0.012 in.)
Side clearance	0.02-0.08 mm (0.001-0.003 in.)
Second ring-taper face	
End gap	0.70-0.90 mm (0.028-0.035 in.)
Side clearance	0.03-0.07 mm (0.001-0.003 in.)
Oil ring	
End gap	0.20-0.70 mm (0.008-0.028 in.)

Table 12 CONNECTING ROD AND PISTON PIN DIMENSIONS

Model F9.9	
Connecting rod bearing clearance (big end)	0.021-0.045 mm (0.0008-0.0018 in.)
Piston pin diameter	13.996-14.000 mm (0.551-0.5512 in.)
Model F15	
Connecting rod bearing clearance big end)	0.021-0.045 mm (0.0008-0.0018 in.)
Inside diameter (small end)	14.015-14.029 mm (0.5518-0.5523 in.)
Piston pin diameter	13.996-14.000 mm (0.551-0.5512 in.)
Model F25	
Connecting rod bearing clearance big end)	0.020-0.052 mm (0.0008-0.0020 in.)
Inside diameter (small end)	15.985-15.998 mm (0.6293-0.6298 in)
Inside diameter color code	A-blue, B-black, C-brown
Piston pin diameter	15.965-15.970 mm (0.6285-0.6287 in.)
Model F40 and F50	
Connecting rod bearing clearance (big end)	0.020-0.052 mm (0.0008-0.0020 in.)
Inside diameter (small end)	15.985-15.988 mm (0.6293-0.6294 in)
Inside diameter (big end)	36.000-36.024 mm (1.4173-1.4183 in.)
Crankpin side clearance (big end)	0.05-0.22 mm (0.0020-0.0087 in.)
Bearing thickness (big end)	Blue–1.494-1.498 mm (0.0588-0.0590 in.)
	Black–1.490-1.494 mm (0.0587-0.0588 in.)
	Brown–1.486-1.490 mm (0.0585-0.0587 in.)
Piston pin diameter	15.965–15.970 mm (0.6285-0.6287 in.)

(continued)

Table 12 CONNECTING ROD AND PISTON PIN DIMENSIONS (continued)

Model F80 and F100	
Connecting rod bearing clearance (big end)	0.023-0.035 mm (0.0009-0.0014 in.)
Inside clearance (small end)	17.965-17.985 mm (0.7073-0.7081 in.)
Inside clearance (big end)	47.025-47.035 mm (1.8514-1.8518 in.)
Bearing thickness (big end)	Yellow–1.499-1.506 mm (0.0590-0.0593 in.)
	Green–1.506-1.513 mm (0.0593-0.0596 in.)
	Blue–1.513-1.520 mm (0.0596-0.0598 in.)
	Red–1.520-1.527 mm (0.0598-0.0601 in.)

Table 13 VALVE SPRING SPECIFICATIONS

Free length	
F15	32.7 mm (1.29 in.)
F25	37.85-39.85 mm (1.49-1.57 in.)
F40-50	37.85 mm (1.49 in.)
F80-100	52.25 mm (2.057 in.)
Tilt limit	
F9.9	1.1 mm (0.043 in.)
F15	1.5 mm (0.06 in.)
F25-50	1.7 mm (0.07 in.)
F80-100	2.6 mm (0.10 in.)
Pressure	
Compressed force	
All 9.9 only	9.0-10 Kg (19.8-22.04 lb.) @ 24.4 mm (0.96 in.)

8

Table 14 ROCKER ARM AND ROCKER ARM SHAFT

Rocker arm inside diameter	
F9.9-F15 and FT9.9 hp	13.000-13.018 mm (0.5118-0.5125 in.)
F25-F50 and FT50 hp	16.000-16.018 mm (0.6299-0.6306 in.)
Rocker arm shaft outside diameter	
F9.9-F15 and FT9.9 hp	12.941-12.951 mm (0.5095-0.5099 in.)
F25-F50 and FT50 hp	15.971-15.991 mm (0.6288-0.6296 in.)

Table 15 OIL PUMP CLEARANCE

F9.9-FT9.9 hp	
Outer rotor-to-housing clearance	0.06-0.11 mm (0.0024-0.0043 in.)
Outer rotor-to-inner rotor clearance	0.02-0.15 mm (0.0008-0.0059 in.)
Outer rotor-to-cover mating surface	0.02-0.07 mm (0.0020-0.0028 in.)
F15 hp	
Outer rotor-to-housing clearance	0.10-0.15 mm (0.004-0.006 in.)
Outer rotor-to-inner rotor clearance	0.04-0.14 mm (0.002-0.006 in.)
Outer rotor-to-cover mating surface	0.03-0.09 mm (0.001-0.004 in.)
F25 hp	
Outer rotor-to-housing clearance	0.03-0.15 mm (0.001-0.006 in.)
Outer rotor-to-inner rotor clearance	0.12 mm max (0.005 in. max)
Outer rotor-to-cover mating surface	0.03-0.08 mm (0.001-0.003 in.)
F40 and F50 hp	
Outer rotor-to-housing clearance	0.09-0.15 mm (0.004-0.006 in.)
Outer rotor-to-inner rotor clearance	0.00-0.12 mm (0.000-0.005 in.)
Outer rotor-to-cover mating surface	0.03-0.08 mm (0.001-0.003 in.)

Chapter Nine

Gearcase and
Drive Shaft Housing

Gearcase failure is usually the result of an impact with an underwater object or poor maintenance. Proper maintenance is essential for optimum gearcase operation and durability. Gearcase maintenance is provided in Chapter Four.

Special tools and accurate measuring devices are required to remove, position and install many of the gearcase components. Makeshift tools may cause irreparable damage to the housing or internal components of the gearcase housing. Part numbers for the proper tools are included in the repair procedures. Contact a Yamaha dealership to purchase these special tools. Some dealerships rent or loan special tools.

GEARCASE OPERATION

The gearcase transfers the rotation of the vertical drive shaft (A, **Figure 1**) to the horizontal propeller shaft (B). The forward and reverse gears along with the sliding clutch (**Figure 2**) transfer the rotational force to the horizontal propeller shaft.

The pinion and both driven gears (**Figure 2**) rotate anytime the engine is running. A sliding clutch (**Figure 2**) en-

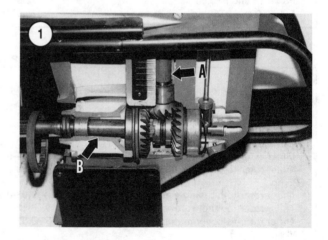

gages the propeller shaft with either the forward or reverse gear.

When neutral is selected (**Figure 2**), the propeller shaft remains stationary as the gears rotate. No propeller thrust is delivered.

When forward gear is selected (**Figure 2**), the sliding clutch engages forward gear. The propeller shaft rotates in the direction of the forward gear as the clutch dogs (raised

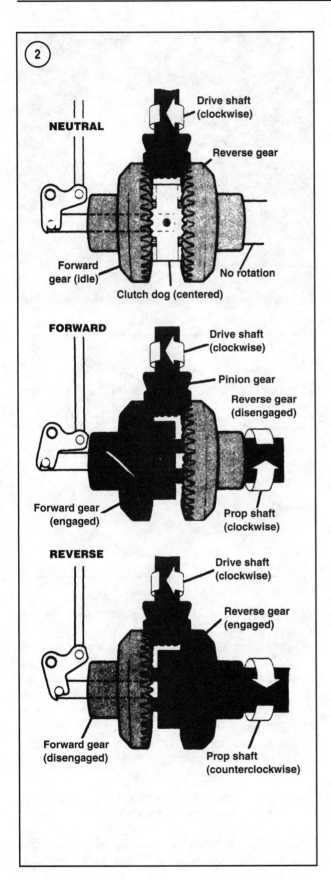

bosses) engage the gear. This provides the clockwise propeller shaft rotation necessary for forward thrust.

When reverse gear is selected (**Figure 2**), the sliding clutch engages reverse gear. The propeller shaft rotates in the direction of the reverse gear as the clutch dogs engage the gear. This provides the counterclockwise propeller shaft rotation necessary for reverse thrust.

GEARCASE IDENTIFICATION

The 9.9 and 50 hp models are available in standard and high thrust designs. Refer to the model designation for the difference. This section provides information that assists with identifying the gearcase used on the various models.

9.9 Hp Models

Both the F9.9 and T9.9 (high thrust) models have a standard 66 mm (2.6 in.) gearcase. This gearcase contains a 13-tooth pinion gear and 38-tooth forward and reverse gears to provide a 2.92:1 final drive ratio.

15, 25 and 40 Hp Models

An 87 mm (3.44 in.) diameter gearcase is used on all model variations. The gearcase contains a 13-tooth pinion gear and 27-tooth forward and reverse gears to provide a 2.08:1 final drive ratio.

50 Hp Models

Both the F50 and T50 models use an 87 mm (3.44 in.) gearcase. The F50 model gearcase contains a 13-tooth pinion gear and 24-tooth forward and reverse gears to provide a 1.84:1 final drive ratio.

The T50 model gearcase contains a 12-tooth pinion gear along with a 28-tooth forward and reverse gear to provide a 2.33:1 final drive ratio.

80 and 100 Hp Models

An optional gearcase is not available for these models. A 108 mm (3.44 in.) diameter gearcase is used. This gearcase contains a 13-tooth pinion gear and 30-tooth forward and reverse gears to provide a 2.31:1 final drive ratio.

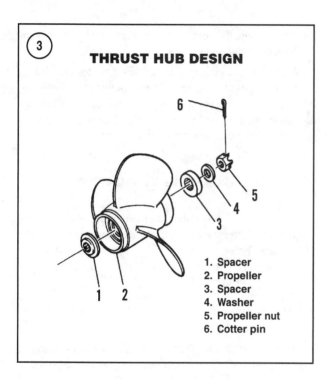

③ THRUST HUB DESIGN

1. Spacer
2. Propeller
3. Spacer
4. Washer
5. Propeller nut
6. Cotter pin

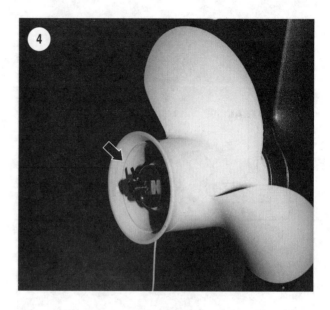

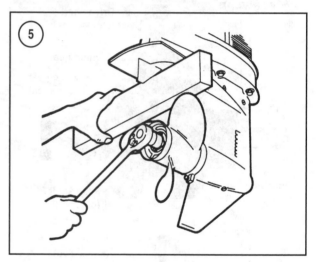

PROPELLER REMOVAL AND INSTALLATION

Refer to **Figure 3** during this procedure.

1. Remove the spark plug(s). Connect the spark plug(s) lead to a suitable engine ground.

2. Shift the engine into neutral. Straighten the ends of the cotter pin (**Figure 4**), and pull it from the castellated nut and propeller shaft.

3. Place a block of wood between the propeller blade and the antiventilation plate (**Figure 5**). Loosen the propeller nut in the counterclockwise direction.

4. Remove the propeller nut, washer (if equipped) and spacer, then pull the propeller from the propeller shaft.

5. Tap lightly on the spacer (1, **Figure 3**) to free it from the propeller shaft. Clean all corrosion and thick grease from the propeller shaft splines, propeller shaft threads and spacer.

6. Apply a coat of Yamaha marine grease, Yamaha A, or a good quality water-resistant grease to the propeller shaft, except the threads.

7. Slide the spacer (1, **Figure 3**) over the propeller shaft with the larger diameter side facing the gearcase. Slide the propeller fully onto the propeller shaft. Make sure the propeller seats against the spacer (1, **Figure 3**).

8. Install the spacer (3, **Figure 3**) and washer (4), if equipped, over the propeller shaft. Thread the propeller nut onto the propeller shaft with the slots facing outward. Place a block of wood between the propeller blade and the

antiventilation plate (**Figure 5**). Tighten the propeller nut to the specification in **Table 1**.

9. Inspect the alignment of the slots in the nut with the cotter pin opening in the propeller shaft. Tighten the nut an additional amount if necessary to align the slot and opening. Install the cotter pin (6, **Figure 3**) through the slot and the propeller shaft, then bend over both ends of cotter pin.

10. Install the spark plug(s) and lead(s). Check for proper shift operation before operating the engine.

GEARCASE REMOVAL AND INSTALLATION

Routine maintenance to the water pump and other gearcase components requires removal of the gearcase.

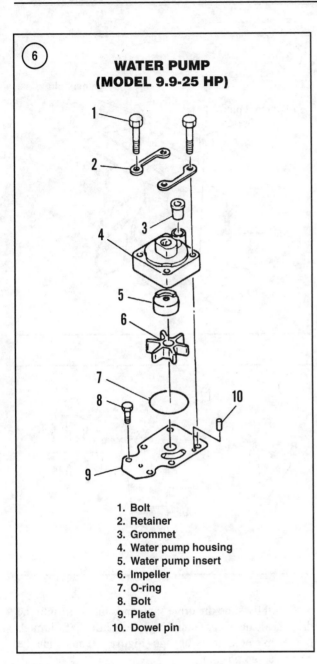

⑥

**WATER PUMP
(MODEL 9.9-25 HP)**

1. Bolt
2. Retainer
3. Grommet
4. Water pump housing
5. Water pump insert
6. Impeller
7. O-ring
8. Bolt
9. Plate
10. Dowel pin

These maintenance items often coincide with the gearcase lubricant change intervals. Change the gearcase lubricant anytime the gearcase is removed. Inspection of the lubricant allows faults to be detected and corrected before they lead to possible gearcase failure.

Drain the gearcase lubricant prior to removing the gearcase if the gearcase requires disassembly. Follow the drain and fill procedure in Chapter Four.

CAUTION
Avoid directing pressurized water at exposed seals or exhaust openings. Pressurized water can blow past seals, and contaminate the gearcase lubricant or possibly damage the seal. Pressurized water can reach the internal power head components if directed into the exhaust openings.

After gearcase removal, clean the drive shaft, shift shaft and all mating surfaces.

Inspect the grommet (3, **Figure 6**) that connects the water tube to the water pump for damage or deterioration. Apply grease to the grommet prior to installing the gearcase.

Inspect the water tube for corrosion or cracks. Replace the water tube if defects are noted. Make sure the dowels or locating pins are properly positioned during installation.

Apply Yamaha marine grease or another good quality water-resistant grease to the drive shaft splines (**Figure 7**) and water pump grommet (3, **Figure 6**) in the water pump housing prior to gearcase installation.

CAUTION
Never apply grease to the top of the drive shaft or fill the crankshaft with grease. The grease may cause a hydraulic lock on the shaft that can cause failure of the power head, gearcase or both. Apply a light coat of Yamaha marine grease only to the drive shaft splines during installation.

CAUTION
Use caution when using a pry bar to separate the gearcase from the drive shaft housing. Remove all fasteners before attempting to separate the housings. Use a blunt pry bar and locate a pry point near the front and rear mating surfaces. Apply moderate heat to the mating surfaces if corrosion prevents easy removal.

CAUTION
Work carefully when installing the upper end of the drive shaft into the crankshaft.

9

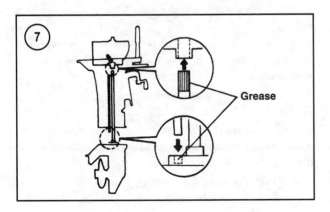

⑦

Grease

The lower seal on the crankshaft may dislodge or become damaged by the drive shaft. Never force the drive shaft into position.

Removal (9.9- 25 Hp Models)

There are four bolts and two dowel pins holding the gearcase to the drive shaft housing. See **Figure 8**.

1. Remove the spark plugs and connect the spark plug leads to a suitable engine ground. Disconnect both cables from the battery, if so equipped.

2. Remove the propeller and attaching hardware as described in this chapter.

3. Shift the engine into NEUTRAL. Tilt the engine to the full up position and engage the tilt lock mechanism.

4. Loosen the shift shaft jam nut (A, **Figure 9**) while holding the coupling to prevent the coupling (B) from rotating. Using a felt tip marker, mark the position of the coupling or count the number of turns while removing the coupling (B, **Figure 9**) from the lower shift shaft. This helps ensure quicker shift adjustment after installing the gearcase.

5. Rotate the shift shaft coupling (counterclockwise) to disconnect the shift shafts (**Figure 9**). Loosen the nut to free the reverse hold down clamp and linkage from the lower shift shaft.

6. Remove the gearcase retaining bolts.

7. Carefully tug or pry the gearcase from the drive shaft housing. Pull the gearcase straight from the drive shaft housing to prevent damage to the shift shaft, lower crankshaft seals and water tube.

8. Place the gearcase in a suitable holding fixture or securely clamp the skeg in a bench vise. Use wooden blocks or padded jaws to prevent damage to the skeg or housing.

Installation (9.9-25 Hp Models)

1. Remove the spark plugs and connect the spark plug leads to a suitable engine ground. Place the engine in the full-tilt position. Engage the tilt lock mechanism. Place the shift selector in the NEUTRAL position.

2. Pull up on the shift shaft until FORWAR gear is engaged. Rotate the drive shaft clockwise to check for proper engagement. The propeller shaft will rotate clockwise (**Figure 2**) if forward gear is engaged.

3. Push down on the shift shaft until the neutral is engaged. Verify neutral gear by spinning the propeller shaft. It must spin freely in both directions.

4. Apply a light coat of water-resistant grease to the splines of the drive shaft and the water tube grommet (**Figure 7**).

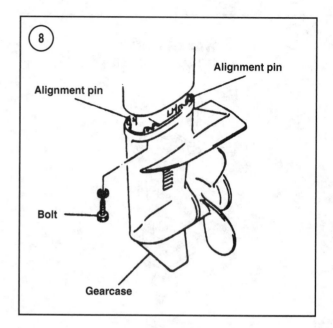

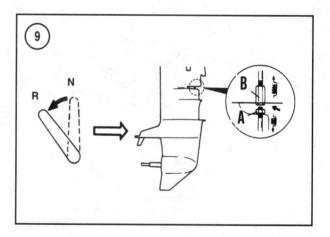

5. Carefully slide the drive shaft and shift shaft into the drive shaft housing. Guide the lower shift shaft through the reverse hold down linkage (**Figure 10**) and slide the gearcase into position.

6. Keep the mating surfaces parallel and align the bolt holes.

7. Make sure the water tube (**Figure 7**) aligns with the water tube grommet in the gearcase and slide the gearcase into position.

8. Align the lower shift shaft with the shift shaft coupling (**Figure 9**).

9. The gearcase should seat against drive shaft housing when the drive shaft and crankshaft splines align. If the housings will not mate, refer to the following:

    a. Drop the gearcase slightly, then rotate the drive shaft clockwise slightly.

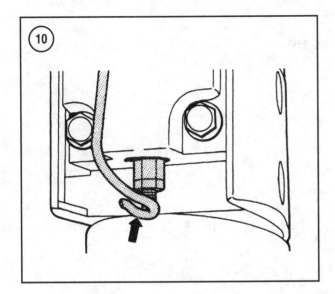

b. Repeat Steps 5-8 until the drive shaft engages the crankshaft. When properly aligned, the gearcase will seat against the drive shaft housing.

c. Align the water tube with the grommet each time installation is attempted.

10. Hold the gearcase in position, and install the mounting bolts. Tighten the bolts to the specification in **Table 1**.

11. Thread the shift shaft coupling onto the lower shift shaft until the mark on the lower drive shaft (made prior to removal) aligns with its reference mark. Prevent the shift shaft coupling from rotating and securely tighten the jam nut against the coupling (**Figure 9**).

12. Adjust the shift and reverse hold-down linkages following the instructions in Chapter Five.

13. Fill the gearcase with lubricant following the instructions in Chapter Four. Install the propeller as described in this chapter.

14. Install the spark plugs and leads. Check for proper cooling and shift system operation immediately after starting the engine.

Removal (40-50 Hp Models)

The gearcase attaches to the drive shaft housing with five bolts (**Figure 11**). Two bolts are located on each side of the gearcase just below the mating surfaces. A fifth bolt is located at the back of the inside the trim tab cavity.

1. Remove the spark plugs and connect the spark plug leads to a suitable engine ground. Disconnect both cables from the battery, if so equipped.

2. Remove the propeller and attaching hardware as described in this chapter.

3. Shift the engine into NEUTRAL. Place the engine in the full-tilt position and engage the tilt lock mechanism.

4. Use a felt tip pen to mark the position of the trim tab on the gearcase (**Figure 12**). This helps ensure quicker trim tab adjustment. Remove the bolt (7, **Figure 11**) and pull the trim tab (8) from the gearcase (10).

5. Support the gearcase and remove all five mounting bolts (11, **Figure 11**).

6. Carefully tug or pry the gearcase from the drive shaft housing. Pull the gearcase straight down from the drive shaft housing to prevent damage to the shift shaft, lower crankshaft seals or water tube.

7. Place the gearcase in a suitable holding fixture or securely clamp the skeg in a bench vise. Use wooden blocks or padded jaws to prevent damage to the skeg or housing.

Installation (40 and 50 hp Models)

1. Remove the spark plugs and connect the spark plug leads to a suitable engine ground. Place the engine in the full-tilt position. Engage the tilt lock mechanism. Place the shift selector in the NEUTRAL position.

2. Verify neutral by spinning the propeller shaft. It must spin freely in both directions.

3. Apply a light coat of water-resistant grease to the splines of the drive shaft and to the water tube grommet (**Figure 7**).

4. Carefully slide the drive shaft and shift shaft into the drive shaft housing. Guide the shift shaft into the coupling of the upper shift shaft and slide the drive shaft into the crankshaft.

5. Keep the housing mating surfaces parallel and align the bolt holes in the housings.

6. Make sure the water tube (**Figure 7**) aligns with the water tube grommet of the water pump and slide the gearcase into position.

7. The gearcase should seat against the drive shaft housing when the drive shaft and crankshaft splines align. If not, proceed as follows:

a. Drop the gearcase slightly, then rotate the drive shaft clockwise slightly.

b. Repeat Steps 4-7 until the drive shaft engages the crankshaft.

c. Align the water tube with the grommet each time installation is attempted.

8. Hold the gearcase in position and install the mounting bolts. Tighten the bolts to the specification in **Table 1**.

9. Place the trim tab into its cavity and align the mark (**Figure 12**). Install the trim tab bolt (7, **Figure 11**). Tighten the bolt to the specification in **Table 1**.

9

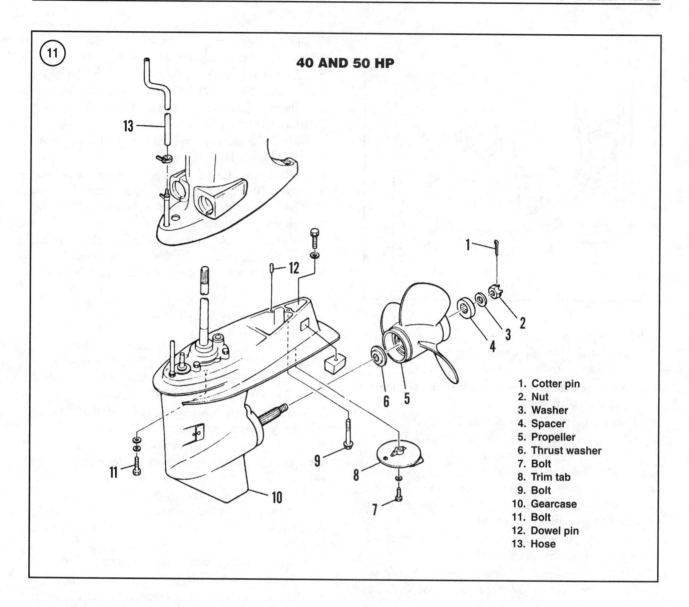

11

40 AND 50 HP

13

12

1
2
3
4

6   5

9

8

11

10

7

1. Cotter pin
2. Nut
3. Washer
4. Spacer
5. Propeller
6. Thrust washer
7. Bolt
8. Trim tab
9. Bolt
10. Gearcase
11. Bolt
12. Dowel pin
13. Hose

10. Fill the gearcase with lubricant following the instructions in Chapter Four. Install the propeller following the instructions in this chapter.

11. Install the spark plugs and leads. Check for proper cooling and shifting system operation immediately after starting the engine.

Removal (80 and 100 hp Models)

The 80 and 100 hp models have a standard long (L) gearcase assembly and an extra long (X), which is an extension (**Figure 13**).

The standard gearcase is attached to the drive shaft housing with five bolts. Two bolts are located on each side of the gearcase. They are located just below the housing

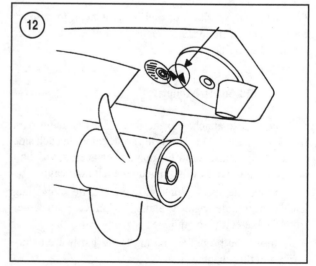

12

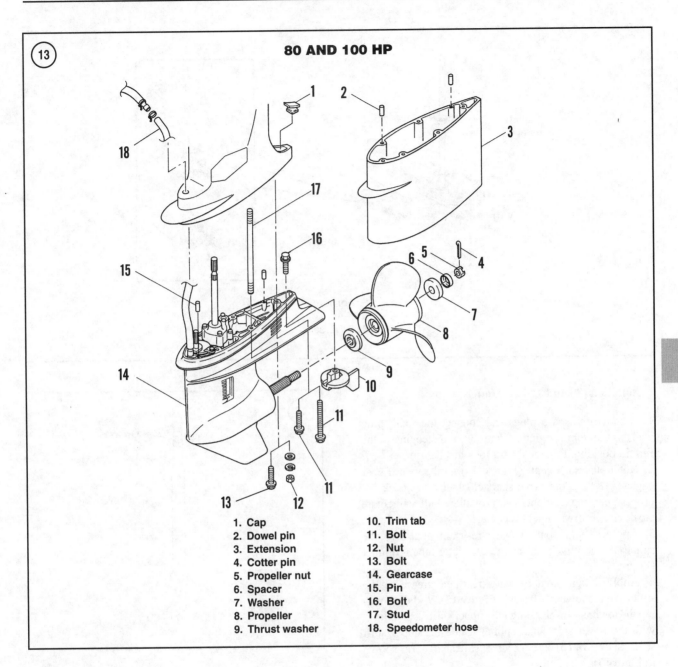

80 AND 100 HP

1. Cap
2. Dowel pin
3. Extension
4. Cotter pin
5. Propeller nut
6. Spacer
7. Washer
8. Propeller
9. Thrust washer
10. Trim tab
11. Bolt
12. Nut
13. Bolt
14. Gearcase
15. Pin
16. Bolt
17. Stud
18. Speedometer hose

mating surfaces. One bolt is located at the back of the gearcase just forward of the trim tab.

The extra long model (X) is attached to the drive shaft housing with four nuts and one bolt. There is also an extension housing, four extension bolts and two locating pins.

1. Remove the spark plugs and connect the spark plug leads to a suitable engine ground. Disconnect both cables from the battery.

2. Remove the propeller and attaching hardware as described in this chapter.

3. Shift the engine into FORWARD gear. Place the engine in the full-tilt position and engage the tilt lock mechanism.

4. Remove all five gearcase mounting bolts (11 and 13, **Figure 13**).

5. Pull the gearcase straight down from the drive shaft housing to prevent damage to the shift shaft, lower crankshaft seals and water tube.

6. Place the gearcase in a suitable holding fixture or securely clamp the skeg in a bench vise. Use wooden blocks or padded jaws to prevent damage to the skeg or housing.

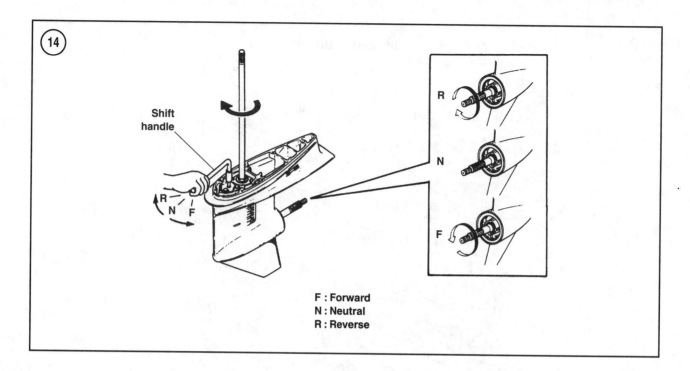

F : Forward
N : Neutral
R : Reverse

Installation (80 and 100 hp Models)

1. Remove the spark plugs and connect the spark plug leads to a suitable engine ground. Place the engine in the full tilt position. Engage the tilt lock mechanism.

2. Rotate the shift shaft (**Figure 14**) until forward gear engages. Rotate the drive shaft clockwise to check for proper gear engagement. The propeller shaft will rotate clockwise if forward gear is engaged.

3. Apply a light coat of water-resistant grease to the splines of the drive shaft and to the water tube grommet (**Figure 7**).

4. Apply a light coat of water-resistant grease to the splines of the lower shift shaft (**Figure 15**). Without rotating the lower shift shaft, align the upper shift shaft splines with the lower shift shaft splines. Slide the upper shift shaft (8, **Figure 16**) onto the lower shift shaft (7) as shown in **Figure 16**.

5. Carefully slide the drive shaft (4, **Figure 16**) into the crankshaft (2). Guide the upper shift shaft (8, **Figure 16**) onto the lower shift shaft coupling (7) and slide the gearcase into position.

6. Keep the mating surfaces parallel and align the bolt holes in the housings.

7. Make sure the water tube aligns with the water tube grommet (5, **Figure 16**) of the water pump and slide the gearcase into position.

8. The gearcase should seat against the drive shaft housing when the drive shaft and crankshaft splines align. If not, proceed as follows:

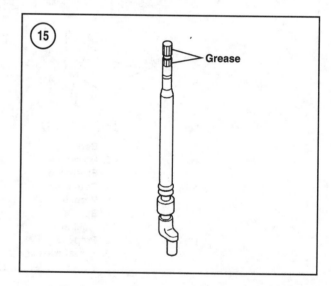

a. Drop the gearcase slightly and rotate the drive shaft clockwise slightly.

b. If necessary, have an assistant move the shift lever slightly to align the shift shaft splines.

c. Repeat Steps 5-8 until the drive shaft engages the crankshaft. When properly aligned, the gearcase will seat against the drive shaft housing.

d. Align the water tube with the grommet each time installation is attempted.

9. Hold the gearcase in position and install the mounting fasteners. Tighten the fasteners to the specification in **Table 1**.

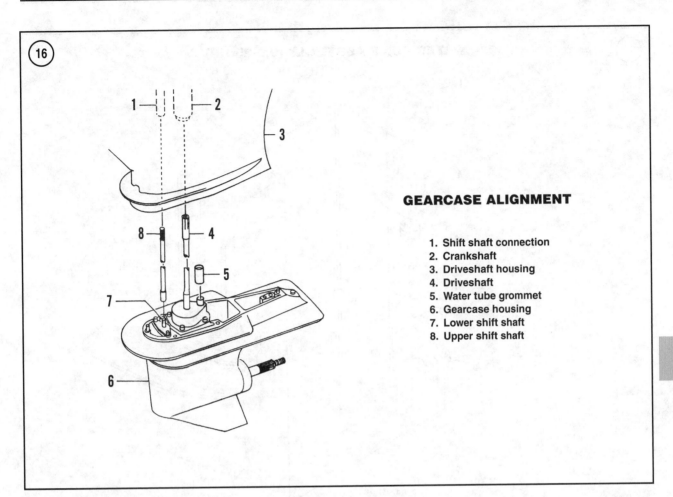

(16)

GEARCASE ALIGNMENT

1. Shift shaft connection
2. Crankshaft
3. Driveshaft housing
4. Driveshaft
5. Water tube grommet
6. Gearcase housing
7. Lower shift shaft
8. Upper shift shaft

9

10. Fill the gearcase with lubricant following the instructions in Chapter Four. Install the propeller as described this chapter.

11. Install the spark plugs and leads. Check for proper cooling and shift system operation immediately after starting the engine.

WATER PUMP

Replace the impeller, seals, O-rings and all gaskets anytime the water pump is serviced. Never use questionable parts. They could compromise the reliability of the water pump. Water pump components are inexpensive compared to damage caused if they fail.

Disassembly (9.9-25 Hp Models)

Refer to **Figure 17** during this procedure.

1. Drain the gearcase lubricant as described in Chapter Four. Remove the gearcase as described in this chapter.

2. Remove the four bolts (1, **Figure 17**), then lift the water pump housing (4) from the gearcase. Pull the water tube grommet (3, **Figure 17**) from the water pump housing (4).

3. Carefully pry the water pump impeller (6, **Figure 17**) away from the wear plate (9). Slide the impeller (6, **Figure 17**) and O-ring (7) from the drive shaft. Pry the impeller from the water pump housing if it is not on the drive shaft. Pull the drive key (11, **Figure 17**) from the drive shaft.

4. Remove the bolts (8, **Figure 17**) securing the wear plate. Lift the wear plate (9, **Figure 17**) from the oil seal housing.

5. Remove the oil seal housing only if removing the drive shaft or shift shaft, resealing the gearcase or if it is damaged.

6. Carefully pry the oil seal housing (14, **Figure 18**) from gearcase. Discard the gasket.

7. Working carefully to avoid damaging the seal housing, carefully pry the drive shaft seals (16, **Figure 18**) and bushing (15) from the oil seal housing.

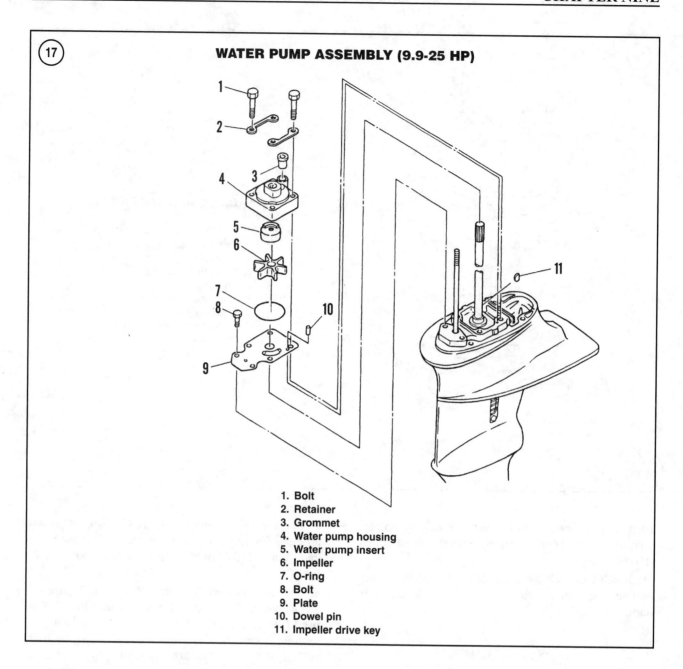

WATER PUMP ASSEMBLY (9.9-25 HP)

1. Bolt
2. Retainer
3. Grommet
4. Water pump housing
5. Water pump insert
6. Impeller
7. O-ring
8. Bolt
9. Plate
10. Dowel pin
11. Impeller drive key

8. Clean the entire water pump using solvent. Carefully scrape gasket material from all components. Inspect all water pump components for wear or damage as described in this chapter under *Component Inspection*.

> **CAUTION**
> *To prevent water or gear lubricant leakage, always replace gaskets, seals and O-rings during assembly.*

> **NOTE**
> *Thoroughly clean all corrosion or other deposits from the drive shaft prior to installing the water pump components. The impeller must slide freely along the length of the shaft.*

Assembly (9.9-25 Hp Models)

Refer to **Figure 17** and **Figure 18** during this procedure.
1. Use a socket or section of tubing as a seal installation tool. The tool must contact the outer diameter of the seal but not the seal bore in the oil seal housing.
2. Apply Yamaha marine grease to the inner diameter of both seals and the bushing. Install the bushing (15, **Figure**

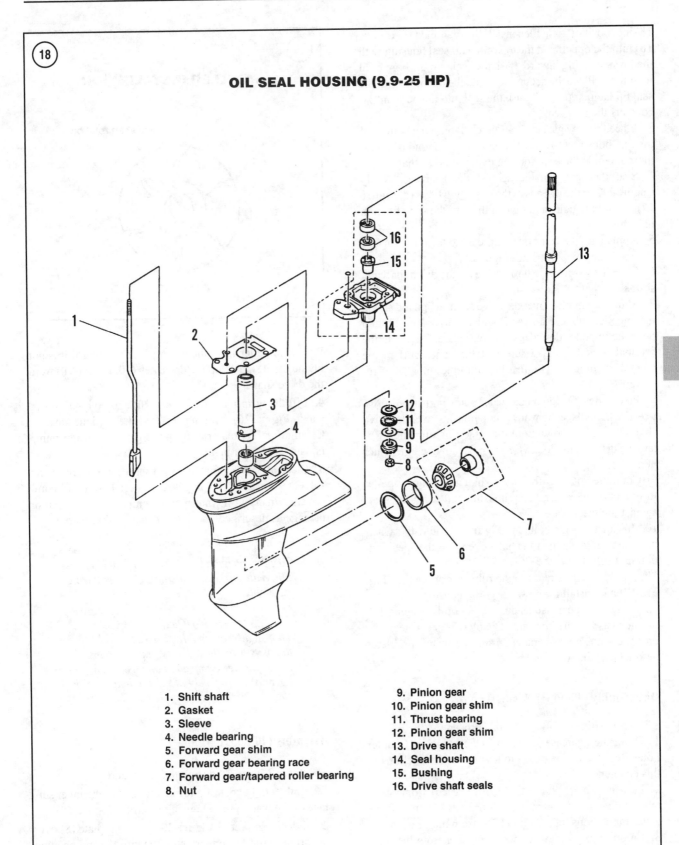

OIL SEAL HOUSING (9.9-25 HP)

1. Shift shaft
2. Gasket
3. Sleeve
4. Needle bearing
5. Forward gear shim
6. Forward gear bearing race
7. Forward gear/tapered roller bearing
8. Nut
9. Pinion gear
10. Pinion gear shim
11. Thrust bearing
12. Pinion gear shim
13. Drive shaft
14. Seal housing
15. Bushing
16. Drive shaft seals

9

18) into position first, then install the first seal (16, **Figure 18**) into the opening at the top of the oil seal housing with the lip side facing inward. Push the seal into the bore until it bottoms. Place the second seal into the opening with the seal lip facing outward. Push the seal into the bore until it contacts the first seal.

3. Place the new gasket (2, **Figure 18**) onto the bottom of the seal housing (14). Gasket sealing compound is not required. Guide the seal housing over the drive shaft.

4. Seat the seal housing against the gearcase. Apply Loctite 242 to the threads of the mounting bolts (8, **Figure 17**). Install the bolts and tighten them to the specification in **Table 1**.

5. Apply a light coat of marine grease to the inner surface of the water pump housing (**Figure 17**).

6. Slide the gasket (9, **Figure 17**) over the drive shaft and shift shaft.

7. Slide the impeller over the drive shaft. Align the slot in the impeller hub (6, **Figure 17**) with the drive key (11) and push the impeller down against wear plate. If reusing the original impeller, make sure that the vanes curl in the clockwise direction (**Figure 19**). Flip the impeller if required.

8. Place a new O-ring on the water pump housing (7, **Figure 17**), then place the water pump housing over the drive shaft and slide it down until it contacts the impeller. Rotate the drive shaft clockwise and push down on the water pump housing.

9. Continue rotating the drive shaft until the impeller fully enters the water pump housing and the body seats against the wear plate.

10. Install the four bolts (1, **Figure 17**) into the water pump housing. Tighten the bolts evenly to the specification in **Table 1**.

11. Apply marine grease to the rubber grommet (3, **Figure 17**) and install it into water pump housing.

12. Install the gearcase as described in this chapter. Fill the gearcase with lubricant (Chapter Four). Check for proper cooling system operation and correct any problems before operating the engine.

Disassembly (40-50 Hp Models)

Refer to (**Figure 20**) during this procedure.

1. Drain the gearcase lubricant as described in Chapter Four. Remove the gearcase following the instructions in this chapter.

2. Pull the water tube seal (13, **Figure 20**) from water pump housing (3). Remove the four bolts (1) and lift the water pump housing (3, **Figure 20**) from the gearcase.

3. Carefully pry the water pump impeller from the wear plate. Slide the impeller (5, **Figure 20**) off the drive shaft.

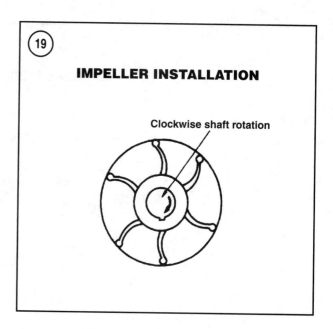

IMPELLER INSTALLATION

Clockwise shaft rotation

Pry the impeller from the water pump housing if it is not on the drive shaft. Pull the drive key (10, **Figure 20**) from the drive shaft.

4. Lift the wear plate (8, **Figure 20**) and both gaskets (6 and 9, **Figure 20**) from the gearcase. Discard the gaskets. Clean all gasket material from the gearcase, water pump housing and wear plate.

5. Clean all water pump and shift shaft components using solvent. Carefully scrape gasket materials from all components. Inspect all water pump components for wear or damage as described under *Inspection* in this chapter.

> *CAUTION*
> *To prevent water or lubricant leakage, replace all gaskets, seals and O-rings during assembly.*

> *NOTE*
> *Thoroughly clean all corrosion and other deposits from the drive shaft prior to installing any water pump components. The impeller must slide freely along the length of the shaft.*

Assembly (40-50 Hp Models)

Refer to **Figure 20** during this procedure.

1. Apply a light coat of marine lubricant to the inner surface of the water pump housing insert (4, **Figure 20**).

2. Slide the gasket (9 **Figure 20**) and wear plate (8) over the drive shaft. Align them with the pins (7) and opening in the gearcase.

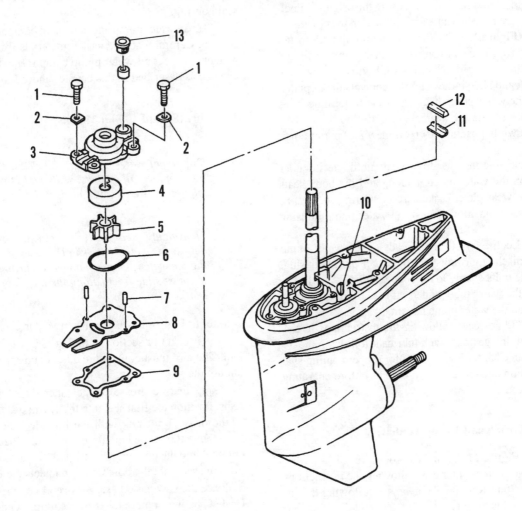

20

WATER PUMP ASSEMBLY
(40 AND 50 HP)

1. Bolt
2. Washer
3. Water pump housing
4. Insert
5. Impeller
6. O-ring
7. Dowel pin
8. Plate
9. Gasket
10. Impeller drive key
11. Seal damper guide
12. Seal damper
13. Water tube seal

9

3. Apply marine lubricant to the drive key and place it (10, **Figure 20**) onto the flat surface of the drive shaft. Make sure the rounded side of the key faces outward.

4. Slide the impeller over the drive shaft. Align the slot in the impeller hub with the drive key, then push the impeller down against the wear plate. If reusing the original impeller, make sure that the vanes are installed in the clockwise direction (**Figure 19**). Flip the impeller if required. Install the O-ring (6, **Figure 20**) onto the water pump housing.

5. Place the water pump housing (3, **Figure 20**) over the drive shaft and slide it down until it contacts the impeller. Position the water pump housing so the water tube faces toward the rear of the gearcase. Rotate the drive shaft clockwise while pushing down on the water pump housing.

6. Continue rotating the drive shaft until the impeller fully enters the water pump housing and the body seats against the wear plate. Make sure the O-ring (6, **Figure 20**) remains in position against the water pump housing (3).

7. Apply Loctite 242 to the threads of the water pump bolts. Install the four bolts into the water pump housing. Tighten the bolts evenly to the specification in **Table 1**.

8. Install the water tube guide/seal (13, **Figure 20**) over its fitting on the water pump housing.

9. Install the gearcase following the instructions in this chapter. Fill the gearcase with lubricant following the instructions in Chapter Four. Check for proper cooling system operation and correct any problems before operating the engine.

Disassembly (80 and 100 hp Models)

Refer to **Figure 21** during this procedure.

1. Drain the gearcase lubricant following the instructions in Chapter Four. Remove the gearcase following the instructions in this chapter.

2. Pull the water tube guide (3) and seal (5, **Figure 21**) from the water pump housing (6). Remove all four bolts (1 and 4, **Figure 21**) and lift the water pump housing (6) from the oil seal housing (13, **Figure 21**).

3. Carefully pry the water pump impeller from the wear plate. Slide the impeller (8, **Figure 21**) off the drive shaft. Pry the impeller from the water pump housing if it is not on the drive shaft. Pull the drive key (17, **Figure 21**) from the drive shaft.

4. Lift the upper gasket, wear plate and lower gasket (10-12, **Figure 21**) from the oil seal housing (13). Carefully scrape the gaskets (10 and 12, **Figure 21**) from the wear plate and oil seal housing (13).

5. Remove the oil seal housing only if removing the drive shaft, replacing the seals or it is damaged. Carefully pry

the oil seal housing off the gearcase. Remove the O-ring (14) from the oil seal housing and remove the gasket (15, **Figure 21**) from the gearcase or oil seal housing.

6. Working carefully to avoid damaging the oil seal housing, pry the drive shaft seals (16, **Figure 21**) from the oil seal housing.

7. Clean all water pump and shift shaft components using solvent. Carefully scrape gasket materials from all components. Inspect all water pump components for wear or damage as described in this chapter under *Inspection*.

Assembly (80 and 100 hp Models)

CAUTION
To prevent water and gear lubricant leakage, replace all gaskets, seals and O-rings when they are removed or disturbed.

NOTE
Thoroughly clean all corrosion and other deposits from the drive shaft prior to installing the water pump components. The impeller must slide freely along the length of the shaft.

Refer to **Figure 21** during this procedure.

1. Use a socket or section of tubing as a seal installation tool. The tool must contact the outer diameter of the seal but not the seal housing.

2. Apply marine grease to the inner diameter of both seals. Position the first seal into the opening at the bottom of the oil seal housing with the lip side facing inward. Push the seal into the bore until it bottoms. Place the second seal into the opening with the seal lip facing outward. Push the seal into the bore until it contacts the first seal.

3. Place the new gasket (15, **Figure 21**) on the gearcase. Gasket sealing compound is not required. Guide the oil seal housing over the drive shaft with the seal side down and place the oil seal housing onto the gearcase.

4. Seat the oil seal housing against the gearcase.

5. Apply a light coat of marine lubricant to the inner surface of the water pump housing insert (7, **Figure 21**).

6. Slide the gasket (12, **Figure 21**), wear plate (11) and upper gasket (10) over the drive shaft. Align the components with the pins on the oil seal housing.

7. Apply marine lubricant to the drive key and place it (17, **Figure 21**) into position on the drive shaft.

8. Slide the impeller (8, **Figure 21**) over the drive shaft. Align the slot in the impeller hub with the drive key and push the impeller down against wear plate. If reusing the original impeller, make sure the vanes curl in the clockwise direction (**Figure 19**). Flip the impeller if required.

WATER PUMP ASSEMBLY
(80 AND 100 HP)

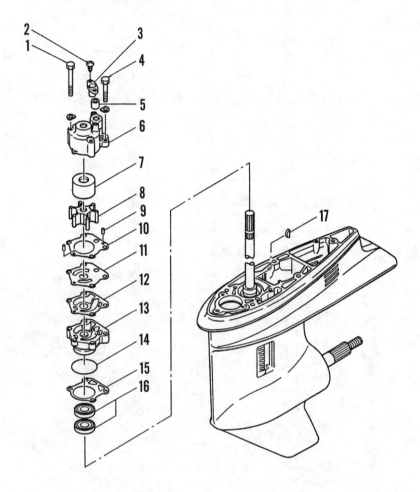

9

1. Bolt
2. Screw
3. Guide
4. Bolt
5. Water tube seal
6. Water pump housing
7. Insert
8. Impeller
9. Dowel pin
10. Gasket
11. Plate
12. Gasket
13. Seal housing
14. O-ring
15. Gasket
16. Drive shaft seals
17. Impeller drive key

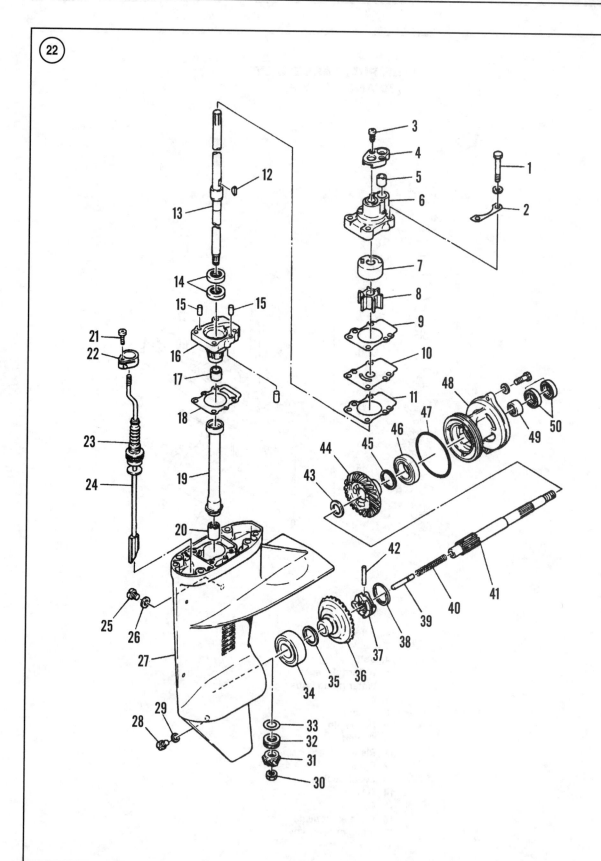

GEARCASE (9.9-25 HP)

1. Bolt
2. Retainer
3. Screw
4. Guide
5. Water tube seal
6. Water pump housing
7. Insert
8. Impeller
9. Gasket
10. Plate
11. Gasket
12. Impeller drive key
13. Drive shaft
14. Drive shaft seals
15. Dowel pin
16. Seal housing
17. Bushing
18. Gasket
19. Sleeve
20. Needle bearing
21. Screw
22. Retainer
23. Boot
24. Shift shaft
25. Oil level plug
26. Gasket
27. Housing
28. Oil drain plug
29. Gasket
30. Pinion nut
31. Pinion gear
32. Thrust bearing
33. Pinion gear shim
34. Tapered roller bearing
35. Forward gear shim
36. Forward gear
37. Clutch dog
38. Cross pin retainer
39. Plunger
40. Spring
41. Propeller shaft
42. Cross pin
43. Washer
44. Reverse gear
45. Reverse gear shim
46. Ball bearing
47. O-ring
48. Bearing carrier
49. Needle bearing
50. Propeller shaft seals

9. Place the water pump housing (6, **Figure 21**) over the drive shaft and slide it down until it contacts the impeller. Rotate the drive shaft clockwise while pushing down on the water pump housing.

10. Continue rotating the drive shaft until the impeller fully enters the water pump housing and the body seats against the wear plate. Make sure the gaskets remain in position.

11. Apply Loctite 242 to the bolt threads, then install the four bolts (1 and 4, **Figure 21**) into the water pump housing. Tighten the bolts evenly to the specification in **Table 1**.

12. Apply marine lubricant to the water tube guide/seal inner surfaces, then push it (5, **Figure 21**) into the water pump housing (6).

13. Install the gearcase following the instructions in this chapter. Fill the gearcase with lubricant following the instructions in Chapter Four. Check for proper cooling system operation and correct any problems before operating the engine.

GEARCASE DISASSEMBLY AND ASSEMBLY

If complete disassembly is not required, follow the disassembly procedures until the required component(s) is accessible. Refer to the corresponding assembly steps to install the component(s).

Proper gear alignment is essential for quiet operation and long service life. Therefore, if the drive shaft, any gears or bearings are replaced, the pinion and drive gears must be correctly positioned inside the gearcase. Special tools are required to check gear and bearing alignment. The tools can be purchased at a Yamaha dealership.

Some of the units use shims to position bearings and gears. Note the location and thickness of all shims as they are removed. Use a micrometer to measure and record the thickness of each shim or spacer removed from the gearcase Wire the shims together, and tag them or place them in an envelope.

Use pressurized water to thoroughly clean the external surfaces of the gearcase prior to disassembly. Pay particular attention to the propeller shaft housing area as debris can easily become trapped in this area.

Mount the gearcase in a suitable holding fixture or a sturdy vise. Use padded jaws or wooden blocks to protect the gearcase. Clamp the gearcase on the skeg (lower fin) when using a vise. Have an assistant provide additional support for the gearcase when removing large or tight fasteners. Refer to **Figures 22-25** (9.9-50 hp) or **Figures 26-31** (80 and 100 hp) as necessary.

9

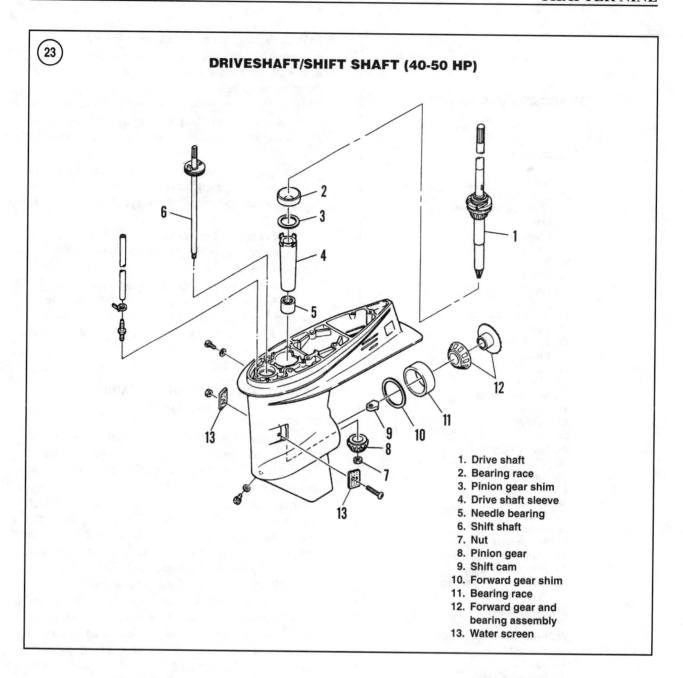

DRIVESHAFT/SHIFT SHAFT (40-50 HP)

1. Drive shaft
2. Bearing race
3. Pinion gear shim
4. Drive shaft sleeve
5. Needle bearing
6. Shift shaft
7. Nut
8. Pinion gear
9. Shift cam
10. Forward gear shim
11. Bearing race
12. Forward gear and bearing assembly
13. Water screen

Disassembly (9.9-50 Hp Models)

NOTE
To ease removal of the propeller shaft housing, use a torch to apply heat to the gearcase near the propeller shaft housing mating surface. Continually move the flame to apply even heat.

CAUTION
If using heat to remove components, keep the flame away from the seals or O-rings. Never heat the housing to the point that the finish is burned. Continually move the flame around the mating surface to apply even heating. Excessive use of heat can distort or melt the gearcase.

Refer to **Figures 22-25** during this procedure. Removal of the propeller shaft housing (2, **Figure 24**) requires a special tool (**Figure 31**). Purchase or rent this tool, Part No.YB-6234 and part No.YB-6117, from a Yamaha dealership.

1. Disassemble the water pump as described in this chapter.

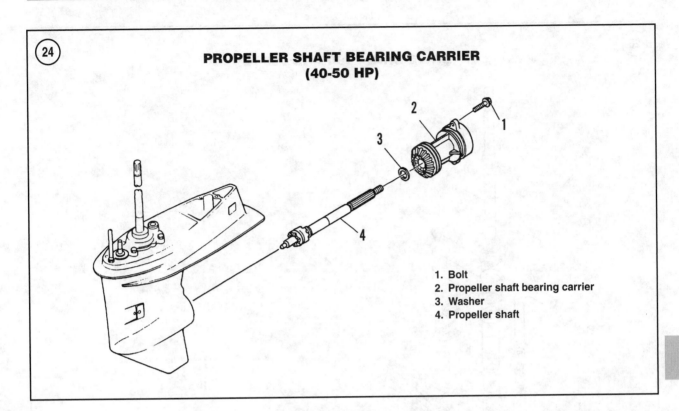

(24)

PROPELLER SHAFT BEARING CARRIER
(40-50 HP)

1. Bolt
2. Propeller shaft bearing carrier
3. Washer
4. Propeller shaft

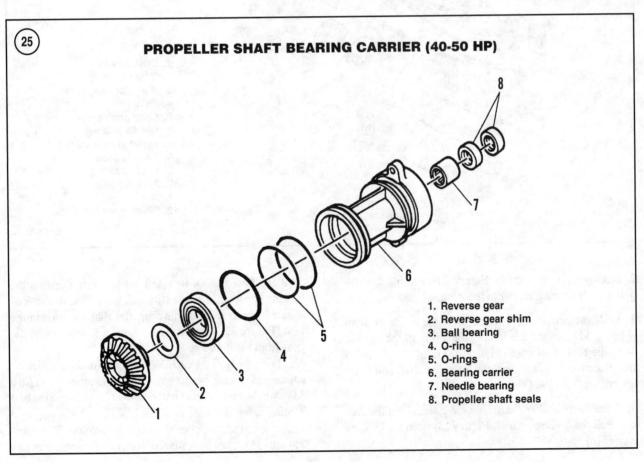

(25)

PROPELLER SHAFT BEARING CARRIER (40-50 HP)

1. Reverse gear
2. Reverse gear shim
3. Ball bearing
4. O-ring
5. O-rings
6. Bearing carrier
7. Needle bearing
8. Propeller shaft seals

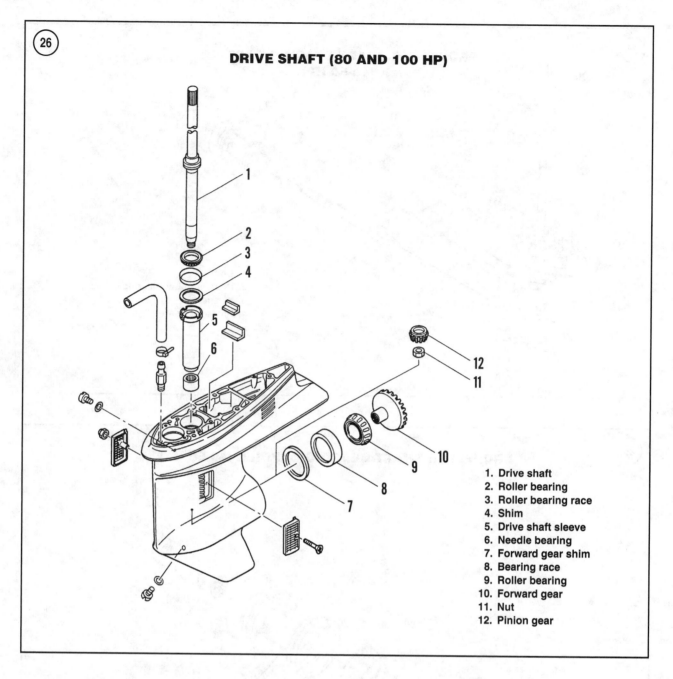

DRIVE SHAFT (80 AND 100 HP)

26

1. Drive shaft
2. Roller bearing
3. Roller bearing race
4. Shim
5. Drive shaft sleeve
6. Needle bearing
7. Forward gear shim
8. Bearing race
9. Roller bearing
10. Forward gear
11. Nut
12. Pinion gear

2. Remove the two bolts (1, **Figure 24**) securing the propeller shaft bearing carrier to the gearcase housing.

3. Slide the carrier removal tool over the propeller shaft (**Figure 31**). Attach the tool to the struts in the carrier. Turn the tool clockwise (**Figure 31**) until the carrier is free from the gearcase. Pull the propeller shaft and bearing carrier from the gearcase.

4. Slide the propeller shaft from the gear side of the carrier. Pull the reverse gear (1, **Figure 25**) from the bearing carrier (6).

5. If the gear cannot be removed by prying, clamp the bearing carrier into a vice with soft jaws. Pass the jaws of a slide hammer through the propeller shaft opening of the gear (**Figure 32**). Use short hammer strokes to remove the gear from the housing.

6. Clamp the bearing carrier in a vice with the smaller diameter side facing up. Engage a slide hammer (1, **Figure 33**) with the reverse gear ball bearing (2). Remove the ball bearing using short hammer strokes.

7. Remove the propeller shaft needle bearing (7, **Figure 25**) only if it must be replaced. Refer to *Inspection* in this

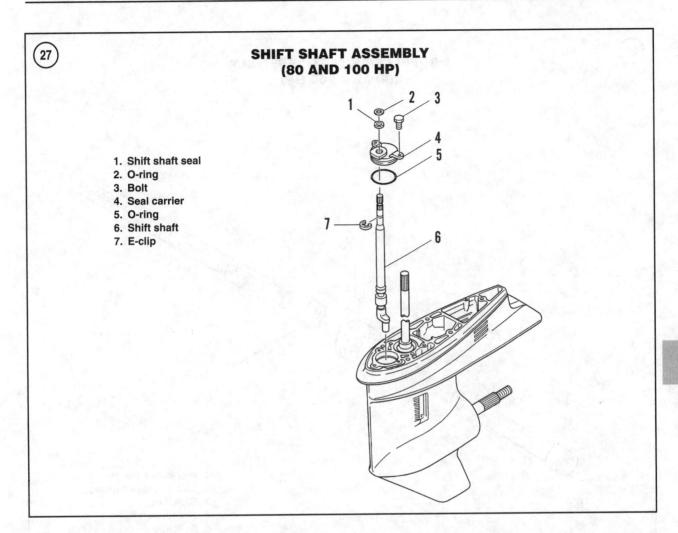

SHIFT SHAFT ASSEMBLY
(80 AND 100 HP)

1. Shift shaft seal
2. O-ring
3. Bolt
4. Seal carrier
5. O-ring
6. Shift shaft
7. E-clip

9

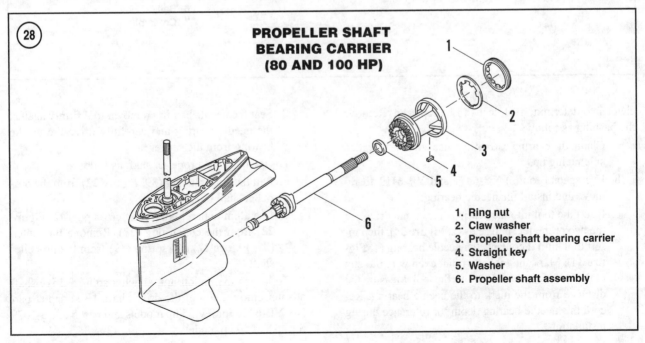

PROPELLER SHAFT
BEARING CARRIER
(80 AND 100 HP)

1. Ring nut
2. Claw washer
3. Propeller shaft bearing carrier
4. Straight key
5. Washer
6. Propeller shaft assembly

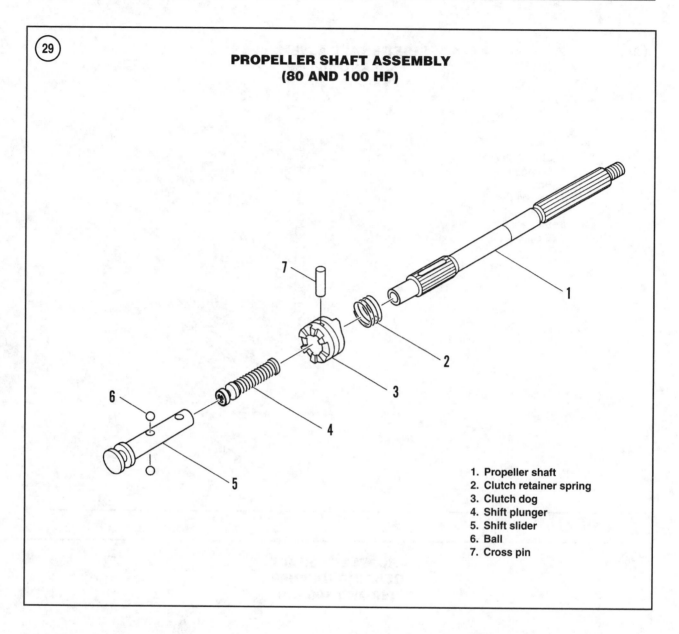

**PROPELLER SHAFT ASSEMBLY
(80 AND 100 HP)**

1. Propeller shaft
2. Clutch retainer spring
3. Clutch dog
4. Shift plunger
5. Shift slider
6. Ball
7. Cross pin

chapter to determine if it needs to be replaced. Remove the bushing as follows:

   a. Clamp the bearing carrier in a vise with the threaded side facing up.

   b. Use special tool(s) YB-6071 and YB-6112 to remove and install the needle bearing.

   c. Insert the tool into the bearing carrier and drive out the two propeller shaft seals (2, **Figure 34**), then insert tool until it contacts the needle bearing (1, **Figure 34**). Mark the tool at a point even with the end of the bearing carrier. Remove the tool. Measure the distance from the mark to the needle bearing. Record this needle bearing depth for reference during installation.

   d. Seat the needle bearing removal tool firmly against the needle bearing and carefully drive the needle bearing from the carrier.

8. Disassemble the propeller shaft as follows:

   a. Pull the shift plunger (39, **Figure 22**) from the propeller shaft (41).

   b. Use a pin punch to drive the cross pin (42, **Figure 22**) from the clutch dog (37). Remove the clutch (37, **Figure 22**) and spring (39) from the propeller shaft (41).

9. To loosen the pinion nut, attach a splined drive shaft adapter onto the top of the drive shaft. Use adapter part No. YB-6228 for 9.9-25 hp models and part No. YB-6079 for 40 and 50 hp models.

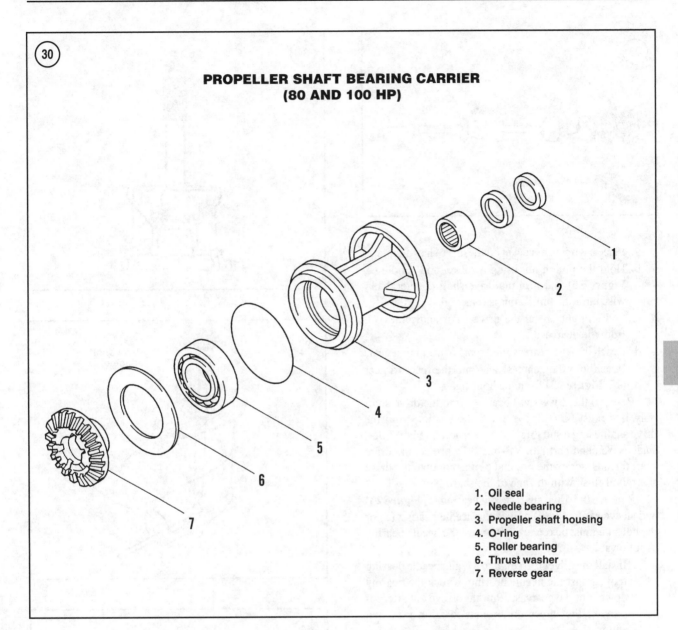

(30)

**PROPELLER SHAFT BEARING CARRIER
(80 AND 100 HP)**

1. Oil seal
2. Needle bearing
3. Propeller shaft housing
4. O-ring
5. Roller bearing
6. Thrust washer
7. Reverse gear

9

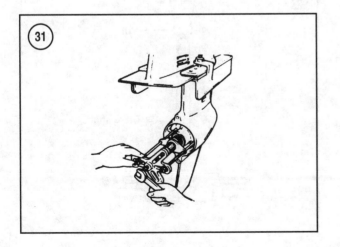

(31)

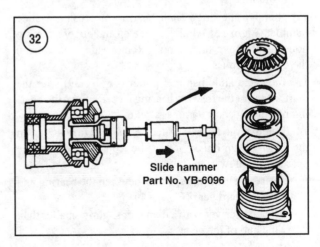

(32)

Slide hammer
Part No. YB-6096

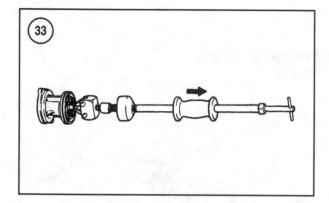

a. Place a wrench or socket on the drive shaft adapter.

b. Hold the pinion nut using a socket and handle (2, **Figure 35**) and turn the drive shaft counterclockwise until the pinion nut is removed.

c. Pull straight up on the drive shaft and remove it from the gearcase.

d. Reach into the gearcase and remove the pinion gear.

e. Reach into the gearcase and pull the forward gear (12, **Figure 23**) from the housing.

10. Remove the drive shaft bearing from the drive shaft only if it must be replaced. Press the bearing from the drive shaft using a suitable bearing separator (**Figure 36**), such as Yamaha part No. YB-6219. To protect the drive shaft threads, screw the original pinion nut onto the drive shaft until flush with the end of the shaft.

11. Remove the drive shaft needle bearing (5, **Figure 23**) and sleeve assembly (4) only if the needle bearing (5) or the housing must be replaced. Remove the needle bearing as follows:

a. Install the driver rod (**Figure 37**) and needle bearing tool against the needle bearing. Knock the bearing down into the gearcase. Pull the sleeve out after removing the upper drive shaft, bearing race and shim.

12. Remove the drive shaft bearing race using a slide hammer (**Figure 38**). Pull the race up and out of gearcase housing. Remove the shim(s). Remove the sleeve from the gearcase housing.

13. Engage a slide hammer puller (**Figure 39**) with the rear surface of the forward bearing race. Remove the bearing race using short hammer strokes.

14. Remove the tapered roller bearing (**Figure 40**) from the forward gear only if it must be replaced. Remove the bearing as follows:

a. Attach a bearing separator between the bearing and the forward gear (**Figure 40**).

b. Select a driver with a diameter slightly smaller than the hub of the gear.

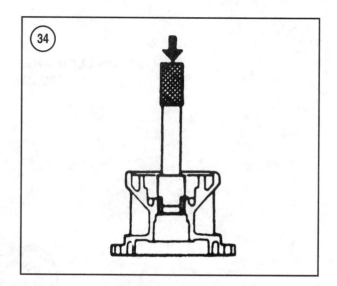

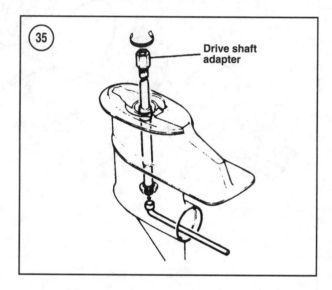

Drive shaft adapter

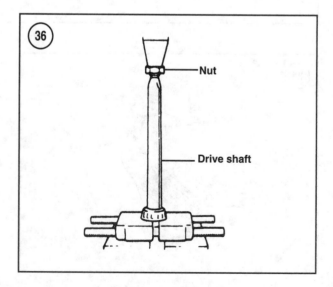

Nut

Drive shaft

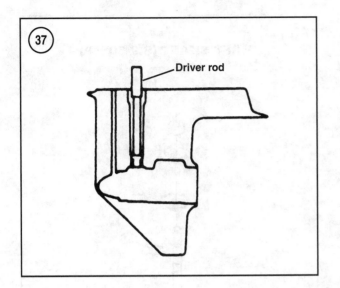

③⑦ Driver rod

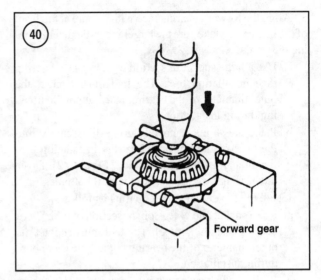

④⓪ Forward gear

c. Place the bearing separator and gear onto a press. Block the sides of the separator to ensure adequate travel for the gear.

d. Place the tool against the hub of the gear. Press on the socket or tubing to remove the gear from the bearing.

15. Remove the shift shaft (5, **Figure 41**) from the gearcase by removing the O-ring (1, **Figure 41**), shift shaft seal (2) and seal housing (3). Remove the seal housing by turning it counterclockwise. Lift the large O-ring (4) from the shift shaft pocket. Lift the shift shaft (5, **Figure 41**) from the gearcase. Reach into the nose of the gearcase and remove the shift cam (9, **Figure 23**), if equipped.

16. Remove the screws and remove the water screen (**Figure 23**).

17. Clean and inspect all components as described in this chapter.

Assembly (9.9-50 Hp Models)

Refer to **Figures 22-25** during this procedure.

1. Install the water screen (13, **Figure 23**) into its opening. Securely tighten the water screen retaining screw.

2. Install the shift shaft as follows:

a. Position the shift cam, if equipped, (9, **Figure 23**) in the forward nose of the gearcase.

b. Install the shift shaft into the gearcase. Align the splines and insert the shift shaft into the shift cam.

c. Install a new O-ring (4, **Figure 41**) into the shift shaft cavity of the gearcase housing.

d. Install the seal housing, shift shaft seal and O-ring. Tighten the seal housing.

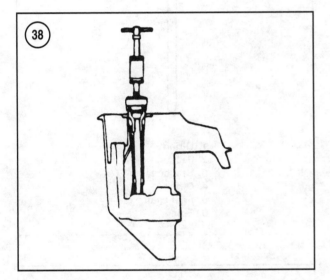

③⑨

Bearing race

3. Align the forward bearing race with its bore at the front of the gearcase. Make sure the larger inner diameter is facing outward.

    a. Use a large socket or section of tubing as a bearing race installation tool. The tool must contact the outer diameter of the bearing race but not the housing during installation.

    b. Place the shims removed during disassembly into the bore of the housing. Seat the installation tool firmly against the bearing race (**Figure 42**). Drive the bearing race into its bore until it bottoms.

4. Install the lower drive shaft bearing as follows:

    a. Use a socket and extension, or section of tubing as a bearing installation tool. The tool must contact the outer diameter of the bearing but not the drive bore during installation.

    b. Position the bearing with the numbered side facing toward the water pump.

    c. Drive the bearing into place (**Figure 43**).

5. Install the drive shaft sleeve and seat it against the lower bearing.

6. Assemble the bearing onto the forward gear as follows:

    a. Place the gear with the teeth side down on the table of a press. Place the bearing onto the hub of the gear with the tapered side facing up (**Figure 44**).

    b. Press the bearing fully onto the gear using a suitable driver.

7. Place the forward gear into the housing. Seat the bearing against the bearing race. Place the shim and thrust bearing (33 and 32, **Figure 22**), then the pinion gear (31), into the housing. Mesh the pinion gear teeth with the forward gear teeth, then align the pinion gear and thrust bearing with the drive shaft bearing. The thrust bearing must be installed directly above the pinion gear with the grooved side facing the gear. Slide the drive shaft into the housing. Slowly rotate the drive shaft to align the drive shaft and pinion gear splines. Place the thrust washer over the end of the drive shaft and rest it against the needle bearing and sleeve.

8. Assemble and install the propeller shaft as follows:

    a. Align the cross pin hole in the side of the clutch (37, **Figure 22**) with the slot in the propeller shaft and slide it over the propeller shaft.

    b. Slide the spring (40, **Figure 22**) into the bore at the forward end of the propeller shaft.

    c. Insert the plunger into the end of the propeller shaft. Push in on the plunger and install the cross pin into the assembly as shown (**Figure 45**).

    d. Install the cross pin into the clutch until it is flush with the clutch surfaces.

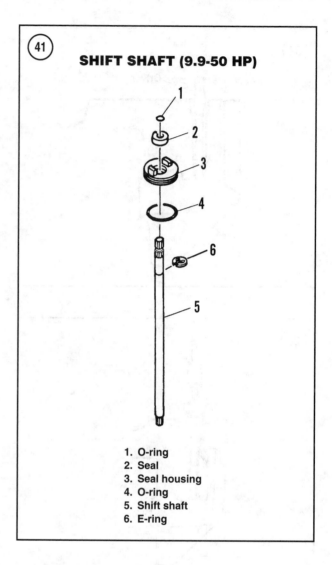

(41)

SHIFT SHAFT (9.9-50 HP)

1. O-ring
2. Seal
3. Seal housing
4. O-ring
5. Shift shaft
6. E-ring

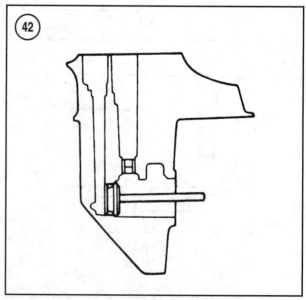

(42)

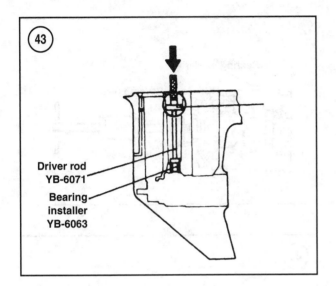

43

Driver rod
YB-6071

Bearing
installer
YB-6063

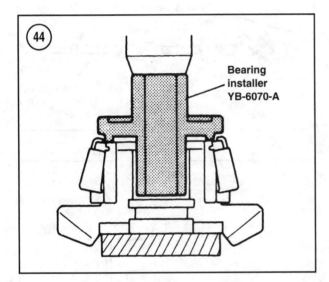

44

Bearing
installer
YB-6070-A

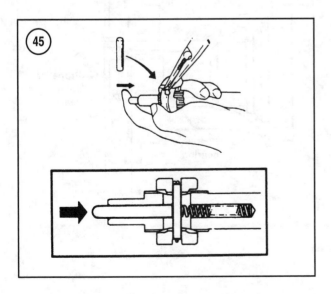

45

e. Apply marine lubricant to the shift plunger and install it with the pointed side out into the end of the propeller shaft.

9. Position the gearcase with the drive shaft pointing up. Slide the propeller shaft with the clutch side first fully into the forward gear.

10. Install the propeller shaft needle bearing into the propeller shaft bearing carrier as follows:

    a. Place the bearing carrier on the table of a press with the threaded side facing up.

    b. Align the needle bearing with its bore and place it in the carrier.

    c. Seat the installation tool firmly against the needle bearing. Stop frequently and press the needle bearing into the carrier to the depth recorded prior to removal.

11. Press the propeller shaft needle bearing into the carrier to the depth recorded during disassembly.

12. Place the bearing carrier on a flat surface with the threaded side facing down. Apply a light coat of Loctite 271 to the outer diameter of the propeller shaft seals. Using a suitable driver, install the inner seal into the carrier with its seal lip facing down. Drive the seal into the carrier until it is just below the carrier surface. Next, position the outer seal onto the carrier with its seal lip facing up. Drive the seal into the carrier until it is just below the carrier surface. Apply a thick coat of marine grease to the seal lips.

13. Place the O-ring (47, **Figure 22**) onto the bearing carrier (48). Apply a thick coat of marine grease to the O-ring and carrier threads.

14. Install the reverse gear (44, **Figure 22**), shim (45) and ball bearing (46) into the bearing carrier.

15. Slide the bearing carrier over the propeller shaft and into the gearcase. Thread the bearing carrier into the gearcase by turning it clockwise.

16. Install the two retaining bolts (1, **Figure 24**) and tighten them to specification in **Table 1**.

17. Install the shift shaft and water pump as described in this chapter.

Disassembly (80 and 100 hp Models)

Refer to **Figures 26-30** during this procedure.

1. Disassemble the water pump as described under *Water Pump* in this chapter.

2. Remove the O-ring (2, **Figure 27**) from the shift shaft (6). Remove both bolts (3, **Figure 27**) and remove the seal carrier (4) from the shift shaft.

3. Shift the motor into NEUTRAL. Lift the shift shaft (6, **Figure 27**) approximately 1/2 in. (12.7 mm), turn the

9

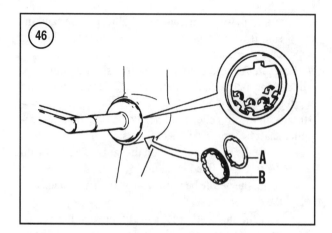

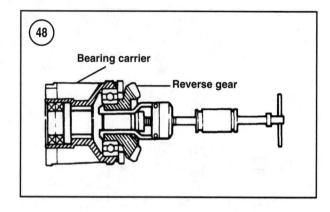

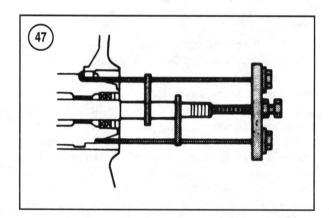

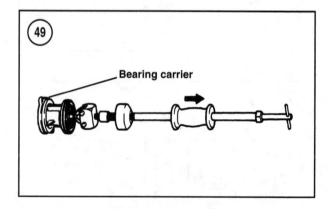

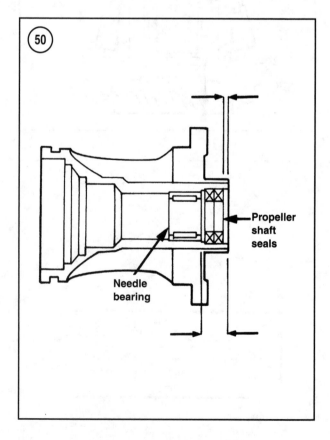

shaft clockwise and remove it from the gearcase. Remove the O-ring (5, **Figure 27**) from the shift shaft.

4. Straighten the tab on the locking tab washer (**Figure 46**) before attempting to remove the ring nut (B, **Figure 46**). Use a ring-nut wrench (Yamaha Part No.YB-34447) remove the nut and tab washer (A, **Figure 46**).

5. Install the bearing carrier puller (Yamaha Part No.YB-6207) (**Figure 47**) and remove the carrier. Pull the propeller shaft from the gearcase.

6. Remove the needle and/or roller bearing (2 and 5, **Figure 30**) from the bearing carrier (3) only if they must be replaced. Refer to *Inspection* in this chapter. Disassemble the propeller shaft housing as follows:

    a. Secure the bearing carrier in a vise with soft jaws. Carefully pull the reverse gear from the carrier using a slide hammer (**Figure 48**).

    b. Note which side faces the reverse gear and remove the thrust bearing (6, **Figure 30**) and ball bearing (5).

    c. Use a slide hammer (**Figure 49**) to pull the roller bearing from the bearing carrier.

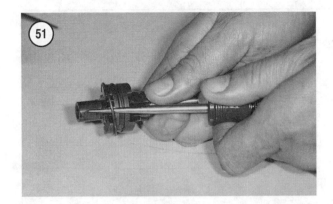

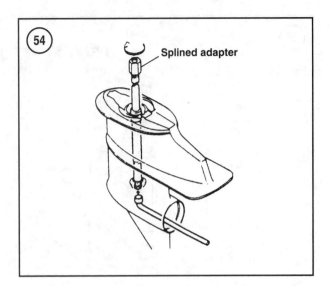

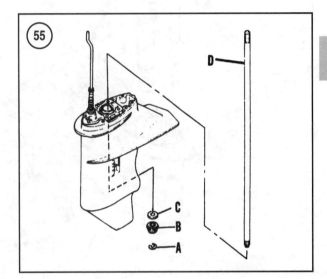

d. Use a driver rod and bearing attachment (YB-6153) to knock the seals and needle bearings (**Figure 50**) from the propeller shaft bearing carrier.

7. Disassemble the propeller shaft as follows:

a. Hook a small screwdriver under one loop of the retainer spring and carefully unwind the spring from the clutch (**Figure 51**).

b. Push the shift slider end (5, **Figure 29**) of the propeller shaft (1) against a solid object, then push the cross pin (7) from the clutch (3) and propeller shaft (**Figure 52**).

c. Pull the clutch from the front of the propeller shaft (**Figure 53**).

d. Slide the shift slider (5, **Figure 29**), ball bearings (6) and shift plunger assembly (4) from the propeller shaft (1).

8. Remove the drive shaft and pinion gear as follows:

a. Use a spline drive shaft holder (Yamaha Part No.YB-6151) to hold the drive shaft. Slip the holder onto the top of the drive shaft.

b. Hold the pinion nut (**Figure 54**) with a socket and handle, and rotate the drive shaft counterclockwise until the pinion nut is loosened. Remove the pinion nut from the drive shaft.

c. Pull straight up on the drive shaft (D, **Figure 55**) to free it from the pinion gear (A, **Figure 55**), washer and shim (C). Lift the drive shaft from the housing.

9

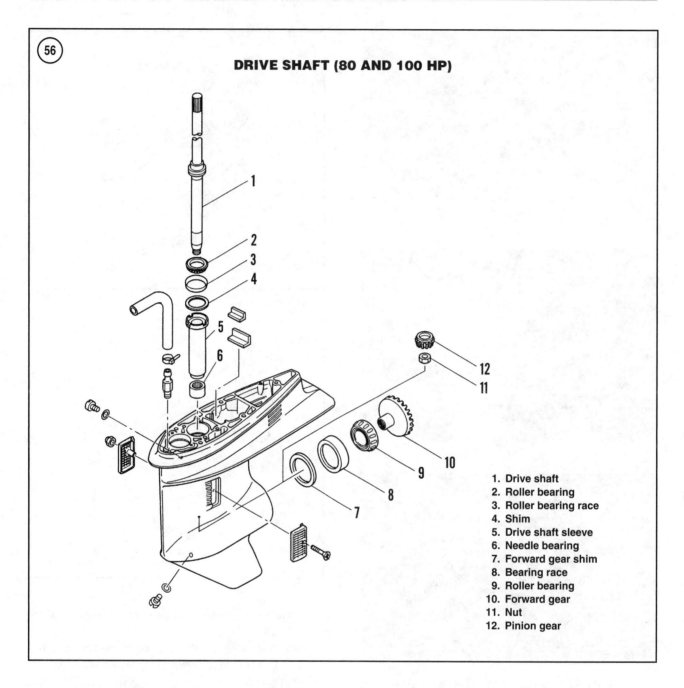

DRIVE SHAFT (80 AND 100 HP)

56

1. Drive shaft
2. Roller bearing
3. Roller bearing race
4. Shim
5. Drive shaft sleeve
6. Needle bearing
7. Forward gear shim
8. Bearing race
9. Roller bearing
10. Forward gear
11. Nut
12. Pinion gear

9. Pull the pinion gear (12, **Figure 56**) and tapered roller bearing from the housing. Pull the forward gear and bearing (9 and 10, **Figure 56**) from the gearcase opening.

10. Use a slide hammer to pull the forward bearing race (A, **Figure 57**) from the gearcase. Remove the bearing race and shim(s).

11. Remove the tapered roller bearing (9, **Figure 56**) from the forward gear (10) only if it must be replaced.

 a. Attach a bearing separator (Yamaha Part No.YB-6219) to the bearing and the forward gear (**Figure 58**).

 b. Place a socket or section of tubing against the hub of the gear. Press the gear from the bearing.

12. Remove the drive shaft tapered bearing race and shim(s) (3 and 4, **Figure 56**) from the housing only if it must be replaced.

 a. Attach a slide hammer with short puller jaws (Yamaha Part No.YB-6096) to the bearing race as indicated in **Figure 59**.

 b. Pull the race from the gearcase cavity.

13. Remove the bearing (2, **Figure 56**) from the drive shaft (1) only if it must be replaced.

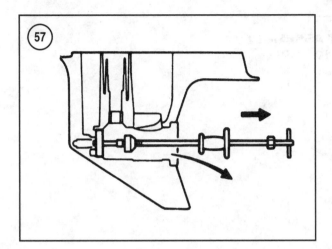

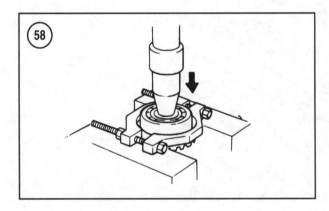

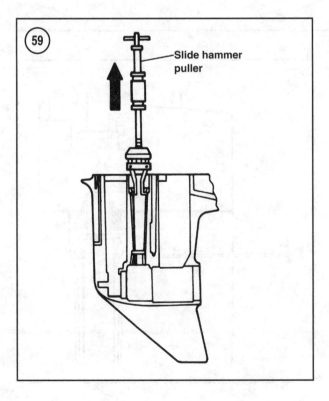

Slide hammer puller

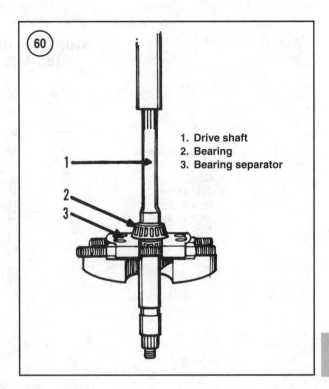

1. Drive shaft
2. Bearing
3. Bearing separator

9

a. Slide the drive shaft (1, **Figure 60**) through the opening in the bearing separator (3) and adjust the separator until it contacts the edge of the race (2).

b. Place the bearing separator and drive shaft on a press as shown in **Figure 60**.

c. Make sure the drive shaft threads are not exposed. Use the old pinion nut and keep it one thread above the end of the drive shaft.

d. Press the drive shaft out of the bearing. Be sure to catch the drive shaft.

14. Clean and inspect all components following the instructions in this chapter.

Assembly (80 and 100 hp Models)

CAUTION
Serious damage to internal gearcase components can occur if the thrust bearing slips from the propeller shaft housing during installation. Do not force the housing into position until all components are in position.

Refer to **Figures 26-30** during this procedure.

1. Assemble and install the shift shaft and shift cam as follows:

a. Use a socket as a seal installation tool. The socket must contact the outer diameter of the shift shaft seal but not contact the housing during installation.

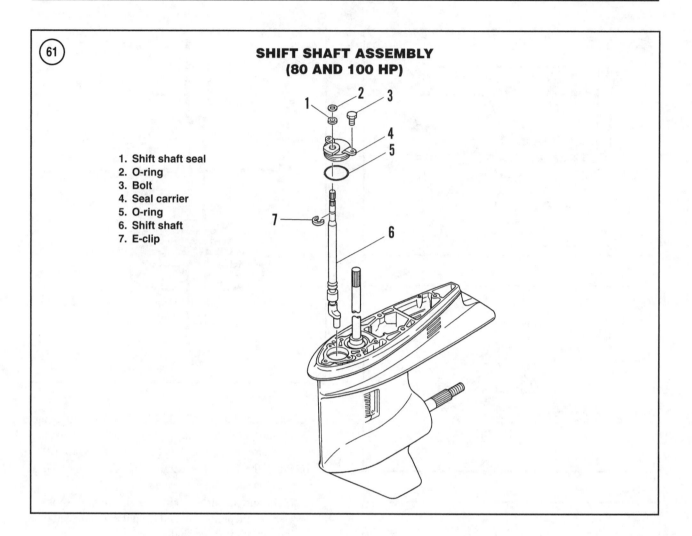

**SHIFT SHAFT ASSEMBLY
(80 AND 100 HP)**

1. Shift shaft seal
2. O-ring
3. Bolt
4. Seal carrier
5. O-ring
6. Shift shaft
7. E-clip

b. Apply marine grease to its outer diameter, then place the shift shaft seal (1, **Figure 61**) into the shift shaft seal carrier (4) with the seal lip side facing down.

c. Use the installation tool to push the seal fully into the shift shaft seal carrier. Apply marine lubricant, then slide the O-ring (5, **Figure 61**) into its groove on the seal carrier (4). Apply a generous coat of the lubricant to the inside lips of the shift shaft seal.

d. Snap the E-clip (7, **Figure 61**) into its groove on the shift shaft (6). Do not install the shift shaft at this time. The propeller shaft must be installed before the shift shaft can be installed (**Figure 61**).

e. Make sure the shift slider and shift control is in NEUTRAL position before installing the shift shaft.

f. Apply Loctite 242 to the threads and install both bolts (3, **Figure 61**). Tighten the bolts to the specification in **Table 1**.

2. Adjust the pinion gear height before proceeding with assembly. The correct pinion gear height is determined by

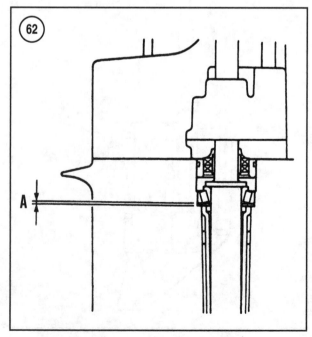

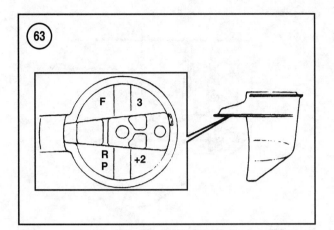

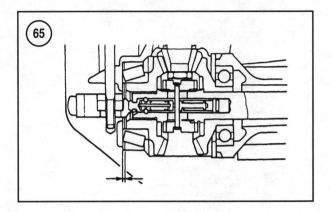

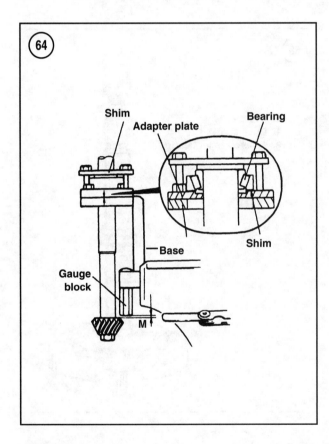

3. Determine the pinion height correction factor. First, refer to the *P* code that is stamped into the housing at the trim tab mounting surface (**Figure 63**). If the *P* code is a positive (+) value, add that value to the standard dimension of 0.20 mm to find the correction factor. If the code is a negative (−) value, subtract the value from the standard dimension to find the correction factor.

    a. If the P code is +3, add 0.03 mm to 0.20 mm. The correction factor is 0.23 mm.

    b. If the P code is −3, subtract 0.03mm from 0.20 mm. The correction factor is 0.17 mm.

4. Install the pinion gear onto the drive shaft. Install and tighten the pinion nut to the specification in **Table 1**. Assemble the shim gauge, drive shaft bearing and original shim as shown in **Figure 64**. If the original shim is not available, install a 0.50 mm shim. Then, using a feeler gauge the same thickness of the correction factor, measure the clearance between the pinion gear and gauge block (**Figure 64**).

5. Vary the shim thickness (**Figure 62**) until a feeler gauge the thickness of the correction factor will slide between the pinion gear and gauge block (**Figure 64**) with a slight interference.

NOTE
Pinion height shims are available in 0.10 mm, 0.12 mm, 0.15 mm, 0.18 mm, 0.30 mm, 0.40 mm and 0.50 mm thicknesses.

6. Adjust the forward gear shim thickness to correctly position the forward gear. The correct forward gear position is determined by the shim located forward of the forward gear bearing race (**Figure 65**). The following Yamaha special tools are required to select the correct shim: base plate YB-34446-1; compression spring YB-34446-3; press plate YB-34446-5; gauge pin YB- 34446-7.

NOTE
*The **F** code indicates assembly line tolerance that varies from the standard dimen-*

a shim (**Figure 62**) located under the tapered roller bearing. The following Yamaha special tools are required to determine the correct shim thickness: gauge block YB-34432-9; adapter plate YB-34432-10; gauge base YB-34432-11-A; clamp YB-34432-17A.

NOTE
*The **P** code indicates assembly line tolerance that varies from the standard dimension of 0.20 mm. The code represents 0.01 mm units.*

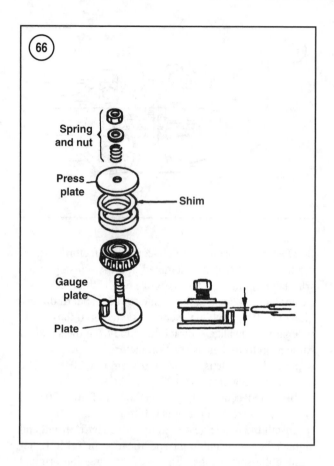

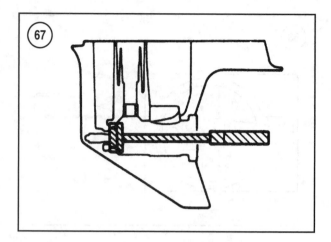

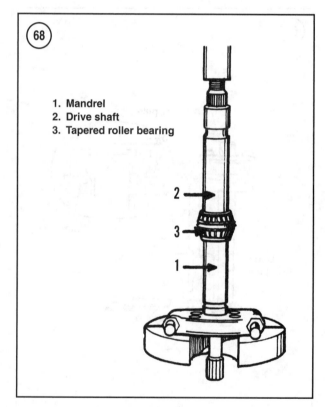

1. Mandrel
2. Drive shaft
3. Tapered roller bearing

sion of 0.69 mm. The code represents 0.01 mm units.

7. Determine the forward gear correction factor. First, refer to the *F* code that is stamped into the housing at the trim tab mounting surface (**Figure 63**). If the *F* code is a positive (+) value, add that value to the standard dimension of 1.69 mm to find the correction factor. If the code is a negative (–) value, subtract the value from the standard dimension to find the correction factor.

  a. If the F code is +3, add 0.03 mm to 0.69 mm. The correction factor is 0.72 mm.

  b. If the F code is –3, subtract 0.03mm from 0.69 mm. The correction factor is 0.66 mm.

8. Assemble the shim gauge, forward gear bearing and original shim as shown in **Figure 66**. If the original shim is not available, install a 0.50 mm shim. Tighten the shim gauge nut until the press plate contacts the spring, then continue tightening the nut four full turns.

9. Insert a feeler gauge the same thickness as the correction factor between the gauge pin and the press plate (**Figure 66**). Vary the thickness of the forward gear shim until the feeler gauge slides between the gauge pin and press plate with a slight interference.

10. Install the forward bearing race as follows:

  a. Use a bearing tool (YB-6276) and driver rod (YB-6071) to install the race. Place the shim(s) (A, **Figure 67**) and bearing race (B) into the housing. Make sure the larger opening of the race faces outward.

  b. Drive the bearing race into its bore until it bottoms. See **Figure 67**.

11. Install the drive shaft roller bearing. Use a bearing separator (YB-6219) and inner race installer (90890) to press the bearing onto the drive shaft (**Figure 68**).

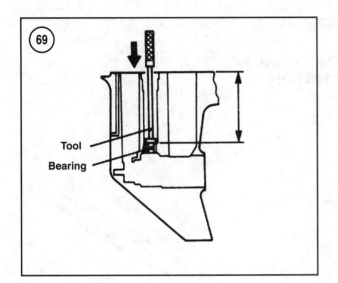

Tool

Bearing

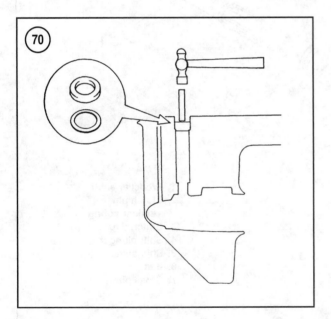

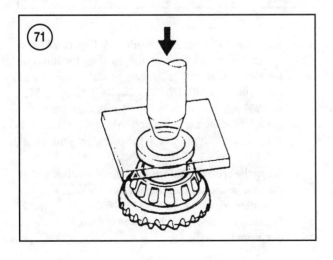

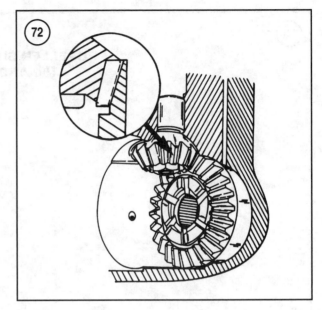

12. Install the drive shaft needle bearing. Use a driver rod (YB-6071), needle bearing plate (YB-34474) and bearing attachment (YB-6155) to drive the needle bearing into the housing (**Figure 69**) to the depth measured during disassembly.

13. Install the drive shaft roller bearing race into the gearcase. Use a driver rod (YB-6071), bearing race installer (YB-6156) and a hammer to seat the race into the gearcase housing (**Figure 70**).

14. Install the forward gear roller bearing onto the forward gear as follows:

   a. Use a suitable tool that will contact the inner bearing race. The tool must not contact the bearing cage or the hub of the gear.

   b. Position the gear, with the tooth side facing down, on a press. Apply gearcase lubricant to the hub of the gear and the inner bore of the tapered bearing.

   c. Place the tapered bearing onto the hub of the gear as shown in **Figure 71**. Place the installation tool onto the inner race of the bearing.

   d. Press the bearing onto the hub of the gear until fully seated. Inspect the bearing to ensure that no damage occurred during installation.

15. Install the drive shaft and pinion gear as follows:

   a. Place the forward gear into the housing. Seat the bearing against the race.

   b. Place the pinion gear into the housing. Mesh the pinion gear teeth with the forward gear teeth (**Figure 72**), then align the pinion gear and bearing with the drive shaft bore. The bearing must fit into its bearing race.

9

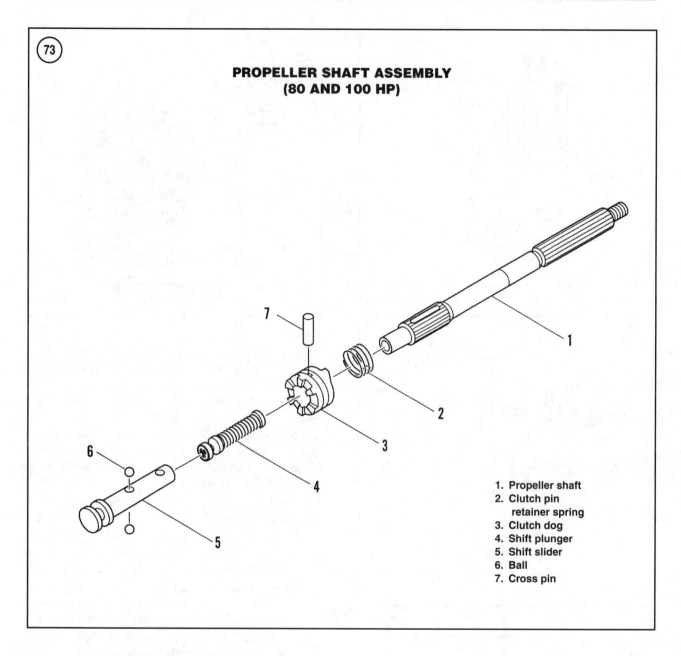

73

**PROPELLER SHAFT ASSEMBLY
(80 AND 100 HP)**

7

1

2

3

6

4

5

1. Propeller shaft
2. Clutch pin
   retainer spring
3. Clutch dog
4. Shift plunger
5. Shift slider
6. Ball
7. Cross pin

c. Slide the drive shaft through its bore and into the bearing. Slowly rotate the drive shaft to align the drive shaft and pinion gear splines.

d. Apply Loctite 271 to the threads of a new pinion nut.

e. Make sure the stepped side of the pinion nut faces the pinion gear, then thread the new pinion nut onto the drive shaft. Place the spline drive shaft holder (Yamaha Part No. YB-6151) onto the top of the drive shaft.

f. Hold the pinion nut with a socket and handle, and tighten the pinion nut to the specification in **Table 1**.

16. Assemble the propeller shaft as follows:

a. Slide the shift plunger assembly (4, **Figure 73**) into the shift slider (5) just enough to align the holes of the shift slider with the recess in shift plunger and install the two balls (6). Slide the shift slider (5, **Figure 73**) into the propeller shaft with the smaller diameter side facing the spring. Align the hole in the shift slider with the slot in the propeller shaft (**Figure 73**).

b. Align the crosspin hole in the side of the clutch with the slot in the propeller shaft and slide it over the propeller shaft (**Figure 73**). Make sure the F stamped on the clutch dog faces toward the front of the propeller shaft.

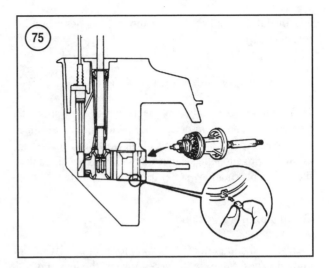

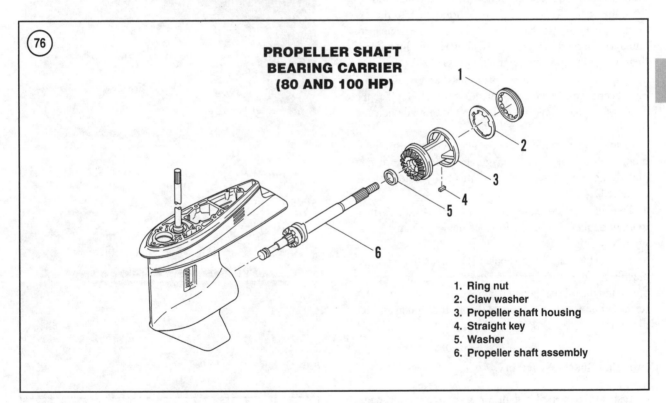

PROPELLER SHAFT BEARING CARRIER (80 AND 100 HP)

1. Ring nut
2. Claw washer
3. Propeller shaft housing
4. Straight key
5. Washer
6. Propeller shaft assembly

c. Slide the cross pin (7, **Figure 73**) through the clutch, propeller shaft and connector.

d. Carefully wind the spring (2, **Figure 73**) onto the grooved portion of the clutch. Make sure the spring loops lay flat and at least three loops pass over each end of the cross pin (**Figure 74**).

17. Slide the propeller shaft into the reverse gear and through the propeller shaft housing. Make sure the propeller shaft seats against the reverse gear. Maintain pressure to ensure the propeller shaft and reverse gear remains in contact with the propeller shaft housing during carrier installation.

18. Lubricate the drive shaft with marine lubricant. Rotate the drive shaft clockwise and slide the propeller shaft housing over the propeller shaft and into the housing. Make sure the UP marking on the carrier faces up.

19. Install the straight key (**Figure 75**) into the carrier, then install the tab washer and ring nut (2 and 1, **Figure 76**) into the carrier and housing. Tighten the ring nut to the specification in **Table 1**.

20. Install the water pump components as described in this chapter.

INSPECTION

Thoroughly clean all components in a suitable solvent. Use compressed air to dry all components, then arrange them in an orderly fashion on a clean work surface. Never allow bearings to spin while using compressed air to dry them. The bearing may suffer irreparable damage.

Water Pump Inspection

1. Inspect the impeller (**Figure 77**) for brittle, missing or burned vanes. Squeeze the vanes toward the hub and release the vanes. The vanes should spring back to the extended position. Replace the impeller if the vanes are damaged, burned, brittle or stiff. Replace the impeller if there is a set in the vanes (curled vanes).

2. Inspect the water tube, grommets and seals for a burned appearance, cracks or brittle material. Replace the water tube, grommets and seals if any of these defects are noted.

3. Inspect the cartridge plate for warpage, wear grooves, melted plastic or other damage. Replace the cartridge plate if a groove is worn in the plate or any other defects are noted.

4. Inspect the water pump insert (**Figure 78**) for burned, worn or damaged surfaces. Replace the water pump housing if any defects are noted.

5. Inspect the water pump housing (**Figure 78**) for melted plastic or other indications of overheating. Replace the cover and the oil seal housing if any defects are noted. Refer to *Water Pump* in this chapter for oil seal housing replacement.

Propeller Shaft Inspection

1. Inspect the propeller shaft for excessive runout, damage or excessive wear. Replace the propeller shaft if defects are noted. Repairing or straightening it is not recommended.

2. Inspect the propeller shaft (A, **Figure 79**) for corrosion, damage or excessive wear. Inspect the propeller shaft splines and threads (B, **Figure 79**) for twisted splines or damaged propeller nut threads. Inspect the bearing contact areas at the front and midpoint of the propeller shaft. Replace the propeller if there are discolored areas, roughness, transferred bearing material or other defects.

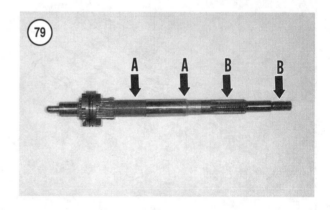

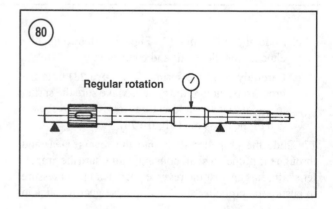

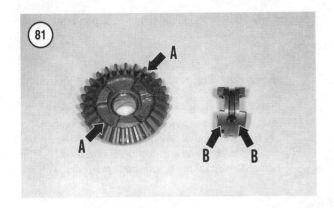

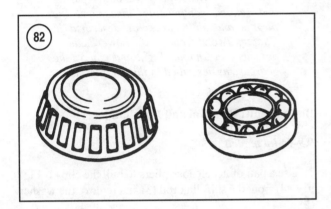

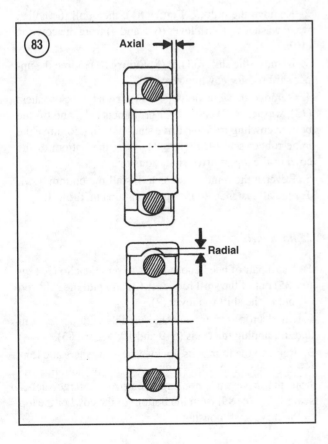

3. Inspect the propeller shaft at the seal contact areas. Replace the propeller shaft if deep grooves are present.

4. Place V blocks at the points indicated in **Figure 80**. Use a dial indicator to measure the shaft deflection at the rear bearing support area. Securely mount the dial indicator. Observe the dial indicator movement and slowly rotate the propeller shaft. Replace the propeller shaft if the needle movement exceeds 0.15 mm (0.006 in.).

Gear and Clutch Inspection

1. Inspect the clutch and gears (B, **Figure 81**) for chips, damage, wear or rounded dogs.

2. Inspect the gears for worn, broken or damaged teeth (A, **Figure 81**). Check for pitted, rough or excessively worn (highly polished) teeth. Replace all of the gears to maintain consistent wear patterns if any of these conditions are found. This is especially important on engines with high operating hours.

NOTE
Replace all gears if any of the gears require replacement. Wear patterns form on the gears in a few hours of use. The wear patterns are disturbed if a new gear is installed with used gears and rapid wear will occur.

CAUTION
*If gears, bearings or the drive shaft is replaced, the gearcase shims usually require changing. Failure to install the correct shims can result in gearcase failure, noisy operation or reduced service life. Refer to **Shim Selection** in this chapter.*

Bearing Inspection

1. Clean all bearings thoroughly in solvent and air dry them prior to inspection. Replace the bearings if the gear lubricant drained from the gearcase is heavily contaminated with metal particles. The particles tend to collect inside the bearing assembly. The particles usually contaminate the gears and bearings during operation.

2. Inspect the roller bearings and bearing races (**Figure 82**) for pits, rust, discoloration or roughness. Inspect the bearing race for highly polished or unevenly worn surfaces. Replace the bearing assembly if any of these defects are noted.

3. Rotate ball bearings and check for rough operation. Move the bearing in the directions shown in **Figure 83**. Note the presence of axial or radial looseness. Replace the bearing if rough operation or looseness is noted.

4. Inspect the needle bearing located in the propeller shaft housing, forward gear, drive shaft seal and propeller shaft housing. Replace the bearing if flattened rollers, discoloration, rust, roughness or pits are noted.

5. Inspect the propeller shaft and drive shaft at the bearing contact area. Replace the drive shaft and/or propeller shaft along with the needle bearing if discoloration, pits, transferred bearing material or roughness are noted.

Shift Cam and Related Components Inspection

1. Inspect the bore in the propeller shaft for debris, damage or excessive wear. Clean the bore of the propeller shaft.

2. Inspect the clutch spring for damage, corrosion or weak spring tension, and replace it if defects are noted.

3. Inspect the cross pin for damage, roughness or wear. Replace if required. Inspect the shift plunger and spring for damage or corrosion. Replace if required.

4. Inspect the shift plunger for cracked, broken or worn areas. Replace any worn or defective components. Inspect the shift slider located at the lower end of the shift shaft for wear, chips, cracks or corrosion. Inspect the shift shaft for a worn, bent or twisted condition. Inspect the shift shaft plate bushing for cracks or shift shaft bore wear. Replace the bushing and/or shift shaft if defects are noted.

Shims, Spacers, Fasteners and Washers

1. Inspect all shims for rust or damage. Replace any shim that is not in like-new condition.

2. Spacers are used in various locations in the gearcase. Some function as thrust surfaces. Replace them if excessive wear is noted, or if they are bent, corroded or damaged. Use only the correct parts to replace them. In most cases, they are of a certain thickness and specified material. Replace any self-locking nut unless it is in excellent condition. Replace the pinion nut during the final assembly.

DRIVE SHAFT HOUSING REMOVAL AND INSTALLATION

A clean engine is easier to work on than one covered with dirt, algae, marine vegetation, grease or other contamination. Using pressurized water, clean the exterior of the drive shaft housing before removal.

Change the engine oil anytime the drive shaft housing is removed. Inspection of the oil allows faults to be detected

and corrected before they lead to possible power unit failure.

CAUTION
Avoid directing pressurized water at exposed seals or exhaust openings. Pressurized water can blow past seals and contaminate the power head lubricant or possibly damage the seal. Pressurized water can reach the internal power head and oil pan if directed into the exhaust openings.

NOTE
Prior to removing the drive shaft housing and related components, disconnect the throttle and shift cables as described in Chapter Twelve, remove the power head as described in Chapter Eight and remove the gearcase as described in this chapter.

Bottom Cowl Removal and Installation

9.9-15 hp models

1. Use a pair of needlenose pliers to pull the clip (1, **Figure 84**) from the shift link rod (3) and remove the washer (2).

2. Remove the bolt (7, **Figure 84**), then pull the collar, wave washer and shift lever (6, 5 and 4) from the cowling (10).

3. Remove the shift rod nut (8, **Figure 84**) to free the upper shift rod for cowling removal.

4. Remove the four bolts (14, **Figure 84**), lockwashers (13), washers (12) and rubber grommets (11), and lift the bottom cowling from the drive shaft housing. Remove the large rubber seal (9, **Figure 84**) from the bottom of the cowl or the top of drive shaft housing.

5. Reverse the removal steps to install the bottom cowl. Torque all fasteners to the specifications in **Table 1**.

25 hp models

1. Use a pair of needlenose pliers to pull the clip (3, **Figure 85**) out of the shift rod lever (2) and pull the shift rod (4) out of the shift rod lever (2).

2. On electric start models and models with power trim and tilt, unplug the leads (6, 9 and 10, **Figure 85**).

3. Remove the four bolts, lockwashers, washers and rubber grommets (12, **Figure 85**), and lift the bottom cowl from the drive shaft housing. Remove the large rubber seal (8, **Figure 85**) from the bottom of the cowl or the top of the drive shaft housing.

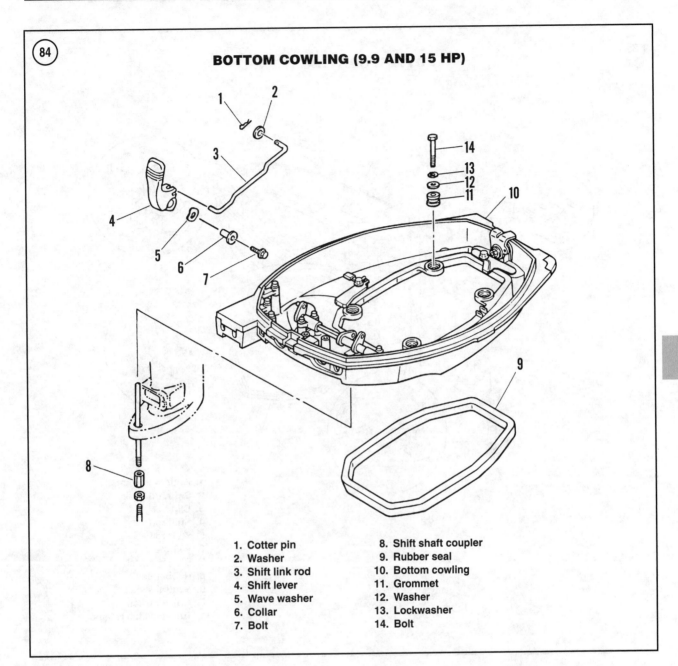

BOTTOM COWLING (9.9 AND 15 HP)

1. Cotter pin
2. Washer
3. Shift link rod
4. Shift lever
5. Wave washer
6. Collar
7. Bolt
8. Shift shaft coupler
9. Rubber seal
10. Bottom cowling
11. Grommet
12. Washer
13. Lockwasher
14. Bolt

9

4. Reverse the removal steps to install the bottom cowl. Torque all fasteners to the specifications in **Table 1**.

40 and 50 hp models

1. On electric start models and models with power trim and tilt, unplug the leads (3 and 13, **Figure 86**).

2. Remove the four bolts, lockwashers, washers and rubber grommets (2, **Figure 86**), and lift the bottom cowl from the drive shaft housing.

3. Reverse the removal steps to install the bottom cowl. Torque all fasteners to the specifications in **Table 1**.

80 and 100 hp models

1. On electric start models and models with power trim and tilt, unplug the leads (21, **Figure 87**). Cut the tie wrap on the water hose (13, **Figure 87**) and remove the hose from the fitting (14) on the cowling.

2. Remove the four bolts (2, **Figure 86**) and lift the bottom cowl from the drive shaft housing.

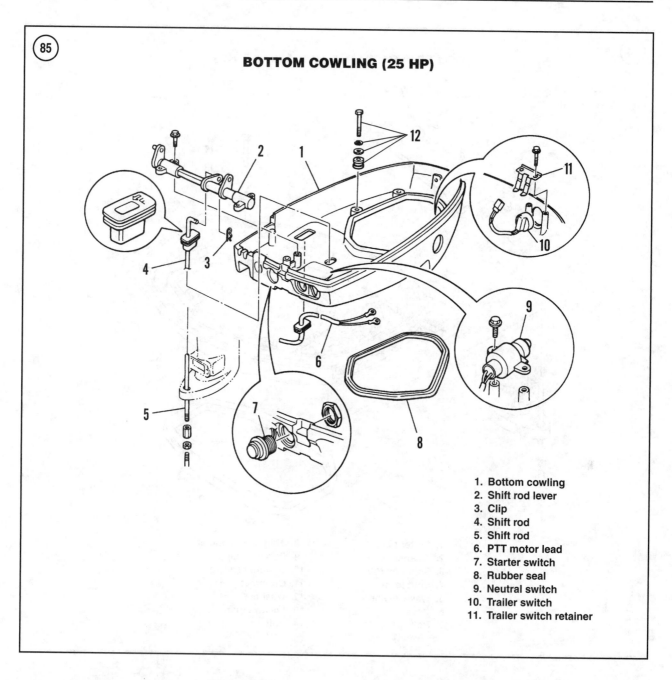

(85)

BOTTOM COWLING (25 HP)

1. Bottom cowling
2. Shift rod lever
3. Clip
4. Shift rod
5. Shift rod
6. PTT motor lead
7. Starter switch
8. Rubber seal
9. Neutral switch
10. Trailer switch
11. Trailer switch retainer

3. Reverse the removal steps to install the bottom cowl. Tighten all fasteners to the specification in **Table 1**.

Bottom Cowl Disassembly and Assembly

9.9 and 15 hp models

Refer to **Figure 88** during this procedure.

1. Remove the three bolts (8, **Figure 88**) securing the fitting plate (7) to the cowl and remove the fitting plate. The

fitting plate holds down the battery cables (23, **Figure 88**) and fuel hose (25).

2. Remove the fuel line, fuel fitting and battery cable from the recessed area of the cowl.

3. Remove the bolts (21, **Figure 88**) and remove the neutral switch assembly (22).

4. Pull the clip (6) out of the upper shift shaft (5) and remove the shift shaft from the shift rod lever (3, **Figure 88**).

5. Remove the four bolts (1, **Figure 88**) from the shift rod lever (3) and lift it from the cowl.

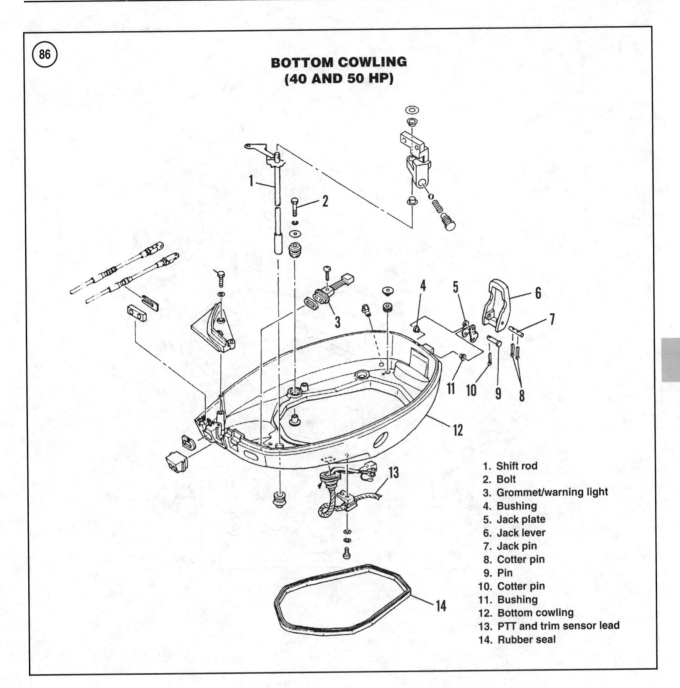

86

BOTTOM COWLING
(40 AND 50 HP)

1. Shift rod
2. Bolt
3. Grommet/warning light
4. Bushing
5. Jack plate
6. Jack lever
7. Jack pin
8. Cotter pin
9. Pin
10. Cotter pin
11. Bushing
12. Bottom cowling
13. PTT and trim sensor lead
14. Rubber seal

9

6. Remove the bolts shown in 9, **Figure 88** and one bolt shown in 14, **Figure 88**, and lift both holding brackets shown in 10, **Figure 88** and the other holding bracket shown in 15, **Figure 88** from the cowl.

7. Remove the bolt (11, **Figure 88**) that holds the locking plate (12) and collar (13) in position on the cowl handle (16). After removing the handle, pull the washer and collar (17 and 18, **Figure 88**) off of handle.

8. Reverse the disassembly steps to assemble the lower cowl. Tighten all fasteners to the specifications in **Table 1**.

25 hp models

Refer to **Figure 85** during this procedure.

1. Pull the clip (3) from the upper shift shaft (4) and remove the shift shaft from the shift rod lever (2, **Figure 85**).

2. Remove the four bolts from the shift rod lever (2, **Figure 85**) and lift it from the cowl.

3. Unplug the power trim and tilt motor leads (6, **Figure 85**)

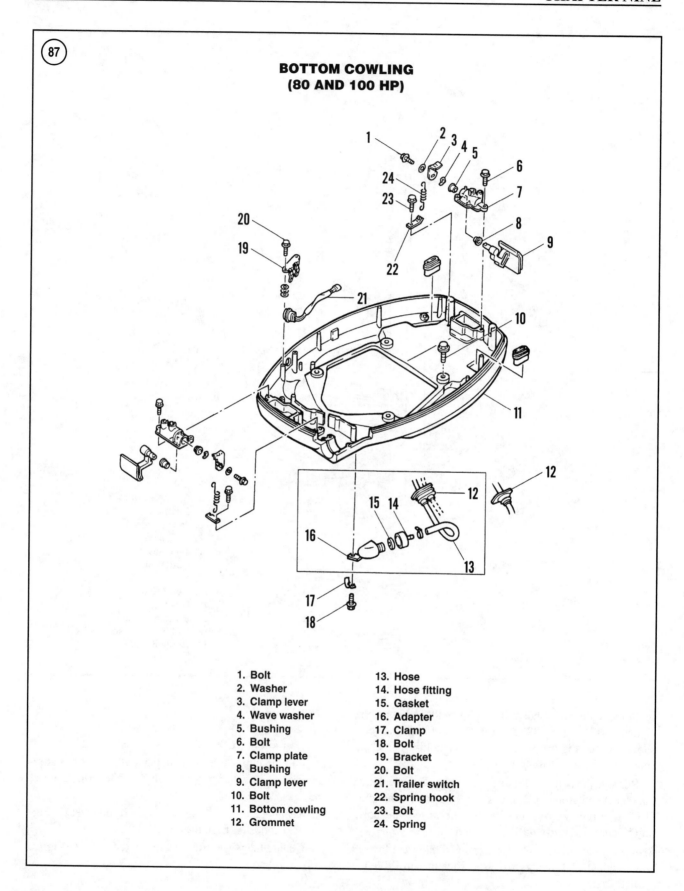

**BOTTOM COWLING
(80 AND 100 HP)**

1. Bolt
2. Washer
3. Clamp lever
4. Wave washer
5. Bushing
6. Bolt
7. Clamp plate
8. Bushing
9. Clamp lever
10. Bolt
11. Bottom cowling
12. Grommet
13. Hose
14. Hose fitting
15. Gasket
16. Adapter
17. Clamp
18. Bolt
19. Bracket
20. Bolt
21. Trailer switch
22. Spring hook
23. Bolt
24. Spring

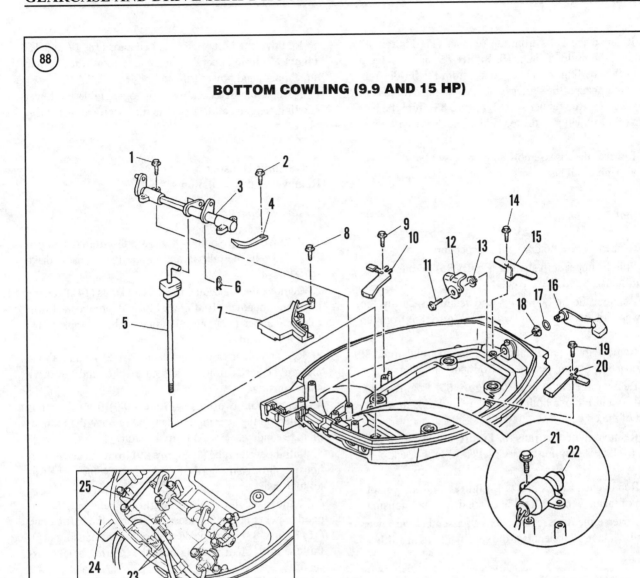

BOTTOM COWLING (9.9 AND 15 HP)

9

1. Bolt
2. Bolt
3. Shift rod lever
4. Spring hook
5. Shift rod
6. Clip
7. Fitting plate
8. Bolt
9. Bolt
10. Bracket
11. Bolt
12. Plate
13. Collar

14. Bolt
15. Bracket
16. Cowling lock lever
17. Wave washer
18. Collar
19. Bolt
20. Bracket
21. Bolt
22. Neutral switch
23. Battery cable
24. Fuel joint
25. Fuel hose

4. Remove the bolts from the retainer (11, **Figure 85**) holding the trailer switch (10, **Figure 85**) and remove it from the cowling. Remove the nut from the inside front cowl that secures the starter switch, if equipped (8, **Figure 85**). Remove the rubber seal (8, **Figure 85**) from the bottom of the cowling or the top side of the drive shaft housing.

5. Reverse the disassembly steps to assemble the lower cowl. Tighten all fasteners to the specifications in **Table 1**.

40 and 50 hp models

Refer to **Figure 86** during this procedure.

1. Pull the upper shift shaft (1, **Figure 86**) from the drive shaft housing and lower cowl.

2. Remove the bolt, washers and retainer securing the power trim and tilt sensor leads (13, **Figure 86**) from the cowl.

3. Remove the screw from the grommet/warning light (3, **Figure 86**), if equipped, at the front port side of cowl.

4. Remove the cotter pin (10, **Figure 86**) from the jack pin (9) and remove both bushings (4 and 11) from each end of the cowl.

5. Remove the cotter pins (8, **Figure 86**) from the jack pin (7) that is securing the jack lever (6) to the jack plate (5).

6. Remove the rubber seal (14, **Figure 86**) from the bottom of the cowl or the topside of the drive shaft housing.

7. Reverse the disassembly steps to assemble the lower cowl. Tighten all fasteners to the specifications in **Table 1**.

80 and 100 hp models

Refer to **Figure 87** during this procedure.

1. Remove the four bolts (6, **Figure 87**) securing the clamp plates (7) to the cowl.

2. Remove the two bolts (23, **Figure 87**) from the spring hook (22), and remove one end of the spring (24, **Figure 87**) from the spring hook (22) and the other end from the clamp lever.

3. Remove the bolts (1, **Figure 87**), one on the front of cowling and one on the back of the cowl, and remove the washers (2) from the clamp lever (3). Remove the wave washers and bushings (4 and 5, **Figure 87**) from the clamp plate (7). Remove the clamp lever (9, **Figure 87**) from the clamp plate (7).

4. Remove the bolts (20, **Figure 87**) from the bracket (19), and remove the spring and trailer switch (21) from the cowling.

5. Remove the bolt, clamp and adaptor (18, 17 and 16, **Figure 87**) from under the cowl that supports the flushing attachment, and power trim and tilt leads.

6. Reverse the disassembly steps to assemble the lower cowling. Tighten all fasteners to the specifications in **Table 1**.

Drive Shaft Housing
Removal and Installation

9.9 and 15 hp models

1. Remove the two bolts (18, **Figure 89**) from the oil pan (17), and pull the oil pan and gasket (6) from the drive shaft housing.

2. Remove the four bolts, washers and nuts (14) from the lower mount cover (10, **Figure 89**), and remove the lower rubber damper (12) and both side rubber dampers (11) from the housing.

3. Remove the grease insert (9, **Figure 89**), and remove the ground leads from the clamp bracket and the drive shaft housing.

4. Remove the two nuts (4, **Figure 89**) from the studs mounted on the steering bracket and remove the retainer plate (3) and washers (7) from the studs.

5. Pull the water tube (1, **Figure 89**) from the drive shaft housing through the upper damper cover. Remove the water tube seal.

6. Remove the three bolts (2, **Figure 89**) and pull the upper damper (5) from the housing. Remove the baffle plate (16, **Figure 89**) from inside the drive shaft housing (15). Pull the drive shaft housing from the steering bracket assembly.

7. Reverse the removal steps to install the drive shaft housing. Tighten all fasteners to the specifications in **Table 1**.

25-50 hp models

1. Remove the four nuts, washers and bolts (8, **Figure 90**) and remove the lower mount covers (7).

2. Pull the two side dampers (6, **Figure 90**) and one front damper (10) from the housing.

3. Remove the grease insert (11, **Figure 90**), and remove the ground leads (9) from the steering bracket and housing.

4. Remove the two drive shaft housing bolts and nuts (1, **Figure 90**) securing the housing to the steering bracket. Remove the three bolts and washers (3, **Figure 90**) that secure the upper damper (4), and pull the damper from the drive shaft housing (5).

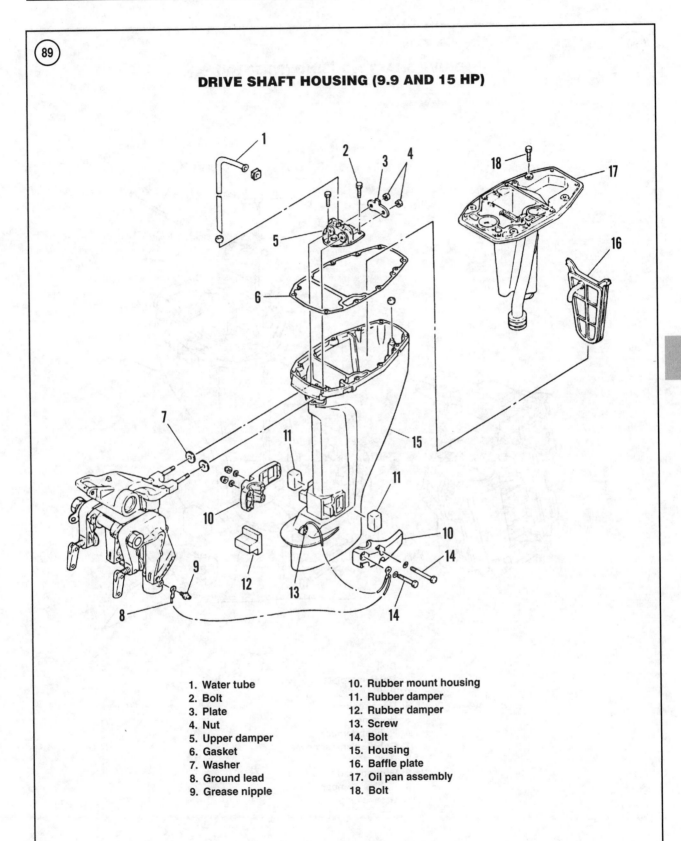

DRIVE SHAFT HOUSING (9.9 AND 15 HP)

9

1. Water tube
2. Bolt
3. Plate
4. Nut
5. Upper damper
6. Gasket
7. Washer
8. Ground lead
9. Grease nipple
10. Rubber mount housing
11. Rubber damper
12. Rubber damper
13. Screw
14. Bolt
15. Housing
16. Baffle plate
17. Oil pan assembly
18. Bolt

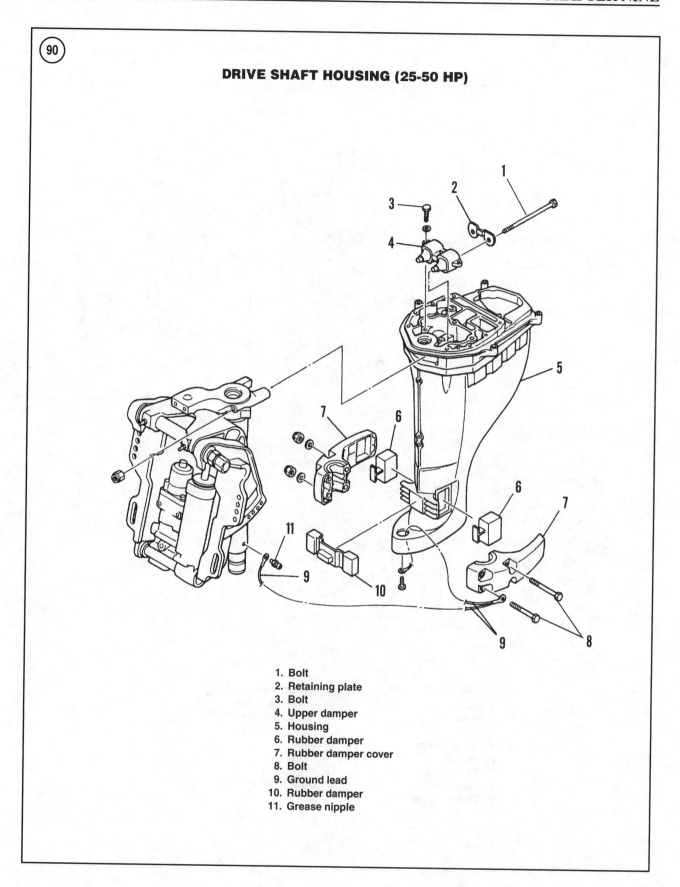

⑨⓪

DRIVE SHAFT HOUSING (25-50 HP)

1. Bolt
2. Retaining plate
3. Bolt
4. Upper damper
5. Housing
6. Rubber damper
7. Rubber damper cover
8. Bolt
9. Ground lead
10. Rubber damper
11. Grease nipple

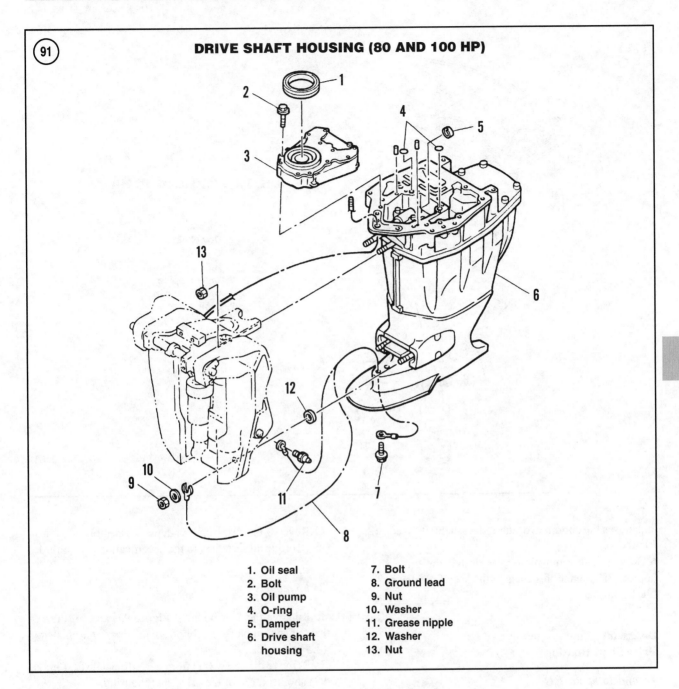

⑨¹ **DRIVE SHAFT HOUSING (80 AND 100 HP)**

1. Oil seal
2. Bolt
3. Oil pump
4. O-ring
5. Damper
6. Drive shaft housing

7. Bolt
8. Ground lead
9. Nut
10. Washer
11. Grease nipple
12. Washer
13. Nut

9

5. The clamp and steering bracket (A, **Figure 90**) is used on models without power trim.

6. Reverse the removal steps to install the drive shaft housing. Tighten all fasteners to the specifications in **Table 1**.

80 and 100 hp models

1. Remove the oil pump (3, **Figure 91**) from the drive shaft housing by removing the six bolts (2).

2. Remove the oil pump seal and O-rings (1 and 4, **Figure 91**) from the oil pump or drive shaft housing.

3. Remove the grease insert (11, **Figure 91**) and remove the ground lead from the clamp bracket.

4. Remove the bolt (7) and the ground lead from the drive shaft housing from the underside (**Figure 91**). The other end of this ground lead is connected to the boat side of the clamp bracket (**Figure 90**).

5. Remove both nuts (13, **Figure 91**) from the backside of the steering bracket. Support the unit so it will not fall

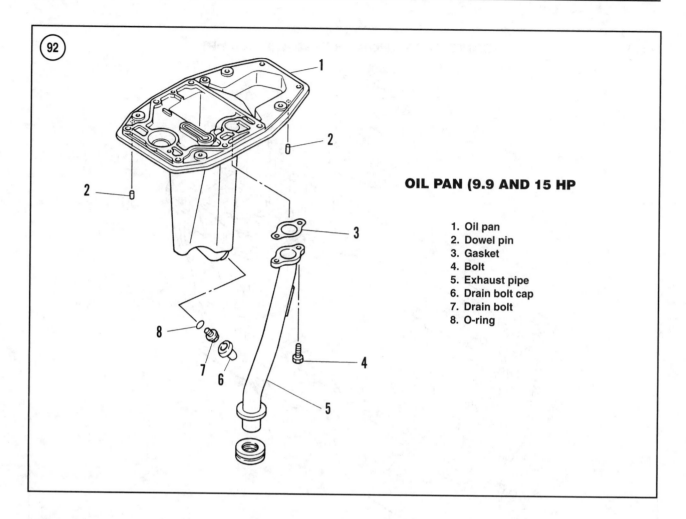

OIL PAN (9.9 AND 15 HP

1. Oil pan
2. Dowel pin
3. Gasket
4. Bolt
5. Exhaust pipe
6. Drain bolt cap
7. Drain bolt
8. O-ring

and loosen the bottom two nuts and washers (9, 10 and 12, **Figure 91**).

6. Reverse the removal steps to install the drive shaft housing. Tighten all fasteners to the specifications in **Table 1**.

Disassembly and Assembly
Drive Shaft Housing

9.9 and 15 hp models

Only the oil pan is not disassembled in the removal of the drive shaft housing.

1. Remove both bolts (4, **Figure 92**) from the exhaust pipe (5), then remove the gasket (3) from the exhaust pipe or the oil pan. Discard the old gasket.

2. Remove the drain plug cap (6, **Figure 92**) and drain bolt (7), then remove the drain plug gasket (8) and discard the gasket. Install a new gasket during assembly.

3. Remove the two dowel pins (2, **Figure 92**) from the oil pan.

4. Reverse the disassembly steps to assembly the housing. Torque all fasteners to the specifications in **Table 1**.

25 hp models

1. Remove the four bolts (3, **Figure 93**) and lift the exhaust plate/oil pan assembly from the drive shaft housing (4, **Figure 93**).

2. Remove the screws (1) from the baffle plate (2, **Figure 93**) and lift it out of the drive shaft housing.

3. Remove the drain plug cap (8) from the drain plug (9), and remove the drain plug and gasket. Discard the gasket. Install a new gasket during assembly.

4. Remove the three bolts (5, **Figure 93**) from the exhaust manifold (6). Remove and discard the exhaust manifold gasket (7). Install a new manifold gasket during assembly.

5. Remove the ten bolts (5) that secure the oil pan (6) to the exhaust guide (2, **Figure 94**). Remove two locating dowel pins (4) from the oil pan.

6. Remove the bolts (8 and 9, **Figure 94**) from the oil strainer (10) and pull the oil strainer from the exhaust

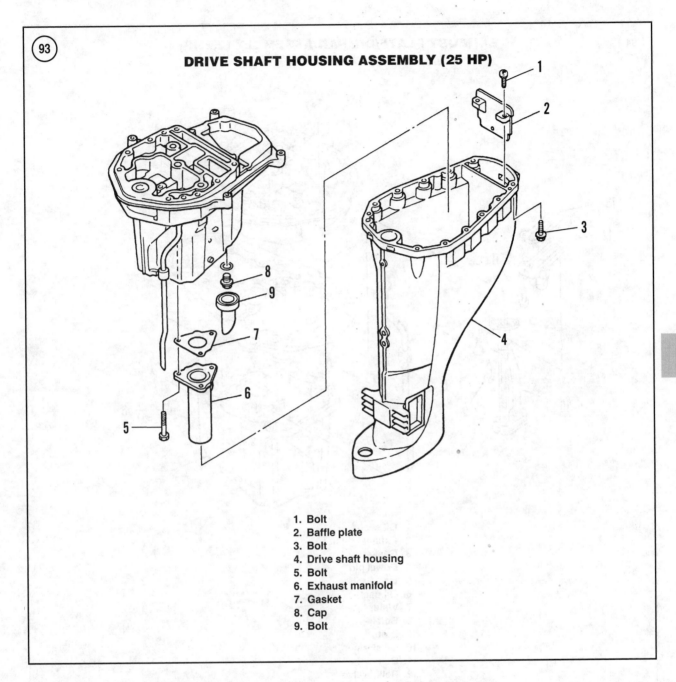

(93)

DRIVE SHAFT HOUSING ASSEMBLY (25 HP)

1. Bolt
2. Baffle plate
3. Bolt
4. Drive shaft housing
5. Bolt
6. Exhaust manifold
7. Gasket
8. Cap
9. Bolt

9

guide (2). Remove and discard the gasket (3, **Figure 94**) from the exhaust guide. Install a new gasket during assembly.

7. Pull the water tube (7, **Figure 94**) from the corner of the oil pan. Remove the three bolts (11, **Figure 94**), and pull the relief valve and gasket (12 and 13, **Figure 94**) from the oil strainer. Discard the relief valve gasket. Install a new relief valve gasket during assembly.

8. Reverse the disassembly steps to assembly the housing. Torque all fasteners to the specifications in **Table 1**.

40 and 50 hp models

1. Remove the four bolts (24, **Figure 95**) from the drive shaft housing (23). Pull the housing (23) from the exhaust guide assembly. Remove the baffle plate (25, **Figure 95**) from the housing by removing the two screws (26).

2. Pull the muffler seal (27) from the bottom of the muffler (28). Remove the rubber seal (29, **Figure 95**) from upper rear of the muffler.

3. Remove the six bolts (31, **Figure 95**) from the muffler (28) and pull the muffler from the oil pan. Next remove

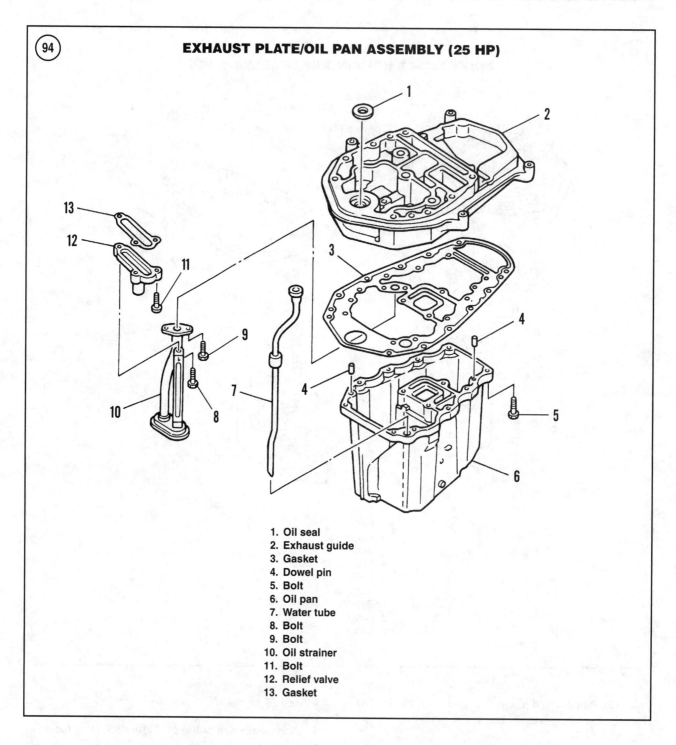

EXHAUST PLATE/OIL PAN ASSEMBLY (25 HP)

1. Oil seal
2. Exhaust guide
3. Gasket
4. Dowel pin
5. Bolt
6. Oil pan
7. Water tube
8. Bolt
9. Bolt
10. Oil strainer
11. Bolt
12. Relief valve
13. Gasket

the muffler gasket (30) from either the top of the muffler or the bottom of the oil pan.

4. Remove the three bolts and washers (21, **Figure 95**), and remove the exhaust manifold (22) and gasket (20) from the bottom of the oil pan (12).

5. Remove the ten bolts (16, **Figure 95**) that secure the oil pan (12) to the exhaust guide (2). Pull the oil pan down

and remove both locating pins (13 and 15) from the top of the oil pan. Pull the water tube (10, **Figure 95**) from the corner of the oil pan, and remove the seal (11) and washer (9) from the water tube.

6. Remove the bolt (7, **Figure 95**) that supports one end of the relief valve (4) to the oil strainer (8). Remove the two bolts (6, **Figure 95**) that secure the oil strainer (8) to

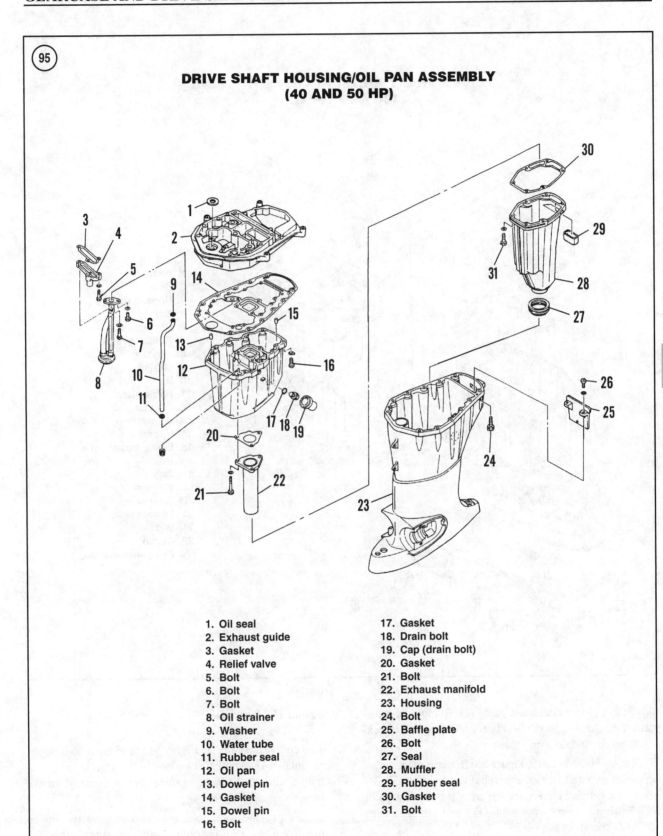

**DRIVE SHAFT HOUSING/OIL PAN ASSEMBLY
(40 AND 50 HP)**

1. Oil seal
2. Exhaust guide
3. Gasket
4. Relief valve
5. Bolt
6. Bolt
7. Bolt
8. Oil strainer
9. Washer
10. Water tube
11. Rubber seal
12. Oil pan
13. Dowel pin
14. Gasket
15. Dowel pin
16. Bolt
17. Gasket
18. Drain bolt
19. Cap (drain bolt)
20. Gasket
21. Bolt
22. Exhaust manifold
23. Housing
24. Bolt
25. Baffle plate
26. Bolt
27. Seal
28. Muffler
29. Rubber seal
30. Gasket
31. Bolt

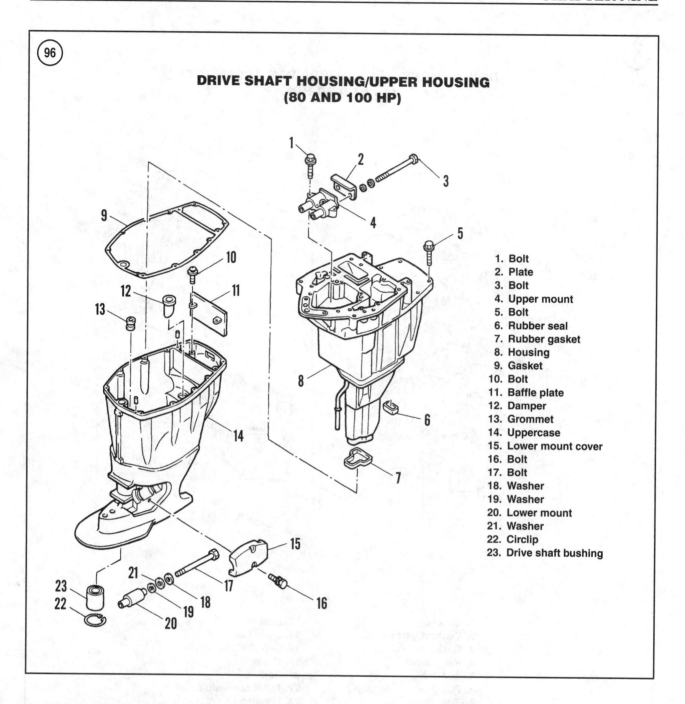

**DRIVE SHAFT HOUSING/UPPER HOUSING
(80 AND 100 HP)**

96

1. Bolt
2. Plate
3. Bolt
4. Upper mount
5. Bolt
6. Rubber seal
7. Rubber gasket
8. Housing
9. Gasket
10. Bolt
11. Baffle plate
12. Damper
13. Grommet
14. Uppercase
15. Lower mount cover
16. Bolt
17. Bolt
18. Washer
19. Washer
20. Lower mount
21. Washer
22. Circlip
23. Drive shaft bushing

the gasket (14) and exhaust guide (2). Remove and discard the exhaust gasket (14, **Figure 95**). Replace the exhaust guide gasket during assembly.

7. Remove both bolts (5, **Figure 95**) from the other end of the relief valve and remove the relief valve gasket (3). Remove the oil seal (1, **Figure 95**) from the exhaust guide (2). During assembly, make sure the seal lips are facing down as shown in **Figure 95**.

8. Reverse the disassembly steps to assemble the housing. Torque all fasteners to the specifications in **Table 1**.

80 and 100 hp models

1. Remove the bolts (1, **Figure 96**) from the rubber upper mount (4). Then pull the two long bolts (3) from the upper mount, and lift the locating plate (2) and mount from the upper housing (8).

2. Remove the four bolts (16) and remove the lower mount covers (15, **Figure 96**) from the drive shaft housing. There are two lower rubber mounts, one on each side of the drive shaft housing, at the lower side of the housing.

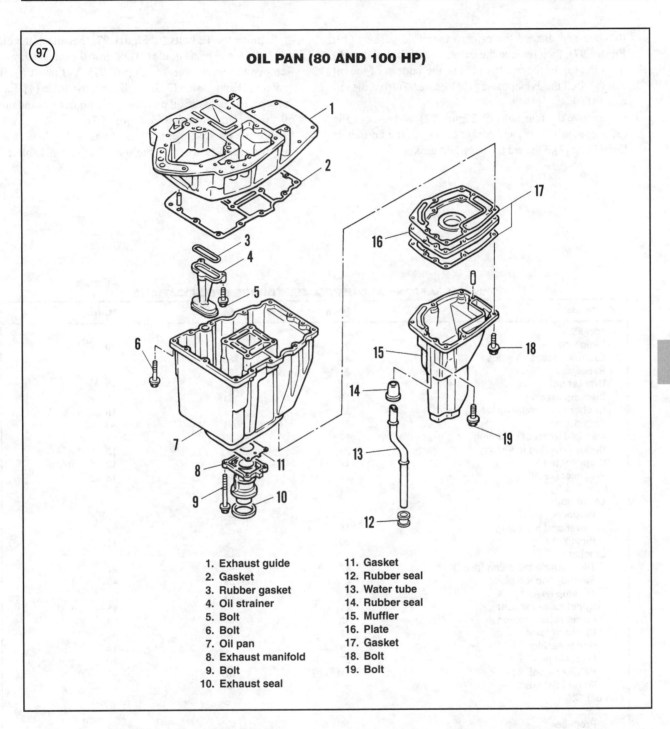

OIL PAN (80 AND 100 HP)

1. Exhaust guide
2. Gasket
3. Rubber gasket
4. Oil strainer
5. Bolt
6. Bolt
7. Oil pan
8. Exhaust manifold
9. Bolt
10. Exhaust seal
11. Gasket
12. Rubber seal
13. Water tube
14. Rubber seal
15. Muffler
16. Plate
17. Gasket
18. Bolt
19. Bolt

Remove the bolts (17, **Figure 96**), washers (18, 19 and 21) and the lower mount (20) from the housing.

3. Remove the four bolts (5, **Figure 96**) that retain the upper housing (8) to the drive shaft housing (14). Lift the upper housing (8) out of the drive shaft housing (14, **Figure 96**). Remove and discard the gasket (9). Remove the rubber gasket and rubber seal (7 and 6, **Figure 96**) from the upper housing (8).

4. Remove the two screws (10) and baffle plate (11, **Figure 96**) from the drive shaft housing (14), then remove the damper (12) and rubber grommet (13, **Figure 96**) from the housing (14).

5. Remove the six bolts shown in 18, **Figure 97** and the one bolt shown in 19, **Figure 97** from the oil pan, and remove the muffler (15). Pull the water tube rubber seals (14 and 12, **Figure 97**) and water pipe (13) from the muffler.

Remove and discard the exhaust manifold gaskets (17, **Figure 97**), then remove the exhaust manifold plate (16) from the top of the muffler (15) or the bottom of the oil pan (7). Pull the exhaust seal (10, **Figure 97**) from the exhaust stack.

6. Remove the four bolts (9, **Figure 97**), and remove the exhaust manifold (8) and gasket (11) from the bottom of the oil pan (7). Discard the manifold gasket.

7. Remove the 12 bolts (6, **Figure 97**) that attach the oil pan (7) to the exhaust guide (1) and drop the oil pan down. Remove the three bolts (5, **Figure 97**), and pull the oil strainer (4) and gasket (3) from the exhaust guide (1). Remove and discard the oil pan gasket (2, **Figure 97**) and the oil strainer rubber gasket (3, **Figure 97**).

8. Reverse the disassembly steps to assembly the housing. Torque all fasteners to the specifications in **Table 1**.

Table 1 GEARCASE AND UPPERCASE TORQUE SPECIFICATIONS

Fastener	N•m	in.-lb.	ft.-lb.
Model F9.9			
Pinion nut	26	–	19
Exhaust mounting guide	10	88	–
Relief valve	8	71	–
Bracket bolt	17	–	12
Steering bracket	13	115	–
Rubber side mount upper	25	–	18
Plug drain	8	71	–
Manifold exhaust mounting	12	107	–
Bottom cowling mounting	21	–	15
Propeller (F9.9)	17	–	12
Propeller (T9.9)	21	–	15
Model F15			
Lower unit			
Propeller	17	–	12
Lower unit mounting	18	–	13
Pinion nut	25	–	18
Bracket			
Tiller handle mounting (pivot)	37	–	27
Steering friction piece	4	35	–
Tilt stop lever	8	71	–
Upper rubber mount	21	–	15
Lower rubber mount	32	–	23
Clamp bracket	12	107	–
Upper casing	18	–	13
Oil drain plug	27	–	20
Exhaust manifold	11	97	–
Water inlet cover	5	44	–
Model F25			
Lower unit			
Propeller	34	–	25
Lower unit mounting	37	–	27
Propeller shaft bearing carrier	11	97	–
Pinion nut	50	–	37
Water inlet	4	35	–
Bracket			
Tiller handle mounting	37	–	27
Tiller handle pivot	13	115	–
Steering bracket adjusting	4	35	–

(continued)

Table 1 GEARCASE AND UPPERCASE TORQUE SPECIFICATIONS (continued)

Fastener	N•m	in.-lb.	ft.-lb.
Model F25			
Bracket			
Upper rubber mount	24	–	17
Rubber mount housing	18	–	13
Upper damper	18	–	13
Lower mount housing	54	–	40
Clamp bracket–upper (manual tilt)	13	115	–
Clamp bracket–lower (manual tilt)	8	72	–
Tilt lock lever (manual)	8	72	–
Clamp bracket–upper (PTT)	23	–	17
Clamp bracket–lower (PTT)	37	–	27
Oil pan	10	91	–
Engine oil drain	27	–	20
Exhaust manifold	9	83	–
Exhaust guide	21	–	15
Grease nipple	3	26	–
PTT mount	18	–	13
Model F40 and F50			
Lower unit			
Propeller	35	–	25
Lower unit mounting	40	–	29
Ring nut (FT 50)	105	–	76
Propeller shaft housing	18	–	13
Pinion nut	75	–	54
Pinion nut (FT 50)	95	–	69
Water inlet	5	45	–
Bracket			
Tiller handle mounting	37	–	27
Steering bracket	37	–	27
Steering friction mounting	20	–	14
Tiller handle pivot	37	–	27
Upper rubber mount	24	–	17
Lower rubber mount	42	–	30
Engine oil pan	11	97	–
Oil drain plug	18	–	13
Exhaust manifold	10	88	–
Exhaust guide	21	–	15
Bracket	23	–	17
Model F80 and F100			
Lower unit			
Water inlet	5	45	–
Lower unit mounting	40	–	29
Pinion nut	95	–	68
Propeller	35	–	25
Propeller shaft bearing carrier ring nut	100	–	74
Apron mounting bracket	4	35	–
Exhaust guide mounting	20	–	14
Exhaust manifold mounting	10	88	–
Grease nipple	3	26	–
Rubber lower mounting	52	–	38
Oil drain	27	–	20
Oil pump cover	4	35	–
Oil pump mounting	10	88	–
Oil strainer mounting	10	88	–
PTT unit mounting	42	–	30
Shift rod friction cap	18	–	13
Sub-exhaust guide mounting	4	35	–
Tapping	10	88	–
Through tube	15	–	11
Upper rubber mounting	52	–	38

9

Table 2 TEST PROPELLERS

Engine	Part No.
T9.9	YB-01627
F9.9	YB-01619
F15	YB-01619
F25	YB-01621
F40-50	YB-01611
F80-100	YB-01620

Table 3 RECOMMENDED GEARCASE LUBRICANT

Model	Oil type	SAE	API	Capacity
T9.9 (MH, EH, ER)	Hypoid	90	–	320 cm (10.82 oz)
F9.9 (MH, EH)	Hypoid	90	–	185 cm (6.25 oz)
F15 (MH, EH)	Hypoid	90	–	250 cm (8.45 oz)
F25 (MH, EH, TH, ER, TR)	Hypoid	90	–	320 cm (10.8 oz)
F40 (TR, ER, TH, EH)	Hypoid	90	GL-4	430 cm (14.5 oz)
F50 (TR, ER, TH, EH)	Hypoid	90	GL-4	430 cm (14.5 oz)
T50 (TR)	Hypoid	90	GL-4	610 cm (20.6 oz)
F80 and F100	Hypoid	90	GL-4	670 cm (22.6 oz)

Table 4 GEAR BACKLASH

Model	Forward gear backlash	Reverse gear backlash
T9.9	0.26-0.76 mm (0.010-0.030 in.)	0.51-1.02 mm (0.020-0.040 in.)
F9.9	0.23-0.69 mm (0.009-0.027 in.)	0.82-1.16 mm (0.032-0.046 in.)
F15	0.19-0.86 mm (0.007-0.034 in.)	0.95-1.65 mm (0.037-0.065 in.)
F25	0.31-0.72 mm (0.012-0.028 in.)	0.93-1.65 mm (0.037-0.065 in.)
F40-50	0.18-0.45 mm (0.007-0.018 in.)	0.71-0.98 mm (0.028-0.039 in.)
F80-100	0.13-0.46 mm (0.005-0.018 in.)	–

Table 5 GEAR RATIO AND GEAR TOOTH COUNT

Model	Gear ratio	Tooth count
F9.9	13:27	2.08
T9.9	13:38	2.92
F15	13:27	2.08
F25	13:27	2.08
F40	13:27	2.08
F50	13:24	1.84
T50	12:28	2.33
F80	13:30	2.31
F100	13:30	2.31

Chapter Ten

Rewind Starter

This chapter provides removal, disassembly, assembly and installation procedures for the manual rewind starter (**Figure 1**).

Table 1 provides tightening specifications for the manual starter and neutral start mechanism. **Table 2** provides general torque specifications. **Table 1** and **Table 2** are located at the end of this chapter.

Cleaning, inspection and lubrication of the internal components are necessary if the manual starter is not engaging properly or the starter is binding. In instances where complete disassembly is not required, perform the steps necessary to access the required component(s). Reverse the steps to assemble and install the starter.

Use only the starter rope specified for your outboard. Other types of rope will not withstand the rigorous use and will fail quickly, potentially damaging other components. Contact a Yamaha dealership to purchase the specified starter rope.

Clean all components, except the rope, in a solvent suitable for composite or plastic components. Use hot soapy water if a suitable solvent is not available. Dry all components with compressed air immediately after cleaning.

Inspect all components for excessive wear or damage, and replace them if necessary. Pay particular attention to the starter spring. Inspect the entire length of the spring for cracks or other defects.

Apply water-resistant grease to all bushings, drive pawls, springs and pivot surfaces during installation. For smooth operation and to prevent corrosion, apply water-resistant grease to the starter spring contact surfaces.

> *WARNING*
> *When servicing the manual starter, wear suitable eye and hand protection. The starter spring may unexpectedly release from the housing with considerable force.*

> *CAUTION*
> *Never use grease containing metal particles or graphite on any manual starter component. It can cause binding and/or incorrect operation of the manual starter.*

Removal (9.9 hp models)

On these models, the starter is mounted in front of the flywheel (**Figure 2**). Refer to **Figure 3** during this procedure.

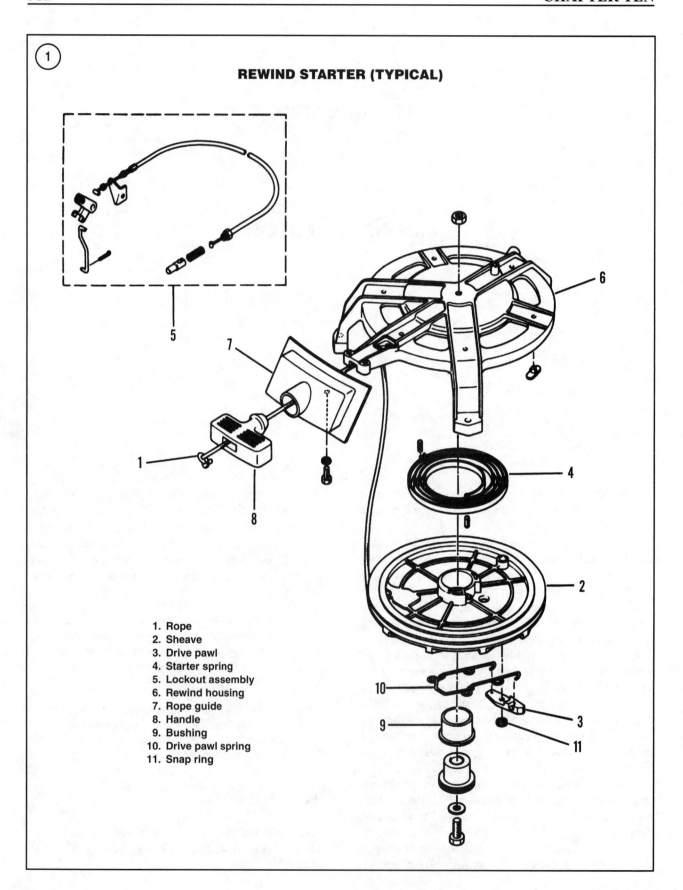

① REWIND STARTER (TYPICAL)

1. Rope
2. Sheave
3. Drive pawl
4. Starter spring
5. Lockout assembly
6. Rewind housing
7. Rope guide
8. Handle
9. Bushing
10. Drive pawl spring
11. Snap ring

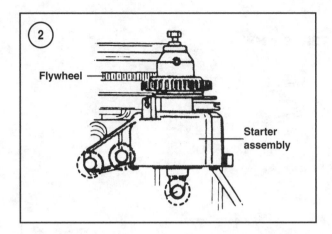

Flywheel —

Starter
assembly

1. Remove the spark plug leads and connect them to a suitable engine ground. Shift the engine into NEUTRAL gear.

2. Pull the starter rope out approximately 12 in. (30.5 cm). Tie a knot in the rope where it exits the starter housing. The knot must be large enough to prevent the rope from pulling back into the starter.

3. Carefully pry the seal (2, **Figure 4**) from the handle (1). Untie the knot and slide the plug and handle from the rope. Carefully slip the neutral start cable (1) from its slot in the neutral start lever (3, **Figure 5**).

4. Remove the three mounting bolts from the starboard side of the starter. Remove the manual starter from the engine.

Disassembly (9.9 hp Models)

1. Loosen the nut (7, **Figure 3**) and remove the bolt (6). Drive the pin (10, **Figure 3**) from the starter pinion (11) and bushing (9, **Figure 3**) using a punch and hammer. Carefully pull the starter pinion (11, **Figure 3**), friction spring (34), bushing (9) and thrust washer (33) from the sheave.

2. Hold the manual starter and the end of the rope as an assistant unties the knot. Hold firm pressure on the rope and allow the rope to slowly wind into the housing.

3. Remove the three bolts (18, **Figure 3**), then lift the cover (20) from the starter.

4. Rotate the sheave (21, **Figure 3**) three complete turns counterclockwise as viewed from the open end to disengage it from the rewind spring (23).

5. Cover the manual starter assembly with a piece of heavy cloth and carefully slide the sheave (21, **Figure 3**) from the housing (25). Unwind the rope from the sheave. Untie the knot from the rope and pull the rope from the sheave.

6. Note the direction the rewind spring (23, **Figure 3**) is wound prior to removing it from the starter housing. Insert a screwdriver into the hole (**Figure 6**) of the sheave and remove the spring from the sheave by pushing the spring. Hold the starter housing with the spring facing downward. Insert a screwdriver into the shaft of the starter housing (**Figure 7**) and push the spring out. Remove the thrust washer (24, **Figure 3**) from the starter housing.

7. Remove the cotter pin (29, **Figure 3**), washer (28), stopper arm (27) and stopper spring (26) from the starter. Remove the lock lever (22, **Figure 3**) from the open end of the starter.

8. Remove the bolt (1, **Figure 3**) and neutral start lever (4) and spring (5) from the starter.

9. Remove the bolt (12, **Figure 3**), then lift the spring washer (13), washer (14), bushing (15) and rope pulley (16, **Figure 3**) from the starter housing.

10. Clean all components, except the rope, using solvent. Inspect all components for excessive wear or damage. Inspect the rope for frayed or damaged areas.

Assembly (9.9 hp Models)

1. Use protective eyewear and gloves when installing the starter spring.

2. Apply a light coat of water-resistant grease to the spring contact areas in the starter housing. Place the thrust washer (24, **Figure 3**) into the spring opening. Align the washer with the pinion shaft opening.

3. When installing a new spring, do not remove the spring retainer until the spring is fully installed. Place the rounded spring end (23, **Figure 3**) into the notched portion of the starter. Make sure the spring spirals in the clockwise direction. Hold the spring firmly in place, then remove the retaining clip. When installing a used spring, place the rounded spring end into the notched portion of the starter.

4. Carefully wind the spring into the housing clockwise until all loops rest against the housing.

5. Slip the rope through its opening in the starter sheave. Make sure the rope passes through to the bottom side of the sheave. Tie a knot in the end of the rope. Make sure the knot is large enough to prevent the rope from slipping through the hole. Wrap the rope seven complete turns, clockwise as viewed from the bottom side, around the sheave.

6. Apply a light coat of water-resistant grease to the pinion shaft. Slide the sheave and pinion shaft into the starter housing.

7. Align the bent end of the spring with the groove on the sheave. Carefully slide the sheave into the manual starter housing.

10

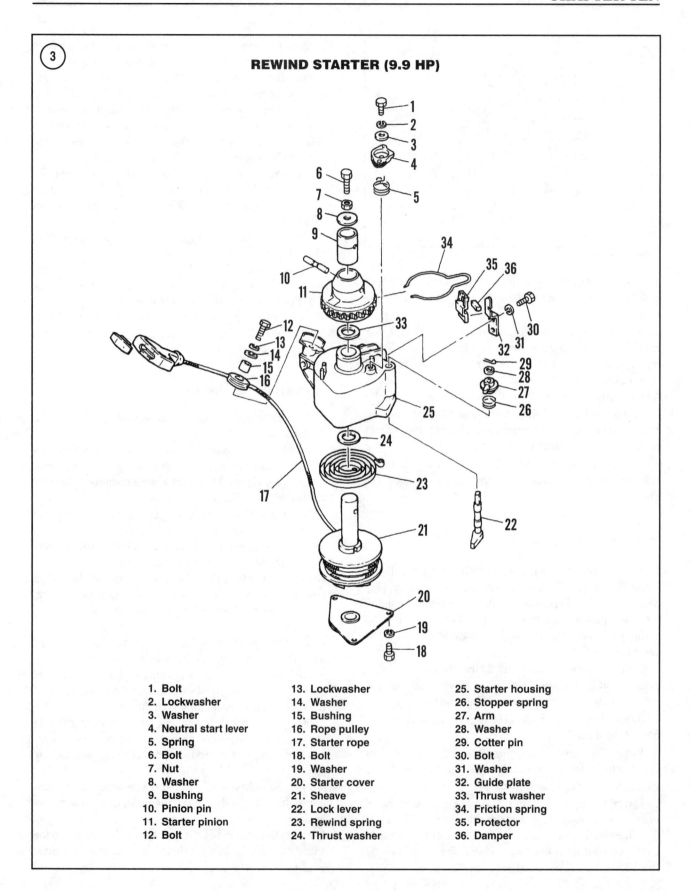

③ **REWIND STARTER (9.9 HP)**

1. Bolt	13. Lockwasher	25. Starter housing
2. Lockwasher	14. Washer	26. Stopper spring
3. Washer	15. Bushing	27. Arm
4. Neutral start lever	16. Rope pulley	28. Washer
5. Spring	17. Starter rope	29. Cotter pin
6. Bolt	18. Bolt	30. Bolt
7. Nut	19. Washer	31. Washer
8. Washer	20. Starter cover	32. Guide plate
9. Bushing	21. Sheave	33. Thrust washer
10. Pinion pin	22. Lock lever	34. Friction spring
11. Starter pinion	23. Rewind spring	35. Protector
12. Bolt	24. Thrust washer	36. Damper

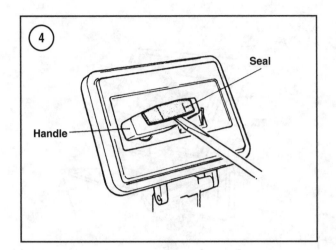

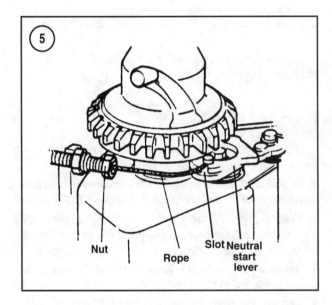

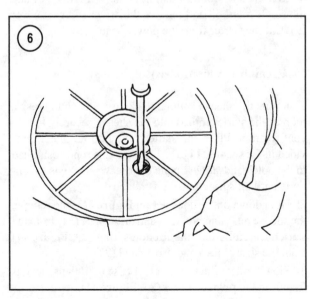

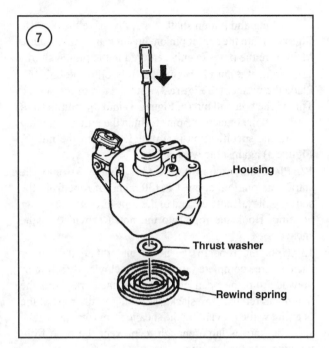

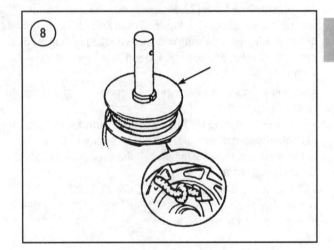

8. Rotate the sheave clockwise and check for spring tension. The presence of spring tension indicates the spring and sheave are properly engaged. Repeat Step 7 if there is no spring tension.

9. Place the free end of the rope into the notch (**Figure 8**) provided in the bottom of the sheave (**Figure 8**). Apply a light coat of water-resistant grease to the shaft bore portion of the starter pinion.

10. Slide the thrust washer (33, **Figure 3**) over the pinion shaft. Seat the washer against the starter housing. Slide the bushing (9, **Figure 3**) over the pinion shaft. Align the pinhole in the bushing with the pinhole in the pinion shaft. Slide the starter pinion (11, **Figure 3**) over the pinion shaft. Align the slot in the starter pinion with the holes in

10

the bushing and pinion shaft. Carefully drive the pin (10, **Figure 3**) into the starter pinion, bushing and pinion shaft. Make sure the pin is evenly centered in the pinion shaft.

11. Install the nut (7, **Figure 3**) fully onto the bolt (6). Place the washer (8, **Figure 3**) onto the top of the starter. Thread the bolt and nut (6, **Figure 3**) into the pinion shaft until the bolt contacts the pin. Tighten the pulley retaining bolt to the specification in **Table 1**. Tighten the nut (7, **Figure 3**) against the washer (8).

12. Place the friction spring (34, **Figure 3**) onto the starter pinion. Pull about 1 ft. (30.5 cm) of rope from the starter pulley. Route the end of the rope through the starter housing. Hook the rope into the notch provided in the sheave.

13. Hold the rope in the notch and rotate the starter sheave three complete turns in the clockwise direction as viewed from the open end. Remove the rope from the notch and remove any slack. Tie a knot in the rope at the opening while preventing the sheave from rotating. Make sure the knot is large enough to prevent the rope from winding into the housing.

14. Slip the lock lever (22, **Figure 3**) into the starter housing. Install the spring (26, **Figure 3**) and arm (27) onto the housing. Engage the spring and arm with the housing, and install the washer and cotter pin. Bend both legs of the cotter pin.

15. Install the cover (20, **Figure 3**). Securely tighten the bolts.

16. Install the spring (5, **Figure 3**) and neutral start lever (4) onto the starter housing. Attach the spring to the slots in the lever and the housing. Install the washers and bolt. Securely tighten the bolts.

17. Install the rope pulley (16, **Figure 3**), bushing (15), flat washer (14), lockwasher (13) and bolt (12) onto the housing. Securely tighten the bolt.

Installation (9.9 hp Models)

1. Position the manual starter onto the powerhead and install the mounting bolts. Tighten the bolts to the specification in **Table 1**.

2. Route the end of the rope through the rope guide and starter handle. Slip the rope through the seal (**Figure 9**) and tie a knot in the rope. Push the knot into the recessed part of the plug, then press the plug into the handle.

3. Untie the knot while an assistant pulls out slightly on the rope. Allow the rope to slowly wind into the starter. Make sure the rope passes next to the rope guide pulley (16, **Figure 3**).

4. Place the end of the neutral start cable into the hole in the neutral start lever (**Figure 5**).

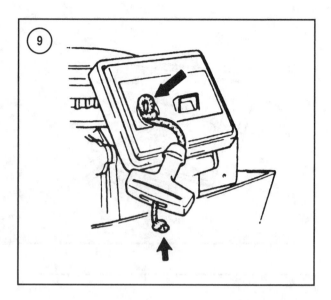

5. Adjust the neutral start cable following the instructions in Chapter Five.

Removal (15 hp Models)

The starter mounts above the flywheel (**Figure 10**). Refer to **Figure 11** during this procedure.

1. Disconnect the spark plugs leads and connect them to a suitable engine ground. Shift the engine into NEUTRAL.

2. Carefully pry the neutral start cable (1, **Figure 10**) from the starter housing. Slip the spring from its notch and lift the neutral start cable and spring from the starter.

3. Remove both screws (1, **Figure 11**) and tilt the starter panel (2, **Figure 11**) forward.

4. Remove the front mounting bolts (2, **Figure 10**) and the single rear bolt and remove the driver sprocket cover (9). Lift the starter from the power head.

Disassembly (15 hp Models)

1. Rotate the sheave counterclockwise enough to grasp a loop of the starter rope. Hold the sheave securely to prevent rotation. Place the starter rope into the notch provided in the sheave (**Figure 12**). Keep the rope positioned in the notch and *slowly* rotate the sheave clockwise. Continue until all spring tension is relieved.

2. Hold down on the sheave (26, **Figure 11**), and remove the sheave retaining bolt (30) and drive plate (31) from the starter. Carefully pull the friction spring (29, **Figure 11**) from the sheave (26) and drive pawl (27).

3. Slowly rotate the sheave clockwise until the sheave is free from the rewind spring (24, **Figure 11**).

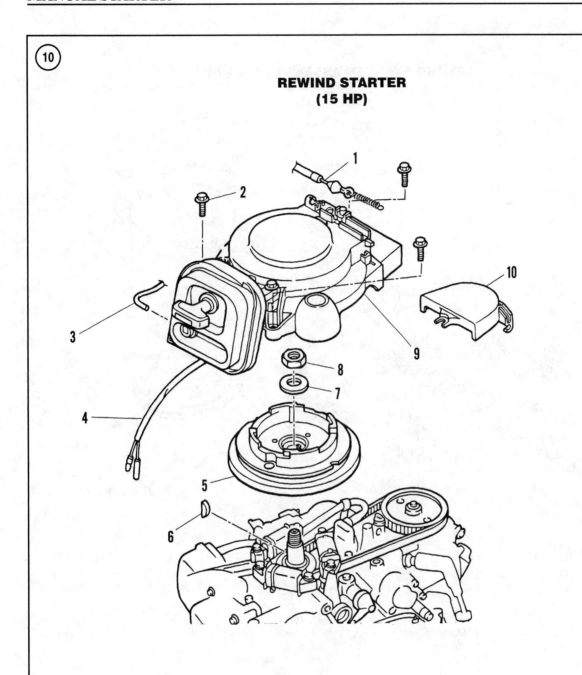

**REWIND STARTER
(15 HP)**

1. Neutral start cable
2. Bolt
3. Choke rod
4. Warning lamp leads
5. Flywheel
6. Woodruff key
7. Washer
8. Flywheel Nut
9. Rewind starter assembly
10. Driver sprocket cover

10

⑪

REWIND STARTER ASSEMBLY (15 HP)

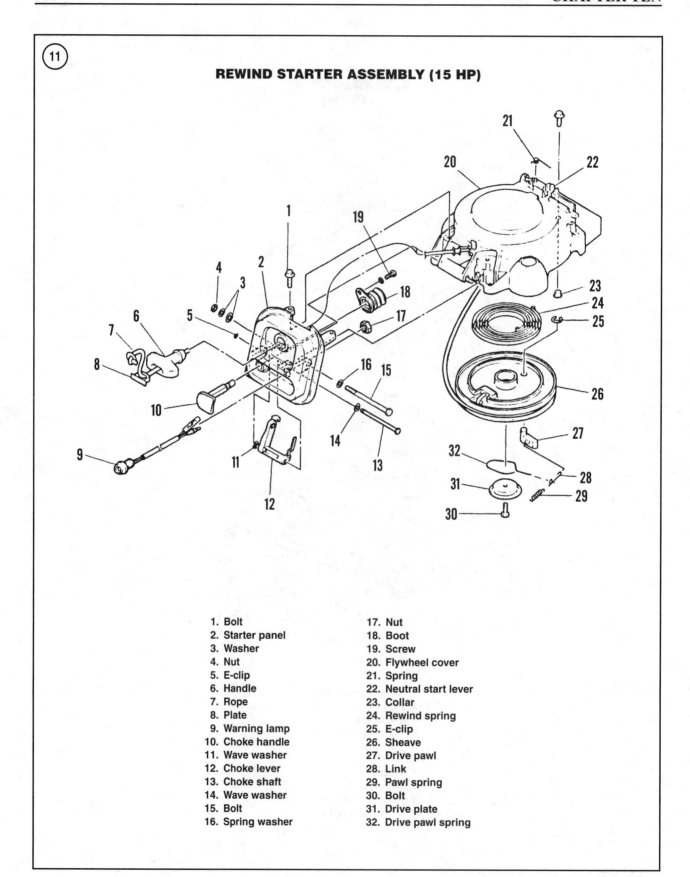

1. Bolt	17. Nut
2. Starter panel	18. Boot
3. Washer	19. Screw
4. Nut	20. Flywheel cover
5. E-clip	21. Spring
6. Handle	22. Neutral start lever
7. Rope	23. Collar
8. Plate	24. Rewind spring
9. Warning lamp	25. E-clip
10. Choke handle	26. Sheave
11. Wave washer	27. Drive pawl
12. Choke lever	28. Link
13. Choke shaft	29. Pawl spring
14. Wave washer	30. Bolt
15. Bolt	31. Drive plate
16. Spring washer	32. Drive pawl spring

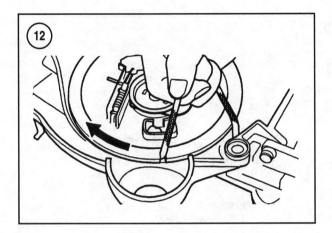

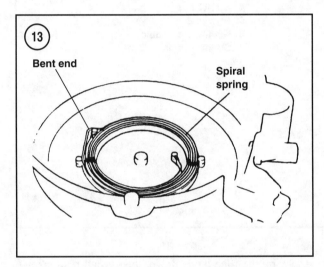

Bent end

Spiral spring

4. Use protective eye wear and gloves when removing the spring or sheave. Carefully lift up one end of the sheave and insert a screwdriver under it to prevent the spring from pulling up as the sheave is lifted. Carefully lift the sheave (26, **Figure 11**) from starter housing.

5. Note the direction in which the spring (24, **Figure 11**) is wound into the sheave (26) prior to removal. Starting at the inner hooked end, carefully remove one loop of the spring at a time. Continue until the entire spring is free from the starter housing.

6. Carefully pull the drive pawl spring (32, **Figure 11**) and link (28) from the sheave. Remove the E-clip (25, **Figure 11**) and pull the drive pawl (27) from the sheave.

7. Pry the handle plate (8, **Figure 11**) from the handle (6). Slip the knot from the handle plate (8) and pull the rope (7, **Figure 11**) from the handle and block.

8. Remove the bolt (15, **Figure 11**) and nut (4), and lift the panel (2) from the starter.

9. Note the orientation of the spring, then carefully pull it (21, **Figure 11**) from the cover (20) and neutral start lever

(22). Gently squeeze the exposed ends of the lever (22, **Figure 11**) and push the lever from its opening.

10. Clean all components, except the rope, using solvent. Inspect all components for excessive wear or damage. Inspect the rope for fraying or damage.

Assembly (15 hp models)

1. Carefully snap the hooked end of the neutral start lever (22, **Figure 11**) into the starter cover (20). Make sure the notched end of the lever faces the starboard side of the housing.

2. Install the spring (21, **Figure 11**) over its mounting boss on the rear upper side of the starter cover. Slip the short end of the spring into the small opening in the housing. Slip the longer end of the spring under the projection on the lock lever.

3. Apply a light coat of water-resistant grease to the drive pawl (27, **Figure 11**) and install it into the sheave. Snap the E-clip (25, **Figure 11**) into the groove on the upper end of the drive pawl.

4. Slip the longer end of the link (28, **Figure 11**) into the drive pawl (27). Connect one end of the spring (29, **Figure 11**) to the shorter end of the link. Place the other end of the spring through the hole in the tab.

5. Place the panel (2, **Figure 11**) into position on the starter housing. Guide the bolt (15, **Figure 11**) through the panel and its mounting bosses. Install the other washers and nut (3 and 4, **Figure 11**). Tighten the rope guide fasteners to the specification in **Table 1**.

6. Apply a small amount of water-resistant grease to the areas of the starter housing that contact the starter spring.

7. Hook the small hooked end of the spring into the slot in the starter housing near the lock lever. Wind the spring counterclockwise one loop at a time until its entire length is in the housing.

8. If a replacement rope is required, cut it to the desired length. Slide the rope through the handle plate (8, **Figure 11**) and handle (6). Tie a knot in the handle end of the rope and slide the knot into the plate. Press the handle plate into the handle.

9. Align the hooked of the spring with the groove on the sheave (**Figure 13**) and lower the sheave into the starter housing.

10. Rotate the sheave slightly counterclockwise to check for spring engagement. If there is resistance, the spring is engaged. Remove the sheave and repeat Steps 9 and 10 until spring is engaged.

11. Place the pointed end of the friction spring (32, **Figure 11**) through the small loop in the link (28). Install

10

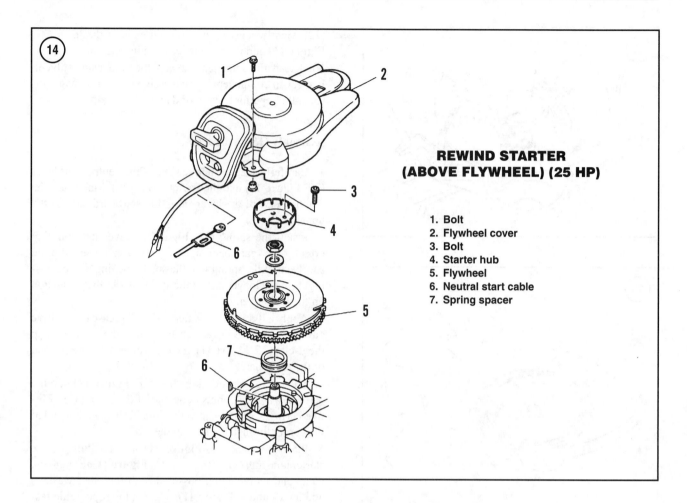

(14)

**REWIND STARTER
(ABOVE FLYWHEEL) (25 HP)**

1. Bolt
2. Flywheel cover
3. Bolt
4. Starter hub
5. Flywheel
6. Neutral start cable
7. Spring spacer

the smaller diameter side of the drive plate (31, **Figure 11**) into the friction spring and place it onto the sheave.

12. Apply Loctite 271 to the sheave retaining bolt (30, **Figure 11**) threads, then install it. Tighten the bolt to the specification in **Table 1**.

13. Rotate the sheave clockwise to align the rope opening in the sheave with the rope guide. Pass the rope through the rope guide and sheave. Tie a knot in the end of the rope.

14. Position the rope into the notch in the sheave (**Figure 12**). Hold the rope in the groove while rotating the sheave three full turns counterclockwise as viewed from the sheave side.

15. Prevent the sheave from rotating and pull the rope from the notch. Guide the rope and allow the sheave to *slowly* wind. The rope winds onto the sheave.

Installation (15 hp Model)

1. Place the manual starter onto its mounting bosses. Install the bolts (2, **Figure 10**) and tighten them to the specifications in **Table 1**.

2. Swing the rope guide down, then install both screws (1, **Figure 11**). Securely tighten the screws.

3. Hook the spring (21, **Figure 11**) into its notch in the starter housing. Pull slightly on the neutral start cable (1, **Figure 10**), then press it into the housing. Check the neutral start mechanism following the instructions in Chapter Five. Release the cable.

Removal (25 hp Models)

The manual starter mounts above the flywheel. Refer to **Figure 14** during this procedure.

1. Remove the spark plug leads and connect them to a suitable engine ground. Shift the engine into neutral gear.

2. Remove the screw from the neutral start cable. Remove the clip and lift the cable from the starter.

3. Remove the nut (12, **Figure 15**) from behind the starter rope guide (6). Unplug the wires and remove the low-oil pressure warning lamp (11, **Figure 15**).

4. Remove the four mounting bolts (1, **Figure 14**) and lift the manual starter from the power head.

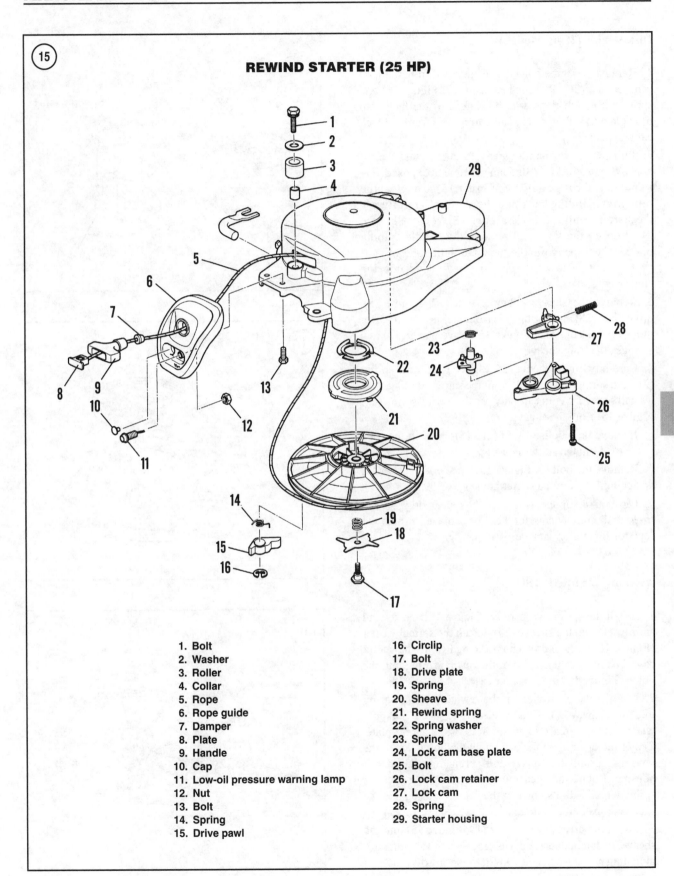

REWIND STARTER (25 HP)

15

1. Bolt
2. Washer
3. Roller
4. Collar
5. Rope
6. Rope guide
7. Damper
8. Plate
9. Handle
10. Cap
11. Low-oil pressure warning lamp
12. Nut
13. Bolt
14. Spring
15. Drive pawl
16. Circlip
17. Bolt
18. Drive plate
19. Spring
20. Sheave
21. Rewind spring
22. Spring washer
23. Spring
24. Lock cam base plate
25. Bolt
26. Lock cam retainer
27. Lock cam
28. Spring
29. Starter housing

10

Disassembly (25 hp Models)

1. Remove the three bolts (25, **Figure 15**) from the lock cam retainer (26). Pull the lock cam (27, **Figure 15**) and spring (28) from the starter housing. Lift the lock cam base plate (24, **Figure 15**) and spring (23) from the lock cam retainer.

2. Pull the starter handle away from the starter until approximately 12 in. (30.5 cm) of rope is exposed. Tie a knot near the rope guide (6, **Figure 15**) to prevent the rope from winding back into the starter. Carefully pry the starter handle plate (8, **Figure 15**) from the handle (9). Loosen the knot and remove the handle, handle plate and damper from the rope. Hold the rope and untie the knot. Allow the rope to *slowly* wind into the starter.

3. Remove the sheave retaining bolt (17, **Figure 15**), drive plate (18) and spring (19) from the sheave (20). Remove both E-clips (16, **Figure 15**), drive pawls (15) and springs (14) from sheave.

4. Carefully lift the sheave (20, **Figure 15**) rewind spring (21) and spring washer (22) from the starter housing. Use a small screwdriver to carefully pry the rewind spring (21, **Figure 15**) from the sheave.

5. Remove both bolts (13, **Figure 15**), then lift the rope guide (6) from the starter housing.

6. Remove the bolt (1, **Figure 15**), washer (2), roller (3) and collar (4) from the starter housing.

7. Clean all components, except the rope, using solvent. Inspect all components for wear or damage. Inspect the rope for fraying or damage.

Assembly (25 hp Models)

1. Install the spring washer (22, **Figure 15**) and rewind spring (21) into the sheave (20). Install the spring washer (**Figure 16**) with its projections facing toward the starter case. Position the inner end of the rewind spring into the notch (**Figure 16**) in the starter case.

2. Position the projection on the rewind spring housing into the cutaway in the starter sheave (**Figure 17**). Apply water-resistant grease to all surfaces of the spring plate. Center the opening in the plate with the bolt holes in the housing. Install the sheave and spring into the starter housing. Rotate the sheave until the raised boss on the spring aligns with its notch in the starter housing and the sheave drops into position.

3. Install the drive pawl springs (14, **Figure 15**) into the sheave. Install both drive pawls (15, **Figure 15**) onto their mounting posts. Attach the ends of the spring over the out-

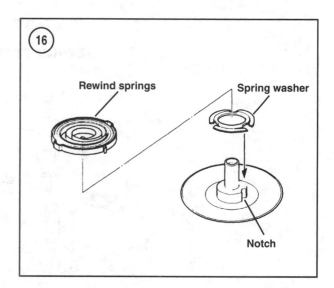

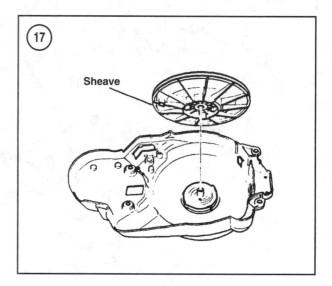

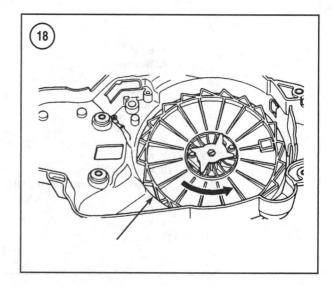

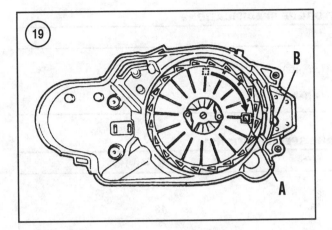

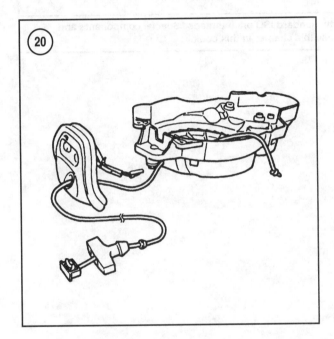

clockwise until the rope hole (A, **Figure 19**) and recoil starter roller (B) align. Hold the starter pulley in that position.

8. If a replacement rope is required, cut it to the desired specification. Route the starter rope through the opening in the rope guide and into the sheave (**Figure 20**). Tie a knot in the end of the rope. Make sure the knot is large enough to prevent it from slipping through the opening. Press the knot into its opening.

9. Grip the rope and release the sheave. Allow the rope to wind into the starter until approximately 12 in. (30.5 mm) of rope extends from the starter. Tie a knot in the rope to prevent the remaining length from winding into the starter.

10. Slip the remaining end of the rope through the rope guide (6, **Figure 15**), damper (7), starter handle (9) and handle plate (8). Place the rope in the plate as shown in **Figure 20**. Carefully press the handle plate into its opening in the handle.

11. Grip the rope and untie the knot. Allow the rope to slowly wind into the starter.

12. Install the lock cam (27, **Figure 15**) over its mounting post in the starter housing. Install the spring (28, **Figure 15**) over the rounded post on the lock lever. Press the other end of the spring into the starter housing.

13. Place the spring (23, **Figure 15**) over the pivot point of the lock cam base plate (24). Carefully slide the lever and spring into the starter housing. Make sure one end of the spring is hooked over the raised pin of the starter housing and the other end is hooked over the cam base plate. Spring installation is correct if there is spring tension as the cam lever is rotated in the clockwise as viewed from the spring side.

14. Apply a light coat of water-resistant grease to the lock lever and cam lever.

Installation (25 hp Models)

1. Position the manual starter onto it mounting bosses with the handle facing forward. Install the four mounting bolts (1, **Figure 14**) and evenly tighten them to the specification in **Table 1**.

2. Place the cable end (11, **Figure 14**) over its post on the cam lever. Install the locking pin (10, **Figure 14**) through the hole in the post to retain the cable end.

3. Retain the cable clamp (12) with its screw and washer (9 and 8, **Figure 14**). Do not tighten the screw at this time.

4. Adjust the neutral start cable following the instructions in Chapter Five.

5. Check for proper operation of the manual starter and neutral only start mechanism.

side edge of the pawls. Install both E-clips (16, **Figure 15**).

4. Place the spring (19, **Figure 15**) into the sheave. Install the drive plate (18, **Figure 15**) onto the sheave with the X mark facing outward. Align the longer ends of the drive plate tabs with the short tabs of the drive pawls.

5. Apply Loctite 271 to the sheave retaining bolt (17, **Figure 15**) threads and install it. Tighten the bolt to the specification in **Table 1**.

6. Install the rope guide (6, **Figure 15**) and secure with the screws (13). Tighten the screws to the specification in **Table 1**. Install the collar (4, **Figure 15**), roller, (3) washer (2) and bolt (1) onto the starter housing. Securely tighten the bolt.

7. Rotate the sheave (**Figure 18**) counterclockwise until the starter spring is fully wound. Turn the starter pulley

10

Table 1 REWIND STARTER TORQUE SPECIFICATIONS

Model	Torque
Shaft bolt	
9.9 and 15 hp	18 N•m (13 ft.-lb.)
Drive plate bolt	
25-100 hp	15 N•m (11 ft.-lb.)

Table 2 GENERAL TORQUE SPECIFICATIONS*

Nut	Bolt	N•m	ft. lb.
8 mm	M5	5	4
10 mm	M6	8	6
12 mm	M8	18	13
14 mm	M10	36	26
17 mm	M12	43	32

*The torque specified in this chart is for standard fasteners with standard ISO pitch threads. Special components and assemblies that require a special torque are covered in the applicable chapter in this book.

Chapter Eleven

Power Trim and Midsection

This chapter provides repair procedures for all power trim and midsection components.

Table 1 provides tilt and trim positions related to the boat transom degree of angle. **Table 2** provides trim and tilt specifications for electric only models. **Table 3** provides tightening specifications for power trim system components. **Tables 1-3** are located at the end of this chapter.

POWER TRIM SYSTEM

Power trim is a factory-installed option on all electric start 25 and 40 hp models. Power trim is standard on all 50-100 hp models.

Disassembly and assembly of the hydraulic part of the system require special service tools and practical experience in hydraulic system repair. Otherwise, have the hydraulic system repaired at a reputable marine repair facility.

Power Trim Relays
Removal and Installation

On 25 and 40-50 hp models, the electric trim motor harness plugs directly onto the mounted relays (**Figure 1**) mounted on the cylinder block.

On 80 and 100 hp models, the trim relays (**Figure 2**) are located beneath the electrical component cover on the front starboard side of the powerhead.

25-50 hp models

1. Disconnect the cables from the battery.
2. The blue wires are attached to the UP relay. The green wires are attached to the DOWN relay.
3. Push down on connector tab and pull the trim harness from the relay. Remove the mounting bolts, (3, **Figure 3**) and pull the relay from the power head.
4. Place the relay onto the power head. Install the bolts and securely tighten them.

5. Plug the trim harness onto the relay. Make sure the locking tab on the connector engages the tab on the relay. Route the wires away from moving components.

6. Connect the cables to the battery.

80 and 100 hp models

1. Disconnect both cables from the battery.

2. Trace the electric trim motor wires to their connections to the trim relays (**Figure 2**). The UP relay has blue wire (11, **Figure 2**) terminals. The DOWN relay has green wire (9, **Figure 2**) terminals.

3. Disconnect all wires from the selected relay.

4. Pull the slots in the rubber relay sleeve from the mounting arms.

5. Align the slots in the rubber relay sleeve with the mounting arms and push the relay into position.

6. Connect the wires to the relay. Make sure the larger diameter wires connect only to the larger diameter terminals on the relay. Verify all terminals are not contacting other terminals, then securely tighten the terminal nuts. Route the wires away from moving components.

7. Connect the cables to the battery.

Trim Switch Removal and Installation (Mounted in Engine Cover)

1. Disconnect the cables from the battery.

2. Disconnect the red, blue/white and green/white engine harness wires from the trim switch (3, **Figure 4**).

3. Carefully slide the retainer (2, **Figure 4**) from the groove in the switch body. Lift the switch (3, **Figure 4**) from the lower engine cover (5). Remove the rubber plugs from the unused terminals.

4. Slide the switch into the engine cover with the switch harness facing downward. Press the switch fully into the cover and insert the locking clip (2, **Figure 4**) into the switch groove.

5. Connect the red, blue/white and green/white switch wires to the engine wire harness. Insert the rubber plugs into unused terminals. Route all wires away from moving components.

6. Connect the cables to the battery.

Electric Power Trim Motor Removal and Installation

Do not attempt to replace the motor without removing the trim system. Proper alignment of the pump coupler, fasteners and sealing O-ring is easier if the trim system is

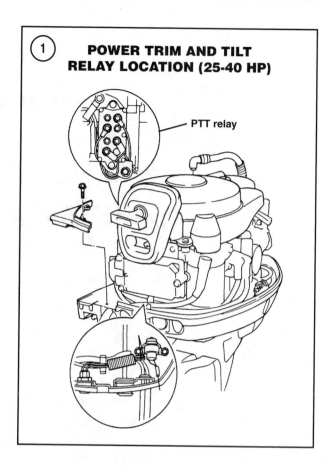

① **POWER TRIM AND TILT RELAY LOCATION (25-40 HP)**

PTT relay

removed. Improper installation can cause water leakage and damage to other trim system components.

NOTE
Always note the orientation of the electric motor and wire harness prior to removing them from the engine. Use a paint dot or piece of tape to mark the wire routing. Never scratch the electric motor or trim housing as it promotes corrosion of the surfaces.

25 hp models

Refer to **Figure 5** during this procedure.

1. Remove the trim system from the engine as described in this chapter.

2. Thoroughly clean the electric motor and the area surrounding it.

3. Remove the four mounting bolts (1, **Figure 5**), then lift the electric trim motor (2) from the trim system.

4. Pull the coupler (4, **Figure 5**) and spring (3) from the hydraulic pump or the shaft of the motor.

5. Align the slot in the coupler with the shaft and place it on the hydraulic pump. Make sure the slot size matches the shaft size.

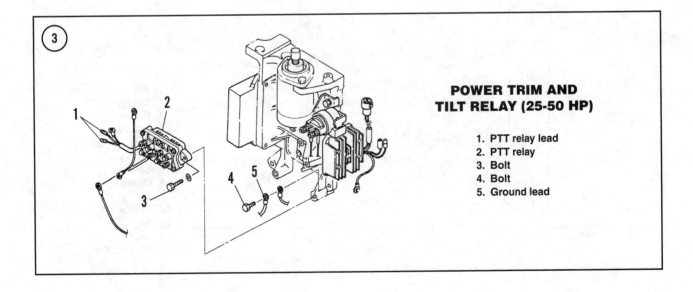

② **POWER TRIM AND TILT RELAY LOCATION (80 AND 100 HP)**

1. Junction box cover
2. Bolt
3. Negative battery lead
4. Positive battery lead
5. Nut
6. Trim meter coupler
7. Tachometer coupler
8. PTT switch coupler
9. PTT motor lead (green)
10. Nut and washer
11. PTT motor lead (blue)
12. Wire harness coupler

Relays

11

③ **POWER TRIM AND TILT RELAY (25-50 HP)**

1. PTT relay lead
2. PTT relay
3. Bolt
4. Bolt
5. Ground lead

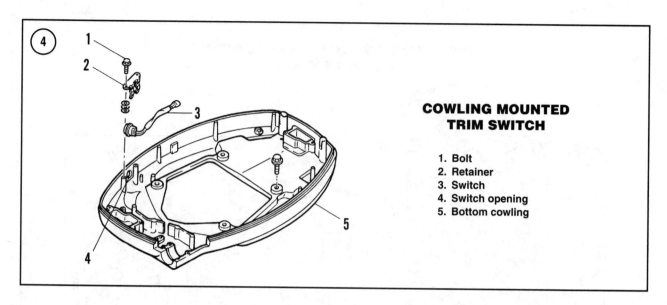

**COWLING MOUNTED
TRIM SWITCH**

1. Bolt
2. Retainer
3. Switch
4. Switch opening
5. Bottom cowling

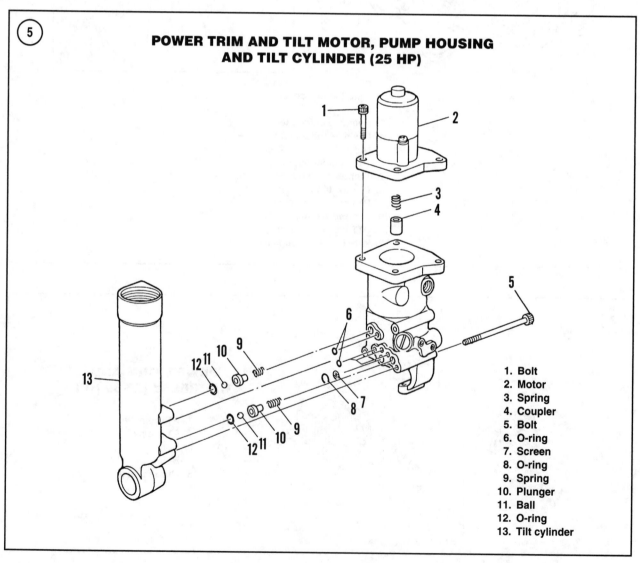

**POWER TRIM AND TILT MOTOR, PUMP HOUSING
AND TILT CYLINDER (25 HP)**

1. Bolt
2. Motor
3. Spring
4. Coupler
5. Bolt
6. O-ring
7. Screen
8. O-ring
9. Spring
10. Plunger
11. Ball
12. O-ring
13. Tilt cylinder

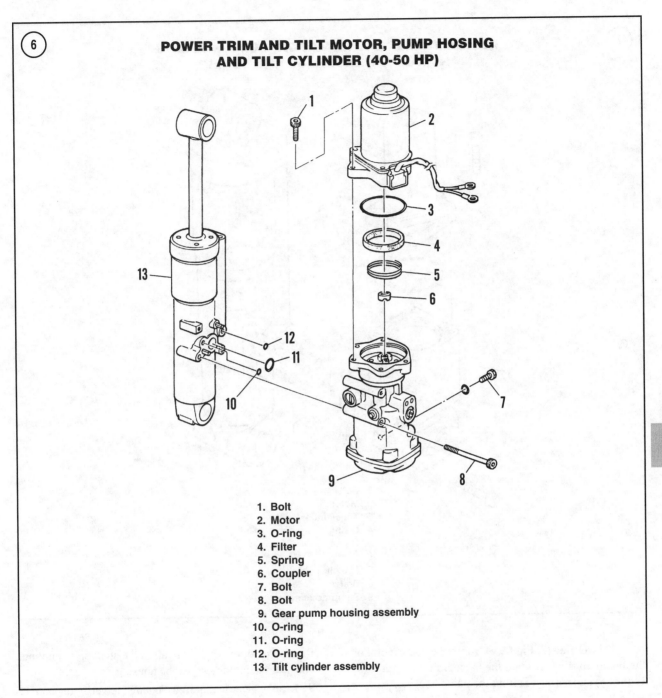

⑥

**POWER TRIM AND TILT MOTOR, PUMP HOSING
AND TILT CYLINDER (40-50 HP)**

1. Bolt
2. Motor
3. O-ring
4. Filter
5. Spring
6. Coupler
7. Bolt
8. Bolt
9. Gear pump housing assembly
10. O-ring
11. O-ring
12. O-ring
13. Tilt cylinder assembly

11

6. Install the spring (3, **Figure 5**) on the armature shaft.

7. Align the slot on the coupler with the shaft of the electric motor and lower it into position on the trim system. Rotate the motor slightly to align the shaft and coupling, then seat the motor against the housing.

8. Install the bolts and tighten them evenly to the specification in **Table 3**.

9. Install the trim system as described in this chapter.

40-50 hp models

Refer to **Figure 6** during this procedure.

1. Remove the trim system from the engine following the instructions in this chapter.

2. Thoroughly clean the electric motor and the area surrounding it.

3. Remove the three mounting bolts (1, **Figure 6**), then lift the electric trim motor (2) from the pump housing (9).

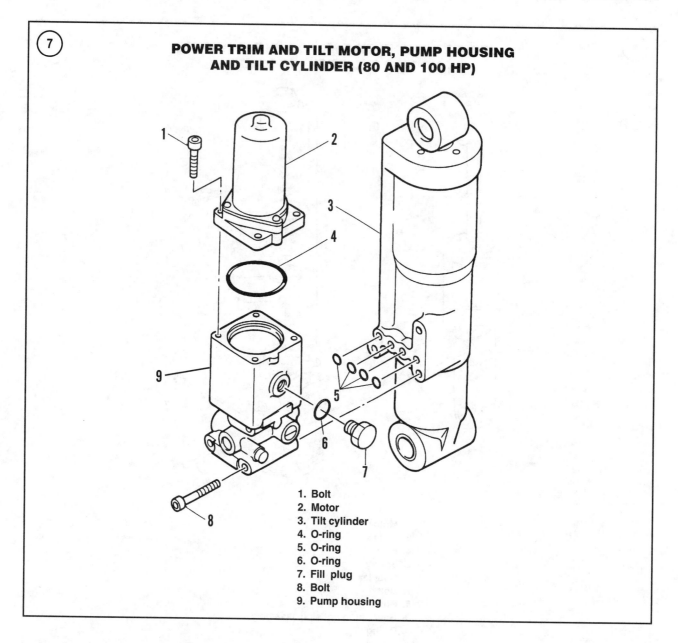

⑦   **POWER TRIM AND TILT MOTOR, PUMP HOUSING
            AND TILT CYLINDER (80 AND 100 HP)**

1. Bolt
2. Motor
3. Tilt cylinder
4. O-ring
5. O-ring
6. O-ring
7. Fill plug
8. Bolt
9. Pump housing

4. Pull the O-ring (3, **Figure 6**) from the electric motor or the pump housing. Discard the O-ring. Pull the filter (4, **Figure 6**) and spring (5) from the pump housing.

5. Pull the coupler (6, **Figure 6**) from the hydraulic pump or the shaft of the motor.

6. Align the slot in the coupler with the shaft and place it on the hydraulic pump. Make sure the slot size matches the shaft size.

7. Install a new oval shaped O-ring (3, **Figure 6**) onto the trim system. Install the spring (5, **Figure 6**) and filter (6) inside the pump hosing.

8. Align the slot on the coupler with the shaft of the electric motor and lower it into position on the trim system.

Rotate the motor slightly to align the shaft and coupling, and seat the motor against the housing.

9. Lift the electric motor just enough to verify the correct position of the O-ring (3, **Figure 6**). Install the bolts and tighten them evenly to the specification in **Table 3**.

10. Install the trim system as described in this chapter.

80 and 100 hp models

Refer to **Figure 7** during this procedure.

1. Remove the trim system from the engine following the instructions in this chapter.

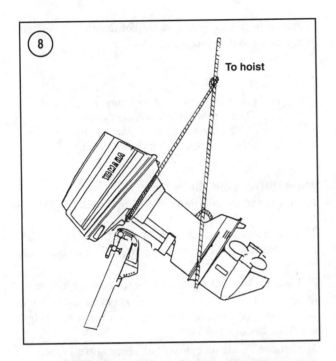

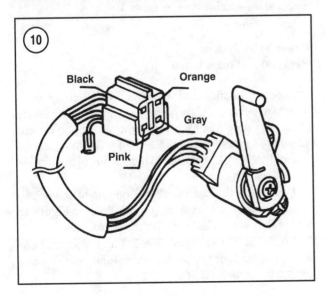

2. Thoroughly clean the electric motor and the area surrounding it.

3. Remove the fill plug (7, **Figure 7**) and O-ring (6) from the fluid reservoir. Place the trim system over a suitable container, then pour the trim fluid from the reservoir.

4. Remove the four mounting bolts (1, **Figure 7**) and remove the trim motor (2) from the pump housing (9).

5. Lift the O-ring (4, **Figure 7**) from the trim motor or pump housing. Discard the O-ring. Note the UP side, then remove the coupling from the electric trim motor shaft or hydraulic pump shaft.

6. Align the notches with the screw holes and place the new O-ring (4, **Figure 7**) onto the pump housing.

7. Place the coupler into the hydraulic pump shaft closest to the pointed end of the pump. Align the electric motor shaft with the coupling and place the motor into position on the trim system.

8. Hold the electric motor slightly away from the housing and rotate the motor enough to align the shaft with the coupler. Position the pump wires toward the starboard side of the system, then drop the motor into position.

9. Install the bolts (1, **Figure 7**). Tighten the bolts to the specification in **Table 3**. Install the O-ring and fill plug (6 and 7, **Figure 7**).

10. Install the trim system on the engine following the instructions in this chapter.

Trim Position Sender
Removal and Installation
(80 and 100 hp Models)

1. Place the engine in the full tilt position. Engage the tilt lock mechanism and support the engine with an overhead hoist (**Figure 8**). Disconnect the cables from the battery.

2. Locate the trim position sender (**Figure 9**) on the upper port clamp bracket. The sensor appearance and wire connections vary by model. The removal and installation procedure is similar. Make a sketch of the sender wire routing and connections prior to removal.

3. Disconnect the sender wires (**Figure 10**) from the harness in the engine cover.

4. Disconnect the black ground wire.

5. Remove the mounting screws and pull the mounting strap from the swivel bracket. Remove the sensor from the swivel bracket. Clean the sensor mounting surface.

6. Align the protrusion on the sensor with the slot and install the sensor into the opening.

7. Slide the sleeve over the terminal or coat the terminals with liquid neoprene after connecting the terminals. Route all wires so they will not become pinched or stretched as the engine tilts or turns. Retain the wires with

11

plastic clamps as required. Install the retaining strap and screws. Securely tighten the screws.

8. Connect the cables to the battery. Disengage the tilt lock mechanism, then remove the overhead support.

9. Adjust the sensor following the instructions in Chapter Five.

Manual Relief Valve
Removal and Installation

Refer to **Figures 11-13** as necessary during this procedure.

After removal, inspect all O-rings for wear or damage. Note the sizes and locations of all O-rings prior to removing them from the valve. Improper trim system operation is likely if an O-ring is installed in the wrong location.

Removal of the manual relief valve is simple if the slotted end of the valve is intact. If it is not, the valve can usually be removed by other means. Never drill the valve out or the machined surface for the O-rings will usually be damaged.

Inspect the O-rings on the valve even if they are discarded. Problems may surface if large portions are missing or torn away from the O-rings. They usually migrate to a pressure relief valve or other component in the trim system. Remove and install the manual relief valve as follows:

1. Position the engine in the full tilt position. Engage the tilt lock lever, then support the engine with an overhead cable (**Figure 8**) or wooden blocks.

2. Place a container under the manual valve of the trim system to capture any spilled fluid.

3. Use needlenose pliers to pull the circlip (12, **Figure 11**) from the valve (11). Rotate the valve counterclockwise until it can be pulled from the housing.

4. Use a light and a pick, small screwdriver or tweezers to remove any remnants of the valve or O-ring from the opening. Avoid damaging any of the machined surfaces in the opening.

5. Lubricate the manual relief valve with Dexron II automatic transmission fluid, then carefully slide the new O-rings, if removed, onto the valve. Lubricate the O-rings with Dexron II automatic transmission fluid and install the valve into the housing. Do not tighten the valve at this time.

6. Rotate the valve clockwise until slight resistance is felt. Rotate the valve 1/4 turn in the closed direction, then 1/8 turn in the open direction. Repeat this process until the manual relief valve is fully seated.

7. Use needlenose pliers to install the circlip (12, **Figure 11**) into the groove in the valve (11). Refer to *Filling and*

Bleeding in this chapter and correct the fluid level and purge air from the system.

> *WARNING*
> *Some manual tilt system components are charged with very high-pressure nitrogen gas. Do not disassemble any part of the system. If the system is faulty, replace it or have it repaired at a local Yamaha dealership.*

Manual Hydraulic Tilt System
Removal and Installation (25-50 hp Models)

1. Disconnect the cables from the battery. Remove the spark plug leads, then connect them to a suitable engine ground.

2. Place the tilt control lever in the tilt position and raise the engine to the full tilt position. Engage the tilt lock lever and support the engine with an overhead cable (**Figure 8**) or wooden blocks.

3. Remove the clamp bracket bolts (6, **Figure 14**).

4. Pivot the bracket spacer (3, **Figure 14**) out of the clamp brackets and carefully drive the lower pin (4, **Figure 14**) from the assembly. Avoid damaging the pivot surfaces or bushings (5, **Figure 14**).

5. Remove the circlip and upper pivot pin from the swivel bracket. Carefully drive the upper pivot pin from the tilt cylinder. Remove the tilt system from the engine. Use an extension, long dowel or section of tubing for a driver.

6. Inspect the circlip for corrosion or weak spring tension, and replace it if its condition is questionable. Inspect all bushings and pins for damage or wear, and replace them as required.

7. Installation is the reverse of removal. Tighten all fasteners to the specification in **Table 3**.

Power Trim System
Removal and Installation

Mark the location and orientation of all components prior to removal to ensure proper assembly. Make a sketch of the trim wire routing before removal. Apply Yamaha all-purpose grease to all bushing and pivot points during assembly. Apply Loctite 242 to the threads of the trim/tilt system fasteners.

1. Disconnect the battery cables from the battery terminals. Disconnect the spark plug leads. Refer to **Figure 15** during the removal and installation procedure.

2. Rotate the manual relief valve 3-4 turns counterclockwise. Tilt the unit to the full tilt position and securely tighten the manual relief valve.

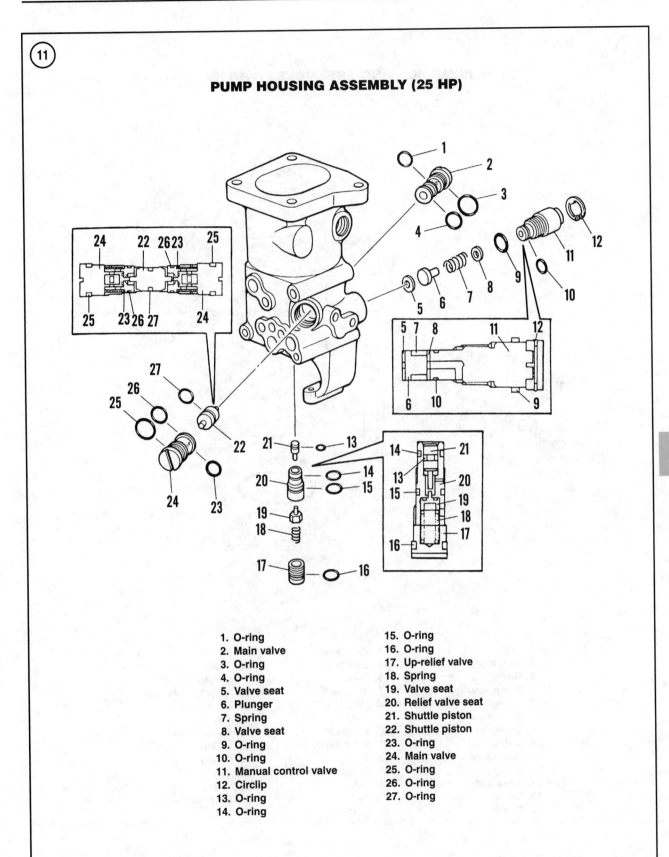

PUMP HOUSING ASSEMBLY (25 HP)

1. O-ring
2. Main valve
3. O-ring
4. O-ring
5. Valve seat
6. Plunger
7. Spring
8. Valve seat
9. O-ring
10. O-ring
11. Manual control valve
12. Circlip
13. O-ring
14. O-ring
15. O-ring
16. O-ring
17. Up-relief valve
18. Spring
19. Valve seat
20. Relief valve seat
21. Shuttle piston
22. Shuttle piston
23. O-ring
24. Main valve
25. O-ring
26. O-ring
27. O-ring

11

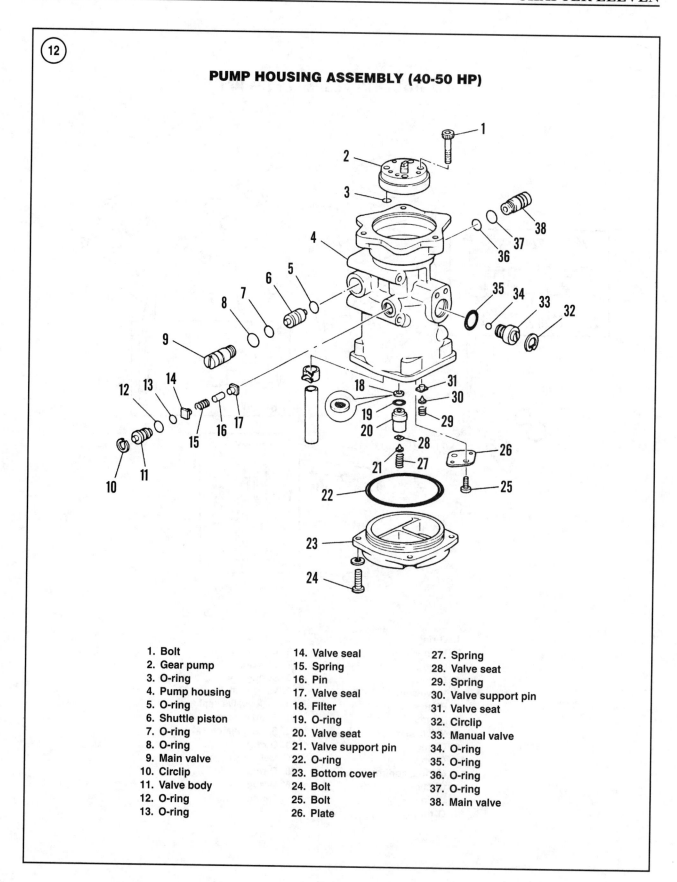

PUMP HOUSING ASSEMBLY (40-50 HP)

1. Bolt
2. Gear pump
3. O-ring
4. Pump housing
5. O-ring
6. Shuttle piston
7. O-ring
8. O-ring
9. Main valve
10. Circlip
11. Valve body
12. O-ring
13. O-ring
14. Valve seal
15. Spring
16. Pin
17. Valve seal
18. Filter
19. O-ring
20. Valve seat
21. Valve support pin
22. O-ring
23. Bottom cover
24. Bolt
25. Bolt
26. Plate
27. Spring
28. Valve seat
29. Spring
30. Valve support pin
31. Valve seat
32. Circlip
33. Manual valve
34. O-ring
35. O-ring
36. O-ring
37. O-ring
38. Main valve

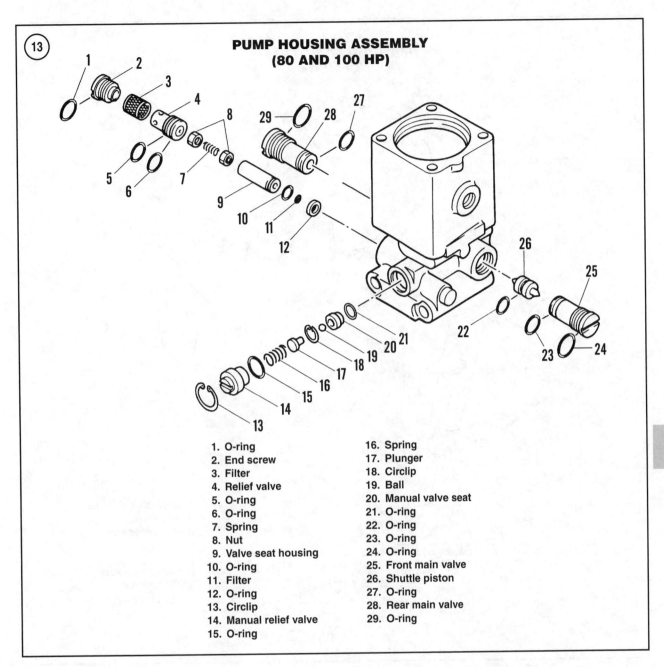

PUMP HOUSING ASSEMBLY (80 AND 100 HP)

1. O-ring
2. End screw
3. Filter
4. Relief valve
5. O-ring
6. O-ring
7. Spring
8. Nut
9. Valve seat housing
10. O-ring
11. Filter
12. O-ring
13. Circlip
14. Manual relief valve
15. O-ring
16. Spring
17. Plunger
18. Circlip
19. Ball
20. Manual valve seat
21. O-ring
22. O-ring
23. O-ring
24. O-ring
25. Front main valve
26. Shuttle piston
27. O-ring
28. Rear main valve
29. O-ring

11

3. Use an overhead hoist or wooden blocks to support the engine as shown in **Figure 8**.

4. Disconnect the wires from the trim system. Route the wires out the cover to allow for removal of the trim/tilt system.

5. Remove the bolt (3 and 5, **Figure 15**) and ground wires (4 and 6, **Figure 15**) from the clamp brackets.

6. Remove the nuts (8 and 13, **Figure 15**), washers and stud bolt (9 and 10, **Figure 15**). Pivot the bracket spacer out of the clamp brackets.

7. Pull the bracket spacer from the trim/tilt system and remove the bushings (12, **Figure 15**).

8. Remove the circlip (14, **Figure 15**). Support the trim/tilt system and carefully drive the pivot pin (15, **Figure 15**) from the swivel housing.

9. Inspect the circlip for corrosion and weak spring tension. Replace it if its condition is questionable. Inspect all bushings and pins for damage or wear. Replace them if required.

10. Lower the trim/tilt system, and remove the bushing and bushing sleeve from the cylinder.

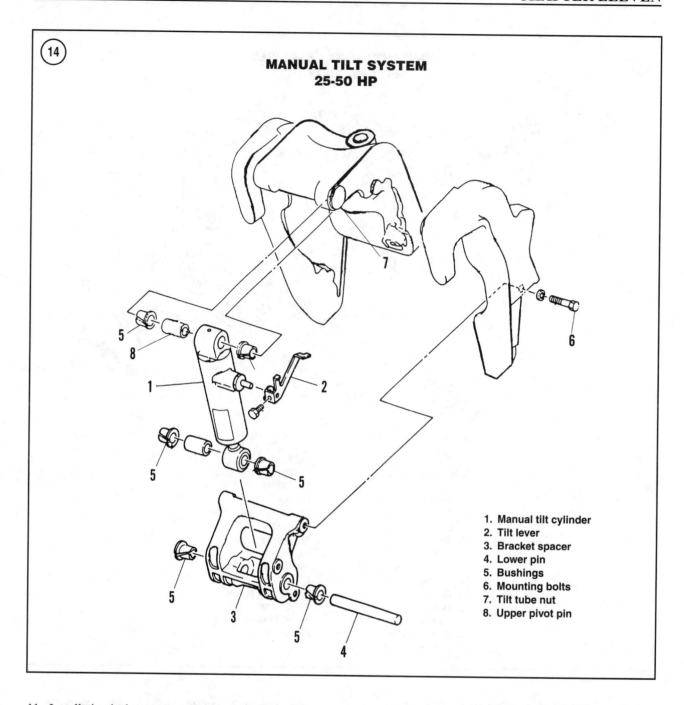

(14)

**MANUAL TILT SYSTEM
25-50 HP**

1. Manual tilt cylinder
2. Tilt lever
3. Bracket spacer
4. Lower pin
5. Bushings
6. Mounting bolts
7. Tilt tube nut
8. Upper pivot pin

11. Installation is the reverse of removal. Tighten all fasteners to the specification in **Table 3**. Route all trim wires carefully to avoid interference with other components. Check for proper operation on completion.

> *WARNING*
> *The trim/tilt system creates very high pressure. Always wear eye protection and gloves when servicing the system. Never disconnect any hydraulic lines or remove any fittings without relieving the pressure in the*

system. Tilt the engine to the full tilt position and provide adequate support. Open the manual relief valve 2-3 complete turns to relieve the pressure.

**Trim System Disassembly,
Inspection and Assembly**

Problems with trim systems are almost always the result of debris in the system or damaged O-rings. Replace all

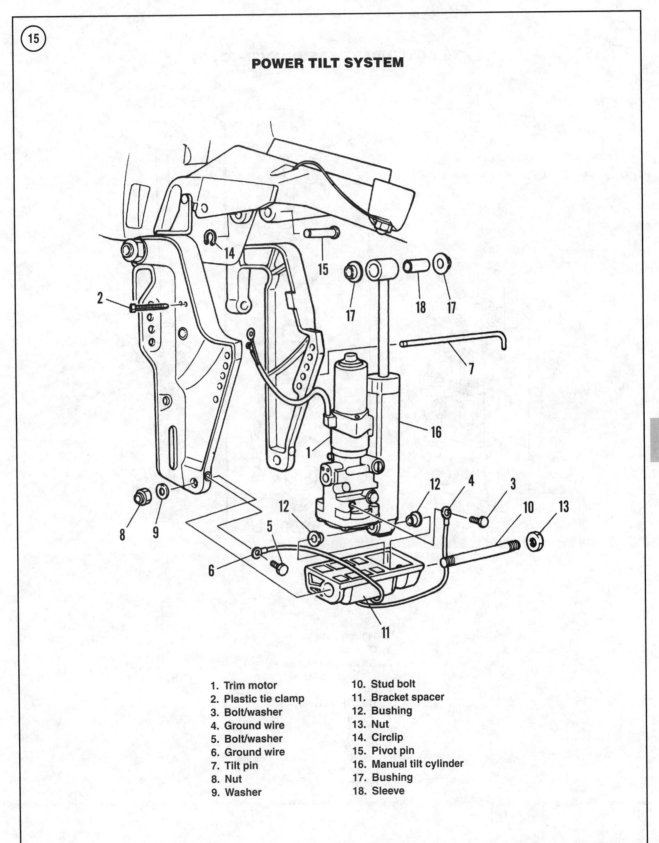

POWER TILT SYSTEM

1. Trim motor
2. Plastic tie clamp
3. Bolt/washer
4. Ground wire
5. Bolt/washer
6. Ground wire
7. Tilt pin
8. Nut
9. Washer
10. Stud bolt
11. Bracket spacer
12. Bushing
13. Nut
14. Circlip
15. Pivot pin
16. Manual tilt cylinder
17. Bushing
18. Sleeve

11

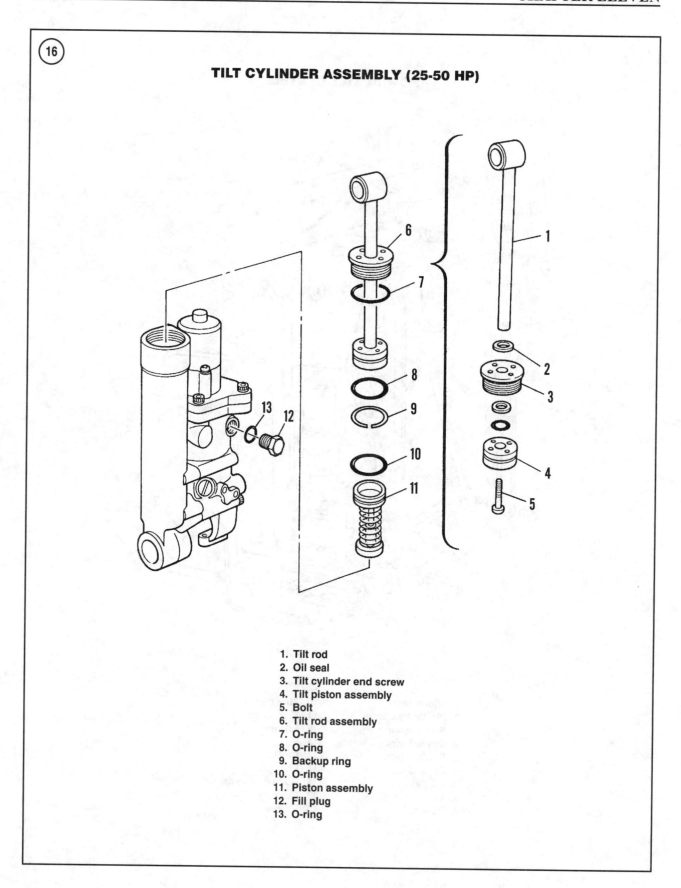

TILT CYLINDER ASSEMBLY (25-50 HP)

1. Tilt rod
2. Oil seal
3. Tilt cylinder end screw
4. Tilt piston assembly
5. Bolt
6. Tilt rod assembly
7. O-ring
8. O-ring
9. Backup ring
10. O-ring
11. Piston assembly
12. Fill plug
13. O-ring

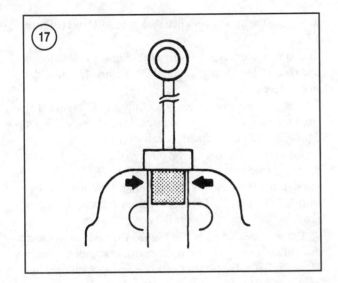

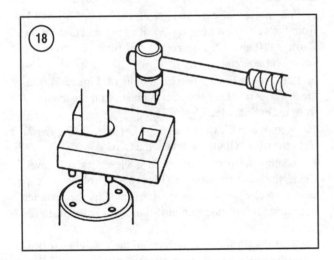

Note the orientation of all springs, plugs, seats and valves as they are removed. Make sure all valves and springs are installed in the original locations during assembly. Refer to **Figures 5-14** for component orientation.

Work in a clean environment and use lint free shop towels when cleaning trim system components. Trim systems must operate with very clean fluid. A minute particle can cause the system to malfunction.

WARNING
Use extreme caution if using air pressure to remove any trim system components. These components can exit the system at extremely high velocity. Use protective clothing and eye protection. Use the lowest possible pressure (10 psi [69 kPa] maximum).

25-50 hp models

WARNING
The trim system contains fluid under high pressure. Always use protective eyewear and gloves when working with the trim system. Never remove any components or plugs without first bleeding the pressure from of the system. Follow the instructions carefully and loosen the manual relief valve to relieve the internal pressure.

A suitable spanner wrench and heat lamp is required to completely disassemble the trim system. Refer to **Figures 5-6** and **11-12**.

1. Remove the trim system, then remove the electric trim motor following the instructions in this chapter.

2. Remove the fill plug (12, **Figure 16**) and pour all trim fluid from the reservoir.

3. Clamp the trim system in a vice with soft jaws (**Figure 17**).

4. Use a spanner wrench to remove the trim cylinder cap (**Figure 18**). Turn the cap counterclockwise to remove the cap from the cylinder. Tap the spanner wrench with a plastic mallet if necessary to loosen the cap.

5. Slowly pull the tilt rod (1, **Figure 16**) from the trim system. Remove the O-ring (7, **Figure 16**), piston assembly (11), O-rings (10 and 8) and backup ring (9) from the cylinder.

6. Clamp the pivot pin end of the tilt rod in a vice with soft jaws. Loosen the tilt piston bolt (5, **Figure 16**). Remove the tilt piston (4, **Figure 16**) tilt cylinder end screw (3) and oil seal (2) from the tilt rod.

7. Locate the main valve (2 and 24, **Figure 11**) on both sides of the pump housing. Using a screwdriver, remove

O-rings and seals when the internal components are removed. Purchase the O-ring and seal kit for the trim system before disassembling the trim system. This reduces the chance of contaminants entering the system while waiting on parts.

Seal and O-ring kits contain numerous sizes and shapes of O-rings. Some of the O-rings have the same diameter, but different thickness. To help ensure correct O-ring placement, remove one O-ring at a time. Find the replacement O-ring of the exact diameter and opening size as the one removed. Install the new O-ring or make notes indicating its exact mounting location.

Scratched or pitted hydraulic cylinder or valve seats cause internal leakage or other hydraulic problems. Very fine scratches occur from system operation and rarely cause hydraulic problems. Replace any components that have scratches deep enough to feel with a fingernail or deep pitting on seating surfaces.

11

both valves by turning them counterclockwise. Remove and discard all three O-rings.

8. Look into the valve opening to locate the shuttle piston (22, **Figure 11**), and remove and discard the O-ring (27). Remove the manual relief valve. See *Manual Relief Valve Removal* in this section.

9. Remove the up relief valve plug (17, **Figure 11**) from the lower side of the manifold. Remove and discard the O-ring (16, **Figure 11**) and pull the spring (18) from the relief valve (17).

10. Remove the valve seat (19, **Figure 11**) and shuttle piston (21) from the relief valve seat (20). Remove and discard the O-rings (13-15, **Figure 11**).

11. Inspect the main valves for wear or damage.

12. Clean all components using clean solvent. Dry the components with compressed air. Direct air through all passages and openings to remove all traces of solvent or debris.

13. Assembly is the reverse of disassembly noting the following:

    a. Replace all O-rings one at a time with the correct one from the repair kit. Lubricate them with Dexron II ATF before installing them.

    b. Lubricate all components with Dexron II ATF during assembly.

    c. Apply Loctite 271 to the threaded portion of the hydraulic ram or the shock piston bolt prior to installing the shock piston.

    d. Fill the hydraulic cylinder 3/4 full of Dexron II ATF prior to installing the hydraulic ram into the cylinder.

    e. Tighten all plugs and fasteners to the specifications in **Table 3**.

14. Install the electric trim motor and pump housing following the instructions in this chapter.

80 and 100 hp models

> **WARNING**
> *The trim systems contain fluid under high pressure. Always use protective eyewear and gloves when working with the trim system. Never remove any components or plugs without first bleeding the pressure off of the system. Follow the instructions carefully and loosen the manual relief valve to relieve the internal pressure.*

1. Remove the trim system and remove the electric trim motor following the instructions in this chapter.

2. Remove the fill plug (7, **Figure 7**). Pour all trim fluid from the reservoir (**Figure 7**).

3. Clamp the trim system in a vice with soft jaws (**Figure 17**).

4. Remove the rear main valve (28, **Figure 13**). Remove and discard the O-rings (27 and 29, **Figure 13**) from the main valve (28).

5. Remove the front main valve plug (25, **Figure 13**) from the pump. Remove and discard the O-rings (23 and 24, **Figure 13**) from the main valve (25).

6. Insert a small probe or rod through the main valve seat opening, then push the shuttle piston (26, **Figure 13**) through the front main valve opening. Remove and discard the O-ring (22, **Figure 13**) from the shuttle piston (26)

7. Remove the end screw (2, **Figure 13**), and remove and discard the O-ring (1) from the end screw. Pull the filter (3) and relief valve (4, **Figure 13**) from the opening. Discard the O-rings (5 and 6) from the relief valve.

8. Pull the valve seats and spring (8 and 7, **Figure 13**) from the valve seat housing (9). Remove and discard the O-rings (10 and 12, **Figure 13**) and filter (11) from the valve seat housing.

9. Remove the three Allen head bolts (8, **Figure 7**) from the lower port side of the trim cylinder. Pull the manifold from the cylinder (3, **Figure 7**).

10. Remove and discard all four O-rings (5, **Figure 7**) from the trim cylinder. Replace the O-rings.

11. Clamp the trim cylinder in a vice with soft jaws. Using the spanner wrench (**Figure 18**), rotate the cap counterclockwise to remove the cap. Tap the spanner wrench with a plastic mallet if the cap is difficult to remove.

12. Pull the tilt rod assembly from the tilt cylinder. Remove the circlip (11, **Figure 19**) from the inner cylinder.

13. Remove the washer (10, **Figure 19**) and two springs (9) from the stopper plate (8). Remove the six balls (2, **Figure 19**) from the inner cylinder, then remove the circlip (7), free piston (4, **Figure 19**) and O-ring (3). Discard all O-rings.

14. Remove the circlip (6, **Figure 19**) and pull the relief valve seal (5) from the free piston.

15. Clean all components using clean solvent. Dry the components with compressed air. Direct air through all passages and openings to remove all traces of solvent or debris.

16. Assembly is the reverse of disassembly noting the following:

    a. Replace all O-rings one at a time with the correct one from the repair kit. Lubricate them with Dexron II ATF before installing them.

    b. Lubricate all components with Dexron II ATF during assembly.

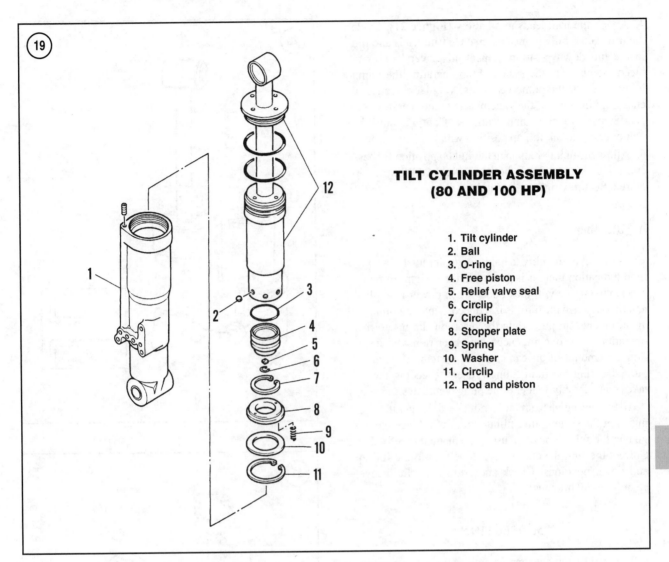

**TILT CYLINDER ASSEMBLY
(80 AND 100 HP)**

1. Tilt cylinder
2. Ball
3. O-ring
4. Free piston
5. Relief valve seal
6. Circlip
7. Circlip
8. Stopper plate
9. Spring
10. Washer
11. Circlip
12. Rod and piston

c. Apply Loctite 271 to the threads of the hydraulic ram prior to installing the shock piston.

d. Fill the hydraulic cylinder 3/4 full of Dexron II ATF prior to installing the hydraulic ram into the cylinder part of the system.

e. Tighten all plugs and fasteners to the specifications in **Table 3**.

17. Install the electric trim motor and trim system following the instructions in this chapter.

FLUID FILLING
AND AIR BLEEDING

Refer to *Fluid Filling* if the system has lost a large amount of fluid or after a major component, such as hydraulic pump or cylinder, has been removed.

Refer to *Air Bleeding* if the trim or tilt system exhibits symptoms of air in the fluid.

Fluid Filling

Refer to **Figure 20** or **Figure 21**. Use Dexron II automatic transmission fluid in both types of trim systems.

1. Open the manual relief valve and position the engine in the full UP position. Engage the tilt lock lever and support the engine with wooden blocks or an overhead cable. Close the manual relief valve.

2. Clean the area around the fill plug. Remove the plug and inspect the O-ring on the plug. Replace the O-ring if it is damaged or flattened.

3. Fill the unit to the lower edge of the fill plug opening (**Figure 20**). Install the fill plug and tighten it securely. Remove the supports and disengage the tilt lock lever.

4. Attach the trim leads to a battery (**Figure 21**). Cycle the trim to the full up, then reverse the trim leads and run to the full down position. Repeat this several times to bleed the air from the system. Stop operating the pump immediately if the pump ventilates. Ventilation causes a change in the tone of the system as the unit operates. Repeat Steps 1-4 if the pump ventilates. Continue until the unit operates to the full up position without ventilation.

5. Allow the unit to remain in the full up position for several minutes, then check the fluid level. Add fluid if required. Securely tighten the fluid fill plug.

Air Bleeding

A soft feel or inability to hold trim under load is a common indication that air is present in the system. In many cases, the engine will tuck under when power is applied and tilt out when the throttle is reduced. Minor amounts of air in the system purge into the reservoir during normal operation. If major components have been removed, a significant amount of air can enter the system. Most air is purged during the fluid filling process. Bleeding the air takes considerably longer if the pump ventilates.

Allow the engine to sit for 30 minutes or longer if air remains in the system after filling with fluid. Place the engine in the full tilt position using the manual relief valve. Correct the fluid level, then cycle the trim to the full up and down positions. Check and correct the fluid level again after 30 minutes.

MIDSECTION

Removal or replacement of major midsection components requires power head and gearcase removal. Power head removal and installation procedures are in Chapter Eight. Gearcase removal and installation is in Chapter Nine.

Clamp Bracket Components
Removal and Installation

Provide overhead support (**Figure 8**) before removing any midsection component. Apply Yamaha all-purpose grease to all pivot points, bushings and sliding surfaces, except the steering friction components, during assembly. Note the mounting locations and orientation of all components prior to removing them from the midsection. Refer to **Figures 22-26**.

1. Position the engine in the full tilt position. Support the engine with an overhead cable (**Figure 8**) or wooden

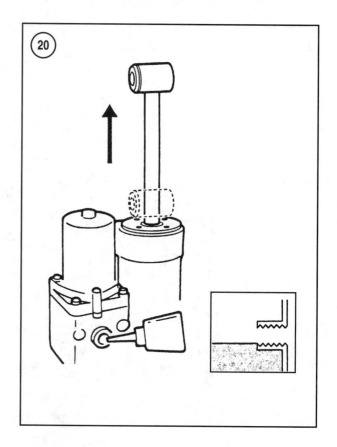

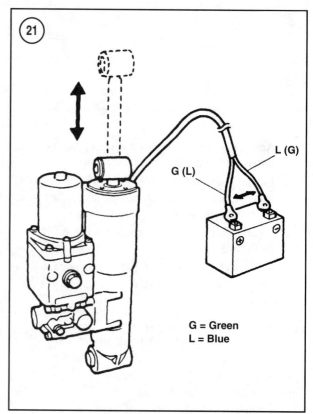

CLAMP BRACKET (9.9 AND 15 HP)

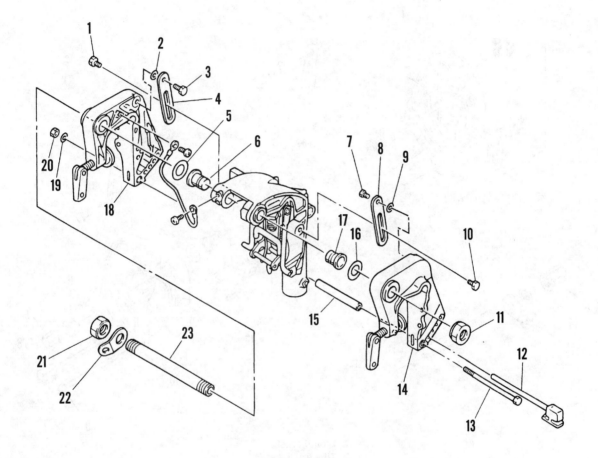

11

1. Bolt	13. Bolt
2. Washer	14. Clamp bracket
3. Bolt	15. Collar
4. Tilt stop lever	16. Washer
5. Washer	17. Bushing
6. Bushing	18. Clamp bracket
7. Screw	19. Washer
8. Tilt stop lever	20. Nut
9. Washer	21. Nut
10. Bolt	22. Clamp bracket plate
11. Nut	23. Through tube
12. Tilt pin	

(23)

CLAMP BRACKET (25 HP)

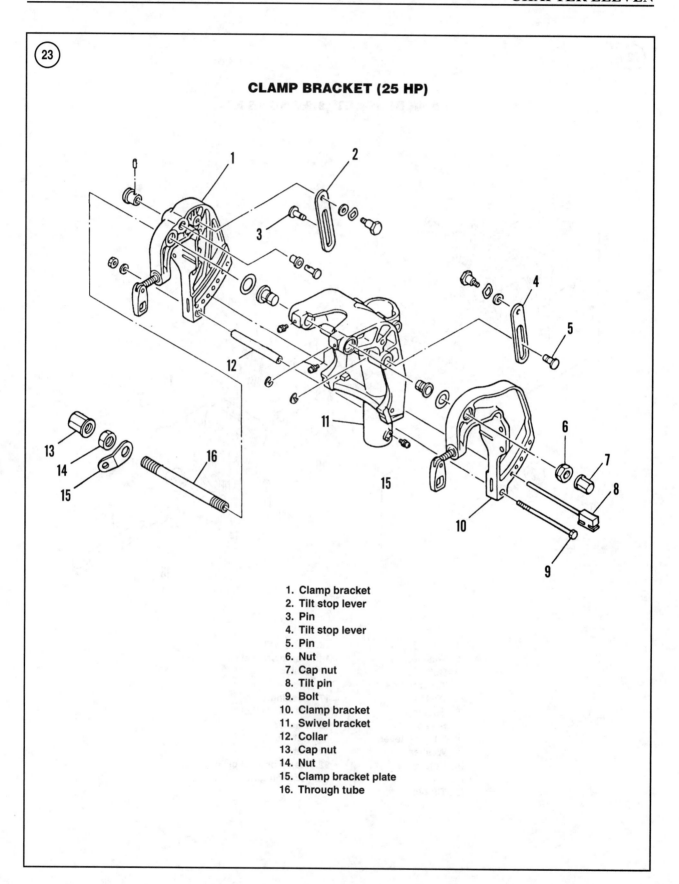

1. Clamp bracket
2. Tilt stop lever
3. Pin
4. Tilt stop lever
5. Pin
6. Nut
7. Cap nut
8. Tilt pin
9. Bolt
10. Clamp bracket
11. Swivel bracket
12. Collar
13. Cap nut
14. Nut
15. Clamp bracket plate
16. Through tube

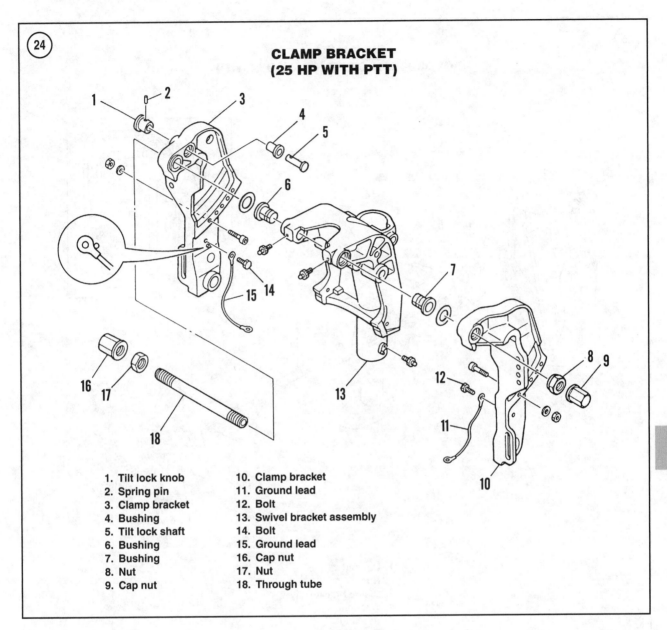

**CLAMP BRACKET
(25 HP WITH PTT)**

1. Tilt lock knob
2. Spring pin
3. Clamp bracket
4. Bushing
5. Tilt lock shaft
6. Bushing
7. Bushing
8. Nut
9. Cap nut
10. Clamp bracket
11. Ground lead
12. Bolt
13. Swivel bracket assembly
14. Bolt
15. Ground lead
16. Cap nut
17. Nut
18. Through tube

blocks to prevent the engine from falling as components are removed.

2. Disconnect the cables from the battery, if so equipped. Remove the spark plug(s), then connect the spark plug lead(s) to a suitable engine ground.

3. Refer to **Figures 22-26** to locate the worn or damaged component(s). Identify which component(s) must be removed to access the required component(s). Remove the trim or manual hydraulic tilt system following the instructions in this chapter prior to removing the clamp bracket or other major components.

4. Note the mounting locations and orientation for all fasteners and components prior to removing them. Disas-

semble the midsection until the required components are removed.

5. Clean all corrosion or contaminants from the components. Inspect them for wear or damage. Replace damaged or excessively worn components. Free play or looseness at a pivot point usually indicates excessive wear.

6. Apply marine sealant to the engine mounting bolts, washers and transom holes prior to installing them.

7. Tighten all fasteners to the specifications in **Table 3**. Install the trim system or manual hydraulic tilt system following the instructions in this chapter.

8. Remove the overhead support (**Figure 8**) and lower the engine. Check for proper operation of the tilt lock, manual

㉕

CLAMP BRACKET (40 AND 50 HP)

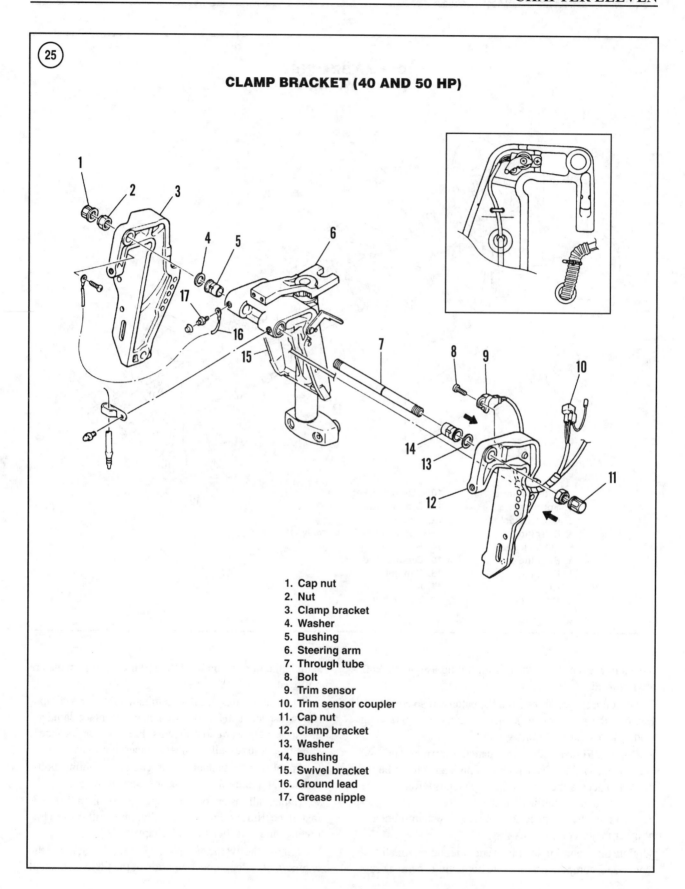

1. Cap nut
2. Nut
3. Clamp bracket
4. Washer
5. Bushing
6. Steering arm
7. Through tube
8. Bolt
9. Trim sensor
10. Trim sensor coupler
11. Cap nut
12. Clamp bracket
13. Washer
14. Bushing
15. Swivel bracket
16. Ground lead
17. Grease nipple

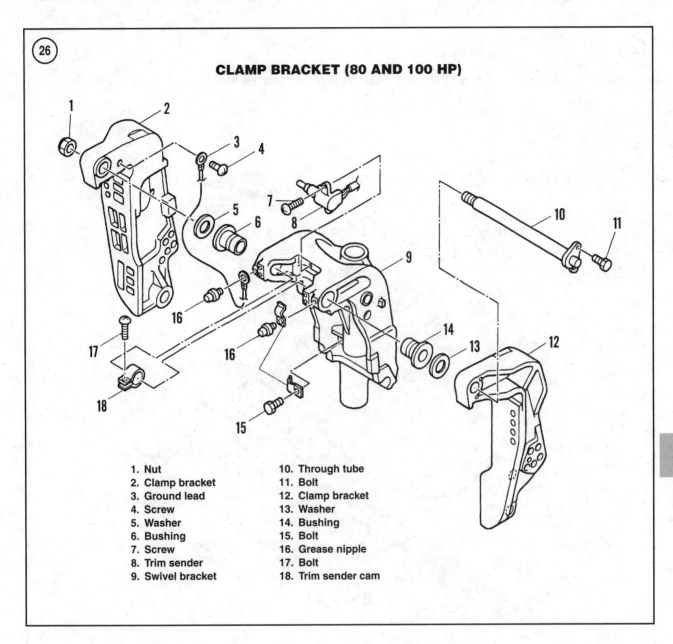

CLAMP BRACKET (80 AND 100 HP)

1. Nut
2. Clamp bracket
3. Ground lead
4. Screw
5. Washer
6. Bushing
7. Screw
8. Trim sender
9. Swivel bracket
10. Through tube
11. Bolt
12. Clamp bracket
13. Washer
14. Bushing
15. Bolt
16. Grease nipple
17. Bolt
18. Trim sender cam

tilt or trim system. Binding during tilt or steering movement usually indicates incorrectly installed components or overtightened fasteners. Correct the cause of binding before operating the engine.

9. On models with an adjustable steering friction mechanism, adjust the mechanism following the instructions in Chapter Five.

Tiller Components

Apply Yamaha marine lubricant to all pivot points and sliding surfaces during assembly. Refer to **Figures 27-29** during this procedure

1. Disconnect the cables from the battery, if so equipped.

2. Disconnect the stop button or switch wires from the engine wire harness.

3. Route the wires through the opening in the lower engine cover. Carefully pry the throttle grip from the front of the tiller arm. Slide the stop button/switch from the tiller arm.

4. Disconnect the throttle cables from the power head throttle lever or wheel.

5. Refer to **Figures 27-29** to determine the locations of the tiller control attaching bolts or nuts. Remove the bolts or nuts, then pull the tiller arm and cables from the engine.

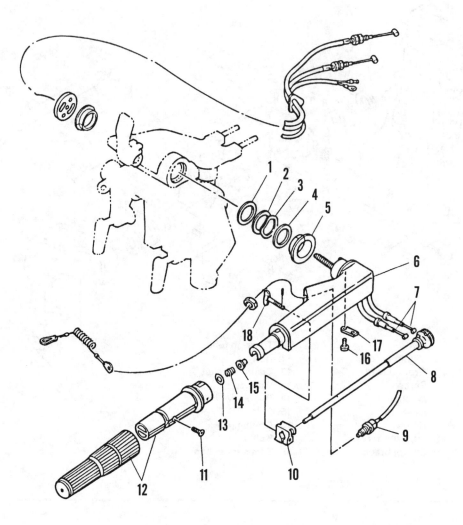

STEERING HANDLE (9.9 AND 15 HP)

27

1. Plastic washer
2. Washer
3. Wave washer
4. Washer
5. Bushing
6. Steering handle bracket
7. Throttle cable
8. Throttle shaft
9. Engine stop switch
10. Friction piece
11. Screw
12. Steering grip
13. Washer
14. Spring
15. Bushing
16. Screw
17. Plate
18. Friction adjusting screw

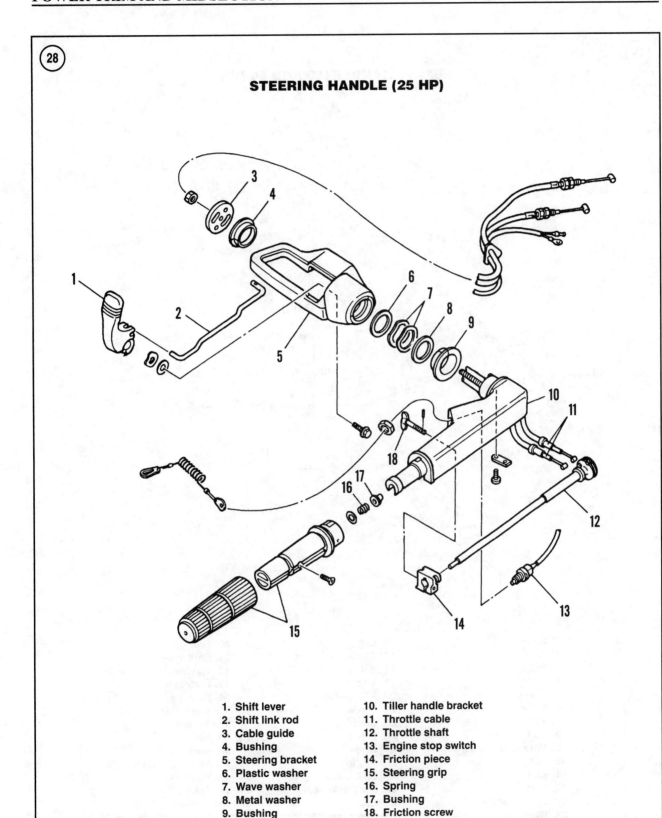

STEERING HANDLE (25 HP)

28

11

1. Shift lever
2. Shift link rod
3. Cable guide
4. Bushing
5. Steering bracket
6. Plastic washer
7. Wave washer
8. Metal washer
9. Bushing
10. Tiller handle bracket
11. Throttle cable
12. Throttle shaft
13. Engine stop switch
14. Friction piece
15. Steering grip
16. Spring
17. Bushing
18. Friction screw

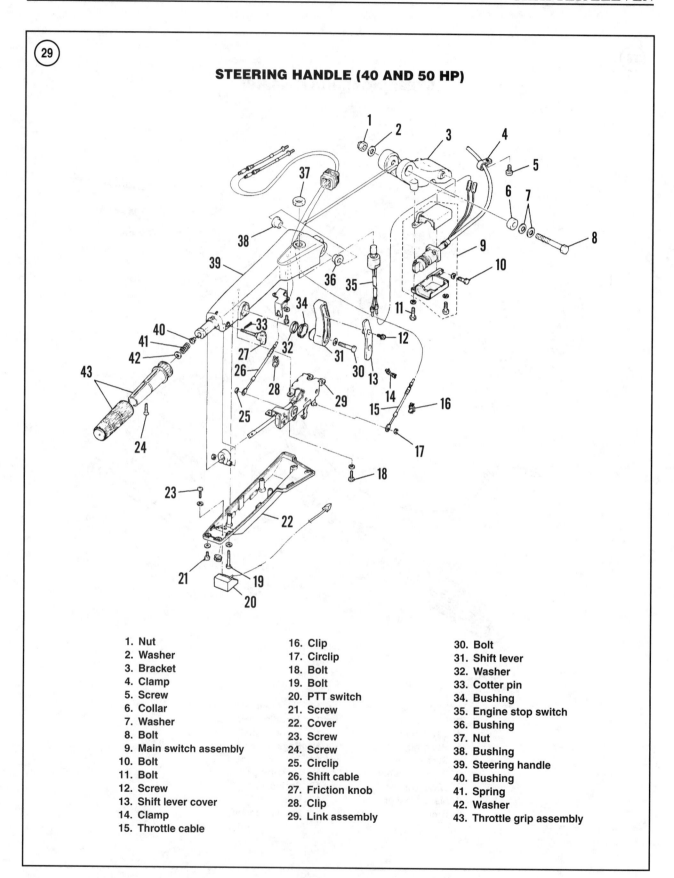

(29)

STEERING HANDLE (40 AND 50 HP)

1. Nut
2. Washer
3. Bracket
4. Clamp
5. Screw
6. Collar
7. Washer
8. Bolt
9. Main switch assembly
10. Bolt
11. Bolt
12. Screw
13. Shift lever cover
14. Clamp
15. Throttle cable

16. Clip
17. Circlip
18. Bolt
19. Bolt
20. PTT switch
21. Screw
22. Cover
23. Screw
24. Screw
25. Circlip
26. Shift cable
27. Friction knob
28. Clip
29. Link assembly

30. Bolt
31. Shift lever
32. Washer
33. Cotter pin
34. Bushing
35. Engine stop switch
36. Bushing
37. Nut
38. Bushing
39. Steering handle
40. Bushing
41. Spring
42. Washer
43. Throttle grip assembly

6. Remove all applicable retainers and pull the throttle shaft from the tiller control. Inspect all components for wear or damage. Replace any worn or damaged components.

7. Assembly is the reverse of disassembly noting the following:

    a. Apply Yamaha marine lubricant to all pivot and sliding surfaces.

    b. Route all wires away from contacting moving components.

    c. Tighten all fasteners to the specifications provided in **Table 3**.

8. Connect the throttle cables to the power head throttle lever or wheel. Adjust the cables following the instructions in Chapter Five.

9. Connect the cables to the battery, if so equipped.

TABLE 1 TILT AND TRIM POSITIONS

Model F9.9, T9.9 and F15	
Manual tilt operation	Tilt angle at 8, 12, 16, 20° on 12° boat transom
	Full tilt-up is 70° on a boat transom of 12°
Model F25	
Manual tilt operation	Tilt angle at 8, 12, 16, 20, 24° on 12 degree boat transom
	Full tilt-up is 64° on a boat transom of 12°
Electric tilt operation	Trim angle at -4 to 20° on a 12° boat transom
	Full tilt-up is 65° on a boat transom of 12°
Model F40 and F50	
Electric tilt operation	Trim angle at -4 to 20° on a 12° boat transom
	Full tilt-up is 69° on a boat transom of 12°
Model F80 and F100	
Electric tilt operation	Trim angle at -4 to 16° on a 12° boat transom
	Full tilt-up is 70° on a boat transom of 12°

TABLE 2 POWER TRIM AND TILT SPECIFICATIONS (ELECTRIC ONLY)

Model F25	
Fluid type	ATF (automatic transmission fluid) Dexron II
Brush	
Length	6 mm (0.25 in.)
Wear limit	3 mm (0.12 in.)
Commutator	
Diameter	16.5 mm (0.65 in.)
Wear limit	15.5 mm (0.61 in.)
Model F40 and F50	
Fluid type	ATF (automatic transmission fluid) Dexron II
Brush	
Length	10 mm (0.39 in.)
Wear limit	3.5 mm (0.14 in.)
Commutator	
Diameter	22 mm (0.87 in.)
Wear limit	21 mm (0.83 in.)
Under cut	1.5 mm (0.06 in.)
Relief pressure up	10.0 MPa (1422 psi)
Relief pressure down	2.0 MPa (284 psi)
Tilt piston relief valve opening pressure	31.0 MPa (4409 psi)
Trim ram stroke	41 mm (1.59 in.)
Tilt ram stroke	110 mm (4.33 in.)
Model F80 and F100	
Fluid type	ATF (automatic transmission fluid) Dexron II
Relief pressure up	18.0 MPa (2560 psi)
Relief pressure down	2.0 MPa (284 psi)
Trim piston relief valve opening pressure	9.5 MPa (1351 psi)
Tilt piston relief valve opening pressure	31.0 MPa (4409 psi)
Trim ram stroke	45 mm (1.77 in.)
Tilt ram stroke	110 mm (4.33 in.)

11

Table 3 TIGHTENING TORQUE

Model	Item	N•m	in.-lb.	ft.-lb.
F25	Fill plug	7	62	–
	Tilt cylinder	9	79	–
	Motor unit	7	62	–
	Cylinder end	90	–	66
	Gear-pump	4	36	–
	Main valve	7	62	–
	Tilt piston	61	–	44
	Manual control	3	26	–
	Up-relief valve	6	53	–
F40-F50	Fill plug	7	62	–
	Tilt cylinder	9	79	–
	Motor unit	4	36	–
	Cylinder end	90	–	66
	Gear-pump	4	36	–
	Main valve	11	97	–
	Bottom cover	7	62	–
	Retaining plate	4	36	–
	Inner cylinder end	80	–	59
F80-F100	Fill plug	12	106	–
	Inner cylinder end	80	–	59
	Main valve	11	97	–
	Manual valve	2	18	–
	Manual valve seat	4	36	–
	PTT motor mounting	7	62	–
	PTT reservoir	6	53	–
	PTT reservoir unit	9	79	–
	PTT reservoir plug	7	62	–
	Outer cylinder end	90	–	65
	Tilt piston	85	–	61

Chapter Twelve

Remote Control

The remote control provides throttle, shifting and other engine operations from a location out of reach of the engine (**Figure 1**). It is the boat operator's link to the engine.

> *CAUTION*
> *Always refer to the owner's manual for specific remote control operating instructions. Become familiar with all control functions before operating the engine.*

Neutral Throttle Operation

Two common types of controls are used on the Yamaha outboard. The most common is the 703 control or *pull for neutral* (**Figure 2**). To activate the neutral throttle function, position the handle in neutral. Pull the handle straight out from the control (**Figure 3**).

The throttle can then be advanced without shifting the engine into gear. This assists with starting and warming up the engine. To return to normal operation, position the handle to neutral and push the handle toward the control.

The other type of control is the 705 control or *push for neutral* (**Figure 4**). To activate the neutral throttle function, position the handle in neutral. Push in and hold the throttle-only button. The button can be released after the

throttle is advanced. The throttle can be advanced without shifting the engine into gear as long as the handle does not reach the neutral position. To return to normal operation, position the handle to the neutral position. The throttle-only button will return to the normal position. Normal operation with shifting can resume.

> *WARNING*
> *A malfunction in the remote control can lead to lack of shift and throttle control. Never operate an outboard if the remote control is malfunctioning. Damage to property, serious bodily injury or death can result if the engine is operated without proper control. Check the control for proper operation before operating the engine, or after performing any service or repair.*

Throttle/Shift Cable Removal/Installation

Throttle/shift cable replacement is required if the cable is hard to move or excessive play occurs due to cable wear. Mark the cables prior to removal to ensure that the throttle and shift cables are installed to the proper attaching points. Remove and attach one cable at a time to avoid confusion.

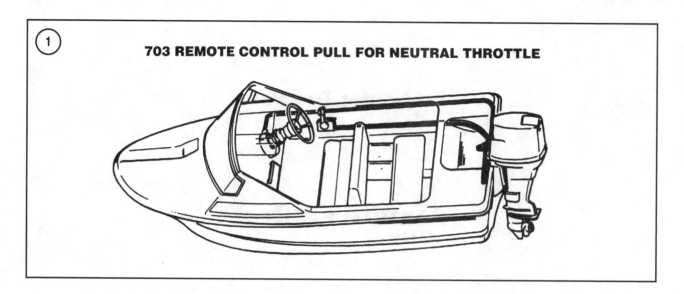

703 REMOTE CONTROL PULL FOR NEUTRAL THROTTLE

703 remote control

1. Disconnect the battery cables from the battery.

2. Remove the screws or bolts attaching the remote control to the boat structure.

3. Remove the cover from the lower side of the control (**Figure 5**).

4. Remove the two screws and the lower back cover from the control (**Figure 6**).

5. Identify the cable that requires replacement. Move the control handle to provide access to the circlip on the cable end (**Figure 7**).

6. Note the location of the cable and cable grommet to the clamp groove (**Figure 8**). Remove the circlip (**Figure 7**), then lift the cable from the clamp groove and pin on the lever. Inspect the circlip for corrosion, damage or lost spring tension. Replace it if any defects are noted.

7. Apply Yamaha marine grease or its equivalent to the threaded end of the replacement cable (1, **Figure 9**). Thread the cable connector (2, **Figure 9**) onto the threaded end until 11.0 mm (0.4 in.) of the threaded end is in the cable connector. Tighten the jam nut (**Figure 9**) securely against the cable connector.

8. Place the cable and grommet into the clamp groove in the control box as indicated in **Figure 8**. Apply Yamaha marine grease to the attaching points of the cables. Position the cable connector over the pin on the lever, then install the circlip. Make sure the circlip is properly installed into the groove in the pin.

9. Repeat Steps 5-8 for the other cable.

10. Install the lower back cover and screws (**Figure 6**). Install the cover (**Figure 5**). Install the control and attaching screws to the boat. Tighten all fasteners to the specifications in **Table 1**. Adjust the throttle and shift cables at

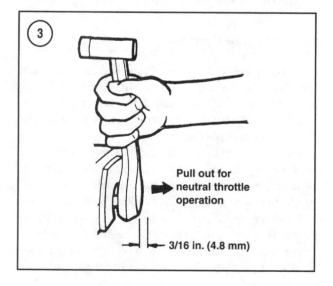

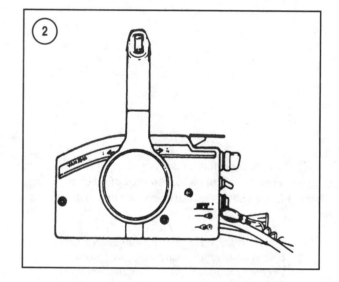

Pull out for neutral throttle operation

3/16 in. (4.8 mm)

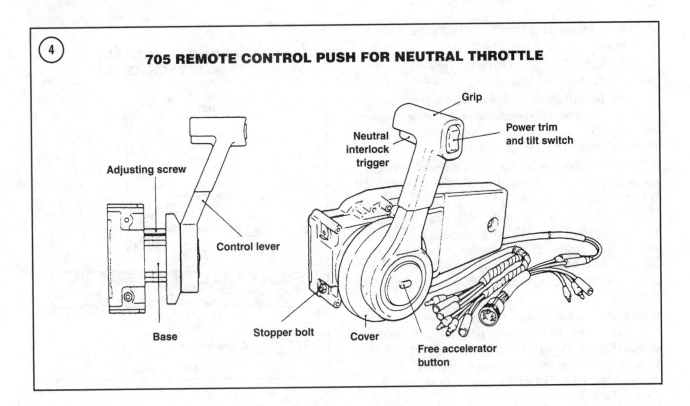

④ **705 REMOTE CONTROL PUSH FOR NEUTRAL THROTTLE**

Grip

Neutral
interlock
trigger

Power trim
and tilt switch

Adjusting screw

Control lever

Base

Stopper bolt

Cover

Free accelerator
button

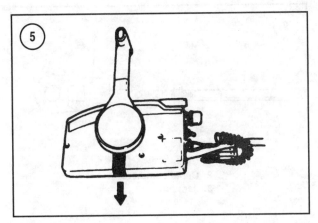

⑤

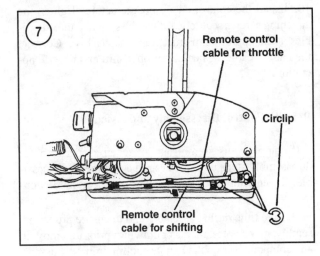

⑦

Remote control
cable for throttle

Circlip

Remote control
cable for shifting

12

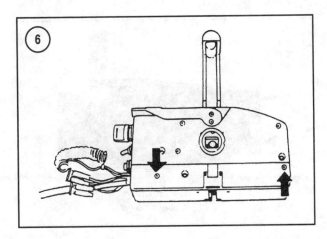

⑥

the engine as instructed in Chapter Five. Connect the battery cables to the battery.

705 remote control

1. Disconnect the battery cables from the battery.
2. Remove the screws or bolts attaching the control to the boat structure.
3. Remove the five screws (1, **Figure 10**) from the back cover. Support the cables and carefully pry the back cover (2, **Figure 10**) from the control.

4. Refer to **Figure 11** to identify the shift cable. Mark it accordingly.

5. Make note of the position of the shift cable and grommet (**Figure 11**) in the clamp groove.

6. Move the shift handle to provide access to the circlip on the cable connector. Use needlenose pliers to remove the circlip from the shift arm attaching pin. Carefully lift the throttle cable from the shift arm and clamp groove.

7. Thread the cable connector onto the threaded end of the shift cable until 11.0 mm (0.4 in.) of the threaded end is in the connector (**Figure 9**).

8. Apply Yamaha marine grease to the attaching points for the cable. Place the cable and grommet ino the clamp groove of the control. Place the cable connector over the pin on the lever or arm. Install the circlip onto the pin. Make sure the circlip is properly installed into the groove in the pin.

9. Repeat Steps 5-8 for the throttle cable. Inspect the cables to ensure that both are properly aligned in the clamp groove (**Figure 11**). Place the back cover onto the control. Hold the back cover firmly in position and install the five screws (**Figure 10**). Tighten all fasteners to the specifications in **Table 1**.

10. Install the control on the boat structure. Tighten the attaching screws securely. Adjust the shift and throttle cables at the engine as instructed in Chapter Five. Connect the battery cables. Check for proper shift and throttle operation.

Remote Control Disassembly and Assembly

If complete disassembly is not required, perform the disassembly steps until the desired component is accessible. Reverse the disassembly steps to assemble the control.

To save time during assembly and to ensure proper assembly, make notes, marks or drawings prior to removing any component from the remote control. Improper assembly can cause internal binding or reversed cable movement.

Clean all components, except electric switches and warning buzzer, in a clean solvent. Use compressed air to blow debris from the components. Inspect all components for damage or wear. Replace any defective or questionable component. Apply Yamaha all-purpose grease or equivalent to all pivot points and sliding surfaces during assembly. Test all electrical components while they are removed to ensure proper operation. Refer to Chapter Three for testing procedures for all electrical switches and the warning buzzer.

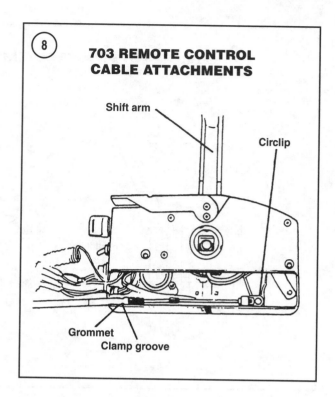

703 REMOTE CONTROL CABLE ATTACHMENTS

Shift arm
Circlip
Grommet
Clamp groove

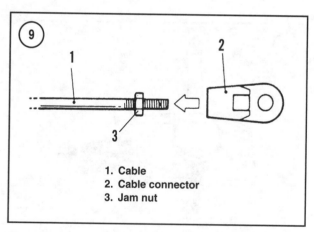

1. Cable
2. Cable connector
3. Jam nut

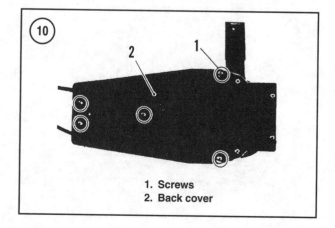

1. Screws
2. Back cover

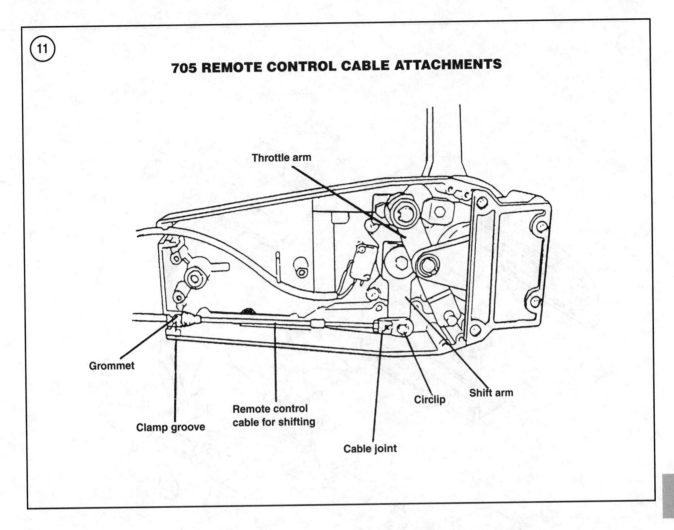

705 REMOTE CONTROL CABLE ATTACHMENTS

- Throttle arm
- Grommet
- Clamp groove
- Remote control cable for shifting
- Cable joint
- Circlip
- Shift arm

12

703 Control Disassembly and Assembly

1. Disconnect the battery cables from the battery.

2. Remove the screws or bolts that attach the control to the boat structure. Mark all wires leading to the control to ensure proper connection on installation. Disconnect all leads. Place the control handle in the neutral position.

3. Mark the cables for reference, then remove the throttle and shift cables from the remote control as instructed in *Throttle/shift cable removal/installation* in this chapter. Place the control on a clean work surface.

4. Remove the back cover plates (18, **Figure 12**) from the control. Remove the throttle-only lever and shaft (19 and 2, **Figure 12**). Remove the retaining bolt, then lift the throttle arm and shift arm from the control. Remove any accessible bushings, grommets and retainers at this point.

5. Remove the retainer (8, **Figure 12**), leaf spring and neutral switch from the control.

6. Note the position of the gear (9, **Figure 12**) and lift it from the control. Remove any accessible bushings, grom-

mets and retainers. Note the trim wire routing and remove the control handle from the control.

7. Remove the neutral position lever from the handle. Note the wire routing, then pull the trim switch and wires from the handle.

8. Note the wire connections and routing prior to removal. Disconnect the wires, and then remove the start switch, lanyard switch and fuel enrichment switch from the control. Note the location and orientation of any remaining components, then remove them from the control.

9. Assembly is the reverse of disassembly. Apply Yamaha all-purpose grease to all bushings, pivot points and sliding surfaces. Apply Loctite 271 to the threads of all bolts and screws during assembly.

10. Install the throttle and shift cables as instructed in *Throttle/shift cable removal/installation* in this chapter. Install both back covers (**Figure 13**). Tighten all fasteners to the specifications in **Table 1**. Reattach all disconnected leads to the control. Install the battery cables to the battery. Adjust the cables at the engine as instructed in Chap-

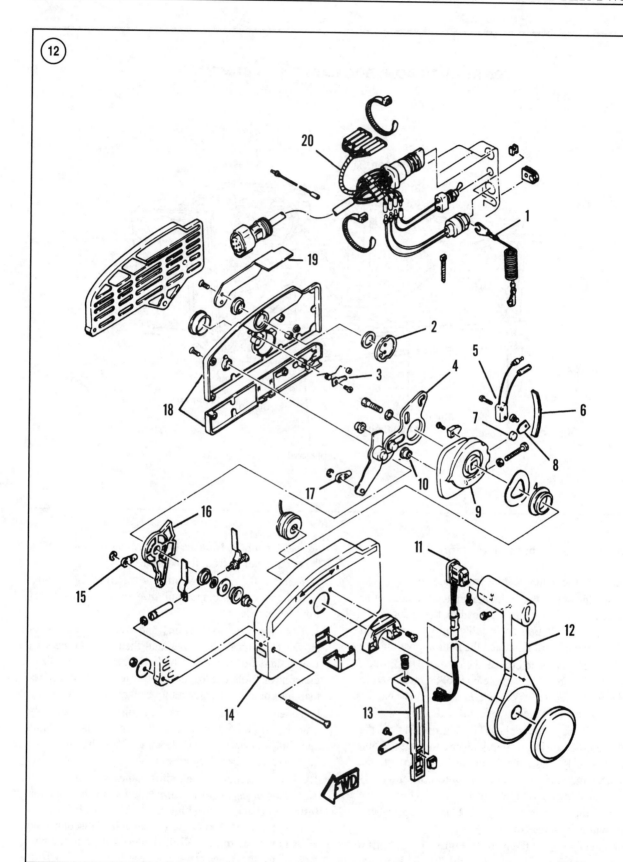

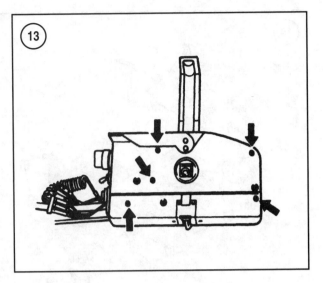

703 REMOTE CONTROL INTERNAL COMPONENTS

1. Lanyard
2. Throttle only shaft/cam
3. Detent roller
4. Throttle arm/lever
5. Neutral switch
6. Leaf spring
7. Throttle only roller
8. Retainer
9. Gear
10. Bushing
11. Trim switch*
12. Control handle
13. Neutral position lever
14. Control housing
15. Cable connector
16. Shift arm
17. Cable connector
18. Back cover plates
19. Throttle only lever
20. Start switch lead connector

* Used only on tilt/trim models

ter Five. Check for proper operation before returning the engine into service.

705 Control Disassembly and Assembly

For component identification and orientation, refer to **Figure 14**. Mark the locations and orientation of *all* components prior to removal.

1. Disconnect both battery cables from the battery.

2. Remove the screws that retain the control to the boat structure. Mark the throttle and shift cable locations. Remove both cables from the remote control as instructed in *Throttle/shift cable removal/installation*.

3. Note all wires and connections leading into the control, then disconnect them.

4. Make drawings of the location and orientation of each component prior to removal.

5. Place the control handle in the neutral position. Remove the circlip (1, **Figure 15**) from the throttle lever pivot. Lift the cam plate (2, **Figure 15**) and dwell plate (3) from the control.

6. Slide the throttle lever toward the back of the control to access the two screws (1, **Figure 16**) that retain the drive plate (2, **Figure 16**). Remove the screws. Note the orientation of the drive arm plate (64, **Figure 14**) and the drive arm limiter (65), then lift them from the control.

7. Count the number of turns it takes to tighten the throttle friction until fully seated. Record the number of turns. Loosen the screw back to its original position. Remove the circlip (1, **Figure 17**). Note the orientation of the components, then lift the washer, throttle arm (3, **Figure 17**), throttle friction plate (4) and bushings (5) from the control. Remove the friction screw (6, **Figure 17**) from the remote control housing.

12

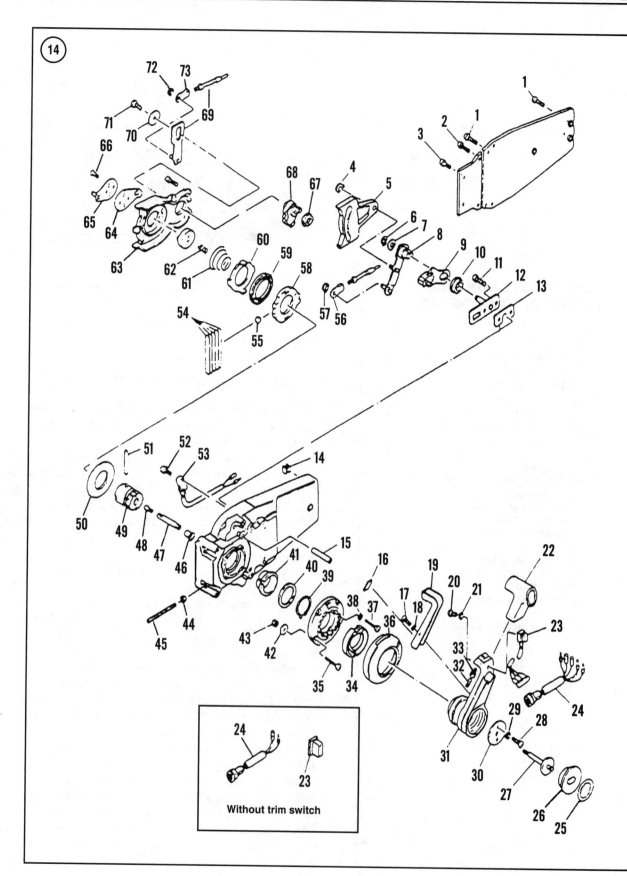

⑭

Without trim switch

705 REMOTE CONTROL
INTERNAL COMPONENTS

1. Screw
2. Screw
3. Screw
4. Circlip
5. Cam plate
6. Circlip
7. Washer
8. Throttle lever
9. Adjusting plate
10. Bushing
11. Bolt
12. Throttle shaft
13. Spacer
14. Cable grommet
15. Friction shaft
16. Cap
17. Screw
18. Washer
19. Neutral lock lever
20. Screw
21. Washer
22. Handle grip
23. Trim switch
24. Trim wire
25. Decal
26. Throttle only cover
27. Throttle only shaft
28. Screw
29. Washer
30. Washer
31. Control handle
32. Spring
33. Screw
34. Neutral lock plate
35. Screw
36. Decal cover
37. Screw

38. Washer
39. Circlip
40. Washer
41. Bushing
42. Washer
43. Nut
44. Locking nut
45. Stopper ccrew
46. Bushing
47. Shaft
48. Screw
49. Drive shaft
50. Washer
51. Pin
52. Screw
53. Neutral switch
54. Spring
55. Throttle only roller
56. Cable connector
57. Circlip
58. Gear
59. Shift plate
60. Lock plate
61. Spring
62. Spring
63. Gear cover
64. Drive arm plate
65. Drive arm limiter
66. Screw
67. Bushing
68. Gear
69. Shift cable
70. Washer
71. Bolt
72. Circlip
73. Cable connector

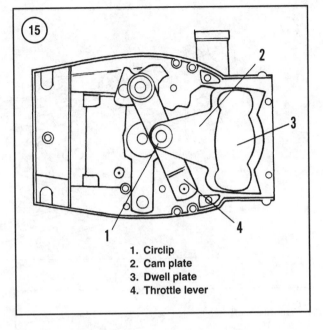

1. Circlip
2. Cam plate
3. Dwell plate
4. Throttle lever

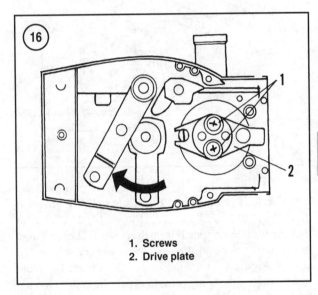

1. Screws
2. Drive plate

12

8. Remove the two hex bolts and lift the throttle shaft (**Figure 18**) from the remote control housing. Note the position of the shift lever (3, **Figure 19**). Install it in the same position as it was removed. Remove the bolt (1, **Figure 19**) and washer (2, **Figure 19**), then lift the throttle lever from the control.

9. Remove the screws (1, **Figure 14**) and carefully lift the gear cover from the remote control housing. Loosen the locking nut (44, **Figure 14**) without turning the stopper screw (45, **Figure 14**). Count the turns while turning the stopper screw clockwise (45, **Figure 14**) until fully seated. Record the number of turns, then remove the screw and locking nut.

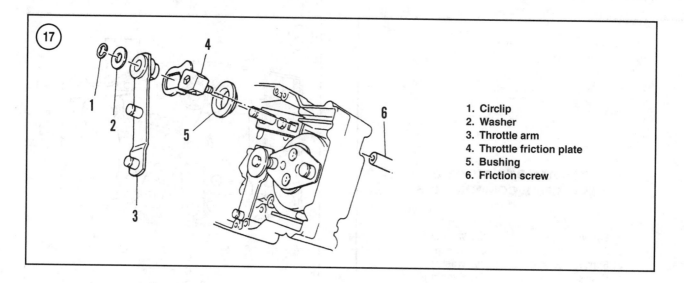

1. Circlip
2. Washer
3. Throttle arm
4. Throttle friction plate
5. Bushing
6. Friction screw

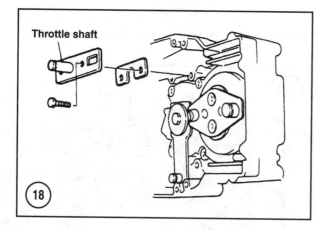

Throttle shaft

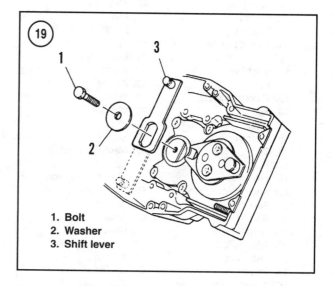

1. Bolt
2. Washer
3. Shift lever

10. Carefully pry the throttle-only cover (26, **Figure 14**) from the throttle-only shaft (27, **Figure 14**). Use pliers to pull the throttle-only shaft from the control. The shaft may break during removal. Remove the screw and washer (28 and 29, **Figure 14**) from the washer (30, **Figure 14**). Note the routing of the trim wires, then pull the control handle and trim wires from the remote control. Disconnect the trim wires from the instrument harness. Remove the decal cover (36, **Figure 14**) and neutral lock assembly (34, **Figure 14**) from the control.

11. Mark all components prior to removal. Remove the screws (35 and 37, **Figure 14**) and the cover/mount from the control. Remove the circlip (39, **Figure 14**) from the drive shaft (49, **Figure 14**). Note the orientation of the lock plate (60, **Figure 14**), shift plate (59) and gear (58), then slide them from the drive shaft. Note the location and orientation of all remaining components, then remove them.

12. Remove the neutral switch (53, **Figure 14**), trim switch (23, **Figure 14**) and leads (24) along with the key switch, enrichment switch and warning buzzer, if so equipped. Refer to Chapter Three for test procedures.

13. Assembly is the reverse of disassembly. Apply Yamaha all-purpose grease to all pivot points and sliding surfaces. Install the throttle friction screw and stopper screws until seated, then back out the recorded number of turns. Tighten the jam nut securely. Apply Loctite 271 to the threads of all fasteners, excluding the throttle friction and stopper screw. Tighten all fasteners to the specifications in **Table 1**.

14. Install the throttle and shift cables into the remote control as instructed in *Throttle/shift cable removal/installation*. Install the control to the boat structure and tighten the screws or bolts securely. Adjust the cables at the engine as instructed in Chapter Five.

15. Check the throttle and shift for proper operation, and correct as required.

Table 1 TIGHTENING TORQUE

Item	N•m	in.-lb.	ft.-lb.
Neutral lock holder (703 control)	1.2-1.5	11-13	–
Neutral throttle lever screws (703 control)	1.5-1.8	13-16	–
Throttle stopper locknut (705 control)	5-8	44-71	–
Throttle lever (705 control)	5-8	44-71	–
Control handle screw (703 control)	6-6.5	52-57	–
Control handle mounting screws (705 control)	3-4	26-35	–
Cover/mount (705 control)	5-8	44-71	–
Drive plate screws (705 control)	5-8	44-71	–
Fastener size			
8 mm nut, M5 bolt	5	44	–
10 mm nut, M6 bolt	8	71	–
12 mm nut, M8 bolt	18	–	13
14 mm nut, M10 bolt	36	–	26
17 mm nut, M12 bolt	43	–	31

12

Index

ELECTRIC START (1985-1991 9.9 HP)

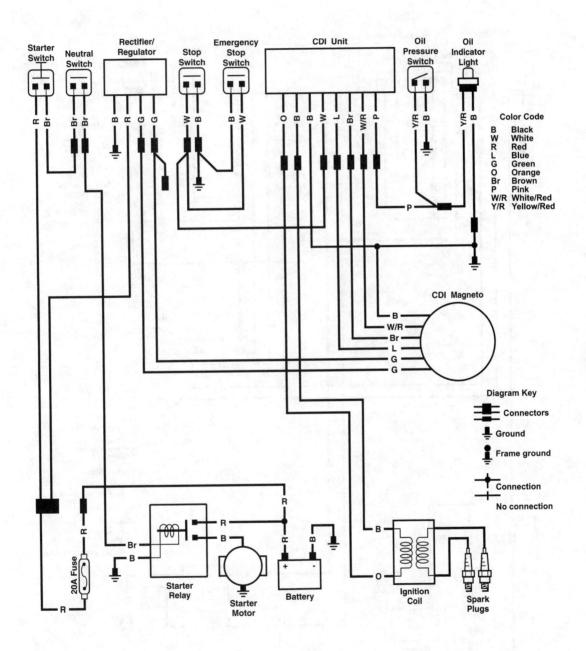

14

MANUAL START (1985-1991 9.9 HP)

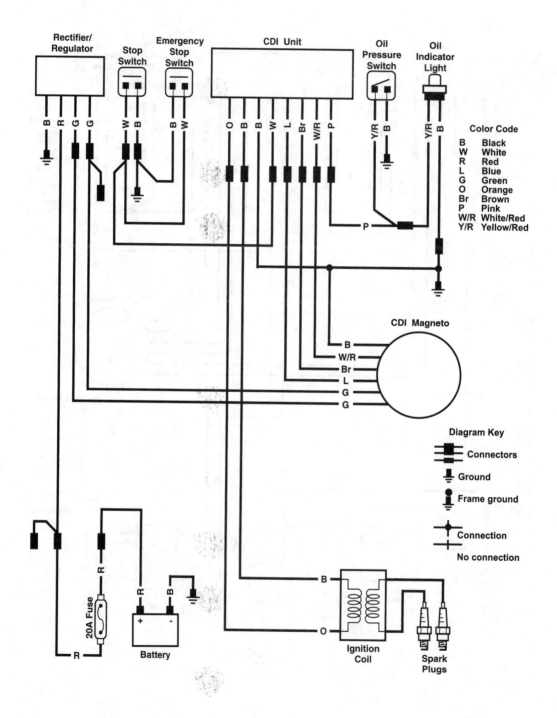

ELECTRIC START/TILLER HANDLE (1992-1999 9.9 HP)

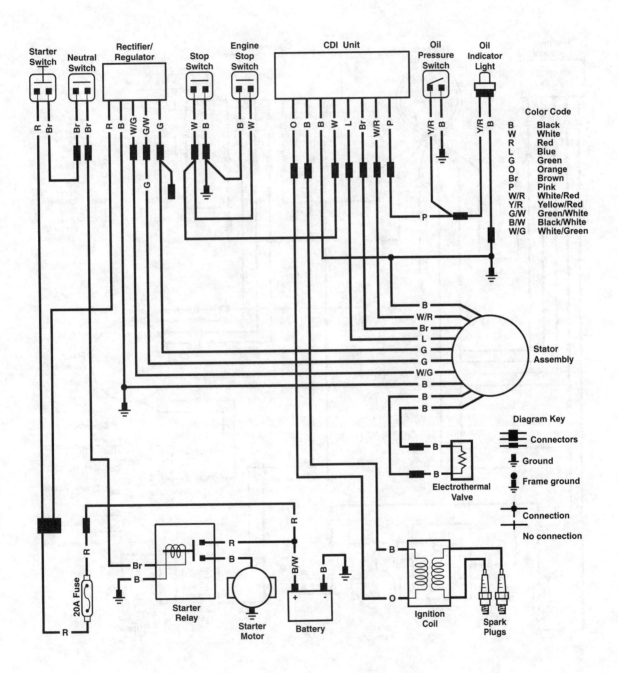

ELECTRIC START REMOTE CONTROL (1992-1999 9.9 HP)

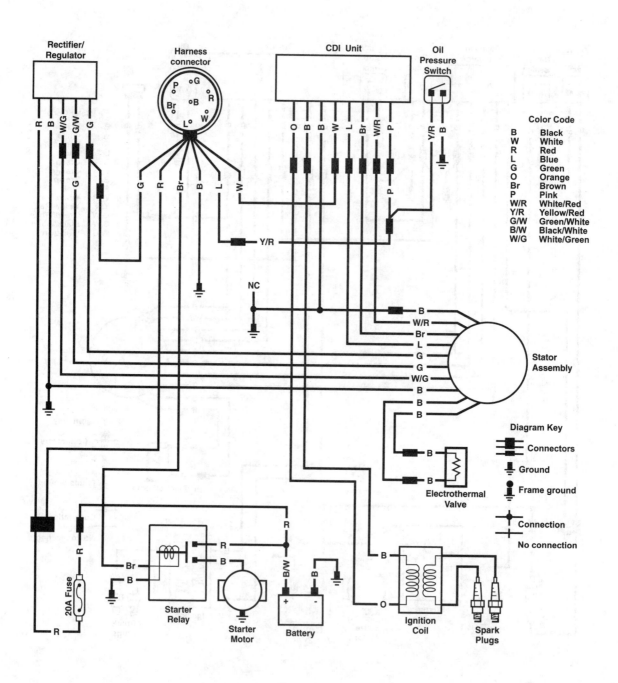

Color Code

B	Black
W	White
R	Red
L	Blue
G	Green
O	Orange
Br	Brown
P	Pink
W/R	White/Red
Y/R	Yellow/Red
G/W	Green/White
B/W	Black/White
W/G	White/Green

Diagram Key

Connectors
Ground
Frame ground
Connection
No connection

MANUAL START/TILLER HANDLE (1992-1999 9.9 HP)

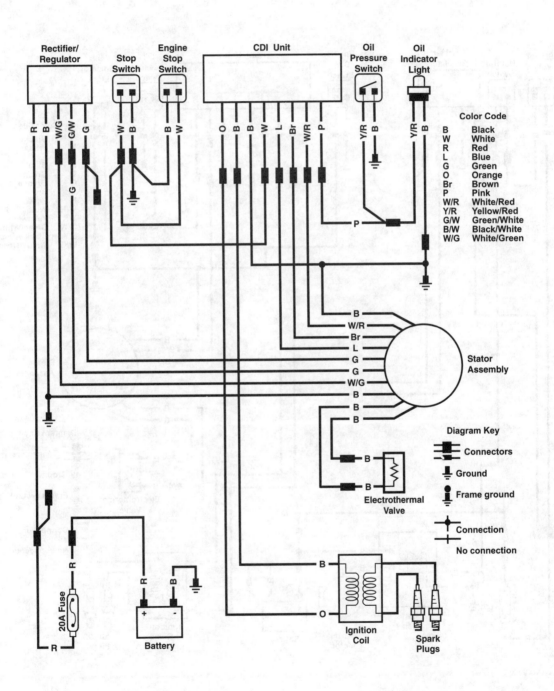

Color Code

B	Black
W	White
R	Red
L	Blue
G	Green
O	Orange
Br	Brown
P	Pink
W/R	White/Red
Y/R	Yellow/Red
G/W	Green/White
B/W	Black/White
W/G	White/Green

Diagram Key

- Connectors
- Ground
- Frame ground
- Connection
- No connection

14

ELECTRIC START/TILLER HANDLE (1992-1999 9.9 HP)

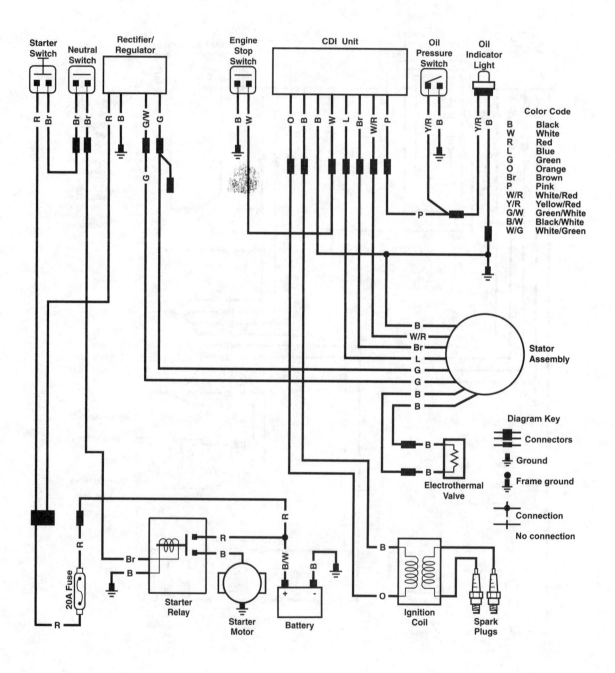

MANUAL START/TILLER HANDLE (1992-1999 9.9 HP)

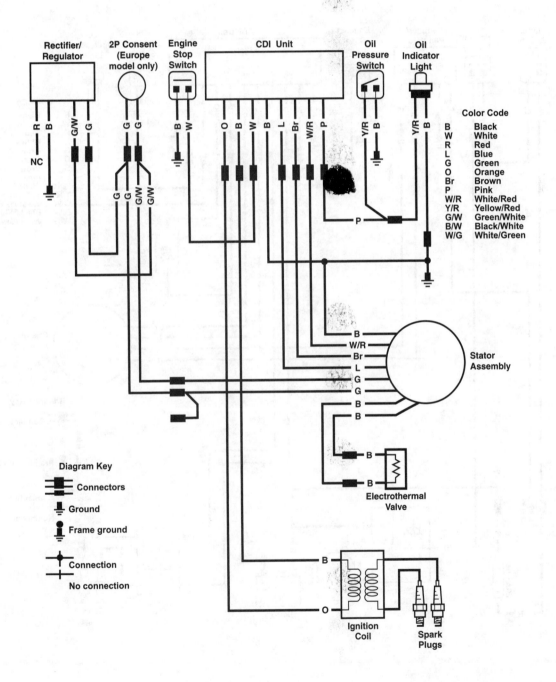

ELECTRIC START/TILLER HANDLE (15 HP)

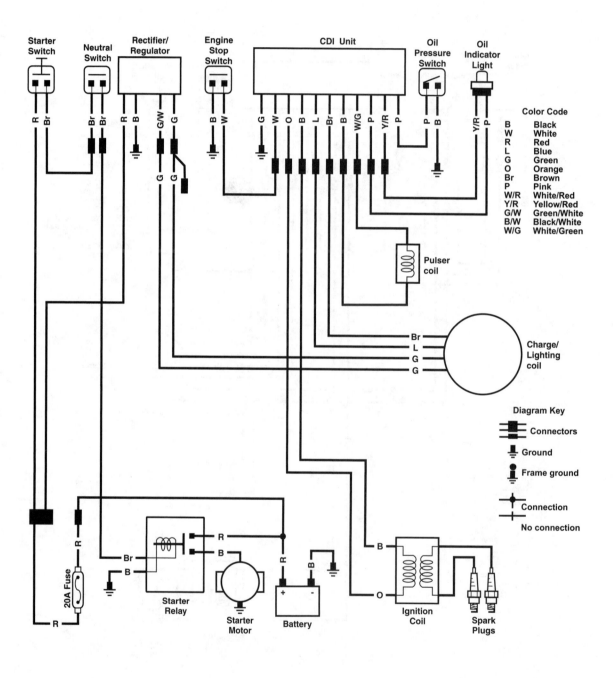

Color Code	
B	Black
W	White
R	Red
L	Blue
G	Green
O	Orange
Br	Brown
P	Pink
W/R	White/Red
Y/R	Yellow/Red
G/W	Green/White
B/W	Black/White
W/G	White/Green

MANUAL START/TILLER HANDLE (15 HP)

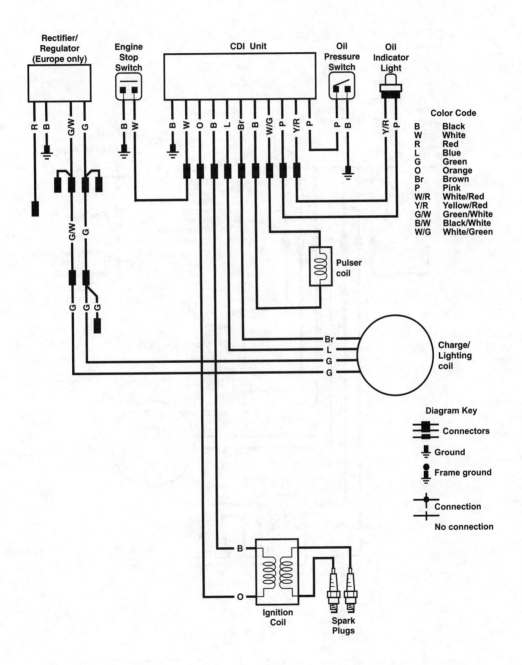

Color Code

B	Black
W	White
R	Red
L	Blue
G	Green
O	Orange
Br	Brown
P	Pink
W/R	White/Red
Y/R	Yellow/Red
G/W	Green/White
B/W	Black/White
W/G	White/Green

Diagram Key

Connectors

Ground

Frame ground

Connection

No connection

IGNITION SYSTEM (15 HP)

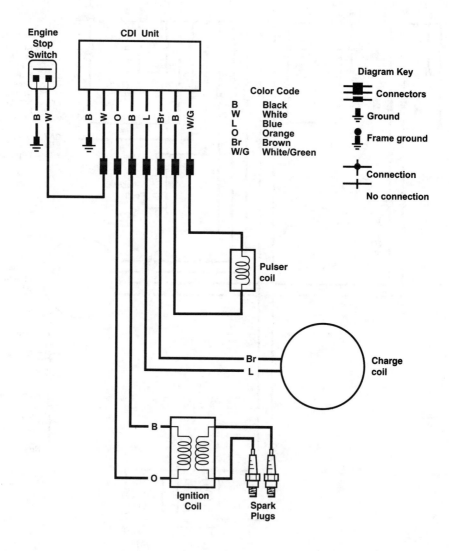

IGNITION CONTROL SYSTEM TILLER HANDLE (15 HP)

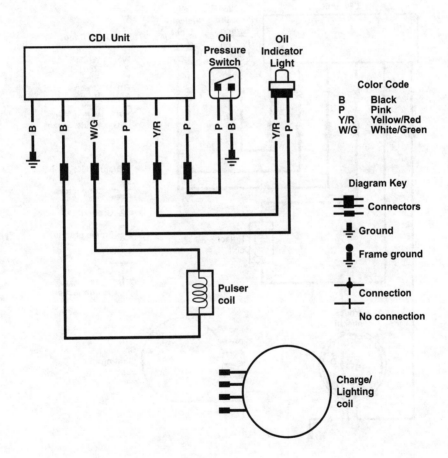

Color Code

B	Black
P	Pink
Y/R	Yellow/Red
W/G	White/Green

Diagram Key

Connectors

Ground

Frame ground

Connection

No connection

14

IGNITION CONTROL SYSTEM REMOTE CONTROL (15 HP)

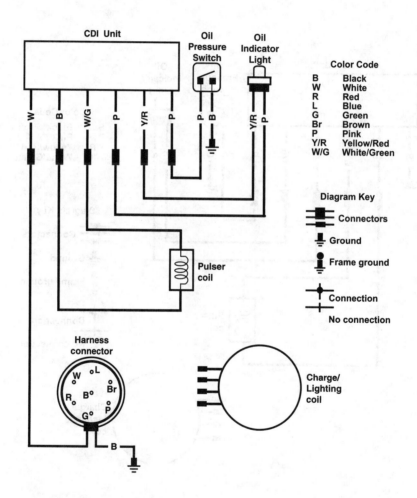

ELECTRIC START/TILLER HANDLE (15 HP)

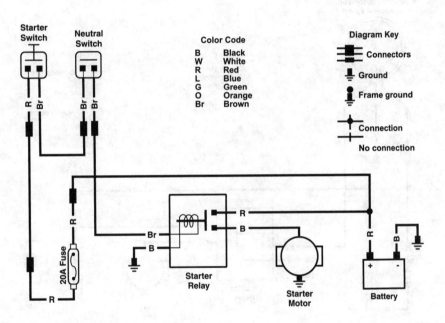

Starter Switch

Neutral Switch

Color Code

B	Black
W	White
R	Red
L	Blue
G	Green
O	Orange
Br	Brown

Diagram Key

Connectors

Ground

Frame ground

Connection

No connection

R   Br   Br   Br

R

Br

B

20A Fuse

R

Starter Relay

R

B

Starter Motor

R

B

+   −

Battery

ELECTRIC START/REMOTE CONTROL (15 HP)

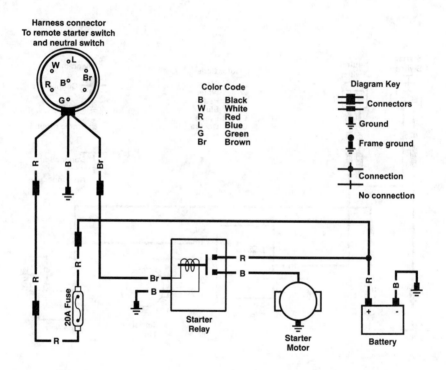

Harness connector
To remote starter switch
and neutral switch

Color Code

B	Black
W	White
R	Red
L	Blue
G	Green
Br	Brown

Diagram Key

Connectors

Ground

Frame ground

Connection

No connection

20A Fuse

Starter
Relay

Starter
Motor

Battery

ELECTRIC START/TILLER HANDLE (15 HP)

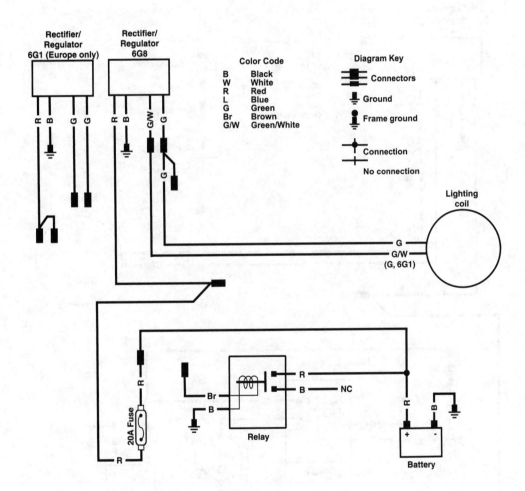

14

ELECTRIC START/REMOTE CONTROL (15 HP)

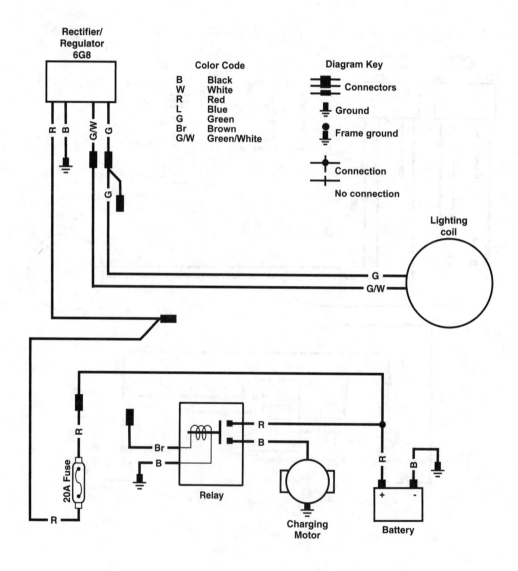

ELECTRIC START TILLER HANDLE (25 HP)

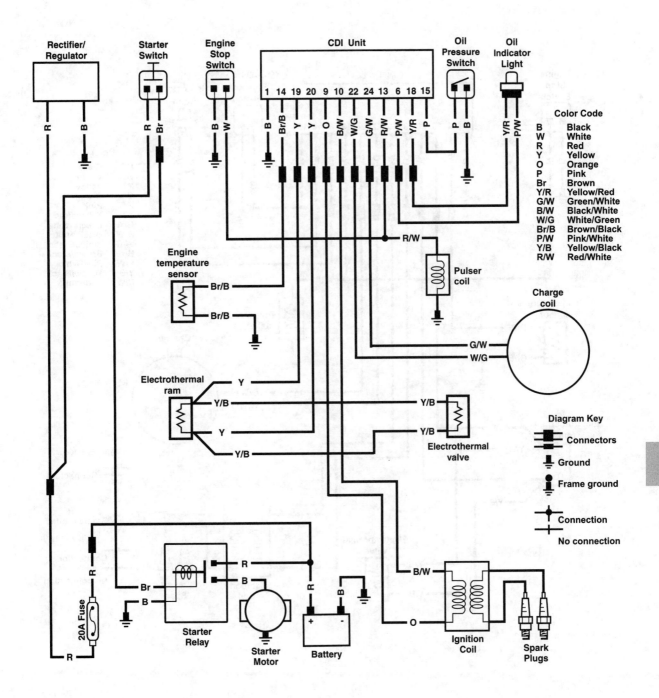

Color Code

B	Black
W	White
R	Red
Y	Yellow
O	Orange
P	Pink
Br	Brown
Y/R	Yellow/Red
G/W	Green/White
B/W	Black/White
W/G	White/Green
Br/B	Brown/Black
P/W	Pink/White
Y/B	Yellow/Black
R/W	Red/White

Diagram Key

Connectors

Ground

Frame ground

Connection

No connection

14

MANUAL START TILLER HANDLE (25 HP)

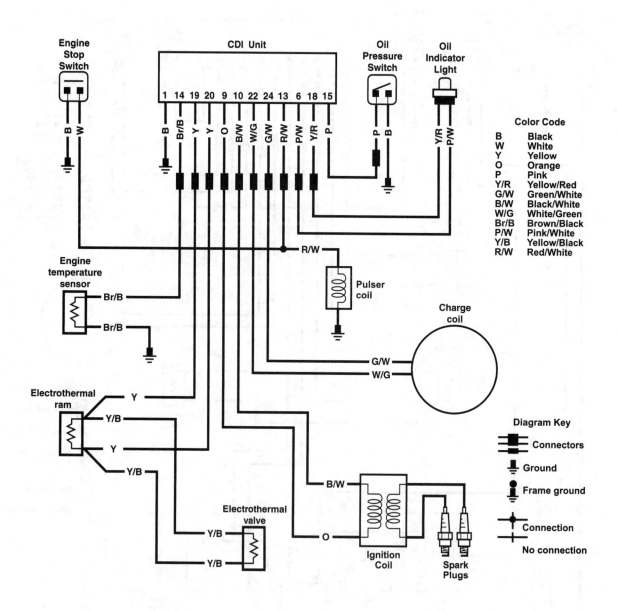

ELECTRIC START REMOTE CONTROL WIRE HARNESS (25 HP)

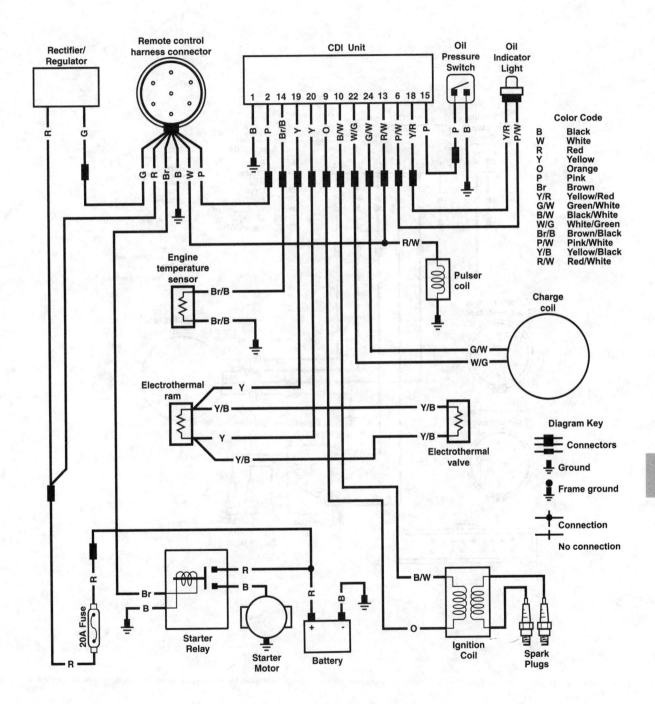

IGNITION SYSTEM (25 HP)

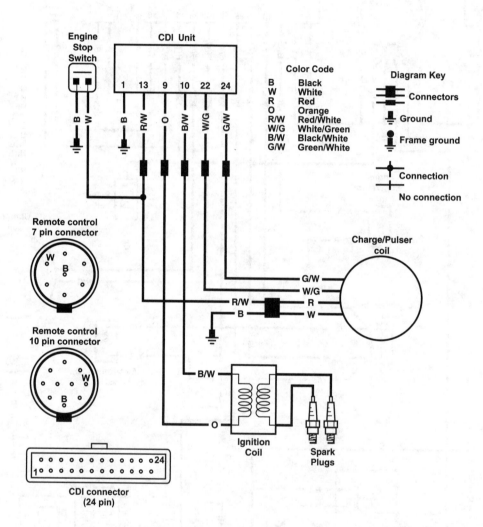

IGNITION CONTROL SYSTEM (25 HP)

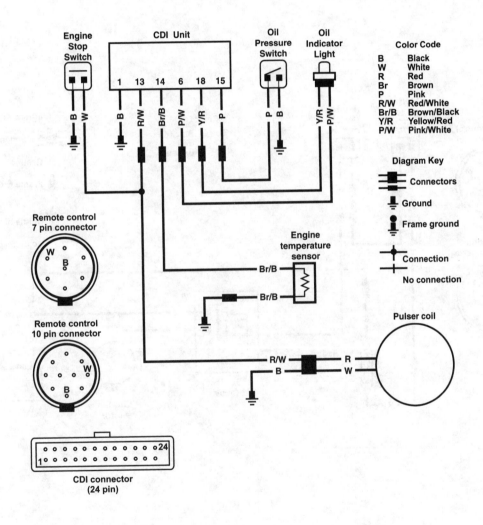

14

STARTING SYSTEM (25 HP)

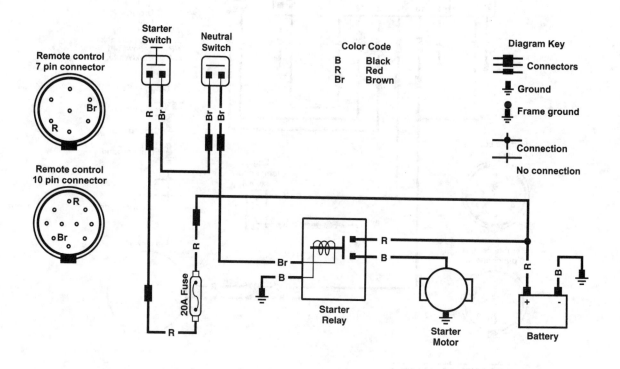

CHARGING SYSTEM (25 HP)

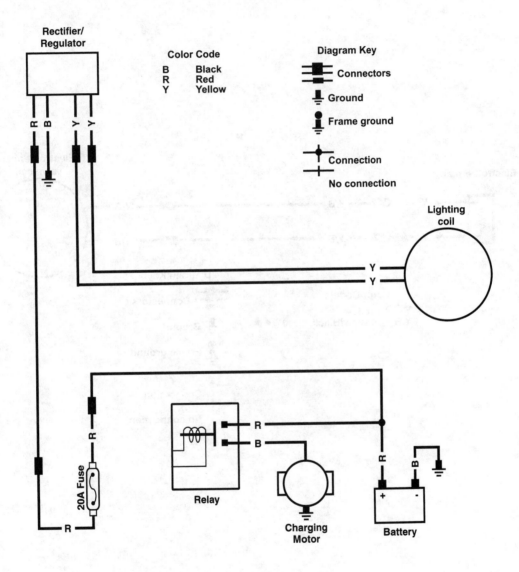

ENRICHMENT CONTROL SYSTEM (25 HP)

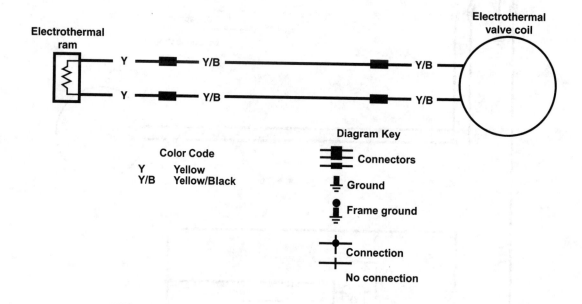

ELECTRIC START REMOTE CONTROL POWER TRIM AND TILT (25 HP)

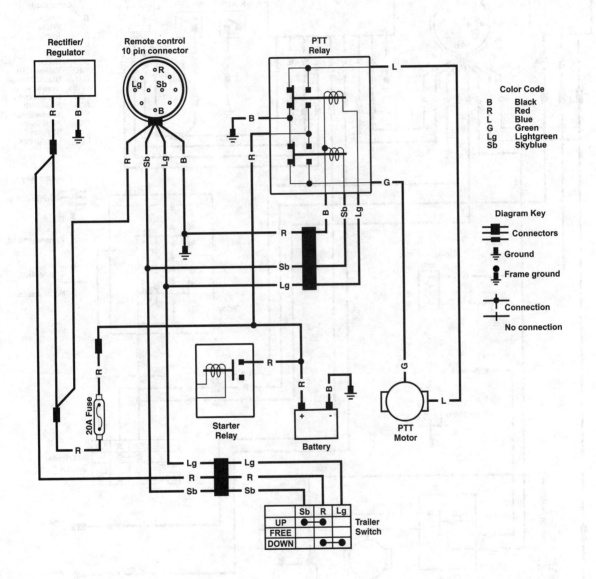

Rectifier/ Regulator

Remote control 10 pin connector

PTT Relay

Color Code

B	Black
R	Red
L	Blue
G	Green
Lg	Lightgreen
Sb	Skyblue

Diagram Key

Connectors

Ground

Frame ground

Connection

No connection

20A Fuse

Starter Relay

Battery

PTT Motor

	Sb	R	Lg	
UP	●	●		**Trailer**
FREE				**Switch**
DOWN		●	●	

14

WIRE HARNESS (40-50 HP)

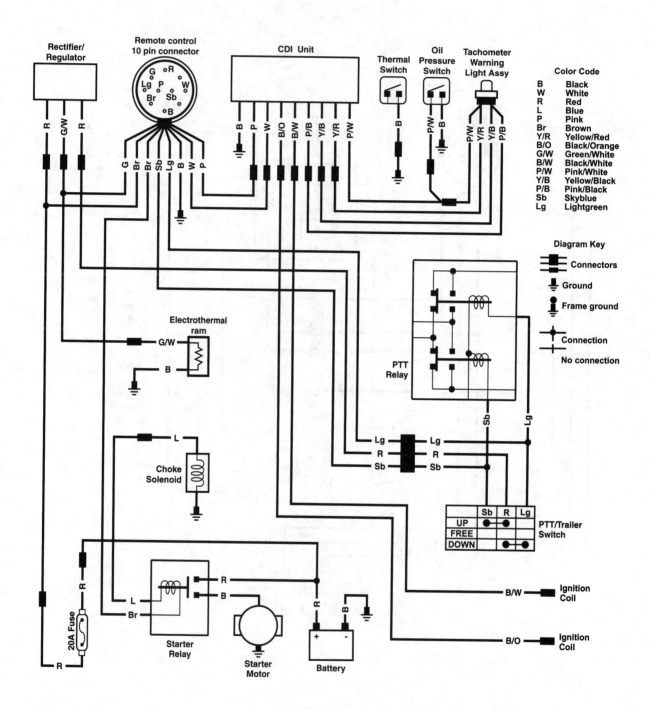

IGNITION SYSTEM (40-50 HP)

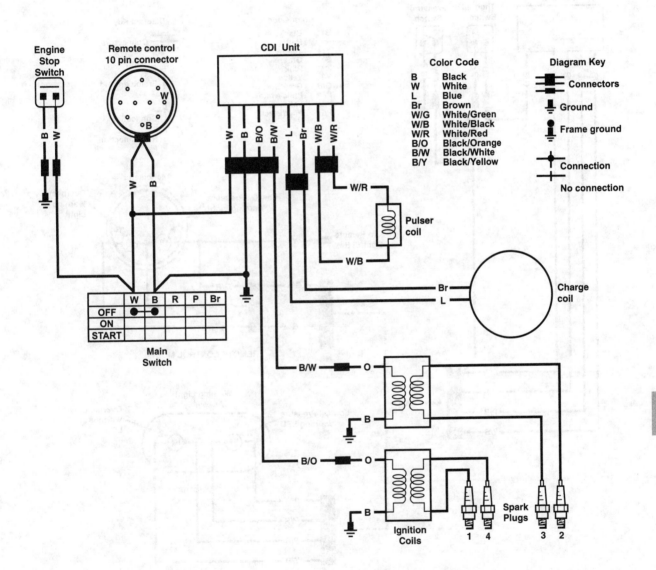

Engine Stop Switch

Remote control 10 pin connector

CDI Unit

Color Code

B	Black
W	White
L	Blue
Br	Brown
W/G	White/Green
W/B	White/Black
W/R	White/Red
B/O	Black/Orange
B/W	Black/White
B/Y	Black/Yellow

Diagram Key

- Connectors
- Ground
- Frame ground
- Connection
- No connection

W B B/O B/W L Br W/B W/R

W/R

W/B

Pulser coil

Br

L

Charge coil

	W	B	R	P	Br
OFF	●	●			
ON					
START					

Main Switch

B/W — O

B

B/O — O

B

Ignition Coils

Spark Plugs
1 4   3 2

14

IGNITION CONTROL SYSTEM (40-50 HP)

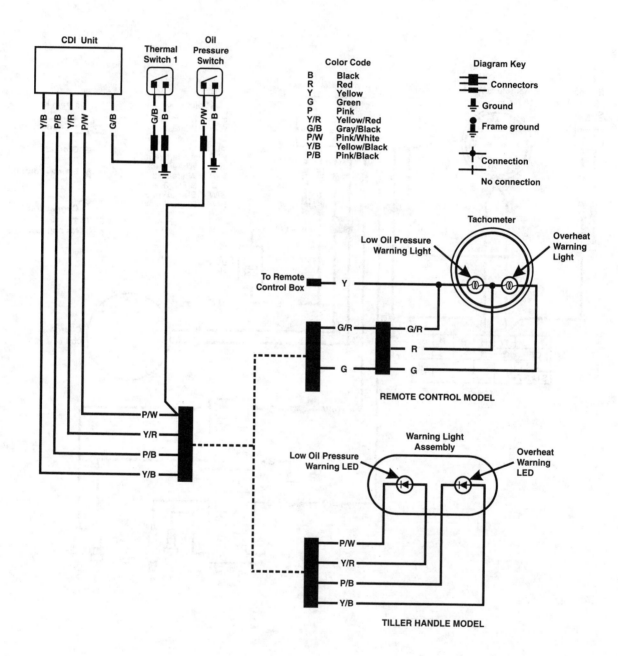

STARTING SYSTEM (40-50 HP)

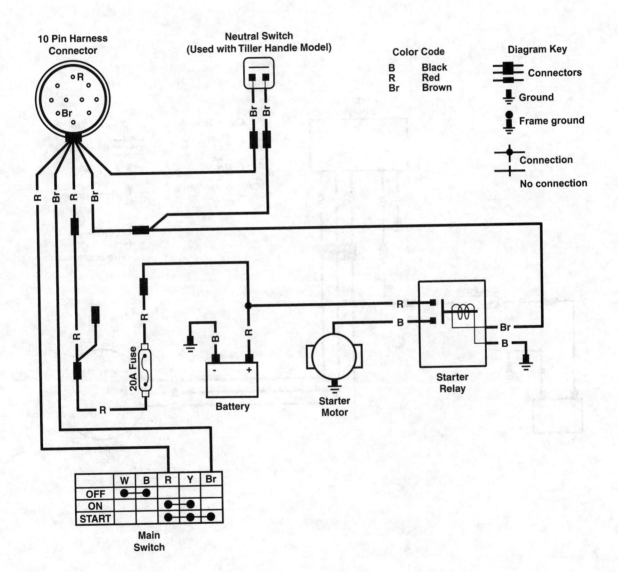

10 Pin Harness Connector

Neutral Switch (Used with Tiller Handle Model)

Color Code

B	Black
R	Red
Br	Brown

Diagram Key

Connectors

Ground

Frame ground

Connection

No connection

20A Fuse

Battery

Starter Motor

Starter Relay

	W	B	R	Y	Br
OFF	●	●			
ON			●	●	
START			●	●	●

Main Switch

14

CHARGING SYSTEM (40-50 HP)

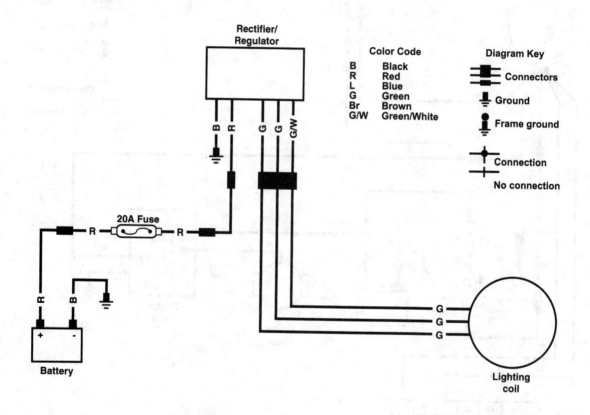

ENRICHMENT SYSTEM (40-50 HP)

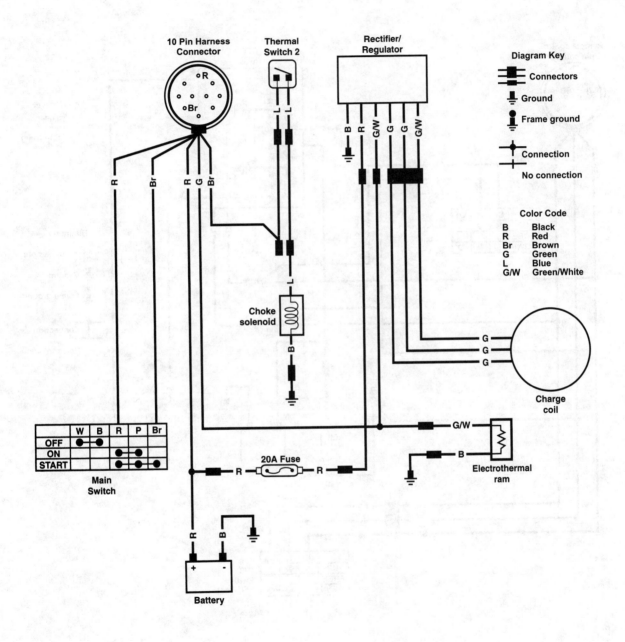

14

POWER TRIM AND TILT SYSTEM (40-50 HP)

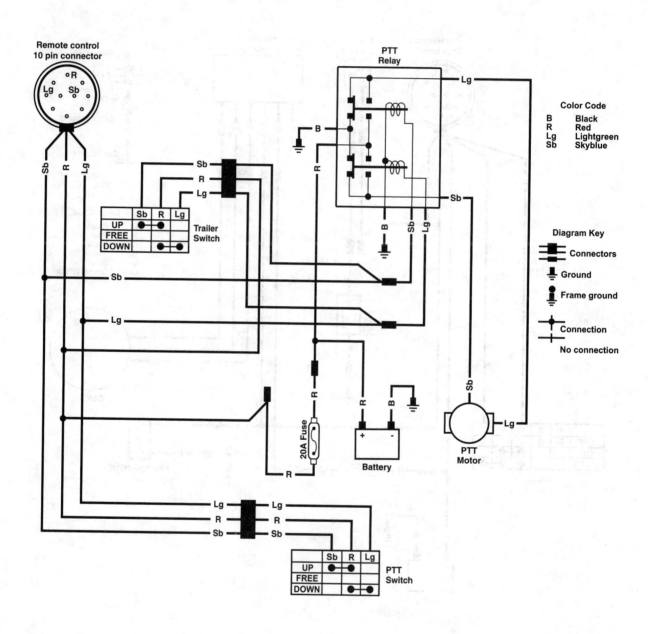

POWER TRIM AND TILT CONTROL SYSTEM (80-100 HP)

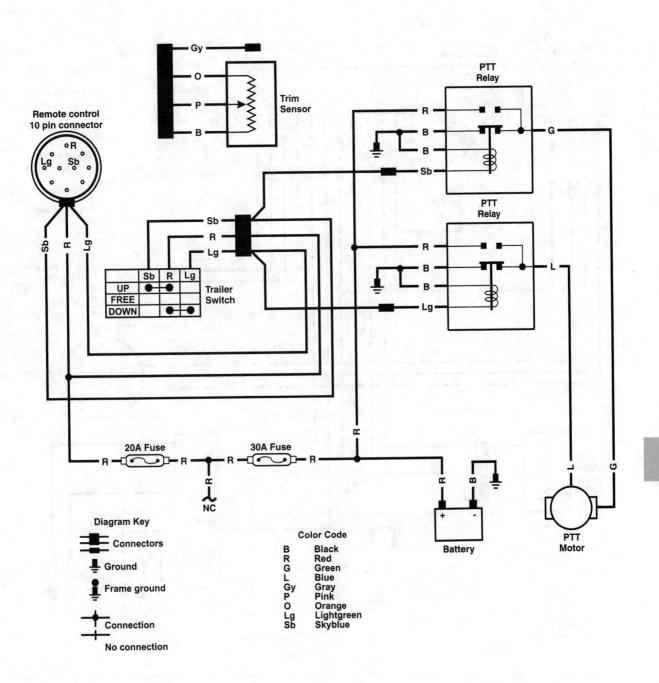

Remote control
10 pin connector

Trim Sensor

PTT Relay

PTT Relay

Trailer Switch

	Sb	R	Lg
UP	●——	●	
FREE			
DOWN		●——	●

20A Fuse

30A Fuse

NC

Battery

PTT Motor

Diagram Key

Connectors
Ground
Frame ground
Connection
No connection

Color Code

B	Black
R	Red
G	Green
L	Blue
Gy	Gray
P	Pink
O	Orange
Lg	Lightgreen
Sb	Skyblue

14

IGNITION SYSTEM (80-100 HP)

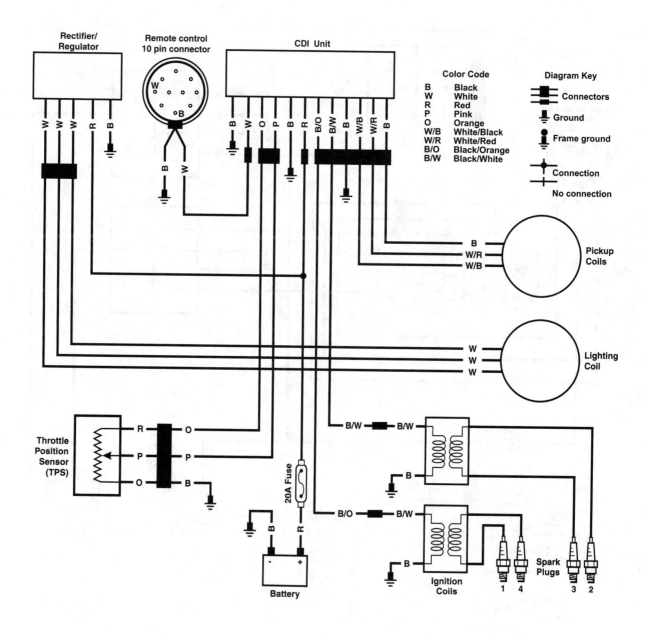

IGNITION CONTROL SYSTEM (80-100 HP)

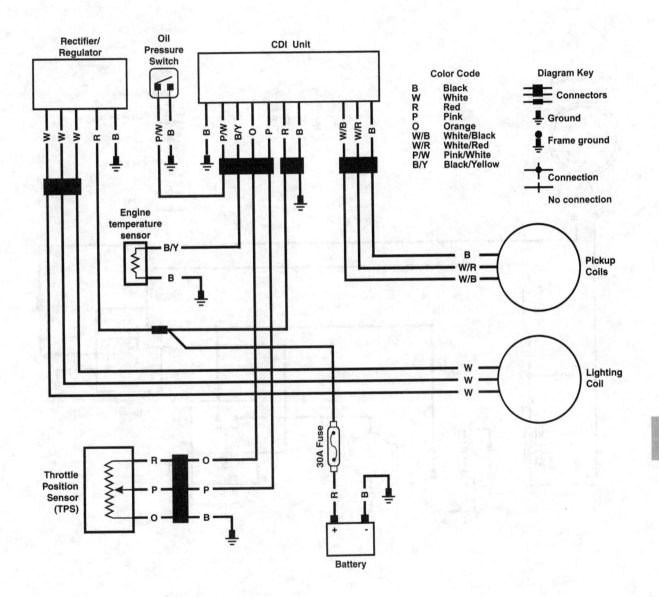

14

STARTING SYSTEM (80-100 HP)

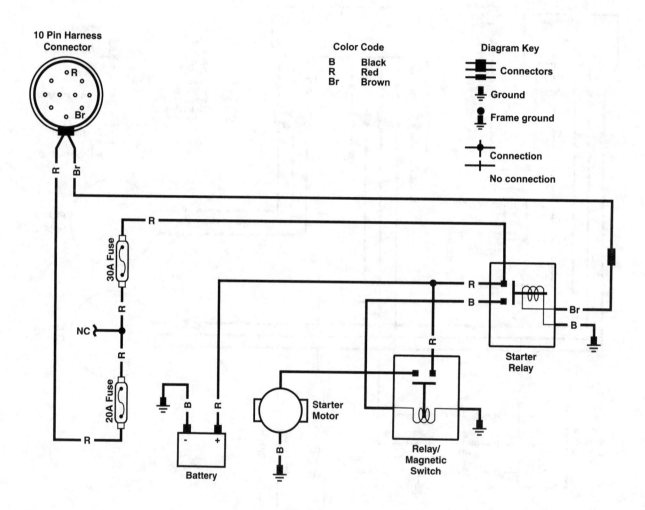

CHARGING SYSTEM (80-100 HP)

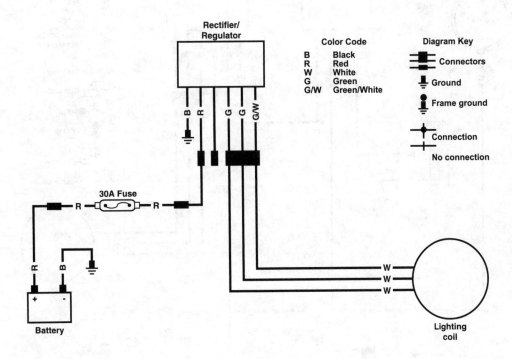

ENRICHMENT CONTROL SYSTEM (80-100 HP)

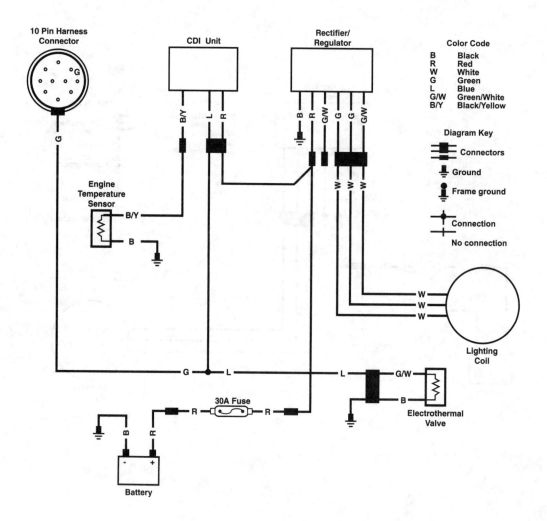

NOTES

NOTES

NOTES

MAINTENANCE LOG

Service Performed	Mileage Reading				
Oil change (example)	2,836	5,782	8,601		